LANCELOT-GRAIL

THE OLD FRENCH ARTHURIAN VULGATE AND POST-VULGATE IN TRANSLATION

LANCELOT-GRAIL

LANCELOT-GRAIL

THE OLD FRENCH ARTHURIAN VULGATE AND POST-VULGATE IN TRANSLATION

Norris J. Lacy, General Editor

VOLUME IX

THE POST-VULGATE QUEST FOR THE HOLY GRAIL
&
THE POST-VULGATE DEATH OF ARTHUR
translated by Martha Asher

D. S. BREWER

First published by Garland Publishing Inc. 1992-1996

This edition published 2010 by
D.S. Brewer, Cambridge

ISBN 9781843842330
(ISBN for ten-volume set 9780859917704)

D. S. Brewer is an imprint of Boydell & Brewer Ltd
PO Box 9, Woodbridge, Suffolk IP12 3DF, UK
and of Boydell & Brewer Inc.
668 Mount Hope Ave, Rochester, NY 14604, USA
website: www.boydellandbrewer.com

A CIP catalogue record for this book is available
from the British Library

The publisher has no responsibility for the continued existence or accuracy of
URLs for external or third-party internet websites referred to in this book, and
does not guarantee that any content on such websites is, or will remain, accurate
or appropriate.

This publication is printed on acid-free paper

Printed in the United States of America.

CONTENTS

THE DEATH OF ARTHUR

PREFACE

NORRIS J. LACY

THE VULGATE AND POST-VULGATE CYCLES

During the second half of the twelfth century, Chrétien de Troyes developed and fixed the form of the Arthurian episodic romance. In the process he popularized King Arthur in French, as Geoffrey of Monmouth had done in Latin, but he also contributed to the legend new characters and themes unknown to Geoffrey. These include in particular the love story of Lancelot and Guenevere and the quest for the Grail. Several texts, notably the works of Robert de Boron, from the end of that century, transformed the mysterious Grail into the "Holy Grail," the Chalice of the Last Supper and the vessel in which Christ's blood was collected after the crucifixion.

Then, between 1215 and about 1235, an anonymous author or group of authors composed the Lancelot-Grail Cycle (also called the Vulgate Cycle, the Prose *Lancelot,* or the Pseudo-Map Cycle) of Arthurian romance. This cycle of five imposing romances can only be termed monumental, owing in equal measure to its enormous length, its complexity and literary value, and its influence. The romances run to several thousand pages of text, and they offer many hundreds of characters and countless adventures intricately interlaced with one another. Most important, they constitute the most extended attempt to elaborate the full story of the Arthurian era and to set that era in a framework of universal history.

The two romances that stand first chronologically were actually composed after the other three. The *Estoire del saint Graal* (translated in this set as *The History of the Holy Grail*) opens the cycle by tracing the early history of the Grail, from Joseph of Arimathea to his son Josephe, who becomes the first Christian bishop, and eventually to Alain, the first Fisher King, who places the Grail in Corbenic Castle and begins the wait for the arrival of the chosen Grail Knight. *The Story of Merlin* depicts the role of the seer and magician in Arthur's conception and birth, in his designation as king following the Sword in the Stone revelation, and in the establishment of the Round Table, a replica of the Grail Table (itself modeled after the table of the Last Supper). Merlin also directs Arthur's major victories over his rebellious barons.

These two romances are followed chronologically (but preceded in order of composition) by the *Lancelot Proper, La Queste del saint Graal* (*The Quest for the Holy Grail*), and *La Mort Artu* (*The Death of Arthur*). The first of these, constituting fully half of the entire cycle, presents Lancelot's youth, his love for Guenevere, and a long series of exploits that he performs in her service. The second depicts the Grail Quest undertaken by a number of knights (Gawain, Bors, Perceval, and others) but finally accomplished by the chosen hero, Galahad. Concluding the cycle, *The Death of Arthur* traces the tragic decline and dissolution of the Arthurian world, due in large part to the sin of Lancelot and Guenevere, and closes with an account of the death of the king.

The Vulgate Cycle was soon followed by an anonymous Post-Vulgate, based on the earlier cycle but characterized by the omission of the *Lancelot Proper* and, consequently, of the emphasis on Lancelot and Guenevere. The second cycle thus focuses squarely on the Grail quest and related pious themes. It includes versions of the other four romances represented in the Vulgate and even borrows the text of the *Merlin* intact; on the other hand, the Post-Vulgate *Death of Arthur* romance is a significantly abridged adaptation of its model. Without a *Lancelot Proper,* the second cycle is far shorter than the first, but it remains daunting nonetheless in its dimensions and in its complexity.

The Post-Vulgate Cycle is further complicated for modern scholars and readers—and this is a complication almost beyond resolution—by the fact that some portions of the Old French text have long since disappeared, whereas others have survived only in fragments or in translations into Portuguese and Spanish. Extraordinary scholarly efforts, especially by Fanni Bogdanow, have made it possible to reconstitute significant portions of the texts.

The importance of the Vulgate Cycle and, to a only slightly lesser extent, of the Post-Vulgate is almost incalculable. Portions of them (most often the Vulgate *Lancelot-Quest-Death of Arthur*) were translated or adapted into a number of other languages. Authors rendered much of the Vulgate narrative into German and Dutch, while the *Quest* was translated into Irish and Welsh. Italian and Hispanic authors too translated it or drew on it, although, as suggested, the Post-Vulgate proved more influential on the Iberian Peninsula than did the Vulgate.

But for English-speaking readers, the importance of the Vulgate is indicated most clearly by its influence on Sir Thomas Malory, who took the cycle as the principal of his numerous sources: although each part of his work has multiple sources, his first, third, sixth, seventh, and eighth tales were drawn largely or principally from the Vulgate Cycle. He even gave his work, *Le Morte Darthur*, a title that indicates his indebtedness not only to related English romances like the *Alliterative Morte Arthure* and the *Stanzaic Le Morte Arthur* but to the final component of the Old French cycle.

THE POST-VULGATE CYCLE

THE QUEST FOR THE HOLY GRAIL AND THE DEATH OF ARTHUR

The revised version of *The Quest for the Holy Grail* gives a greater role to Perceval, and introduces a number of knights not found in the Vulgate; but the largest change is that much of the story of Tristan (and of his rival Palamedes) is incorporated into the story. The achievement of the Grail quest centres on Galahad's healing of Pellehan, which has to be accomplished before the knights can reach the Grail itself. *The Death of Arthur* is little more than a relatively brief postscript, bringing the story of the adventures of the kingdom of Logres to an end;m Lancelot and Guenevere are revealed as lovers, and Arthur fights both Lancelot and then the Romans. Despite this victory, he is betrayed and killed by Mordred, as has been foreshadowed from the outset of the new material. The romance ends with King Mark of Cornwall's death when he attempts to kill Lancelot and Bors at the hermitage to which they have retreated.

See the introduction in volume VIII for a full discussion of the Post-Vulgate Cycle. The volumes in the set are listed opposite the title page. A complete chapter summary of the cycle and an index of names is to be found in volume X.

THE POST-VULGATE, PART II
THE QUEST FOR THE HOLY GRAIL

TRANSLATED BY MARTHA ASHER

THE QUEST FOR THE HOLY GRAIL

73. GALAHAD IS KNIGHTED.[*]

On the eve of Pentecost, a large crowd was assembled at Camelot, so that one could see a great throng of finely attired knights and ladies. The king, who was very happy about this, honored them and had them well served, and he had everything done that he thought would make the court more delightful.

On that day of which I am telling, just when they wanted to lay the tables—it was the hour of nones—a beautiful, well-dressed maiden arrived and entered the palace on foot as a messenger. She began to look around on all sides throughout the palace, and they asked her what she was seeking.

"I'm looking for Sir Lancelot of the Lake," she said. "Is he here?"

"Yes, my lady," said a knight. "See, he's at that window, talking to Sir Gawain."[†]

She went to him at once and greeted him. As soon as he saw her, he greeted her well and embraced her, for she was one of the ladies who lived on the Isle of Joy,[‡] the one King Pelles's daughter Elaine loved more than any other lady of her company.

[*] Corresponds to Augusto Magne, ed., *A Demanda do Santa Graal* (Rio de Janeiro: Institute Nacional do Livro, 1955), I, 3-9, hereafter abbreviated as Magne; Fanni Bogdanow, ed., *La Version Post-Vulgate de la "Queste del Saint Graal" et de la "Mort Artu,"* Société des Anciens Textes Francais (Paris: Picard, 1991-), II, 11-18, hereafter abbreviated as Bogdanow 1991; Joseph-Maria Piel, ed., *A Demando do Santo Graal* (Lisbon: Imprensa Nacional, 1988), 3-5, hereafter abbreviated as Piel. This translation is from Magne, although the corresponding pages from the other two editions are given in the first note of each chapter. Since the Bogdanow edition is established where possible from French fragments, whereas the other two are from the Portuguese translation, there is often considerable variation in wording; variants are used only if they are of unusual significance or modify the story content.

[†] The *Lancelot's Madness* fragment as we have it (chapters 60-72) does not relate Lancelot's return to court, but he is there at the beginning of the Grail Quest section.

[‡] See chapter 65.

How the maiden told Lancelot to come with her.

"Oh, my lady," said Lancelot, "what fortune has brought you here? For I know that you haven't come without reason."

"My lord, that's true, and I ask you, if you please, to come with me to the forest of Camelot; you'll be back here at the dinner hour tomorrow."

"Certainly, my lady," he said, "that pleases me greatly, for I'm bound to serve you in every way I can." Then he asked for his arms.

When the king saw that he was having himself armed in such haste, he went to him with the queen and asked him, "What? Do you want to leave us at such a feast, when knights from all over the world come to court, more to see you than for anything else—some to see you and some to have your company?"

"My lord," he said, "I'm only going to the forest with this maiden who has asked me, and at tierce tomorrow I'll be back here."

How Lancelot went with the maiden.

Then Lancelot went out of the palace and got on his horse, and the maiden got on her palfrey. She had two knights and two maidens with her.

When she returned to them, she said, "I've accomplished what I came for: Sir Lancelot of the Lake is coming with us."

Then they set out and entered the forest. They had not gone far when they arrived at the house of the hermit who used to talk with Galahad. When he saw Lancelot and the maiden go by, he knew at once that they were going to make Galahad a knight. He left his hermitage in order to go to the convent, for [5]* he did not want Galahad to leave before he saw him, since he knew that once Galahad had gone he would not return, for as soon as he became a knight he would have to enter into the adventures of the kingdom of Logres. Therefore, it seemed to him that he had lost Galahad and would see him but rarely, and he feared that, for he took great pleasure in Galahad, who was a holy creature.

How Lancelot arrived at the abbey.

When they arrived at the abbey, they took Lancelot to a room and disarmed him. The abbess came to him with four ladies, bringing Galahad with her. Galahad was a marvelously handsome boy, as well dressed as he could be.

The abbess wept with pleasure as soon as she saw Lancelot and said to him, "My lord, for God's sake, dub our new knight, for we don't want him to be knighted by anyone else's hand. For no better knight than you could make him a knight, and we truly believe that he will yet be so good that you will think well of him, and it will be to your honor to knight him. If he doesn't ask it of you, you should do it anyway, for you know well that he is your son."

"Galahad," asked Lancelot, "do you want to be a knight?"

Galahad answered enthusiastically, "My lord, if it pleases you, I do truly want to be one, for there's nothing in the world I desire as much as the honor of knighthood

---

*   This is a parallel text edition; the even-numbered pages are facsimile reproductions from the manuscript.

and to become a knight at your hand; I wouldn't want to become one at anyone else's, for I have heard you praised for chivalry so much that no one you knighted could, in my opinion, be bad or cowardly. And this is one of the things that give me the greatest hope of being a good man and a good knight."

"Son Galahad," said Lancelot, "God has made you strangely beautiful. So help me God, if you did not intend to be a good man and a good knight, it would be a great loss and misfortune."

Galahad said, "If God made me beautiful, He'll give me the goodness, if it pleases Him, for otherwise I would be worth little. And He'll want me to be good and a credit to those from whom I come. I've put my hope in Our Lord, and therefore I ask you to make me a knight."

Lancelot answered, "Son, since it pleases you, I'll make you a knight. And may Our Lord, who can do it if it pleases Him, make you as good a knight as you are beautiful."

The hermit replied to this, "Sir Lancelot, have no doubt of Galahad, for I tell you that in the excellence of his chivalry he'll surpass the best knights in the world."

And Lancelot answered, "May God make it so, for I wish it."

Then everyone there began to weep with pleasure.

How Galahad promised the hermit what he asked.

Lancelot remained there that night, and he had Galahad keep vigil in the church. The hermit, who loved Galahad exceedingly, stayed awake all that night and never stopped [7] weeping, because he saw that Galahad had to leave him.

When morning came, he said to Galahad, "Son, holy and honored creature, flower and praise of all young men, grant me, if you please, to keep you company for the rest of my life, as long as I can follow you, after you leave King Arthur's court, for I know well that you won't stay there more than one day, since as soon as you get there the quest for the Holy Grail will begin. I ask you for your company, as you have heard, because I know your goodness and your holy life better than you do. And I know nothing in the world that could comfort me, from now on, as much as to see what a holy knight you will be and to see the marvels you will see and accomplish. For God, who caused you to be born in such sin, as you know, in order to show His great power and might, granted you—because of His own pity and because of the good life you have led from childhood until now—power and strength, skill at arms and courage surpassing all the knights who now bear arms in the kingdom of Logres, so that you will accomplish all the marvels and adventures in which the others will fail. And therefore, I want to know all the deeds you will do, who were conceived in such sin, that the others may not attain who were conceived in legal wedlock. And I want to keep you company, as I know that Our Lord never in our time performed such beautiful or famous miracles as He will perform for you. I want to know this better, to see the great adventures and miracles that God will do for you. And I'll put down in writing all the marvels that God will show in this quest for love of you. Son, grant me what I ask of you. May God make you a good man."

And Galahad granted it to him.

How Lancelot knighted Galahad.

That day at the hour of prime, when Mass had been said, Lancelot made his son Galahad a knight according to the custom. And know that everyone there was pleased with the way he looked, and it was no wonder, for no man at that time could find in all the kingdom of Logres a young man so beautiful or so well made. In every way he was such that no one could find anything in which to censure him, except that he was exceedingly gentle in his bearing. Lancelot, when he made him a knight, could not keep from weeping, because he knew that Galahad was as excellent as he could be in all qualities; he saw such meager celebration and such slight festivity at his knighting, and he could not believe that the boy could attain to such great things as he later did. He had a well-formed physique, and his bearing was meek.

How Lancelot met Bors and Lionel, who had followed him.

After [9] Lancelot had done everything appropriate to the making of a knight, he said, "Son Galahad, now you are a knight. God grant that knighthood be as well employed by you as by the rest of our line. Now tell me: will you go to King Arthur's court, where many good men come from all parts of the world and all the knights of the kingdom of Logres are assembled for today's festival?"

Galahad said, "My lord, I'll go, but not with you; another will conduct me there."

"When?" asked Lancelot.

The other knights, who were with him, said, "My lord, since he's already a knight, he'll go to court more quickly than you think, for he'll be there very soon."

"Then I commend you to God," said Lancelot, "for I want to go to court, as I'm to be there at the hour of tierce."

Then he took his arms and mounted, and as he prepared to leave the monastery, he saw outside a room Bors and Lionel, armed and also seeking to mount.

As soon as they saw him, they went to him, and he said to them, "What chance brings you here? I thought you were at court."

"My lord," they said, "we left because we feared for your life, for you wouldn't have left except for some great need. Therefore, we followed you this far and concealed ourselves the best we could. When we knew that you wanted to return to court, we armed ourselves to return with you and for no other reason."

"Then mount, and let's go," he said.

Then they mounted, and as they were going along the road, Bors asked, "My lord, who's that knight you knighted just now?"

"You'll know soon," said Lancelot. "For now, stop asking about him."

Then Lionel said, "Whoever he may be, he's the most beautiful youth of his age I ever saw, and if he's as good a knight as he is beautiful, Our Lord will do well for him.'"*

74. THE ADVENTURE OF THE BURNING KNIGHT; THE SWORD IN THE STONE; ERIC AND HELAIN SEATED AT THE ROUND TABLE.[†]

How Lancelot, Bors, and Lionel arrived at Court.

Talking in this way, they arrived at Camelot, and everyone at court was very happy about it, for the celebration was much greater for it and would have been much poorer if they had not been there. The king, richly attired, went to hear Mass in the church with a great company of knights, which you would have been amazed to see, and so many ladies and maidens accompanied the queen that it was a wonder. They heard Mass and went to the palace.

Meanwhile it happened that men, going about, looking at the seats of the Round Table, found, HERE SHOULD SIT SUCH A ONE, and HERE SUCH A ONE. And when they came to the Perilous Seat, they found there newly-written letters, which said, FOUR HUNDRED FIFTY-THREE YEARS AFTER THE DEATH OF JESUS CHRIST, ON THE DAY OF PENTECOST, THIS SEAT MUST HAVE A LORD.

"By God," said Lancelot when he heard of this marvel, "then it must have a lord today, for from the death of Jesus Christ to this Pentecost it's been four hundred fifty-three years.[‡] And I'd like [11] very much, if possible, to have no one see these words until he comes who's to fulfill them."

They said, "We will certainly await him." Then they covered the seat with a piece of red silk, just as the others were covered.

When the king came from church, the queen went to her quarters with her ladies and her company. The king asked if it was time to eat.

"My lord," said Kay, "it's time to eat, for it's already nearly midday, but if you want to observe the custom that you have kept in all the great feasts up to now, it doesn't seem to me that you can eat, for at such a great feast as this one, no adventure has yet occurred, and at any great feast you're not in the habit of eating until some adventure happens to you."

"That's true," said the king. "I've always observed that custom since I became king, and I'll observe it as long as I live. Because of the great adventures that happen at my court, they call me the King of Adventures.[§] Therefore, I'll support adventures, for after the time when they stop happening, I know well that it won't

---

* Literally, "Our Lord will make him good."
† Corresponds to Magne I:9-17; Bogdanow 1991 18-26; Piel 5-9.
‡ The Vulgate gives 454 years. See *The Quest for the Holy Grail,* chapter 1.
§ See Merlin's "King of Adventures" speech in chapter 27 and Arthur's reference to this concept in chapter 158.

please Our Lord for me to reign long. But however adventures usually happen at the great feasts, I know that they won't fail today; rather, there will happen the greatest and most marvelous that have ever happened, for my heart divines this. It doesn't bother me if we wait a little, for truly I know that our feast today won't be without adventure, but I had such great pleasure at the coming of Lancelot and his cousins that I forgot the custom."

How the knight fell crying from the window.

While the king was saying that, Sir Lancelot and many other knights were watching some windows that overlooked the river, and they saw a noble knight sitting there, a native of Ireland and a good knight at arms, of great fame and well dressed. He was thinking so hard that no one could rouse him from his thoughts, so that his mind was not on the feast or the court.

As he was thus brooding, he uttered a cry, "Ah, wretch, I am dead!" and he let himself fall out the window and broke his neck. The knights who were there went to him, to see what it was, and they found flames coming out of his mouth and nostrils as strong as from a lighted oven. He held in his hands a letter, which fell from them, and the knights took it.

The king came with his knights to see this marvel. Because the knight was a companion of the Round Table, the king, when he saw that he was dead, ordered them to take him out of the palace, for he did not want his court to be upset. They took him outside with great difficulty, for he was burning so hotly that all his clothing was turned to ashes, and no one could get near him without being burned. After he was out of the palace, they began their celebration as before, but everyone was grieved for the knight, because he had been highly respected. The king [13] was deeply grieved, but he did not dare show it, for fear the court would be sadder.

When he knew that the knight was in the church, he said, "Knights, now you may eat, and you won't fail to eat for lack of a marvelous adventure, for this adventure seems very strange to me."

How the squire told the king news of the stone.

While they were speaking about this, a squire came and said to the king, "My lord, I bring you the most marvelous news you ever heard."

"And what news is that?" asked the king. "Tell us."

"A block of marble, in which a sword is fixed, has just landed at your palace, and in the air over this stone is a scabbard. And I tell you that I saw the stone float on top of the water as if it were wood."

The king thought it was a jest and asked if he could see this stone.

The squire said, "Many knights of your company are already there to see this marvel."

As soon as he heard this, the king went at once with his company of good men. Lancelot followed them, as soon as he knew what it was; and Hector and Perceval, who had already seen it on another occasion,* wanted to see if, in such a large company as was assembled, there would be someone who would accomplish the adventure at this time.

When the king reached the bank and saw the stone and the sword that had been fixed there by Merlin's spell, just as the story has already told,† and a scabbard near it in the air, and the letters Merlin had caused to be written, he was completely amazed.

"Friends," he said, "I'll tell you something. Know that by this sword the best knight in the world will be recognized, for this is the test by which he's to be known, and no one except the best knight in the world will be able to draw the sword from this stone."‡

How the king told Lancelot to draw the sword from the stone, and Lancelot would not.

When the knights heard this, most of them drew back, for they did not want to be tested.§

The king said to Lancelot, "Sir Lancelot, take this sword, for it's yours by testimony of all men here, who think you the best knight in the world."

When he heard this, Lancelot was deeply embarrassed and answered, "My lord, these men think me the best knight in the world, but certainly, I'm not the one who should have this sword, for a much better knight than I am will have it, and it grieves me that I'm not as good as you think."

Many were sad at what Lancelot said, and most of all those of King Ban's line, who thought him the best knight in the world.

The king, who understood that he was sad, said, "You must try it, for you won't be blamed if by chance you fail."

"My lord," he said, "saving your grace, I won't approach it, for, God help me, I'm not worthy to lay [115] a hand on the weapon of such a man as he will be who is to bear this sword."

How Gawain tried the sword at the king's command.

Then the king said to Gawain, "Nephew, since Lancelot has refused the sword, you try it, and we'll see what will happen."

"My lord," he said, "I'll try it to fulfill your command, but I know that it's nothing I can accomplish, for you and everyone here know well that when Sir Lancelot leaves something because of a lack of knightly qualities, I will accomplish nothing there, for he is a much better knight than I."

"Nevertheless," said the king, "try it to please me."

Then Gawain drew near, took the sword by the hilt, and pulled on it as hard as he could, but however hard he pulled he could not draw it from the stone.

---

* Not in the Post-Vulgate as we have it.

† At the end of the adventure of Balan and Balin; see chapter 23.

‡ This sword-in-the-stone test echoes the one by which Arthur was known to be the rightful king (see *The Story of Merlin,* chapter 5). By this parallel the author brings to the audience's attention the similarities and differences between Arthur and Galahad.

§ Literally, "for they wanted to try to draw it." This reading is not supported by what follows.

Then he left it, saying to the king, "My lord, now you may seek someone else to try it, for I won't lay a hand on it again, since I see clearly that God will not grant it to me."

"Sir Gawain," said Lancelot, "the king did as he pleased when he ordered you to try it, but you shouldn't have entered into this adventure; harm will come to you from it before long, for because of this you'll receive a great wound, of which you will die or come very close to dying."*

"Friend," he said, "I can't help that, for even if I thought I would die on the spot, I wouldn't fail to obey the king's command."

"Since it is done," said the king, "the fault is mine alone." Then he asked all the others, "Friends, is there anyone here who wants to try this sword?"

They all kept silent.

When the king saw that they would do no more, he said, "Now let's go eat, for it's already time, and may God bring us the one who will accomplish this adventure, for indeed, it would please me very much to see him soon."

How the priests found letters on two seats.

After this they went to the palace and ordered the tables laid. The priests who undertook to keep watch over the seats of the Round Table—which was their task—went from one place to another, and they found that on two seats the letters were not what they had been before but were new. On one seat was written the name of Eric, and on the other was that of Helain the White; and Eric's was the seat of the knight who had died, as the story has just told. The other seat was that of a knight from Scotland named Dragan, whom Tristan had killed that week before Joyous Guard because Dragan had asked Queen Iseut for her love (but the chronicle of the Holy Grail does not tell this, for it does not pertain to this book, but the great chronicle of Sir Tristan tells it in that book).

How Eric and Helain were given [17] *the seats.*

When the priests saw the seats furnished with new names, they realized at once that their former owners were dead and that it would please God for others to take their places. And they found other names on the seats, those of Eric and Helain the White. Then they went to the king and told him what they had found. The king thanked Our Lord, who had given them so much counsel in the matter of the Holy Grail and the Round Table. Everyone was very glad about Eric and Helain. But know that everyone of King Ban's line was especially pleased about Helain the White, for Helain was the son of Bors of Gaunes, and King Arthur had made him a knight that very day.

King Arthur loved Eric dearly and valued him for chivalry because of his reputation, of which he had heard, so that he valued no other knight of his age so much.

---

* In chapter 110 Gahahad wounds Gawain with the sword from the marble block. In chapter 84 he wounds him, and as far as we know it is with that sword, but the author does not mention the fact.

When he saw that this honor had come to Eric, he said with great pleasure, "Let my friend Eric, son of King Lac— and such that no one in this court should value a young man of his age more for chivalry—come to me, and we'll confirm him in the high place that Our Lord has given to him and no one else."

Then they went for him to the queen's room, where he was sitting talking with the maidens. The king took him by the hand and seated him in the seat at the Round Table, where his name was written.

As he seated him, he said to him, "Eric, may God make you as good a knight from now on as you've been up to now."

Then he went to Helain the White and said to him, "Son, you are very beautiful, but may God by His goodness make you resemble in chivalry your relatives, King Ban's kindred."

When they saw that he had thus gained a seat at the Round Table by Our Lord's pleasure, they were marvelously happy, and Lancelot said, "Helain will yet go on to great deeds."

And may all who hear this story know that Helain the White was the son of Bors of Gaunes, who begat him on a daughter of the king of Britain. However, before this took place, Bors had promised Our Lord to keep his virginity for Him. But she liked him as soon as she saw him, and she loved him from then on; then she tricked him by enchantment, and he lay with her and that night begat Helain, who was later emperor of Constantinople. And if Bors broke his vow, it was not willingly but because of the enchantment the girl cast on him, and afterwards he made up for what he had done, for he kept his chastity all the days of his life.

75. THE PERILOUS SEAT; GALAHAD ACHIEVES THE ADVENTURE OF THE STONE; TOURNAMENT AT CAMELOT.*

How those who were watching the seats found them.

That same day that Eric and Helain were seated in the seats of the Round Table, as I have told you, the king ordered the tables spread, for it was already time to eat. [19] The king went to sit in his high seat. Then the companions of the Round Table went to sit each in his place, and the others, who were not of such great reputation, sat each where he should.

At that time, before they were given anything to eat, the king ordered a count of the companions of the Round Table— how many had come to that feast and which were missing. Those who counted found all one hundred fifty seats filled except two, and they said so to the king.

The king held up his hands toward the sky and said, "Jesus Christ, Father and Lord of all things, may You be praised for letting me live to see the Round Table

---

* Corresponds to Magne I:17-27; Bogdanow 1991 26-36; Piel 9-15.

complete, for only two are missing from it." Then he said to those who were appointed to watch the seats, "Which are missing?"

"My lord," they said, "Tristan and the Perilous Seat, which isn't filled."

"Don't let that worry you," said the king; "it will soon be filled, for I've had so many people come to my court for no other reason but to see the marvels that will occur at this table; today my court will be named for all time the Court of Adventures."

How Galahad entered the palace and accomplished the Perilous Seat.

While they were speaking of this, they looked and saw that all the doors and windows of the palace had closed; however, it did not become dark in the palace because of that, for a ray of light entered and extended through the whole building. Then a great marvel took place, for everyone in the palace lost the power of speech; they looked at one another and could say nothing. There was no one there so brave that he was not frightened, but no one left his seat while this lasted. Then Galahad entered, armed in hauberk, armpieces, and helmet, with two insignia in red silk. After him came the hermit who had asked to accompany him, and he carried a mantle and a robe of red silk on his arm.

But this much I tell you, that no one in the palace could see where Galahad had entered, for the doors did not open at his coming, nor did they hear door or window open, but I cannot say as much of the hermit, for they saw him enter by the great door.

As soon as Galahad was in the middle of the hall, he said so that they all heard, "Peace be with you."

The good man put the clothes he carried on a red woolen cloth, went to King Arthur, and said to him, "King Arthur, I bring you the desired knight, the one who comes of the high lineage of King David and Joseph of Arimathea, by whom the marvels of this land and others will come to an end."

The king was happy at what the good man said; he answered, "If that is true, you are welcome, and the knight is welcome, for if he's the one who is to bring to an end the adventures of the Holy Grail, never was mortal man [21] so honored in this court as he will be by us. Whoever he may be, I wish him well, since he comes from such a high lineage as you say."

"My lord," said the hermit, "soon you will see him make a good beginning." Then he had Galahad put on the robes he carried and sit in the Perilous Seat, and he said, "Son, now I see what I have greatly desired, when I see the Perilous Seat filled."

When they saw Galahad in the seat, all the knights suddenly regained the power of speech, and they cried out all with one voice, "Sir Galahad, you are welcome!" They already knew his name, for the hermit had spoken it.

The knight of whom Merlin and all the prophets had spoken.

As soon as the king saw in the Perilous Seat the knight of whom Merlin and all the other prophets in Britain had spoken, he knew that this was the knight by whom the adventures of the kingdom of Logres would be accomplished, and he was so joyful that he praised God and said, "God, may You be praised, since it has pleased You to let me live to see in my house the man about whom all the prophets of this and other lands have prophesied for so long. Now Sir Tristan alone is missing from the Round Table," he said. "Cursed be Iseut's beauty, because of which we've lost him, for were it not for her, he would never fail to come to such a great feast."

How a youth gave the queen news of Galahad.

Thus the king spoke about Tristan with great sorrow because he did not come to court. However, the others were not grieved by this but were as happy as possible that the Perilous Seat had just been achieved, and they honored and served Galahad as well as they could, for they knew that he was to bring to an end the marvelous adventures of the kingdom of Logres. But Lancelot was happier than all the others, for he saw clearly that, if Galahad lived, he would surpass in goodness and chivalry everyone else in the kingdom of Logres.

This news went from one part of the court to another until it reached the queen, for a youth said to her, "My lady, a great marvel has just now taken place in the palace."

"And what marvel is that?" asked the queen. "Tell us."

"My lady," he said, "the Perilous Seat has been filled; a knight sits there."

"Indeed?" she said. "God has sent a beautiful adventure. For of the many who have sat there, never was there one who didn't die or wasn't wounded.[*] And what age may he be?" asked the queen.

"My lady," he said, "eighteen years."

She was amazed at what she heard of him. Then she said, "A marvel may come of him, and I [23] didn't know him. Do you know from what lineage he comes?"

The youth said no, except that everyone said he looked more like King Ban's kin than any other. She began to think, and at once it occurred to her in her heart that this was Lancelot's son, for Hector had told her that Galahad was already a tall young man and would soon be a knight.

The queen asked the youth, "Young man, do you know his name?"

"My lady," he said, "his name is Galahad."

When she heard the name, she immediately knew for certain that he was Lancelot's son, for she had known for a long time what his name was.

Then she said to the ladies with her, "I'm not greatly amazed if he's a good knight, for he comes of good knights on both sides, so that he couldn't fail to be better than another knight."

"My lady," they asked, "who is this, who's better than all other knights?"

"You'll find out," she said, "but not from me."

How Galahad accomplished the adventure of the stone.

That day there was great joy among them, and the king commanded that food be given to them.

---

* "or wasn't wounded" added by Bogdanow 1991 (30).

As soon as they had eaten, the king asked everyone in the palace, "What do you think of what's happened to us? For there was a time, before Galahad came, when I couldn't speak?"

And they all said that the same thing had happened to them.

"By God," said the king, "this was a great marvel. Can you understand why it happened?"

"No," they said.

"By God," he said, "that grieves me greatly."

Great was the joy and pleasure they all felt.

The king stood up from his table and went to the table where Galahad was sitting. He saw his name written there and was glad, and he said to Gawain, "Nephew, now you may see Galahad, the exceedingly good knight, whom we have so long awaited and so much desired to see."

The knights of the Round Table spoke more than all the others, and they said, "Since God has brought him to us, we'll serve and honor him while he's among us, for he won't stay with us long because of the quest for the Holy Grail, which will soon begin."

"So help me God," said Gawain, "we should certainly serve him, for God has sent him to us to deliver the land from the great marvels and strange adventures that have been occurring so frequently and for such a long time."

Then the king went to Galahad and said to him, "My lord, you are welcome, for I've long desired to see you. Thanks be to God and to you that you wanted to come here."

"My lord," he said, "I've come here because I had to, for from this spot everyone must set out who wants to go on the quest for the Holy Grail, and I know well that it will soon begin."

"My lord," said the king, "your coming is beneficial to us because of many marvelous [25] adventures that we can't bring to an end. And I say this to you because of one that happened to us today. Come see it, if you please."

Galahad said he would go gladly. Then the king took him by the hand and led him to the bank of the river, where the stone was, and everyone from the palace went with them to see what would happen. When the queen saw that the king was leading Galahad by the hand to the stone, she came out with a large company of ladies and maidens.

The king said to Galahad, "Will you draw this sword from this stone? For no one, of all those here, wants to try it, for they say the adventure isn't for them. Try it, if you please, for if you don't try it we won't find a knight who will."

Then Galahad grasped the sword by the hilt and drew it as easily as if nothing were holding it. He took the scabbard, put the sword in it, and quickly girded it on himself.

Then he said to the king, "My lord, now I have the sword, but I have no shield."

"Friend," said the king, "since God and adventure have given you the sword, the shield won't long delay."

How a maiden gave the king news.

While they were speaking of this, they saw a maiden coming along the riverbank on a white palfrey. When she reached them, she asked if Lancelot was there.

He stood in front of her and said, "My lady, what is your pleasure?"

She said, "I bring you the most marvelous news you've heard in a long time, and for your grief, not your pleasure. Know that your name has been diminished since this morning, for then he who called you the best knight in the world spoke the truth, but now it isn't so. And this you can see clearly by the test of this sword, for you see that a better knight than you are has won it."

"My lady," he said, "you tell me nothing I haven't known for a long time to be true, for I saw this sword on another occasion* and didn't dare try it."

Then the maiden turned to the king and said to him, "King Arthur, Nascien† the hermit sends you word that on this very day there will come to you the greatest marvel and honor that ever came to you. And it will come not for your sake but for another's."

As soon as she had said this, she reined her palfrey and turned back. There were many there who wanted to know more about her, but she would not wait, no matter who asked, or tell more about herself.

How Arthur had a tournament prepared in the field of Camelot.

Then the king said to those who stood beside him, "Friends, the start of the quest for the Holy Grail is the true signal that you will soon go. And because I know truly [27] that I'll never again see you gathered in my house as I see you now, I want a tournament to be begun now in this field of Camelot such that it will be recounted after my death and will give our descendants something to talk about."

They all agreed to that. They returned to the city, asked for their arms, armed themselves, and returned to the field. And the king had done this only in order to see something of Galahad's skill at arms, for he knew well that the youth would not stay long at Camelot.

How Galahad jousted, and how the king stopped the tournament.

That day Lancelot asked his son Galahad to bear arms in that tournament with the insignia of the house of King Ban, and he did it willingly, for he feared nothing his father commanded him, but he did not want to bear a shield. When they were assembled in the field of Camelot, they began to strike each other with lances in such a way that you would have seen many fall there, and there were many who did very well. Galahad, entering the field, began to break lances and knock down knights and do so many marvels that they all said they had never seen a knight so good at jousting. For, without doubt, he reached no skillful knight, however brave, without laying him on the ground. He did so much there that everyone who saw him said that never had a knight so nobly begun to knock down knights. And this was

---

* Not narrated in the Post-Vulgate as we have it.

† "Nascien" added by Bogdanow 1991 (33); Magne has "the hermit."

fully apparent in what he had done that day. For of all those who were companions of the Round Table, there were only a few whom he did not knock down.

This tournament lasted until the hour of vespers. Then the king ordered them to stop, for he feared to see it develop into a real fight. He told them to go disarm and had Galahad's helmet taken and given to Bors of Gaunes, who took it, for Galahad trusted Bors, who was always ready to honor and aid him.

76. Tristan Arrives; The Round Table Is Complete; The Holy Grail Appears; The Knights Vow to Seek It.*

How the king and the knights saw Tristan coming.

The engagement was not yet finished when they saw a knight coming along the river bottom on a horse so good that there were few better on the field, and he rode as fast as if all the devils of hell were after him. He bore no arms but a sword and a shield.

The king looked at the shield, pointed it out to Lancelot, who was beside him, and said, "Now we're happy, for I see Tristan approaching, King Mark's nephew of Cornwall. I know that shield well, and I haven't seen it since it gave me much grief."†

Lancelot began to strike his horse [29] with his spurs and ride toward Tristan, and he called to him from as far away as he thought he could hear, "Welcome, Sir Tristan."

Tristan, recognizing Lancelot, greeted and embraced him; then he asked, "Friend Lancelot, is it true that Galahad, the Very Good Knight, has come to court, he who is to achieve the Perilous Seat and put an end to the adventures of the kingdom of Logres?"

"Indeed, friend," said Lancelot, "he has come to court and achieved the Perilous Seat and accomplished the adventure of a sword on which no knight of the Round Table dared lay a hand. But how did you know that he was to be here today?"

"I'll tell you another time," said Tristan, "not now."‡

Meanwhile, the king came to meet Tristan, for he was very happy at his coming, and he said to him, "Sir Tristan, you are welcome," and Tristan greeted him most correctly.

The king said to him, "Sir Tristan, I'm very happy at your coming, for none of the companions of the Round Table was missing but you."

---

* Corresponds to Magne I:27-35; Bogdanow 1991 35-41; Piel 14-18.
† Allusion to an incident not in the Post-Vulgate as we have it.
‡ A promise not kept in the Post-Vulgate as we have it.

How the king spoke with Tristan, and about the knights' joy.

When the knights saw that it was Tristan with whom the king was speaking, they went to him, pleased at his coming, for they greatly prized his chivalry and courtesy.

As soon as they saw his shield, they said to one another, "We were deceived the other day, for this was the knight who was taking the lady away and who knocked down the knights of this place."*

Great were the joy and pleasure they all felt at Tristan's presence. He asked the king to point out to him Galahad, the Very Good Knight, and the king told him that Galahad had gone to the city with some of King Ban's kindred.

"Oh, my lord," said Tristan, "arrange for me to see him, for I came here for no other reason."

"Gladly," said the king.

Then they went to the palace and dismounted. When they entered the palace, they found Galahad with his kin, who had already disarmed him.

The king took Tristan, led him to Galahad, and said to him, "Friend Tristan, you see here what you seek."

"In the name of God," said Tristan, "he is welcome, for I'm very happy at his coming." Then he fell to his knees before Galahad and said to him, "My lord, blessed be the day on which you were born, since God gave you such grace."

Galahad would not let him remain thus at his feet, and he raised him and kissed him as a sign of friendship and brotherhood. He had already heard it said that this was the best and most renowned knight of the Round Table except for Lancelot.

How the knights of the Round Table received the grace of the Holy Grail. [31]

Great were the joy and pleasure of the knights of the Round Table that day when they found themselves all together. And know that never, since the Round Table had been founded, had they all been thus assembled, and they would never be again, but that day unquestionably it happened that they were all there.

Toward night, after vespers, when they had seated themselves at the table, they heard a storm coming, so frightful that it seemed to them that the whole palace would fall down. Immediately after the storm struck, there entered such a great light that it made the palace twice as bright as it had been before. Everyone in the palace was immediately filled with the grace of the Holy Spirit, and they began to look at one another, and for a great while they saw one another more beautiful than they usually were. They were amazed at what had come to pass, and there was no one there who could speak for a long time, but they were silent and looked at one another. And while they were sitting like this, the Holy Grail came into the palace, covered with a piece of white silk, but no one saw who bore it. As soon as it entered, the whole palace was filled with fragrance, as if all the spices of the world were there. It went through the palace, from one side to the other, around the tables, and wherever it went, at once all the tables were filled with such food as each man desired in his heart. And after each one had had what was necessary to his pleasure,

---

*   Allusion to an incident not included in the Post-Vulgate as we have it.

the Holy Grail went out of the palace, so that no one knew what had become of it or where it had gone out. Those who could not speak before spoke then, and they gave thanks to Our Lord, who did them such great honor and who had thus comforted them and given them in abundance the grace of the Holy Vessel. But above all, King Arthur was the happiest, because Our Lord had shown him greater favor than to any king who had reigned in Logres before him. Everyone there was amazed at this, for it certainly seemed to them that God had remembered them, and they spoke at length about it.

The king said to those near him, "Indeed, friends, we should be glad, for God has shown us this great sign of His love, that at such a high feast as that today of Pentecost He has given us to eat from His holy granary."

How Gawain began the great quest far the Holy Grail.

Gawain, who was serving* in the king's presence, said, "My lord, there's yet more to this than you know. Know that there is no knight in the palace who hasn't had as much to [33] eat as he imagined in his heart. This never happened in any other court, except in the house of King Pelles. But we were deceived to this extent, that we only saw it veiled. And therefore, with all my heart, I now swear to God and to all knighthood that in the morning, without waiting,[†] I'll enter into the quest for the Holy Grail, so that I'll follow it for a year and a day and perhaps longer; and I further say that I'll never return to court, whatever happens, until I see better and more to my pleasure what I've just seen, but if that may not be, then I'll return."

How those of the Round Table began the quest far the Holy Grail.

When the knights of the Round Table saw that it was Gawain and heard what he said, they waited until after they had eaten, but as soon as the tables had been taken up, they all went to the king and made the same vow Gawain had made, saying that they would never cease wandering until they saw that table and those savory foods, laid out the same way as those they had eaten that day, if it were something that might be granted to them through effort and labor that they could endure.

How the king spoke harshly to Gawain.

When the king saw that they had all made this vow, he felt great grief and bitterness in his heart, for he saw that he could in no way change their minds.

He said to Gawain, "You've shamed and slain me, for by this vow you've made, you've taken from me the best and most loyal company that ever was in the world, the company of the Round Table. Once they leave here, I know well they won't soon return, but a great number of them will die in this quest, for it won't be completed as soon as you think. Therefore, I'm grieved, for I've always honored them as much as possible, and I've wished and do wish them well, as if they were my brothers or my sons. For this reason their departure is grievous to me, and when

---

* "serving" as in Bogdanow 1991 (39) and Piel (17). Magne has "sitting."
† "without waiting" as in Bogdanow 1991 (39). Magne and Piel (17) have "if God will heed me."

I, who am used to seeing them and having their company, see them no longer, I'll suffer great hardship and sorrow."

After he had said this, the king began to brood, and, as he was brooding, tears began to run from his eyes down his cheeks, so that everyone there saw them.

After a while he said, so that they all heard him, "Gawain, Gawain, you've put such grief into my heart that it will never come out again until I see the end of this quest, for I'll have sorrow and fear of losing my friends in it."

"Oh, my lord," said Lancelot, "what are you saying? A man such as you should have no fear but courage and good hope. [35] Indeed, if we all died in this quest, it would be greater honor to us than if we died elsewhere."

"Oh, Lancelot!" said the king, "the very great love that I have always had for you and for them makes me say this. It is no wonder if I feel great sorrow, for never a Christian king had or will have so many good knights at his table as I have had today. Therefore, I fear that they won't ever again be gathered, here or elsewhere, as they are now."

77. THE TEST OF THE BLOODY SWORD; THE UGLY MAIDEN PROPHESIES THAT GAWAIN WILL KILL MANY KNIGHTS ON THE QUEST.*

How the ugly maiden arrived at the house of King Arthur.

Gawain did not know what to reply to what the king had said, for he knew well that the king spoke the truth, and he would gladly have changed his mind if he could, but he could not because of the others who had already promised, just as he had, and, what is more, because the queen and all the ladies and maidens already knew that the quest for the Holy Grail had begun, and those who were to go on it were to set out in the morning. Then the ladies began to make a great lamentation, and they started to go into the palace like madwomen. The king was in sympathy with this crying and tumult that the ladies were making in the queen's house. He was sitting with his barons, brooding sorrowfully. Suddenly a maiden entered on foot, bearing a sword that had a rich, beautiful pommel and an elegantly worked scabbard.

She recognized the king, went to him, and said, "King, don't brood, for your brooding does no good, but receive this that I bring you and do with it what I will command you. I tell you that you'll see something happen that you'll think amazing."

How the maiden had the sword drawn.

Then the king raised his head and said to her, "What are you saying, my lady?"

---

*   Corresponds to Magne I:35-39; Bogdanow 1991 42-45; Piel 19-24.

"I'm telling you to take this sword and have each of your knights of the Round Table draw it from its scabbard, and you'll see that a great marvel will come of it. Afterwards I'll advise you what to do about it."

He took the sword and drew it from the scabbard, and he found it very beautiful.

The maiden said to him, "Now you may give it to someone else, for you aren't the one I seek."

"Now tell me, my lady," said the king, "what marvel may come of it, and we'll believe you more when we see it."

"I'll tell you," she said, "since you wish to know. Know that this sword, which you now see so beautiful and clean, will be all stained with hot, red blood as soon as that man takes it in his hand who will kill more knights [37] in this quest than any other. I've brought this sword here to find him out and make him stay here, for, without fail, if he goes on the quest, so much harm and grief and the death of so many good men will come of it that at his return you'll call yourself a poor king, deprived of good noblemen."

"By God, my lady," said the king, "it would be better for me to lose him than for so much harm to come to me from him. And it would be better for everyone to stay here."*

"Then see which one he is," she said, "for you may know and recognize him by what I tell you."

Then the king gave the sword to Galahad; he drew it from the scabbard, and it did not change from what it had been.

The king said, "You're not the one."

Galahad gave it to his father, who drew it, and nothing appeared. Then to Bors of Gaunes and Hector and Perceval of Wales and Eric, son of King Lac, and Gaheriet, but nothing appeared with any of these. Then Gawain took it, and as soon as he drew it from the scabbard, it was all covered with blood on both sides, as hot and red as if they had drawn it from the body of a man or from a wound.

How the king forbade Gawain to go.

When the men of the palace saw this, they said, "This is one of the greatest marvels we've seen in a long time."

The king said to Gawain, "I ask you not to go on this quest, for great harm may come of it. My lady, do you believe that this is the man you seek?"

"I don't believe it, I know it to be true," she said; "if he goes, he'll cause such great loss among the knights here that all his kin won't be able to conceal it."

The king believed firmly that she was telling the truth, and he said to Gawain, "Nephew, I ask you to stay here and not go on this quest."

Gawain, exceedingly sad at what had happened among so many good men, answered, "My lord, you shouldn't believe everything they tell you. Know that it's all illusion and deceit, the greatest you've seen in a long time. Don't you remember

---

*   "better for everyone to stay here" as in Piel (19). Magne has "better to test everyone."

when you saw Queen Morgan and all her company turned into stone?* Therefore, you shouldn't believe this."

The maiden said, "This is not illusion, so help me God, but honest truth. By God, if you go, such great harm will result that you won't be able to conceal it, nor will King Arthur here." [39]

To this the king replied, "My lady, I've seen such a sign of his going that, so help me God, I know truly that evil will come of it. And therefore, I order him as his lord not to go but, no matter what, to remain."

"What, my lord," said Gawain, "do you believe this lady more than me?"

"I believe what I see," said the king, "and therefore I forbid you absolutely to go on this journey."

"My lord," he said, "it seems to me that you're considering not my honor but my loss and shame, for if I don't go I'm forsworn and false; after that, no one should think me a knight."

"I don't know what you'll do," said the king, "but if you go, it will grieve me most exceedingly."

78. Preparations for the Quest.[†]

How the queen grieved for Lancelot.

Gawain, who was very sad about this, left the king's presence and went to his lodging.

The queen said to the young man who had told her the news of the quest, "Now tell me, were you there when the knights swore to seek the Holy Grail?"

"Yes, my lord,"[‡] he said.

"Gawain and Lancelot are to go?"

"My lord," he said, "Sir Gawain swore it first, and after him Lancelot, and after him all the others of the Round Table."

"Was it so?" she said. "In an evil hour was this undertaking begun, for many good men will die of it, and great loss will come of it to the kingdom of Logres." Then she felt such great sorrow for Lancelot that tears came to her eyes, and she said, "Indeed, this is an especially great loss, for this quest will not be completed without the death of many good men, and I am amazed that the king allows it, for the best knights in the world will leave him, and his land will be much poorer because of it." Then she began to weep hard, and the ladies and maidens also.

---

*   See chapter 40.

†   Corresponds to Magne I:39-51; Bogdanow 1991 45-55; Piel 20-26.

‡   The young page addresses his queen with the masculine form. Perhaps this implies that the queen holds feudal lordship over the vassal in her own right, not simply as wife of the king.

The ugly maiden, who was still in the palace—the king having given Sir Gawain the sword and the latter having left there in anger—spoke to the king about Sir Gawain's going: "Know that much evil will come of it."

He said, "No knight will go whose going will not grieve me, but his going will grieve me much more, for I know well that much evil will come of it."

"Then, my lord," she said, "I ask you to make him stay here."

"I tell you," he said, "that he won't be so bold as to try to go, for I forbade him to, and you heard me."

"Many thanks," she said. Then she went away with her sword. [41]

How the courtiers learned that Galahad was Lancelot's son. How they read the letter.

That evening, most of the people of King Arthur's household knew that Galahad was Lancelot's son, for the facts about such a great man as Galahad could not be concealed for long. The king and the queen spoke a great deal with Galahad that night, and also the nobles who were there and his own kin, who loved him dearly. When night came, the king had not forgotten the marvel of the knight who had burned that morning, and he asked who had the letter the man had been holding in his hand when he burned.

Then a knight from North Wales said, "My lord, here's the letter he held in his hand."

King Arthur took the letter in his hand, read it, and found that it said this:

> Archbishop of Canterbury, holy man, wise, and clean living, counsel me in my misfortune and sin as I will tell it to you. Know truly that I reveal it to God and to you, for I am the greatest of sinners, for I lay with my mother and my sister and then killed them both at the same time because they would not comply with my wish. And afterwards, as I was standing looking at them where I had killed them, my father, king of the Isle of the Gate, came on the scene. When he saw that slaughter, he took his sword, and I took mine, and I killed him. And as I was standing looking at him, my brother, the count of Geer, arrived, and he wished me ill, and I killed him. All this evil I have told you I did in just one day. Now advise me, my lord father, for however great penance you give me, I will do it.

The letter that the knight had held when he died said all this.

After the king had read the letter, so that Galahad and the other good men with him heard it, he said, "Now we may know why this knight died so cruelly. Know that this was the vengeance of Jesus Christ."

And the others said that that certainly seemed to be the truth, according to what the letter said. Then the king had the letter put in an abbey, that of St. Stephen, which was the chief church of Camelot; he had a rich monument made for the knight and had written on it, HERE LIES THE KNIGHT WHO IN ONE DAY KILLED HIS FATHER AND HIS MOTHER AND HIS BROTHER AND HIS SISTER.

This inscription was made after the knights went on the quest for the Holy Grail.

How the old man said that no one should take his lover with him on the quest.

After that the king sent for the queen and the maidens and ladies to come to him. Once they were in the palace, each one of the knights went to be with his wife or his betrothed or his beloved.

There were some who planned [43] with their ladies to take them along, and so it would have been had there not been an old man there, who came dressed in the robes of a religious order, and who said so loudly that they all heard him, "Knights of the Round Table, hear me. You have sworn to the quest for the Holy Grail. Nascien the hermit has sent you word by me that no knight of this quest should take with him lady or maiden, unless he would commit a mortal sin. And let no one enter on the quest unless he is clean confessed, for no one should enter into such high service of God as this unless he is well confessed and communicated and clean and purged of all misfortunes and mortal sin, for this quest is not of such deeds but is a quest for the secrets and hidden things of Our Lord, who will reveal them clearly to the fortunate knight whom He will choose for His servant over all other earthly knights, to whom He will show the great marvels of the Holy Grail, and He will reveal to him what mortal heart cannot imagine nor the tongue of man say."

How the queen questioned Galahad.

Because of this speech, it was left that no knight would take his beloved with him. The king commanded them to see to the good man carefully and asked him about himself, but the good man told the king little, for his heart was elsewhere.

The queen came to Galahad, sat down beside him, and said, "Friend, where are you from and of what lineage?"

He told her part of it, but he did not tell her that he was Lancelot's son or that Lancelot had fathered him on King Pelles's daughter, something he had heard his mother speak of many times.

Nevertheless, because she wanted to know the truth about it, she asked him again, saying, "Tell me, who is your father?"

"My lady," he said, "I really don't know."

"Oh, my lord," she said, "you're hiding it from me; why are you doing that? So help me God, you should have no shame in recalling your father to mind, for he's the most beautiful knight in the world, and he comes on both sides from kings and queens and the noblest lineage in the world, and he has a reputation as the best knight in the world. Therefore, truly, you should surpass all the best knights in the world."

How the queen told Galahad that he was Lancelot's son.

When he heard this, he was deeply embarrassed and answered, "My lady, since you know it so well, you can tell it to me as well as I to you. And if he is the one I believe, I won't deny it to you, but if he's not the one you tell me, I won't reveal another." [45]

"Since you don't want to tell me," she said, "I'll tell you. Your father is Sir Lancelot of the Lake, the best knight at arms and the handsomest, the most gifted, and the most desired and loved of all those who have been born in our time. All these virtues your father has. Therefore, it seems to me that you shouldn't deny him to me or to anyone else, for you couldn't be the son of a better father or a better knight."

"My lord,"* he said, "since you already know this so well, why should I tell it to you? For men will know it well from now on."

How King Arthur thought about the knights who were going on the quest.

That night the king had Galahad sleep in a room where he himself usually slept, in his very bed, for he had a great desire to honor him. And all those of King Ban's lineage slept in the king's house for love of Galahad. It was a very grievous thing to them that they had to separate so soon, for all that family loved each other very much, and they would rather have lived together than apart. Without question, there were then in the king's house nineteen knights of that lineage,† and all were very good. All were so fortunate that there was not one who was not a companion of the Round Table. Therefore, that lineage was so honored and respected that no one ever spoke of another lineage in the kingdom of Logres but that one. That night, when King Arthur saw that King Ban's kin—who were at that time flower and praise of the knights of the world— stayed in his house for love of Galahad, he began to look at them and to think that in all the world these were the men who had done most for him most times and who had avenged him best on his enemies. And when he also thought that they wanted to go in the morning to a place from which he did not think they would ever return, he was so sorrowful that he could not comfort himself, for this was the lineage he loved most in the world after his own. He went then to lie alone in a room, and he began to make the greatest lamentation in the world and to curse his nephew Gawain roundly. He said that the hour was cursed in which he had first seen Gawain, who would soon take from him all the good knights and men because of whom he was feared more than any other king in the world.

How the king mourned for his knights, and how their going grieved him.

Thus the king mourned and lamented for his knights who were leaving him. As soon as it was light, he got up as quickly as he could, for he was greatly concerned over what he had to do, but, though he had [47] risen early, he found more than sixty knights of those who were to go on the quest already putting on their hauberks and girding on their swords. The king, who was sadder than anyone could imagine at this, was so troubled when he saw them standing this way that he had no power to greet them, and his heart was about to fail him in its great grief.

He saw Gaheriet and said to him, "Gaheriet, your brother has killed me, because he has taken away from me all the good men I had in my house. If King Ban's kindred, at least, were left to me, I wouldn't be so sad."

---

*   See note 2 preceding.
†   See the list at the end of this chapter.

When Gaheriet heard this, he kept silent, for he was well aware that the king spoke the truth. That day the king helped arm Galahad, and after he was armed except for his helmet and sword, he and his kin went to hear Mass in the king's chapel. Afterwards they returned to the palace and found the others who were to go on the quest already there, for they were awaiting no one else. They sat down together.

Then King Bademagu stood up and spoke loudly so that they all heard him. "My lord," he said to King Arthur, "since this undertaking is thus irrevocably begun and those who are to go are only waiting for you, I would advise that the Holy Gospel come here and the knights swear such an oath as men should swear who go on such a noble quest."

"I agree," said the king, "since it can't be otherwise."

Then they sent for the priests, and they brought the book on which were sworn the oaths of the court. They placed it at the king's high seat.

The king called Galahad, because he considered him the best knight there, and said to him, "Galahad, you are like a leader of the knights of the Round Table and the best. Come forward and take the oath of this quest."

Galahad said that he would do it gladly. He went and fell on his knees before the book and swore that, if God guided him and kept him from harm, he would follow this quest a year and a day, and more if necessary, and that he would never return to court until in some manner he learned the truth about the Holy Grail. Then Lancelot and Tristan swore, too. Know that of all the hundred fifty knights of the Round Table, there was not one who did not swear this oath except Gawain. He was not there, for he had already gone forth fully armed, just after dawn, to await the others in the forest of Camelot, for he knew well that if he tried to leave with the others, the king would not let him but would make him stay behind.

The roll of the hundred and fifty knights of the Round Table; [49] *their names.*

For this reason Gawain had departed at dawn from the court. And the king, because of the sorrow he felt when he received the oath, never remembered Gawain, so numerous were the others.

But because the history does not give the names of those who went on the quest for the Holy Grail, it is fitting that I list[*] here the names of those who were companions of the Table and took the oath. Of the hundred fifty knights who took the oath of this quest, Galahad was the first; after him Tristan and Lancelot and Bors of Gaunes and Blioberis and Lionel and Hector of the Fens; Brandinor his brother, and Helain the White; Banin, the godson of King Ban; Aban, a marvelously good knight; Gadran, Laner, Tanri, Pincados, Lelas the Ruvho, Crinides the Black, Ocursus the Black, Acantan the Agile, Danubre the Brave. All these knights except Tristan were of King Ban's lineage and had come to King Arthur's court for love of Lancelot; because of their good chivalry and conduct, they were companions of the Round Table and were praised by the knights over all the other knights of King Arthur's house; because of the virtues of these, who were knights errant, the

---

[*] The list is occasionally corrected from Bogdanow 1991 (54-55) when her version seems to make more sense.

lineage of King Ban was famous, just as I tell you. Others, who were not of King Ban's lineage, were Gawain and Gaheriet, Agravain, Guerrehet, and Mordred; these were brothers. Others were Agloval and Perceval, Corsidares, Maidairos, his first cousin, and Persives de Langaulos; Eric, son of Lac, Cujeram, his brother, and Deganaor, a very good knight at arms, but marvelously arrogant. Others: Kay the Seneschal, and Sagremor the Unruly, and Girflet, son of Doon; Lucan the Wine steward, and Dondinax the Wild; Calogrenant; Yvain, son of King Urien; Yvain of the White Hands; Yvain of Canelones of Germany, Gures the Younger; Guares the Black, the ugly, burned one; Garnaldo his brother; Mador of the Gate, the tall knight; Craidandos; Isaias; King Bademagu; Patrides his nephew; Madam his cousin; the Youth of the Ill-Made Tunic, of whom the *Tale of the Cry* speaks a great deal; Dinadeira, his brother, a marvelously good knight who did a great deal in the kingdom of Logres; Gar of the Mountain; Clamadeu, who had only recently won a seat at the Round Table; Taulat the Great of Desert, Senela his brother, Caradan, Damas, and Damcab who were his first cousins. All these were such good knights that one could find no better in the kingdom of Logres unless they were of King Ban's lineage. These last five wished ill to that lineage from envy, because people did not pay them [51] as much honor as to the others. In addition, Lambeguen, who was Bors's and Lionel's chamberlain; Sinados; Artel; Bagarim; Sanasesio; Arnal the Handsome; and the Knight of the Field; Angelis of the Vaaos; Baradan the Young, his brother; Marat of the Tower; Nicorant the Well-Made, valued for his sword work; Alain of the Meadows; Martel of the large shield; Meles the tall; Dinas his brother; Codias Longhand; Pinabel of the Island; Daniel the Believer; Gandaz the Black and Gandin of the Mountain, who were brothers; Ataz; Calendin the Younger; Utrenal; Raface; Conais the White; Agregam the Angry; Guigar, Gawain's son, of whom the *Tale of the Cry* speaks; Anarom the Fat; Amatin the Good Jouster; Canedam the Thin; Canedor of the beautiful lover; Arpian of the Strange Mountain; Saret; Dinados; Peliaz the Strong, who was a native of Logres; Alaman; Ganadal; Lucas of Camelot; Brodan; Endalan; Melian; Julian; Galiadan; Cardoilen of London, a very good, brave knight; Delimaz the Poor, Asalim the Poor, Caligante the Poor—these three were brothers; Hecuba and Eladinan his brother. All these, whose names I have told you, were of the Round Table, and there was no one of them who was not a chosen, tested knight. King Arthur was unquestionably of the Round Table also, and with him, certainly, they were a hundred fifty.*

---

*   In fact, rather fewer than one hundred fifty names are given. Since punctuation is supplied by the editor, the count can be increased by taking as separate individuals epithets that the editors attach to proper names.

79. Departure; Gawain's Slaughters Foretold; The Suicide.*

How the queen grieved for Lancelot, who was going on the quest.

After they had taken the sacrament[†] and eaten a little, for the sake of the king, who begged them to, they put their helmets on their heads, commended the queen to God,[‡] and took leave with tears and weeping. The queen began a lamentation as great as if she saw all the world dead before her. So that they would not hear her, she returned to her room. She let herself fall on her bed and began to lament so that anyone who saw her would have marveled. When Lancelot was fully armed, he felt as sad as he could for his lady, and he went to the room where he had seen her go.

As soon as she saw him, she said, "Oh, Lancelot, you've killed me, leaving the king's house to go to strange lands, so that you'll never return unless by a miracle."

"Oh, my lady," he said, "I will return, God willing, much sooner than you think."

"My heart tells me otherwise," she said, "which fills me with such dread and [53] anxiety as a lady never felt for a knight before."

"My lady," he said, "I will go with your blessing when it pleases you."

"It could never please me," she said. When she saw that there was nothing else to do, she said, "Go with the grace of God Our Lord; may He guide you and bring you back safely and give you honor in this quest."

"My lady," he said, "may God do so, if it pleases Him."

How the king went a little way with the knights.

Then Lancelot left the queen, went to the king's palace, and found that they were all mounted already, except him, because they were awaiting him. He went to his horse and mounted.

The king, seeing Galahad without a shield, said to him, "Friend, I think it's unwise for you not to take a shield like these others."

"My lord, I'd do wrong if I took one from here. Know that I will bear no shield until adventure gives me one, may it be in God's name."

How the knights were going happily to the quest for the Holy Grail.

Then they left the palace and went through the village. You never saw such a great lamentation as the knights of Camelot made and the other people who remained behind, but those who were to go gave no sign that they cared anything about it; rather it would have seemed to you, had you seen them, that they were happy and joyful, and unquestionably they were.

---

*   Corresponds to Magne I:51-59; Bogdanow 1991 56-63; Piel 26-31.

†   "the sacrament" as in Bogdanow 1991 (56) and Piel (26). Magne has "the oath."

‡   "commended the queen to God" as in Bogdanow 1991 (56) and Piel (26). Magne has "commended themselves to the queen and God."

How the ugly maiden told Gawain to turn back, for he would do much wrong in this quest.

When they reached the edge of the forest, near the castle of Vagan, they all stopped at a cross.

Then Lancelot said to the king, "My lord, turn back; you've come far enough with us."

"So help me God," said the king, "this turning will be grievous to me, for I leave you most unwillingly, but because I see that I have to do it, I'll turn back."

Then Lancelot took off his helmet, and the others, too, and the king embraced them and kissed them, weeping freely from his heart, and the others did the same. After they had tied their helmets back on, they commended one another to God and wept from the heart.

Then the king left them and returned to Camelot, and they entered the forest. They rode until they arrived at the castle of Vagan, where they were well served with all they needed. This Vagan was a good knight, who had led a good life, and when he saw the knights of the Round Table and knew they were going to seek the adventure of the Holy Grail, he received them well and thought himself fortunate that God had brought him so many good men and that he could shelter them. That night they lodged with Vagan and were so well served with all they [55] needed that they wondered how he had so quickly prepared the means to do such honor to such a large company. In the evening, when they were eating, there came the ugly maiden, the one who I told you had insulted Eric and who had struck Lancelot with the bridle.*

She saw Gawain standing and went to stand in front of him, saying in anger, "Gawain, Gawain, false knight, how are you so bold as to go on this quest when you know that so much evil will come of it, and most to these knights of the Round Table.† If you remember the death of Lamorant‡and his brother Brian of Monjaspe, and the treachery you committed then, you should now keep yourself more than another knight from doing anything disloyal, for you did enough of it on that occasion. You want to go on this quest like the others, but see what will come of it. Know that Sir Galahad here—he is now the best knight in the world—won't do as much good in this quest as you will do evil, for you with your own hand (which in an evil hour first took a sword) will kill a good eighteen of these companions of yours, such that they are better knights than you. And this will happen because of you in this quest. Now see how they should refer to your coming and curse it."

How Gawain escaped and how the maiden said that some would believe her later who did not believe her then.

Gawain was deeply ashamed at what the maiden said to him, and he answered, "My lady, if I believed that so much evil would happen in this quest because of me,

---

    *   Not narrated in the Post-Vulgate as we have it.

    †   "and most to these knights of the Round Table" as in Bogdanow 1991 (59). Magne has "will come of it, and these knights of the Round Table ask you if you...."

    ‡   Chapter 66.

I'd turn back, but because I know truly that not everything that one says comes to pass, therefore I don't believe what you tell me."

"No?" she asked.

"My lady, no."

"You don't believe me? You'll believe me when you see that everything I have told you will happen to you. I'm concerned to break up this undertaking, not for your sake but for that of the wisest man in the kingdom of Logres, whom you will kill." Then she turned to King Bademagu and said to him, "King Bademagu, I'm greatly grieved that you are going on this quest, for you'll die on it, and that will be a great loss for two reasons, first because you are a very good knight, and second because you are the wisest man in the kingdom of Logres. Know that one single knight will kill you[*] and your nephew Patrides[†] and Eric[‡] and Yvain[§] and so many of these others that it was an evil hour in which that sinner was born who will do so much evil, and it would be better if he were still unborn, for by his arms many kingdoms will be orphaned of good knights and lords for more than one hundred years after his death."

Then she turned to Gawain and said, "Gawain, believe that you and your brother Mordred were born only to do bad and dolorous deeds. If those who are here knew it as I know it, they would cut out your hearts, for you will yet make them die with sorrow and suffering. And those who don't believe what I say now will believe it when they can't do anything about it." [57]

How the knight told Galahad to kill him or he would kill Galahad.

As soon as the maiden had said this, she left them and went off as fast as she could. They remained so dumbfounded that they did not know what they should believe. Then they stopped talking about it, for the sake of King Arthur and Gawain, whom they loved.

While they were sitting like this, suddenly a knight entered, unarmed except for his sword, and he was big and strong.

As soon as he saw Galahad, he fell to his knees and said to him, "Galahad, fortunate knight, chosen over all who have borne arms in Britain, I beg you, by the great faith that you owe to all knighthood, to grant me a favor, for no one has asked one of you since you received the order of chivalry, and if you don't do it, you will commit a great sin."

Galahad looked at the knight who pleaded with him so courageously, and he did not know what to reply, because he believed it was a serious matter; he said to him, "Stand up, knight. I'll give you what you ask of me, if it's something I can and should give."

"Many thanks," said the knight. "I beg you, then, to cut off my head with this sword that I bear, for I desire nothing so much as to die by the hand of such a good knight as you are, for I know well that I couldn't be killed by a better knight." Then

---

[*]   Chapter 113.
[†]   Chapter 89.
[‡]   Chapter 121.
[§]   Chapter 92.

he drew the sword from the scabbard and, putting it on the table, said, "Galahad, take this sword and do what I ask of you."

Galahad looked at him and began to cross himself because of what the knight had said to him, for he thought it amazing.

He answered, "Oh, sir knight! Ask something else of me, for I won't kill you or any other knight except in defense of my person or my lord."

"Indeed," said the knight, "you won't, at the beginning of your career as a knight, fail to keep your promise to me, for you'd be the worst knight in the world and the most forsworn, if you began like that."

"It won't do you any good to ask such a thing of me," said Galahad, "for there's nothing in the world for which I'd kill you this way."

"No?" he said. "You won't keep your promise to me?"

"Another promise to you I'd keep," said Galahad, "but this I wouldn't do for any power that could be."

Then the knight stood up, took the sword in his hand, and said, "Now I'll give you another choice: either you kill me or I'll kill you. Now choose which you want."

Galahad began to smile and crossed himself, he thought this so amazing. "See here, knight, by good faith," he said, "you are the maddest and most foolish man I ever heard of, if you want to force someone to kill you."

"If you don't kill me," said the knight, "someone else will kill me in the morning; no one but God could protect me, [59] for he is the one man in the world to whom I wish worst and whom I respect the least. Therefore, I would have you kill me, so they won't find me alive tomorrow."

"Whatever may happen," said Galahad, "I won't kill you for any reason."

"No?" he said; "then I want to kill you."

Then he raised the sword and made a pretense of wanting to kill Galahad, but Galahad, who had never felt fear, did not move, for he had never dreaded anything that might happen.

When the knight saw that he could not frighten Galahad, he said, "Galahad, now I see clearly that you'll accomplish the adventures of the kingdom of Logres, for I see you strengthened more than I ever thought anyone could be. It was for this that I tested you; because you are braver than any other, I won't kill you, for it would be a great loss if you died at such a time. Nevertheless, since I have to die tomorrow, I won't postpone my death because of you." Then he put the sword through himself and fell in his death agony, saying to Galahad, "My lord, pray to God for me."

As soon as he had said this, he died. Everyone in the house was amazed. Then knights and squires came and dragged him out of the palace where they were eating. The knights told the lord of the castle to have him buried and to ask about his name and his deeds and have them written on his monument, so that those who came after him would know about this marvel.

At that time they decided to leave in the morning, each one to go his own way, for if they went on together it would be considered wrong and cowardly of them.

How the knights separated.

The next day at dawn they heard Mass, and after that they mounted, commended their host to God, and thanked him warmly for the generous hospitality he had shown them. Then they went out of the castle, and as soon as they arrived at the forest, each one went off where he found a road or a path, and they wept hard at the parting.

But now the story stops speaking of the knights and turns to Galahad.

80. GALAHAD WINS HIS SHIELD; MELEAGANT ASKS TO BECOME A KNIGHT.*

Now the story tells that when Galahad left his companions, he wandered three days without finding an adventure to tell about, and he bore no shield. And know that the hermit followed him always on foot, for he did not want to get on a mule. The fourth day, at the hour of vespers, it happened that Galahad reached an abbey of white monks.† The brothers received him very well, for they recognized him as a knight errant, and they made him dismount, took him to a room, and disarmed him. He looked and saw two [61] knights of the Round Table: one was King Bademagu and the other was Yvain the Bastard. As soon as they recognized one another, they were happy and embraced one another, and they were certainly bound to do so, for they were like brothers, since they were of the Round Table.

That evening, after they had eaten, they went out into a garden to relax, and Galahad asked what chance had brought them there.

King Bademagu said, "We've come to see a marvelous adventure here."

"And what adventure is that?" asked Galahad.

"I'll tell you," said King Bademagu. "There is a shield here that no man can hang at his neck and bear a day's journey from here without being killed or badly wounded. Sir Yvain came here to see it, and I want to try it and to bear it away, whatever may happen."

"By God," said Galahad, "you speak of a great marvel; this is one of the greatest marvels I have seen, and I think it's good that you try it. If you can't bear it away, I'll take it, if I can, for I have no shield."

"My lord," said Bademagu, "if you try the adventure first, I believe you'll accomplish it, but let me take the shield, and we'll see if what they say is true."

How the monks told Galahad and the others about the adventure of the shield.

That night the knights were well served with everything the monks had, and they paid much honor to Galahad because of the good they heard the other two knights tell of him. In the morning, after they had heard Mass, King Bademagu asked a

---

*   Corresponds to Magne I:59-75; Bogdanow 1991 64-76; Piel 31-38.

†   Cistercians.

monk to tell him where the shield was about which men spoke so much throughout this country.

The monk said, "Why do you ask?"

"Because I want to see if I can take it away, and I'll see if it has such power as they say."

"I wouldn't advise it," said the monk, "for I think you'll gain dishonor by it."

"Don't let that worry you," said Bademagu, "but, if you please, show it to me."

"Gladly," he said. Then he took them to the altar and showed them the shield, which was behind the altar, and the shield was white and bore a red cross. The monk said to them, "Here's the shield you are seeking."

They looked at it, and it seemed to them that it was the richest and most beautiful they had ever seen, and it gave off a good fragrance, as if all the spices in the world were there.

When Yvain the Bastard saw the shield, he said, "So help me God, I say this much about this shield, that no knight but the best should hang it at his neck. And, indeed, I won't be the one to try it, for I don't feel myself such that I should do it."

"In the name of God," said King Bademagu, "I want to take it away from here, whatever may happen to me as a result."

Then he took it and hung it at his neck, [63] saying to Galahad, "My lord, if you please, I'd like you to await me here until we see what may come of this adventure. If harm comes to me from this shield, I'd like you to try it, for I know well that you won't fail."

"I'll await you willingly," said Galahad.

The monks gave Bademagu a squire who would accompany him, take the shield if Bademagu could not bear it, and return to the abbey with it.

How King Bademagu was wounded.

Thus Galahad remained, and Yvain with him, and King Bademagu rode away. After they had gone as much as two leagues, they saw coming out from the direction of a hermitage a knight with white armor. He came on toward King Bademagu as fast as his horse could bring him, his lance under his arm. The king, who saw him coming, turned toward him and broke his lance on him, but the knight, catching Bademagu in an unshielded spot, struck him so hard that he broke through his hauberk and put the point of his lance through under his right shoulder, throwing him to the ground.

Then he dismounted, took the shield from him, got back on his horse, and said to him, "You were very foolish, knight, when you took this shield, for it is granted only to one single man, and he must be the best knight in the world. He who takes vengeance sent me here to take vengeance on you for the great sin you committed."

After he had said this to King Bademagu, he turned to the squire and said to him, "Take this shield, and bear it to the servant of Jesus Christ, the one they call

Galahad. Tell him that the High Master commands him to bear it, for it will always be as fresh and beautiful as it is now, and this is a great thing, because of which one should love it greatly. Greet him on my behalf."

"My lord," said the squire, "who are you?"

"This you may not know now or later," said the knight.

The squire said, "Since you won't tell me your name, I ask you, by the thing you love most in the world, to tell me the truth about the shield and who brought it to this land, for I've never seen a knight hang it at his neck without harm coming to him."

"Now you've asked me in such terms," said the knight, "that I'll tell you, but I won't tell you alone. I want you to bring here the knight to whom you are to take the shield, and [65] I'll tell you in front of him, and tell him from me that if he wants to know the truth, he should come speak with me, for he'll certainly find me here."

Then the squire went to King Bademagu and asked him if he was badly* wounded.

"I think I'm mortally wounded," said the king.

"Can you ride?" asked the squire.

"I'll try," he said, "for only harm can come to me from staying here."

Then he stood up the best he could and got on his horse with great difficulty, with the squire behind him to hold him.

How the squire gave the shield to Galahad.

Thus they left that field and returned to the abbey, where the monks took King Bademagu, carried him to a room, and busied themselves with treating his wound, which was very large.

Galahad asked a monk who was treating Bademagu's wound, "Do you think he can be healed? Indeed, it would be a great pity if he died for such an adventure, for I've heard him highly praised for breeding and for knighthood."

"My lord," said the monk, "have no fear that he will die. In any case, no one should be sorry for him, for we told him that if he took the shield he'd receive harm from it."

Then the squire came to Galahad and said to him in the presence of everyone there, "My lord, the good knight of the white armor sends you greetings. He says to tell you that he sends you this shield and that you must bear it, for he says there is no one in the world now who deserves it as much as you. And he says that if you want to know where the shield comes from and how many marvels have come of it, come to him, and he'll tell you. And I'll take you where he is."

When the monks heard this, they bowed deeply to Galahad and said, "Praised be this news, and praised be God, who brought him here, for now we know that by this man the marvelous adventures of the Kingdom of Logres will be accomplished."

Yvain the Bastard said, "Sir Galahad, hang this shield at your neck. Thus my wish will be to some extent fulfilled, for, so help me God, I never desired anything so much as to see the Good Knight who is to be lord of this shield."

---

* "badly" added by Bogdanow 1991 (68).

Galahad said he would do it, since they sent it to him, but that first he wanted to have his armor, and they brought it to him. After he was armed and mounted on his horse and had hung his shield at his neck, he commended the monks to God and rode away. Yvain the Bastard, who was already armed and ready to mount, said he would keep him company; Galahad [67] thanked him warmly but said that he did not want anyone with him except the squire and the hermit.

Without fail, the hermit followed him always, sometimes closely, sometimes at a distance, and told him each day the lives of the Holy Fathers and the old stories. He told Galahad where he was from and of which lineage and of which knights, and he told him about Joseph and King Mordrain and Nascien, what kind of men they were and what kind of knights and with what kind of love Our Lord loved them. This was the thing that Galahad heard most gladly in the world and that most comforted him, and he had such a great desire to hear it that nothing in the world pleased him so much.

*How the knight** told Sir Galahad the truth about the shield.*

When Galahad arrived at the hermitage where the knight with the white armor was awaiting him, the squire who accompanied him said to Galahad as soon as he saw the knight, "My lord, you see there the knight who sent you the shield."

The knight, as soon as he saw Galahad, came out to meet him and greeted him, and Galahad did the same to him.

"My lord," said the squire, "now tell Sir Galahad what you said you would tell him in my presence."

"With great pleasure," he said, "for there's no one in the world to whom I should tell it more willingly than to him, for he is now the Chosen One, who has no peer among all the knights who now live or who have lived for a long time." Then he said to Galahad, "Know that the squire asked me to let you know the truth about this shield and why so many marvels have come from it to those who, because of their foolish boldness, against Our Lord's prohibition, hung it at their necks— why so many misfortunes have come to them, as they know in this land. All this he asked me to tell you, for it is not right that anyone else know it before you, but since you've come here, I'll tell you in his presence and that of this hermit who accompanies you and who has already told you a part of it."

"My lord," said Galahad, "indeed, this is something I've wanted to know."

"Then I'll tell it to you," said the knight, "everything just as it happened."

Then he began to tell it to him just the way the book will now tell it to you.

How the white knight told Galahad about his lineage.

"Galahad," he said, "it happened, a long time ago now, that sixty-two years after the death of Jesus Christ, Joseph of Arimathea came to the city of Sarras,† just as the High Master arranged it according to His will. When he arrived at the city [69] of Sarras with his kin, who were then newly servants and disciples of Jesus Christ, the

---

*   Corrected by translator; all three texts have "hermit."

†   Sarras is the city to which Galahad, Bors, and Perceval will take the Holy Grail when it leaves Britain (see chapters 151-152).

king of the city, whose name was Evelac and who was then a pagan, received them well. The king was then sad and troubled about Tolomer, a neighboring king, richer and more powerful than he was, who was making war on him, and he would easily have been defeated, for his men were failing him, had it not been for Josephus, Joseph's son, who said to him,

"'King Evelac, if you will believe me, I'll advise you in such a way that you will rejoice over all your enemies. And what is more, I'll make you win never-ending joy.'

"The king was happy at this news and asked him what sort of man he was.

"'I am a Christian,' said Josephus.

"When the king heard this, he was amazed, and he commanded them to call his priests at once, so that they might debate with him about the law of the Christians. When they were assembled, Josephus, who, inspired by the Holy Spirit, spoke eloquently,* defeated them all, so that there was no one else there who spoke. When the king saw Josephus so wise, he believed.

"And when it happened that the king wanted to go against Tolomer, who was entering into his land, Josephus said to him, 'King, have your shield brought to me.'

"The king had it brought at once. Josephus took a piece of red silk, made a cross of it, and nailed it to the shield with good, little nails.

"Then he said to the king, 'Do you see this sign?'

"'Yes,' he said, 'it's very good.'

"'Indeed,' said Josephus, 'There's no peril in the world from which he who perfectly believes in this sign may not escape, because we pray to this sign. Therefore, I want you to bear it. When you are in such peril that you don't think you can ever escape, then uncover it and say, "God, who received death on this sign, return me whole and happy to receive Your grace," and know truly that, if you call on Him with a good heart, you won't die but will have joy and honor.'

"Then Josephus covered the shield with a cloth."

How Evelac saw the test of the shield and how he captured Tolomer.

"Then the king believed that Josephus might well be telling the truth, and although he still had some doubts, he had the shield carried with him to the battle he was to have with Tolomer. He left Sarras and went against Tolomer, and the two nations joined battle. It happened that Evelac was defeated and captured and taken toward a forest where those who had captured him wanted to kill him. When Evelac saw himself being taken away from his people, he thought he would never be able to escape if those who had taken him were to put him in the forest. Then he removed from the shield the cloth with which it was covered. He saw on the cross [71] an image of the Crucified, and it seemed to him that drops of blood fell from His feet and hands. When he saw this, he felt in his heart wondrously great pity for him. Then he said in his heart, 'Lord God, who received death on this sign, make me return whole and happy to my city, that I may receive Your holy faith and that others may know from me that You are truthful and powerful in all things.'

---

*   Could also be translated, "who spoke eloquently about the Holy Spirit."

"By these words I tell you," said the white knight to Galahad, "was King Evelac delivered from the peril he was in, for Our Lord sent me there to help him, and I helped him so well, with the power that He who sent me there gave me, that I freed him from those who held him prisoner, and as a result of what I did there, Tolomer was captured and all his people destroyed.'"*

How Evelac defeated his enemies.

"After King Evelac defeated his enemies, he returned to Sarras and received baptism because of the great miracles Our Lord had shown him, for he saw that a knight who had had his arm cut off was healed at once as soon as he touched the shield. And yet another marvel happened, for the cross disappeared from the shield and appeared on the knight's arm. When the king saw this, he ordered the shield well guarded, for he was deeply moved by the miracles Our Lord was showing him by its means. And later, when he came to this land and delivered Joseph from prison, he went with Josephus, Joseph's son, for whom Our Lord worked a wondrously good miracle."

How the knight told Galahad how the cross was made on the shield.

"After Evelac had stayed in this land a great while with Josephus, the latter had to end his life. When the king saw that Josephus was to die, he begged him in God's name to leave something by which he would remember him always.

"'King,' said Josephus, 'have brought to me, then, your shield, on which you saw the sign of the True Crucified, by which you were saved from Tolomer's hands.'

"The king had the shield brought. At the very moment that they brought the shield into Josephus's presence, so much blood flowed from his nostrils that they could not stanch it. Josephus took the shield and with his blood made this cross on it, just as you see it now, and this is the shield about which I am telling you.

"And after he had made the cross, just as you can still see it, he gave the shield to the king and said to him, 'You see here the memento that [73] I leave you of myself, for you know well that this cross is made of my blood. Know that it will always be as fresh and red as you see it now, as long as this shield lasts, and it will last no little time, because harm will come to every knight who hangs it at his neck until the coming of the Good Knight, Galahad, last of Nascien's line, who will hang it at his neck. Therefore, I tell you that no one will be so bold as to hang it at his neck except the one to whom Our Lord has granted it. And just as more marvels will come from this shield than from another, so there will be more skill at arms and holy living in the one who is to bear it than in another knight.'

"'Since it is so,' said the king, 'and you're leaving such a good memento of yourself, tell me, if you please, where shall I leave the shield? For I would very gladly have it put in such a place that the Good Knight will find it when he comes.'

---

*   For an expanded version of these events, see *The History of the Holy Grail* chapters 8-10.

"'I'll tell you how to do it,' said Josephus. 'Where you see that Nascien has himself put at his death, leave the shield there. And the Good Knight will come there promptly on the fifth day after he receives the order of chivalry.'

"And so it happened," said the white knight to Galahad, "that on the fifth day after you became a knight, you came to this monastery where Nascien lies, and you found the shield here. Now I've told you why the great and terrible adventures happened to the knights who, through their foolish boldness, against this prohibition, wanted to take the shield that was granted only to you."

How the squire asked Galahad to make him a knight.

As soon as he had told Galahad this, he disappeared in such a way that Galahad never knew what had become of him or in which direction he had gone.

When the squire, who was beside Galahad and had heard all this, saw that he who had told it all to them had disappeared, he dismounted, went and fell on his knees before Galahad, and said to him, weeping, "Oh, my lord, I beg you, for the love of that Lord whose sign you bear on your shield and who received death on that sign, to receive me as your squire and to make me a knight."

"Friend," said Galahad, "if I wanted the company of a squire, I would not refuse yours, but the fact is that I have sent my squires away from me because I don't want anyone's company, except by chance, if I find myself with someone so that I can't do anything about it."

"My lord," he said, "make me a knight, for God's sake, for I tell you truly, not to praise myself but to follow God, that, with God's help, knighthood will be well [75] used by me, according to the strength and courage that are in me, and God, of His goodness, will make me do my deeds well."

81. GALAHAD RETURNS TO THE ABBEY AND DRIVES A DEMON OUT OF A GRAVE.*

How Galahad granted the squire's request.

Galahad looked at the squire and saw him weeping as hard as if he saw the man he loved most in the world dead before him, and he was seized with great pity. Therefore, he agreed to make him a knight.

"My lord," said the squire, "since you have agreed to make me a knight, I ask you to take me back to the abbey, for there I'll have horse and arms, but return there not so much for my sake as to see an adventure that you'll think the greatest marvel you ever saw, and I think you'll accomplish it, for there has never been a knight who could accomplish it. Therefore, it would be well for you to return there."

---

* Corresponds to Magne I:75-83; Bogdanow 1991 77-85; Piel 38-42.

Galahad said he would go with a good heart. Then they returned to the abbey. The monks came out to meet them and received them well, asking the squire why the knight had returned. He said that Galahad was returning to make him a knight and to see the adventure there. As soon as Galahad had dismounted, he asked if he could see the adventure.

"My lord," said a good man, "you may certainly see it, and you never heard of such a marvel. For a long time there has been near here a graveyard where lie the bodies of many good and holy men. It happened that a pagan was buried there, the falsest knight anyone ever saw in Britain and the most devilish person in the world. As soon as he was buried, everyone in this abbey immediately saw devils over his grave, and a voice began to come out of it, so evil that anyone who heard it would lose consciousness for a long time. Because of this marvel, many good men came here on many occasions, and there was never one of them who didn't suffer great harm, for, as soon as he heard the voice, he had no power to raise himself from the spot. There were some who died here, and some who lived—but these were few."

"I want to see that grave," said Galahad.

The monk said he would show it to him. He took him out of the apse of the church, and they passed through a graveyard.

Then he showed him a tall tree standing in a large, uncultivated field and said to him, "Under that tree is the grave from which comes the voice, such that any man who hears it loses consciousness and remains unconscious forever, and if you want to go there and God wants you to be able to raise the stone, you will find some marvel there under it, which is a very great truth." [77]

How Galahad achieved the adventure of the monastery.

After this Galahad waited no longer but went quickly to the grave. As soon as he reached it, he heard a voice amazingly full of sorrow, and it said, "Oh, Galahad, servant of Jesus Christ, don't come near me, for you'll make me leave this place, where I've been until now."

Although Galahad heard this, he was not frightened, being stronger than any other knight, and he went to the grave and tried to raise the stone. He saw smoke come out, as black as pitch, then a flame, then a figure in the semblance of a man, the ugliest and strangest thing a man ever saw, and he crossed himself, for it certainly seemed to him a thing of the devil.

Then he heard a voice, which said to him, "Oh, Galahad, I see something holy in you; I see you encircled with angels, so that I cannot stand against you. Therefore, I leave you my place, in which I have rested for a long time."

When he heard the voice, he thanked Jesus Christ fervently, and he crossed himself and cast the stone far from the grave. He saw lying in the grave the body of a knight, fully armed with a sword beside him and everything necessary to a knight except horse and lance.

When he saw this, he called the monks and said to them, "Come see what I've found here, and tell me what to do with it, for I'll do more here if I should."

They came and saw the body lying in the grave, and they said, "My lord, you've done enough here. It isn't necessary for you to do any more, for we don't think this body will be moved from here."

"Yes, it will be," said an old man who was there. "This man must be removed from this grave, for such a false and evil body as this was shouldn't lie in blessed, consecrated ground."

"Friends," asked Galahad, "have I done all I should about this adventure?"

"Yes, my lord," they said, "for that voice from which so much harm has come won't ever be heard again."

"And what may be the significance of this voice and this adventure?" asked Galahad. "For it couldn't be without great significance."

"My lord," said a good, old man, "I'll tell you, and you should certainly hear it, for it's a marvelous thing."

How Galahad made Meleagant a knight.

Then they left the grave and returned to the monastery. Galahad said to the squire, "Friend, since you'll become a knight tomorrow, keep vigil tonight according to the true custom." [79] The squire did just as Galahad commanded and instructed him.

The good man took Galahad to a room, had him disarmed, then had him lie down on the bed and said to him, "My lord, you asked me for the significance of this adventure that you brought to a conclusion today. I'll tell you gladly. There were three problematic things in this adventure. One was the stone of the grave, which wasn't easy to raise; the second was the knight's body; the third was the voice, such that everyone who heard it lost consciousness and the strength of his body and his limbs. I'll tell you the significance of these three things."

Significance of the stone.

"Know that the stone that covered the grave stood for the hard hearts that Our Lord found in the world when He came here, for He found only hard hearts in the world. It was very apparent, for son didn't love father nor father son, and for this reason they were all going to hell. When the Father of the heavens saw that there was such great hardness of hearts in the world, that men wouldn't heed the words of the prophets, and that they made themselves new gods, He sent His Son into the world, so that the great obduracy of their hearts might be softened and* to renew men's hearts and make them obedient. After He came into the world, He found the hearts so hard and so wrapped up in mortal sins that it was as hard for Him to turn them to Himself as it would be for a man to soften a large stone. Wherefore He said through the mouth of His prophet David, 'I am alone in my Passion,' which is as much as to say, 'Father, I will have converted a very small part of this obdurate

---

*   "He sent His Son ... softened" as in Bogdanow 1991 (81) and Piel (40). Magne has "He sent His Son, who could soften that great obduracy of their hearts, into the world ..."

people before my death.' Now it happened that that sending, in which the Father sent His Son onto the earth to deliver the people, is now renewed. For just as strife and folly fled at His coming and the truth was known through Him, in the same way Our Lord has chosen you over all other knights, to send you through strange lands, to undo serious adventures, and to make known how they came about and in what manner they were begun. And therefore one should see your coming as figuring Jesus Christ's in semblance, but not in degree. And just as the prophets, a long time before the coming of Jesus Christ, prophesied His coming and that He [81] would deliver the people from the pains of hell, so the holy hermits and many good men as well prophesied your coming a long time before you came. And all have certainly said that the adventures of the kingdom of Logres would never end until you came. And we have awaited you, and now, thanks be to God, we have you."

Significance of the knight; what he stood for.

"Now tell me," said Galahad, "what do you say about the knight? For you've already shown me clearly what the gravestone stood for."

"I'll tell you," said the good man. "The body of the knight makes us think of the people, who for a long time had lived under this hardness of heart, so that they were killed and damned for many mortal sins that they had brought on themselves and increased from day to day. And it certainly appeared that they were all damned when Jesus Christ came on earth. For when they saw the King of Kings and the Savior of the world come among them, they didn't know Him, but they thought Him a sinner and such as they were, and they believed in the voice of the devil more than in other speech, and they put His flesh to death on the commandment of him who has commanded all evil: the devil, who was at their ear all day. For that reason, they committed a deed for which later Vespasian disinherited and destroyed them, as soon as he knew the truth about that prophet whom they had put to death so treacherously. Thus they were all killed and damned, because they believed the advice of the enemy. Now we must understand how this present manifestation and that earlier one are similar. This stone here stands for the great hardness of the hearts that Jesus Christ found in the Jews; and the knight's body stands for the Jews and all their descendants, for they all died for their mortal sins, which they couldn't give up. The voice that came out of the grave stands for the dolorous words they said to Pilate, when they said, 'Let His blood be on us and on our sons.' Because of these words, they were lost and destroyed, and they were unbelievers for all time."

Significance of the knight in terms of the Passion of Jesus Christ.

"Thus you can see in this adventure a figuration of the Passion of Jesus Christ and a reminder [83] of His holy life. And something else happened here on many occasions, for knights errant came here and wanted to enter the grave, and the devil, knowing them for sinners wrapped up in their sins, frightened them so with the terrible cry he uttered that they lost the power of their bodies and their limbs, and this force they lost they could never recover."[*]

But Robert de Boron did not dare translate this from Latin into French, because he did not want to reveal the secrets of the Holy Church, for it is not right that a layman know them. And, for another thing, he feared to reveal the secrets of the[†] quest for the Holy Grail, just as the true Latin history tells it, lest men of little knowledge, in reading it, fall into error and contempt for the faith. Because of this, it might happen that his book would be forbidden, so that no one would make use of it or read it, which he did not want. Therefore, he promised that a third part of his book would report the quest for the Holy Grail, the knightly deeds and exploits that the knights of the Round Table did on that quest, and the marvels they found there, and how the Holy Grail went away from England to the city of Sarras. And may everyone know that what is not appropriate, he does not want to tell, for he would be blamed by the Holy Church. But whoever wants to know that, let him try to see the book in the Latin, which will make him understand and know completely the marvels of the Holy Grail. For we must respect the secrets of the Holy Church; nor will I say more, if I can help it, than what is appropriate to the story, for it is not right for a man to reveal the secrets of the High Master.

82. GALAHAD KNIGHTS MELEAGANT, WHO IS WOUNDED.[‡]

How Meleagant asked to accompany Galahad.

After that man had explained to Galahad the significance of the adventure he had accomplished, Galahad said it was much the best explanation he had ever heard. That night the brothers served him well, for they respected and loved him. Before the hour of prime, Galahad made the squire a knight, just as the custom was at that time. Then he asked him his name, and the squire said his name was Meleagant and that he was son of the King of Denmark.[§]

"Friend," said Galahad, "since you come from such a noble line,[¶] take care to use knighthood well, so that you advance the honor of your lineage. Indeed, when a king's son reaches the age to receive the order of chivalry, he should surpass all other knights in knightly skill and prowess, just as a ray of the sun surpasses the stars."

---

[*]   All three editors run the text on at this point, as if what follows were part of the monk's explanation to Galahad.

[†]   "the secrets of" added by Bogdanow 1991 (84).

[‡]   Corresponds to Magne I:83-95; Bogdanow 1991 85-96; Piel 42-48.

[§]   "of Denmark" added by Bogdanow 1991 (85). This person is not to be confused with Meleagant, son of Bademagu in the Vulgate (see *Lancelot,* chapter 76). In the Post-Vulgate, Bademagu's son is not named (see chapter 113).

[¶]   "come from such a noble line" as in Bogdanow 1991 (85). Magne has "have great knowledge."

Meleagant said that he would not diminish the honor of his lineage, for, whatever physical labor he had to undertake, he would not fail to be a good knight. [85] Then Galahad asked for Meleagant's arms, so he could leave. They brought them to him, and he armed Meleagant.

Meleagant said to him, "Galahad, my lord, you've made me a knight, through your grace and God's. Because of that, I have such great pleasure in my heart that I could hardly tell it to you. For, without question, the best knight in the world has given me arms. You know the custom, that he who makes a new knight can't excuse himself from granting a favor, if he sees that it's right."

"That's true," said Galahad.

"Then, my lord," he said, "I ask you by your mercy to let me go with you on this quest until chance separates us, and if chance keeps us together, not to take your company from me."

Galahad granted him that gladly. Then he asked for his own arms and, after he was armed, mounted his horse and commended the monks to God. They rode that day and the next without finding an adventure. Thus on Monday morning it happened that they arrived at a cross where two roads diverged. That cross stood at the edge of a large field.

The cross was made of very old wood, and they found on it letters that said, LISTEN, KNIGHT ERRANT, YOU WHO GO SEEKING ADVENTURE. HERE ARE TWO ROADS, ONE TO THE RIGHT AND THE OTHER TO THE LEFT. THE ONE ON THE LEFT I FORBID TO YOU, FOR HE WHO WOULD TAKE IT MUST BE AN ESPECIALLY GOOD KNIGHT, FOR IF HE IS NOT GOOD HE CANNOT COME OUT OF IT WITHOUT GREAT HARM. I DO NOT SAY AS MUCH TO YOU ABOUT THE ONE ON THE RIGHT, FOR THERE IS NOT SO MUCH PERIL THERE; NEVERTHELESS, IF YOU TAKE IT AND ARE NOT A GOOD KNIGHT, YOU WILL ACCOMPLISH NOTHING THERE.

When Meleagant saw the letters, he said to Galahad, "My lord, of your courtesy, let me have this road on the left, for, if you please, I want to see if there's anything in me for which I should have a reputation for chivalry."

"Indeed," said Galahad, "I would go that way, for I'd know better how to bring some adventure to an end. I think I'd pass that way more easily than you."

But Meleagant said that he wanted to go that way anyway, and Galahad agreed, since the young man begged very hard for it. Then they embraced each other, commended each other to God, and parted, and each went his own way.

But now the story stops speaking about Sir Galahad and turns to Meleagant.

The story tells that Meleagant left Galahad and rode for a while until he had passed through that field and reached an ancient forest, which was two days' journey across. He rode through it until he reached a river bank, where he found many huts constructed and two beautiful tents erected, well [87] made of red silk. In the middle between the tents there was a beautiful, rich chair, and on that chair sat an old man. I do not know if he was a knight or not, but he had a crown of gold, as beautiful and rich as if it had been made for some emperor. Know that he was sleeping as hard as if he had never slept before, but there was nobody with him nor any other thing except the tents. When Meleagant saw this, he approached the chair, just as he was on horseback, and it seemed to him the most beautiful he had ever seen. When he saw that the good man was sleeping, he wondered how he could wake him up, for it would have pleased him greatly to know about him before he left.

He said in a loud voice, "Friend, my lord, who are you? Tell me, if you please."

The man replied nothing at all. Meleagant called again in a louder voice than before, but the old man was sleeping so hard that he did not wake.

Then Meleagant said to himself, "Oh, God! What if this man is a king? I never saw a king sleep like that, and because of the fault I see in him, I want to take his crown from him, for I don't think this man was ever king except of sleep."

Then he took the crown from him and put it on his left arm, and he left him sleeping and rode through the forest as fast as his horse could go.

How Meleagant took the crown and how he took the maiden from Amador of the Lovely Home.

As Meleagant was going through the forest, he came upon a maiden making a great lamentation over a knight who had been wounded shortly before. The maiden was very beautiful, and Meleagant was pleased with her and asked her why she made such a great lamentation for this knight. She said that another knight had just wounded him mortally, so that he could not ride and get out of that forest.

Meleagant said to her, "My lady, the knight is dead, and you can't take him away. It would be better for you to leave him and go to some place of safety, for I know that if you stayed here in this forest, harm could soon come to you."

"My lord," she said, "I'll do great wrong by leaving him. I'll do it reluctantly, for he loved me very much, but since only harm would come to me from staying, and no good would come to him, I'll go with you, for I'm afraid to wander lost through this forest." [89]

"My lady," he said, "I'll guide you and bring you to safety."

"My lord," she said, "if I knew that, I'd go with you, for I see clearly that I can have no help for this knight."

Then Meleagant said, "He seems to me near to death, but his soul is still in him."

Then the damsel went to her palfrey, which she had tied to a tree, and mounted, leaving the knight's horse beside him, for he was still holding it by the reins, and he had his shield and lance beside him. He was not so badly wounded that he could not still recover, if he had someone to treat him, for Bors of Gaunes had certainly struck him so hard that he lay unconscious, but the wound was not so large. The knight heard clearly everything Meleagant and the maiden said, and he knew that the knight with whom she was going away was not Bors. He was deeply aggrieved that the girl had left him so quickly, before she knew if he was dead.

How Amador followed Meleagant.

Then he got up from where he lay, laced on his helmet, wiped his eyes, which were full of blood, and armed himself the best he could, being a man of strength and courage, got on his horse, and went after Meleagant to avenge himself.

He caught up with Meleagant and called to him, "You'll have to give up the maiden, for it was an evil hour in which you saw her."

Then he lowered his lance. When Meleagant saw him coming, he put the crown in a tree, turned toward the knight, and struck him so hard that he put his lance through him, and the knight, who was very strong, struck Meleagant so hard that he broke through his shield and hauberk and put the point of the lance into his left side. They fell to the ground so badly wounded that they both required rest and someone to treat them.

Then the knight picked himself up, for he was strong of heart, and when he saw that he was mortally wounded, he took his sword, went to the maiden, and said to her, "I'm dying because of you, and it's right that you die because of me, for otherwise my death would be poorly avenged."

Then he raised the sword and cut off her head. After he had done this, he had not enough strength to get on his horse or go to Meleagant but fell to the ground so badly wounded that he doubted he would recover.

But now the story leaves off speaking about Meleagant and turns back to Galahad.

When Galahad had parted from Meleagant, he went all that day without finding an adventure worth the telling. That night he arrived at the house of a widow who lived in the middle of a forest, and she lodged him very well. [91] That night the hermit told him the lives and deeds of his ancestors, how they were loyal servants* of Jesus Christ and the great love Jesus Christ showed them because of their service. In the morning he heard Mass and took leave of the lady, mounted, and rode until midday.

Then he met a maiden riding on a black palfrey, and she asked him, "My lord, are you a knight errant?"

"Yes, my lady, I am. Why do you ask?"

"Because of a great marvel," she said, "which I will now tell you about, which I found just now in this forest."

"What marvel is that?" asked Galahad.

"Just now I found two dead knights and a young lady with her head cut off, and all three lay in the middle of the road. If you want to go along this road by which I've come, it will take you to them."

"Is it far?" he asked.

"No," she said, "it isn't more than three bowshots."

How Galahad found Meleagant wounded.

Then Galahad went toward where the maiden had told him and found what he was seeking. When he recognized Meleagant, he was very sad, for he thought that he was dying, and he dismounted and asked him how he was feeling.

---

* "servants" added by Bogdanow 1991 (91) and Piel (45).

Meleagant raised his head, happy to see him, and said, "Oh, my lord Sir Galahad, you are welcome. For God's sake, take me to some abbey where I may have the rites of the Holy Church, for I know well that I'm mortally wounded."

"That grieves me greatly," said Galahad. "Who wounded you this way?"

"My lord," he said, "that knight who lies there, and I believe that he's badly hurt, as badly as I am or worse."

"And that maiden—who killed her?" asked Galahad.

"That knight, because she was coming with me," he said.

Then Galahad went to the knight and took off his helmet, for he wanted to know who he was, if he could.

After he had taken off the helmet and iron cap, the knight opened his eyes, which were full of blood, and spoke to Galahad: "Who are you, who take off my helmet?"

"But who are you," asked Galahad, "who were so cruel to this young lady?"

"I did less than I should have done, for I'm dying, and because of my death many will be very sad."

"Who are you?" asked Galahad. "By chance are you of King Arthur's house or of the Round Table?"

"Yes, I am," he said, "and I started with the others on the quest for the Holy Grail; but because of my sins this happened to me, and I'm dying; may God give better fortune to the others than He gave to me."

When Galahad heard that he was of the Round Table, he was very sad, afraid [93] the knight might be of his own kindred, King Ban's line.

Therefore, he asked him, "What's your name?"

The knight said, "My name is Amador of the Lovely Home."

Galahad knew that this was the last knight who had started on the quest for the Holy Grail, and his death grieved him deeply, for he had heard him praised a great deal in the court for knighthood and courtesy.

He said, "Amador, I'm sorry about your death, for you were a good knight."

As Galahad was saying this, Amador stiffened in his death agony, saying, "Oh, Jesus Christ, Father of Pity, look not at my sins but, as a father has pity on his son, if he goes astray, have pity on me as Your creature and Your son, however much of a sinner I may be."

Then he lay a great while, and Galahad was so sad that he began to weep.

Amador spoke to him again, "Holy creature, holy knight, pray for me to the King of Kings, that He may have mercy on such a sinner as I am, for I'm certain that, if you ask it, He'll have mercy on me, for He receives the petitions of the just."

As soon as he had said this, his soul went out of his body. When Galahad saw that he was dead, he took off his own helmet and kissed him, and he did this because he was of the Round Table.

When he saw that Amador was dead, he closed the man's mouth; then he went to Meleagant and asked him what he should do for him.

"My lord," said Meleagant, "take me to an abbey near here, and if I am to die, may I die there rather than in the wilderness, and if I am to recover, I'll be healed quickly."

Then Galahad disarmed him, drew the lance point out of the wound, and bandaged him the best he could. As he was trying to get him on the horse, Yvain the Bastard arrived. As soon as he saw Galahad, he recognized him, went to him and greeted him, and asked him who had killed the knight and the girl. Galahad told him the truth as it had happened.

Yvain marveled and was sorry about the knight, and he said, "Indeed, King Arthur will be sad when he knows about the death of this knight, for, unquestionably, Amador was one of the most famous knights for skill at arms in the court of King Arthur."

Galahad said, "Now I'm more grieved by his death than before, for all men should grieve at the death of a good man and, moreover, for such a good knight as this one and because he was a companion of the Round Table."

How Galahad defended Meleagant against the knights.

As they were saying this, suddenly two armed knights rode up and asked which was the knight who bore the white shield with the red band.

Galahad said, "Here he is," [95] and he pointed to Meleagant, who was there.

The knights said, "We're looking for him because he has done us so much wrong that if he isn't dead we'll kill him."

"Really?" said Galahad. "Indeed, you won't, for I'll defend him the best I can."

Then he drew his sword, and they, seeing him on foot, said to him, "Knight, you are mad, deliberately trying to kill yourself. Do you think you can oppose us, we on horseback and you on foot?"

Galahad made no reply to what they had said. He struck the first one he came to so hard that he cut through his hauberk and cut off his leg at the thigh, so that his body fell on one side and his leg on the other. When the other knight saw this blow, he had no heart to await Galahad; moreover, he saw that it would certainly be folly to await a blow from a man who struck like that. He went to the crown, which he saw hanging in the tree, took it, turned, and began to ride away as fast as he could.

Galahad put Meleagant on his horse and then, riding behind him, took him to the house of a religious order, which stood in a valley and was surrounded by moats and stone walls because they were afraid of robbers, of which there were many in the forest. Yvain the Bastard did the same to Amador of the Lovely Home, for he brought him to that place in order to have him buried in consecrated ground. They left the maiden, because they could not carry her, and the story speaks no more of her, but it says of the knight that he was buried and his name written on the headstone.

Galahad asked the monks if there was anyone there who knew how to heal wounds.

"Yes, my lord, there is," they said, and they brought an old man, who had been a knight. At once he looked at Meleagant and told him that, with God's help, he would heal him quickly. Galahad was very happy and stayed there three days after that.

83. GALAHAD AND YVAIN THE BASTARD ARE GUESTS OF DALIDES'S FATHER; DALIDES AND HIS FATHER KILL THEMSELVES.*

How Galahad and Yvain the Bastard were guests of the lord of the castle.

After Galahad had left Meleagant, it happened that he arrived at a castle that stood on a mountain, for the road went that way, and Yvain the Bastard was traveling with him.

When they started up the castle road, suddenly an old knight, who was lord of that castle, came to them and said, "My lords, are you knights errant?"

"Yes," they said, "but why do you ask?"

"I ask," he said, "for your honor and benefit. Since you are knights errant, I beg you to be my guests. Know that you'll be honored and served to the best of my ability, as if you were in King Arthur's house." [97]

"My lord," they said, "we won't stay with you, but we commend you to God, and we thank you very much for all you have said to us."

"What?" he said, "do you intend to go away so casually that you won't stay one night with me? May God never help me if that happens, for it would be my shame and dishonor. You show clearly that you don't respect me, when you won't do what I ask you in my own castle."

When they saw that he held them in such great esteem, they did not know how to excuse themselves from him, and they had to grant him what he wanted.

How they went with the lord of the castle and saw Dondinel prisoner.

Then the lord of the castle took them to the fortress. They dismounted, and he had them disarmed, and he did them so much honor that they marveled at it.

He said to them, "My lords, if I take pleasure in your company and honor you, don't be surprised, for, indeed, I do it with a good heart, and I should certainly do it, for I have a son who is a knight errant. I myself was King Pellinor's companion, in his time the best knight I knew in the kingdom of Logres or any other place, but with all this I have a son who is a knight errant, who pleases me more than anything else in the world."

They asked his son's name.

---

*   Corresponds to Magne I:95-109; Bogdanow 1991 97-107; Piel 48-55.

"My lords," he said, "his name is Dalides. I don't know if you know him."

Galahad said he did not know him, but Yvain the Bastard said he knew him well, for he had seen him in many places.

"What shall I tell you?" said the father. "In this land they think him a very good knight."

"Whoever said otherwise would tell a great falsehood," said Yvain the Bastard, "for, God help me, I think him one of the best knights I know, for no one has seen as much of him as I have or can say more good of him than I."

The father was happy at that, for he loved that son as much as possible. When night came, they sat down to eat in a meadow. The host entertained them well and was happy. As they were sitting talking about that knight, whom his father could not get out of his mind, suddenly a squire arrived on foot, coming quickly like a messenger.

When the good man saw him, he asked, "What news do you bring of the tournament?"

"My lord, good news."

"What?" he asked.

"My lord, your son won the tournament, so that the honor is all his from both sides."

"Praised be such news, and praised be God, who has given me such a son, who seems to me the honor and prize of chivalry." [99]

"My lord," said Galahad, "where was this tournament?"

"My lord," he said, "six leagues from here, near a castle that is called The Dark Castle, but they changed its name at the wish of Sir Lancelot of the Lake, because he accomplished an adventure at that castle."*

As he was saying this, a man came quickly and said to him, "My lord, your son is coming with a large company of knights, and he's here."

When he heard this, he went to the palace, where he found his son with a large company of knights, who were coming from the tournament with him.

The son went to his father, kissed his hand, and said to him, "My lord, you see here a knight whom I'm bringing to be your prisoner, one of those of the Round Table, with whom I fought after leaving the tournament."

How Dondinel and Dalides arrived.

The father asked him what the quarrel had been between them, and he said, "There were words between us that grieved me, for he said that the man who had won this tournament had no great skill at arms. I said to him, 'Speak no more of it,[†] for no one could do more than I did,' and he answered, 'I don't know what you did there, but I know one knight such that, if he faced four knights such as you in the field, he would defeat them in one hour of the day; this would be very quick, and I say it to you only because I know it's the truth.' When I heard this, I charged at him and did so well at arms that I defeated him, and he has given his word to me that he'll

---

*   This episode is not narrated in the Post-Vulgate as we have it.

†   "'Speak no more of it'" as in Bogdanow 1991 (100) and Piel (50). Magne has "'You would have done no more there.'"

never leave my captivity until he shows me that knight about whom he spoke so much to me."

How Dondinel told Dalides that it was Galahad.

When the father heard this, he said, "Son, son, leave this matter to me, for this knight will go with me to where there are two knights of the Round Table, who are my guests today, but not willingly."

"My lord," said his son, "do what you like with him."

His father thanked him warmly for that and then asked the knight his name.

The knight replied, "My name is Dondinel the Wild."

"In the name of God," said the host, "I've often heard of you, and you're very welcome. I've heard so much good of you that you'll find no one here who won't do you more honor than in King Arthur's house."

He thanked him for it warmly. Then squires came from all around and disarmed them, Dondinel and those who had come from the tournament with him. Then there was great joy in the palace. The lord of the [101] castle led them into the meadow where he had left Galahad and Yvain the Bastard. When they saw Dondinel, they immediately came to meet him, and they received him well.

When he saw Galahad, he said at once, "My lord, you are welcome, for you've freed me from captivity. I promised this knight, son of this good man, that I'd show him the knight of whom I had told him, and when I had done this I'd be free of captivity." Then he said to Dalides, "See here this knight, whom I said I'd show you. Now I'm free."

When Dalides heard this, he began to look hard at Galahad, and he saw him to be so young that he could not believe it was true.

Dalides said to Dondinel, "As of now I release you from captivity for the love of him of whom you have said so much good. I free you here, before him."

Dondinel thanked him for that.

How Dalides did not believe that Sir Galahad was so good.

That night there was great joy among the foreign knights and those of the castle. But however the others felt, Dalides kept watching Galahad, for he prized him for his beauty over all the knights he had ever seen, but he could not believe that he was such a good knight as Dondinel had said, for he did not have such a build or such a face.

Dalides kept saying in his heart, "So help me God, I don't see anything in him to make me think I couldn't defeat him."

Truly, Dalides* was one of the good knights of the world, and he had no bad habits, except that he thought very well of himself, so much so that he did not think there was a better knight than he in the kingdom of Logres.

The next morning Galahad went with his company to hear Mass in a chapel there. After they had heard Mass, they armed themselves and had their company

---

*   "was saying this in his heart" repeated in the text.

assemble; they commended to God the lord of the castle and his son and all his people, and they went away, riding together until adventure might part them.

How Dalides asked for his arms in order to follow Sir Galahad.

They rode out of the castle, and they were not three bowshots distant when Dalides asked for his arms. His father asked why he wanted them.

He said, "I won't for anything fail to go after Galahad, whom those other knights praised so much for his chivalry, for [103] I think they said it out of flattery, and I know there's no way he can be such a knight as they say, and* I can make them admit that what they said is a lie."

"Oh, son," said his father, "for God's sake, have pity on me, who am so old and feeble and infirm. Don't go, for I, who take pleasure in you, loving you so much, am dead if I don't see you."

"Father," said Dalides, "have no fear for me against Galahad, for I want them to cut off my head if I don't defeat him before the hour of tierce."

"Son," said his father, "you don't know Galahad as I do. Even if you were a greater and better knight than you are, you should stay, since I ask you, for you shouldn't disobey your father's command."

"My lord," said Dalides, "I wouldn't stay for anything in the world, and if you force me, I'll kill myself with my own hands."

When his father heard this, he was afraid and said, "This is bad news, for I fear that harm will come to you and to me, but since I see that it means so much to you, may God guide you."

Then they gave Dalides his arms, and, after he was armed, he parted from his father, leaving him very sad. Two knights and two squires of his father's house went with him.

How Galahad knocked down Dalides.

After they had left the castle, they rode until they caught up with Galahad. Dalides took his shield and lance, which a squire was carrying, and called to Galahad, "Galahad, defend yourself against me, for you must fight."

Galahad turned toward him and struck him so violently that he broke through his hauberk and shield and put the point of his lance through his left side, but the wound was not so great that it could not heal. After that he knocked him to the ground, for he made him fall from between the cantle and the pommel, and Dalides was thoroughly bruised by the fall. When the others saw him fall to the ground, they charged at Galahad and broke their lances on him, but they did not move him from the saddle or do him any other harm, for he was of great courage and stronger than anyone else. Galahad charged at one of them and struck him so hard that he knocked him from his horse to the ground, badly wounded, and his lance splintered. Then he drew his sword and wanted to attack the other man, who, when he saw Galahad coming and saw that he had struck two such blows, would not wait for him but began to flee toward the castle. Galahad, who had no desire to follow

---

*   "'there's no way ..., and" added by Bogdanow 1991 (102) and Piel (51).

him, turned to Dalides, who was already back on his horse. Dondinel and Yvain the Bastard would not [105] lay a hand on him, because of the honor his father had done them. When Dalides saw that one of his knights lay badly wounded, he was so sad that he wished he were dead, unless he could avenge himself.

The battle between Galahad and Dalides. *

Then Dalides drew his sword and said to Galahad, "Knight, just because you've knocked me down, I'm not, therefore, defeated. I summon you to a sword fight, and if you don't come, I won't consider you a good man."

Galahad said, "It's pointless and without profit for you to call me to battle. I see no reason for it, for I never disliked or wronged you."

Dalides said, "Either admit yourself defeated by me or defend yourself against me, for this matter won't rest here."

Then he went to Galahad and gave him the greatest blow he could, but Galahad's helmet was good, and Dalides did him no harm. Galahad, unable to get away from him, raised his sword, which was good, and struck Dalides so hard that he cut through his shield and his helmet, and Dalides, who could not endure it, fell unconscious to the ground. Blood came out of his nostrils and his mouth, for he was badly hurt by the blow and the fall.

When Dondinel saw Dalides lying on the ground, he said to Galahad, "My lord, what are you waiting for? Dismount and cut off his head and be done with him, for I never saw a more arrogant man."

Galahad said, "God willing, I won't lay a hand on him, for to kill such a knight would be the greatest iniquity in the world. But let's leave here, for I've already done more than I wanted."

"You're right," said Yvain the Bastard, "and, indeed, if you listened to Dondinel the Wild, you'd do many devilish deeds, which, God willing, you won't do."

Then all three started on their way.

How Dalides's father went after his son.

Dalides had left his father, and his father loved him very much, as a father loves a son. He grieved for him, as he should, and he did not dare reveal this to any of his vassals for fear they would think it cowardice in him, but he ordered one of his men to saddle his horse. Then he left the castle by a postern, and he did not want anyone to come with him. He found the tracks of the others and followed them.

How Dalides killed himself with his own sword.

Dalides lay unconscious a long while. Then he got up and found his companion, where he lay badly wounded, and asked him how he felt.

"My lord," he said, "I'm mortally wounded." [107]

---

* "and the knight who was with him" omitted, as the remaining companion knight does no more fighting.

"Is it so?" asked Dalides. "God help me, I'm sorry about that. Would that I were mortally wounded, for I'll never have honor in anything I do; this knight has shamed me forever. Therefore, I'd rather be dead than alive."

Then he disarmed himself, threw his weapons away, and swore that he would never bear arms again, since he had received the greatest shame he could ever have.

He began to lament loudly and said with such grief that the tears ran down his cheeks, "Friend, you and I were companions at arms; believe that I die more of grief than of wounds and that I don't want to live any more, such a great desire do I have to die. What's more, I'm badly wounded. But I ask, by the friendship we have shared, that, as soon as my soul leaves my body, you take me to the Strange Castle, which belongs to that lady I have loved, as you know." Then he drew his sword from its scabbard and said, "My lord,* for whom I have suffered so much hurt and whom I have always served since I became a knight, I ask the God of Love, as I have loved you faithfully, to put it into your heart not to forget me and to love no other after my death unless he is as good a knight as I."

Then he raised his sword and stabbed himself through the chest so that the blade appeared on the other side, and he said he would rather die thus than be dishonored a second time by one single knight. Then he fell dead to the ground.

When the other knight saw this he said, "Oh, how wretched I am! What harm and loss I have known today!" Then he fainted.

The lamentation of Dalides's father.

After this it was not long before Dalides's father arrived, but he bore no arms except a sword.

When he saw his son dead, he said, "Oh, I'm a dead man! My son is dead!"

Then he let himself fall from his horse to the ground and lay unconscious a great while. When the other knight saw him lying thus, he took off his helmet and did his best to revive him.†

When the good man recovered consciousness and saw his son dead before him, the sword stuck through him, he said, "Oh, my son! What's this I see, my lord?" At once he went to kiss him, covered with blood as he lay, and said, "Son, by God, I've guarded you poorly. Son, you were a good knight; beautiful son, handsome son, brave son, strong son, it's my fault you are dead, for if I hadn't granted you what you asked of me this morning, [109] you would even now be alive and well. This land will be diminished by your death, and it will turn to suffering and poverty, for it will have no one to defend it or maintain it in peace. Indeed, son and friend, if I live any longer after you, I will live in tears and suffering, for I have no hope of joy, since you are dead, and if I did otherwise in this situation, all the world should wish me ill and stone me for it. Therefore, it is better, oh my lord and son, for me to die immediately after you than to live a long time, for life would be grief and torture to me, and death will be rest and comfort. Moreover, son, if I die now, my soul cannot fail to be with yours, in paradise or in hell."

---

*   Although addressing his lady, he uses the masculine form. See note on p. 21.
†   "to revive him" supplied by translator.

Then he asked the knight who lay wounded, "Friend, how did my son die?"

"My lord," he said, "however he died, there's no profit to you in my telling you and none to him if you lose heart, but for God's sake I beg you not to torment yourself, to have pity on yourself, and not to think of the great loss that has come to you but to put your mind on God."

"That I can't do," said the good man, "but, for God's sake, tell me how my son died."

He begged so hard that the other agreed to tell him, just as the story has already related, how he killed himself in grief because Galahad, who was a better knight, had disgraced him, "and you may well see it by the sword with which he killed himself, for you gave it to him not long ago."

Then the father took his sword and drove it through himself and at once fell dead beside his son.

84. ADVENTURES OF GALAHAD, GAWAIN, DODINEL, BORS, AND KAY; THE BIZARRE BEAST; THE WHITE STAG.*

When the knight saw this, he said, "Oh, God! Did anyone ever see such great misfortune as for two such men to kill themselves with their own hands?"

As he was saying this, a knight arrived, fully armed, and if anyone asked me who it was, I would tell him that it was Gawain, who had gone from Pentecost until that day without finding an adventure worth the telling. When he saw the father and son lying dead and the knight wounded, he was amazed and asked the wounded man what had happened. He told Gawain everything as it had taken place, but he did not say that it was Galahad; rather he said that it was a knight who bore the white shield with the red cross.

That knight asked the other, "What is your name?" [111]

"My name is Gawain."†

"In that case," he said, "you should avenge him, for this is Dalides, one of the knights you loved most in the world, according to what you said. And this is his father, who did you much service and honor. You know well that if Dalides were just as you say, he would rather lose his head than not avenge you to his satisfaction. So help me God, this is the knight who loved you most in the world, of those who were not your kin."

When Gawain saw Dalides lying dead, he recognized him and was deeply grieved, for he loved him very much, and he asked the knight which way the one who had killed him had gone, and the knight told him. When he had heard it, Gawain waited no longer but began to ride very fast after him.

---

* Corresponds to Magne I:109-125; Bogdanow 1991 108-126; Piel 55-62.

† At this point Bogdanow 1991 (109) switches to a French fragment. The wording of this French text varies considerably from the Portuguese translation, but these variants will be noted only if used to correct Magne or if they change the story.

Here the story tells that after the three knights who were traveling together had left Dalides, when Galahad had knocked him down, they had not gone a league when they came to a forest that was a day and a half s journey across. After this they had not gone far when they came to a cross where three roads parted. Then the knights drew together to take counsel about what they would do, since they had come to three separate roads, for they had to separate because they were all three of the Quest.

While they were preparing to part, they saw the Bizarre Beast—the one King Pellinor had once hunted—come out of the underbrush, and it was the one King Arthur saw when he was sitting pensively beside the spring,* the very one that bore inside itself the dogs that barked.

When the beast came near the knights and they heard the barking, they were sure there were dogs coming after the beast, but when they listened carefully and saw that nothing was with it but that the nearer it came the nearer the barking came, they began to cross themselves in wonder, for they saw clearly that the barking was coming from inside it.

Then Galahad said, "By God, friends, this is a beautiful and marvelous adventure, and it seems to me that he would be fortunate who found out where those cries that lie hidden here are coming from."

"My lord," they said, "that is the truth."

The beast passed by them. [113]

Then Yvain the Bastard said, "Sir Galahad, I ask you, by the faith you owe to King Arthur, that you for your part let me follow this beast until I know where these cries are coming from. I assure you that I won't quit until I know the truth, if it is something I can do."

Galahad and Dodinel agreed when they saw that he had such a mind to it.

Then Yvain the Bastard said, "Now we must go by our separate roads."

How Galahad, Yvain† and Dodinel saw the white stag.

Then they embraced one another and took their leave, commending one another to God. Coming from another direction they saw a stag, white as snow, with four lions guarding it, two before and two behind.

When Dodinel and Yvain the Bastard saw this, they said to Galahad, "By God, we should certainly perceive this as one of the greatest marvels anyone ever saw, lions guarding a stag. And it seems to me that whoever wanted to have the stag would first have to kill the lions."

"So help me God," said Galahad, "that is exactly the case. I tell you truly that this is one of the adventures of the Holy Grail. You will grant me this adventure, if you please, and I will labor in it gladly. If you please, grant it to me."

"My lord, gladly," they said, "for we know well that we could not achieve it as easily as you."

* Chapter 1.
† "Yvain " added by translator.

How Galahad, Yvain, and Dodinel parted.*

After the stag had entered the forest by a narrow path, with such company as I have told you, and Galahad was preparing to leave them, they looked in another direction and saw, coming on a large horse, an armed knight, who was very large of body and bore before him a knight armed in hauberk and helmet, badly wounded with many wounds. And know that the wounded knight was of the Round Table, and his name was Asgares the Sad. He was a native of the city of Carduel and was a good knight at arms, and the man who carried him was even better. And if anyone asked me who that knight was, I would tell him that it was Tristan, nephew of King Mark of Cornwall. He had done this because he did not recognize Asgares.†

When they saw this, they said, "By good faith, we are fortunate. Here are three adventures, and we are three knights. God has shown us mercy, sending each one his own."

Dodinel said, "My lords, each of us has his adventure, and I am the third and should have [115] the third. Therefore I ask you to grant me this one." And they granted it to him.

How Galahad went after the white stag.

Then they commended one another to God and parted. Sir Yvain the Bastard went after the Questing Beast and Galahad after the stag to learn the truth about such a great marvel, and Dodinel the Wild followed Sir Tristan to take the knight from him, if he could.

But now the story leaves off speaking of Dodinel and says that when Galahad parted from Yvain the Bastard and Dodinel the Wild, he went after the stag as fast as he could in his desire to catch him. He had not gone far when he listened and heard coming after him a knight on a horse, riding as hard and making as much noise as if he were ten knights. And if anyone asked me who the knight was, I would tell him that it was Sir Gawain, who was following Galahad to avenge the death of Dalides, but Gawain did not know that it was Galahad, or he would never have meddled with him. The shield Galahad bore, which Gawain had never seen, caused Gawain to proceed against him.

How Sir Galahad wounded Gawain.

When Gawain caught up with Galahad, he called to him and said, "Faithless and brutal knight, defend yourself against me."

When Galahad heard the knight calling him faithless, he was amazed, and when he saw that he could not leave him without a fight, he turned to him and struck him so hard that neither shield nor hauberk kept him from putting the point of his lance through Gawain's left side, but he was fortunate in that the wound was not mortal. Galahad, who was of great heart and strength, knocked him to the ground so hard that Gawain could not get up. Galahad drew his lance from Gawain unbroken, and

---

*   "Yvain" added by translator.

†   There seems to be a sentence missing. We learn in the next chapter that Tristan has wounded Asgares in a fight that would not have taken place had they recognized each other.

when he did so, Gawain fainted. Galahad did not look at him again but left him lying in the road and went off after the white stag.

How Bors went after Galahad to avenge Gawain.

While Gawain was lying on his face in the road, along came Bors, who arrived there by chance. When he saw Gawain's shield, he recognized him by it and was very sad, for he had always loved him.

Bors threw his lance and shield to the ground and said in great sorrow, "Who has hurt you so?" Then he dismounted from his horse and said, [117] "My lord, Sir Gawain, how do you feel? Do you think you will recover?"

Gawain opened his eyes and did not recognize him, and asked him* who he was. "I am a friend of yours," said Bors, "who is grieved by your misfortune. For God's sake, tell me how you feel."

"And what is your name?" asked Gawain.

"I am Bors of Gaunes," he said.

"Oh, my lord, you are welcome! Indeed, I would feel neither wrong nor wound if you avenged me on the most brutal and treacherous knight in the world. He is riding along that road, and he is so near that you will catch him if you go right after him. I feel wronged less for myself than for a knight he killed who was unquestionably the best knight in this world, and his name was Dalides. I think you knew him."

"That is true," said Bors, "but if I don't avenge him, I will avenge you for the dishonor he did you. Now tell me what shield he was bearing, for I won't stop until I catch him." Gawain said that it was the white shield with the red cross.

How Sir Galahad knocked Bors down.

Bors waited no longer but took his shield and lance, got on his horse, and went along the road Gawain had shown him. He had not gone far when he caught up with Galahad near a hermitage. Galahad was riding slowly, thinking.

As soon as Bors saw the white shield and the red cross, he recognized at once that this was the knight of whom Gawain had complained, and he called to him, "Turn, sir knight. I defy you, for you have earned my mortal hatred."

When Galahad heard that he could not get away from him, he turned and struck Bors so violently that he knocked both him and his horse to the ground. Bors was badly bruised in the fall, for his horse fell on him.

How Bors followed Galahad.

After Galahad had done this, he neither looked at Bors again nor said anything to him but went off in peace after his stag. As soon as Bors's horse got up off him, he stood up at once, being of great strength and courage. After this, he got on his horse and said that he would not abandon this matter until he had avenged his and Gawain's disgrace, for if the other knight had found him inadequate with a lance, he would not think to find in the whole kingdom of Logres anyone who would wield a sword better than he.

---

*   "asked him" as in Bogdanow 1991 (117). Magne has "Bors told him."

How Sir Galahad was about to kill Bors.

After Bors got on his horse, he hurried to catch up with Galahad, [119] which he did soon, saying, Turn, knight; don't say that you have defeated me just because you have knocked me down, for that would be a double honor, but come test me with the sword, and then I will see that you are a knight."

When Galahad heard that against his will he must fight with Bors and that he could not do anything else without it being held against him, he drew his sword and said, "Knight, you wrongfully make me fight with you against my will."

Then he raised his sword and struck Bors with all his strength so hard that he cut through his shield, the pommel of his saddle, and the horse's withers, so that half the horse fell one way and half the other in the middle of the road, and Bors was left on foot, holding his naked sword and half his shield, the other half having fallen in the road.*

When Galahad had struck this blow, he said, "Knight, you're fortunate that you aren't wounded, and I, too, am fortunate, God help me, for I certainly think that you're a good knight. Now I ask you to release me and let me go, and I'll release you of whatever quarrel I have with you, which I wouldn't do if I didn't want to, since you attacked me first."

How Bors recognized Galahad.

Bors, who was so frightened by the blow that he did not know what to say, saw clearly that this was the best knight in the world and answered, "My lord, I attacked you foolishly, and I find myself the worse for it, for I see clearly that harm and shame have come to me because of it. And I see by this blow that you're the best knight I ever saw. Therefore, I'd like to ask you to tell me your name, for you may be such that I'll release you from this quarrel† or such that I won't."

"Indeed," said Galahad, "you've shown me friendship, and for this reason I want peace with you, and in order to free myself of your quarrel, I'll tell you my name: Galahad."

When Bors heard Galahad's name, he threw what remained of his shield to the ground, fell to his knees before him, and said to him, "Oh, Sir Galahad! For God's sake, forgive me, for I've wronged you only through not recognizing you."

"Who are you," asked Galahad, "that you're so distressed to have offended me?"

"I'm Bors," he said, "your father's first cousin."

When Galahad heard this, he was very happy and, dismounting from his horse, went to Bors and embraced him, saying, "My lord, you are welcome. What chance brings you here after me?"

Bors told him how he had found Gawain wounded and how he had followed Galahad to avenge Gawain.

"What," asked Galahad, "did I hurt Gawain?"

"Yes," said Bors.

---

* "and Bors was left on foot ... fallen in the road" added by Bogdanow 1991 (119).
† "from this quarrel" added by Bogdanow 1991 (120).

"Gawain attacked me wrongfully," said Galahad. "However, I'm sorry that harm came to him. If I'd recognized him, [121] I would have avoided him as much as I could. But now tell me about my father: do you know or have you heard any news of him since you left him?"

"No," said Bors.

How Kay killed the knight in Sir Galahad's presence.

As they two were talking about this, suddenly a knight came galloping toward them as fast as his horse could go.

When he reached them, he said to them, "My lords, have mercy on me and defend me against a knight who wants to kill me without any reason."

"Who is he?" they asked. "Do you know him?"

"No," he said, "but he bears a black shield with a silver lion."

They realized that it was Kay the Seneschal and answered, "We cannot support or defend you against him except by good words, for he is our companion of the Round Table."

As they were speaking, along came Kay.

Just as they were, on foot, they said to Sir Kay, "Spare this knight and do him no harm."

Kay made no reply to what they said to him but charged between them and struck the knight so hard that the lance passed through his shield and hauberk, through his body, and out the other side, and he knocked him to the ground, so badly wounded that he needed no doctor.

When Galahad saw this, he said to Bors, "Kay has mocked us by killing this man in our presence, to our disgrace and shame."

"My lord," said Bors, "we can't do anything about it, for he's our companion of the Round Table. If we lay a hand on him for anything he does to us, except in peril of death, it won't turn out well, for we'll be forsworn and false and will lose our seats at the Round Table. We have to let him go." Then he said to Kay, "You've done us a greater dishonor than we would have done to you. If you'd asked us as we asked you, we would have granted your request."

Kay, who had looked at Bors's shield, recognized him and said, "Oh, my lord, mercy, for I have wronged you greatly. God help me, I didn't recognize you; forgive me."

"Kay," they said, "we pardon you, since we can't do anything else."

Then Bors took the knight's horse, because his own horse had recently been killed, and the knight needed no horse. [123] Then they asked Kay why he had killed the knight.

How Kay told why he had killed the knight and asked who Galahad was.

Kay said, "I killed him because I found him in a valley where he would have beheaded Lucan the Wine Steward; he had wounded him badly, and he certainly

---

*   "Heading as in Piel (61). Magne has "How Sir Galahad complained of Kay, who had killed the knight."

would have cut off his head, for he hated him, if I hadn't arrived at that moment. I arrived and defeated him, just as you see. And that should please you, for by it you've gained a horse that you didn't have before."

Then he looked at the blow Galahad had inflicted on the shield and the horse and asked Bors for the truth. Bors told him everything, just as it had happened, and Kay crossed himself and said that he had never seen anything close to such a blow and that no wise man would stand to await one who gave such a blow, for that blow was not of man but of the devil. Then he asked Bors who had given him such a blow. Bors pointed out Galahad to him.

"And what's his name?" asked Kay.

Galahad, who did not want Kay to recognize him, said, "Kay, I'm a stranger and a knight, and you may not know more at this time."

"My lord," said Kay, "that grieves me, so help me God, for you're the best knight I know."

Galahad made no reply to anything Kay said, for he was very angry about the knight Kay had killed in his presence, and if it had not been for the guileless and exceedingly great love that Galahad had for Bors, the knight would certainly have been avenged at once, to Kay's loss.

How Kay went to meet Gawain.

Then Kay asked Bors, "Have you seen anyone from the Round Table, then, or have you see Sir Gawain?"

"You may find Gawain near here, for he needs your help."

Then he told Kay where to find him, and Kay got on his horse and rode to where Gawain lay, making a great lamentation. Kay dismounted from his horse near Gawain and asked him how he was feeling.

"I'd be well," said Gawain, "if I were in a place where I could have my bleeding stopped. But what have you done to the knight who did this?"

He asked this because he thought it was Bors.

Then Kay understood that Gawain did not recognize him, and he said, "My lord, I don't know what knight you mean."

Then Gawain opened his eyes, saw Kay, and said, [125] "I thought you were Bors, who left me a little while ago to go after the knight who did this to me."

"What shield did this knight bear?" asked Kay.

He told him.

"My lord," said Kay, "I found them, that knight and Bors; and don't wait for Bors to return, for he won't come here."

"Do you know who that knight is?" asked Gawain.

"No, indeed," said Kay. "Although I asked him several times, he didn't want to tell me anything about himself, and that distresses me greatly, not because of anything else so much as because of a blow that Bors told me the knight had given him." And he told him about it.

"Ah," said Gawain, "I've been deceived today. That's Galahad or Lancelot or Tristan, for there's no other knight in the world who could perform such a prodigy."

Then Kay removed Gawain's helmet, took off his hauberk, and got him to his horse the best he could. Gawain mounted with great difficulty, and Kay took his weapons and armor. They rode until they reached a monastery that King Arthur had founded when he began to reign. As soon as they arrived at the monastery, the monks came out; they welcomed Gawain and saw to his wounds.

And know that it was almost two months before he could bear arms.

85. YVAIN THE BASTARD AND GIRFLET WOUNDED BY THE KNIGHT OF THE QUESTING BEAST; DODINEL AND ASGARES THE SAD WOUNDED BY TRISTAN.[*]

But now the story leaves off talking about Galahad and turns to Yvain. Now the story tells that after Yvain the Bastard left Galahad and Dodinel to go after the Questing Beast, he rode all that day without finding an adventure worth the telling. That night he arrived at a hermit's house, where there was very little luxury. There was nothing to eat but vegetables, which the good man had gathered in the garden he kept, and he drank of the water of the spring. After Yvain had eaten of what the hermit had, the good man asked him where he was from, and Yvain told him the truth about it.

"And what adventure brings you here, to such a strange and distant place?" the good man asked.

Yvain said, "I'll tell you the truth. I've been following the Questing Beast, and I'll follow it until I know where the barking comes from; once I know what cries they are that issue from it, I won't follow it any more."

When the good man heard this, he bowed his head, and tears ran down his cheeks. When he had brooded sadly for some time, he said, "Oh, my lord, you are going to your death, for that beast you seek is a beast of the devil. That beast has done me so much harm that I will always lament it, for I had five handsome sons, the best knights in this land, and as soon as they saw the beast, just as you did, [127] they longed to know what you want to know about it, and they set out to seek it, just as you are now doing. I was then a knight errant, just as you are now, and I went with them."

How the hermit told Yvain about the marvel of the beast.

"One day it happened that we were beside a body of water, and we saw the beast totally surrounded, so that there was no way it could escape.

"The oldest of my sons was holding a lance, standing nearer to the beast than his brothers, and the youngest of my sons called to him, 'Strike! strike! And we'll see what it carries in its body, from which these cries emerge.'

---

[*]   Corresponds to Magne I:125-139; Bogdanow 1991 127-141; Piel 63-69.

"He heeded his brother and the others, who were saying the same thing, and he struck the beast through the left thigh, for he couldn't strike it anywhere else. When it felt itself stricken, it gave a frightful cry, after which there came out of the water a man blacker than pitch, with eyes red as live coals, who took the lance with which the beast had been stricken and struck the one of my sons who had struck it with such a great blow that he killed him. And the second, then the third, then the fourth, then the fifth. And then he went into the water, so that I never saw him again. This affliction about which I've told you happened to me in one hour because of that beast you are following. After I saw that there was nothing more I could do about it, I had my sons brought here and had them all five laid in one grave in a chapel that stands here. For love of them I stayed here, leaving the pleasures of the world's riches, and I want to serve God forevermore for their sake and for my own. I tell you this," said the hermit, "because I would advise you not to seek the beast. If you started the quest in folly, free yourself of it in wisdom, for, so help me God, I expect you to die in it rather than to live, for this is a thing not of God but of the devil."

"Indeed," said Yvain the Bastard, "since I've begun it, I won't abandon it, for those who knew about it would criticize me, and I'd rather die than abandon it thus."

"Do as you like, " said the good man. "I don't think good will come of it for you."

How the hermit told Yvain that he would not tell him where to find the beast.

That night Yvain the Bastard was in great disquiet at what the good man [129] had told him, for it was something that frightened him badly and would have made him give up the quest. Nevertheless, he knew well that he would never have honor at court if he did so.

In the morning, as soon as he had heard Mass, he mounted, commended the good man to God, and said to him, "For God's sake, I ask you to tell me where I may find the beast most quickly."

"For God's sake, friend, I won't tell you, for if I did I'd bring about your death."

"My lord," said Yvain the Bastard, "since you don't want to tell me this, I commend you to God; may He maintain you in His service."

Then he left him and went where chance took him, not knowing where to find the beast. He rode thus from one place to the next, until he found some men herding cattle, and he asked them if they had seen the Bizarre Beast, telling them what it was like.

"We know very well what you're seeking; you're seeking the Questing Beast. Go to the top of that mountain, and you'll find a field, and in that field you'll find a tall tree, and under that tree a large spring, and under that tree, beside that spring, the beast is accustomed to go to rest, and I saw it go there a little while ago."

How Yvain was wounded by the Knight of the Beast.

When Yvain heard this, he was very happy, and he went to the top of the mountain. When he reached the tree, he saw a knight under it, fully armed and riding a good horse, and he had with him thirty beautiful dogs, good to all appearances.

"Friend," said Yvain the Bastard, "can you give me news of the Questing Beast that often comes here?"

The knight asked him, "Why do you ask about it, and what do you want with it?"

"I would gladly find it," said Yvain the Bastard, "for I'm going about looking for it, and I'm not going to leave off until I know why it is so strange."

"Indeed," said the knight, "you're mad and foolish to involve yourself in such a quest, for such a quest as this is not for you. A much better knight than you is needed here, and I, who am the most famous knight in this land, have been following the beast more than twelve years, with all the dogs you see here, and have never been able to catch it or kill it or know more about it than [131] you do. And you're a stranger and hope to catch it alone? Indeed, you're chasing folly."

"Whatever folly it may be," said Yvain the Bastard, "I have to continue with it, since I've started it."

"Proceed no farther in this quest," said the knight, "for I forbid it to you; for, indeed, you're not of such power or virtue that you should hold to such an exalted quest any longer. And what's more, I tell you that if you were the best knight in the world, I wouldn't permit you to follow my quarry, which I have hunted for so long and for which I have endured so much hardship and effort; rather, I'd fight you to the death, and if you killed me, you would follow the quarry, but while I live, I won't permit it to you or to anyone else."

"You can't stop me," said Yvain the Bastard, "nor can you prevent me from following it or killing it, and if I find it in a place where I can kill it, I will do so."

"It will be very ignoble of you to do this," said the knight. "By my faith, I'd rather cut off your head than have you do any more about this."

"Is that so?" said Yvain the Bastard. "Know, then, that I won't abandon the quest because of you."

"No?" he said. "On my word, you will."

Then he charged toward Yvain as fast as the horse could carry him and struck him so hard that he broke through Yvain's shield and hauberk and put the lance through his chest, but Yvain was fortunate in that the wound was not mortal. He threw Yvain off his horse to the ground, and in the fall the lance broke and the point remained in him.

After he had Yvain on the ground, the knight said, "Sir knight, now you'll leave my quarry to me; for this month, at least, you won't be able to go hunting it. God help me, were I not ashamed, I'd cut off your head, because you undertook something that wasn't for you."

How the Knight of the Beast wounded Girflet.

As they were speaking of this, suddenly the beast came to the spring to drink. As soon as the dogs saw it, they went to it to kill it. When it saw the spring held by its enemies, it began to flee.

Girflet, who had just arrived, began to follow it as soon as he saw it, and when he saw it go down the mountain, with the dogs after it, he crossed himself at the agility he saw in it, of which he later said in Camelot to King Arthur, who asked him for an account of it, "My lord, when the arrow leaves the bow it does not go as fast as I saw the beast run." [133]

When Girflet saw the chase begun, he began to follow the beast, and he called to the dogs and urged them on. When the knight came down off the mountain and saw this, he was not pleased, for it seemed to him that Girflet wanted to take his hunt from him.

He said to Girflet, "Turn back, or you are a dead man."

Girflet did not want to turn back because of him, for he greatly desired to bring this hunt to an end. When the knight saw that Girflet was not turning back, it seemed to him that Girflet was acting from disdain, that he did not respect the knight enough to be willing to turn back for him. Then the knight drew his sword and charged at Girflet. He was large, strong, and experienced and very skillful at arms, and he struck Girflet on top of his helmet so hard that he drove the whole sword through it, so that he lifted his scalp right down to the forehead and, when he withdrew the sword, Girflet fell stunned to the ground, so that he, for his part, did not know whether it was night or day.

When the knight saw Girflet on the ground, he said, "Now you'll leave my quest, for you have to. You'd have been better off to go to your companion, who is lying on the mountainside."

He said this because he assumed Girflet was of King Arthur's household, and after he had said this, he went after the beast, leaving Girflet lying on the ground.

How Girflet went to meet Yvain the Bastard.

Thus the knight went off after the beast, having clearly shown the two companions from King Arthur's house that he did not want anyone to follow his quarry. When Girflet got up, he went to his horse and mounted, and he thought he would go to the mountain where the other knight was lying. He did that; he went there and found Yvain the Bastard, who had already come to and drawn the iron point out of himself. He had lost so much blood that he was surprised he was not dead; nevertheless, when he recognized Girflet, he was as happy and full of energy as if he were whole.

He said to Girflet, "Friend, welcome."

Girflet dismounted and went to him, asking how he was.

"Very bad," he said, "for I certainly think I'm mortally wounded, because I've been stricken by a lance through the chest."

Saying this, he fell to the ground unconscious, because of the quantity of blood he had lost. When Girflet saw this, it grieved him, for, unquestionably, Yvain the

Bastard was one of the best knights in King Arthur's house. Had he been as strong of body as he was of heart, he would have been marvelously respected.

Yvain the Bastard lay [135] three months with that wound, so that he could not ride, and he lay in a convent of nuns on that mountain. Girflet, who was not so badly wounded, was laid up only fifteen days, and when he was able to ride, he started on his quest as before.

But now the story leaves off speaking of Girflet and turns to Dodinel, saying that when Dodinel left Galahad and Yvain the Bastard, he went after Tristan. Tristan was riding only at a walk, for the horse was carrying two knights, and since it was going at a walk, you know that it was not his own horse, which they called "Bastard," but another. Dodinel rode fast and caught up with him. When he reached Tristan, he did not know him, for Tristan had that day broken his shield and left it in a tent not far from there. That was why Dodinel did not recognize him.

He called to Tristan, "Knight, you must leave what you're carrying, for in my opinion you've no right to it. And if you don't want to, I'll strike you with this lance, and all the loss and dishonor will be yours."

How Tristan recognized Dodinel and Asgares the Sad.

When Tristan heard what Dodinel was saying, he took his shield on his arm and his sword in his hand and turned to him. Dodinel gave him a great blow with his lance, so that he broke through Tristan's shield and broke the lance on his chest, but he did him no other harm, nor did he move him from the saddle. And Tristan, who was very strong, struck him on top of the helmet so hard that he knocked him to the ground unconscious, so that Dodinel did not know if he was dead or alive. Tristan gave Dodinel no other blow, but that one blow was such that the blood came out of his eyes, his nostrils, and his mouth. After he was on the ground, Tristan looked at him and recognized him, and he was very sorry; he thought certainly that if he had killed Dodinel, he would lose his seat at the Round Table, if they found out, and he would be forsworn. Then he dismounted, tied his horse to a tree, and went to Dodinel; he took the helmet from his head, and when he saw him so badly hurt, he was very sorry. When Dodinel found himself relieved of his helmet, he got up and wiped his eyes, which were full of blood.

Tristan said to him, "Friend, how do you feel?" [137]

Dodinel looked at him, and when he saw him on foot, he* realized that it was he who had knocked him down.

Then he answered, "Knight, I am well, but why do you ask?"

"If I've offended you, it grieves me greatly," said Tristan.

"Why does this grieve you? And who are you?" asked Dodinel.

"I'm Tristan, your companion of the Round Table, and it grieves me that I laid a hand on you. Know that, if I'd recognized you, there is no man or thing in the world for which I would have laid a hand on you."

Tristan removed his helmet, fell to his knees before Dodinel, and begged his pardon. Dodinel pardoned him, and he took him by the hand and raised him.

---

*   From here down to "why does this grieve you?" from Magne, 1944 edition, 1:150; the passage represents gaps in the manuscript that are filled by the editor from the Spanish *Demanda*.

How Tristan asked Asgares and Dodinel to pardon him.

When Asgares the Sad, who was badly wounded, saw Dodinel's shield, he recognized him and Tristan, and as soon as Tristan took off his helmet, he was very happy, for he saw clearly that they were both companions of the Round Table.

Then he got up and went to them and said, "Sir Tristan, you've hurt me wrongfully, and you shouldn't have done it."

Then Dodinel took off his helmet and recognized Asgares; he went to him at once, embraced him, and said to him, "Friend Asgares, you are welcome. How do you feel?"

Asgares said, "I am well, thanks be to God, but Sir Tristan here has almost killed me, and for a very slight offense."

When Tristan heard that Asgares was of the Round Table, he was as sad as he could be, and he called himself wretched and star-crossed and said that he would never have honor, and he should not have it, as he was forsworn and faithless to those of the Round Table. He went to his horse, got on it, and went galloping off as fast as the horse could carry him, lamenting as if he saw dead before him the person he loved most in the world. When they saw Tristan going off like that, lamenting and riding as fast as if they were chasing him, the others, who remained together, spoke at length of it.

Dodinel said to Asgares, "Now you can see the knight's good will and moderation, and you may well believe that it grieves him to have offended you without reason, for he did it through lack of recognition. For no one ever saw a knight go off in such grief. But where did he find you, and how did this anger arise between you and him?"

"Indeed, because of a small thing, and I'll tell you how it was, if you wish."

How Asgares the Sad told about his sadness.

"Near here in a castle there's a [139] young lady who has loved me for a long time, but because I loved another lady, richer and more beautiful, I didn't want to do what she asked of me. Today I happened to be passing near that castle, and a knight came out to me, fully armed, and told me to enter, for the young lady wanted to speak with me, but I didn't want to go. When he saw that I wouldn't go, he challenged me, and before I had gone very far, he fought with me. I happened to kill him, and after that I fled. Before I had gone far, I saw Sir Tristan coming after me, and if I had known that it was he, the matter wouldn't have been as it was. He asked me to turn back, but I wouldn't turn back for his asking, for I didn't recognize him. We began to fight, but the battle was soon over, for I was powerless against him. He reduced me to such a state as you saw, put me before him, and carried me, and he would have carried me to the young lady if you hadn't arrived. I would rather have been dead than taken there."

"Are you badly wounded?" asked Dodinel.

"Yes," said Asgares, "but I think I'd certainly get well if I were in a place where they would see to my wounds."

"I'll take you where you may be healed," said Dodinel. "Near here is a friend and relative of mine who will do you all the good he can."

"Then there's nothing more to say," said Asgares.

Then they both mounted Dodinel's horse and went to the knight's house.

But now the story stops speaking of them and turns to Galahad and Bors.

86. GALAHAD AND BORS IN THE HOUSE OF KING BRUTUS, WHOSE DAUGHTER KILLS HERSELF FOR LOVE OF GALAHAD.[*]

How Galahad and Bors joined company.

When Kay the Seneschal had left[†] Galahad to go to Gawain, Bors mounted the horse belonging to the knight Kay[‡] had killed and left the knight dead in the road, and he would not take anything from him except his horse and his shield, to replace his own, which Galahad had cut in two.[§]

After they had started,[¶] Bors said to Galahad, "It pleases me that I've found you here, for I greatly desired your company in this quest, and I won't part from you until chance parts us."

Galahad said this pleased him.

"My lord," said Bors, "which way do you want to go?"

"So help me God," said Galahad, "I don't know. This morning we were three companions of the Round Table, Yvain the Bastard, Dondinel the Wild, and I. We happened to find a crossroad, and as [141] we prepared to separate, three marvelous adventures happened to us." Then he told what they were. "After we parted, we found each his own. 'I want to go by this road,' I said, 'for the stag that the four lions were guarding went this way.'"

How Galahad and Bors were guests of King Brutus.

When Bors heard this, he said, "So help me God, you were fortunate, for it's been a long time since I've heard of three such adventures taking place. And among such as I've heard of, the best happened to you. But now may it please God to let me be there when you accomplish it."

"I don't know if you'll be there," said Galahad. "From now on I won't stop seeking it, if chance doesn't stop me, until I know the truth about whatever it signifies."

Talking thus, they rode all that day. After vespers, when it began to grow dark, it happened that they found a castle in a little field. Its name was "Castle Brut," after

---

*　　Corresponds to Magne I:139-159; Bogdanow 1991 142-159; Piel 69-78.

†　　"Kay the Seneschal had left" as in Bogdanow 1991 (142). Magne has "he wanted to leave."

‡　　"Kay" as in Bogdanow 1991 (142). Magne has "he."

§　　"and his shield ... cut in two" added by Bogdanow 1991 (142).

¶　　"started" as in Bogdanow 1991 (142). Magne has "entered the field."

Brutus, who had built it. The men of Troy had plundered and usurped this castle after they had been overcome by the Greeks, defeated because of Helen the Fair.

How King Brutus's daughter fell in love with Galahad.

That castle was named "Brut" and would have been well situated if it had had enough water. The lord of that castle was a king, and his name was Brutus, after the man who first settled there. And know that the rule of that castle extended a day's journey in all directions. That Brutus who reigned at that time was one of the good knights of the world and marvelously rich. He had conquered a great deal by his knightly deeds, and he had a daughter fifteen years old, who was the most beautiful girl in the kingdom of Logres. At the moment when the knights came, the king was leaning out a window in his palace. When he saw them coming, armed thus and without company, he knew that they were knights errant, and he was happy about them, for he had always loved chivalry and those who labored in it. He sent word to them by two knights that they should come stay with him, for he did not want them to stay with anyone else. When Galahad and Bors heard his command, they thought him courteous and generous [143] and, thanking him warmly for it, went with the knights. After they were inside and disarmed, the king honored them by seating them at his side; he began to ask them about themselves, and they told him something of what he asked. King Brutus's daughter, a very beautiful creature, looked at Galahad for a long time, and he seemed to her so handsome and well built that she loved him with all her heart, so that she had never loved anything in the world so much, and she did not take her eyes off him. The more she looked at him, the more she liked him and the more she loved him.

How the nursemaid asked the girl why she was crying.

Thus the maiden loved Galahad; however, she had never seen or known what love was. She looked at Galahad and in her heart esteemed him more than anything, more than a woman ever esteemed a man. Therefore, it seemed to her that if she did not have her way with him, she would die. She hoped to get him the more easily because the knight was young and beautiful, and she believed that he would willingly agree to such a thing because she was one of the most beautiful women in the kingdom of Logres. It comforted her that he was a young knight; because of that, she thought she would sooner accomplish her desire. But if she employed any deception in order to love him, she feared that it would be thought bad of her if people knew it, and if she did not do anything, how would she have the man she desired—because of this she was so sad in her heart that she could not bear it. The maiden was thinking about this while her father was talking with the knights. After she had thought as much as she could, she went to her room, let herself fall on her bed, and began to lament as if she had her father dead before her. However, she made no noise but wept inwardly, so hard that it was a marvel. As she was mourning thus, her nursemaid entered, a lady of great consequence who had raised her since she was little and loved her like a daughter.

When she saw the maiden weep so silently, she wondered what it was and asked, "Oh, my lady, what's wrong with you? Has someone grieved you? Tell me, my lady, why you're crying, and I'll give you some help, for I won't ever be happy while you are sad."

The young woman did not want to tell her why she was weeping. The nurse began to comfort her, saying, [145] "In any case, tell me what's the matter and what's the cause of your grief."

The maiden fell silent and stopped crying. The nurse said to her, "If you don't tell me what's wrong, I'll tell your father. Therefore, it will be better if you tell me, for if the thing is to be hidden, have no fear that I'll ever give you away."

How the maiden promised her nurse that she would not love Galahad.

When the maiden saw that her nurse wanted to tell her father, whom she feared because he was brutal and domineering, she was badly frightened. "Oh, lady! For God's sake," she said, "don't go. Rather, I'll tell you what you ask me, but on your oath that you won't give me away."

"Have no fear," said the nurse, "for since it's a thing to be hidden, I'll hide it for you very well."

Then the maiden said, "I love one of the visiting knights errant so much that, if I don't have my way with him, I won't see tomorrow but will kill myself with my own hands."

When the lady heard this, she was so sad that she did not know what to do, for she knew well that if the maiden had her way with the knight, the king would know about it, sooner or later, and when he knew that the knight was with her, he was so brutal that he would kill his daughter and all who had helped her.

How the nurse answered the maiden.

Then the lady said to her, "Go on, mad, miserable, wretched creature, what's this that you tell me? Either you've lost your mind or you're bewitched, you who are a young lady of great consequence and so beautiful, and set your heart on such a poor, foreign knight whom you don't know? If he's here tonight, he won't be here tomorrow, nor would he stay here if your father gave him all his land. Be careful what you say and think and what may happen to you. Go on, foolish thing, how did you dare imagine this? Indeed, if your father knew, all the world couldn't help you, but he'd cut off your head."

When the maiden heard this, she was so frightened that she really wished she were dead, for there was no way she could detach her heart from the knight, but she would try to have what she wanted by any means. Also, her father's brutality worried her considerably. Thinking about these things, the maiden [147] wept without stopping.

When she spoke, she said, "Cursed be the hour in which I was born, star-crossed, wretched, and most cursed person in the world!"

"Now tell me," said the nurse, "does the advice I gave you seem good to you, that you detach your heart from that knight?"

"Yes," she said, "for one who could do what she wanted with her heart."

"You must do it," she said, "if you don't want to be disgraced."

"Lady," she said, "I'll do it, since I see that there's no alternative at this time."

How the maiden spoke with herself about her love for Galahad.

The young woman said this to protect herself, but she had something else in her heart, and she showed it that evening after both the knights had lain down in a room. Thinking for sure that they were already asleep and knowing which was Galahad's bed, the maiden got out of her own bed in her chemise, although much embarrassed and with great sorrow that she had to do against her will what love commanded. To her misfortune, she planned to seduce the knight. When she came to the room where they lay, she went inside, and she was so frightened that she did not know what to do. Nevertheless, she returned to her first plan, which love had suggested to her, and against her will she made herself strong. She went to Galahad, raised the coverlet, and lay down beside him. Galahad, who was sleeping soundly because of the hard day he had had, did not wake up. When the maiden saw that he was sleeping, she did not know what to do, for, if she woke him up, he would think it madness and assume that she was in the habit of acting this way with everyone who came here, and he would be angrier and more startled when he saw that she had undressed herself thus without his asking.

Then she said to herself in a low voice, "Wretch, I'm shamed and debased, and I won't ever have honor in anything I do, since, in sin, of my own deed and without being asked, I've come to lie with this stranger who knows nothing about me." Then she said, "Mad, foolish girl, what are you saying? Nothing you can do for this knight will be shame and dishonor to you, for he's the handsomest knight you ever saw."*

Then she thought that she would wake him gently and tell him how she felt and why she had come;† since she was lying beside him, he would satisfy her [149] desire, and there was no way she could imagine, since she was so beautiful and important, that he would be so ignoble as not to do her will. Then she drew closer to him than before and gently put a hand on him to wake him.

But when she felt the hair shirt he wore—for he was never without the hair shirt, day or night—she was so dismayed that she said at once, "What's this I see?

---

* "Nothing you can do ... for he is the handsomest knight you ever saw" as in Bogdanow 1991 (149). Magne has "You can do nothing for this knight that will not be shame and dishonor to you."

† "she would wake him ... why she had come" added by Bogdanow 1991 (149).

He isn't one of the knights errant, who they say are lovers, but he's one of those whose life and joy are always in penitence, because of which great good comes to them in the other world, and God pardons them whatever offenses they may have committed against Him. And in no way," she said, "can I accomplish what I would with him. However joyful this knight may appear, greatly does he torment his flesh, and he shows clearly that his heart is thinking of one thing and my miserable and wretched flesh of something else. Wretch! I have lost everything I planned. This is one of the true knights of the quest for the Holy Grail, and it was an evil hour for me when he became so beautiful." Then she began to weep and lament as softly as she could, so they would not hear her.

How Sir Galahad found the maiden in bed with him.

After a while, Galahad woke up and turned toward the young woman, and when he felt her, he was amazed and opened his eyes.

When he saw that it was a maiden, he was startled and angry, and he drew away from her the full width of the bed, crossed himself, and said, "Oh, my lady, who sent you here? Indeed, he gave you bad advice. I thought you were of a different kind. I ask you, of your courtesy and honor, to go away, for I will certainly not, God willing, regard your mad intention, for I should fear peril to my soul rather than do your will."

How the maiden threatened Galahad.

When the young woman heard this, she was so sad that she did not know what to do, for this answer from Galahad, whom she loved excessively, made her lose all sense and reason.[*]

He said to her, "My lady, you're badly advised. Think of your situation and the nobility of your ancestors and your father, and act so that they aren't dishonored because of you."

When the maiden heard this, she replied like a woman out of her mind, "My lord, nothing else matters. Since [151] you value me so little that you have refused me, you have brought me to a quick death.[†] I'll kill myself with my own hands, and you'll have greater sin from it than if you kept me here with you, for you'll be the cause of my death, and you could prevent it, if you wanted."

Galahad did not know what to say, for, if the maiden killed herself as she threatened, he would be the cause of her death. On the other hand, if he did what she wanted, he would break the vow he had made when he became a knight, to remain a virgin all his life and to die a virgin.[‡]

---

[*]   "all sense and reason" as in Bogdanow 1991 (150). Magne has "her head and all her heart."

[†]   "you have refused me ... a quick death" as in Bogdanow 1991 (151). Magne has "you only want to kill me one way or another. Death will soon be with me, for...."

[‡]   "for, if the maiden ... die a virgin" as in Bogdanow 1991 (151). Magne has "and he said to the girl that if she killed herself as she said and for such a reason, she should understand clearly that he cared nothing about her death, and, on the other hand, he said to her that if she were the most beautiful woman Our Lord ever made, he would pay no more attention to her. He told her it would be better for her to remain a virgin, for if others did as much to her as he would, it could well be that she would die a virgin."

The maiden seemed completely mad,* when she saw that she could not have her pleasure with Galahad, and said, "What, knight, are you so ignoble? Will you do nothing for me?"

"No," he said. "I tell you truly, and you may well be certain of it."

"By my faith," she said, "this will be folly, for you'll die for it before you get out of here."

"I don't know what will happen," he said, "but if that were the case, I'd rather die acting honorably than escape death by doing wrong."

How the maiden killed herself for love of Galahad.

After she heard this, she waited no longer but got out of bed and went running to Galahad's sword, which was hanging at the door of the room.

She drew it from the scabbard, seized it in both her hands, and said to Galahad, "Sir knight, you see how I've been deceived in my first love. In an evil hour were you made so beautiful, since your beauty costs me so dearly."

When Galahad saw that she already held the sword in her hand and wanted to strike herself with it, he got out of bed, badly frightened, and cried to her, "Oh, noble[†] maiden! Wait a little! Don't kill yourself this way, for I'll do all your pleasure."

Deeply tormented, she answered in anger, "Sir knight, you are late in saying that to me."

Then she raised the sword and stabbed herself with all her strength through the chest, so that the sword passed through and appeared on the other side, and she fell dead to the ground without speaking another word.

How Bors was amazed.

When Galahad saw this, he was deeply shocked, and he dressed himself [153] as quickly as he could and said, "Oh, Saint Mary, what's this I see?"

At this Bors woke up, got out of bed, and said, "My lord, what's this?"

"By God, Bors," said Galahad, "this is the greatest marvel you ever saw. This maiden has killed herself with my sword for no reason."

When Bors heard this he said, "The devil made her do it. Now I don't know what we should do, for her father won't believe us but will say that we killed her."

"Don't worry so much," said Galahad, "for God is just and will help us."

Thus it happened to the maiden, as I have told you, that she killed herself for love of Galahad.

Next to the room[‡] where the young woman lay dead there lay two sick ladies. When they heard what the knights were saying, they got out of bed in their chemises and went there. When they saw the maiden dead, they began to lament loudly.

---

*   "mad" as in Bogdanow 1991 (151). Magne has "paralyzed."

†   "noble" as in Bogdanow 1991 (152). Magne has "good."

‡   "room" as in Bogdanow 1991 (153). Magne has "house."

How King Brutus came out to the tumult.

The king, who was lying in his room some distance away, got up, thoroughly startled, when he heard the uproar and went there.

When he found his daughter dead, he was very angry and said, "Oh, God! Who has caused me this loss?"

"My lord," said those who were there, "who could have caused it except these knights whom you invited in yesterday."

"Ah!" said the king, "they've killed me. Take them for me, for I will never be happy until I take such vengeance on them as my court will adjudicate."

When Bors heard this, he did not lose heart, for he was very powerful and had been in danger many times. He went to his sword, drew it from the scabbard, and said to Galahad, "My lord, take your weapons and plan to defend yourself, for it seems to me that you need to. I'll defend you until you are armed."

Galahad went running to his armor, which was beside his bed, and armed himself as well and as quickly as he could. Then they wanted to attack Bors at once and take him, but they could not, for he defended himself so marvelously with his sword that he cut off their heads and their arms, knocked down some here and others there, and cleared the room of them so well that in a little while nobody remained but the two of them and the maiden's body, unless it was a dead knight or one so badly wounded that he could not get away. After Bors had done this, he locked the door of the room tightly, went to take his armor, and armed himself well.

As soon as they were both fully armed, Bors said to Galahad, "It's too bad this maiden [155] has killed herself, for in a little while we'll have to pay dearly for her death. Nevertheless, since I see you already armed, I have no fear of them."

"If God wishes," said Galahad, "we'll get out of here in one piece, since He knows we have no guilt in this maiden's death."

Then he drew the sword out of her and wiped the blood off it. He went to the door of the room and said, "We didn't come here to become prisoners."

He opened the doors, and they both went into the palace.

When the others, already armed to fight with them in the room, saw Bors and Galahad come out so actively, prepared to strike and to defend themselves, they were thoroughly frightened, and they all said, "Light!"

A great light was made in the house, for they all brought either candles or lighted torches. When the king, who was already armed, saw only two taking on all the men of the palace, well over fifty armed men, he marveled that it could be and realized that they were the best two knights he had ever seen, or else they were the most insane. And the king, who was a good knight and fiercely courageous, told his men to draw aside until he had spoken with those knights.

How the king and Bors argued about the king's daughter.

Then the king came forward and said, "Knights, I have reason to complain of you, who, in my own house, where I had received you very well for the honor of chivalry, killed my daughter. Indeed, I'll be deeply grieved if I don't have vengeance for this treachery according to my wish."

Bors replied to this, "My lord, you are a king, and a king who lies shouldn't wear a crown—is not worthy to wear a crown. Indeed, you should carefully avoid saying anything you don't know to be true."

"I know well," said the king, "that one of you two killed her. If it pleases you, I'll prove, on whichever of you you like, that it's so."

"Indeed," said Bors, "either one of us would defend himself against you and against the best man you have, were it not for one thing."

"What thing is that?" asked the king.

"I'll tell you," he said. "You know that you have lodged us and done us much honor and kindness while we've been with you. Therefore, since you did us so much honor without our deserving it, it would be thought wrong and brutal of us if we killed you now."

"Oh!" said the king, "this ploy will do you no good; either defend yourself against this accusation, or [157] I'll consider you a traitor."

"And if I can defend myself successfully against you," said Bors, "will we be safe from you and from all the others?"

"Yes, indeed," said the king, "so that you'll find no one who will grieve you afterwards."

"On that condition," said Bors, "I won't fail you."

The battle between Bors and King Brutus.

After this exchange there was no further delay, and they charged at each other with their swords raised and gave each other as great blows as they could. The king, wildly angry at the death of his daughter and believing that they had killed her, thought he could avenge himself all alone, for he felt strong and excited. He charged at Bors and gave him a blow on the helmet, the hardest he could, but he did him no great harm, for the helmet was very good. And Bors, who had delivered many* a hard blow and who did not want to deceive him, struck him so hard on the helmet that the king was stunned, so that he could not keep his feet but fell on his hands and knees on the ground, and his sword fell from his hand. Bors turned to him again and struck him such a blow that he knocked his helmet some distance from his head, so that the king's head was uncovered and unprotected except for his iron skullcap. The king fell to the ground badly hurt, but he got up as quickly as he could.

Then Bors said to him, "Now you see how it is. If I'd wanted to, I would already have killed you, but I don't want to until I know if we may have peace with you. It seems to me that you need peace more than war, for you see clearly that you are without weapons and that I can kill you easily if I wish."

The king replied, "Indeed, knight, I recognize that you speak the truth, and I see that you, Bors, can kill me if you wish, but your courtesy won't let you. Therefore, I acquit you of this matter, and I do it more because of your excellence as a knight than anything else, for it would be a great outrage if, after the death of my daughter,

---

*   "delivered many" as in Bogdanow 1991 (157). Magne had "given him."

whom I can't get back, I killed such a good knight as you. But I beg you, for God's and courtesy's sake, to tell me how or why you killed my daughter."

"My lord," said Bors, "on all [159] my faith and on all the honor of knighthood and by the faith I owe to my lord and brother Lancelot, I swear to you that we didn't kill her."

"Then how did it happen?" asked the king. "I must know."

"My lord, I'll tell you, and without lying in any detail."

Then he began to tell it just as the story has already done. When the king heard that his daughter had killed herself with her own hands, he said, "Oh, God! How unfortunate this was!" Then he said to his men, "Go disarm yourselves, for, so help me God, such good men as these, who have deserved no harm from me, will receive none, for this misfortune and this shame have come to us only because of our own great sin."

87. GALAHAD AND BORS CHASE THE QUESTING BEAST AND MEET PALAMEDES AND HIS FATHER, ESCLABOR THE UNKNOWN.*

How Galahad and Bors saw the Questing Beast.

The knights who were in the king's presence disarmed themselves at once when they heard their lord's command. By that time day was already dawning.

When Galahad and Bors saw that it was already light, they said to the king, "My lord, if you please, have our horses brought to us, for we have so much to do that we may not remain here."

The king commanded that the horses be brought to them at once. They took their leave and started on their way, saying that the encounter had ended well, after a bad beginning. When they had left the castle, where they had found honor—as well as grief, because of the maiden they were thought to have killed—they rode together until midday. Then it happened that they saw the Questing Beast coming out of a valley. It came alone and seemed very tired, for it had been chased a great deal that day.

As soon as Galahad saw it, he recognized it and pointed it out to Bors, saying, "Bors, here's a marvelous adventure." Then he told him what had happened to Yvain the Bastard, who had gone after it. "It seems to me," he said, "that he has abandoned it."

"My lord," said Bors, "this thing is so marvelous that I'm sure it isn't granted to every man to know it, and I firmly believe that the truth about it will never be known if not by you, for, indeed, this adventure is only for you."

"I don't know," said Galahad, "but I would certainly like God to grant it to me, for it's something I would gladly know."

---

*   Corresponds to Magne I:159-169; Bogdanow 1991 159-168; Piel 78-83.

While they were saying this, they were going [161] directly toward it, but as soon as it heard them, it turned in the other direction and began to run so swiftly that no animal in the world could have caught up with it. And in a little while it had gone so far away from them that they did not know which way it had gone.

Galahad said, "Now I fear that we've lost it."

"We must consider it lost," said Bors, "for there's nothing in the world fleet or light enough to catch it, and by everything I see, they who seek it labor in a foolish task. Therefore, I, for my part, will never exercise myself to follow it, except insofar as I'll go with you if you want to go after it."

"Don't worry," said Galahad, "for if God, in whose strength we act, wishes, we'll know the truth about it in a very short time."

How Galahad and Bors found Palamedes, the Knight of the Questing Beast.

As they were speaking of this, there appeared coming toward them a knight armed in black armor, the one who had knocked down Yvain the Bastard and Girflet.

He rode a very good horse and had more than thirty dogs, and as soon as he reached them he asked, without greeting them, "My lords, did you see the Questing Beast pass by here?"

"Yes," said Bors, "but why do you ask?"

"Because it's my quarry," he said, "and I'm following it and will do so until fortune wants me to catch it."

"Then," said Bors, "you may now go with us, for we have begun to follow it, and we won't leave it until we know the source of these cries that emerge from it."

"It's madness," said the knight, "for you to have begun such a quest, for you aren't worthy. There is perhaps in this land a knight who, if he knew you wanted to go after the beast, would make you leave it, to your dishonor, for he has hunted it so long that he wouldn't have anyone else hunt it."

Then Bors began to laugh and said, "I know no knight in the world because of whom I'd leave it, if he weren't of the Round Table."

"Indeed," said the knight, "he was never of the Round Table, but he has been in King Arthur's house many times. I tell you that there isn't in Great Britain a knight so good that this one wouldn't expect to defeat him before the day was out."

"If I believed that," said Bors, "I'd be very foolish, for, indeed, there are better knights than he in King Arthur's house, and because of what you tell me I promise God, before Sir Galahad here, to continue this quest in order to see if that knight of whom you've spoken to me is so [163] mad that he would forbid it to me."

"Now we'll see," said the other, "what you'll do about it, for I tell you truly that if you want to do as you say, harm will come to you, and would even if there were no other knight in the world except you and him."

After he had said this, he began to ride as fast as he could toward where he thought the beast was. Galahad and Bors did the same,* and they rode all that day until the hour of vespers. Then it happened that they met an old knight, riding

---

*   As the next few pages make clear, the stranger rides off alone, as he is not with Galahad and Bors when they meet Esclabor.

unarmed except for his sword, and they greeted him and he them, and he asked them where they were from. They said they were from King Arthur's house.

"And are you of the Round Table?" he asked.

"Yes," they said.

"Then you are welcome," he said, "for I'm very happy about your coming, the more so because it's time to take shelter, for now by your kindness you will keep me company and stay with me in a beautiful, luxurious fortress of mine, which is very near here, where you'll be lodged and entertained to your liking, and I ask you to go there."

They agreed to this, since they realized that it was time for them to take shelter.

How Galahad and Bors were guests of Esclabor the Unknown.

They went with him, and when they arrived at the fortress that evening, they were well received. After they had eaten, the knight took them out to a meadow to relax and asked them what they were seeking in this land.

Bors, who was older and more talkative, answered their host, "We've recently started on a quest for a beast that we are following." And he told him which one.*

When the knight heard this, he began to brood, and, brooding, he wept hard; if he had been happy before, he now became very sad, saying, "Oh, God! Cursed be the hour in which that beast was born, for because of it I have lost the best knight, in my opinion, who ever bore arms in Great Britain."

After he had said this, he returned to brooding, weeping as before, and the others did not speak to him, for fear of grieving him.

After he had brooded a great while, he rallied himself, trying to present a better countenance to them, and said, [165] "My lords, for God's sake, don't think it wrong of me that I appear sad, for I can't do otherwise; for the account you now give me of this beast confounds me each time I hear it and remember the beast. I'll tell you how it is, and you'll consider it a great marvel, and I'm not telling you so that you'll help me, for you can't."

How Esclabor told Galahad and Bors about himself.

"The truth is, and God and men know it, that I'm a native of Galilee. I was a pagan and am a good enough knight. To see the prowess of Great Britain and test its knights, whose great fame had spread throughout the world, I came here a little while before King Arthur was crowned. One day I came to King Arthur's court, when he was at the start of his reign, with a knight who had been my companion at arms for more than three years. He thought I was a Christian, but I wasn't, and King Arthur and many good men who knew me, who thought me a good knight, all thought that I was a Christian. On the day I'm telling you about, it happened that knights brought to court a very beautiful maiden, daughter of a giant they had killed that day on a mountain. When they gave her to the king, they asked her if she wanted to become a Christian and said they would give her rich land and a good knight as a husband. She said she would rather die by any death at all than become

---

* Bogdanow 1991 (163) switches back to the Portuguese manuscript at this point.

a Christian. Therefore, there was no knight there who wanted to ask her of the king, except myself, who wasn't a Christian.

"The king said to me when I asked for her, 'What will you do with her, since she doesn't want to become a Christian?'

"'My lord,' I said, 'I like her better like this than if she became a Christian, for I'm a pagan like her, and, therefore, I ask her of you.'

"The king, who knew me well, for he had seen me many times in many tournaments, said, 'What? Aren't you a Christian?'

"'No, my lord,' I said.

"'By God,' he said, "I have not known you well. And, therefore, I name you Esclabor the Unknown.'

"Just as the king named me then, so have I been called ever since, and because I asked for the lady, he gave her to me, saying, 'Now may she be yours, since you are both of one law, but I'd have loved you better if you'd been a Christian.'

"Once I had the lady, I left the court happily, and I lived with that lady twelve years, and we had twelve sons, all of whom I subsequently saw [167] great, strong knights and very brave, until no one knew of any other knights in Great Britain of such fame. Thus God blessed me with a company such as I tell you; everyone knew that they were pagans, but they were honored wherever they went, as if they were all King Arthur's sons."

How Esclabor told Galahad and Bors how he had lost his eleven sons.

"One day it happened that I was with my wife and sons in a castle that King Arthur had recently given me. After we had eaten (for it was midday) we first heard of the Questing Beast, for one of our squires told us that it was then passing near the door of my castle. Then we took our arms, and all my sons were with me except one who was sick. When we had mounted, we went after it, and as soon as we caught up with it at a lake, where it had entered to drink—the lake was not very big—we surrounded it on all sides, so that it could only come out past one of us. When it saw itself thus surrounded, it stood still as if it didn't want to move, and then I told one of my sons to strike it. He struck it so that the lance head appeared on the other side of its leg. It uttered a cry so agonized and frightened that there's no knight in the world who wouldn't have been terrified, had he heard it. What shall I tell you? The cry was so strange and eerie that not one of us could hold himself in the saddle, and we all fell unconscious to the ground."

How Esclabor praised his son Palamedes.

"When I regained consciousness, I found myself struck through the body by a lance stroke such that I thought I would die at once. And when I looked around me, expecting help from my sons, I found them all eleven dead.* What shall I tell you? This became known throughout the whole land, and everyone was deeply grieved. And I, who wasn't mortally wounded, got on my horse and sent for my sons and had them buried. My son who had stayed in the castle was the oldest. When he

---

*   Esclabor's loss parallels that of the hermit who lost five sons to the Beast (chapter 85).

saw what had happened to us, he was so grieved that he swore he would never stop following the beast until he killed it or it him. In this manner my son began this hunt, which he has continued until now and still continues."

"What arms does he bear?" asked Bors. Esclabor told him. "By my faith," said Bors, "we [169] saw him today."

"Know, then," said the other, "that you saw a good knight when you saw him. And if he weren't my son and I knew him as I know him now, I'd say that he was the best knight who ever was in Great Britain, but he's lacking in that he isn't a Christian."

"What?" asked Bors, "are you now a Christian?"

"Yes," he said, "because of one of the most beautiful adventures that ever happened to a sinner, and I'll tell you about it."

How Esclabor told how he became a Christian.

"It happened one day, six years ago now, that I was going through a forest with six pagan knights, very good knights at arms and famous in this land. It was late, so that night came on us in the forest, and we had to stay there and camp in a clearing near the road in a hut we found there. Then a storm began, as violent and strange as if all the world were about to founder, and it lasted until midnight. Then a bolt of lightning fell from the sky and killed all the knights who were with me; I lost consciousness—but it did me no other harm— and I lay like that until full day."

How they spoke of the deeds of the Questing Beast.

"While I was lying unconscious, there came a voice above me, which said, 'Wretched man, poor in wisdom, twice already have I saved you from the peril of death, and never have you rewarded Me for it. I will cast down My vengeance onto you, if you do not submit to Me, and that vengeance will be so marvelous that it will be known throughout the world.'

"This much the voice said to me and no more. Know that I was at once converted, because I knew the voice spoke the truth, so that I was baptized that very day with my whole company. My son, who was hunting the beast, adamantly refused to be baptized; he told me he would never on any account become a Christian until he knew the truth about the beast. This happened to me as I've told you through the cursed beast, for because of it I lost my sons, and I therefore become so sad, whenever I hear speak of it, that I can't for a long time afterwards show a cheerful face."

"Indeed, that is no great wonder," they said, "for your loss has been very great. But however great your loss may be, we must follow the beast, since we have begun. For if we leave it, men will think it wrong of us."

"God give you help and grant that better come to you from it than came to me. Indeed, no one ever involved himself in this matter who didn't come to harm at the end."

After they had said this, they went to lie down, and in the morning, when they got up, they armed themselves, took leave of their host, and went off. [171]

88. YVAIN OF CENEL DIES; GAWAIN ESCAPES, IS BLAMED BY YVAIN'S SISTER.*

But now the story leaves off speaking of Galahad and turns to Gawain, telling that after Gawain was healed of the wound Galahad had given him and felt he could ride, he mounted and went on his way. As he was riding one day, he happened to meet Yvain of Cenel, a good and brave knight who was of the Round Table. Gawain greeted him as soon as he reached him, and Yvain did the same to him, but they did not recognize each other, for they had both changed their arms. As they were going along the road, they began to question each other. When they recognized each other, they were very happy, and at last they agreed that they would not part, since God had brought them together, until chance separated them.

How Gawain turned away and Yvain went to the castle.

That day they rode together, speaking of many things, and the next day they arrived at a strong, beautiful castle standing on a river bank, but it seemed deserted. When they arrived at the gate, they found on a block of stone letters that said, HERE LIES LAMORAT, WHOM GAWAIN, KING ARTHUR'S NEPHEW, KILLED BY TREASON.† After that they found other letters that said, THE INHABITANTS OF THE CASTLE FORBID ANYONE OF KING ARTHUR'S LINEAGE TO BE SO BOLD AS TO ENTER, FOR IF HE BUT ENTER HERE, ALL THE WORLD WILL NOT BE ABLE TO SAVE HIM FROM DEATH.

After they had read the letters, Gawain, who knew well what had happened, turned his horse's head and said, "Let's turn away, Sir Yvain, for if we enter here, we're dead men."

The other, who was so brave that he would not fear death if he saw it coming, said, "God forbid I should ever turn away for fear of death, for people would think it wrong and cowardly of me."

"Let them," said Gawain, "for I want to turn away, since I see my death clearly if I go forward."

"Then I commend you to God," said Yvain, "for I want to go in there, whatever happens to me."

How a youth told Yvain that harm must come to him, since he was of King Arthur's lineage.

Then they parted, and Gawain went away by another road. And Yvain, who was so brave and such [173] a good knight that there were few better in the world, entered the castle. As soon as he had passed through the castle gate, the portcullis fell.

He understood at once that he could not return by that route, but he was still not frightened, for his great courage comforted him. Immediately after this, he heard a horn blown.

---

* Corresponds to Magne I:169-179; Bogdanow 1991 169-178; Piel 83-87. Bogdanow switches back to a French manuscript at this point.

† See chapter 66.

Then a squire came to him and said, "Knight, tell me who you are. Don't lie to me, by the faith that you owe to all the knights of the world."

He answered, "You've asked me in such terms that I wouldn't for anything lie to you. My name is Yvain of Cenel, and I'm of King Arthur's house and lineage."

"Indeed," said the squire, "much grief will come to you today, for you'll meet a painful death because of our love of that lineage."

"I don't know what will happen," said Yvain, "but if death must come to me, I'll defend myself as well as I can."

How Yvain of Cenel was captured in the castle.

Then they parted, and the squire went running to the fortress.

After a little while, Yvain of Cenel saw coming toward him ten armed knights, who said all with one voice, "Now at him!"

Then they charged at him, killed his horse, and encircled him on all sides. When they saw him on foot, although he was defending himself marvelously well, they captured him, for they were all good knights; they disarmed him, and they found on him ten wounds so large that another man would expect to die of the smallest.

After that, they asked him what his name was, and he said his name was Yvain of Cenel, "and know that much harm will come to you from my death, as soon as King Arthur knows about it, for you'll all be destroyed because of my death."

"We won't worry about that," they said, "as long as we're avenged for the death of Lamorat, whom your cousin Sir Gawain killed treacherously."

How Yvain of Cenel was burned.

After this they took Yvain of Cenel and carried him [175] to the fortress, shaming him as much as they could. There was a beautiful, rich chapel there, where Lamorat lay, and it had been made for him in honor of Saint Mary, so that Saint Mary would plead for him with Her Blessed Son. And know that Lamorat's sepulchre was so rich and beautiful that one could hardly find better in the world.

When they came before the altar, they had a pit made seven feet deep, and when the pit was made they took Yvain of Cenel, showed him Lamorat's sepulchre, and said to him, "Yvain, here lies Lamorat, whom Gawain your kinsman killed by great treachery. Everyone should do him harm because of it. He has destroyed and confounded us and reduced us to poverty, and may God, the Great Avenger, grant us such vengeance as we desire for it."

Then they began to lament so that no one in the world, seeing them, however hard of heart he might have been, could have kept from weeping.

After a while, they said, "Oh, Lamorat, good knight, man of great heart, son of a king and a queen and of ancestors of great consequence, how badly the man who killed you has injured us!" After this, they fell on their knees before the monument, kissed it, and said, "My lord, what fortune has shamed and killed you, taking you away so early?"

After they had made their lamentation, they drew Yvain aside, tied his hands behind him, and threw him into the pit. They took dry wood, threw it on top of him, and set fire to it, and it burned, so that he turned to ashes.

How King Arthur came to destroy the castle after Perceval's death.

Thus was Yvain of Cenel burned for Lamorat's death. He could have escaped this death, had he wanted, but his great heart and his inability to perform any cowardly act would not let him. When King Arthur knew this, he was deeply grieved, so much so that he later destroyed the castle because of it, but not while Perceval was alive. And know that Gawain was later greatly dishonored and considered a coward because he had left Yvain in such a great predicament, for he should not for any fear have left him at such a time as that.

But now the tale leaves off speaking of Yvain and turns to Gawain, saying that after Gawain left the castle where he had seen the letters on the stone, [177] he had not gone far when he found another road, going toward a mountain. He took this road and went along thinking hard and with great sorrow, for it seemed to him that he had been wrong, because from fear of death he had abandoned his companion. As he was riding along like this, it happened that he met a maiden escorted by two squires.*

As soon as she saw him, she stopped, for she saw clearly that he was a knight errant; however, she did not know that he was Gawain, and she said, "Sir knight, you are welcome."

"My lady," he said, "God give you joy. Who are you, and whom are you seeking?"

"I'm a foreigner," she said, "recently come to this land, and I'm seeking one of the knights of the Round Table."

"Which one?" he asked.

"Yvain of Cenel," she said.

"I'll tell you such news of him as I know," he said. "Go to a castle that is a short league from here, and there you'll find him. This is the road, and it goes that way and will take you to the castle."

"May you be blessed," she said, "for you couldn't tell me anything else as pleasing as this news; but I ask you, of your courtesy, to tell me your name."

He gave his name.

She said, "I love you dearly, for I am your close relative."

He looked at her and recognized that she was the sister of Yvain of Cenel, and he told her he would serve and honor her in every way he could.

How Yvain's sister found him.

Then they parted, Gawain going toward the mountain and the maiden toward the castle. She hurried to reach the castle, and, as soon as she entered, she happened to pass before the chapel where they had burned her brother.

---

*   "escorted by two squires" added by Bogdanow 1991 (175) and Piel (86).

When she saw the fire, which was still large, and the people standing around it, she asked a good man, "Friend, can you give me tidings of a knight who came in here?" And she described to him the arms he bore.

"Why do you ask?" asked the good man.

"Friend," she said, "because I'd like to see him, for I came here for no other reason."

"Then you may turn back without taking any more trouble," he said, "for you'll never be able to see him." [179]

Then he described to her how and why they had burned him. "And know," he said, "that they would have done as much to the other man who was traveling with him, who left him at the entrance of the castle."

How the maiden mourned for her brother.

When the maiden heard this, she felt such grief that she fell unconscious from her palfrey to the ground and lay a great while, so that everyone there thought she was dead. They all ran to her and asked her squires what kin she was to that knight, and they said that he was her brother and that they who had killed such a knight had done a great wrong and a disloyal act and that his death would be avenged as soon as King Arthur knew about it.

"We care nothing for what King Arthur may do to us," they said, "as long as we have done some harm to the lineage of King Lot,* for the great traitor Gawain, his son, has offended us and all our company."

After a while the maiden came to, and when she could speak she said, "Oh, Sir Yvain, my friend and my brother, what a great loss I have sustained today. Those who killed you have destroyed me, for they've put such grief into my heart that it will never leave me."

Then she mounted her palfrey and went away with her squires. She went along the main street, lamenting and cursing the castle and all who lived there, wishing that evil lightning would strike it.

After they had emerged from the castle, she said, "Let's turn back in the direction from which we came and see if we can find the traitor Gawain, who in his cowardice left my brother to die. I'll never be happy until I'm avenged and make him die a hard death, for he has deserved it."

---

*   "Lot" as in Bogdanow 1991 (178) and Piel (87). Magne has "Lac."

89. Gawain Kills Patrides.*

How Patrides promised his help to Yvain's sister.

Then they started on their way and hurried along. The maiden went very fast in order to catch up with Gawain. They rode like that until vespers, the maiden lamenting constantly. Along the way it happened that she met Patrides, King Bademagu's nephew, a good knight and wonderfully brave. He was fully armed, but at that time he was badly wounded, for he had fought with Yvain, son of King Urien, and had almost succeeded in defeating him, for he would have killed him, but God made [181] them recognize each other, and so the battle ended. When he met the maiden, he was riding at a walk, as he was in great pain with two bad wounds.

When he got to her and saw her lamenting, he said to her, "For God's sake, my lady, and by your courtesy, tell me why you're lamenting so. I promise you to help you the best I can."

"Oh, my lord!" she said, "I'm right to lament so, for all the world couldn't make good to me the loss I've sustained today, that of one of the best knights in the world, my brother, whom they've just killed."

"And who was he?" asked Patrides.

"My lord," she said, "he was Yvain of Cenel."

"Yvain is dead?" he asked.

"Yes, my lord," she said, "unquestionably."

"And who killed him?" he asked. "Tell me that much, for, so help me God, I'll avenge him if I can. And if I didn't, all the world would think it wrong of me, for he was my companion at arms for a long time."

"My lord," she said, "a knight who is riding along here had him killed, and if I were avenged on him I'd ask no more."

"What arms did he bear?" asked the knight, and she told him.

"By God," he said, "I just met him back there, and he wouldn't even speak to me. I don't know if it was from anger or something else."

"Oh, my lord!" she said, "if you ever loved Yvain, avenge him on that man, for Yvain died because of him."

"By my faith," he said, "I'll do everything in my power to see that he's avenged, although I have more need to rest than to fight, for I'm badly wounded."

Then he rode on quickly. He climbed to the top of the mountain and found Gawain, who had stopped on his horse before a hermitage where he was just about to dismount in order to lodge there that night; however, he had not yet dismounted.

As soon as Patrides saw him, he said to the young lady, "Is this the man you were complaining about?"

"Yes, my lord, God give me vengeance on him, and I'll have everything my heart desires."

Patrides waited no longer but said to him, "Knight, defend yourself against me, for I defy you."

---

* Corresponds to Magne I:179-185; Bogdanow 1991 179-184; Piel 87-90.

When Gawain heard this, he charged at Patrides, and they gave each other such great lance strokes that their lances splintered, and they fell to the ground wounded. Gawain was badly hurt [183] by the blow, which he received in his left side, and the point of the lance remained in him. Patrides was not so badly wounded, for he was one of the best men in the world and jousted more wisely, but he was already so badly wounded that he was only slightly less severely stricken than Gawain. They both got up, and they took no notice of the hurts they had, so great was their anger and so much they both desired to be avenged. Both drew their swords and struck each other with such great blows that, had you been there, you would have seen sparks fly from their helmets. Gawain, who had endured much in the first encounter, drew the spear point from himself; he was not as badly hurt as Patrides and, after they had rested a little, attacked him again, for it seemed to him that people would think it bad of him if he did not avenge himself on a man who had attacked him for no reason. He raised his sword and gave Patrides such a great blow on the helmet that he knocked him to the ground unconscious, so that Patrides did not know if it was night or day. As soon as Gawain saw him on the ground, he went to him and took off his helmet and iron cap in order to cut off his head.

When the maiden saw this, she let herself fall to the ground, crying out like a madwoman, "Oh, Gawain, brutal and faithless! Don't kill such a good knight as this, for you'll knowingly commit a great treachery, at the very least because he's of the Round Table, as you are."

When Gawain heard this, he checked his blow, for he was greatly afraid it might be one of his brothers or other kin, and he asked the maiden, "Who is he?"

"Patrides," she said, "King Bademagu's nephew, a good knight, as you know."

"By God," he said, "I don't care about that, for he attacked me without reason, and he has wounded me, perhaps fatally. I wouldn't for anything fail to kill him. After I'm through with him, he won't attack another good man without reason."

Then he cut off Patrides's head and threw it away. After that he turned to the maiden and said to her, "My lady, see what the arrogant man gets for his arrogance and for believing such as you."

How the maiden reviled Gawain and threatened him.

When she saw that Gawain had killed the knight, she was so grieved about it that she would rather have been [185] dead, and she said in her anger, "Oh, God! Why do You suffer this treacherous and traitorous knight to go about killing all the good men through such mischance? Oh, Gawain! Never has your treachery been known as it is here today. Never would I have believed this, nor could anyone have made me believe it, that there is in you such great treachery as I see now, for you've killed my brother, and you've killed Patrides. God give us such vengeance for it as will give us pleasure, vengeance through which your treachery may become known."

After she had said this, she got on her palfrey. He asked her to stay, for it was already time to take shelter, but she said she would never stay with such a faithless knight as he was, for no man or woman who was not his adversary would ever remain with him.

"And do you know, Gawain," she said, "why I'm going from here so quickly? Know that I'll go straight to the court of the king, your uncle, and tell him and the others the great treachery that lies in you and the terrible deeds you're doing in this quest. After I tell all your evil ways to the people, I'll seek your death, and I'll have done to you what you did to him whose head you cut off."*

As soon as she had said this, she rode away, dark as it was, and Gawain stayed in the hermitage. In the morning he left there before hearing Mass, for he did not want anyone from King Arthur's house to find him there or know what he had done with Patrides.

90. FURTHER ADVENTURES OF HECTOR OF THE FENS, HELAIN THE WHITE, GAWAIN, KING BADEMAGU, YVAIN'S SISTER, AND THE KNIGHT OF THE QUESTING BEAST.†

How Gawain met Hector of the Fens.

All that day Gawain rode, much troubled by his wound, which he had not had cared for well the night before. At midday he reached the house of a knight he knew, with whom he stayed for a whole week, and the knight took such good care of him that soon he could ride. When he felt himself healed, he went on his way as before, and he rode until he met Hector of the Fens. After they had talked together and recognized each other, they were overjoyed, for it was a long time since they had seen each other.

"Sir Hector," said Sir Gawain, "how have you been since I left you?"

"Very well," he said, "thanks be to God, for I'm healthy and happy. But I've found no adventures since then, and I'm much amazed, for in the quest for the Holy Grail I thought I would find more adventures and marvels than in another quest"‡

"I tell you exactly the same of myself," said Gawain, "but do you have any news of your brother Lancelot?"

"No," he said.

"Or do you know anything of Galahad or Perceval or [187] Bors?"

"No, indeed," he said. "Those four are so thoroughly lost that no one knows their whereabouts."

"Do you know anything of Tristan?"

"No," he said, "but God protect them all, wherever they may be."

"Indeed," said Gawain, "if they fail at the adventures of the Holy Grail, there is no one who will succeed, for they're the best men in the quest."

---

* She never gets real revenge, but she meets him right after he has been refused admission to the Grail Castle and revels in his humiliation (chapter 144).

† Corresponds to Magne I:185-197; Bogdanow 1991 184-196; Piel 90-95.

‡ "quest" as in Bogdanow 1991 (184). Magne has "land."

After this Hector said, "Sir Gawain, until now you've been riding alone, and I also, and we've found nothing. Now let's ride together, and we'll see if we'll be more fortunate."

"That's a good idea, and I agree. Now let's go together, and may God guide us to where we may find something of what we're seeking."

"In the region from which I've come," said Hector, "we'll find nothing, nor in that from which you've come, but let's go by another road."

And Gawain agreed to this.

How Hector and Gawain met Helain the White.

Then Hector chose a road that wound through the forest. They looked before them and saw the fresh tracks of a horse, and they saw the ground stained in places with blood.

"Doubtless," said Gawain, "some knight seeking adventures is riding through here, and he's badly wounded."

"Truly," said Hector. "Let's go after him, for we'll see who he is."

Then they followed the tracks. They had not gone far when they overtook the knight, who was riding alone at a walk, complaining bitterly and saying, "Oh, God! How brief my career as a knight has been!"

And if anyone asked me who he was, I would say that he was Helain the White, Bors's son. As soon as they caught up with him, they recognized him, for he had not changed his arms since he had started on the quest.

Hector said to Gawain, "You see here the knight we've been following by the trail of blood; he's badly wounded."

"That distresses me," said Gawain, "for he's our good friend."

As soon as they caught up with him, they greeted one another, and he asked who they were. They gave their names.

"Oh, friends," he said, "you are welcome."

They asked, "Who has wounded you so?"

"By God," said Helain, "a knight who is going this way. I'm following him to see if I can avenge myself. If I can, I won't care what happens to me afterwards."

"Who is the knight?" asked Hector.

"I don't know," he said, "except that he's hunting with a great company of dogs after a beast, and it's the most grotesque beast I've ever seen."

"Which way is he going?" asked Hector.

"Along this road," said Helain.

"Sir Gawain," said Hector, "now I [189] ask you to stay with him and keep him company, for I'm afraid he is mortally wounded, and if he stayed alone, harm could come to him. I'll go after the knight, to see if I can avenge him."

"I'll stay," said Gawain, "since it pleases you."

Then Hector asked Helain, "What arms did the knight bear who did this to you?"

"My lord," said Helain, "he had black armor, but he had a red lion on his shield."

Then Hector said to Helain, "Ride at a walk, and rest in the first place you can."

How Hector went after the knight.

Then Hector rode off as fast as he could toward where he thought he could most quickly find the knight, and he had not gone far when he met a maiden who was making such a great lamentation that it was a marvel.

"My lady," said Hector, "have you met a knight with black armor?"

"Oh, my lord," she said, "by God, I met him, but in an evil hour for me, for he killed a brother of mine, who was a very good man and a very good knight, and I left him lying there beside a spring."

"Why did he kill him?" asked Hector.

"Because it pleased him," she said. "I know no other reason."

"Now don't torment yourself," he said, "for, God willing, you'll soon be avenged, for this isn't the first wrong he has done. Do you think he can have gone far?"

"No," she said.

Then Hector started down the road as fast as he could go, at a trot and a gallop, and he had not gone far when, beside a spring, he overtook the knight, who had just dismounted and laid aside his shield, lance, and helmet and was drinking from the spring.

As soon as Hector saw the shield, he knew at once that this was the man he sought, and he called to him, "Sir knight, take your arms and mount; you must defend yourself against me, for I defy you."

How the Knight of the Questing Beast knocked down Hector of the Fens.

When the knight saw that he had a battle on his hands, he stood up briskly, went to get his arms, mounted, and said to Hector, "Sir knight, consider, if you please, that you could well dispense with this battle, since I don't believe I've ever wronged you so that you should attack me."

"You have so wronged me," said Hector, "that there's no man in the world I hate so much. [191] Therefore, defend yourself."

"I certainly will," he said, "since I must."

After that, without saying anything more, they charged at each other, striking each other so hard that both were badly hurt with great wounds. Hector fell to the ground, together with his horse, for the knight who struck him was very strong.

When the knight saw Hector on the ground, he said to him, "Knight, you've wounded me without cause, and if it wouldn't be seen as villainy on my part, I'd avenge myself. But I won't do it, and I'll leave it more for courtesy's sake than for yours."

After he had said this, he left Hector and went off, wounded as he was, as fast as the horse could take him.

When Hector found himself on the ground and realized that he was badly wounded, he said in his heart, "By the faith I owe to God, the knight who is riding away is good, and I know well, from all I've seen, that he's a better knight than I am. Therefore, I'll leave him this time, for I see clearly that I'm not of such skill at arms that I could defeat him."

Then he went to his horse and got on it, wounded as he was, and he returned to where he hoped to find Gawain and Helain.[*]

But now the story leaves off speaking of Hector and turns to Gawain.

Here the story says that Gawain and Helain, who was badly wounded, rode along together. As they were riding, they happened to meet Yvain's sister. She had King Bademagu with her and had told him how Patrides had been killed, but she had not named Gawain as the one who had killed him, for she doubted that Bademagu would fight with Gawain, since they were both of the Round Table. All this she did to bring about Gawain's death, if she could, for she greatly desired his death.

The fight between King Bademagu and Gawain.

As soon as she saw Gawain and recognized him, she said, "King Bademagu, now you have a chance to avenge your nephew's death. Here's the man who killed him. Now we'll see what you'll do, if you're so bold that you dare attack him."

The king saw that they were two and asked the maiden, [193] "Which is the one who killed him?"

She said, "The one who bears the white shield with the red lion."

"So?" he said. "May God never let me wear a crown if I don't avenge my nephew Patrides, the person I loved most in the world." Then he cried out to Gawain, "Defend yourself against me, knight, for I defy you."

When Gawain heard that Bademagu was defying him, he charged at him, and they struck each other so violently that they both fell to the ground, their horses on top of them and their lances splintered. They got up briskly, however, for they were both of great heart and strength. Next they took their swords and began such a brutal battle that any man in the world who had seen it would have thought them both very good knights, and he would soon have been able to see which of them was better, had chance not brought Hector of the Fens there, wounded as I have told you by the huntsman knight. When he saw the two knights fighting so hard, he recognized Gawain at once but not King Bademagu. Nevertheless, because he saw him so skilled at arms, he immediately suspected that he was of the Round Table and that he was fighting with Gawain because he did not recognize him.

He came up to them and said to Gawain, "My lord, stop this battle until I speak with you and with this knight, who's fighting with you."

And Gawain left off at once.

How the battle ended.

Then Hector said to King Bademagu, "Sir knight, I beg you, by your love and courtesy, to tell me who you are."

"I'll tell you," he said. "My name is King Bademagu."

When Gawain heard that it was King Bademagu with whom he had been fighting, he was amazed, and because he felt that he had wronged him by what he had done to his nephew, he went and fell to his knees before him, saying, "Oh, my lord! I

---

[*]   Bogdanow 1991 (191) switches back to the Portuguese manuscript at this point.

hold myself defeated in this battle, since you are King Bademagu. Now do with me what you like, for never, God willing, will I fight with you." Then he took his sword and gave it to him.

The king, who saw that he had not defeated the knight, marveled at what he was saying and, in order to find out who he was, drew a little aside and said to him, "Tell me who you are."

"My lord," he said, "I am Gawain, King Arthur's nephew."

"Oh, Gawain!" said the king. "In truth, is it you?"

"Yes, my lord," he said.

The king, who realized that Gawain was [195] a man on whom he could not be avenged at will, was so deeply grieved that he took the sword and threw it as far away as he could.

Then he said, "Gawain, you've shamed and slain me by killing my nephew, the man I loved most in the world. Know that I'd avenge his death if you weren't my brother of the Round Table, but I can't do it without being forsworn. Therefore, I'll leave it, and I'll be more loyal to you than you were to him. May God reward you for it."

"Oh, my lord!" said Gawain. "Know that if I killed him, it was through lack of recognition, and, therefore, no one should blame me for it."

"You weren't fortunate in this," said the king. "God will take his vengeance for it, for if you do evil deeds, God will do evil to you for it."

Then he went to take his sword from where he had thrown it and climbed on his horse.

Hector went to him and said, "My lord, for God's sake, forgive Gawain, for he wronged you through lack of recognition."

Then the maiden arrived and asked, "My lord, who are you?"

"I'm Hector of the Fens," he said.

"My lord," she said, "you are welcome. If you knew how this matter had developed, as I know it, you wouldn't, for anything in the world, fail to kill him with your own hand, for this is the most faithless knight I've ever heard of, according to what I've seen of him."

"Oh, my lady," said Hector, "what's this you say? However the others blame him, you should defend him, for you know well that this is the Knight of Maidens."

"This is the knight of the devil," she said, "for this is not a knight in whom God has any part."

Then she told him how Yvain of Cenel was killed because of Gawain's abandonment, and how she had seen him kill Patrides, after having made him known to Gawain.

"Oh, my lord," said Gawain, "for God's sake, don't believe this maiden, for I'd rather have my head cut off than do such deeds as she says."

"My lord," said Hector, "I wouldn't believe it for anything, nor will I ever believe it unless I see it, for afterwards you wouldn't deserve to be called a knight, unless it was a disloyal and treacherous one."

Then King Bademagu said, "Even if I'd seen you kill Patrides and had the power to kill you for it, I wouldn't, for I wouldn't do a treacherous act for any man on earth. And if you've done the treacherous deed this young lady tells us, may God take His vengeance for it."

Then he left them and would not stay for all that Hector asked him. At his [197] departure the maiden said to Gawain, "Gawain, you have defeated me. But I'll never be happy until I have vengeance on you and see you die as cruel a death as I saw Patrides die."

As soon as she had said this, she left them and went off after King Bademagu.

91. HELAIN, HECTOR, AND GAWAIN SEE VISIONS IN THE ANCIENT CHAPEL.*

How Helain, Hector and Gawain slept in the field.

The three knights—Gawain, Hector, and Helain—started on their way, and Gawain asked Hector if he had found the knight who was hunting the Bizarre Beast.

"Yes," he said, "truly, I found him."

"And how did the two of you part?"

Then he told him everything that had happened. "And by everything I saw of his skill," he said, "I know truly that there are in all the quest only four such knights as he: Gawain, Tristan, Lancelot, and Bors. Therefore, I gave up the battle, for I saw clearly that there was nothing to be gained by pursuing it."

When Gawain heard this, he crossed himself, thinking it a marvel. Speaking of this, they rode until the hour of vespers, and then they reached an ancient chapel, where apparently neither man nor woman lived. That chapel stood in the middle of a large, secluded field, and they went that way in order to rest there that night, whatever might happen, for they were far from castle or village, and they preferred to lie under cover rather than in the open field, whatever the weather might be. When they got there, they took the bridles and saddles off their horses, so they could graze; after that they went into the chapel and disarmed themselves. They contented themselves with what they could find, for they had nothing to eat, and they saw to Helain's wound, which they found to be large.

No one who came there could enter the apse, for it was locked with a good iron grille. In the middle of the apse, before the altar, there was a marvelously rich, large sepulchre.

Hector, seeing how rich it was, said to Gawain, "How can we get in there?"

"It doesn't seem to me that we will get in there," said Gawain, "unless we break the grille, but this wouldn't be courteous or good, for it certainly seems that those who made it here didn't want every man who came here to enter, and, therefore, it's good that you leave it."

Hector agreed to this. [199]

---

*   Corresponds to Magne I:197-209; Bogdanow 1991 197-208; Piel 95-101.

How Helain saw great marvels in the chapel.

As soon as it was dark, they all lay down, for they were very tired. Because of the pain of his wound, Helain did not fall asleep, for he was badly wounded. When the other two were in their first sleep, it happened that the whole chapel began to shake as violently as if it were about to fall into the abyss. Then there came a great noise, as of a storm, so that Helain, who was not asleep, was stunned by it, and a little while after this a light entered the apse, as great as if a hundred lighted candles stood there.

With the light came many voices, all of which said, "Joy and honor and praise be to the King of the heavens." At their coming the chapel was filled with a good fragrance, as if all the spices in the world were there. After the voices had sung sweetly a great while, four men appeared in the semblance of angels, so beautiful that Helain was amazed. They came to the stone, took it by the four sides, lifted it up a full lance length, and held it there. After they had done this, a man in the semblance of a bishop descended onto the altar.

He was seated in a rich chair, and after he had descended onto the altar, he said so that Helain could hear him clearly, "Come forth, holy woman, and receive your daily bread."

After he had said this, he took a Mass wafer between his two hands. Then there came out of the sepulchre from which they had raised the stone a very old woman, completely naked, covered by nothing but her hair, which fell to the ground and was white as snow.

She went and fell to her knees before the man on the altar and said so that Helain could hear her clearly, "My lord, give me that by which I live, if you please."

He bent down at once and gave her the Host he held, saying to her, "Here is your Savior."

After she had received it, she kissed the foot of the man who was sitting in the chair, and after that she went back into the sepulchre, and at once the stone was put over it, so that it seemed it had never been removed. Then the voices stopped singing, and he who was sitting in the chair, who had come with such a great light, went away with it, and the chapel was dark as before.

How Gawain and Hector spoke of the marvels Helain had seen.

After this had happened as I have told you, [201] Helain, who had seen everything, was suddenly healed of all his wounds. Then he understood that those things were spiritual and holy, and he thanked God fervently for the good He had done him, for permitting him to see that, and for having the mercy to heal him by such power.

Then the others woke up and asked him, "Friend, what is it?"

"I feel such great joy as I never thought to feel all the days of my life."

"Praised be God," said Hector, "for just as a beautiful miracle happened to you, so did it happen to me. Know that I'm healed of the wound the huntsman knight gave me. I'm certain that some body lies here because of which these miracles occur."

"That's true," said Helain. "If you'd seen what I saw, you'd think it the greatest marvel in the world."

"Oh, God," said Gawain, "what beautiful marvels there are here! Truly they are signs from Our Lord, high marvels of the Holy Grail, and great secrets of Holy Church. Indeed," said Gawain to Hector, "by what God showed Helain we should understand that we're in mortal sin and that God doesn't love us as He does him, but he's more fit to be a knight of the Holy Grail than we."

How their host told them about adventures.

They spoke a great deal about what Helain had told them. The next morning they threw themselves into their orisons, praying that Our Lord would help them so that they might understand His life in such a way that they might be rightful questers in the quest for the Holy Grail. After each one had lingered in his prayers as long as he pleased, they went to take their arms, got on their horses, and started on their way, and, before the hour of tierce, chance brought them to a cross where the road split into three ways.

"Now we separate," said Gawain, "since we find three separate roads, and we are three knights."

Then they embraced one another, commended one another to God, and parted, and Gawain went to the right, Hector to the left, and Helain by the middle road. But they had not gone far after this when the roads Gawain and Hector were following met.

Gawain said to Hector, "Welcome! Now I see that Our Lord doesn't want us to part so soon, since He has reunited us so quickly."

"So it seems to me," said Hector.

Speaking of this, they rode all that day without finding an adventure worth the telling. At night they arrived at the house of a nobleman, who lodged them well because of Hector, whom he knew.

They asked him, [203] "My lord, is there in this land some adventure or marvel where knights go to prove themselves?"

"Indeed, marvels enough and many adventures happen in this land."

"And where do they happen more?" asked Gawain.

"Indeed, my lord, I don't know," he said, "except that near here there's a mountain, and on the mountain there's a chapel, which they call the Perilous Chapel. Knights go there day and night, mostly those of the Round Table, and, without exception, no man I ever heard of ever went there without finding an adventure so marvelous that he thought himself badly hurt or wounded or frightened by what he saw."

"And where can we find this chapel?" asked Gawain.

"Along a road that goes toward the rising sun," he said. "This road will certainly take you there."

Then they stopped speaking about it.

How the maiden told the news of Gaheriet's battle.

In the morning they left their host and went to the hermitage, and they would have arrived there quickly were it not for a maiden they met, who told them news they did not like at all. They met this maiden at the edge of a field, and a squire was traveling with her. Gawain greeted her and she him.

"My lady," he said, "can you give me news of any of the knights of the Round Table?"

"I don't know," she said, "except that yesterday I saw a knight defeated; he was a very good knight at arms and of great reputation, and they called him Gaheriet."

"Oh!" said Gawain. "What bad news this is!"

And Hector said the same.

Gawain, who was so grieved by this that tears came to his eyes, asked the maiden, "Did you see the battle?"

"Yes," she said.

"How was it?" he asked.

"By God," she said, "Gaheriet remained on the ground, so badly wounded that I think he must be dead by now, but I never saw anything at which I marveled as much as at that battle, for, without question, three times I saw Gaheriet bring the other knight close to defeat. Each time the knight left the battle so badly wounded that, had you seen him, you'd have thought he must die at once, and each time he returned after a little while as whole and healed as if he had never had a wound.[*] Thus he went to the battle three times, each time healed of the wounds Gaheriet had given him, and in this way Gaheriet endured until finally he was defeated, so that I truly believe that he's now already dead, and he endured more than any other knight could endure."

"Oh, God!" said Gawain. "And who was the knight who has inflicted this loss on me?"

"So help me God," she said, [205] "I don't know, except that he bears two diagonal red bands on his shield, and the field is green."

"And where was the battle?" he asked.

"At the edge of the Forest of the Serpent," she said, "right before the giant's castle."

"Oh, Sir Gawain," said Hector, "don't torment yourself, for I will never be happy until I know how this matter turns out."

"Oh, Hector," said Gawain, "he who killed such a brother of mine has destroyed and shamed me, for Gaheriet is the best knight of my kin."

Then they parted from the young lady with marvelously great sorrow. They went toward where they might most quickly find Gaheriet, but they had not gone far when they lost their way, and they wandered from place to place as chance guided them. In this way it happened that they arrived at the chapel about which their host had spoken to them.

When Gawain saw that they could not find what they wanted at that time, he said to Hector, "Alas, friend! Alas! friend, we have lost everything! I'll never get to where my brother lies dead or know who killed him."

---

[*] See chapters 146 and 150 for an explanation of the Spring of Healing.

"Friend," said Hector, "don't grieve so, for, so help me God, my heart tells me that it isn't as bad with Gaheriet as the young lady said."*

"May Our Lord grant that it's so, for He can," said Gawain.

Of the vision Gawain saw.

Then they dismounted, for the night was already very dark, and they saw to their horses the best they could and went into the chapel, where they saw nothing, for there was no light there from a candle or anything else. They were deeply grieved by the news the maiden had told them, but they were tired, and they fell asleep as soon as they lay down. And as they were sleeping, each one saw a marvelous vision, which we must not omit.

What Gawain saw was this. It seemed to him that he stood in a green meadow, where there were many flowers. And in that meadow there was a corral where there were one hundred fifty bulls, which were arrogant and lustful. They were all spotted except three. Of these three, one was not really spotted, yet not without a spot, because he appeared white and yet he had a spot. Two of them were as beautiful and white as they could be. These bulls were tied with strong, tough leather thongs.

All the other bulls said among themselves, "Let's go from here to seek another pasture, better than this one."

And the bulls left there. Then they wandered in the wasteland, not in the meadow, [207] and they stayed there a long time. When they returned, they were fewer than before, and those who returned were so thin and tired they could hardly stand. Of the three who were without a spot, one came back and two remained. And when they had all returned to their corral, they were greatly troubled by hunger, for their pasture failed them, and they had to leave, some here and the others there.

Of the vision that Hector of the Fens saw.

This vision Gawain saw, but Hector saw another, marvelous and different from Gawain's, for it seemed to him that he and his brother Lancelot came down off a single chair and got on two large horses.

They said to each other, "Let's go seek what we won't be able to find."

Thus they rode many days, until Lancelot fell off his horse, and a man knocked him down, then made him get on a donkey, stripping him of his clothes and everything he had. After he had got on the donkey, he rode for a long time, until he arrived at a spring, the most beautiful and desirable he had ever seen. He dismounted to drink from it, but when he tried to drink, the water receded from him. When he saw that it receded from him, he returned to where he had come from. Hector, who was riding all the while, wandered aimlessly here and there until he came to the house of a rich man, who was holding a great wedding feast.

Hector came to the door and said, "Open up." The rich man said to him, "Seek another lodging, for no man enters here who goes riding on a large horse as you

---

*   In fact, next time we see Gaheriet (chapter 98), he is fine.

do." Then he returned with great sorrow* to the seat he had left in his land. Hector was so frightened by this dream that he awoke in distress and turned from one side to the other. Gawain, who was not sleeping and who had also been awakened by his dream, said to Hector when he saw him turning over, "Friend, are you sleeping?"

"No," said Hector. "A marvelous dream woke me up."

"Just the same happened to me," said Gawain, "and I'll never be happy until I know what it means."

Of what Gawain and Hector of the Fens saw in the chapel, at which they marveled.

As they were speaking of this, they saw a hand enter the chapel; it appeared up to the elbow, covered with red silk, and from that hand hung a rich bridle. The hand bore in its fist a lighted candle, which gave a great light, and it passed in front of them and entered the apse. After that, [209] they did not see it again.

Then a voice said, "Knights of little faith and small belief, these three things, which you have seen here, you lack, and, therefore, you cannot succeed in the quest for the Holy Grail so as to have honor from it."

When this was said, they were so frightened that for a long while they did not know what to say.

Gawain spoke first and said, "Hector, do you understand these words."

"No," he said, "but I heard them clearly."

"In the name of God," said Gawain, "we've seen as much asleep as awake. The best thing I can see in our situation is to go seek some good man or hermit who may tell us the significance of our dreams and of what we've heard. Then we'll act according to what he advises us, for otherwise we'd be traveling in vain."

Hector said that there was only good in this suggestion.

Thus it happened to the two knights in the chapel, and they could not sleep again that night. When day came they went to their horses, put the bridles and saddles on them, armed themselves, mounted, and left the chapel. When they reached a nearby valley, they met a youth.

"Friend," said Gawain, "could you tell us of some inhabited hermitage near here or the house of a religious order?"

"My lord," said the youth, "there on the mountain you can find Nascien, a hermit, the best man I know in this land and the wisest, the one who best knows how to advise all men who go to him. A little path to the left, which you'll find ahead of you at a crossing, will take you directly there."

"Now we commend you to God," said Gawain, "for you've shown us well what we were seeking."

---

* "sorrow" as in Bogdanow 1991 (206). Magne has "pleasure."

92. GAWAIN KILLS YVAIN THE BASTARD; GAWAIN'S AND HECTOR'S VISIONS EXPLAINED.*

How Gawain killed Yvain the Bastard.

Then they left him and began to ride. After they had gone a little way, Gawain said to his companion Hector, "Oh, Hector! I'm a dead man! In this matter we've forgotten my brother Gaheriet. What shall we do about him?"

"Whatever you like," said Hector, "but I think we should first speak with some good man and then go seek Gaheriet until we find him."

Gawain readily agreed to this. When they had gone forward a little, they met a fully armed knight who asked a joust of them.

"In the name of God," said Gawain, "it has been a long time since I met a knight who asked me [211] to joust, and so I won't fail him in this request."

"Friend," said Hector, "let me go."

"I won't," said Gawain. "Forgive me, but I'll go first, and if he knocks me down, you go, as you're a better knight than I am."

Then he took his lance, put his shield on his arm, and rode toward the other knight—and the knight toward him—as fast as the horse could carry him, and they struck each other so hard that they cut links from their hauberks. The other knight[†] was wounded in the chest so badly that the lance appeared on the other side, and both fell to the ground and, in falling, broke their lances. The other knight felt that he was mortally wounded and could not get up. Gawain stood up briskly, drew his sword, threw his shield before his face, and prepared to show great skill at arms, as he had much of it. But when he saw that the other knight could not get up, he thought at once that he was mortally wounded.

He went to him and said, "Either admit yourself defeated or I'll kill you."

"My lord," said the other, "You can't kill me more than you have. You can certainly make my death painful, if you like, but for God's sake and by your courtesy, do one thing that I ask of you."

Gawain said that he would do it gladly, if he could.

"I ask you," said the knight, "to take me to some abbey near here, where I may receive the rites of Holy Church, as a Christian should do at the end of his life."

"So help me God," said Gawain, "I don't know a place near here where I can take you."

"Then do this much for me," said the knight. "Take me up before you, and I'll guide you."

Then Gawain took him, laid him across the saddle, and got on behind to hold him, giving Hector his shield to carry. They rode until they reached an abbey in a nearby valley. After they had taken him down, they put the knight in a room.

At once he asked for his Savior, and they brought Him to him. When he saw Him coming, he began to weep hard, held out his clasped hands toward Him,

---

*   Corresponds to Magne I:209-225; Bogdanow 1991 208-220; Piel 101-108.
†   The other knight" as in Piel (102). Magne has "Gawain."

and confessed at once to God, before everyone there, all the things of which he felt himself guilty before his Creator, and he begged mercy of Him, weeping marvelously. After he had told everything he remembered, the priest gave him his Savior, and he received Him humbly. After he had received Him, he told Gawain to [213] draw the lance point from his chest. Gawain asked him where he was from and of what land.

"My lord," he said, "I'm of King Arthur's house and a companion of the Round Table. My name is Yvain the Bastard. I'm King Urien's son,* and I started on the quest for the Holy Grail with others of my companions. But this has happened to me for my sins, that you've killed me. I forgive you with the best heart I can, and God pardon you."

When Gawain heard this, he said with great sorrow, "Oh, God! What bad luck this has been! By God, Yvain, I'm deeply grieved by your death."

"My lord," he asked, "who are you?"

"I'm Gawain," he said, "King Arthur's nephew."

"Then I don't mind dying," he said, "since I die at the hand of such a good knight. But I beg you, for God's sake, when you return to court to greet my companions for me, those you find alive (for I know that many have entered upon this quest who won't return from it), and ask them to remember me as a brother in their prayers."

Then Gawain began to weep, and Hector and Yvain, too, and Gawain put his hand on the lance head and drew it out of Yvain's chest. When he drew it out, Yvain stiffened from the pain, and his soul at once left his body. Gawain and Hector made a great lamentation for him, for many times had they seen him do good, knightly deeds. They had him wrapped in a rich silk cloth, which the brothers brought them as soon as they knew that Yvain was a king's son. They sang Masses for him and had his sepulchre put before the high altar, and they put him in it and wrote on it his name and that of the man who had killed him.

How they reached the hermitage.

Then Gawain and Hector left the abbey in great sorrow and rode until they reached the hermitage. They tied their horses to two large oak trees they found there and hung their shields on the branches. They went along a narrow path by which they climbed the slope to the hermitage. It was stony and exceedingly hard to climb, and when they got to the top, they were tired. After they got to the top, they found a [215] hermitage, which people called Nascien's, a small, poor house, and a small chapel. The good man was beside the chapel, gathering herbs for his meal, for it had been a long time since he had eaten anything else. When he saw the armed knights coming, he thought at once that they were knights errant riding in the quest for the Holy Grail, about which he had heard tidings some time ago. He left off gathering his greens, went toward them, and greeted them. They bowed deeply to him and greeted him.

He asked them, "Why have you come here?"

---

* The Vulgate *(The Story of Merlin,* chapter 19) identifies him as the other Yvain's half-brother, son of King Urien and his seneschal's wife.

"My lord," said Gawain, "because of our desire to speak with you, to have counsel where we're without counsel, and to be sure where we're in doubt."

When Nascien heard what Gawain said, he understood at once that he was knowledgeable in worldly matters,* and he said, "Indeed, my lord, I won't fail you in anything in which I have ability and knowledge."

Then he took them to his chapel and asked them who they were, and they introduced themselves, so that he knew well who each one was. Then he told them to tell him what they needed counsel about and that he would help them if he could.

Gawain said to him at once, "My lord, yesterday it happened to me and to this knight that we arrived at a chapel and took shelter there. After we had lain down and fallen asleep, I dreamt my dream."

Then he told him what it was, and Hector also told his dream. Then they told about the hand they had seen and what the voice had said to them, and after they had told him everything, they begged him for God's sake to interpret that dream and voice to them.

How the hermit explained to Gawain the vision of the meadow and the hundred fifty bulls.

When the good man heard why they had come to him, he answered, saying to Gawain, "By the meadow you saw, where there was a corral, we should understand the Round Table, for just as the corral was divided by fences, which separated the stalls of the cattle, so in the Round Table pillars separate some of the seats from the others. By the meadow, which was green, we should understand humility and patience. In the corral you saw the hundred fifty bulls, which went out, not into the meadow [217] but into the wasteland; you should understand that if they had gone into the meadow they would have been humble and obedient. The bulls were arrogant and spotted, except three. For the bulls you should read the companions of the Round Table, who by their fornication and evil ways have fallen into pride and mortal sin, so much so that their sins cannot be concealed inside them but appear on the outside, so that they are all spotted. Of the three bulls who were without spot you should understand that the two that were white and beautiful are without sin. Beautiful and white are those who are perfect in all the virtues. The two bulls who were white stand for Galahad and Perceval, who are white, for they are clean virgins and without a spot. The third, on whom there was a mere trace of a spot, was Bors, who sinned against his virginity a long time ago but has since made up for it, for he has guarded his chastity so well that that sin has been totally pardoned. The bodies of the three bulls were bound: they are these three knights who are so bound by humility that pride can never enter into them. The other bulls, who said, 'Let's go seek a better pasture than this,' are the companions of the Round Table, who said on the day of Pentecost, 'Let's go on the quest for the Holy Grail, and we'll be heaped with worldly honors and with the heavenly food that the grace of the Holy Spirit sends to those who sit at the table of the Holy Grail. There's a

---

*   The rhetorical embellishments of Gawain's speech reveal his education and gain Nascien's respect.

good pasture; let's leave this and go there.' And they left the court and went into the wasteland, not into the meadow, for they didn't go to confession, as he should do who enters into the service of Our Lord, nor did they start with humility or patience, which we understand in the green meadow, but they went into the dry wasteland, where there was neither leaf nor flower nor fruit. This was the road to hell, where all things are dry. And when they returned, most of them were missing; by this you have to understand that, at the end of this quest, many will be missing, for they will die there. The bulls who returned were so thin and tired that they could hardly stand. These are the knights who will escape from the quest and return to court, who will be so stained and involved with sin that some will kill others, and they will have no goodness or virtue in which they can stand, to keep them from falling into hell. Of the three without spot, one will return, and the other two will stay; by this is meant that of the three [219] good knights one will return to court to tell about the good pasture that those in mortal sin have lost; the other two will remain, because they will find such great delight in the food of the Holy Grail that they will never leave it, once they have it at their will. Our Lord's final words," he said to Gawain, "I won't tell you, for evil, not good, could come of it."

"My lord," said Gawain, "I'll make do without it, if you please. And I should certainly do so, for you have made everything clear to me, so that I see all the truth of my dream."

How the hermit unraveled Hector's dream.

Then the good man said to Hector, "It seemed to you that you and Lancelot descended from one chair. The chair stands for nobility. The nobility from which you descended is the great honor of the Round Table, from which you have descended, for you left it when you departed from King Arthur's house. You climbed onto two large horses; the two horses are pride and arrogance. Then you said, 'Let's go seek what we cannot find.' This was the Holy Grail. These are the secrets and hidden things of Our Lord, which won't be revealed to you, for you aren't such as you should be. After you parted one from the other, Lancelot rode until he fell off his horse. This means that he will fall from pride and be abased in humility. Do you know who will knock him down from his pride? He who knocked down pride from heaven, and that is Jesus Christ, who has abased Lancelot and stripped him of his sins so that he recognized himself, and he saw himself naked of all the virtues that a Christian should have.* He begged for mercy, and as soon as he asked for it, Our Lord clothed him. And do you know with what? With chastity, humility, patience, and moderation. These were the garments He gave him.

"Then He made him get on an ass; this is the beast that stands for humility. It became clear a long time ago that by the ass we should understand humility, for on the day of branches† Our Lord, who was King of Kings and to whom all riches belonged, entered into the City of Jerusalem. And he came not on a horse or a palfrey but on the lowliest beast He could—He came on an ass—in order to [221] teach from that time on, to the rich and the poor, the way of humility. On such a

---

* See chapters 99-100.
† Palm Sunday.

beast you saw Lancelot riding in your dream. After he had ridden thus a long time, he came to a spring, the most beautiful he had ever seen, and he dismounted to drink. And when he wanted to drink, the water fled from him. When he saw that he couldn't drink, he turned back to where he had come from. The spring was beautiful and was made in such a way that however much water one drew out, it was never diminished. This delightful spring is the word of the Gospel. The heart of one who finds himself sick of the sins he has committed has such a great desire that the more he drinks, the more he wants to drink. This is the grace of the Holy Ghost and of the Grail that, the more abundantly it gives, the more remains in it, and because it is never diminished, it should be called a spring. When he came to the spring and dismounted, it showed that he had come close to the Holy Grail, and he will stand there and be changed until, in the presence of that Holy Vessel, he won't consider himself a man, because he has fallen into sin. When he bent down to drink and the water fled from him, this means that he will fall to his knees before the holy Vessel, in order to see something of the secret things that are there. Then the Holy Grail will hide itself from him, for he will lose the sight of his eyes, because he has turned them to worldly filth, and he will lose the power of his body because for a long time he has served the devil's power, and this vengeance will last twenty-four days, because for twenty-four years he has been the enemy's servant.*

"After he has been like this for twenty-four days, without eating or drinking or moving hand or foot, it will seem to him that he is in as good condition as before he lost the sight of his eyes. Then he will tell part of what he has seen, and at once he will leave that land and go to Camelot. And you, who all the while were riding on the large horse, this shows that you will remain in a state of sin—in pride and envy—and you will go here and there, so astray that you will arrive at the Fisher King's house, where good men and knights will be feasting and celebrating the great things they have found. When you get there and expect to enter, they will tell you that they care nothing for a man in mortal sin—in pride and arrogance.† Then you will return to Camelot, and you won't be able to boast about your part in the quest. Now I've explained to you a great part of what is to happen to you."

The explanation of the hand that Hector saw.

"Now I must tell you what [223] is meant by the hand you saw pass before you, covered, that bore the candle and the bridle, and afterwards the voice said to you that you were lacking these three things. By the hand you should understand charity; by the red silk with which it was covered you must understand the fire of the Holy Spirit, from which comes charity with burning, and whoever has charity in himself has heat and is red and burns with the love of his Lord Jesus Christ. By the bridle you should understand restraint, for just as the knight guides and commands his horse wherever he wants by the bridle and makes him stop when he wants, so does restraint, when it is firm in the Christian's heart; it holds him so strictly that he cannot fall into mortal sin or move according to his will, except to move in the path of good works. By the candle that it bore, which gave light, we should understand

* See chapter 144.
† See chapter 144.

the truth of the Gospel, which speaks of the Son of God, which gives light and brightness to all those who turn aside from the way of sin and return to the straight way, which is that of Jesus Christ. Thus you saw charity and restraint in the chapel. And for this God came to His chapel, for He did not make it so that sinners and evil men should enter but so that truth would be fixed there. And when He found you there, He went at once to the place that you had desecrated only by your gaze.

"And when He was ready to go, He said to you, 'You, knights of little faith and small belief, you are lacking these three things, and, therefore, you may not attain the great adventures of the Holy Grail.'"

How the good man told Gawain that he would accomplish nothing in the quest while he was in mortal sin.

"Now I've explained to you the meaning of your dreams and of the hand."

"Indeed," said Gawain, "you've explained it in such a way that I see clearly that it's so. Now I beg you to tell me why we aren't finding as many adventures as we're used to."

"I'll certainly tell you that," said the good man. "The great adventures that are now happening are the signs of the Holy Grail. But the signs and lessons of the Holy Grail don't appear to a sinner or a man who is wrapped up in earthly pleasures. Therefore, they aren't appearing to you, for you're a treacherous sinner. We shouldn't think that the adventures that are now abroad are to kill knights or other men. Nobody will see adventures come of that; rather, adventures are things that show to good men the meaning of other things, for heavenly things are hidden, so that the mortal heart will never [225] be able to know them except through the Holy Spirit."

"My lord," said Gawain, "according to what you tell me, it seems to me that, being in mortal sin, I will labor in vain in this quest, for I won't accomplish anything."

"Indeed," said the good man, "you speak the truth, and all who go on it will receive nothing but harm."

"By my faith," said Hector, "if we believe you, we'll return to Camelot."

"Indeed," said the good man, "I've told you and tell you again that while you are in mortal sin, you'll do nothing on the quest from which you'll receive honor."

When they had heard this, they commended him to God and left him.

When they had gone a little way away, the good man called Gawain, who returned to him, and he said, "Gawain, Gawain, it is now a long time since you first became a knight, and, since you received the order of chivalry, you've served your Creator only a little. And now you're such an old tree that there remains in you neither branch nor leaf nor fruit. From now on take care to this extent, that Our Lord may have your bark and pith, since the devil has taken your branches and leaves and fruit."

"My lord," said Gawain, "if I had leisure, I'd talk with you gladly, but you see, that other knight, whose companion I have been for some time, is going away. Therefore, I must leave, whether I want to or not. But as soon as I can, I'll return, for I have a very great desire to speak with you in complete privacy."

How Hector and Gawain left the hill where the hermitage stood.

Then they departed, and the two knights climbed down the hill where the hermitage stood and came to their horses.

They mounted, took their arms, and rode until nightfall. At night they arrived at the house of a mountaineer, who lodged them well as soon as he recognized them. In the morning they left him and started on the quest; they rode a long time together without finding an adventure worth the telling.

93. BORS CLEANSES HIMSELF SPIRITUALLY AND CHOOSES TO SAVE A STRANGE MAIDEN RATHER THAN HIS BROTHER LIONEL.*

But now the story stops speaking of them and turns to Galahad and Bors, saying that, after they had left Esclabor the Unknown,† they rode that day until nones without finding any adventure. Then they happened to find, at the edge of the forest through which they had passed the day before, that same knight who for such a long [227] time had been following the Questing Beast.

Bors said to Galahad, "Now you may see the knight whom his father praised to you for skill at knighthood over all the other knights of Great Britain."

"Indeed," said Galahad, "it's quite apparent that he's a good knight, but I would certainly think there is someone better in the kingdom of Logres."

"I don't know what will happen to me as a result," said Bors, "but I'll never be happy until I see for myself if he is such a knight as his father says."

"You'll do as you like about it," said Galahad, "but I fear you may come to grief."

How Galahad and Bors met the Knight of the Questing Beast and how he jousted with Bors and knocked him down.

As soon as the knight reached them, he said, without greeting them, "My lords, what are you seeking?"

Then Bors replied, "We seek what you seek: the Questing Beast."

"What?" said the knight. "You seek and follow my quest, at which I have been laboring so long and at which I forbade you to labor any more? Indeed, this is ignoble and foolish, and you'll regret it, if I have my way."

Then he put his hand under the arm piece and his shield before his chest, and Bors did the same when he saw that he had a joust on his hands. The knight, who was agile and skilled at arms, struck him so violently that he broke through Bors's shield and hauberk, giving him a great but not mortal wound in the chest and throwing him and his horse to the ground, for he was a man of exceptionally great strength. In that fall Bors was badly hurt, for the horse fell directly on top of him. After the

---

*   Corresponds to Magne I:225-239; Bogdanow 1991 220-233; Piel 108-115.
†   At the end of chapter 87.

knight had struck this blow, he did not look at Bors again but started into the forest, and he went away so fast that it seemed lightning was chasing him. When Galahad saw Bors on the ground, he was greatly afraid the latter was mortally wounded.

Therefore, he let the knight go and went to Bors, who had already stood up, being of great heart and strength, and asked him, "Friend, how do you feel?"

"Well enough, my lord," he said. "Thanks to God, I'm not hurt."

He said this to comfort Galahad, but he felt a great deal otherwise than he said.

"You see," said Galahad, "I told you before. Know that this is one of the best knights in the world."

"I already consider it proved, so that I won't test it again, because of the great ability that I know is in him. I say that it's a great sin and wrong that he isn't a Christian."

"That's true," said Galahad. "But [229] since you're my companion and of the Round Table, and he knocked you down in front of me, I'll avenge you the best I can; otherwise he'd think me a cowardly knight. Now you stay and ride at a walk, and I'll follow him until I catch up with him, God willing."

As soon as he had said this, he started into the forest and went where he thought he would find the knight, as fast as the horse could carry him.

How Galahad went after the Knight of the Questing Beast in order to avenge Bors.

When Bors saw Galahad go, he got on his horse and went after him, for, if he could, he wanted to see what would come of it. Thus wounded, he rode hurriedly, and he had not gone far when he met a man dressed in the habit of a religious order. He was riding on an ass, reciting the vespers of St. Mary as he rode, for it was already the hour for it. When Bors reached him, he greeted the good man, and the latter left off what he was saying and greeted Bors. Then they both stopped.

"My lord, did you see a knight with a red cross on a white shield pass by here?"

"Yes," he said. "He's going so fast that you won't be able to catch up with him today. Therefore, I'd advise you to stay with me today, for it's time to take shelter, and, what's more, you seem to be to be wounded. I'll take you to a place where they'll care for you well and serve you."

Bors agreed to this, for it was already time to take shelter, and the other seemed to him a good man.

How Bors remained with the hermit, and how the hermit counseled him and explained to him what the quest for the Holy Grail was.

Then they began to speak of many things, until the good man asked him, "My lord, who are you?"

"I'm a knight of King Arthur's house," he said.

"And what do you seek in this land?" he asked.

"I seek what, in my opinion, will hardly be found," said Bors, "into which many men have already put and are putting great effort: the Holy Grail. We started on this quest on Pentecost, one hundred fifty knights, all good men and of great renown."

"What?" asked the good man. "Has the quest for the Holy Grail begun?"

"Yes," said Bors.

"And are you a companion in it?" he asked.

"Certainly," said Bors.

"Indeed, you involve yourself in a great matter by seeking the hidden things of Our Lord and searching for the greatest marvels in the world."

"My lord," said Bors, "it's so."

"Now tell me," said the good man, "how you expect to accomplish such a noble undertaking." [231]

"My lord," he said, "I started on it by chance, like my companions, and, if it pleases God that good come to me, it will please me. And if something else happens to me because of it, I'll endure it."

"What is your name?" asked the good man.

"My lord," he said, "my name is Bors, and I'm son of King Bors of Gaunes."

"Indeed," said the good man, "I know your father and your mother, and by rights you should be a good man, for the scriptures say that a good tree yields good fruit, and the tree from which you've come was good, because of which you'll be good, if sin and evil do not take you from it. But tell me this: how did you start on this quest?"

"My lord," said Bors, "as my companions did."

"By God!" said the good man, "you started on it foolishly, and I'll tell you how. But tell me this first: do you know what the quest for the Holy Grail is?"

"Not very well," said Bors.

"I'll tell you what it is," he said; "to seek the Holy Grail is as much as to seek the marvels of Holy Church and the hidden things and marvels and great secrets that Our Lord doesn't want to let a man find who is in mortal sin. The quest for the Holy Grail, then, is that He separates the good knights from the bad, as the grain from the straw. And when He separates the sensuous knights from the good ones, then He'll show to these good and fortunate knights the marvels of the Holy Grail that they're seeking. Then He'll heap them with the good of the Holy Grail, with His holy grace, and with the blessed food of which the prophets and good men of this earth—who already knew what was to come—have spoken plainly.*

"This will happen when they'll secretly be given in abundance this blessed food,† which is called the grace of the Holy Grail—they, the good knights who follow this quest, who will confess truthfully, lament their sins, and keep themselves pure in such a great undertaking as this, which obviously is the service of Our Lord. To those who go to it in sin, it will happen as the Evangelist says happened to the man who was without wedding clothes at the rich man's wedding. For he said that there was a rich man, and he was holding a very great wedding; he cast an eye about the

---

* "—who already knew ... have spoken plainly" as in Bogdanow 1991 (225). Magne has "good men of this earth have spoken, who already knew this and who spoke plainly of the things that were to come."

† "food" as in Bogdanow 1991 (225). Magne has "quest."

palace, where they were sitting at the table, and saw among the others a man who was not dressed in wedding clothes, and he ordered him to be taken and his hands and feet tied, and he had him thrown into a prison.

"This, which the Scriptures say, I say to you, for you and your companions: just as that rich man invited one and another [233] to his feast and his table, so Our Lord invited all the companions of the Round Table to see the marvels of the Holy Grail and to enjoy that sweet food with which they were served on the day of Pentecost, if they started on this quest equipped as they should be, like those who enter into God's service. But if they started in sin and sensuality as before, they labor in vain, for they'll never enjoy it but will suffer loss and disgrace, because they call themselves knights of the quest for the Grail, which is to say knights of Our Lord, and they aren't. They'll leave it with dishonor and disgrace, just like the man who went to the rich man's wedding without wedding clothes. Know well, Sir Bors, that if you were the best knight now in the world, your knighthood would only harm you until you were clean confessed and had received the Body of God. But if you've done this and have stopped sinning mortally[*] since you've started on the quest for the Holy Grail, I believe, because of the good there is in you, of which I've heard a great deal, that you'll have honor and joy in this quest, more than your heart could imagine. Now take thought about what I've told you, for, indeed, if you act in any other way, you've started on the quest in vain, in my opinion."

How Bors told the good man that he would be better because of what he had told him and that he would make his confession at once.

When Bors heard this, he replied, "Indeed, my lord, you've corrected so much in me by what you've told me that I hope to be a better man because of it all the days of my life, and I realize that you've told me the truth. I truly believe that any man who starts on this quest, if he is not clean confessed, is failing in his service to Our Lord and will be shamed in it. And I am one who won't continue on it unless I first make my confession the best I can and receive my Savior. After I've done this and have in my company such a noble guide as the Savior of the world, then I'll be able to ride confidently and seek in all directions the adventures of the Holy Grail."

"That's true," said the good man.

How Bors left the good man, and how he found his brother Lionel being led away prisoner, and how a knight was taking a maiden away against her will.

Speaking about [235] this, they rode until at nightfall they arrived where the good man lived. Bors did not sleep that night, thinking about what the good man had told him, for he saw clearly that he had told him the truth.

In the morning, before he heard Mass, he received the Body of God, and the good man said to him, "Bors, you've given shelter to your Savior. Now watch yourself, that you don't take away His resting place from Him. Know that if you keep yourself

---

[*]   "But if you ... since you started ..." as in Bogdanow 1991 (227). Magne has "But if you do this and stop sinning mortally, good will come to you. And since you have started ..."

from sinning mortally in this quest, such great honor and joy and good fortune will come to you that you won't be able to believe it until you see it."

Bors answered at once, "May God permit me to do Him such service in this quest as pleases Him."

"Just as I desire, so may you always act," said the good man.

Then he gave Bors his blessing, and Bors took his armor, armed himself, got on his horse, and took leave of him. He went away thinking hard about what the good man had told him. He quickly made a vow that throughout that quest he would eat only bread and water, and he subsequently kept that vow very well. All that day he rode without finding an adventure worth the telling, and he asked everyone he met for news of the knight who bore the white shield with the red cross. But he never met anyone with any news of him.

The next day it happened that he was going through a great forest, and two marvelous adventures happened to him, both together. He found a road that divided into two paths. Two knights were riding along that road, bearing his brother, Lionel, disarmed and severely wounded; they wanted to take him to a denser part of the forest in order to kill him, and as they went along they were giving him great blows with the flats of their swords. That was one adventure. The other was that a knight was carrying off a maiden before him, going by the other path; she was weeping and making such a great lamentation that it would certainly have seemed to you that she would rather have been dead than alive, for the knight had abducted her from her father's house and wanted to take her into the forest, to her grief, in order to have her virginity.

As soon as the maiden saw Bors, she recognized clearly that he was one of the knights of the Holy Grail, those who would not fail a maiden in distress for anything that might happen, and she cried to him as loudly as she could, "Oh, good knight, for God's and pity's sake, help me; deliver me from this traitor who wants to shame me, if you're one of the good knights who are seeking the Holy Grail."

Thus the maiden asked Bors to help her, and Lionel, who recognized his brother, called to him, [237] "Oh, brother Bors! Don't let me die here, but help me; deliver me from these traitors, who are taking me to the mountains near here to kill me."

How Bors prayed to God to keep his brother and how he helped the maiden instead of his brother.

When Bors heard this, he did not know what to do; if he did not help his brother, it would be the greatest evil in the world. On the other hand, if he did not help the maiden, he would be false in God's eyes and the world's, for he had promised God and the men of the Round Table that he would never fail to give aid to a maiden who asked it of him.

And she was asking it of him, saying, "Oh, good knight, for God's and pity's sake, have mercy on me; don't let me be shamed."

When Bors heard her begging him so humbly, he was so troubled in his heart that he raised his hands toward heaven as high as he could and said, "Father Jesus Christ, if You please, keep me and keep my brother, that he may not die, for I'll try to help this maiden. But I beg You that my brother may not die before I can help him."

Then he struck his horse with his spurs and went after the maiden, who was already some distance away. He commended himself fervently to God, and he had not gone far when, in a valley, he saw the knight, who had dismounted and held the maiden underneath him, in order to lie with her. She was crying out as loudly as she could.

When Bors heard this, he charged at the knight, crying, "Sir knight, leave the maiden, for in an evil hour have you seized her."

When the knight heard this, he stood up quickly and said, "Knight, you aren't courteous to meddle in things that don't concern you, for she's mine, and I'll have all my will with her in spite of her wish and yours."

"So help me God, my lord," said the maiden, "it isn't so, for I never belonged to him or anyone else, but he seized me today in my father's house."

"So, knight," said Bors, "do you hear what she says? Indeed, you'll be the worse for what you've already done, if I have anything to say about it."

Then he dismounted, tied his horse to a tree, drew his sword, and charged. The other, seeing him coming, realized that Bors was a good knight, and he drew aside a little to find out who he was.

He said to Bors, "Sir knight, I ask you to tell me who you are."

Bors said, "I'm Bors of Gaunes."

When the knight heard that this was Bors of Gaunes, one of the best and most famous knights [239] in the world, he threw down his sword and said, "My lord, now you may do as you like with me, for I won't fight with you for anything, since I know well that harm would come to me at the end."

Then he fell to his knees before him and said, "My lord, I put myself at your mercy, but I beg you, for mercy's and courtesy's sake, to give me this maiden, whom I have loved so long and for whom I have endured so much labor. I'll take her to be my wife and hold her in such great honor as the son of a king and a queen should do to the daughter of a king and a queen."

"This I'll by no means do," said Bors, "at least without knowing from her if it pleases her."

Then he asked the maiden, and she answered at once, "Sir Bors, I know truly that he has wanted me for a long time, and I recognize truly that* he is of as high rank as I, but I won't do this without the advice of my friends, for I would be the more blamed, since I'm a virgin."

"My lady," said Bors, "since he wants to do you such great honor as to take you to be his wife, and since he loves you so much, I ask you to take him, and, indeed, I tell you that you'll gain honor from it. If there's blame in it, let it be mine and the honor yours."

---

*   Here Bogdanow 1991 (231) switches back to the French manuscript.

"My lord," said the maiden, "you are thought to be a very good knight and a very good man; for God's sake, don't make me do something from which dishonor may come to my family."

"I know that it won't grieve them," said Bors, "and that it will be to their honor, and, therefore, I ask you to do it."

"My lord," she said, "I'll do it, since you press me so hard."

The knight promised her that he would take her to be his wife. Then Bors said, "Now you may go together, and I'll go elsewhere, where I have much to do."

Then he went to his horse and mounted; he left the knight and the maiden, who, indeed, later did all they had promised. And may all those who hear this story know that of that knight and that lady there later came Licanor the Great, the good knight, who killed Meraugis of Portlegues after King Mark's death,* just as the story will later tell at the end of our book. But it speaks no more of them at this time.

How Bors went to help his brother Lionel.

When Bors left the knight and the maiden, he went as quickly as he could to where he thought he could most quickly find his brother, but he tried in vain, for the farther he penetrated into the forest, the farther from Lionel he went. But since I have not told you who the two knights were who were taking Lionel away captive, I want to explain it to you, just as the true history tells it. [241]

94. THE LADY OF THE TENT; LIONEL SAVED BY BORS'S PRAYER.[†]

How Lionel reached the tents, where he found the lady alone.

That very day Lionel had left the house of a nobleman, where he had lain that night. After he had started on his way, just like the others, chance brought him at the hour of prime to a tower, which stood in a clearing in the very forest where Bors, passing by, saw him.[‡] When he reached the tower in the middle of a meadow, he saw two beautiful, rich tents set up, and before each one were two shields and two lances. As soon as Lionel saw the shields, he went eagerly in that direction, for it had been a long time that he had been riding on the quest, and he had not found anything that had pleased him much. When he reached the tents, he looked inside, but he saw nothing except a lady who lay there sleeping in a bed. Nevertheless, she woke up because of Lionel's horse, which began to whinny. When he saw the lady alone, he dismounted in order to rest and ask her something about herself. He put his lance and shield on the ground, tied his horse to a tent pole, and went inside.

---

*   Chapter 160.
†   Corresponds to Magne I:241-249; Bogdanow 1991 233-241; Piel 115-120.
‡   "the very forest where Bors, passing by, saw him," as in Bogdanow 1991 (233). Magne has "that very forest."

The lady, who was very courteous, received him well and said to him, "My lord, are you a knight errant?"

"Yes, my lady," he said, "but why do you ask?"

"My lord," she said, "in order to do you as much service and honor as I can. But since you're a knight errant, sit now and rest, if you please, for, indeed, I'm very happy at your coming."

"Thank you, my lady," he said.

How the lady recognized Lionel, and how her husband and his father wanted to kill her.

Then he sat down beside her, and she said to him, "My lord, where are you from?"

"My lady," he said, "I'm from King Arthur's house."

"My lord," she said, "it seems to me from your language that you're a native of the kingdom of Gaunes or that you have lived there a great deal."

"Indeed," he said, "and you also seem to me to be from there."

"Truly, I am," she said, "and from the kingdom of Benoic and of good enough lineage. But when King Arthur went to Gaunes to destroy King Claudas, who had entrenched himself in the city of Gaunes, then I was given to a knight of the kingdom of Logres, who asked me of King Arthur as a reward for his service and took me for his wife. After he brought me to this land, he made this tower, which you see. But I beg you, since you're a knight errant and from the kingdom of [243] Gaunes, to tell me your name."

He gave her his name. When she heard it, she fell to her knees before him and wanted to kiss his foot, but he did not want her to and raised her up quickly.

She said to him, "Oh, Lionel, you are welcome. For God's sake, how is it with my lord Sir Lancelot, the best knight I know, whom I would very much like to see?"

"Indeed," he said, "I haven't seen him in a long time; however, I believe that he's well, for not long ago a knight of our company gave me good news of him."

"God give him health," she said, "for, certainly, when he dies, knighthood will be sadly diminished."

Then Lionel asked her, "These tents, whose are they?"

"They belong to the man who took me as his wife," she said.

"And the shields," he asked, "whose are they?"

"This white shield is his," she said, "and that black one his father's, and those other two belong to his brothers."

"And where are they?" asked Lionel.

"They have gone on foot to amuse themselves in the forest," she said, "and they'll be back soon."

As they were speaking of this, the lady's husband and his father suddenly appeared, coming toward the tents. When the husband saw the armed knight inside the tent and saw that his wife entertained him so happily, he was greatly shocked by it and so deeply grieved that he did not know what to do or say. He drew aside and began to brood.

His father, seeing him brooding, asked him, "Son, what's wrong with you?"

"What's wrong with me?" he said. "Don't you see my treacherous, disloyal wife, who has had a strange knight come here to shame me while we went to walk in this forest? Now the knight has already done all he wanted to her, and then he has taken his arms in order to make it appear to us that he came here for no harm."

"By God, son," said the father, "I do think that you speak the truth. Now do whatever you have in your heart about it, for I will back you."*

"I don't know how I can better avenge myself on them," said the son, "than to kill them. First I'll kill her, who made him come here, and after that him, who came here for my harm."

How the lady's husband killed the lady in front of Lionel, and how Lionel mortally wounded the father.

Then he drew his sword and went straight to the tents, saying to the lady before she could say anything to him, "You've shamed me, and I'll shame you, for you've deserved it of me."

Then he raised the sword and cut off her head, and he said to Lionel, "I've done this to your dishonor, for you've shamed me in the thing I loved most in the world, and I'll shame you in the thing you love most in the world, your person. Defend yourself against me, for I promise you only death."†

Then he and his father charged at Lionel, unarmed as they were, so great were the anger and resentment they felt.

Lionel, who was also [245] very angry and deeply grieved by the dishonor he had received, said, "Knight, you've shamed me by killing this lady so wrongfully, to my dishonor. So help me God, if you weren't unarmed, I'd avenge myself in such a way that you'd never lay a hand on anyone else, for if I, armed as I am, attacked you, who are unarmed, people would think it ignoble of me. Therefore, I advise you not to attack me, for you know without question that I'll kill you, however ignoble people think it of me."

Angry and aggrieved, they did not stop what they had begun. When Lionel saw that he could not escape without defending himself, he raised his sword and struck the father, who was annoying him more, so hard that he cut off his left shoulder, and the man fell to the ground at once. When the son saw this, he thought that Lionel would kill him if he attacked him any more, and he drew aside a little.

Lionel said to him, "Knight, you've severely dishonored me, and I'd avenge myself well on you if you weren't unarmed. But I tell you truly that wherever I may find you armed, you'll give me your head there, if I have my way."‡

How the lady's husband and his two brothers went after Lionel, and how Lionel killed the lady's husband with his first blow and the two brothers captured Lionel.

The knight made no reply to anything Lionel said to him, seeing himself in danger of death, but he went out of the tent. Lionel put his sword in its scabbard, went to his horse, mounted, and started on his way with great sorrow over the lady's death.

---

* "I will back you" as in Bodanow 1991 (236). Magne has "I recommend it to you."
† "I promise you only death" as in Bogdanow 1991 (237). Magne has "there is only death ahead."
‡ Literally, "If I am able."

He had not gone far when he heard knights coming after him, and he looked and saw three, sons of the man he had killed.

They were coming fast, and as soon as they reached him, they said to him, "Defend yourself against us, treacherous knight; you are facing death, for you have truly deserved it."

When he saw their shields, he realized who they were, and he saw at once that he could not get away from them without a perilous battle. Then he turned toward them and put everything at hazard. He lowered his lance and struck the first man so hard that he drove his lance through his chest and threw him to the ground. The fall broke the lance, and the knight was mortally wounded. And you may know that this was the one who had killed the lady. The other two brothers, who feared Lionel not at all, struck him so hard that one gave him a great but not mortal wound, and the other killed his horse, so that against his will he was forced to the ground. However, he got up nimbly, for he was agile and light, and he drew his sword and [247] prepared to defend himself, for he saw clearly that he had great need. The others, angry and deeply grieved, went to him just as they were on horseback, took his sword from him by force, and captured him, for they were both good knights.

They uncovered his head, and one of them wanted to cut it off, but the other said to him, "Don't kill him, but let's take him to our father, and if we find him alive, we'll then take such vengeance as he asks of us."

Then they returned to the tents, and there God performed a beautiful miracle for Bors, who had prayed to Our Lord to keep his brother from death, since he himself was going to help the maiden, for love of her and in order not to break the oath he had sworn at the Round Table, that he would help any maiden in distress. Because of this, for love of Bors, God brought it about that both the knights who were leading Lionel fell dead at the edge of the field where those two tents and the three knights' shields were.

How Lionel left the place where God had delivered him from the knights who had taken him prisoner and cursed Bors as he went.

When Lionel saw this adventure, he was very happy. He went to the tents, provided himself with a horse and arms the best he could, and started on his way, although he was so badly wounded that he had more need to rest than to ride. He rode with especially great sorrow because his brother had failed him in such distress, so that he conceived for Bors such a great, mortal hatred that he said he would cut off his head, if he could defeat him in battle, for never had one brother committed such an offense against another. Preoccupied with his anger, Lionel rode all that day, and at night he arrived at a monastery of white monks, where there were many good men living a holy life. That monastery stood on a large body of water called Celeca. There Lionel was received honorably and well served, and they cared for his wounds; the brothers did this for him gladly, because two knights errant had recently built that monastery. Lionel lay there as long as he liked, until he saw that he could ride, but he did not try to ride while he was still so badly wounded. He confessed to one of the best brothers there, telling him the harm he wished his brother and how he had escaped death. The good man knew Bors, who had confessed to him the week before, and he knew his [249] goodness* and believed truly that Our Lord loved him marvelously well.

He replied to Lionel, "Sir knight, you've told me about one of the most beautiful adventures I ever heard of, and I want you to know that this was a great miracle by Our Lord, but this happened not because of your goodness or any love Our Lord has for you, but because of some petition that Bors made to Our Lord on your behalf, for I truly believe that he is a holy person and one of the knights Our Lord loves most in the world, because I know his life and behavior to be such."

"My lord," said Lionel, "you may say what you like, but I don't believe that if he were such as you say he would have left me in such peril as he did, and, therefore, truly, I will never be happy until I avenge myself on him fully."

95. LIONEL'S REVENGE; CALOGRENANT'S DEATH; BORS RIDES TO THE SEA.†

How Lionel arrived where the tournament was to be and how he found his brother Bors.

When Lionel saw that he was able to ride, he armed himself, mounted, and rode away. He traveled until he reached a castle named Cidela, where there was at that time a great crowd of people, both outside and inside, because there was a tournament planned there for the next day, and many good knights of the Round Table and from many lands were gathered there. When Lionel knew that there was to be a tournament there, he thought that some knights of the Round Table would certainly come, and if his brother came, he could avenge himself there for the offense Bors had done him.

Then he asked a youth, "Do you think I could find lodging in this castle, if I went there?"

"No," said the youth, "for there are so many there that they won't all fit inside."

When he heard this, he went away from in front of the castle gate. Being a foreigner who did not know the land, he rode about near the castle seeking lodging where he could take shelter, until he arrived at a hermitage, dismounted, and thought that he would stay there that night, that he would rest better there than in the open. After he was disarmed, he took the saddle and bridle off the horse and threw himself down to rest under an oak that stood in front of the hermitage door. As he was lying there, he saw coming toward him his brother Bors. As soon as he recognized him, he immediately recalled the peril in which Bors had left him, and he began to seethe with anger and ill will. He stood up to meet him—not to greet him but to do him harm and grief if he could.

---

* "goodness" as in Bogdanow 1991 (240). Magne has "mind."
† Corresponds to Magne I:249-261; Bogdanow 1991 241-251; Piel 120-125.

When Bors realized that it was his brother Lionel, he was more joyful than one could tell, and he quickly dismounted from his horse and said, "Friend and brother, you are welcome! How long ago did you get here?"

Lionel would not reply to this but said to him, "Bors, it's no thanks to you that I escaped death the other day, when you saw that the two knights were taking me away and [251] you wouldn't help me but helped a maiden you didn't even know. Never did a brother commit such a disloyal act as you committed at that time, and for that deed I defy you to the death, for never will I be happy until I avenge myself for all you've done to me."

How Lionel injured his brother Bors and how he killed the hermit who asked him not to kill his brother.

When Bors saw his brother so angry, he was deeply grieved, and at once he fell to his knees before him, clasped his hands, and begged mercy of him, asking him to pardon that wrong.

Lionel answered, "May God never help me if I pardon you. Defend yourself against me, for indeed I'll do to you what one should do to a treacherous and disloyal knight, for you're certainly the most treacherous I ever saw."

Then he took his weapons and got on his horse. He said to Bors, "Defend yourself against me, for, so help me God, I'll kill you. If the whole world spoke to me on your behalf, I wouldn't spare you."

When Bors saw how the matter stood and that he must fight with his brother or die, he did not know what to do, for he would not for anything fight with him if he could help it, for Lionel was his elder brother, to whom he owed submission and fealty. And because he did not want to hurt him in any way, he thought he would try again to see if he could find mercy in him.

Then he took off his helmet, fell to his knees before the feet of his brother's horse, and wept hard, saying, "Friend, good brother, have mercy on me and don't kill me, but pardon me this offense and remember the great love there should be between you and me."

Lionel did not give a straw for anything Bors said, for he was a man possessed by devils who were filling him with the desire to kill his brother. All the while, Bors was on his knees before him, hands joined, begging him for mercy. When Lionel saw that Bors would not get up for anything he said, he spurred the horse and struck Bors with the horse's chest so hard that he knocked him to the ground. Bors was badly hurt in the fall, and Lionel rode over him so many times that he completely crushed him. Bors was in such pain that he thought he would die there without confession. As soon as Lionel saw that Bors could not get up, he dismounted, having a great desire to cut off his head. As he was preparing to behead him, the hermit came out of the hermitage, a [253] man of great age, who had clearly heard all that had been said between the brothers.

When he saw that Lionel was prepared to cut off his brother's head, he went running there, badly frightened, threw himself down on top of Bors, and said, "Oh, good knight, have mercy on me and on your brother, for, if you kill him, you'll be in mortal sin, and you'll never be worth anything, and the death of such a man will be a great loss."

"So help me God, good cleric," said Lionel, "if you don't get up from there, I'll kill you. And that won't prevent me from doing to him what I've begun."

"Indeed," said the good man, "I'd rather you killed me than see him die before me."

Then he lay full length on top of Bors, holding him by the shoulders, and said to Lionel, "Now you may do what you like, for I want to receive death for him."

When Lionel heard this, he did not delay at all, for he was very angry, and he gave the good man one blow such that he split him completely down to his teeth.

How Calogrenant arrived where Lionel wanted to cut off Bors's head, and how he fought Lionel for Bors.

Although Lionel had done this, the anger he felt was not at all diminished; rather, he ran to his brother and gave him with the pommel of his sword such a blow on his head that he made the blood come out in seven places, and he would certainly have killed him if at that moment Calogrenant, a knight of the Round Table, who was going armed to the tournament, had not come that way. When he reached them and saw the good man dead, he was amazed. Then he saw the knight who held the other one underneath him and wanted to cut off his head, and when, after looking hard at them, he recognized them both, he was deeply grieved.

He got off his horse, took Lionel by the shoulders, drew Bors away from him, and said, "What's this, Lionel? Are you mad, that you want to kill your brother, the best knight and the best man I know? Certainly, I wouldn't permit you to do this to any good man."

"What?" asked Lionel. "Would you take him away from me? By my faith, if you meddle further with this I'll leave him and occupy myself with you."

When Calogrenant heard this, he was frightened and said to him, "Is it true that you want to kill him?"

"I want to kill him," said Lionel, "and I won't spare him for you or for anyone else, for he has greatly deserved that from me."

Then he raised his sword to strike Bors on the head. Calogrenant put himself [255] between the two and said that if Lionel wanted to strike again, he had a fight on his hands.

When Lionel heard this, he took his shield and asked him who he was, and Calogrenant gave his name.

Lionel said to him, "You're of the Round Table, but, God help me, that won't keep me from fighting you, because you're preventing me from taking vengeance on the man to whom I wish the worst in the world, and I defy you at once."

Then he quickly gave him the hardest sword stroke he could on his helmet. When Calogrenant saw that the fight was beginning, he went running to his shield, which he had thrown on the ground, took it, and drew his sword. He was a good knight and very brave and defended himself briskly, and the battle lasted so long that Bors sat up, so badly hurt that he never expected to bear arms again unless God laid His hand on him. When he saw that Calogrenant was fighting with his brother, he was deeply grieved, for, if Calogrenant killed his brother in front of him, he would never be happy, so much did he love him from his heart, and if his brother killed Calogrenant, the dishonor of it would be his, for he knew well that Calogrenant had begun this battle because of him. He was especially sad about that and would gladly have gone to part them if he could, but he couldn't for anything, for he was in great pain. He waited until Calogrenant was getting the worst of the battle, for Lionel was very brave and strong. Calogrenant had already had his helmet cut to pieces, and his shield and his hauberk, so that he awaited only death. He had already lost so much blood that he could no longer stand, and he was greatly afraid that he was going to die.

He looked and saw Bors, who had just stood up with great effort, and he said to him, "Sir Bors! Why don't you come rescue me from death? I ran this risk to save you, who were as near death as I am now or nearer. Indeed, if you let me die, everyone who hears about it will blame you, and the dishonor will be yours and the loss mine."

"All that will do you no good," said Lionel. "You are to die right now, and all the world can't save the two of you from death at my hands."

When Bors heard this, he was not very confident, for, after Calogrenant's death, his brother would kill him, if he found him unarmed. Therefore, he went to his helmet and tied it on.

When he found the hermit dead, he was very sad and said, [257] "Oh, God! What misfortune and what a sin!"

Calogrenant called out again, "Oh, Sir Bors! Will you let me be killed this way? If it pleases you that I die, it pleases me well, for, indeed, I couldn't now or later meet death for a better man than you."

How Lionel killed Calogrenant.

At this Lionel raised his sword and struck Calogrenant so hard that he knocked his helmet off. When Calogrenant saw his head unprotected and saw that he could not escape, he said, "Oh, Lord and Father Jesus Christ, who let me start on this quest less prepared and less free from sin than I should have been, have mercy on my soul, so that the pain that I will suffer here for the good and charity that I wanted to do may be comfort and penance to my soul."

He threw his helmet away and laid himself down in the form of a cross, and while he was saying this, Lionel, who was wild with anger, struck him so hard that he killed him. At that a beautiful miracle occurred, just as the true history explains, and we will not fail to relate it. The miracle was like this: when Lionel wounded him in the head, instead of the blood that should have flowed* from the wound, which was very large, there flowed milk as white as snow; as much as half a barrel flowed from it, and it was true that it flowed from his body. From that blood, which was so white, from which the ground could not be fully clean, it happened that flowers grew before half a year had passed after his death, and still every year at that season there are flowers that grow from those, and all summer one may find them. Those flowers are called calogres, and they serve even now someone who is bleeding because they stanch the flow, but if an animal eats them, it dies

---

*   Here Bogdanow 1991 (287) returns to the French manuscript.

at once. Just as I have told you, Calogrenant died, and the beautiful miracle that I have described happened because of it And that hermitage, beside which he died and where he was buried, was called "the hermitage of Calogrenant" and never afterward changed its name.

How Our Lord sent fire between Lionel and Bors, so they would not kill each other, and how a voice told Bors not to stay with his brother.

After Lionel had killed Calogrenant, he did not look at him again or at the miracle that had been performed but charged at his brother and gave him on top of the helmet such a great blow that he made him fall face down. Bors by his nature loved humility, and [259] he still begged Lionel for God's sake to stop this battle, "for if it happens, brother, that I kill you or you me, this will be the greatest betrayal that ever happened in the kingdom of Logres, and we'll die in a state of sin. Therefore, I ask you for God's sake to give it up."

"May God never help me," said Lionel, "if I have mercy on you, as long as I can do more than you, for I wasn't kept from death by you."

Then Bors drew his sword and said, "Lord and Father Jesus Christ, don't count it a sin against me if I defend myself against my brother."

Then he raised the sword, but when he wanted to strike his brother on the helmet, he heard a voice, which said to him, "Bors, my son, don't strike him, for you'll kill him!"

Then there came down between them a sheet of fire in the semblance of lightning so hot that it completely burned their shields. They were in such pain from it that they fell to the ground and lay unconscious a great while. After they had stood up, they looked around and saw all the ground between them scorched by the fire that was burning. But when Bors saw that his brother was not hurt, he raised his hands toward heaven and thanked God for it fervently.

Then a voice said to him, "Bors, stay with your brother no longer, but go directly toward the sea; do not delay, for Perceval is waiting for you there."

When he heard this, he held out his hands and said, "Father of the heavens, may You be praised, who are pleased to call me to Your service."

Then he went to Lionel and said to him, "For God's sake, brother, pardon me."

Lionel said that he pardoned him gladly.

Then Bors said further to him, "Brother, you've done wrong in killing Calogrenant, your companion of the Round Table, and also in killing the good hermit."

But he still did not realize the marvel that had happened about Calogrenant, for God did not want him to delay any longer in going to where Perceval awaited him.

Lionel answered, "I'm deeply grieved by all I have done, but my sin and misfortune made me do it. Now tell me what I should do about it."

"Brother," said Bors, "I can't stay here any longer, but you stay. I commend you to God, for I don't know if I'll see you again, and I ask you, for God's sake and for the honor of your lineage, never again to commit such brutal cruelty as you have done, for no good can come to you of it, but all evil."

And Lionel said that Bors would never see him like that again.

How Bors went toward the sea and found Perceval, just as the voice had told him.

Then Bors went to his horse and mounted, badly hurt as he was, and Lionel stayed to have those he had killed buried. After Bors had mounted, [261] he went toward where he thought he would most quickly come to the sea, and he rode day after day until he arrived at an abbey, which stood on the shore of the sea. He slept there that night and was well served with whatever the good men had.

At the hour of midnight a voice said to him, "Bors, get up and go to the sea, for Perceval is already there and awaits you at the shore."

When he heard this, he got up quickly, crossed himself, and asked Our Lord to guide him. He did not want to wake anyone, so they would not know he had left at such an hour. He went to saddle and bridle his horse; he took his armor, armed himself, and left the abbey by the gate that was open toward the sea, and he left there in such a way that no one heard or saw him.

96. PERCEVAL SAVES THE GOOD MAN FROM SUICIDE, LEARNS MORE ABOUT THE QUEST.*

But now the story leaves off speaking of Bors and turns back to Perceval.

Perceval, his story says, rode a great while without finding an adventure to please him. Everywhere he went he asked about his companions, Lancelot, Hector, and Tristan, and his brother Agloval—for he remembered and loved them the most—and he was so fortunate that everywhere he went he obtained news of one or another. This comforted him. And I tell you truly that in that quest he led a very good life, for he spent more time in prayers than anything else. No day passed without his fasting, and most days he lived on bread and water, and he met no hermit or recluse to whom he did not confess and with whom he did not take counsel about his soul. God showed him special mercy: he seemed so beautiful and joyful that there appeared to be no knight in the world who rejoiced more in delights and pleasures, and of the experienced among the knights errant of this time it seemed that no one had loved more than he or thrown himself more into the desires of the world. But he was different than he seemed.

How Perceval arrived at the hermitage.

One day a marvelous adventure happened to him, having to do with a man of a religious order who was very high born and of King Uther Pendragon's lineage. That nobleman had been a knight of great skill [263] at arms and good in another

*   Corresponds to Magne I:261-275; Bogdanow 1991 252-263; Piel 125-132.

respect, for he had entered a hermitage for the love of Our Lord and had lived thus a full thirty years or more. This hermitage stood in the middle of a great forest, on top of a mountain, far from all people, in a very distant place. When Perceval arrived there, there was no one else in the good man's company except one knight who had recently come there. Perceval arrived at the hermitage on a Friday at the hour of prime, and he came there not by anyone's instruction but as chance brought him. When he arrived and saw the house so poor, he knew at once that it was a hermitage, and he dismounted, being accustomed to speaking with holy men on the subject of his soul. After he had put his shield and lance on the ground and taken off his helmet and sword, he entered the hermitage.

As he entered, he crossed himself, asking Our Lord to help him, and as he was making the sign of the Holy Cross, he heard, in a little chapel there, the voice of a man who said to him,* "Come forward, Perceval, holy, blessed creature; praised be God who has brought you here. Your coming has delivered me from the death of hell. Truly, you are among the true knights and the fortunate ones who are to accomplish the quest for the Holy Grail."

When Perceval heard this, he was amazed and wondered what it could be, who it was who knew him but had not yet seen him.

The other called repeatedly, "Oh, Perceval! Holy knight, give me your blessing, for you are among the fortunate ones who will see the Holy Vessel openly."

When Perceval arrived at the door of the chapel, he saw before the altar an old man, white-haired, thin, and poor; he wore a long robe and had such a long beard that it brushed on the ground, and he had around his neck a thick rope, like someone being taken to be hanged.

As soon as he saw Perceval near him, he fell to his knees before him and said to him, "Oh, Perceval! You are a friend of God; you are welcome, for you have delivered me from an evil and painful death. However, you didn't do it, but Our Lord did it for love of you."

How the man Perceval found in the hermitage asked Perceval to bless him.

Perceval was completely dumbfounded when he saw that the other fell to his knees before him.

He wanted to raise him up, but the old man would not rise and said to him, "I'll stay here unless you give me your blessing, for I know you for such a good man and such a holy knight that your blessing is necessary to me and will be able to heal me of the power of the devil."

"Oh, my lord," said Perceval, [265] "mercy! I'm no bishop or priest of the Mass who can give you a blessing. Rather I'm a knight, much more sinful and wretched than I should be."

"Perceval," said the good man, "do what I ask of you, or I will never move from here."

"My lord," said Perceval, "for God's sake, mercy. I've already told you that I'm not a prelate of Holy Church who can give you a blessing. And I say it to you again: what you ask of me is a great marvel."

---

*   Here Bogdanow 1991 (254) returns to the Portuguese manuscript.

"Perceval," he said, "I'd rather have your blessing than that of all the prelates I now know, for you are a good man in God's eyes and a holier person than you think. Therefore, I still beg you to do what I ask of you, or I promise you that I'll never move from here, not for death or anything else."

Then he seized the edge of Perceval's mail coat with both his hands and said, "Now make me stay here as long as you please."

When Perceval saw that it meant so much to him, he did not know what to do or say, for at that time it was not the custom that knights errant were asked to give their blessing, for, unquestionably, there were few who were not in a state of mortal sin and sensuality, for there were very few who did not have carnal relations with their ladies.

How Perceval blessed the good man and how the good man kissed his foot.

With the good man like this, as I tell you, Perceval said, "I'll do what you ask of me, but not willingly, for it is certainly not the custom in the kingdom of Logres that a knight meddle in such a matter." Then he raised his hand and said, "May the King of Kings give you His blessing, for that of such a poor knight as I am cannot help you; but may this help you."

Then he made the sign of the cross over him in the name of the Father and the Son and the Holy Spirit, and the good man came closer to him and kissed his foot. Perceval was completely dumbfounded at what he had just seen him do.

How the good man said to Perceval that he would tell him the marvel God had done for him.

Then the good man stood up and said to Perceval, "Praised be God, who brought you here at this time, for indeed, I had great need, as I'll tell you. Now sit down, and I'll tell you the greatest marvel that has happened to a sinner in a long time. This marvel happened to me today."

Perceval sat down at once, as he greatly desired to know about that man. And the good man began to tell it in this manner. [267]

How the good man told Perceval the marvel that had happened to him.

"Friend Perceval, I was born a long time ago, a good hundred twenty years ago and more, and I wouldn't consider those days poorly used had I spent them in good works, but I was such a sinner, boy and man, that I consider all my days wasted, for I did little good and much evil. I was king of a large, rich land, and I was a companion of Uther Pendragon and of this King Arthur, when he began to reign. But because of one sin that happened to me, in which I felt myself guilty before Our Lord, I retired here to save my soul, and my brother, who was a very good knight, left the world for my sake and came here to keep me company. He had lived with me twenty-nine years, such a life as God knows, when he died not yet two years ago. He died, I believe, in such great penitence, after such a good life, and amid so many tears, begging mercy of Our Lord, that I believed firmly that as soon as his soul left his body it went immediately before God's face with a great company of angels and archangels. I remained alone a full year and had no company but God's. It was not half a year ago that a knight came here and remained with me to do penance for two of his sons, whom he had killed. He said he would live always in penance, but it didn't seem to me that he suffered the penance with a good heart; I thought that he would rather return to the world than remain, were he not ashamed. Thus he stayed with me a full three months, and it didn't seem that he did anything for which God should reward him. It is three days ago now that he died, and something happened in my presence at which I am much amazed, and I'll tell you what. At the moment when his soul was ready to leave his body, he said to me, 'Friend, pray for me, for I think that your prayer will do me good in God's sight, and I promise you that, if I can possibly do it, I'll come to see you on the third day from today, and I'll give you news of your brother and about how long you have to live.'

How the good man told Perceval how he had news of his coming from his companion, who had died there shortly before and who told him how long he had to live.

"Saying this, he passed away, ardently begging mercy of Our Lord, and I marveled because he told me what I didn't ask him. I doubted that what he had promised could ever be, but nevertheless it came to pass, for, where I was saying my prayers before the altar, he appeared to me, so beautiful and with such [269] a great light that I could hardly see him. Nevertheless, all the while I knew it was he, and he said to me, 'Friend, I bring you marvelous news. Your brother is in the pain and torment of Purgatory, and he will be there three years yet, before he completes his penance, but it is not so with me, God be thanked, for as soon as I departed from this world, at once my soul went to the delight of Paradise that will never fail. Now take good care what you do, for you'll leave this world seventeen days from now; then you'll have what you have deserved. I can't stay here any longer, but you'll see Perceval the fortunate and glorious, who is coming here to see you."

How the good man told Perceval in what manner God had delivered him.

"In this way, as I've told you, my companion appeared to me, and then he went away, and I didn't know when. I remained brooding and amazed at the good life I had seen my brother lead, and the long penance he had had, and it seemed to me that he had found little mercy in his Creator and little reward for the great hardships he had suffered for Him. Then I began to think about the fact that I had been so long in that hermitage, and I said in anger that it was folly for a man to exercise himself so much for an uncertain reward, for the evil man will receive as much good after his death as the good one and more. And I said this because of my brother, who deserved to go to Heaven as much as my companion or more.

"Thus I fell into despair and, brooding on this, heard a voice that said to me—but I know now it was the devil who wanted to entrap me—'You can expect the same for yourself as for your brother, or worse. And this will be the reward you'll have for your labor.'

"As soon as I heard this, I said in anger, 'Ah, wretch! I am deceived in the life I've led so long. I've used my labors poorly; I'll never again* exercise myself to serve God, since I see the reward is like this.'

"Then I was so beside myself and so wrathful that I planned to kill myself with my own hands. At once I took this rope and put it around my neck, as you see, and I thought I'd hang myself from that beam you see there, so that I'd heal all my hurts with one stroke. Thus I prepared [271] my death, as I've told you and as the demon had me do; but it seems to me that it didn't please Our Lord for me to die such a dishonorable death. Rather he wanted to help me by your coming, whence such a miracle happened that, as soon as you came through the door and crossed yourself, the demon left me—as near to death as I have told you—for he had no power to endure the holy sign made by the hand of such a holy man as you. At once I returned to my right mind and recognized how the devil had wanted to make me lose body and soul. I know truly that I was delivered by your coming, and I thank Our Lord for it. Indeed, if you weren't a holy man, leading a holy life and filled with the grace of Our Lord, such a beautiful adventure would never have taken place through you. For that reason I asked you for your blessing, as soon as you entered, for I know you and your goodness much better than you yourself."

Perceval did not know what to reply to this, as he desired no earthly praise; nevertheless, he said to him, "Our Lord has kept you from such a great sin; thanks be given to Him alone, for I certainly tell you that this didn't come about through me but through Him who made you and didn't want to lose you."

How Perceval asked the good man to tell him what the quest for the Holy Grail could be.

Then the good man took off the rope and threw it away. He began to talk with Perceval, and each asked the other about himself.

After they had talked a long while about their affairs, Perceval asked him, "My lord, what do you think about this quest for the Holy Grail, which we have recently begun? Do you think we can accomplish it?"

"Indeed, I don't know," said the good man, "but for love of you I'll ask Our Lord in the secret prayers of the Mass to show me, through His mercy, what may come of it, and you also ask Our Lord to show me something about it, for I know that your petition can help a great deal."

Perceval said he would do so.

How the good man told Perceval everything that would happen to him in the quest for the Holy Grail and how he would die in penance.

That day and night Perceval remained with the hermit, and in the morning, when the hermit was clad in the armor of Jesus Christ and had sung the Mass with the secret prayers, at that moment a letter fell onto the altar, but they did not see who had thrown it down, for spiritual things do not [273] show themselves in all places where they happen, except to whom God wishes.

---

* "again" supplied by the translator.

After the good man had said the Mass and taken off his vestments, he took the letter and said to Perceval, "Friend, Our Lord has heard your prayer; see here a letter, which He has sent you. I think you'll find written here what you asked me about."

Then he opened the letter and, after he had read it, said to Perceval, "Friend Perceval, of the quest for the Holy Grail I tell you truly that you will have much pleasure and good fortune and much labor and hardship, and that you will reach the house of the Fisher King in order to have the sacred food of the Holy Grail. There you will be twelve companions of those who are good in the sight of God and the world, and there you will have greater joy and pleasure than you have ever had before. After you leave there, you will suffer great labor and hardship keeping the Holy Vessel company. Then Our Lord will guide you—you and Galahad and Bors of Gaunes—to an alien land, far from the kingdom of Logres, and in that land you and Galahad will die in the service of Our Lord."

"May everything be according to the will of Him who made me," said Perceval, "for I don't much care where I die, as long as I die in good works and my soul is saved. But tell me this, if you please: do you think I'll ever again see the company of the Round Table assembled as I saw it at Pentecost?"

"No, indeed," said the hermit, "you'll never see it together like that again except on the Day of Judgment, for be certain that in this quest there are already many dead, and still more will die in it."

"And about my brother Agloval," said Perceval, "do you know if I'll see him?"

"No, indeed," said the good man, "you'll never again see him alive, for the man who has killed so many of your friends will kill him."

"Who is that?" asked Perceval. "Who will kill him?"

"That I won't tell you," said the good man, "for much evil could come of it to you and to the one who is to kill him."

"Whatever happens to my brother, death or life," said Perceval, "may Our Lord have mercy on his soul and make him know Him well at his death, for in the death of a man is everything."

"Now," said the good man, "ask me no more, for I won't tell you."

How Perceval took leave of the good man and rode away, deep in thought.

After [275] they had spoken together of many things, Perceval said to the hermit, "My lord, I must go after my companions, and I ask you, for God's sake, to remember me in your prayers, for I'm a sinner just like any other man."

"I'll pray for you," said the good man, "and you also pray for me."

Perceval said he would do so. After that he went to his horse and put the saddle and bridle on him. Then he armed himself, mounted, and took leave of the hermit, asking him to see that he continued what he had begun.

The hermit answered him, "Perceval, be sure that I won't ever leave the service of Jesus Christ; rather I'll serve him much better than I have until now, for I have great need of it, since my remaining days are so few, and great evil would come to me if in seventeen days I lost what I've gained in thirty years of great effort."

Perceval commended him to God and then went. He rode all that day without finding an adventure worth the telling, thinking hard about what he had seen and heard from the good man and about the fact that so many good knights of the Round Table were to die in this quest.

97. PERCEVAL AND THE KNIGHT OF THE QUESTING BEAST.[*]

How Perceval found the Questing Beast.

The next day at noon, he found the Questing Beast[†] in a valley, and when he saw it and knew that it bore within itself the source of the barking, he marveled more than at anything he had ever seen and said, "Truly this is the beast that my father followed so long and for which he labored so hard.[‡] Indeed, I want to follow it to know if God will give me better luck with it than He gave my father."

Then he left the road and went after it. He had not gone far when he lost sight of it, for the beast was fleet and went at a great pace, as if chased by lightning. Perceval followed it at a walk, for he did not want to tire his horse. While he was riding like that, there suddenly appeared the pagan knight who had been hunting the beast so long; he was armed all in black and rode on a good horse, also all black, from which he had knocked down Gaheriet, Gawain's brother.

How Perceval met the pagan knight, who forbade him to follow the Questing Beast any more.[§]

As soon as the knight reached Perceval, he asked without greeting, "Did you see the Bizarre [277] Beast pass by here, and thirty dogs after it?"

"I didn't see any of the dogs," said Perceval, "but truly I saw the beast, and it was going so fast that nothing could have caught it; by now it's probably a full league from here."

The knight answered, "May the beast and the dogs go to the devil, for that beast will make me die of grief!"

Then the knight who had inquired after the beast asked Perceval, "Who are you?"

He said, "I'm a knight errant of the house of King Arthur and a companion of the Round Table."

"What's your name?"

"Perceval of Wales," he answered.

---

[*]　Corresponds to Magne I:275-281; Bogdanow 1991 263-267; Piel 132-134.

[†]　The author alternates between *bêsta ladrador,* which I have translated "Questing Beast" (out of deference to Malory scholars, although "Barking Beast" might be better modern English), and *bêsta desassenulhada,* which I have translated "Bizarre Beast" (might also be "Grotesque Beast").

[‡]　Perceval's father, King Pellinor, was hunting the beast in chapters 1 and 2.

[§]　From here on, these brief headings, found in the manuscript, appear less frequently and regularly.

"In the name of God," said the knight, "I've often heard men good at chivalry speak of you and praise you highly. But tell me this, as God may help you: what are you seeking alone in this country?"

"Indeed," said Perceval, "I take no companion with me because it isn't the custom of the knight errant to take company, unless he finds it by chance, for men would think it cowardice in him."

"And what are you seeking?" asked the knight.

Perceval said, "I ride in the quest for the Holy Grail, like the other knights of the Round Table, and I've been working at it for a long time now and haven't done anything by which I'm worth more or less. But now truly I left the road to go after this beast you are seeking."

"And what do you want with it?" asked the knight. "Why were you following it?"

"I followed it," said Perceval, "because my father, King Pellinor, hunted it a long time and couldn't catch it, and he was such a good knight that still today they speak of him throughout the whole world. And I, who am not of such great reputation, wanted to see if I could accomplish that at which he failed."

"Indeed, Perceval," said the knight, "you've labored at folly; you're a good knight but not so good that you should concern yourself with such a great thing as this, and I ask you, as you value your life, to meddle in it no more but keep to your great quest for the Holy Grail, for you may be sure that if I find out that you're hunting this beast again, we'll have a fight. [279] By force or by blow of lance or sword I'll show you that you shouldn't usurp my quest, for I'm a better knight than you, and I've already followed it for so long that men would think me more than lacking if I didn't forbid it to you."

Perceval considered what the knight said proud and arrogant, because he praised himself so much, and Perceval could not believe that the other was such a good knight as he said.

Therefore, he said to him, "Sir knight, it may well be that you're a better knight and more valiant than I am, but be assured that, if you were a still better knight than you are, I wouldn't leave this quest because of your prohibition until I was forced to do so."

"No?" he said. "By my faith, I think I'll make you leave it against your will. Now defend yourself against me, for I'll soon show you who's the better knight, you or I."

"What?" said Perceval. "Are you asking for a battle?"

"Yes," said the knight. "We won't part in any other way, you and I, since you won't willingly do what I ask."

After this, without delay, they charged at each other as fast as the horses could carry them, and they struck each other so hard that neither shields nor mail shirts kept them from being badly wounded, one more and the other less. Perceval was badly wounded with a great wound in his chest, but it was not mortal, and the other was wounded, but not so much. He was strong and knew everything there was to know about jousting, and he pushed against Perceval with his shield and body so hard that Perceval could not hold himself in the saddle because of the other's strength and because he was wounded. He fell from his horse to the ground, so badly bruised that he could not get up. The knight ran to Perceval's horse, which was running away, brought it to a tree, and tied it, so that Perceval would find it when he wanted to ride; after that he went as fast as he could go after the Questing Beast. Perceval, who had been knocked down just as I have told you, lay on the ground only the least possible time, as he was great of heart.

But when he did not see the man who had knocked him down and gone off with all the honor of that fight, he felt such sorrow that he did not know what to do, and he stood up quickly and said, "Oh, God! What shall I do? This knight who is going away from here has mortified and shamed me. Wherever I go from now on, if they know [281] I was knocked down by one knight, they'll neither like nor honor me. Oh, God! Who can he be? I never expected to find such excellence at arms in a foreign knight who wasn't of King Arthur's house. Oh, God! And where shall I be able to find him? I don't know," he answered himself; "what you ask is poor sense, for he has taken from you all honor and left you great shame."

98. GAHERIET TAKES PERCEVAL TO BE HEALED; PERCEVAL FINDS LANCELOT DREAMING.*

Perceval greatly lamented this adventure that had happened to him; nevertheless, when he looked and saw his horse, which the knight had tied to a tree for him, he thought at once of the other's great courtesy, and he checked his ill will a little and said, "Oh, God! How You make all things equal according to Your justice and reason!"

He said this because of the knight's courtesy and chivalric ability. Then he took his shield and mounted his horse, and he was so impatient and angry that he cared nothing about his wound. He began to follow the knight's tracks, saying that he should not leave so freely and that if he had had the better of the joust with lances, Perceval did not think the other knight would find him so bad with a sword, for he knew himself to be one of the best swordsmen in the world, and so he was. Thinking like this, Perceval went after the knight who had knocked him down, deeply concerned about his loss of honor.

He had not gone far when he met Gaheriet. As soon as they saw and recognized each other, they went to embrace each other with marvelous rejoicing.

"Sir Gaheriet," said Perceval, "what adventure has brought you here, or what are you seeking alone here in this land?"

"Indeed," said Gaheriet, "I'm seeking a knight with black armor who is hunting a beast, the most grotesque I ever saw."

"Why are you seeking him?" asked Perceval.

"I'll tell you," said Gaheriet, "and I won't withhold any of it from you, because if I hide it from you now, you'll be able to find it out in the end. It happened this morning that I met the Questing Beast and a good thirty dogs, which were chasing

---

* Corresponds to Magne I:281-287; Bogdanow 1991 267-273; Piel 135-138.

it, and when I saw it was so strange, I decided to go after it until I found out what its secret was. As I was following it, I saw behind me the knight about whom I told you, and he asked me so importunately what I was seeking [283] that I told him. When he heard that I was following the beast, he told me that I wasn't such a knight as should undertake such a noble struggle, and at once he challenged me so that we had to joust. We jousted, but the shame was mine, for he knocked me down and took my horse, because it was better than his. And when I was on the ground and saw that the knight was going, taking my horse, I didn't know what to do, for I wasn't used to going on foot so heavily armored. But this much good happened to me, that where I stood like that there came a strange knight—I don't know who he was—and he had no more than this one horse, but he gave it to me, because of I know not what kindness he said my uncle King Arthur had once done him, so that he remained on foot. I took the horse and went after the knight to see if I could catch up with him, in order to see how he wields a sword, since I already know how he handles a lance. I've told you what I'm seeking. Now tell me why you've come here."

"Indeed," said Perceval, "I'm here for the same reason as you. I, too, am seeking the knight, for the same thing happened to me today with him as happened to you: he knocked me down."

Gaheriet thought it such a great marvel that he crossed himself, and he said, "God help and save me, the knight is good!"

"God help me," said Perceval, "much better than I thought."

Then Gaheriet looked at the ground and saw how much blood was coming from Perceval's wound; he said to him, "You're badly wounded. Who wounded you?"

"That knight we're seeking," he said.

"And how do you feel?" asked Gaheriet.

"Poorly, for I'm badly wounded. However, I know I can be quickly healed of it as soon as I reach somewhere where I can rest."

"Let's turn back," said Gaheriet, "to the house of a friend of mine, which is near here, and we'll stay there until you're whole, for if you try to ride very far, it can only be your death."

Perceval said that he could not stop following the knight, since he had begun it; however, Gaheriet begged him so much that they turned back to the knight who was Gaheriet's friend. There Perceval remained until he was healed, but not Gaheriet, as he wanted to find the knight; but because he did not find him, the story speaks of him no more but tells of Sir Perceval. [285]

When Perceval was healed, he mounted, took leave of his host, and rode away. Everywhere he went he asked about the men of the Round Table, and sometimes he got good news and sometimes bad. One day chance brought him to the edge of the forest, and he found there, under an oak tree, a knight sleeping on his shield. He had his helmet and his sword and lance beside him, and his horse was grazing. Perceval stood and looked at him and could not recognize him by his face, which was stained by his armor; nevertheless, he seemed so well made that any man who saw him would have to respect him. While he was looking in this way there came a maiden on foot, and she was very beautiful.

When she saw Perceval, she said to him, "Friend, go your way and let the knight sleep. Indeed, you aren't such as should even look at him."

"What?" asked Perceval. "Is he so bad that a knight shouldn't look at him?"

"It isn't like that at all," she said. "Rather he's so worthy and of such great goodness that no knight should look at him who isn't much better than the others, and, therefore, I forbid you to look at him, for simply because you've already seen him, I fear that harm may come to him."

When Perceval heard this, he was dumbfounded, for he wondered if the maiden had seen him perform some evil act, since she said such an insulting thing. He kept silent, but all the while he looked at the knight.

The maiden said to him further, "God save you, knight, go your way, for it would certainly be a very ignoble act for you to awaken such a man."

"My lady," he said, "you praise him very highly. As God may help you, tell me who he is."

"I won't," she said, "for I don't know and can't find out, and I've worked very hard at it."

"No?" said Perceval. "Then how can you know that he is as you say?"

"I know it well," she said, "for I've kept him company for three days now, and during these three days I've seen him do so many deeds of arms and escape with honor from so many perilous adventures by means of his skill, that he couldn't have done it were he not the best knight in the world. And for this reason I have praised him so much to you."

"Now tell me why you don't know his name," said Perceval, "since you've traveled with him so long."

"By God," she said, "it isn't my fault, but he never would tell it to me, or anything about himself."

"And who do you think he is?" asked Perceval.

"God help me," she said, "I don't know what to think, and for that reason I can't tell you anything about him." [287]

"May God never help me," said Perceval, "if I leave here before I know who he is, provided he will tell it to a strange knight. That he is traveling incognito and is such a good knight as you say gives me a greater desire to know him than anything else."

"Since you want to stay here for this," said the maiden, "I ask you, by the faith you owe to all knighthood, to tell me his name as soon as you know it."

Perceval said he would gladly do so.

"Now dismount," she said.

He dismounted, laid aside his lance and shield, but not his helmet, and went to sit down in front of the knight who was sleeping. He began to look closely at him in order to recognize him, and he put his mind to it so much that finally he realized that it was Lancelot.

Then he stood up, drew the young lady aside, and said to her, "My lady, now I know this knight, and, indeed, if you praise him it's no wonder, for, God help me, there's more in him to praise than you or I could tell, for this is without doubt the knight in the world who has done most since he took arms."

"Oh, sir knight!" said the maiden; "by God and the True Cross, since you know his name, tell me, for there's nothing in the world I so much desire to know."

"Don't trouble yourself," said Perceval. "I'll tell it to you before we part."

"Many thanks," she said.

Then they sat down and talked of many things. The man who was sleeping (after he had been asleep for a long while) began to lament loudly, and he thrashed about and, heaving great sighs, began to weep so hard that his cheeks were all drenched with tears.

When the maiden saw this, she said to Perceval, "My lord, for God's sake, let's wake him up, and he'll thank us for it, for he is deeply troubled."

"Don't interfere," said Perceval, "for it would give him great grief."

Then she fell silent. Lancelot, sleeping, mourned and groaned and sighed so hard that it seemed that his soul wanted to leave his body. And if anyone asks me why he grieved so in his dream, I will tell him that it is because of a great vision that he saw, and I will tell you which one. [289]

99. LANCELOT'S DREAM.*

The vision that came to Lancelot was this. It seemed to him that he came to a river, the ugliest and most fearsome he had ever seen, and that no man could enter it without dying. He looked at the river and did not dare enter it, for he saw it full of snakes and vermin, so that any man who tried to drink of it would die at once, so poisoned was the water by them. And he stood, looking at the river, and crossed himself at the marvel he saw. While he was standing there, he saw a man emerge, wearing a rich crown of gold on his head, and he was encircled with stars. Then he saw another emerge from it, similarly crowned, who seemed a marvelously good man and a good knight. Then he saw a third emerge, and then a fourth, and then a fifth, and then a sixth, and then a seventh, and all were crowned with golden crowns, so that he thought it the greatest marvel he had ever seen. Then he saw another emerge, thin and wretched, poor and tired, who had no trace of a crown, so poorly dressed and so ill-equipped that, if the others, who had emerged from the river before, seemed rich, this one seemed poor and unfortunate and in need of all that is good. Nevertheless, poor as he was, he went toward where the others stood in order to enter their company. But the others did not want to receive him into their company but kept him at a distance. After these eight† who had already emerged, Lancelot saw one emerge, but he was more beautiful and worthy, it seemed, than all

---

*   Corresponds to Magne I:289-295; Bogdanow 1991 273-279; Piel 138-141.

†   All three editors have "seven."

the others. And as that one drew away from the river a little, Lancelot saw coming from the direction of heaven a company of angels bearing a rich, beautiful golden crown; they put it on his head and rejoiced around him as if he were one of the noblest martyrs of heaven. After they had sung a great while and given praise to the Creator of the world, they went all crowned toward heaven. But with no one did they rejoice as with the one who emerged last. Thus were all the crowned ones taken toward heaven, but the ill-equipped one remained.

When he found himself alone, he cried out, "Oh, my lords, I am of your lineage, and you leave me* poor and so wretched? For God's sake, when you go to the House of Joy, remember me and pray to the High Master for me, that He may not forget me."

They all answered with one voice, "You cause yourself to be forgotten, and you've done that for which you'll be forgotten; you'll deserve [291] a reward only according to your labor."

Then he called himself ill-starred and wretched and made a great lamentation; after that he disappeared, so that Lancelot did not know where he went.

After this vision, he saw another marvelous one, for it seemed to him that he saw before him Morgan, King Arthur's sister, ugly and fearsome; she seemed to him as if she had just emerged from hell, and she wore no clothing except a wolf's pelt, which covered her poorly. She groaned as if she were wounded, and Lancelot, who recognized her easily as Morgan, looked at her and saw that more than a thousand devils were with her, and each one laid a hand on her to hold her better.

One said to another, "Let's go as fast as we can."

But however they tormented her, she seized Lancelot by the hands and gave him to those who guarded her, saying, "Keep him well, for this is one of your knights."

As Morgan commanded, so they did, and they took him and went very fast with him. They took him to a deep, dark, black valley, where there was only a little light. In that valley there was so much weeping that a man could not hear an echo return from anything thrown down there.

He heard more than a hundred thousand voices, all saying together, "Ah, ah, wretches! Ah, wretches! Why do we deserve this great disgrace and wretchedness and such great sorrow, passing all sorrows!"

Lancelot, hearing these sorrowful voices, was so frightened that he thought he would die of fear, and he asked those who were taking him to let him go, but they would not; rather they were taking him to a pit, dark and black and full of fire that smelled marvelously bad. He looked into the pit and saw a great chair of fire, alight as if all the fire in the world burned there. In the middle of that fire stood the chair, in which Queen Guenevere was sitting naked,† her hands before her breast; she sat there disheveled, with her tongue hanging out of her mouth, and she was burning as brightly as if she were a fat candle. She had on her head a crown of thorns, which burned marvelously, and she herself was burning all over, sitting there. [293] She was making such a great lamentation and uttering such sorrowful cries that it would

---

*   "my lords, I am of your lineage, and you leave me ..." as in Bogdanow 1991 (274). Magne has "lords of our lineage! Do you leave me ...."

†   Here Bogdanow 1991 (276) returns to the French.

certainly seem to anyone who heard her that she was heard throughout the whole world.

Sitting there in such great torment, when she saw Lancelot, she could not refrain from saying to him, "Oh, Lancelot! How evil was the day on which I first knew you! Such are the rewards of your love! You've brought me to this great torment in which you see me. I'll bring you to as great, or greater, and that grieves me, for although I'm lost and cast into the torments of hell, I don't want the same to happen to you. Please God, I'd have it happen only to me."

Queen Guenevere said this to Lancelot, or so it seemed to him in his sleep, and he felt such grief as a result that he would rather have died on the spot. After this it seemed to him that he was fortunate enough to escape whole and happy from the power of Morgan and her company, and he went into a garden, the most beautiful and delightful he had ever seen. He saw beautiful, well-dressed people, and it seemed to him that they were all as happy and delighted as if each one had all he could desire. Everyone there had on his head a beautiful, rich golden crown. He looked from one to another, and they were thinking only of rejoicing and pleasure. In that company he saw a man of great age, who had on his head a rich, beautiful golden crown, and written on it was, "This was King Ban of Benoic." Beside him was a lady, also crowned, and there were letters on her crown that said, "This is Elaine, who was Queen of Benoic."

When Lancelot, who had often heard that his father's name was King Ban of Benoic and his mother's Elaine, saw the letters, he asked the king, "My lord, weren't you my father?"

The king answered, "Yes, you were my son. I'm sorry for it, because you've left the Savior of the world and me, who was your father, and have placed yourself in the service of the devil and in his trap. You've no business here, where we are, for your place is in hell with Queen Guenevere, who has brought you to eternal death, both of you, unless you both abandon the sin that until now you've been committing [295] in the sight of God and the Holy Church. In vain have you entered into the quest for the Holy Grail, and you'll find there only shame unless you free yourself of this sin."

As soon as his father the king had said this to him, his mother Queen Elaine approached and said to him, "Son, in an evil hour I bore you, since with all the goodness and all the good qualities God gave you, you've served the devil until now.* Son, God has made you beautiful and more gifted than any other knight, but your beauty and gifts are wasted, for you placed yourself entirely in the devil's service when you coupled with Queen Guenevere, who was born in an evil hour. For a long time you've been with her against God and right. That sin will cast you into torment as great as you saw inflicted on Queen Guenevere or greater. Son, you're condemned to shame and death, and that ugly sin in which you persist will cause you to die in such great dishonor that all those of your lineage who are alive will be dishonored by it. Know that no mortal heart could imagine the sorrow and misery you'll suffer for it, for the slight pleasure you've had from it, for such is the penance for this sin, that the pleasure is brief and the torment and sorrow are

---

* "until now" added in Bogdanow 1991 (278).

unending, unless Our Lord does something about it. Therefore, I tell you, beloved son, beautiful creature, to leave that sin, for, indeed, you've greatly offended God and the world by it, and I greatly fear that you'll be damned for it."

100. PERCEVAL AND LANCELOT AT THE HERMITAGE OF THE RED OLIVE TREE; LANCELOT CONFESSES.*

These marvels Lancelot saw in his dreams, as a result of which he felt such great sorrow that the tears ran down his cheeks, and he sighed and lamented. After he had seen this vision, he awoke as tired as if he were emerging from a battle, and then he uttered a cry of great sorrow and opened his eyes.

When he saw Perceval sitting in front of him and recognized him, he got up and said to him, "Friend, you are welcome." However, he was very sorry that Perceval had found him sleeping.

"Friend," said Perceval, "you were having great trouble in your sleep, and, therefore, we had wanted for some time to wake you up, but we feared to grieve you."

Lancelot said, "I [297] wouldn't for anything in the world have had you wake me, for you'd have kept me from seeing the greatest marvels a knight ever saw in his dreams, and because of this dream I think I'll be a better man all the days of my life."

"Indeed," said Perceval, "I never saw a man experience so much distress in his dreams."

"If I was distressed," said Lancelot, "it's no wonder, for I saw all the misery and distress that the human heart can imagine, and all the good things of the world, too. What shall I tell you? I saw the most marvelous things. I saw everything I desired to see, for I saw clearly my death and my life and more than I could have imagined while I lived. And if ever I succeed in seeing some of the marvels of the Holy Grail, it will be because of this, for otherwise I would have involved myself in it in vain, for the labor would be lost. Now let us mount and go to some hermitage, for I will never rest until I know the truth about my dream."

Perceval agreed to this.

Then they took their weapons and whatever of that sort they were lacking and mounted, and the maiden said to Perceval, "My lord, tell me what you promised me: the name of this knight."

He thought a little, and then he drew Lancelot aside and said to him, "I'm bound to tell your name to this maiden, for I promised it to her."

"Then you may certainly tell her, if you wish," said Lancelot. "However, she wouldn't know it from me, now or ever, for she is one of the most ignoble and irritating girls I ever met, and it would please me greatly if she wanted to relieve us of her company."

---

*   Corresponds to Magne I:295-311; Bogdanow 1991 280-293; Piel 141-148.

"Don't worry," said Perceval, "for I'll get rid of her." Then he returned to the maiden and said to her, "My lady, I'll tell you what you asked me if you'll promise me something that won't cost you anything."

She agreed.

Perceval said to her, "This is Sir Lancelot of the Lake."

She said, "By my faith, that grieves me, for now I see that I won't be able to accomplish what I desire most in the world, and I consider myself mad and wretched to have given my heart to one so high."

Immediately she turned back by that road by which Perceval had come, lamenting as if she saw all her friends dead before her, calling herself wretched [299] and ill-starred, miserable and unfortunate, saying that she would never know joy since the thing she desired most in the world would not be hers.

Then Perceval said to Lancelot, "It seems to me that we're free of this girl."

"Her going pleases me greatly," said Lancelot.

Then they started on their way, speaking of little, for Lancelot continued to brood on the marvels he had seen and was so frightened that he would have liked never to have seen anything of Guenevere, for truly it seemed to him that no other sin had wounded him so much, to the perdition of body and soul, as that one, and that because of it they were both lost. Thus he went along brooding, so frightened that he did not speak a word, and Perceval was so sorry for him that he did not know what to say.

However, after a great while, Perceval said, to draw him out of his sorrow, "Lancelot, be comforted, and don't distress yourself so greatly, for it isn't for such a good knight as you are to be terrorized by a dream he saw."

"Oh, friend, spare me!" said Lancelot. "Don't say that to me. God help me, if you saw the marvels I have seen, I don't think you would ever know pleasure again. And these are the greatest and most terrifying marvels that a sinner ever saw in a dream."

"Whatever it may be," said Perceval, "You must take comfort, since for a man to feel grief and wrath this way can only bring him harm. Perhaps God showed you this wonder so that you would amend your life and to take you from some mortal sin, if you are guilty of any."

Lancelot did not answer him, but it occurred to him that Perceval was right.

That day the companions rode, and they had neither joy nor pleasure, for Lancelot was deeply grieved. At night they happened on the Hermitage of the Red Olive Tree. They called that olive tree red because its leaves were red both in winter and in summer, but the tree was not red; rather it was the same color as any other olive tree. When they saw that it had red leaves and green wood, they thought it a great wonder.

Lancelot spoke first and said to Perceval, [301] "Friend, what do you think of this tree?"

"Friend," said Perceval, "it only seems to me that the Lord of marvelous works is marvelous. You may be sure that this happened through some miracle of Our Lord, for, unquestionably, nature couldn't work so marvelously. God help me, it pleases me greatly that I've seen it, for I've heard many knights speak of it, and I couldn't believe that it was true."

"I never saw it before," said Lancelot, "nor heard of it."

"Know, then," said Perceval, "that this is the red olive tree, and this hermitage that you see is the hermitage they call that of the Red Olive Tree. I believe that in the chapel lives one of the best men in Great Britain—one of the most virtuous— and that he will best counsel you to the profit of your soul, for I've heard many knights speak of his goodness."

"Indeed," said Lancelot, "I'm very glad of that, for I have great need of him."

As soon as they reached the hermitage, they dismounted. The good man who lived there came out when he heard the noise of the horses. When he saw the armed knights, he understood at once that they were knights of adventure, and he greeted them and asked them to rest in his house, such as it was. They told him that they had great need to do so, for it was already quite dark. After they had seen to their horses the best they could, they entered the good man's house, which was small and beside which there was a very plain chapel. Inside they disarmed themselves to rest a little, but you never saw a man so sad or thoughtful as Sir Lancelot, for he could not, try as he might, forget what he had seen in his dreams. Nor for anything Perceval or the good man said would he be comforted, nor would he eat or do anything but brood. And if anyone asked me what he was thinking about, I would say, about two great matters; one was whether he would leave his lady the queen; the other, whether he would reveal himself and tell in his confession how he had loved such a noble lady, for there was [303] no way he would reveal* this love unless a great power made him do it, and this was because he loved the queen more than himself. These two things confused him so much that he did not know what he could do.

When the good man saw him thinking so, and because he already knew that he was Lancelot of the Lake, the knight who was at that time the most famous in the world, he asked Perceval, "My lord, what's wrong with Lancelot, that he broods so?"

"I don't know," he said, "so help me God. However, I'll tell you what I know, because with God's help you'll give him counsel."

Then he began to tell how he had found him sleeping and what he had seen of it, and what Lancelot had said, that he had seen in his dreams the greatest marvels a sinful knight had ever seen.

"Indeed," said the good man, "I don't know what this may be."

"Nor I, indeed," said Perceval.

Then the good man bowed his head toward the ground and fell into thought apparently as deep as Lancelot's,† or deeper, so that Perceval was more amazed than before.

---

*   "reveal" as in Bogdanow 1991 (285). Magne has "leave."

†   "apparently as deep as Lancelot's" as in Bogdanow 1991 (286). Magne has "as deep as before and as deep as Lancelot's."

After a while the good man said, "Perceval, knight good in the sight of God and the world, holy creature, holy body, holy flesh, pure and virgin, I know you are such a holy man and such a loyal servant of Our Lord that, if you ask, He will reveal to you what Lancelot is thinking about, and you'll know the whole truth about his life, so that you'll be able to give him counsel in his trouble, and I, who am a priest of the Mass, will help him as much as I can."

In that manner the two knights passed the evening with the hermit, and they neither ate nor drank. When it was completely dark, they lay down, each in his place, meditating and with great sorrow. Lancelot fell asleep very quickly, for he had labored hard that day. When he was ready to go to sleep, he commended himself fervently to Our Lord, made the sign of the cross over himself, and said such prayers as he knew. And as soon as he fell asleep, a marvelous vision came to him, for it seemed to him that he saw before him Yvain the Bastard, completely naked, such an ugly, repulsive, horrible creature that it was a marvel. He was wholly engulfed in fire, so that he burned all over as clearly as a well lighted candle. After him came a crowned lady, with such great sorrow and so tearful that it was apparent that she was experiencing trouble and distress, and the lady had written on her forehead, "This is [305] Catanance, the queen of Ireland,* wife of King Caradoc Shortarm." After her he saw another queen, similarly crowned and sad, and he looked at her and realized that she was Queen Iseut. After her came a knight uttering cries and lamenting, suffering the strangest distress a knight ever suffered, encircled by fire on all sides; Lancelot looked at him and realized that he was Tristan the Handsome.

Queen Iseut was saying to Lancelot, "Oh, Lancelot, such is my reward for loving; you can have such or worse, if you don't stop the madness you commit with Queen Guenevere."

Lancelot, amazed at what he saw, could not help saying to Iseut, "Is this fire with which you're surrounded or an illusion?"[†]

"It's no illusion," said Iseut. "Rather, it's a torment and fire from hell, and you'll learn how it burns, since you don't want to castigate yourself for your sins."

Then she drew near and struck him on the thigh with one finger. And Lancelot awoke and uttered a cry so full of pain that it was amazing, for he felt that his thigh was burning so badly—the fire was so well lighted and so harsh and painful—that he had never felt any anguish but this was a hundred times worse.[‡]

He cried in a loud voice, "Oh, Perceval, good friend! Save me, for I'm dying the most painful death a man ever died."

At these cries Perceval awoke and found a letter in his hand, but he did not know what was there, for it was dark, and he put it into his breast, as he wanted to know what it was all about.

---

* Magne has *[I]rlanda.* Bogdanow, working in French, has *Horlande.* Piel has *Orlande.*

† "Is this fire ... or an illusion?" as in Bogdanow 1991 (288). Magne has "This fire ... is an illusion."

‡ "the fire was so well lighted and so harsh and painful—that he had never felt any anguish but this was a hundred times worse" as in Bogdanow 1991 (288). Magne has, "the fire there was already so well lighted—that he had never felt any anguish so bad."

He ran to Lancelot in great sorrow at his pain and said, "Friend, where did this pain strike you?"

"In the right thigh," he said. "Know that there's fire there, the sharpest and hottest a man ever felt."

Perceval was horrified at what he heard and put his hand where Lancelot said, and, as soon as he laid his hand on Lancelot, a beautiful miracle happened, as the true history tells, for, by Perceval's goodness and the love Our Lord had for him, the fire was immediately quenched and the pain relieved.

Then Perceval asked Lancelot, "Friend, how do you feel?"

Lancelot answered, sighing, "How? Good friend Perceval, I am very well, for Our Lord has had mercy on me because of your goodness, for he has taken away from me the greatest pain and anguish a knight ever felt."

"Be sure that he did it not from love," said Perceval, "but to correct you. If until now you've been in a state of mortal sin, make your confession and take care not to return to it, remembering this miracle that [307] Our Lord has shown you. Indeed, I believe that if you had been confessed after you started on this quest, which is a quest for Our Lord and for His great marvels, this adventure wouldn't have happened to you."*

Lancelot answered, badly frightened, "Indeed, friend Perceval, if worse had happened to me it wouldn't be any wonder, and if Our Lord takes greater vengeance on me than on another man, I'm not surprised, for, without doubt, since I became a knight I never did the slightest thing that wasn't against Him and against my oath as a knight."

The good man said to him, "Indeed, Lancelot, this is a great loss, for you were bound to serve Our Lord more than many others, for God gave you more talent and ability than any other knight of whom anyone has heard in a long time."

"My lord," he said, "it's so, for I've served Him poorly, and I can expect a bad reward unless I amend the wrong I've done Him."

"You can amend it only by true confession, contrition, and penance," said the good man.† "Be sure that if you lack even one of these three things, you've started on the quest for the Holy Grail in vain."

Lancelot said that he would do all three, since God had shown him such a miracle and had relieved his suffering so quickly.

Talking this way they passed the night, and the good man admonished them constantly, for he truly believed that Lancelot would not confess his sin with the queen, for many good men had told him in confession what they truly thought about it.

In the morning Lancelot looked at his thigh, and he found it as black as if it had lain in the fire two or three days. He could not use it as well as before; on the

---

*   "return to it, remembering this miracle that [307] Our Lord has shown you. Indeed, I believe ... marvels, this adventure would not have happened to you" as in Bogdanow 1991 (290). Magne has "... return to it. Think of this miracle that [307] Our Lord has shown you, and, indeed, I believe ... marvels, there would not have happened to you as much as has happened."

†   "...'by true confession, contrition, and penance,' said the good man" as in Bogdanow 1991 (290). Magne has "...'by confession,' said the good man, 'and by grieving for the evil you have done and obeying the commandment of your abbot.'"

contrary, it hurt a great deal, and a bad odor came from it. The good man, looking at it, marveled at the heat that had come from it, and Perceval did, too. And all three said that truly that was a miracle from Jesus Christ.

Then Perceval drew the letter from his breast and gave it to the good man, saying, "This letter was given to me last night. I don't know where it came from, but I received it at the moment Lancelot began to cry out. Now see what's in it and tell me, if it's something I should hear."

The good man thanked God for this adventure and said, [309] "Oh, Perceval, let's rejoice, for Our Lord has heard our petition."

Then he opened the letter and found that it said, "Lancelot, vile creature, evil knight, son of hell, abode of the devil's darkness, forsworn and disloyal to your king and earthly lord! Why don't you correct yourself after the beautiful marvels I have shown you? For I have shown you all torment and all sorrow, all pleasure and all joy. Either leave your sinful ways or I'll make you dwell in sorrow with Iseut and with Tristan, who will deserve to be lost forever if they don't give up their sin. And you, son Perceval, who keep your flesh so pure, as knights of the Holy Church should do, who have never been touched by the fire of sensuality because you never desired that fire of misfortune, I will now do you honor, for the fire I cast onto the sensuous man in vengeance for his sensuality will die down as soon as you place there your hand, which never lowered itself to such a sin. And I do you this honor because of the good life I see you leading among the vile and the evil, who think you are other than you are."*

After the hermit had read the letter, he said to Perceval, "friend, son, holy creature, now I see and understand clearly the goodness and grace that God has granted you and the disloyalty of this other knight. Now hear the letter, and I'll read it to you in such a way that this false knight, who won't leave his unfortunate ways for either the miracle or the goodness that Our Lord has shown him, will be able to comprehend his madness and his evil."

Then he read the letter, so that they both heard him, and after he had read it he said further, "Lancelot, now you can see that you are deceived and that you'll die in shame and sorrow if you don't leave the sinful life you've led until now, and yet Our Lord has shown good will to you more than to any other man, for He calls you thus by such beautiful miracles and signs."

That's true," said Lancelot, "and because of the great love He has just shown me, I promise Him that I won't ever return to leading such a life."

He confessed all his sins at once to the good man, in Perceval's hearing, and know that at that time he hid nothing from them of his relationship with Guenevere, for he knew Perceval was so loyal and good that he would not reveal it to anyone.

After Lancelot had made his confession, the good man said to him, "Lancelot, are you deeply sorry for this [311] sin you have just confessed?"

"Yes, my lord," he said, "and I have the idea that I would certainly like not to have to take arms because of any pledge I might have made, for I know well that this sin more than any other has made me an enemy of Our Lord. And for this reason I leave it completely, so that I will never return to it."

---

*   Here Bogdanow 1991 (292) returns to the Portuguese.

101. PERCEVAL AND LANCELOT SEEK TO LEARN WHY THE OLIVE TREE HAS RED LEAVES; THE ADVENTURE OF THE MAN IN THE CHAIR.*

How Lancelot and Perceval asked the good man the reason why the hermitage's olive tree had red leaves, and he told them what he knew.

In this way, as I have told you, Lancelot recognized his sin and the queen's, because of the great marvels that had happened to him, by which he had been badly frightened. That day the good man put the letter Perceval had given him on the altar, and at night, when he wanted it, he could not find it, although he looked hard for it.

Lancelot and Perceval stayed there a week, and when Lancelot felt himself healed so that he could bear arms, he mounted, and Perceval with him. But the day before they left, they asked the hermit for the truth about the red olive tree.

"So help me God, you're asking me something I don't know, and I'd certainly like to know it as much as you."

"Then how may we find out about it?" asked Perceval.

"I don't know, so help me God," said the hermit, "but I'll tell you one thing I do know. Near here there's a cloister on a low mountain, and there's a small but rich chair there, in which there sits a very old man—I don't know if he was a king or a prince. It is already a great while since he died, but he sits in the chair just as if he were alive. He holds a letter in his right hand. Many good knights have gone there to take it from his hand, but they couldn't."

"Why did they want to?" asked Perceval. "I would gladly know that."

"My lord," he said, "all the people of this land say, and I firmly believe it's the truth, that the man who can take the letter from his hand will learn the truth about this tree, for the truth is in the letter, and from the letter one could also find out who he is who sits in the chair, but not otherwise."

"So help me God," said Lancelot, "I would very gladly see this, for it seems to me that a knight who heard about such a thing and didn't try to see it would not be very enterprising. Therefore, we ask you to take us there, so we may see this marvel, for if we may not take the letter, we'll speak about it in the Court of Adventures when it pleases God that we go there together."

How Perceval and Lancelot found the man who was sitting in the chair and could not draw the letter out of his hand.

All three agreed to this, and they went to the cloister on foot. The cloister stood exactly halfway up the side of the mountain. It was square, made with hewn corners, and was [313] sixteen yards long and sixteen yards wide.† Exactly in the middle stood a chair, as beautiful and rich as if it were made for King Arthur himself. In

---

* Corresponds to Magne I:311-315; Bogdanow 1991 293-297; Piel 148-150.

† Twenty-eight *côvados*, or twenty-eight cubits. One cubit is between seventeen and twenty-two inches. Therefore, twenty-eight *côvados* is about sixteen yards.

the chair there sat a man with completely white hair. He had his sword girded on, and he sat so well in the chair that if his color had not changed you would have thought that he was alive. He held the letter in his right hand. He was still armed with his sword and arm pieces, his white shield leaning against the chair near his shoulders.

When the good man came inside and showed them who was sitting in the chair, he said, "My lords, how does it seem to you?"

They said that it was one of the greatest marvels they had ever seen.

Then after a great while Lancelot said to Perceval, "Friend, King Pellinor, your father, was just like this on an island where I went once, a long time ago, and if this man had a crown like your father, I'd believe that it was he and that they had moved him from there to here." Then he told Perceval under what circumstances he had seen him and said, "Never will he change from what he is* until Gawain is dead."

"What does Gawain have to do with it?" asked Perceval.

Then Lancelot fell silent, because he did not want to reveal such a thing, knowing that great harm could come of it, for he feared that Perceval would kill Gawain if he knew the truth.

Perceval asked the question again, and then Lancelot answered, "Friend, don't ask me anything about this, for I will neither tell you the truth nor lie."

Then Perceval fell silent, as he could not possibly believe that Gawain had killed his father, although he had heard it said several times, but he thought it a lie.

"Friend," said Lancelot, "what shall we do about this letter? We must see if we can get it, for otherwise people would not think us adventurous knights, if we didn't try to experience all adventures."

Perceval said, "We've come here for nothing else."

Then he grasped the letter to draw it out of the hand of the man who held it, and he could not.

When he saw that he could not, he drew aside and said to Lancelot, "Now you may go try it."

Lancelot himself grasped it and could do no more than Perceval, and he drew aside with grief, for he would rather have been dead, and said with great anger, "Oh, God! How long has the world been duped and deceived!"

"Friend," said Perceval, "why do you say this now?"

"Because," he said, "all the world thought that I was the best knight in the world, and I'm not, and I deceived them when they thought I was better than I am."

The good man said to him, "My lord, if you've failed in this adventure, don't be dismayed, for this [315] adventure is granted only to one knight, and he must be the best knight of all who now bear arms in the kingdom of Logres or who will come after him."

"I'll keep still," said Lancelot, "since it is so, and I won't speak of it again, except that I beg Our Lord to bring here soon the man who is to be successful in this adventure, that we may know from him the truth about the red tree."

---

* That is, he will remain perfectly preserved.

"May God grant* it," said the good man, "for I certainly want to know it as much as you."

102. PERCEVAL AND LANCELOT MEET GALAHAD AT PERCEVAL'S AUNT'S CELL.†

In this manner they left the cloister. They stayed all that day with the good man. The next day they took their weapons, left him, and rode, and subsequently they rode for many days without finding an adventure worth the telling. One day as they were riding along, talking of many things, they came to the edge of the Waste Forest, where they found a cross in front of a cell and stopped. Know that in that cell was a very beautiful lady who had been queen of a great and rich land—she was Perceval's mother's sister—but because of her grief at the death of Lamorat her nephew, whom she had loved dearly and valued for his knighthood above all other knights in the world, she had shut herself up there, so that no man or woman of her family knew where she was. They had already sought her in many places, and if they had known that she was there, they would not for anything in the world have let her stay there. The lady had been there a long time, and she lived such a good and holy life that it would have seemed a marvel to you, had you seen her. She never had any other clothes than those in which she had originally come there, so that she no longer had anything with which to cover herself except her hair, which was marvelously long and all white.

How the wounded knight reached Lancelot and Perceval and asked them to defend him against a knight who was following him.

After Lancelot and Perceval reached the cross that stood before the cell, they stopped while Perceval said to Lancelot, "Now if it pleased God, I wish we would find some marvelous adventure."

As soon as he said this, they saw a knight coming, armed but without lance or shield, badly wounded, and he was coming as fast as his horse could bring him.

As soon as he saw the [317] knights, he called to them, "Oh, my lords! For God's sake, are you knights errant?"

They said, "Yes, but why do you ask?"

"So that I may have your help," he said, "for there is a knight coming after me who wants to kill me, and you shouldn't fail me at such a time, for every knight errant should help all those who ask him for help."

"Don't be afraid," they said, "for we take you under our protection against the knight, whoever he may be."

He said, "Now I'll stay with you."

---

* All three editions have "know."
† Corresponds to Magne I:315-319; Bogdanow 1991 298-302; Piel 150-152.

He stayed, and he said, "You will both have to joust with him, for he's such a good knight at arms that neither of you alone will prevail against him."

When he said this, Perceval said, "By my faith, I don't know."

He said, "Believe me, he is just as I tell you."

They wondered greatly who he could be.

Then after a while they saw Galahad, the exceedingly good knight, emerge from the forest, but they did not recognize him.

"Now," said the knight, "you may see the man I was telling you about. Know that this is the best knight I ever saw."

Lancelot said at once to Perceval, "Friend, let's go to him."

Galahad, who was riding with his lance lowered, came on very fast and struck Perceval so hard that he knocked him and his horse to the ground, and he wounded him badly in the left side. After he had knocked Perceval to the ground, he did not look at him but charged at his father, whom he did not recognize because Lancelot had changed his armor, for many occasions had come to him for changing it, especially since he had started on the quest. Galahad's lance was still whole, and he gave his father such a great blow with it that he knocked him to the ground, on his face in the road, but he did him no other harm, for his lance was very good. After that he passed by him in order to go to the knight he was following, but that man, who knew Galahad's skill at arms, did not await him at leisure but let himself fall from his horse as soon as he saw Galahad close to him.

He fell to his knees on the ground, lifted his clasped hands toward Galahad, and said, "Oh, excellent knight! Mercy, for God's and pity's sake, don't kill me, for I put myself at your mercy."

When Galahad saw that the other had so abased himself, he said, "Knight, you have greatly offended me, [319] but since you ask mercy of me, I'll release you from my complaint, for it is right that he who asks for mercy should find it."

Then he rode back toward the forest as fast as if chased by lightning.

When Lancelot and Perceval had seen this adventure, they were greatly amazed. They walked a considerable distance to catch their horses, which had taken fright.

They caught them and mounted, and Lancelot said to Perceval, "God heard your prayer, for as soon as you asked for adventure He gave it to you."

Perceval said, "That's true, but I had wanted something else, for I see that we are shamed by a good knight. In King Arthur's house they would hardly be able to believe that this happened to us."

"Now leave me," said Lancelot, "for, by the faith I owe to all knighthood, I swear that I'll never be happy until I avenge this dishonor, and if a knight knocks me down with his lance, may I knock him down with my sword or never wear a sword again. Now I'm going after him, and I won't rest until I catch him."

"It would be wasted effort at such an hour," said Perceval, "for night is coming on quickly, and he has been gone for some time, as you see, so that if it were still broad daylight we couldn't catch him unless he stopped somewhere, and, therefore, it would be highly advisable for us to turn aside and take shelter somewhere, and we'll follow him in the morning."

Then Lancelot said, "We won't rest until we avenge this dishonor, and he who did it to us is not yet far away. May God never help me if I agree to your proposal; rather, I'll go after him, and when it becomes completely dark, I'll stay where night overtakes me, and then no one will blame me."

"Friend," said Perceval, "You'll do what you like, but I'll stay near this cell, and in the morning I'll go after him."

"Then I commend you to God," said Lancelot, "for I don't know why I should stop following him before I know who he is, and if he isn't of King Arthur's house, I'll have a battle with him, as long as I can strike with this my sword."

103. Lancelot Follows Galahad and Stays with Two Hermits.*

Thus Lancelot and Perceval parted. Perceval went toward the cell, for he wanted to stay, and Lancelot, who was thoroughly amazed at what had happened to him, followed Galahad along the road through the dense forest. He rode until he reached a deep valley, and he rode through it until he reached a hermitage in which there lived two good men, brothers and good knights, kin to Perceval. Know that at that time there were in the kingdom of Logres [321] a great number of hermits everywhere, which was not without its amazing side, and there were few who were not knights or noblemen. At that time, by God's grace, all the knights of that kingdom, after they had borne arms thirty or forty years, left their lands and their riches and their families and went to the mountains, to the most secluded places they could find, and there performed penance for their sins and sensuality and for the great desires that existed within these large groups of knights, and I tell you that there were many who did this because of their distress and sorrow at the misfortunes of their friends and relatives, and because of this the kingdom of Logres was well furnished with monks and hermits.

Now the story says that Lancelot arrived at the shelter of those two hermits who were kin to Perceval. Know that as soon as they recognized him, they did him all the service they could, for they prized him for knightly skill above all the other knights they knew in the world except only Galahad, and they already knew Galahad well. That evening they began to ask Lancelot what adventure had brought him there at such an hour. He told them everything, just as it had happened to Perceval and him with the knight who bore a white shield with a red cross.

"And because of the dishonor he did us, I've followed him, for I expected to catch up with him, but I couldn't, for night came on too soon."

"Indeed," said one of those hermits, "God did you a favor that you didn't catch up with him, for truly, although you're one of the best knights in the world, we know that he's such a good knight that he's better than all others, so that you couldn't

---

* Corresponds to Magne I:319-325; Bogdanow 1991 302-36; Piel 153-155.

escape him, neither you nor any other knight who now bears arms, if it came to sword play, for this is his pleasure, and he doesn't fear others better than you."

When Lancelot heard this, he was amazed and asked who that good knight was who passed all others in skill.

They said, "We can't tell you his name, for he asked us not to reveal it [323] to any knight errant, but we tell you this much truly, that he is of King Arthur's house and a companion of the Round Table."

Lancelot fell silent when he heard this, for suddenly he felt in his heart that it was Galahad, his son. That night he thought long about the adventures that had happened to him and the visions he had seen in his dreams. The next day, after he had heard Mass, he told the hermits about them, for he truly believed that they were such good men in Our Lord's sight that they would know how to advise him. This they certainly did, for they told him about his lineage, about King Mordrain* and Nascien† and Celidoine‡ and all those about whom the story has already told you, and they told him frankly that he was shamed because of Queen Guenevere and the queen because of him.

"And know," they said, "that if you don't give up this sin, it will cause you to die by the lance by misadventure, and you will make such a bad, degraded end that all your accomplishments will be diminished and turned to nothing."

When Lancelot heard this, he answered in great sorrow, "It grieves me deeply to have come this far and to find myself in such a bad state that I'd rather never conquer at arms than that people should see me, for I have already promised the Lord never to return to my sin, and I promise it again."

The good men said, "Good will always come to you, and know that you won't leave this quest without honor, if you keep to this course."

Lancelot said that he believed it firmly and intended to do that, with God's help.

At once one of the brothers took a rough hair shirt and gave it to Lancelot, saying, "I want you to wear this garment next to your skin in the name of penance while you ride in the quest for the Holy Grail."

He took it, put it on, and wore it, and he never took it off until he returned to King Arthur's house, when he went back to committing his old sin, as he had been doing before.

After he had confessed fully to the good men, they admonished him strongly, telling him to give up that sin, draw himself away from it, and put all his faith in God, who desired his honor, and he would succeed in the quest for the Holy Grail, and he promised that he would do everything they said. After that, he left them and started on his quest, just as before, and rode many days without finding [325] any adventure. And know that most of the time he was saying his prayers and begging Our Lord to pardon him, for he felt himself guilty of nothing so much as of his sin with the queen, for it seemed to him that he was a traitor and disloyal to King Arthur, whose vassal he was and who had always honored him more than any other man.

---

*   Mordrain is the same as Evelach; see the Vulgate *History of the Holy Grail,* chapters 18 ff.

†   See *The History of the Holy Grail,* chapters 12 ff.

‡   The text has *Cilodormes,* which is probably the same as Celidoine, Nascien's son. See *The History of the Holy Grail,* chapters 23 ff.

104. Lancelot Gives His Only Food to a Maiden and Has His Horse Killed by a Black Knight.*

One day it happened that Lancelot was going through the Waste Forest wearily, having ridden now here, now there, without eating or drinking, for his fortune was such that in four full days he had not found a place to take refuge but had ridden aimlessly through this forest, which was very large; he never complained but said that it was Our Lord's will that he suffer in the quest for the Holy Grail. After the fourth day he happened upon a spring, which rose in the middle of a valley at the foot of an oak tree. The spring was very beautiful, he was very hungry and thirsty, and it seemed to him that if he did not drink of the water he would die, because his thirst and hunger would be greater. He dismounted and drew water in his helmet, and he saw a roebuck coming to drink at the spring. He took his lance, thinking that if he could kill it he would eat of it, one way or another, to kill his hunger. Then he threw his lance and struck it, so that he killed it instantly, and he was very happy. As he wanted to take it toward the spring, there appeared a maiden, riding on her palfrey, and she came so quietly that he never saw her until she got right up to him.

The maiden was very beautiful, and she said to him, "Oh, knight! Grant me a gift."

He looked at her and said, "My lady, ask and you will have it, if it isn't something against my oath."

She answered, "Many thanks. Now give me this roebuck, for I came here for nothing else."

"Oh, my lady! For God's sake, ask another gift of me, for at this time I couldn't give up this roebuck, because it's a long time since I've eaten. In spite of that, if you want the roebuck, take as much of it as you want; leave me only enough to satisfy my hunger."

"By God, I'll either take it all [327] or none of it, and I ask you, by the faith you owe to God, to give it all to me."

Then he said, "I give it to you, for after such an appeal I wouldn't refuse it to you or anyone else."

"And I ask you, by the faith you owe to God, to give it to me at once."

"Take it," he said.

"Many thanks," she said. "Know that He for whose love you gave it to me will know how to reward you for it well and soon."

At once she took the roebuck up on her horse, and when Lancelot saw that she wanted to leave, he said to her, "Oh, my lady, for God's sake, look: are you willing that I keep you company and that you take me somewhere where I can find something with which to kill my hunger?"

She answered quickly, "You think of only one thing, but you won't reach town or shelter until it pleases God, and this won't be as soon as you think."

---

* Corresponds to Magne I:325-329; Bogdanow 1991 306-310; Piel 155-157.

Then the maiden went away from him at once, so that in a very short while he had lost sight of her.

When Lancelot saw that the maiden was going away in a great hurry, he thought she was not going far and that she had said that to him to frighten him. At once he took his helmet, shield, and lance, got on his horse, and thought that he would go after her, and when he found her he would beg her so hard that she would get him to some place where he could find relief from his misery. Thus he followed the maiden, and he rode until he reached a valley between two tall, wild precipices. He looked and saw before him the river men called Marcoisa,* which divided the forest in two. When he saw this he did not know what to do, for if he wanted to get to the other side, he would have to ford the river, which was so perilous that he truly believed that no man who entered it could escape. Nevertheless, he put his hope and faith in his Lord, so that he completely lost his fear and thought that, with God's help, he would cross safely. As he was thinking this, he saw a strange and marvelous adventure happen, for he saw coming out of the water a large knight armed in black armor, riding on a mulberry-black horse; he charged at Lancelot without saying anything to him and struck and killed his horse, but he did not kill Lancelot. After that [329] he went away through the forest so fast that in a little while Lancelot could not see him anywhere. When he saw that his horse was dead, it did not grieve him greatly, for he understood that everything was happening to him because of his sin. Therefore, he gave praise to Our Lord and did not look at the horse again but went to the bank of the river. When he saw that he could not pass, he stopped, took his lance, shield, helmet, and sword, and put them all beside a cliff, saying that he would stay there until Our Lord sent him some guidance. Thus Lancelot was closed in on three sides, by the water in one direction and by the two cliffs in two others, and he knew no way to satisfy his hunger, for if by chance he started into the forest, he would wander a long time without finding man or woman who would help him, for this was the strangest and most pathless forest he had ever entered, and if he went into the river, it was so perilous that if a thousand men went into it, not one would come out, unless God drew him out with His own hand. These three things made him stay on the bank and pray to Our Lord, asking Him for pity's sake to comfort him and give him help, so that he would not fall into despair or the devil's temptation.

But now the story stops speaking of Lancelot and turns to Perceval.

105. PERCEVAL AT HIS AUNT'S CELL.†

The story says that after Perceval parted from Lancelot, he went to the cell, not because he thought anyone lived there but to give shelter to his tired horse. As soon as he reached it, he dismounted, and when he saw that he could not put the horse

---

*   'Bogdanow 1991 (309) and Piel (156) both have *Martoisa.*
†   Corresponds to Magne I:329-335; Bogdanow 1991 311-317; Piel 157-160.

inside, he tended it the best he could. He disarmed himself in order to rest a little, and when the lady in the cell saw him alone and disarming himself, she understood at once that he was one of the knights errant who were seeking the adventures of the kingdom of Logres, and she had a great desire to speak with him, to hear news of Agloval and Perceval.

She put out her head the best she could and said, "Oh, sir knight! As God may help and save you, speak with me."

Perceval looked, and he was amazed when he saw that she was walled in; he said, "Willingly, my lady."

Then he went to sit down near her, and she asked him where he was from.

"My lady, I'm from King Arthur's house and a companion of the Round Table."

"In the name of God," she said, "now I'm sure you'll be able to give me news of two knights errant, relatives of mine, who are of this court."

"And which are they?" asked Perceval.

She said, "One is Agloval and the other Perceval, sons of King Pellinor; they're my [331] nephews, my sister's sons, and I'd like to hear good news of them, especially of Perceval, who was a small boy, and now I hear him praised for his knighthood, for I've heard many good men speak of his abilities."

"My lady," he said, "it's a long time since I've seen Agloval, but I left him healthy and happy when I departed. He started on the quest for the Holy Grail with the other knights of the Round Table."

"God be praised," she said, "and God keep him in that goodness in which he has begun, for I've heard much good of him since I came here. And you, my lord, what is your name?" she asked.

He answered timidly, "My lady, I'm that Perceval you're seeking."

"Is that true?" she asked. "You are welcome! Praised be the Holy Spirit who let me see you before my death, for this was the thing I desired most in the world."

She raised her hands toward heaven and gave thanks to Our Lord for having fulfilled her desire, and then she remained a long time in prayer.

Finally she turned to Perceval, so happy that tears of joy ran down her cheeks, and said to him, "Nephew, how is it with you?"

He said, "Very well, my lady, thanks be to God."

"And how is it with you in matters of chivalry?" she asked.

"My lady," he said, "as with other knights errant: sometimes good and sometimes bad, as adventures and fortune come to us."

"Nephew," she said, "may Our Lord in His pity give you better fortune than your father and your brothers, who died in great pain. Each time I remember the death of your brother Lamorat, who was killed by treachery, my sorrow has no reckoning, for the man who killed him reduced you and all your kin to misery. For his goodness was all your lineage famous."

"That's true," said Perceval. "Indeed, if I knew truly who had killed him, I'd do everything in my power to avenge his death."

"You can't do that without being forsworn," said the lady, "for the man who killed him is of the Round Table, and you know well that you may not lay a hand on him for anything."

"My lady," he said, "because he killed my brother I may kill him."

"You may not," said the lady, "for you'd be forsworn and faithless. Just because he did wrong does not mean you should do it, for you should look not at another's treachery [333] but at your own truth, for you know well that you have to go on being as true as you were at the beginning. If you do so, you'll ascend into honor much greater than you can imagine. Therefore, never strive for the death of your companion, for you could fall into disgrace because of a little thing, and all the good you've done could turn to your dishonor. Therefore, I beg you not to concern yourself with such a matter, but if one of them, against his oath, offends you, suffer it, for God, who is the Great Avenger, will avenge you better than you could avenge yourself."

"Then, my lady," he said, "I'll put myself in God's hands and concentrate on the vengeance of the Great Avenger."

"Do so," said the lady, "and I tell you that good will always come to you."

Immediately he promised her that he would do so gladly.

Thus the lady and Perceval talked that evening, and they were both very sad when they reckoned up the great loss to their lineage.

After they had wept a great deal, the lady said to Perceval, "Nephew, what adventure brings you here alone?"

He said, "I had as my companion today Lancelot of the Lake, one of the best knights in the world, but, because of an adventure that happened to us, he left me, angry and sorrowful."

Then he told her how it had been and how Lancelot had gone off after the knight who had knocked them down, and how he had remained there. "And I know that, if he can find him, the battle will be fierce, for Lancelot is the best knight I ever saw with a sword, and the other one is also very good. I know this well, and I don't know what to say, but as soon as it's light I'll go after them, and if I find the knight he won't be able to leave me until I defeat him or he me."

"What arms does he bear?" she asked.

He said, "His badges are red, and he has a white shield with a red cross."

"Stay away from him, nephew," said the lady. "You don't know what you're beginning. Don't imagine defeating him or even encountering him, for know that there is no way you can prevail against him, you or any other knight now alive, for this is Galahad, the knight who at Pentecost accomplished the adventure of the Perilous Seat; this very knight is the one who will bring to an end the adventures of the kingdom of Logres; this is he who, because of his goodness, will see the marvels and secrets of the Holy Vessel; this is he against whom no earthly power can prevail."

"What, lady?" asked Perceval. "This is Galahad, whom God placed over all the knights of the Round Table?"

"Yes, unquestionably," she said, "and you should realize that clearly by what you saw him do, for no knight could deliver in one hour two such blows as you saw him give."

"My lady," he said, "you speak the truth. From now on I give up this project, for I know well that he's a better knight than any other man I now know. But now I'm worried [335] about Lancelot more than I've ever been before, for I know well that if he finds him he won't leave him without a battle, and if because of their sins they don't recognize each other, it will be an exceedingly great loss."

"Have no fear of that," she said, "for Sir Galahad is a knight of Our Lord, and he won't in any way sin mortally against his father."

They talked much that night about their family, and it pleased them to talk about it, for many were the men who had gone forth to great deeds. Perceval ate nothing that night, for there was nothing for the lady to give him, as she lived on raw greens more than anything else. And if anyone asked me who gave them to her—for even if she had wanted to get out of there she could not—I would tell him that a hermit gave them to her, one who lived nearby and came to see her and comfort her each day and to speak with her about confession. This lady lived thus ten and a half years without ever eating anything but raw greens, and when she died, there occurred a beautiful miracle, for the very hour that she passed away, King Arthur in Camelot, a full ten days' journey from there, knew it, and we will tell how.

The truth is that she had been one of the most beautiful ladies in the world and such a friend to God and Holy Church that all those who knew her spoke about it; her great goodness was the reason that King Arthur loved her and asked her for her love, but she, who was such a good woman that no better could be found, did not want his love in any form, and therefore she hated him more than any other man in the world, so that she never forgot him, because of which it happened that the very day and hour she died she appeared to King Arthur, where he lay sleeping in his room at Camelot. She came crowned, and she was such a beautiful creature and so joyful that anyone would have longed to see her.

Standing there she said joyfully to Arthur, "King Arthur, I'm going to paradise, which you wanted to take from me by your sensuality; my chastity has brought me to joy, but your sensuality will bring you to great suffering, if you don't correct yourself."

In this way King Arthur knew about the lady's death. This was the very year in which the quest for the Holy Grail ended,[*] right at the beginning of April. And because of the great goodness that he sensed in the lady, he went to the Waste Forest with a large company of knights and had the cell broken and the lady's body taken out. He took it to Camelot and had it buried with great honor in the Church of St. Stephen, which was then the largest church. But because we will certainly be able to return to this matter when it is necessary, we will be still about it for now.

---

[*]   "the very year ... ended" as in Bogdanow 1991 (317). Magne has, "on the eve of Pentecost, the anniversary of the day on which the quest for the Holy Grail had begun."

106. GALAHAD RESCUES PERCEVAL AND A MAIDEN; PERCEVAL REFUSES TO KNIGHT AN UNKNOWN BOY WHO LATER TURNS OUT TO BE ARTHUR THE LESS.*

Perceval passed that night [337] with his aunt, speaking of many things, she admonishing him to serve his Creator and go often to confession.

"Know, nephew," she said, "that if you forget Our Lord, He will forget you, and He won't give you honor for anything you do for him if you leave His service."

"My lady," he said, "thank you for all the good things you've said to me, such that I'll be a better man because of them for as long as I live."

The next day, when it was light, he took his arms, climbed on his horse, commended his aunt to God, and went away.

They both wept freely on parting, and she said to him, "Nephew Perceval, pray to God for me, for I know you'll never see me again nor I you until the terrible day when each man must account for his deeds before the Great Judge. Then you'll see me and I you, and God grant that it be to our profit."

Then Perceval went away through the forest, weeping with sorrow for the lady whom he previously had seen so comfortable and now had seen in such great distress and suffering. That day he rode here and there until he reached the main road. Then he fell into deep thought, which cut him to the quick, for he thought about Gawain, who, he had heard it said, had killed his father and his brothers, and he thought about how he could have done it.

"For I know well," he said, "that my father and my brothers were better knights than he, and since they were better knights, how could he kill them? I don't know how this could have been, unless by treachery, and I don't know how such a good and courteous knight could commit treachery. There's no way this could be so."

As he was riding along brooding like this, he looked to his right and saw an armed knight seated sadly beside a spring; beside him a beautiful lady sat weeping. When he saw the young lady weeping, he went there to learn the reason for her sorrow and to give her all the help he could, for this was the duty of the knights errant, to help all unknown ladies. When he reached them, he greeted the knight first. The knight was sitting in such deep thought that he said nothing to Perceval.

Then Perceval said to the young lady, "God give you joy, for it seems to me that you have great need of it."

She answered weeping, "May God be aware of my situation."

"My lady," he said, "would you tell me the reason for your sorrow? I promise you as a knight that I'll give you all the help I can."

"My lord," she said, "who are you, who promise to do so much for me?"

"I'm a knight errant," he said.

"And where are you from?" she asked.

He said that he was of King Arthur's house.

"And are you of the Round Table?" she asked.

"Yes, certainly."

---

* Corresponds to Magne I:335-349; Bogdanow 1991 318-329; Piel 161-168.

"Then I ask you to tell me your name," she said.

He gave his name, and as soon as the other knight heard it, he stood up joyfully and said, [339] "Oh, Sir Perceval! You are welcome. Your help is much needed here at this time."

"And who are you?" asked Perceval.

"I am Gansonais, and I'm of the Round Table like you."

"In God's name," he said, "I know you well. Tell me your problem, for I'll give you the best help I can."

"For God's sake," said Gansonais, "I'll hide nothing from you. Yesterday I happened to reach this maiden's farmhouse, which is at the edge of this forest. After I had dismounted— for it was already time to rest—I saw two of our companions coming, also to rest, one from one direction and the other from the other. When we recognized one another, we were very happy, and we all three stayed with this maiden. At night, after we had dined, she asked us to keep her company as far as a castle located ahead there, where a brother of hers lies sick, as they had told her. We asked her if she was afraid of anyone who lived in that forest.

"'Yes,' she said, 'a cousin of mine, my father's first cousin, has inherited everything there was except for one castle that he couldn't get, and if he could capture me, I'd never escape from his hands until he had taken back his land.'

"We assured her that we'd take her to safety. This morning, as soon as it was light, we armed ourselves, and she mounted, and we entered this forest. We rode until we reached a valley, and, where we had expected nothing to fear, suddenly there appeared ten knights who came against us. There began a fierce battle between us, with great losses on both sides, so that my two companions were killed there, and I was badly wounded, and of the ten others, none remained alive except one,[*] who fled, badly wounded. And this was the lady's cousin. When I saw him, I recognized him. I saw him flee; I went after him, and I would have overtaken him, I think, but my horse grew weary and fell down near this spring, so that he seemed dead. As I was looking, I saw the maiden following me, not daring to stay in the forest for fear that someone might capture her. So it happened to us in the matter of this lady, but we have not yet done anything of any value for her, for she is more afraid now than she was before."

"Why?" asked Perceval. "Didn't her cousin run away?"

"Yes," said Gansonais, "but know that he will soon return with a larger company than before, and therefore she would like to return to her house, if there were someone who would take her back there. I'd gladly take her, but I can't, for I'm badly wounded, and I have an exhausted horse. Therefore, I ask you to take her there, for love of me and in order to keep the lady from harm."

Then Perceval said to the maiden, "Where do you want to go, to your house or where your brother lies ill?"

"My lord," she said, "if it may be, rather where my brother lies ill."

"Mount, then," he said, "and you will go with me, for, so help me God, I'll do everything in my power to take you there in safety."

---

[*]   "one" as in Bogdanow 1991 (321). Magne has "myself."

"Go with you?" she said. "Three knights came with me and could not [341] protect me, and you would protect me? I'd have to be mad to go with you."

"Oh, my lady," said Gansonais, "never doubt him, for he alone is worth more than twenty knights from this land."

Perceval said to her further, "My lady, don't be afraid, for I'll do all I can to bring you in safety to where your brother is."

"Not under any circumstances," she said, "would I go there in the protection of one lone knight, for I know well that harm would come to me."

"I won't take you anywhere else," he said, "for if I turned back out of fear of words, any man who dared speak of it would consider it cowardice."

"Oh, my lady," said Gansonais, "since Perceval wants to guide you, put yourself in his protection, for I tell you that he will take you to safety."

"I'll do so," she said, "since you advise me to."

"And you," Perceval asked Gansonais, "what will you do?"

"My lord," he said, "I'll stay here, and you'll go with your young lady, and God guide you well."

Then Perceval went with the maiden, and she, very much afraid, said to him, "My lord, we should have gone by another way, for they can see us more easily on this one than on another."

"Have no fear," said Perceval, "for I certainly won't go out of my way from fear."

In this manner Perceval went with the lady, she badly frightened and he very valiant, for he was marvelously brave. They had not gone far like this when they met Galahad, who was riding alone deeply puzzled.

As soon as Perceval saw him, he recognized him, and he said to the maiden, "Now you may see the best knight in the world."

"Who's that?" she asked.

"That man who's coming here; he's unquestionably the best knight who ever was in Great Britain."

"In the name of God," she said, "he's welcome, and may God be praised, who has brought him here at such a time, for his help is very necessary to us."

Then Perceval spurred his horse in order to reach Galahad more quickly, and after he had reached him, he said to him, "My lord, you are welcome; blessed be the hour in which you were born."

Then Galahad came out of his thoughts and made a bow, and he wondered why Perceval had said that to him. He also greeted the maiden.

The girl said at once to Perceval, "Sir Perceval, now you may go where you wish, for I want to go with this knight, who will guide me more safely than you."

"Oh, my lady!" said Perceval, "why are you leaving me?"

"Why?" she asked. "Because if I can have my choice of two good knights, wouldn't anyone think me ignorant and foolish if I didn't choose the better? And therefore I leave you and want to take him, who's better than you, as you yourself have said."

Galahad was amazed at this and asked who she was. The lady told him her whole adventure, just as she had told it to Perceval, and after she had told the whole adventure, Perceval said to Galahad, [343] "My lord! I beg you of your courtesy and moderation, because you are a better knight than I am, not to take from me what I've begun, for it would be attributed to cowardice on my part and would become a matter of shame for me, and you'd have no honor from it either. I've undertaken to escort this young lady; leave her to me, if you please."

The maiden drew closer and said to Galahad, "My lord,* you are the best knight in the world, and I'm a poor, helpless maiden; since I ask your aid, for God's sake, don't fail me at this time, for if you do, I'll be disgraced, and the dishonor will be yours, for you know well that you're bound by the oath of the Round Table to help any maiden who asks you."

He said, "That's true, but if another knight undertakes it, I shouldn't hinder him, unless he fails at what he has begun, for they would say to me that I wanted to do it because I thought the knight wasn't such that he could accomplish it. Therefore, I leave you to this knight, and know that if one lone knight can accomplish what he has begun, he will accomplish it, and I give you good advice: that you not ask for better protection than his, for you could easily get worse rather than better."

When the maiden heard this, she began to weep hard and said with great anger, "Oh, God! How chivalry is brought low today and turned to nothing! My lord, what will the ladies of this kingdom do from now on? How will they find aid from the knights of the world, when the best knight in the world fails to help me in the greatest distress I've ever known?"

"My lady," said Galahad, "I'm not failing you, for if I took over what this knight has started, I'd be committing the lowest act in the world."

"A low act?" she said. "Rather it would be a great courtesy, and I'll tell you how. Aren't you bound to help ladies you don't know as well as those you do?"

"Yes," he said.

"And if one of your companions starts something he can't finish, aren't you bound to help him with all your might?"

"Yes," said Galahad.

"Then I tell you," she said, "that it's necessary for you to follow us, for I know well that from a castle that stands ahead here a full ten knights will emerge who will want to capture me. If they come when Perceval is alone, how will he get free of them without being killed or captured? If ten knights attacked you, and you could defend yourself—you who are the best knight in the world—certainly it would be a great thing; tell me, then, what he would do. He will be killed or captured, for more than ten knights will attack him, and I'll be taken and dishonored; and all this evil will be your responsibility, for if you wanted to help us, he would remain healthy and happy at this time and I happy." [345]

"My lady," said Galahad, "have no fear, now, but go confidently with Perceval, and I tell you that, if they attack you, God will give you such aid that you'll leave the place happy and with honor."

"I'll do it," she said, "since you tell me to, and God grant that no harm come to me."

After this, with no further delay, they parted from Galahad, and Galahad, worried by what he had heard, followed them slowly and at a distance, so they would not

---

* "My lord" added by Bogdanow 1991 (324).

see him, but if he saw that they needed his help, he would help them. Perceval and the maiden rode until they came to a little valley.

Then they saw knights appear from all directions, saying to Perceval, "Knight, you're a dead man; you can't defend her."

When the maiden saw this, she said to Perceval, "Oh, Perceval! You've betrayed and killed me. Now I see clearly that I won't get away from here without dishonor, for you can't defend yourself against so many knights."

He made no reply but charged them all. He struck the first so hard that no armor kept him from putting his lance point through the other's left shoulder and making him fall from his horse to the ground. The others, who came after him, struck Perceval with seven lance blows and killed his horse, but he got up briskly, for he was agile and lively. He drew his sword, put his shield over his head, and gave every appearance of a man who would defend himself.

When the maiden saw Perceval on foot among so many of his enemies, she began to cry out in a loud voice, "Help! Help!"

And she did this because she was sure Galahad was following to help them.

When Galahad, who was not far behind, heard this cry, he knew that Perceval was in a battle, and he rode up as fast as he could. He found that they already had the maiden prisoner and were taking off Perceval's helmet, preparing to cut off his head.

When Galahad saw this he raised his voice and said, "Let the knight go, evil people; you're all dead men or captives!"

He went in among them and began to knock them down and give them such great blows with his biting sword that there was no man he reached whom he did not knock to the ground, nor was there any whose helmet or armor was good enough to endure against his sword. He was so lively and agile that it seemed to them that he was not one man but more than twenty, because there was no one of them who had not within a brief time received a blow. Therefore, they gave up and began to flee toward [347] where the forest was thickest, in order to recover there. After Galahad had defeated them, he did not want to follow them any more, for he had no desire to kill anyone.

He returned to Perceval, who had already taken a horse from among those who had fled, and Perceval said to him, "My lord, you are welcome, for we had great need of your help at this time."

"That pleases me very much," said Galahad. Then he said to the maiden, "Do you think you're now safe from your enemies?"

"My lord," she said, "why do you ask?"

"I ask because I would go away, if you please, for I have much to do elsewhere, more than here."

"Indeed," she said, "from now on I won't fear anything, since these men have been defeated. You may go where you wish, and may Our Lord guide you."

"And you, Sir Perceval, will go with this young lady, whom you have to protect, and I'll go where I have to go, and I commend you to God."

"My lord," said Perceval, "God guide you."

In this manner they parted.

Galahad entered the forest by another way, not the one by which he had come. Perceval went with the maiden until they reached a little castle that stood on a riverbank.

"My lady," asked Perceval, "is this the castle where your brother lies sick?"

"My lord," she said, "this is it, truly."

"Since you're safe," he said, "I'll go now."

"Oh, my lord!" she said, "this discourtesy shall not be; since you've come this far with me, why won't you come inside?"

He said, "I certainly won't do that, but I commend you to God."

He turned away at once, and she entered the castle, very sad because he had not wanted to come with her, for she had wanted to do him service because of the great knightly ability she had seen in him.

When Perceval left the maiden, he rode through the forest until evening, wounded as he was, and he arrived by chance at the house of a widow, who lodged him well and saw to his wounds, as she knew much about him, and once she knew that he was Perceval, she took great pains and made him rest in her house twenty-two days.

When she saw that he was healed and could ride and bear arms, she said to him, "I ask you, in payment for the service I've done you, to make a knight of this young man of mine who's here with me."

"Who is he?" asked Perceval.

"So help me God," she said, "I don't know, for I found him in this forest more than fifteen years ago, near a lake, wrapped in silk cloths, and it wasn't more than three days since he had been born. From that time to this I've brought him up and taken care of him, and he's a very handsome young man, large, strong, [349] and so lively and agile that there's no youth in this land with his ability. I ask you to knight him because I think that he will use knighthood well."

"What," asked Perceval, "don't you know anything else about him or from where or of what lineage he is?"

"Indeed," she said, "I know it no more than you do, except by looking at him, but because I see him so lively, I think he must be a good man, and I want him to be a good man and a knight."

"My lady," said Perceval, "You say what you like, but indeed, since you know nothing about his family, I have no reason to want to make him a knight, for I'm afraid he might be of low birth, and I ask you not to be grieved by it."

"Although I am grieved," she said, "I'll have to endure it, since I see that you won't do what I ask for all my asking."

107. PERCEVAL AND GAWAIN, DEFEATED BY THE UNKNOWN KNIGHT (WHO IS ARTHUR THE LESS)[*]

Thus Perceval parted from the lady, who had served him well and made him comfortable in her house, and he rode day by day as chance took him, until one day he met Gawain by a spring at the edge of a forest. Gawain had removed his helmet and was resting there, for he was marvelously tired.

When Perceval saw him, he was very happy and said to him, "God be with you."

He dismounted at once. Gawain did not recognize him, for Perceval had changed his armor many times since he had started on the quest.

However, he stood up to meet him, and Perceval said to him, "Gawain, don't you recognize me?"

"No," he said, "so help me God, but don't let it grieve you."

Perceval promptly lowered his helmet, took it from his head, and pulled off his iron coif.

As soon as Gawain recognize Perceval, he threw himself on him with open arms and said, "Oh, Sir Perceval, you are welcome! If I didn't recognize you, I shouldn't be blamed for that, for I never saw you bear these arms before."

Great was their joy and pleasure. After they had welcomed each other, they sat for a long time beside the spring, and they began to speak of many things. They asked each other about the adventures that had happened to them since they had started on the quest, and, sitting there, they related many of them. But know that Gawain did not tell Perceval the whole truth about what had happened to him on the quest or about the companions of the Round Table, of whom he had already killed many. While they were talking this way, Perceval began to think so hard that he heard nothing of what Gawain was saying to him, and he was so distressed by these thoughts that [351] tears rolled down his cheeks. Gawain immediately understood what he was thinking and, falling silent, began to look at him. After Perceval had brooded a great while, he gave a sigh and raised his head.

Gawain said to him, "Friend, you were brooding deeply on that thought. God grant that good come of it to you."

Perceval's face began to darken, and he looked at him.

Gawain was sad to see him brooding like this, and he said to Perceval, "It grieves me greatly that you've fallen into such pensiveness, for I have done neither better nor worse than any other."[†]

After a while Perceval said to Gawain, "Sir Gawain, so help you God and by the faith you owe to all the companions of the Round Table, tell me the truth about what I'll ask you, and by the faith I owe to God and to all knighthood, harm will never come to you from it."

Gawain, who was very perceptive and who had already come through many such perils, realized at once that Perceval wanted to ask him about the death of his father

---

[*]   Corresponds to Magne 1:349-361; Bogdanow 1991 330-340; Piel 168-174.
[†]   This phrase makes little sense in all three editions, and the verb appears to have been miscopied.

and brothers, and he was so frightened that he did not know what to do, for if he told him the truth, he thought Perceval would harm him, for he considered Perceval a better knight than himself; if out of fear he concealed it from him, no man would ever hear of it who would not think it wrong of him. However, he finally thought it better to conceal than to tell, for even if Perceval did him no harm then or later, he would always hate him.

Then Gawain replied, "Sir Perceval, ask what you will, for I won't conceal from you anything I know, even if I think harm will come to me."

"Indeed," said Perceval, "harm will never come to you through me or another, for it's such a thing that I'd want to hide it more than you yourself." Then Perceval said, "Sir Gawain, I've heard many men say that you killed my father and my brothers, but because I can't believe it, I've been angry with the men who said it.* If you killed them without recognizing them, I forgive you for it, and you need never fail to talk about it, for I wish you no ill for it, and after I know that you killed them, no good man will wish you ill for it."

Gawain, who was very much afraid that Perceval was saying this to see if he could uncover Gawain's evil and treachery, said at once, "Oh, Sir Perceval! How could I kill† your father and your brothers, whom I loved so dearly that there was not one of them but I'd have risked death to save his life? Never think it, and so that you'll believe me much better, I'll swear to you on the Holy Gospels. There's no knight in the world so good that, if he accused me of this treason, I wouldn't defend myself successfully against him, because I know that I never did such a thing."

When Perceval heard this, he said, "Indeed, Sir Gawain, you've said enough, and you've said it in such a way that [353] I'll always believe you. For God's sake, forgive me for having until now thought less well of you than I should."

And Gawain forgave him. Speaking thus, they stood by the fountain a great while, and, when they saw that the hour of nones was passing, they took their arms, got on their horses, and started on their way.

Gawain said to Perceval, "Friend, do you know a place near here where we could take shelter?"

"No," said Perceval, "but don't be impatient, for God will help us."

As they were riding and talking, they looked behind them and saw a knight coming, armed all in white.

"It seems to me," said Gawain, "that that is Lancelot, for he bore such arms when he first became a knight, and because of it everyone called him the White Knight."‡

Before he had finished speaking, the other knight caught up with them, and they greeted him and he them.

"My lords," he said, "where are you from?"

They said they were knights of King Arthur's house and companions of the Round Table.

The knight asked Perceval, "Can you give me news of Perceval?"

"What do you want with him?" asked Perceval.

---

*   Literally, "wished ill to many knights because of it."

†   "How could I kill" supplied by Magne.

‡   Not in the Post-Vulgate; see the Vulgate *Lancelot,* chapters 23 ff.

"I'd certainly be able to tell him if I saw him," said the knight.

Then Perceval answered, "I'm the one you seek; what do you want with me?"

"You are? So help you God?" said the knight.

"Certainly," said Perceval, "I never heard of another Perceval."

"In the name of God," said the knight, "it pleases me greatly that I've found you so soon, since I'm free of a great task, for I would never have ceased to wander until I found you. Now defend yourself against me, for I won't ever be happy until I do battle with you."

"What?" asked Perceval. "You've followed me to fight with me?"

"Yes," said the knight.

"What quarrel is there between you and me," asked Perceval, "because of which battle must be done? For I wouldn't fight with you or anyone else without a reason, and if I've offended you so badly that you wish me mortal harm, I'd rather make it up to you as Sir Gawain dictates."

The other replied, "That won't serve you; you can't leave me without a battle. Now defend yourself against me if you wish."

"I'll do so," said Perceval, "since I see that I have to."

After this, without further delay, they charged at each other, striking each other so hard that they were both badly hurt. Perceval fell to the ground and was badly bruised in that fall, for the horse fell on top of him, and the knight passed over him without looking at him. When Gawain saw this blow, it grieved him greatly, and he did not know what to do about it, for if he wanted to avenge Perceval, he did not think he could, for he knew well that [355] Perceval was a better knight than he was. All the same, he said he would risk it, for people would think it great cowardice in him if he did not do what he could.

Then he said to the knight, "Defend yourself against me."

The knight turned to him and struck him so that he broke through Gawain's shield and hauberk and drove the point of his lance into Gawain's left side, although the wound was not mortal. He knocked Gawain to the ground, and in the fall his lance broke. After he had struck this blow, he turned to Perceval, who had already stood up, full of sorrow at what had happened to him.

Perceval went toward the knight and drew his sword, saying to him, "Sir knight, I summon you to battle, for just because you've knocked me down, you haven't defeated me. Therefore, you must fight until you defeat me or I you."

The other answered, "I won't fight, for I don't want to. I believe I've done a great deal, since I've knocked down you and Sir Gawain."

"What?" asked Perceval. "Do you think that you can go off like this and gain the victory so easily?"

"I want to go like this," said the knight, "for we who are outsiders and who haven't yet won the honor of the Round Table have an advantage over you that you don't have over us, for we can summon you to battles and jousts at our pleasure, and you can't do that without people thinking it wrong of you, but if you summon us, we can excuse ourselves without guilt, unless we are summoned because of treachery or treason. Am I right?"

"Yes, indeed," said Perceval, "but since I've tested you at jousting and you had the better luck, if I subsequently summon you to battle and you won't consent, I'll think it cowardice, say what you like."

The other man said, "I won't fight with you for anything you say, and I call you quit."

Perceval said, "But know that you're more dishonored than I."

"Let it not concern you," said the knight. "May the honor and the dishonor be mine."

As they were speaking of this, Sir Gawain, wounded as he was, got on his horse, and when he saw that the knight wanted to depart without doing anything more, he was very angry and said, "What, recreant knight, do you intend to go away like this? I summon you to battle; if you want to defend yourself, do so, for I'll do all I should and can to kill you."

"Sir Gawain," said the knight, "don't be so angry. Indeed, if this is to be, I believe I can defend myself well."

"Then defend yourself," said Gawain, "for you have great need," and he took his sword.

"What?" asked the knight. "Do you want me to fight with you?"

"Come on!" said Sir Gawain.

Then Perceval said, "Sir Gawain, it may not be. Since [357] the knight doesn't want to fight, let him go, for you can't do otherwise according to the custom of the Round Table."

"Such a custom might be cursed," said Gawain, "along with anyone who would now observe it; if you weren't here, I'd avenge myself on this recreant knight."

Then the knight answered angrily, "What, Sir Gawain, do you think me such a bad knight that you expect to defeat me that easily?"

"Yes," said Sir Gawain, "since because of cowardice and lack of skill you don't dare fight with Sir Perceval or me."

"Let's see how cowardly I am," said the knight. At once he took his sword and gave Gawain such a heavy blow on his helmet that he made him worse off than he had been. Gawain struck him wherever he could reach him with such great blows that anyone who saw it, knowing that Gawain was wounded, would have said that he knew well how to wield a sword. No one who saw him giving and receiving blows at that time would have thought him cowardly or lazy. I can truly tell you that the other knight was lighter and more agile than Sir Gawain, but Gawain was bolder and knew better how to cover himself. It was already some time since they had dismounted from their horses, in order not to kill them, and they fought on foot.

When they were so tired that they had to stop and draw apart to rest, Perceval, who was afraid for Gawain, because it seemed to him that they would kill each other, said, "Sir knight, I don't know your rank, but I see you conduct yourself so well against such a good knight as Sir Gawain that, so help me God, I respect you greatly, and because of the skill that I see in you, it seems to me that it would be a great loss if you were crippled or killed in this fight. You can't escape it if you continue, for if you kill Sir Gawain—which can't be done so easily, for I truly think he is a better knight than you—then you'll have to fight with me, and I am rested, so that you couldn't withstand me at all, but I'd kill you quickly."

"What?" asked the knight. "If I defeat or kill Sir Gawain, will I have to fight with you?"

"Yes, indeed," said Perceval, "and I'll tell you why. The custom [359] of the Round Table is such that if I see my companion defeated or killed, I must avenge him before I leave and must kill with my own hands the man who fought him, unless both are companions of the Round Table."

"This is a bad custom," said the knight.

"Take care, then," said Perceval, "for if you continue this fight, you can't leave this place without great hurt."

"No?" he said. "Then I'll give it up, for you're a better knight with a sword than I am."

Then he said to Gawain, "Sir Gawain, I ask you, for your good and mine, to call yourself quit of this battle."

"I'll do it," said Gawain, "if you own yourself defeated by me."

"I own myself defeated?" said the knight. "You'll have no honor from it, for know that you haven't yet defeated me and that I leave this battle only for the love of Sir Perceval."

"By the Holy Cross," said Gawain, "I'll make you say otherwise before we part. You won't escape me like this, for I'm not so easy as you think."*

Then Perceval approached and said to Sir Gawain, "Friend, give up this fight, since the knight asks you, and I ask you by the faith you owe to your uncle King Arthur."

"Friend, you ask me in such a way that I'll give it up, although I leave it to my dishonor; but know truly that if people blame me for it, I'll put the blame on you."

Then he put his sword in its scabbard and got on his horse. The other knight did the same, and Perceval said to him, "I ask you to tell me why you fought with me today. In what way have I offended you, that you bear me so much ill will?"

"I'll tell you," said the knight. "I am the boy of fifteen, whom the lady asked you, as a reward for her services, to make a knight, but you wouldn't because you thought I was of low birth. So you kept me temporarily from receiving the order of chivalry, but Sir Tristan didn't do so—a better and more courteous knight, for [361] as soon as my lady asked him, he did me all honor and you dishonor. Therefore, I've hated you until now and would still hate you, had I not found you a better knight than I thought, and, therefore, I pardon you for whatever offense you've done me. It isn't more than twelve days since Sir Tristan made me a knight," he said.

Perceval was amazed and said to him, "You've made a good beginning, and God grant that the end be as good. Know that I refused to make you a knight, not because of any fault in you but because of the honor of all knights. However, tell me this much, if you please: what is your name?"

---

*   Literally, "I am not there whence you think."

"My name," he said, "is 'The unknown knight.'* Tristan gave me this name when he made me a knight, because he didn't know my name."

"And what are you going to do?" asked Perceval.

"Indeed," said the knight, "I want to go to King Arthur's court, if by chance he'll take me, for a wise man told me that there I'd learn my name and lineage. However, I tell you truly that when I left my lady's house I left only in order to kill you because you wouldn't make me a knight. But now I've seen so much good in you and have heard you praised so much for chivalry that I wish you no ill but would help you with all my might whenever I saw you had need."

Perceval thanked him warmly for that.

"Now tell me," said Perceval, "do you know where we might lodge today?"

"No, indeed," he said.

"Then what will you do?" Sir Gawain asked. "Will you go to some lodging yet today?"

"Indeed," said the knight, "I won't; I'll never enter a village, except by chance or if my horse fails me, until I arrive at King Arthur's house, for there I'm to find out the thing I desire most in the world to know, my name and lineage."

"By God!" said Perceval, "it's a long way from here to there, for it's at least six days away. God bring you there to your salvation."

"Amen!" said the knight.

108. PERCEVAL, GAWAIN, AND CLAUDIN.†

So they parted, and the knight went away in one direction and Gawain and Perceval in another. That night they lay in a forest, poorly sheltered, and they had [363] nothing to eat or drink. The rain fell on them all night, and the weather was bad in every way, for winter was approaching. The next day, when they saw the light, they were very happy, for they truly thought that they would always find more good adventures by day than by night. Then they started on their way as before. At the hour of midday, they arrived at a beautiful tower, which stood near some lakes, and they went inside to rest a little. They were well and honorably received, as soon as they were known. When they left that place, they took to the main road in order to find adventures more easily. They had not gone far when they met Claudin, son of King Claudas, king of the Land Laid Waste. This Claudin was a marvelously good and brave knight, endowed with many good qualities, and he had just recently left the kingdom of Gaunes and come to Great Britain, because he had heard that the great quest for the Holy Grail had begun, and he wanted to join it like the knights of the Round Table. And know that he had already done many knightly deeds since he had come to Great Britain and had accomplished many beautiful adventures of which the tale does not speak because he was not of the Round Table.

*   In Chapter 123 we learn that this is Arthur the Less.

†   Corresponds to Magne I:361-369; Bogdanow 1991 341-346; Piel 174-178.

When Gawain saw him coming, he said to Perceval, "Oh, Sir Perceval, you see here the arms of one of the best knights I ever saw, and if this is the knight I saw bear those arms previously, I tell you truly that he's one of the knights in the world whom I have seen endure most labor at arms and most pain and suffering in mortal battles."

"What's his name?" asked Perceval.

"We call him Claudin," said Gawain. "He's the son of King Claudas of the Land Laid Waste."

While they were going along, speaking of Claudin, Claudin stopped in the middle of the road and began to call to them to ask if they wanted to joust. Perceval, who never failed or refused any adventure, put his shield before his head and chest and lowered his lance.

Gawain said to him, "Oh, my lord, for mercy's sake, give up the joust, for you don't know the knight."

Perceval did not say a word but charged toward Claudin and gave him such a blow that he knocked him off his horse, although he did him no other harm, for [365] Claudin's hauberk was good.

When Claudin found himself on the ground, he got up quickly and angrily, took his sword, and said to Perceval, who had already passed on by, "Knight, defend yourself against me, for, since you knocked me down with a lance, I never want men to think me a knight if I don't reward you with a sword."

When Gawain heard this, he thought at once that this was Claudin, and he approached a little and said to him, "Friend, so help you God, tell me who you are."

"Why should I tell you?" he asked. "I'm from a land so distant and have come here so recently and am so little known that I know you've never heard of me, and you wouldn't know me if I told you my name."

"All the same," said Gawain, "I ask you to tell me your name. Know that no harm will come to you."

Then he said, "I'll tell it to you. Know that my name is Claudin. I'm a native of the kingdom of Gaunes, and I was once richer and more powerful than I am now."

When Gawain heard this, he dismounted from his horse, put his shield and lance on the ground, and ran to embrace him, saying, "Sir Claudin, you are welcome. So help me God, you're one of the foreign knights I value most in the world for chivalry. I was speaking to Sir Perceval of this just now, when I saw your arms."

"My lord," said Claudin, "who are you who do me so much honor?"

"I'm Gawain," he said, "King Arthur's nephew. You've seen me on occasion in Gaunes, where I saw you do so well at arms in many places that I remembered you as soon as I saw your arms."

When Claudin saw that this was Gawain, he fell to his knees on the ground and said to him, "For God's sake, my lord, forgive me for having challenged your companion, for know that I wouldn't even have glanced at him, except for good, as soon as I knew that he was of King Arthur's house."

Then he went to Sir Perceval, fell to his knees, laid down his sword before him, and said, "My lord, I hold myself defeated and yield myself your prisoner in order to amend the folly I've committed against you."

Perceval raised him up and forgave him everything. After that they went to their horses and mounted.

"Sir Claudin," said Gawain, "now tell me what adventure brings you to this land."

"My lord," he said, "I'm a poor knight like any other, but I was rich and abundantly provided for before my father was disinherited. After this Pentecost, when I heard that the quest for the [367] Holy Grail had begun, I wanted to come here and join the company of the knights of the Round Table, and I did so, for I came as quickly as I could. I've labored to seek adventures, and good has come to me in many places, but now I must leave the quest, like it or not,* and I'll tell you why. This week it happened that I was riding through a forest seeking adventures as a knight errant should do. Then at the hour of tierce a knight caught up with me, riding alone as I was. We rode on a little, and he asked me what I was seeking. And I told him I was seeking what the knights of the Round Table were seeking.

"'What?' he asked; 'are you a companion of the Round Table?'

"'No,' I said, 'for I've never been in King Arthur's house.'

"'What?' he asked; 'you haven't been in King Arthur's house and aren't of the Round Table, and you say you are a companion in the quest for the Holy Grail? You're the most brazen knight I ever met, to meddle in such a noble quest. Watch yourself, now, that you never speak of it before a knight again until you're a companion of the Round Table, for they'll think you mad.'

"Then I answered him, 'I'm certainly engaged in such a noble quest, for I'm a better knight than some from the Round Table who have begun it.'

"Then he said to me, 'So help me God, if you're a better knight than some from the Round Table, I'll see what kind of a knight you are.'

"So the fight began, but it ended quickly, for he was without doubt the best knight and the best swordsman I ever met, except for Lancelot of the Lake. After he had defeated me, he made me promise that I'd never pursue this quest until God and fortune gave me the honor of one of the seats of the Round Table. After I'd promised this, he commanded me to go to court and stay there until it pleases King Arthur to receive me as his knight.

"I asked him, 'My lord, after I'm there, who shall I say you are who sent me there?'

"'Tell King Arthur that Tristan, King Mark's nephew, sent you to him.'

"So I left Sir Tristan with great sorrow at having met him, for I'd never met another knight who defeated me, and therefore [369] I'm so sorrowful, for never before did anything so bad happen to me."

"Then," said Gawain, "because of this are you going to King Arthur's court?"

"Yes, my lord," he said. "I'll never be happy until I get there."

---

*   "but now I must leave the quest, like it or not" added by Bogdanow 1991 (344).

"Now I ask you," said Gawain, "to greet King Arthur and Queen Guenevere for me and tell them that you found me with Sir Perceval and that we are healthy and happy but haven't yet found anything of what we seek."

He said that he would deliver that message well. Then they parted, and Claudin went in one direction and Perceval and Gawain in another.

That day they rode until night, when they arrived at a castle that belonged to a beautiful lady, a relative of Perceval. As soon as the people of the castle saw them armed, they knew at once that they were knights errant and were seeking adventures, and they received them well, but when the young lady saw Perceval and recognized him, she was so happy that I do not know what to tell you. Thus they were lodged and pampered as if they were in King Arthur's house. The next day they took leave of the lady and rode until they arrived, at midday, at a cross at which two roads parted.

Perceval stopped and said to Gawain, "Friend, here we must part, for this cross tells us so."

"By God," said Gawain, "that grieves me; I'd rather have your company than leave you."

Then they embraced and took leave of each other, and each went his way. Gawain went one way, happy at leaving Perceval, for he was greatly afraid that Perceval would kill him because of the death of his father and brothers. Perceval went the other way, and he rode until he reached the sea without finding an adventure.

109. THE TEMPTATION OF PERCEVAL.[*]

When Perceval reached the sea, he looked around him and saw a rich, beautiful tent. He went toward it, firmly expecting to find someone there, and he dismounted at the entrance, for he would never respect himself again if he did not see what was inside. Then he tied his horse to a tree, leaned his shield and lance against it, and went inside. Sleeping on a bed—the most beautiful and rich he had ever seen—he saw a young lady. She seemed to him more beautiful than Queen Guenevere and Queen Iseut and the beautiful daughter of King Pelles, for it seemed to him that since the world was made there had not been another woman [371] so beautiful, nor had he seen one except perhaps that Virgin who was virgin and mother and Queen of Queens. After he had looked a long while in amazement at her beauty, he drew back a little, thoroughly abashed, for it seemed to him that if all the beauties in sinful women were assembled in one, she would not be as beautiful as this one.

The lady opened her eyes, and when she saw him near her, she got up as if startled and said, "Oh, my lord, who are you who enter here armed like this?"

"My lady," he said, "I'm a knight errant, and chance has brought me here. Have no fear of me, although I desire to stare at you like this. It's no wonder if I stare at you, for, God help me, you're the most beautiful creature I ever saw."

---

[*] Corresponds to Magne I:369-375; Bogdanow 1991 347-352; Piel 178-181.

The maiden said to him, "I never saw a knight errant."

"No?" he said. "Then where are you from?"

She said, "I'm from a land very far from here and strange, but such chance and bad luck have brought me here now that you could hardly believe it. And even worse has happened to me since I came here than before."

"So help me God," he said, "that grieves me very much, and if it pleases you to tell me about yourself, I'll do all I can to help you."

"Really?" she said. "I'll tell you in order to see if you are as courteous as you seem. Now sit down beside me, and I'll tell you my misfortune and grief."

And he did as she commanded.

"Sir knight, I'm a native of Athens, a city of Greece, and I'm daughter of a king and a queen. Because he had heard of my beauty, the emperor of Rome sent word to my father to send me to him, and he'd make me his wife. My father, thinking himself fortunate, had a ship prepared and put me into it with a large company of knights, ladies, and maidens. After we had put to sea, such a bad storm came upon us, lasting fifteen days, that all of us, even the strongest, had more expectation of death than of life. The bad weather passed, and we landed and found ourselves in Great Britain. This grieved us very much. We had this tent set up, just as you see it, so we could rest after the torment we had had at sea. The next morning it happened that our company got into one of the ship's boats, in order to take rest and relaxation on this sea. [373] As soon as they got into it, a wind arose so strong that it sank them, so that I saw them all die before me. And in this manner, my lord, my misfortune came upon me, so that I've lost all my father gave to me and all my company, and I'm poor and alone and helpless, for I have nothing but what you see. Therefore, I ask you to help me, as you promised, for you never saw a maiden of such high station so bereft."

Perceval looked at the maiden, who seemed to him far more beautiful than anyone else he had ever seen. Then his heart began to change violently, so that he forgot the habit of a lifetime, for he had never before looked at a maiden in love or with desire for her flesh, but now he was so troubled by love that he desired nothing else in the world. As soon as he had seen this maiden it had seemed to him that he would call the day of his birth lucky if he could have her love.

She said to him, "My lord, what help will you give me in what I've told you?"

And he replied, as the devil taught him, to satisfy his desire, "My lady, I don't know what to say to you, but if you'll do what I tell you, I'll help you in such a way that you'll think yourself well satisfied."

"My lord," she said, "there's nothing in the world I won't do for you, as long as it is honorable."

He made no reply to that but asked her for her love, saying that if she would be his lover, he would take her as his wife and make her queen of a rich and good land.

She said that she would not do it; however, he persisted with her so long that she finally granted everything he asked, as long as he did what he had promised.

And as he was standing talking of this, suddenly such a great sound came from the direction of heaven as if it were a thunder clap, and there arose such a great whirlwind, as if the earth had moved, that Perceval shook all over with fear.

Frightened, he got to his feet, and he heard a voice, which said, "Oh, Perceval, what a mistake you are making!* You're trading all pleasure for all sorrow, grief, and misfortune."

And it seemed to him that that voice was so loud that everyone in the world should hear it, and he fell stunned to the ground and lay there a long time. Then he came to and looked around him, and he saw the [375] maiden laugh, because she saw that he had been afraid. And when he saw her laugh, he was amazed and understood at once that she was a demon who had appeared to him in the semblance of a maiden in order to entrap him and lead him into mortal sin.

Then he raised his hand and crossed himself, saying, "Oh, True Father Jesus Christ, don't let me be trapped or sent to eternal death! If this is a demon who wants to take me from Your service and remove me from Your company, reveal it to me."

As soon as he had said this, the maiden turned into a demon so ugly and frightening that the bravest man in the world would have been terrified. Perceval was so frightened that he did not know what to do, except that he said, "Oh, Jesus Christ, True Father, Lord, be with me."

Then he saw the tent and everything there fly through the air, followed by a blackness, as if all the inhabitants of Hell were there, and he was so frightened by what he saw that he did not know what to do. He looked around and saw nothing but his arms and his horse, just as if everything before had been a dream. As he was standing in amazement, he saw a ship coming across the sea toward him as briskly as any ship could come when a good wind directed it and as fast as if a hundred galleys were chasing it. When it got close, he saw that it was very beautiful, covered with white silk. He had not looked for long when it landed near him, and he wondered how it could navigate, for there was no sailor nor anyone else to steer it; but in every other way it was marvelously well equipped.

As he was thinking about this, he heard a voice that said to him, "Perceval, you have won; enter this ship and go where it takes you. Don't be afraid of anything you see; God will guide you wherever you go, and this much good will happen to you, that you'll find the two companions you love most in the world, Bors and Galahad."

When he heard this, he felt the greatest joy possible, and he thanked Our Lord fervently. He took his arms and entered the ship, leaving his horse on the bank. The wind struck the sail and drove him from the shore so fast that in a little while he had lost sight of land.

But now the story leaves off speaking of him and turns to Bors of Gaunes.

---

* Literally, "what bad counsel is here."

110. BORS AND PERCEVAL ON THE MYSTERIOUS BARK; GALAHAD AT A TOURNAMENT.*

When Bors left the abbey,[†] a voice told him to go to the sea, for Perceval was waiting for him there, and he went, just as the story has already told. When he reached the shore, a beautiful ship covered with white silk [377] landed. Bors dismounted, commended himself to Our Lord, and went on board, leaving his horse behind. As soon as he got on board, he saw that the ship left the shore as fast as if it flew. He looked around the ship and saw nothing, for the night was very dark, and he leaned against the bulkhead and asked Our Lord to guide him to where he could save his soul. After he had said his prayers, he lay down to sleep. In the morning, when he awoke, he saw on the ship a knight armed with hauberk and arm pieces. After he had looked at him, he recognized him, and at once he took off his helmet and went to embrace him joyfully. Perceval was amazed when he saw Bors coming toward him, for he could not understand when he had come on board the ship. Nevertheless, when he recognized him, he was as happy as he could be. He stood up and embraced him, receiving him as he should, and they began to tell each other their adventures, what had happened to them since they had started on the quest. Thus the friends found themselves in the bark God had prepared for them, and there they awaited whatever adventures He wanted to send them. And Perceval said that nothing was missing from what was promised him except Galahad.

But now the story leaves off speaking of them and turns to Galahad, for it has been silent about him for a long time.

The story tells that after the Good Knight left Perceval, having delivered him from the twenty knights who were chasing him because of the young lady,[‡] he started down the main road through the forest. He rode for many days, now here, now there, just as chance took him. After he had ridden for a long while through the kingdom of Logres, to many places where they told him there were adventures to accomplish, he was moved to head for the sea.

One day chance brought him near a castle where there was a great and marvelous tournament. There were many people there on both sides, and there were many of the Round Table, some helping those on the inside and others those on the outside, and they did not recognize one another because they had changed their arms. By the time Galahad got there, those on the inside had been so badly beaten that they awaited only death. Tristan, whom chance had brought to that tournament and who was helping those defending the castle, had already suffered so much there that he had four very large wounds, for all those attacking the castle were on top of him to capture him, because they saw that he was a better knight than any of the others, and none of them did him as much harm as Gawain and [379] Hector, who were on the other side and did not recognize him. Nevertheless, he defended himself so briskly that all who saw him were amazed. Galahad was already very near the gate, and

---

*   Corresponds to Magne I:375-381; Bogdanow 1991 353-359; Piel 181-184.
†   At the end of chapter 95.
‡   See chapter 106.

he saw before him a badly wounded knight who had emerged from the tournament and was making the greatest lamentation you ever heard. Galahad reached him and asked him why he was lamenting so.

"Why?" he repeated. "Because of the best knight in the world, whom I see dying by great misfortune, for everyone is against him, just as you see, and still he won't leave the tournament."

"Which one is he?" asked Galahad.

The knight pointed him out.

"By God," said Galahad, "truly he's a very good knight. God save you, tell me his name."

"My lord," said the other, "his name is Sir Tristan."

"In the name of God," said Galahad, "I know him well. Now people would think it bad of me if I didn't go help him."

Then he charged at them and knocked Girflet to the ground, then Hector, then Sagremor, then Lucan. When his lance broke, he took his sword, as he knew well how to use it, and, going where the press was greatest, began to knock down knights and horses and perform such great feats that all who saw him were amazed.

Gawain said to Hector and his other companions, who had already mounted, "On my soul, this is Galahad the Good Knight. Now, the man would be mad who awaited him further, for no armor can withstand his blow."

As he was saying this, it happened that Galahad reached him and gave him a sword cut that sliced through his helmet, his iron cap, his scalp, and his flesh to the skull, and he was fortunate that the wound was not mortal. Gawain let himself fall to the ground, in the firm belief that he was being killed, and Galahad, who could not check his stroke, caught the horse across the front of the saddle and sliced it through the withers, and the horse fell dead beside its lord.

When Hector saw this blow, he marveled and drew aside, for he realized that it would be madness to wait for more.

Then Sagremor said, "By my faith, now I can truly say that this is the best knight I ever saw. Never believe me in anything if this isn't Galahad, the Very Good Knight, the one who is to put an end to the adventures of the kingdom of Logres."

"Unquestionably, it is," said Hector.

As they were speaking of this, Galahad saw that those on the outside were beginning to flee, and those of the castle were chasing them, capturing them at their pleasure. When Galahad saw that those [381] of the outside were so badly beaten that they could not recover, he departed so secretly that no one saw him except Tristan, who followed him at a distance, because that day he had seen in him such great knightly skill that he said he would never be happy until he knew who he was. Thus both went away so covertly that the people in the crowd did not know what had become of them.

Gawain, who had been so badly hurt by the blow that he did not expect to live, said to Hector, "By God, Sir Hector, now I see that it was true, what Lancelot said to me before you all at Pentecost,* that if I tried to draw the sword from the stone, I'd bring harm on myself before the year was out, and it would be by that very

---

*   See chapter 74.

sword. Unquestionably, he struck me with that very sword, and I see that it has happened to me as was prophesied."

"Are you badly wounded?" asked Hector.

"I'm not so badly wounded that I can't be healed," he said, "but fear hurts me more than anything else. But what can we do?"

"It seems to me that we'll stay here," said Hector.

"You won't stay," he said, "but I'll stay until I'm healed."

As they were speaking of this, the men of the castle reached them. When they knew that it was Gawain, there were many there who were grieved. They took him up and bore him to the castle, disarmed him and put him in a dark room, far from people, and had a very good doctor look at his wound, one who knew a great deal about such doctoring and who assured them that he would soon make him whole. Thus Gawain remained in the castle and Hector, too, who would not leave Gawain until he recovered.

The others went away, and when they had left the castle, they began to speak about Galahad and said, "What shall we do? That good knight isn't far; let's go after him until we find him, and if God wills us to find him, let's keep him company while we can, for we'll certainly have marvels from him."

They agreed on this, and wherever they went they asked after Galahad, but because they did not find him this time, the story is now silent about him and returns to Gawain.

111. GAWAIN AND HIS BROTHERS IN MORGAN'S HOUSE LEARN LANCELOT'S SECRET.*

At this point the story says that after Gawain left the castle where he had lain sick with the wound Galahad gave him, he rode a long time without finding an adventure worth the telling. Wherever he went, he asked about Galahad and Perceval and Bors, and he often had news of them but could not find them.

One evening it happened that he met an armed knight, coming as fast as he could on his horse.

When he reached Gawain, he said to him, "Oh, sir knight! If ever there was in you courtesy or goodness, help me! Defend me against a knight who's following me and who wants to kill me wrongfully."

The moonlight was very bright, so that he could see a long way, for he was in a [383] large field. Gawain looked at the knight and saw him so bloody and badly wounded that he took pity on him. Therefore, he promised him his help and said that he would defend him the best he could. As they were speaking of this, they looked far ahead and saw, a bowshot away, a knight coming on a white horse, sword in hand.

---

* Corresponds to Magne I:381-393; Bogdanow 1991 359-369; Piel 184-190.

"My lord," said the knight, "you see the knight I'm telling you about. If you don't help me, I'm a dead man."

"Have no fear," said Gawain.

Immediately he charged at the knight who was coming with the sword, and he broke his lance on his chest but did not move him from the saddle. The knight, who was very strong, struck Gawain's horse in front, close to the saddle, so that he sliced it through the withers. They both fell, the horse one way and Gawain the other, but Gawain stood up quickly, being lively and light, and drew his sword.

The knight turned to him and asked, "Sir knight, do you want to defend this treacherous knight against me?"

"I don't know if he's treacherous or true," said Gawain, "but I'll defend him with all my might, since he has remained with me in the hope of my help."

"Then we're now in a fight," said the other. "But so that no one will think it bad of me to fight you, you on foot and I on horseback, I'll dismount."

He dismounted and tied his horse to a tree. When the knight who had previously been fleeing saw the other one on foot, it seemed to him that he could easily do him harm, and he struck him with his horse's chest so violently that he laid him flat on the ground.

"Knight," said Gawain, "You've shamed me! This knight was safe from everybody but me, since he was fighting with me, and you, on top of this, attacked him with your horse. Indeed, you've committed the greatest wrong in the world, and know that if you do any more of it I'll leave him and occupy myself with you."

"Shut up!" said the knight. "What are you saying? I won't forbear killing him for anything, since I have the advantage, for he has offended me greatly, more than you could believe."

"I forbid you to touch him again," said Gawain, "and if you do it, defend yourself against me, for I defy you."

"By my faith," said the other, "if you don't shut up I'll kill you."

Then he spurred and went to strike the other knight; he knocked him down again and rode his horse over his body so that he crushed him badly. The knight fainted, thinking he would die, such great agony he felt.

When Gawain saw this he said, "Oh, God! How this knight I was to defend has mortified me, for he has killed this knight with whom I was fighting."

Then he went to his horse to get on it, to be safer. When the knight saw this, he was afraid that after Gawain was on his horse he would kill him. And when Gawain would have put his foot into the stirrup, the other knight charged at him and struck him so [385] hard with the horse's chest that he knocked him flat in the middle of the field. Then the horse charged over him so many times that Gawain was badly hurt. After the knight had done this, he returned to the knight from whom he had fled, dismounted, took off the other man's helmet, and then drew his sword, as he had a great desire to cut off his head. And he would have cut it off, had it not been for Gawain, who had just stood up the best he could. He went there with great sorrow because of the knight who had killed his horse, who was in danger of dying. Gawain had no sword, for it had fallen from him there, but he did not fail because of that to go to the other knight; he seized both his arms and squeezed and pulled him so hard that he got him underneath. He took him by the fist in which he held his sword and took it away from him by sheer force. With it he cut the straps of the other knight's helmet; he threw it away and gave him great blows with the pommel of the sword, so that he drove the links of his cap into his head.

When the knight saw himself so badly hurt, he begged mercy and said, "Oh, good knight who took me under your protection, if you kill me it will be a very faithless act. For God's sake, have mercy on me, and I promise you that I'll do your will in everything."

"Indeed," said Gawain, "you well deserve to die a dishonorable death, for, so help me God, you're the falsest knight I ever saw, and I see so much treachery in you that I'm near to killing you. But because I detained you and received you into my protection, I'll let you live. Take your sword, for I give it to you as to the worst knight I know in the world."

Then he got up and went to the other knight, finding him so badly hurt that, although Gawain called to him, he could not speak, for he was completely crushed. Gawain mourned over him and said that this was an especially great loss.

The knight lay unconscious a long while, so that Gawain did not know if he would die. He removed the other knight's iron coif, so that he could get some air, and then seated himself beside him for, if he could, he would gladly have learned who he was.

After a great while the other man uttered a cry of pain and opened his eyes; he saw Gawain sitting sadly before him and said as well as he could, "Oh, good knight, for God's sake, if you know any hermit or priest of the Mass here, get him for me, for I'm greatly afraid that I'll die soon."

"Indeed," said Gawain, "I know of no hermitage or house of a religious order near here."

"Oh, God!" he said, "can it be that I won't have the rites of Holy Church at my death? Oh, King Arthur! What great sorrow you'll feel when you know about this death."

When Gawain heard this, he was sorrier than before, for he realized at once that this man was from King Arthur's house, and he said to him, weeping, [387] "Sir knight, for God's sake, tell me where you're from and what's your name."

"My lord," he said, "I'm from King Arthur's house, and my name is Gaheriet; I'm brother to Sir Gawain, and I have three other brothers, very good knights, who will be deeply grieved by my death."

When the other knight heard this, he let himself fall on him and said, "Oh, brother! What strange news we have here!" and he felt such sorrow that he fainted.

Gawain looked at him and realized that it was Mordred, and he crossed himself in amazement and said sorrowfully, "Ah, wretch! Will I now lose two of my brothers?"

Then he began to make such a great lamentation that it was a marvel, and he drew off his helmet and said to Gaheriet, "Oh, brother, what a loss I suffer today in you!"

Gaheriet realized from his words that this was his brother Gawain, the man he loved most in the world, and he was so glad that he said to him, "Have no fear, for I have in my heart such pleasure at seeing you that I know I will soon be healed."

"Oh, brother," said Gawain, "do you know who this is you were following, to kill him?"

"No," he said.

"Then know," said Gawain, "that it's Mordred, your brother. And we're fortunate that he narrowly escaped being killed either by you or by me."

"Cursed be the hour he escaped death," said Gaheriet, "for he has richly deserved it, and know that I am one who, from now on, won't look on him as a brother because of the treacherous act I saw him commit today."

"Whatever he may be," said Gawain, "he's our brother, and we must love him, however much others hate him."

Mordred understood very well what Gaheriet said, and were it not that he feared Gawain, he would have killed Gaheriet at once, for he was one of the falsest knights then in the world. Gaheriet felt such joy to be with his brother Gawain that he said he felt he had no injury. It was not so, and yet the joy he felt made him forget somewhat the pain of his wounds.

All night they stayed there, for want of horses, since they had only Mordred's, for Gaheriet's had fled to a forest nearby. That night they stayed there, and they neither ate nor drank, for they had nothing. They spoke of many things, until Gawain asked Gaheriet where he had met Mordred.

"I met him yesterday," he said, "in this forest, where he was dragging a maiden at his horse's [389] tail, so that he had almost killed her. Never before did a man of our lineage commit such a false act, and because of the brutal act I saw him commit, I attacked him, for I didn't recognize him. He defended himself against me a great while, leaving the maiden. The battle lasted a long time, and it would have lasted longer, but, because he saw no advantage in it, he fled."

"Brother," said Gawain to Mordred, "since when are you so faithless and brutal, when they used to think you such a good knight and so faithful?"

"My lord," he said, "don't believe what Gaheriet tells you. This isn't the first bad thing he has said about me."

"I can't say good things about you unless I want to lie," said Gaheriet, "for you've become the most treacherous knight I know today."

That night both brothers thought ill of Mordred for what they had seen him do. The next day at dawn, when the sun had already risen, it happened that Morgan the Fay passed that way with a large company of ladies and maidens, knights and squires. When she saw the three brothers on foot and wounded, she asked them where they were from, and they introduced themselves.

When she knew that they were Gawain and his brothers, she was as happy as she could be and said to them, "Friends, do you know who I am?"

"No," they said.

"Know that I'm Morgan the Fay, your aunt," she said, "and I'm sister to King Arthur."

As soon as they heard this, they were very happy, and they went to embrace her, for it was a long time since they had seen her. She asked them about themselves, and they told her how they would have killed each other, had they not learned each other's identities by chance.

"Now," she said, "however much labor you've had, I'll take you to my castle, where you'll rest until you're healed of your wounds."

And they thanked her warmly. She had horses given to them, and they mounted at once and arrived, at the hour of tierce, at Morgan's house, where Lancelot had been prisoner two winters and a summer.*

When they dismounted, she ordered them laid in a room, and she saw to their wounds and injuries, as she knew a great deal about it, so that before eight days had passed they were much better. On the eighth day it happened that Mordred entered by chance into the room where Lancelot had been prisoner. Lancelot's deeds were painted there, and when Mordred entered, he had a great desire to look around the room, which was especially beautiful and luxurious and well painted. After he had looked at the story and read the letters, which in [391] every scene told the names, he wondered greatly, for he saw clearly that the story was about King Arthur and the queen and Lancelot, but he could not understand it.

After he had looked a great while and had seen that he could not interpret it by himself, he called Gawain and Gaheriet and said to them, "My lords, come see what's here."

They looked at the room and said that it was especially beautiful, and they were marvelously well pleased, but they could not understand the story. When they saw that they could not interpret it by themselves, they called Morgan and asked her to explain it to them.

"I won't do it," she said, "for you'd be more deeply shocked than by anything else you ever heard, nor would it please you, for you'd find your dishonor there openly."

They said, "All the same, we want to know."

Then she held our her hands toward a chapel there and said to them, "Nephews, so that you'll more readily believe me in what I want to tell you, I swear to you on these holy things that I won't lie to you in whatever I tell you about this story."

Then she began to tell the story of Lancelot and the queen, how they two loved each other.

"And, therefore," she said, "I've hated him mortally since I knew it, and I'll hate him as long as I live, for he couldn't cause me greater grief than by bringing shame on such a noble man as my brother and by loving his wife and lying with her. And because of the great love he felt for her, when I held him in prison here a year and a half, he painted with his own hand all his deeds, from the time he became a knight until he was imprisoned here. Each morning, as soon as he got up, he embraced and kissed the queen's hands with as much emotion as if she had been real. I saw this many times, and I'm true witness to you. Because he isn't true to King Arthur,

---

* Not in the Post-Vulgate. See the Vulgate *Lancelot,* chapters 95-102.

his lord, I hate him and will always hate him, and you should hate him even more mortally, for you, to the extent that you are of higher rank, are more dishonored by this."

When Gawain heard this, he was so shocked that he could not speak for a long time, and when he spoke he said, "My lord.* I don't know what to say to this, except that I can't possibly believe that such a good knight as Lancelot would commit treason, and if he has offended in this regard, I know well that it was because of the great strength of love, which would easily make a traitor of the most loyal knight in the world."

Gawain said this of Lancelot because he could not believe that Lancelot loved the Queen carnally unless he learned about it other than by hearsay.

"Know that he is sleeping with the queen," said Morgan, "for which you would long ago have avenged the king, if you were good knights."

"By God," said Gawain, "never [393] will I meddle in it or believe it unless I see it."

"However," she said, "when you arrive at court, you'll have to tell all your adventures, and there you'll tell everything you saw and heard in this room."

And they said they would have to do this, for otherwise they would be forsworn.

"By God," said Gawain, "I never heard of any knightly deed Lancelot did that isn't painted here."

Then he pointed out Dolorous Guard to them and told them the marvelous feat Lancelot had performed there.†

The three brothers stayed in Morgan's house until they were healed; then they told her they wanted to go.

"Since it's so," she said, "I conjure you by the faith you owe to me and by the thing you love most in the world to tell my brother the truth about Lancelot and the queen. You should do it, for you're his sworn vassals, and if you hide it from him any longer, you'll be forsworn and faithless. And if he's so mad or of such a good disposition that he won't believe you, you're such close friends to him that you should avenge him for it as soon as you can."

"So help me God," said Gawain, "I'm one who will never believe it until I know it more truly than by these paintings. Therefore, I will yet keep silent."

"I, too," said Gaheriet.

"And I tell you," said Mordred, "that as soon as I can find more dependable evidence than this, I won't keep still but will tell King Arthur."

"That would be very foolish," said Gawain, "and greater harm could come of it to you than you think."

They spoke about this a great deal and many times, and then they parted from Morgan, well provided with horses and weapons, and they went all that day without finding any adventure. At night they took shelter with a hermit who served them well as soon as he knew who they were. The next day, after they had heard Mass,

---

*   See note in chapter 78.
†   Not in the Post-Vulgate. See the Vulgate *Lancelot,* chapter 24.

they left, and they had not gone far when they came upon a way that divided into three paths.

"Brother," said Gaheriet to Gawain, "there are three paths here. Each one should go by his own."

Mordred agreed, and they separated at once, each taking his own way. But now the story leaves off speaking of Gawain and Gaheriet and turns to Mordred to tell what happened to him.

112. MORDRED BRUTALLY KILLS A MAIDEN; BADEMAGU WOUNDS MORDRED; GAWAIN WOUNDS BADEMAGU MORTALLY.*

Here the story tells that after Mordred left his brothers, he rode for a long time without finding any adventure to tell about. One day, at the beginning of winter, when it was already somewhat chilly, it happened that he met a knight, unarmed except for his sword, and riding with him were a maiden and a [395] squire, his brother and sister. When they saw Mordred armed, they realized at once that he was a knight errant. As soon as they reached him, they greeted him, and he greeted them but very unwillingly, as he was bad-tempered and uncouth.

After they had passed by him, he said, "What a mistake I made just now, that I didn't take that girl and have my pleasure with her! If I were such a knight as they call me, she wouldn't have escaped me."

Then he turned quickly and went to the maiden; he took her reins and said to her, "You must turn back and come with me, for that's my pleasure."

"By God," she said, "I won't go, God willing, for there has never been anything between you and me because of which I should do it."

"By God," he said, "you will go, like it or not."

And he pulled her by the reins in order to take her away by force.

When the knight saw this, he took his sword and charged at Mordred, unarmed as he was. The squire, who had a lance, struck Mordred's horse in the chest and knocked him and the horse to the ground. Mordred got up quickly, as he was lively and agile; he took his sword and struck the squire so angrily that he laid him dead on the ground. They he went to the knight and struck him so that he cut off his right arm and knocked him from his horse. Then he went to the maiden, knocked her off her horse, dragged her to some bushes nearby, and took off his mail shirt.

She had never married, and, seeing herself about to be dishonored unless God helped her in some way, she wept and lamented and cried as loudly as she could, "Help! help!"

When he saw that she was crying out this way, he struck her and shamed her as much as he could. He seized her by the hair, dragged her toward a path, and insulted her as badly as he could, for he was one of the most brutal knights in the world. She cried out more and more, so that King Bademagu, who was seeking

---

*   Corresponds to Magne I:393-401; Bogdanow 1991 370-376; Piel 190-194.

adventures like the others, heard her and went in that direction to see what it was. He approached and found Mordred, who had the maiden on the ground and was inflicting so much grief and misfortune on her that it was surprising she was not dead, and she cried out more and more for help. [397]

King Bademagu, when he saw Mordred holding the maiden this way, did not recognize him, for his face was stained by his armor, which he wore all the time, and Mordred did not recognize him, because the king had changed his arms some time ago in order to be less easily recognized. The king, who was very courteous and benevolent, asked Mordred for the sake of God and courtesy not to do any more harm to the maiden.

When she saw the king, she called to him, "Oh, good knight, for the sake of God and your honor, take me from the hands of this treacherous knight, who has killed my two brothers without reason and wants to have me by force."

"What, my lady?" asked Bademagu, "aren't you his?"

"So help me God, my lord," she said, "as far as I know, I never saw him before, nor he me."

"Knight," said King Bademagu, "is she telling the truth?"

"Even if she is telling the truth," said Mordred, "what concern is it of yours?"

"It's this concern of mine," said King Bademagu, "that if you lay a hand on her again, unless I know the reason for it, you'll be sorry."

"How little I fear your threats!" said Mordred. "By my faith, because of your meddling, I'll kill her in front of you!"

At once he drew his sword and struck off her head, saying, "Sir knight, now you may see how I fear you, and if it hadn't been for you, she wouldn't have died."

When Bademagu heard this, he was grieved, and in his wrath he could not keep himself from attacking Mordred—although it was a base deed, for Mordred was unarmed and on foot, while he was armed and on horseback—and striking Mordred in the chest so that the lance emerged on the other side. He knocked Mordred to the ground so badly hurt that he expected to die, and Mordred shed so much blood that all the ground around him was covered with it. When the king saw him like this, he thought he was dead and therefore did not want to strike him again, and he left him and went away with great sorrow for the maiden who had died because of him.

King Bademagu rode away, more sorrowful than he had been in a long time. He could not have gone far when Gawain reached the place where Mordred lay wounded.

When he looked at Mordred, he recognized that it was his brother, and he dismounted to see if he was mortally wounded or could be healed, for he saw clearly that he was not dead.

He asked, "Brother, who has wounded you? Do you think you can be healed?"

When Mordred heard himself called, he opened his [399] eyes and recognized Gawain; he was happy to see him and said, "Brother, I'll recover quickly if you avenge me on the falsest knight I ever met, who wounded me, as you see, treacherously, for he was armed and on horseback and I unarmed and on foot."

"Which way did he go?" asked Gawain.

"My lord," said Mordred, "I think he went that way," and he pointed to the right path, as chance had it. "And he bears a red shield with a white lion on it."

While they were talking about this, Yvain arrived, and when he had recognized Gawain and Mordred, he remained with Mordred to take him to an abbey nearby, where he could be healed of his wound. Gawain got on his horse and rode until he overtook King Bademagu, who was riding along and brooding sorrowfully over the maiden who had died because of him.

When Gawain was near enough to be heard, he said to him, "Filthy traitor, turn and joust, for you must."

When the king heard himself called a traitor, he was not pleased, and he turned to him and said, "Sir knight, whoever you are, I'll defend myself very well against you, God willing, against a charge of treason."

He had no lance, for he had broken it on Mordred, and he took his sword. Gawain, who was coming as fast as the horse could bear him, struck Bademagu so hard, putting all his strength into it, that neither shield nor sword kept him from giving Bademagu a great wound in the left side. The lance splintered, and Gawain collided with Bademagu so hard with shield and body that the king could not hold himself in the saddle, for he was badly wounded, and he had to fall. Nevertheless, with all this injury and pain, he got up as quickly as a man of his age might do. Gawain, who hated him mortally, dismounted from his horse, tied it to a tree, and then drew his sword, put his shield over his head, and charged at King Bademagu. The king, who was a very skillful knight, defended himself marvelously, although he was wounded, so that Gawain was completely taken aback. Then there began a battle between them so great and perilous that any man who saw it would have thought them very good [401] knights, and it lasted until both of them had lost a great deal of blood, for both swords were very good. Wielding their swords, they pressed each other now here, now there, as each in turn caught his breath.

Thus the battle lasted, cruel and brutal, from midday until the hour of nones. By then they were badly wounded, but King Bademagu had ten wounds such that a lesser man would expect to die of the least of them. Gawain thought his opponent very good and valued him so highly for his knightly skill that he wondered greatly who he could be. He pressed him all the while more and more and struck him so often with his trenchant sword that he cut the helmet from his head. Then he struck such a blow on top of Bademagu's head that he gave him a mortal wound, and if the sword had not turned in his hand, he would have split him to the shoulders. King Bademagu was so stunned by this blow that he fell to the ground, and his sword fell from him on one side and his shield on the other. When Gawain prepared to cut off his head, he looked at him and recognized instantly that it was King Bademagu, and he was so deeply grieved that he did not know what to do or say.

He blamed himself, cursed the hour he was born, and said in self-condemnation, "Oh, God, what a great misfortune this is! By mishap I've killed the best man in the world!"

While he was making such a lamentation, it happened that a very old man passed that way on foot, dressed in white clothes. When he saw Gawain lamenting so, and did not recognize him—although he knew that Gawain was a knight errant and was grieving for the knight who lay on the ground—he went there to learn who those two knights were.

Gawain, who was deeply grieved by this misfortune, said to King Bademagu, "My lord, how do you feel? Do you think you can recover?"

The king, who knew that he was mortally wounded and that his life was already nothing, said, 'Who are you who ask me if I can recover after you've killed me?"

"Oh, my lord," said Gawain, "if I've killed you, it grieves me deeply, for at the death of such a good man all the world should weep, and, so help me God, if I'd known you before as I do now, I wouldn't have laid a hand on you, even if you had offended me more than you did. I ask you, for God's and pity's sake, to pardon me, for, God forgive me, I didn't recognize you."

113. THE DEATH OF KING BADEMAGU; MERAUGIS FIGHTS GAWAIN; ERIC MAKES PEACE.*

When the king, who was in such pain that he realized that death was near, heard Gawain speak in this manner, he realized that he was a companion of the Round Table, but he never guessed that it was Gawain, because the latter had changed his arms. And Gawain, who was on his knees before the king, begged him all the while for God's and pity's sake to forgive him for causing his death.

"Who are you?" asked the king. "Tell me your name, so I may know who has killed me."

Gawain, who was deeply grieved, answered weeping, "My lord, I'm Gawain, your friend whom you loved so much. And, so help me God, I'm as deeply grieved by this misfortune as if it had been one of my brothers."

When the king understood what Gawain was saying, he answered the best he could, "Oh, Sir Gawain, are you the one who has killed me, and I loving you as I have since first I saw you? Your friendship has brought me harm. But all the same, since it's so, I pardon you with a good heart. May God pardon me my sins the same way. And I ask you, by the companionship there is between you and me, to greet Sir Lancelot, the most loyal knight I ever met, for me, but of this misfortune that has happened to us, say nothing to him or to anyone else as long as you can conceal it."

After he had said this, he fainted from pain. Gawain thought that he was dead and began to weep and to mourn his goodness and faithfulness.

After a while the king regained consciousness and opened his eyes; he raised his hands toward heaven and said as well as he could, "Father of heaven, true Pardoner, have mercy on this wretched king, and don't consider my misfortune or

---

*   Corresponds to Magne II:3-14; Bogdanow 1991 376-387; Piel 194-201.

the bad deeds I have done while I reigned on earth, unfortunate sinner among other sinners. My Lord, who are pity and unfailing compassion and who call to Your pity every sinner who repents of his sin, You who see all things hidden and known, protect me in this my last day and hour, in which the soul, poor and stripped of all good deeds by the bad company of its host, must depart from its lodging and go to the dark house of sorrow, unless Your compassion directs it to the house of joy. My Lord, shelter it as the wise and fore-sighted father shelters his son, when [5] the son recognizes his error; and however it may be, Lord, with my poor soul—which I think will pay dearly for the errors of the flesh, if Your great pity doesn't look out for it—watch over the good knight, son of King Bademagu.* However he may have offended You more than he should, pardon him, if You please, and grant my soul to be with his after my death and his, wherever they may be, for this is the thing I most desire, that my soul be with his after my death, either in torment or in joy, just as we were in life, if it is something that may be granted to a sinner."

As soon as King Bademagu had said this, he laid his hands on his breast in the form of a cross. When Gawain saw that he was dead, he began to lament and complain and curse himself. When the good man who was there saw Gawain making such a lamentation, he immediately understood that the knight had died and that he was a man of consequence; furthermore, he had heard Gawain say that he was a king.

Then he said to Gawain, "My lord, why are you lamenting so? Your weeping won't help you. This man is already dead. May God have mercy on his soul. But, if you please, tell me who he is and what's his name; I greatly desire to know it because I saw him bemoan his sins so well."

Gawain, who was so deeply grieved that he did not know what to say or do, replied weeping, "Know that this was one of the best and wisest men in the world, and such a good knight as all the world may know. He is King Bademagu of Gorre."

"Bademagu?" said the good man. "I knew him well. You've done ill in killing him, for because of this death so many lands will be reduced to poverty and destruction that neither you nor all your kin could conceal the harm that will come of it except by a miracle."

"Indeed," said Gawain, "I'm more sorry about his death than I can tell you. And I consider myself so much at fault that there is nothing except death that I wouldn't suffer if it could only be undone. But since it is so, I ask you to tell me some place where we may bury him, for he's so good and of such great consequence that he should be buried honorably."

"Indeed," said the good man, "I don't know any abbey or hermitage near here, for I'm not of this country but from another, foreign place, but a brother of mine who lies sick in this land summoned me here in a great hurry."

"Since that's so," said Gawain, "I'll go seek a place, near or far, to bury him, and [7] I ask you to stay with him to keep him company until I come."

He agreed, for he was very sorry about the death of the king.

---

*   His son is not mentioned elsewhere in the Post-Vulgate as we have it. In the Vulgate *Lancelot,* chapter 76, he is called Meleagant, not to be confused with the Meleagant of the Post-Vulgate, chapter 82.

Gawain got on his horse and rode as chance guided him until he reached a hermitage that stood on a mountain in a place far from the road and people. There were many good hermits there who had been knights and men of great consequence, but to amend their lives they had come there at the end of their years. When they heard from Gawain that he wanted to bring King Bademagu's body there and learned how the king had died, they felt sorrow and pleasure—sorrow at his death and pleasure to have the body of such a man in their hermitage.* They told Gawain that they thanked him warmly and to go for Bademagu, that they would receive him with good will and pay him all the honor they could. Gawain left at once. When he arrived where the body of King Bademagu lay, he found there a fully armed knight who gave all the appearance of a man in great sorrow. The knight was on a black horse, and his arms and devices were all black.

The knight was brooding deeply and looking at the body. When his horse, which was resting, saw Gawain's horse coming, he began to whinny so loudly that the knight had to abandon his meditation.

When he saw Gawain coming toward him, he asked the good man, "Is this the knight who killed the king?"

"Yes," said the other man.

"Then I'll avenge him, for they wouldn't consider me a knight if I didn't do my best to avenge such a good man."

"I don't advise it," said the good man, "for this is such a good knight at arms that you'd never have the victory in this engagement, unless you were of exceptionally great skill at arms. Therefore, I advise you not to do anything about it."

The knight answered that he would rather be killed than not do what he had in mind, and he called to Gawain, "Gawain, Gawain, I challenge you. You've certainly deserved death for having killed such a good king as King Bademagu."

When Gawain, who was weary from the battle with the king, saw that he would have to fight, it did not please him at all, for he did not need a fight. Moreover, he had no shield or lance.

He said to the [8] knight, "Sir knight, since you wish me to fight with you, although I need no fight, I ask you now for courtesy's sake to let me take my shield, which lies before you, and then you'll have greater honor in attacking me."

The knight agreed, and Gawain took his shield at once. He slung it at his neck and said to himself that if he had a lance he would be better satisfied, and this troubled him greatly. The knight who had challenged him charged at him, and Gawain took his sword, for he had nothing else with which to defend himself. The knight struck him with the lance in such a way that he breached his shield, but Gawain's hauberk was good, and none of its links broke. The knight was so strong that he knocked Gawain to the ground, and Gawain was badly bruised by that fall. However, he got up with agility, for he saw clearly that his need was great, and he prepared to defend himself.

When the other knight saw him on foot, prepared to fight, he said to him, "Gawain, wait a minute; since you're on foot, I'll dismount, for men would think it bad of me to attack you this way."

---

*   "the body of" added by translator.

Then he dismounted, tied his horse to a tree, and leaned his lance against it. He went to Gawain with his sword raised and gave him on the helmet the hardest blow he could, so that Gawain was badly hurt by it. However, he was not yet so tired that he could not defend himself well, for he saw clearly that death was at hand if he did otherwise. The knight, who wished him great harm—a very good knight at arms and whole and agile—began to drive him with his trenchant sword, now here, now there, more or less at his will, so that anyone who saw the battle would have understood at once that Gawain was getting the worse of it and the other the better.

While Gawain was fighting, as I am telling you, so unequally that he feared death and disgrace,* suddenly chance brought that way Eric, the son of King Lac, the knight who never knowingly broke a promise or told a lie.

When he saw the battle, he stopped to look at them, but he did not recognize either.

However, because he thought that they were both good knights and perhaps from King Arthur's house, he went to the knight with black armor and said to him, "Sir knight, I ask you for courtesy's sake to stop this battle until I find out who you both are." [9]

The knight stopped as soon as he saw that the other asked it from his heart; he drew away from Gawain a little and said to Eric, "Sir knight, I'll tell you my name, since you ask me so pressingly. My name is Meraugis of Portlegues, and I'm from Cornwall, not yet of much fame, for it isn't long since I became a knight."

"And of what lineage are you?" asked Eric.

"I don't know," he said, "so help me God. I never knew who my father or mother were, nor have I met, as far as I know, any man of my lineage, and, therefore, I came to this land and started on this quest where the knights of the Round Table are going, for a good man told me, on the day on which I first became a knight, that I wouldn't learn the truth about my lineage unless I went on the quest for the Holy Grail, but there I'd hear the truth if I stayed with it a long time. And, therefore, I started on it after the others."

"And who's this knight you're fighting with?" asked Eric.

"He's Gawain," he said, "King Arthur's nephew, and I'm fighting with him because he killed King Bademagu, whom you see lying there dead."

When Eric heard the news of King Bademagu's death and saw him lying dead, he was very sad and angry, for he had especially loved and respected King Bademagu for his wisdom and chivalry. If he had not loved Gawain as much as he did, he would have avenged King Bademagu's death at once. Yet he could not have done it for another reason, for he would have been faithless and forsworn, and since he was of the Round Table he also could not let Gawain be killed in his presence without being forsworn.

He said to Meraugis, "If Sir Gawain did this through failure to recognize him, he shouldn't be held as guilty as if he did it on purpose. I'm sure and I believe that it grieves him more than you, and therefore I ask you, before harm comes of it to

---

* "and disgrace" as in Bogdanow 1991 (381). Magne has "... death, and the other knight on the point of receiving all honor."

both of you,* to stop this fight, for I won't for anything permit harm to come to Sir Gawain, and even if you were a much better knight than he, if you wouldn't stop at my request, you and I would have to fight."

"And who are you," asked Meraugis, "who want to force me to leave off this fight?"

"I'm Eric," he said. "I don't know if you've heard of me."

"Eric?" said Meraugis. "You're the one who never breaks a promise or tells a lie? So help me God, I've heard you praised in all [11] matters so much that I'll grant your request, for you may well believe that I wouldn't do it for any other knight."

And at once each put his sword into its scabbard.

When the battle had been interrupted as I have told you, Eric dismounted, took off his helmet, put his shield and lance on the ground,† and went to King Bademagu.

He lamented over him and wept a great while, and he said to Gawain, "What can we do with this body? Indeed, everyone should do him honor; he was a very good man."

"Near here," said Gawain, "there's a hermitage where I was planning to take him when this knight attacked me. There he'll be received with great honor. Moreover, they told me that men of his lineage founded that hermitage."

"Then let's take him there," said Eric.

Then they made a bier and tied it to their horses; they laid the king on it and followed him on foot with great sorrow and lamentation. They went to the hermitage, and they buried him there with as much honor as possible. But he had a richer tomb later, for King Caradoc Shortarm, whom chance brought that way, made his tomb so rich, with gold and silver and precious stones, that if the richest king in the world lay there he would lie in honor. He had letters made on top of the stone, which said, HERE LIES KING BADEMAGU OF GORRE, KILLED BY GAWAIN, KING ARTHUR'S NEPHEW. Lancelot later found that inscription and was deeply grieved at the news and very angry about King Bademagu's death, for he had loved him greatly in his lifetime.‡

The knights rested there three days, and Eric frequently asked§ Meraugis about himself, but he could learn nothing, for Meraugis himself did not know from what lineage he came. The reason for this is told in the story of Tristan, and this story touches on it¶ a little and passes by it briefly,** for Meraugis was unquestionably a good knight and brave, one of the most courteous of his age in all the land. He was a native of Cornwall, son of King Mark, Iseut's husband, but he was born not to her but to [13] Ladiana, Aldret's sister and niece of this same King Mark, who had her virginity by force and fathered Meraugis on her. Afterwards, when he saw that she was pregnant, for fear that they would be found out and talked about before everybody, he had her put into a tower until she had the child. When that

---

* "to both of you" as in Bogdanow 1991 (383). Magne has "I ask you and him."
† "put his shield and lance on the ground" added by Bogdanow 1991 (383).
‡ Here Bogdanow 1991 (384) returns to the French.
§ "days, and Eric frequently asked" as in Bogdanow 1991 (384). Magne has "... days. One day Eric asked ..."
¶ This is the only place in the Post-Vulgate where the story of Meraugis is discussed.
** "briefly" as in Bogdanow 1991 (384). Magne has "the best it can."

time arrived, he took her to a well hidden place, far from people, and, after she had had her son, he killed her, for fear that his niece would reveal his identity to the boy when he grew up. Thus King Mark killed his niece there, when she was still in great pain from having given birth, and this was not the first treacherous act he had committed. Doubtless he had a little more pity on the boy, because he was his son, than on the mother, but he had less compassion for him than a father should have for his son. He demonstrated this clearly, for when he left his niece lying on the mountain, where wild beasts later ate her, he took the boy before him, brought him to the road, and hung him by the feet from a tree, so the beasts could not touch him. He thought that someone would come along the road who would find him and take him, and he cared nothing whether he lived or died as long as he never saw him again.

Thus King Mark departed and left the little boy hanging in a tree. But God, taking pity on him because he had nothing to do with his father's evil, took care of him, for, as soon as the king had left, one of the men who guarded his forest* arrived. When he reached the baby and saw him thus suspended, he was sorry for him and cut him down quickly, wondering who had hung him there. He saw that the baby was beautiful for his age, and he took him home and showed him to his wife, who was good and wise.

She said, "I don't think he's a Christian yet.† It would be good to take him to church and baptize him."

"My dear," said the good man, "this boy is very beautiful, and I think it would be good to take him to the king, our lord; then we'll do with him what he commands."

"That seems good to me," said his wife. [14]

They did as they had said and took the son to his father, where he sat in his palace with his barons, and the good man told how he had found him.

The king, who recognized his son plainly, said, "By my faith, you've made a rich find!"

He ordered him to be baptized, and he was named Meraugis of Portlegues, after a knight who was called that, who gave him his name. And know that Portlegues was the castle where Merlin's mother died. King Mark, who pretended not to recognize his son, told the mountaineer to keep him and raise him until he was grown, and that he would yet be a good man, for perhaps he was noble. The man did just as the king commanded, for he raised the boy until he was old enough to become a knight. King Mark made him a knight on Easter Day.

But people throughout the household were saying that Meraugis resembled King Mark so closely that he could very well be his son. As soon as King Mark heard the rumor, he said that he did not want a man without a father to live with him. Meraugis, who was a man of great heart, felt insulted when he heard this and took his leave of the courtiers. He left Cornwall and said he would never stop riding and seeking adventures, as long as he had his health, until he found someone who would tell him whose son he was, if it was something a man could know. In order

---

* "forest" as in Bogdanow (386). Magne has "door," but on the next page he calls the man a mountaineer, which indicates that he is in fact a forester rather than a gatekeeper.

† "yet" added by Bogdanow 1991 (386).

to seek this adventure, he started on the quest for the Holy Grail. But now the story stops speaking of him and turns to another adventure. And if anyone wants to know what happened at the end of his quest and how he found out how he had been hung from the tree, and how he learned about his father and how he had killed his mother, let him take the great history of Tristan, for there he will be able to find complete the truth of all these things.*

114. ERIC AND MERAUGIS WITH A MAIDEN FREE CASTLE CELIS AND ERIC'S SISTER.†

Now the story says that Gawain, Eric, and Meraugis stayed at the hermitage three days after they had buried King Bademagu. On the third day Eric and Meraugis went away, and Gawain remained, because he was badly wounded. The others rode together for two days without finding any adventure worth the telling.

On the third day they happened to meet a maiden, riding alone on a white palfrey. When she reached them, she greeted them and they her. [15]

"My lords," she said, "can you give me any tidings of a knight of the Round Table I've been seeking for a long time?"

"My lady," they said, "tell us what his name is, and perhaps we'll give you some tidings."

"My lords," she said, "his name is Eric, he who never breaks a promise or tells a lie."

"Eric?" he said. "Why do you seek him?"

"I seek him," she said, "because he is bound to give me a gift when I ask it of him, and I would have him give it to me."

He looked at the maiden, and he kept his eyes on her so long that he realized that she was the one who had brought him to Perceval's sister's island,‡ and because she had guided him there he had promised her the first gift she would ask of him.

He could no longer conceal his identity from her, for it would be thought wrong, and he said, "My lady, I'm that Eric you seek. What's your pleasure?"

"Take off your helmet," she said, "so I may see you, for in no other way will I tell you anything of what I want."

---

*   In fact, Meraugis gets this information in chapters 122-123 of the Post-Vulgate.

†   Corresponds to Magne II:14-25; Bogdanow 1991 388-399; Piel 202-207.

‡   The Post-Vulgate has no mention of Eric going to Perceval's sister's island. There was a maiden (chapter 64) to whom he promised a gift/favor in return for telling him where Lancelot was and where his father lay wounded. This episode may have become confused with that (chapter 67) in which Perceval promises a favor to a maiden who takes him to his sister's island where Gaheriet is imprisoned; later (chapter 70) the maiden appears and demands Gaheriet's head, but the situation is resolved without loss of life.

He took it off, and she recognized him immediately and said to him, "My lord, you are welcome. I've been seeking you for a long time; thank God I've found you. Now come with me,* for I have great need of your help."

He granted it. The maiden turned back, taking Eric with her, and they followed a path that intersected the way on which Eric and Meraugis had been riding before.

"Oh, my lord,"† said Meraugis, "I'm still a new knight and of little reputation, and I ask you for God's sake to let me come with you until I see if you need company, for my heart tells me that some harm is to happen to you."

"God willing, that won't happen," said Eric.

"All the same," said Meraugis, "I ask you to let me go with you." And he let him. Then all three together started on their way.

In Meraugis's presence, the maiden said to Eric, "Eric, you are bound to give me what I ask of you."

"That's true," he said.

"And will you break your promise to me because of anything that happens?"

"No," he said, "so help me God; I'd rather die."

"I ask no more," she said.

Then she asked Meraugis, "Sir knight, what's your name?"

And he gave his name.

"You are welcome," she said. "I'm glad that you've heard this, for if he breaks his promise to me, you'll be my witness in King Arthur's house."

"So help me God," he said, "I've heard such testimony given about him—that he's so faithful—that I firmly believe that he won't [17] break his promise to you."

"I don't know," she said, "but you'll soon be able to see."

Thus they rode all that day, and they talked about nothing else, except that Eric kept saying he would keep his promise, but he wondered greatly what it was that she wanted to ask.

When they wanted to stop for the night, it happened that they arrived at a beautiful, rich castle, which stood on a large river called the Celise, and the castle's name was Celis because it stood on the Celise. The moon had already risen when they reached the castle.

The maiden said to Eric, "Do you know this castle?"

He said, "I know it. My father, King Lac, was lord of this castle, and here they killed him by treason. It should have been mine, but the traitors who killed my father are still there. And since God has brought me here, I won't leave until I avenge him, and either they kill me or I them."

Then he went inside, and he crossed himself on entering.

The maiden said to him then, "Eric, I ask of you the head of a maiden who is up above there, whom I'll point out to you, and then you'll be free."

Eric said, "Oh, my lady! For God's sake, ask something else of me, for it isn't my custom to lay a hand on lady or maiden, nor will it be, God willing. For this is the basest thing a knight can do."

"You have to do it," she said, "since you promised me."

---

* "come with me" as in Bogdanow 1991 (389). Magne has "believe me, my friend."

† "my lord" as in Bodanow 1991 (389). Magne has "my lady," but what follows indicates that Meraugis is speaking to Eric.

"It grieves me," he said, "but since I have to do it, I'll do it, but know for certain that it's very much against my will."

They rode through the village, speaking of many things, until they arrived at the fortress, a little tower, very well situated in the middle of the castle, and they met no one who spoke to them.

"Sir Eric," said Meraugis, "I heard you say just now that here you were among your enemies. You're a better knight than I, but all the same I tell you, if you want to perform some feat of arms here, don't stop just because they are many, for I think you are such a good knight that, with the little aid I'll give you, they won't stop us unless they are extremely numerous."

Eric said he would not fear as long as he had his soul in his body.

Speaking thus, they arrived at the fortress and found the door open, for the people from inside were not yet lying down but were walking for relaxation through a meadow that lay around the tower. But because this book has not yet [19] told how King Lac died, we will tell it to you as briefly as we can, just as the true history tells it. The truth is that King Lac and Dirac were natives of Greece and brothers with the same father and mother, sons of King Canan of Saloliqui. King Canan was descended not from kings but from poor knights; however, he did so much by his prowess that he became king, for he conquered a large, rich land. There were in his land many people who hated him mortally, but they dared not show it, and they plotted how they would bring him to death, if they could, but they could not, for he had himself well guarded. Then it happened that he fell a little sick at the beginning of one summer, and one day when he was sitting in his meadow, he asked for something to drink. Certain members of his household, who were especially close to him and secretly wished him ill, then prepared poison, which they gave him to drink. However, they were not so bold as to give it to him themselves, but they sent it to him by Dirac, his son, who was yet a boy, for he was not more than ten years old.

They said to him, "The king is dying of thirst. Take this drink and give it to him, for it will be very beneficial to him in his illness."

The boy, suspecting no poison, took what they gave him and carried it to his father, and, as soon as his father drank it, he died.

When the king was dead, just as I tell you, the barons, who had not loved the father and did not love the sons, said among themselves, "If these boys live and become kings, they'll want to avenge their father's death, and harm could come to us. But we'll soon fix that: let's kill them as we killed their father, and thus no harm will come to us from them."

To this most of the barons of the kingdom agreed, and they would have done it had it not been for the boys' tutor, a good man and loyal, who took them one night with great wealth and fled to the sea. They went on board a ship so secretly that they were not recognized and went to sea. The wind was good, and God protected them, so that before a month was over, they had landed in Great Britain.

How King Arthur ordered King Lac's sons to be brought up.

King Arthur, who was then a young man and had recently begun to reign, was hunting that day near the sea and found the bark, which had just landed. When he saw the boys, who were very handsome, he was greatly pleased with them, for they seemed to be of high rank. He asked about [20] them, and the tutor told him the whole story. When the king heard about the treason of the men of Greece, it grieved him deeply, and he took the boys and ordered them raised. When they were old enough, he made them knights and gave them land, and later by their own deeds they both became kings and won as wives two of King Pelles's sisters. King Dirac's wife bore her husband three sons and a daughter. King Lac's wife had a son and a daughter.[*] King Dirac's three sons, when they were grown knights, were very jealous of King Lac, because he was more famous than their father and more skilled in everything, and from this they conceived an amazingly great dislike of him.

Therefore, when Eric, who knew nothing of this, was already a knight and had left his father in order to go to King Arthur's court, it happened that, one evening when King Lac went to see his brother in that castle I have told you about, King Dirac's sons, who hated their uncle, rose up against him and killed him. King Dirac, his brother, was deeply grieved, although not as deeply as he should have been, and all the barons of Great Britain thought it treachery. A little while before the quest for the Holy Grail began, King Dirac's sons took Eric's sister, one of the most beautiful women in the world, and imprisoned her, because they thought certainly that if Eric knew it, he would come there by some means or other, and if he came there, they would kill him, so that King Lac's land would be theirs.

How Eric and Meraugis entered the castle, killed Dirac's sons, took the castle, and released from prison Eric's sister and the others who lay there.

Thus, as I have told you, King Lac was killed and his daughter captured. Eric had certainly heard about his father's death, but the company of King Arthur's house pleased him so much that he could think only of chivalry, and he did not know that his sister was a prisoner.

When the maiden who had asked the gift of him led him into the fortress, and he saw that Meraugis wanted to keep him company, he said, "Sir Meraugis, there are a great many people here who could quickly do great harm to two knights better than you, and I've never done so much for you that you should risk death for me. Therefore, so help me God, I would wish you to turn back, for if you died here with me, your death would be a great pity, and I wouldn't gain anything by it."

"So help me God," said Meraugis, "what you say isn't good, for, God save me, I'd rather [21] die now with you than go away alive and well from here without you."

"Then may God now come to our aid," said Eric.

Then Eric asked the maiden, "Do you think that King Dirac's sons are here?"

"Yes, unquestionably," she said. "I'll soon show them to you."

"Oh, God, may You be praised!" said Eric.

As soon as they reached the palace, they dismounted, for they could not enter on horseback.

---

[*]   This sentence supplied by Bogdanow 1991 (394), not in Magne.

As soon as they were inside, the maiden cried out, "Come forward, my lords, come forward. Behold here Eric, son of King Lac, whom I bring to you."

There was a great light in the palace, so that one could see almost as well as if it were day. After the maiden had uttered the cry, it was not long before the palace filled up completely with knights and men at arms, but they bore no arms, and the three brothers who were King Dirac's sons did not recognize Eric when they saw him armed.

The maiden called to them again, "You see here what you have asked for so long. Now we'll see what you'll do about it."

They were frightened when they saw that they stood unarmed before Eric, who was armed and whom they considered their mortal enemy, a very good knight and of great fame.

Eric, who hated them mortally, took his sword as soon as he recognized them and called to them, "False traitors, you killed my father by treachery. Tonight the hour of your reward will come."

Then he raised his sword and struck the oldest so hard that he split him to the shoulders, and Meraugis killed another. When the third saw this, he wanted to run away, but Meraugis killed him beside the others. Then great cries were raised and an uproar throughout the palace, and all the other inhabitants of the palace wanted to flee, but the two knights, who were good and lively, did not want them to escape in good health. [23] They struck on all sides and killed and wounded many and made others jump out through the windows. They accomplished so much in a short time that the wounded and dead were more than sixty, and they afflicted them so greatly that no one remained alive and uncaptured in the palace except the three of them—Eric, Meraugis, and the maiden.

The uproar throughout the castle was very great, for some were crying, "To arms! To arms!" and others, "Help! Help!" and they all rushed to the palace to fight with whoever was inflicting such loss on them. However, as soon as they heard that it was Eric, King Lac's son, who by right should be lord over them and over the castle and many others, they lost their anger and drew aside.

Those who were wiser began to say to the people, "My lords, what do you want to do? Know that God has performed a miracle and sent us the most beautiful adventure He ever sent to a people, for He has sent us our natural lord, who by his prowess has delivered us from the great servitude in which these men held us by force. Now we have no reason to delay further. Let's go to him and ask his mercy and make him lord of this castle, just as he should be. This will turn to our honor, and we'll be thought loyal."

How the inhabitants of the castle were greatly pleased with Eric.

They all agreed to this and sent to the palace the one they found wisest and best spoken among them. In a short time he managed to speak with Eric and Meraugis, so that peace was made between the people of the castle and Eric. Eric was well satisfied with the settlement. He received the men of the castle as his men, and they received him as their lord. They had the dead taken out of the palace, and Meraugis had them thrown into ditches outside the village, for he said that traitors should be buried not honorably but like dogs.*

After they had [25] done this, their joy was great, and the old, good men, when they recognized Eric, wept with emotion and said, "Lord God, may You be praised for having guided our lord here, for greater joy or good fortune couldn't come to us in such a short time."

Then they had his sister, whom the traitors had held captive, come before him, and as soon as she saw her brother and recognized him, she felt such joy as no tongue could tell, and rightly so, for she loved him more than anything else in the world. He also was very happy when he saw her and praised God who had brought him there, because He had showed him his sister.

Great was the rejoicing of the castle's inhabitants that night, and they made a bed for Eric, the richest they could, and another near it for Meraugis. After Eric had lain down and gone to sleep, he dreamt a very frightening dream, and I will tell you what it was. It seemed to him that he was standing in an empty field, in which there was neither grass nor tree nor flower nor fruit nor anything on which a man could live. And as he was standing in that field, badly frightened by what he saw, he saw coming toward him a wolf bitch who carried a lamb in her mouth.

She said to him, "Eric, kill this lamb, for you have to."

He killed it, but very unwillingly, and he went away at once and left the wolf. Then after a little while, there came after him a male wolf who attacked him, tore him into more than a hundred pieces, and ate him.

115. Eric Kills His Sister.†

How the maiden asked Eric for his sister's head.

Such was the dream that Eric dreamt that night. He was so badly frightened that he woke up and crossed himself many times, saying a prayer to God and Saint Mary and all the saints to protect him from misfortune and sin.‡ He thought about this so much all night that he could not sleep. When it was light, he and Meraugis got up and went to hear the Mass of the Holy Spirit. That day, when all were sitting eating with great [26] joy, and Eric's sister, who was beautiful and delightful, was sitting

---

*   "like dogs" as in Bogdanow 1991 (398). Magne has "like this."
†   Corresponds to Magne II:25-32; Bogdanow 1991 399-407; Piel 208-212.
‡   Literally, "misfortune and mischance," but both words carry implications of sin.

beside her brother, it happened by ill luck that the evil maiden*, the one who had brought Eric and Meraugis there, entered.

When she saw Eric sitting beside his sister, she went to him and said, "Eric, you owe me a gift, of which I reminded you yesterday, and I want everybody here to know it."

"That's true," he said, "and, God willing, I won't break faith with you."

"Then," she said, "I'll wait until the time is right to ask for it."

"I'm willing to have you wait as long as you please," he said, "for if I fail to give you the gift I've promised you, I wish that God may fail me when I call Him."†

Thus Eric spoke, and so much evil came to him later that he would rather have died, for as soon as the tables were cleared away, the evil maiden came to Eric and said, "Eric, I ask of you the head of this maiden who is sitting beside you."

When he heard this, he was so frightened that his heart failed him, and he said, "Oh, my lady, for God's sake, mercy! Take pity on me and on her, for if I killed my sister—and, what is more, such a beautiful and delightful maiden—this would be the greatest treachery a knight ever committed in this land. At least if you won't have pity on her for God's sake and for mine, have mercy because she's so beautiful, for I don't think you have ever seen such a beautiful maiden."

"I'm not concerned about her beauty," she said, "for she's the person I hate most in the world, and I want you to keep your promise to me."

How Eric asked the maiden not to make him kill his sister.

When Eric heard this, he stood up, from his full height let himself fall at her feet, and said to her, weeping, "Oh, my good lady, have mercy on my sister, and I'll become your servant and all those who hold land from me. Let her go, for, if she dies now, the loss will be great, and I'll be disgraced by it, and you, my friend and my lady, will gain nothing from it."

All the people of the palace said the same thing, and they called out and cried mercy in such a way that no one who saw them could fail to have pity on them.

They said to the maiden, with tears and weeping, "Mercy, mercy, fortunate lady! Don't let such a beautiful creature as this maiden die."

But pity had never entered into her heart, and when she saw them beseeching her [27] so fervently, she became more brutal and arrogant and said, "You're wasting your time. I won't grant your petition. Either I'll have this maiden's head or Eric will have broken his promise to me."

When Eric saw that he could get nothing else out of her, he replied, weeping hard, "Oh, false and treacherous maiden, in an evil hour was this promise made, for I'll be more disgraced than any other knight ever was, and you won't gain anything by it, for, God willing, you will yet die a terrible death for this."

"Don't worry about that," she said, "but do what you must, for I won't let you off in any other way."

---

*   Her behavior leads us to suspect that this may be Dirac's daughter, although the author never says so.

†   "I wish that God may fail me when I call Him" as in Bogdanow 1991 (400). Magne has "I wish that you may fail me when I call you."

"No?" he said. "That grieves me greatly. Indeed, I'd have preferred death to this."

How Eric's sister asked her brother not to kill her, and all the people of the castle asked him.

Then he stood up, so sorrowful that he fervently wished he were dead, and said to his sister, "Sister, beautiful creature, what shall I do about you? For I can't avoid killing you. Cursed be the adventure that brought me here, to my sorrow and death, where I thought to come to my welfare and honor."

When the maiden heard this, she was not a little frightened, for she feared death as much as anyone, and she let herself fall at his feet and said, weeping, "Brother, have mercy on me and remember that I'm your own sister, of the same father and mother, and that I haven't deserved death from you. Recollect what you should rightfully do, for if you kill me, you'll commit the greatest sin and the basest act a knight ever committed. If for no other reason, you shouldn't do this because I'm a maiden, and such a knight as you are should not lay a hand on a maiden for any reason."

Then the people of the palace said with one voice, "Oh, my lord, have mercy on your sister. Don't do the brutal act that this false maiden tells you to do."

Then he said, "What are you saying, my lords? I can't escape from this unless you kill me, for while I live I won't get out of a promise [29] I make, but if you kill me, she'll be spared. Now do whichever you think better: either you kill me or I'll kill her. I want with all my heart to die this death, for otherwise I will never again be a true knight; after I do this cruel deed, I won't be worth a straw."

How Eric cut off his sister's head and gave it to the maiden.

Those who were in the palace did not know what to say, for they would not for anything kill their lord, and they thought him such a good knight and good man that he could attain greater honor than the maiden.[*]

Meraugis, who was so deeply grieved that he could not think what to do, said to Eric, "Oh, Sir Eric, you'll be shamed for the rest of your life if you kill your sister this way for a false maiden."

Then Eric said, "What shall I do about what I promised?"

Then he went to a room and took his sword. He returned to the palace with great sorrow, wishing lightening would fall from the sky and strike him. When he reached his sister, he drew his sword.

She begged him all the while for mercy, saying, "Oh, brother Eric, for God's sake, mercy! Consider the fact that I haven't deserved death. If you won't spare me for the sake of God and your knighthood, at least consider the fact that I'm a maiden, beautiful as you see, and I'm praised for my beauty above all other maidens of Great Britain."

---

[*]   "than the maiden" added by Bogdanow 1991 (403).

He replied with great sorrow, "Sister, all this will avail you nothing; you have to die. But what you say to me will make me die of grief, if a knight can die of grief."

Then he raised his sword and turned his face away, unable to look at such great suffering. She was already totally senseless, so that she could not defend herself against the blow, and he struck her hard, so that he made her head fall more than a lance length away, and her body fell to the ground.

At once he said to the maiden, "Cursed, godless girl, the most treacherous girl who ever mounted a palfrey, now take your promise, and may God give you such pleasure as you've given me."

She went at once to the head, took it, and said, "Now I have what I wanted."

Then she said to Eric before everyone, "You accuse me of treachery, but, indeed, you're more to blame than I, for if you weren't a more [31] treacherous knight than any other, you wouldn't have killed your sister this way for a simple promise you had made me."

Then she left the palace, took the head, and mounted her palfrey. But you never heard such a lamentation as they were making after her, when they saw she was taking the head, and, if they had dared kill her, they would not for anything have failed to tear her into a hundred pieces. But at that time it was the custom in Great Britain that no one would lay a hand on a maiden who was a messenger unless he wanted to lose honor for all the days of his life or unless he was a knight possessed of the devil.

How the maiden who took the head was burned by lightning.

Thus the evil maiden went out of the castle as quickly as she could, for she feared that the people of the castle would follow her and harm her. But she had not gone more than three bowshots from the castle when a marvelous adventure happened to her, and it was without doubt a miracle, for there came from the sky a cloud full of fire and flame, which placed itself over the maiden and her palfrey. When she saw that the fire was catching her, she uttered loud cries of agony, so that the people of the castle heard them, but her cries soon stopped, for within a short while she was burned, and the cloud departed from her, so that the people of the castle saw her and her palfrey lying there burned.

How they found Eric's sister's head unburned.

As all the people of the castle had seen this marvel, they came and found the evil maiden and her palfrey burned, but Eric's sister's head was so untouched that not even one hair of it was burned.

They all said, "Oh, God! What a miracle this is, and a beautiful display of power! Now the truth of our young lady and the treachery of this other one are apparent."

Then they made a great lamentation and wailing over the maiden's head, and they gave thanks to God for the beautiful vengeance He had taken on the evil maiden.

When Eric, who was still in the palace mourning, heard this, he said to Meraugis, "What do you think about this?"

He answered, "I think that Our Lord isn't very happy with what happened to your sister [32] when you killed her, and if harm doesn't come to you soon because of it, I won't ever believe anything my heart tells me."

Eric, who was so sad that he did not know what to do, replied, "Indeed, friend Meraugis, if Our Lord's vengeance comes as quickly as my heart desires, it won't delay, for, indeed, I wish lightning would come strike me just as it did the evil maiden, and that all the people of this castle would see the vengeance of it."

Then Meraugis replied, "Sir Eric, death comes not at the wish of the sinner nor of the one who desires it, but as God wishes."

"Wretch!" said Eric; "how badly I have erred! How badly I have sinned! How wrongly I have killed!"

"All this was your fault," said Meraugis. 'You wouldn't yield to my petition or that of the good men of this palace, and I certainly think that harm will come to you."

"As much harm can't come to me as I deserve," he said.

Then he asked for his arms, for he did not want to stay there any longer. The people of the castle gave them to him unwillingly, for they did not want him to leave them so quickly. Meraugis, when he saw him arming, said that he had come here for Eric's sake and with him he wanted to go away, and he armed himself, mounted his horse after Eric had mounted his, and left the castle.

116. Eric Mourns His Sister.*

Eric's grief and suffering because he had killed his sister.

Thus Eric left his castle, where he had killed his sister. He rode all that day, weeping and lamenting so that anyone who saw him would have thought him mad. That day, when it began to get dark, they arrived at the edge of a forest. They entered it and rode until they arrived at a deep valley, full of dense wood and hard to ride through. They found beside the road an old, deserted house, mostly fallen down. Eric was riding in the greatest possible sorrow, and he had just left off mourning because of something he was thinking. He was thinking that he would leave Meraugis, if he could, and if he left him he would always ride alone and lament and mourn until perforce he died, whether from fasting, wakefulness, or mourning, nor would he ever keep Meraugis or any one else company. This, Eric said, would be the vengeance he could exact for his sister whom he had killed.

---

*   Corresponds to Magne II:32-38; Bogdanow 1991 407-413; Piel 212-216.

How Eric left Meraugis in order to mourn. [33]

Eric was riding along thinking about this when he saw the deserted house. He thought they would stay there and, as soon as Meraugis slept, he would leave and go someplace where Meraugis could not find him even if he searched, and thus he would be able from then on to travel alone and do what he planned.

When they got there he said to Meraugis, "Friend, I feel so tired already that I would gladly dismount, if it pleased you, and rest here a little. What's more, it's already nearly night, and it isn't good to ride at night."

Meraugis was happy at this, for he truly thought Eric said it in order to rest, not knowing what Eric was really thinking. They dismounted at once and laid aside their shields, lances, and helmets in order to rest better. They let the horses go graze and threw themselves down on the grass. Eric did not sleep, for he was planning something else, but Meraugis fell asleep quickly, for he had no suspicion that Eric would leave him. When Eric was sure that Meraugis was asleep, he bridled his horse, threw the saddle on him, took his arms, and mounted, returning by the main road by which they had come. All night he rode, wandering where he saw the forest thickest, for he did not want them to find him. He desired to ride alone and to lament and mourn his sister, and he planned not to eat and always to inflict suffering on himself, for he truly imagined he could sooner die in this way. And that he would gladly do, for it seemed to him that in this way the death of his sister would be truly avenged.

How Eric arrived at the recluse's house when he had not eaten for five days.

Thus he rode all that day and the next, wandering now here, now there, and on the fifth day he chanced upon the house of a recluse. This was at night, just before dawn. He was then already very tired and weak, which was not surprising, for it was five days since he had eaten or rested, mourning as he went, and his horse was so tired it could hardly bear him. When Eric reached the cell, he did not think there was anyone there, man or woman. Nevertheless, because he felt tired and saw that his horse was failing him, he dismounted and let it go graze where it wished. He laid aside his shield and helmet, threw himself down on the grass before the recluse's window, and fell asleep. He was so afflicted with fatigue and [35] grief that he slept until noon the next day.

How Eric lamented his sister whom he had killed, and how the recluse comforted him.

At midday Eric awoke. He recalled his sister and the grief he was unable to forget, and he began to lament so loudly that anyone who heard him would have been amazed. The recluse, who had studied him at length while he slept, wondered when she saw him lamenting so loudly what it could be, for she had not seen anyone afflict him to make him lament.

Then she called out to him, "Oh, knight! What a lamentation you're making! God save you, speak to me* and tell me, if you may, the cause of your sorrow, and, if it's something about which I can advise you, I'll do so."

When he heard someone speaking, he was amazed, for he had not thought there was anyone there, man or woman, and he looked around as if frightened.

When he saw the recluse, he left off mourning and said, "My lady, what's your pleasure?"

"For God's sake," she said, "tell me something about yourself and the cause of your grief, for I'd gladly know it."

"My lady," he said, "I'll tell you. I'm a wretched and unfortunate knight, the most disloyal of whom you ever heard, for I've committed the greatest treachery a knight ever committed."

And he told her everything.

After he had told her, the lady was deeply sorry and said to him, "Sir knight, since this has happened to you and you see that it can't be otherwise, you have to comfort yourself the best you can and pray to Our Lord to pardon you, for, indeed, only evil will come to you from mourning as you have been, nor will God thank you for it, and no man was ever thought so unfortunate as you will be if you die in this manner."

How the recluse told Eric that his death was approaching.

The lady said so much to him and admonished him so much that he somewhat abated his mourning. However, Eric said that he would never be happy; then he said further to the lady, "My lady, if I'm visited by bad intentions, it isn't surprising, for, indeed, the night before that day on which I killed my sister, there came to me a dream—I never heard of a similar one—and I was so badly frightened [37] that I woke up." Then he told her what the dream was.

The lady said, "If I knew how to interpret it as others do, I'd interpret it for you, but it doesn't please God that His secrets be revealed to me.[†] However, I dare tell you this much, that your death is rapidly approaching, and, therefore, I advise you truly to make a good confession and, both with mouth and with heart, ask mercy of Our Lord. A brutal, treacherous knight will kill you, and this event is not far off."

How the recluse gave Eric something to eat, and he left her.

When he heard this, he began to brood more than before, for she frightened him when she described his death. However, after a while he said, "My lady, for God's sake, do you know who it is who is to kill me?"

"Indeed, no," she said. "I know no more than I've told you."

"Then," he said, "may everything be as Our Lord wills. However, since my death is to be by arms, I know that I couldn't die in greater service of God than in the quest for the Holy Grail, for if I die as well confessed as I am now and with as

---

*   "to me" as in Bogdanow 1991 (410). Magne has "speak, friend."
†   "to me" added by Bogdanow 1991 (411).

great sorrow for my sins, I know well that Our Lord will have mercy on me, and my kindred will have greater honor from such a death than if I died in some other manner. And, therefore, I'll leave off mourning as much as I can and enter into the quest for the Holy Grail with my companions. However, because I'm wearier than I should be, for it's five days since I've eaten, I ask you to give me something to eat."

She gave him a loaf of dark barley bread, hard and unpleasant to eat for such a man as Eric, but he ate it quickly all the same, for he was tormented by hunger. After he had eaten the bread, he went to his horse, mounted, and commended the lady warmly to God and she him. Then he rode through the forest rather slowly, because of his horse, which he realized was not as vigorous as usual. In this way he rode for a while without finding an adventure worth the telling. But now the story stops speaking of him and turns to Meraugis, to tell how he and Hector [38] became companions and how they later found Eric in the land of the Dolorous Field, from which no good knight could depart without grief.

117. MERAUGIS AND HECTOR LOOK FOR ERIC.*

The story tells that after Eric left him, as the tale has already told, Meraugis slept the whole night. In the morning, when the sun rose, he awoke and looked around. When he did not see Eric, he got up quickly and went looking for him on every side, and when he could not find him, he realized at once that Eric had left him in order to mourn in seclusion and die far from people in dishonor and disgrace.

Meraugis was so sad at this torment of Eric's that he did not know what to do. He began to mourn and lament for Eric, because of the great goodness he knew in him, and he said, "Oh, good man, good knight, good at arms, good in courage, good in courtesy, educated, moderate, honest, polite, endowed with the best grace a knight ever had! Now I see that you've left me in order to mourn and to go mad and kill yourself, so that I may not see your torment or your death and you may not see my grief at them. Well have you demonstrated your courtesy!"

Thus Meraugis spoke to himself with as much grief at Eric's departure as if he had been his brother.

As Meraugis was standing in the path where Eric had left him, suddenly a knight appeared, fully armed, coming through the middle of a field, and I tell you that this knight was Hector of the Fens. When Meraugis saw him approaching, he thought he would only ask to joust, and he took his shield and lance, got on his horse as quickly as he could, and waited in the middle of the path, so that if the other wanted to ask it of him, he would be ready to defend himself.

When Hector saw Meraugis waiting thus in the road, he said in his heart, "This knight asks only to joust; he will think me bad and cowardly if I go away without doing more."

---

* Corresponds to Magne II:38-41; Bogdanow 1991 414-418; Piel 216-218.

He called out to Meraugis, and Meraugis, who thought himself very brave and bold, answered, "Since you ask me for a joust, I won't fail you if I can help it."

Then they charged at each other and [39] struck each other so violently that their lances splintered. Meraugis fell to the ground badly bruised, for he took a mighty fall, and Hector, too experienced to fall easily, remained on his horse. When Meraugis found himself on the ground, he stood up quickly, deeply ashamed of this adventure, took his sword, and prepared to give the best account of himself he could, for he saw clearly that the man who had knocked him down was no boy. When Hector saw that Meraugis was preparing to fight as he was on foot, he respected him more than before and thought that he was one of the knights of the Round Table.

Therefore, he wanted to know who he was before doing anything more, and he said to Meraugis, "Sir knight, you're on foot, and I'm on horseback, and still with such fortune you want to fight?"

Meraugis said that he truly wanted to, for otherwise he would be dishonored.

"So?" said Hector. "Then I ask you, by the faith you owe to all knighthood, to tell me who you are and what you're seeking, for you may be such that I'll fight with you, and you may be such that I won't."

"My lord," said Meraugis, "my name won't be hidden from you, since you ask it of me. Know that my name is Meraugis, and I'm from Cornwall. I haven't yet done as much as my heart desires, neither that with which I might be satisfied nor that from which I might have great reputation. Nevertheless, I had recently become the companion of a knight, because of the great goodness that I saw* in him."

Then he told him everything as it had happened and what his companion's name was, and Hector gave his own name. As soon as Hector heard about Eric, his adventure and fortune, he was very sad, for he loved Eric greatly, as the story has told you.

Then he said to Meraugis, "You're seeking a man whom I love more than all the knights of my kindred, and since you love him as much as you tell me, I wouldn't fight with you for any reason except mortal hatred. Therefore, I forgive you this battle, for, God willing, I'll speak of it no more, and I yield myself defeated." Then he dismounted, drew his sword, and said, "Sir Meraugis, take this sword, which I give you, and, if you please, I hold myself defeated in this battle."

"My lord," said Meraugis, "God willing, I won't receive this honor, for, indeed, you're a better knight than I."

"Now tell me," said Hector, "what you want to do about Eric."

"My lord," he said, "I want to leave as quickly as I can and seek him until I find him." [41]

"Then I ask you," said Hector, "please to let me keep you company in this search, for, if you don't want to seek him, I'll seek him until I find him, in order to console him for this ill fortune that has happened to him."

Meraugis said he was very glad of Hector's company.

In this way Hector and Meraugis became companions in the search for Eric.

---

*   "I saw" as in Bogdanow 1991 (417). Magne has "was."

After they had mounted, Hector asked Meraugis, "Do you know which way he went?"

"No," he said, "for I don't see his trail, nor do I know when he left me."

"Then let's go where chance takes us," said Hector, "and may God bring us to where we may find him."

"May God grant it," said Meraugis.

Then they started out and rode for a long time as chance guided them without finding any adventure worth the telling. But now the story stops speaking of them and returns to Eric, in order to tell how he died.

118. Eric Incurs the Enmity of Gawain and Agravain.*

When Eric left the recluse, he rode a long time, as the story tells, without finding an adventure worth the telling. One day at the beginning of August, chance brought him to a forest near a castle that stood on a plain. The inhabitants of the castle were celebrating a great feast that day, it being a week since their king had taken the crown, and there was such a competition—because they knew that knights errant passed by the castle each day—that if any knight of the land dared undertake to joust with everyone who passed by there that day and knocked them all down, they would give him as a reward a crown as rich as their lord's and a maiden, the most beautiful he could choose in all the land.

Gawain had come to that competition the previous day. As soon as he saw the maiden who would be the prize for the man to whom God gave the honor of that competition, he was very much taken with her, for she was exceptionally beautiful. He waited until a knight of the land learned about the competition they had set, and when he saw that the knight was taking his arms in order to win the prize of the day, Gawain went there incognito, as if he were a poor knight, and asked him for a joust. The knight jousted with him without question, and it happened that Gawain knocked him down and wounded him mortally. The festival organizers came to him and asked him who he was, and he gave his name. When they heard that he was Gawain, one of the bravest knights in the world, they said that he would have the honor the other knight had sought and that he should defend all day against the knights who would [43] pass by. Gawain said he would do it if no knights of the Round Table came that way. So he stood in that festival in the hope of having the maiden he had seen. When the hour of nones came, and they were all saying that Gawain would have that honor, suddenly Eric arrived, alone and as sad, tired, and tormented as I have told you. Gawain, who did not recognize him because he had changed his arms, demanded a joust of him.

When Eric realized that he was required to joust, he said he did not need that, for his horse was already so thin and tired that it could hardly stand.

---

* Corresponds to Magne II:41-45; Bogdanow 1991 419-426: Piel 218-222.

Nevertheless, he said, "Since it can't be otherwise, I'd rather joust than go away in shame."

Gawain was on a large, beautiful, good horse. The inhabitants of the castle gave Eric, who had no lance, a very good one. Then they charged at each other, and Gawain struck Eric with all his might so hard that he splintered his lance, but he did him no other harm. Eric, who was stronger than Gawain, struck him so hard that he knocked him from his horse to the ground, but he did him no other harm. His lance broke, and the people in the field, who had seen all this, began to jeer and hoot so on all sides that no one would have heard it thunder, had it done so.

When Eric saw Gawain on the ground, he did not recognize him from his arms, which Gawain had changed many times since he had started on the quest for the Holy Grail. Eric went to Gawain's horse and got on it, leaving his own, from which he had been getting little use. When Gawain saw him going, he was so grieved and ashamed that he did not know what to do.

When an unarmed knight from among those who were guarding the festival saw Eric going off this way, he said to him, "Oh, sir knight, if you please, wait a little while I speak with you."

Eric stopped then, and the knight asked him, "My lord, why are you going? Indeed, if you knew what you have won in this joust, you would gladly remain, and you'd be happy about it when you knew."

Then he told it all to him, just as the story has already described.

When Eric heard this he said, "My lord, let not what I say grieve you. [44] Know that I wouldn't now take the most beautiful maiden in the world, if they gave her to me, for so much wrong and grief have come to me recently because of a woman that there is no maiden in the world I would take. Therefore, I commend you and all your company to God, for I'm in a hurry, because I have much to do elsewhere."

"What?" said the knight. "Do you reject this honor God has given you?"

"Yes," he said, "I reject it completely."

"At least," said the knight, "by your courtesy, tell me your name."

"My name is Eric," he said, "son of King Lac."

And immediately they parted. Eric left and went toward the forest as fast as he could ride, for he would gladly have already been in it. The knight returned to his companions and told them the news he had learned. When Gawain heard that it was Eric who had defeated him in front of so many good men, he felt such grief and shame that he would rather have been dead than alive, for he had not believed that Eric could be such a good knight, and he thought that he would avenge himself on him as no knight ever avenged himself on another. Nor because he was a companion of the Round Table would Gawain spare him or fail to cut off his head, and he conceived toward Eric such anger that no man ever hated another more mortally. That day he stayed in that castle with greater sorrow than he showed, and the next day, when he left, they gave him a very good horse in exchange for his own, which he had lost, for they saw clearly that Eric's was worth nothing. After he was armed, he left them and rode to the forest by the path by which he had seen Eric go, but be sure that he rode with such grief and anger that he said he would never be happy until he found Eric.

As he was riding along thus in his grief, he met Agravain, his brother. They did not recognize each other by their arms, which they had changed, nor did they challenge each other, for both were preoccupied.

As soon as they reached each other, Gawain asked, after he had greeted him, "Sir knight, have you seen today or yesterday a knight who bears white arms with a red lion?"

Agravain recognized his brother as soon as he heard him speak and said to him, "Oh, my lord, you are welcome, for I've been seeking you for a long time."

As soon as Gawain recognized his brother he embraced him, and Agravain embraced Gawain.

Gawain said to him, "Brother, why were you seeking me?"

"My lord," he said, "because they told me that you lay wounded in an abbey."

"It isn't so, thanks be to God," said Gawain, "but can you give me any news about the knight I'm [45] asking you about?"

"Yes," he said, "I met him yesterday, in an evil hour for me."

"Why?" asked Gawain. "Did he do you some harm?"

Agravain said, "Very great harm: he knocked me down so violently that even now it pains me."

"And which way did he go?" asked Gawain.

"My lord," said Agravain, "he went by the main road of the forest. But since you're seeking him, I know well that it isn't without reason, and I beg you to tell it to me."

And Gawain told him the whole story.

"Since it's so," he said, "I want to turn back with you, and we'll take such vengeance as you like."

Gawain agreed to this.

Then the two brothers turned and went after Eric, and Agravain asked Gawain, "My lord, do you know who the knight we are following is?"

"Yes," he said, "he's Eric, the son of King Lac."

As soon as Agravain heard this, he pulled on the reins, drew aside, and said, "By God, you won't follow him, by my counsel."

"Why not?" asked Gawain.

"It's this way," said Agravain. "I don't know if you know it, but I know for a truth that you are fated to die at the hands of a knight; I don't know his name, but I do know that it will be either Lancelot or Eric.* And, therefore, I wish you would keep yourself away from these two."

"Who told you this?" asked Gawain.

"My lord," he said, "I won't reveal that for anything, but know this much for sure, that it will happen just as I have told you, if you don't keep yourself away from these two."

"I won't keep myself from one of them," said Gawain, "for, were it necessary, he'd risk his life to save mine, and that's Lancelot. And I know that the other isn't

---

*   In chapter 156 Gawain dies of a wound inflicted by Lancelot.

such a knight that, at the last, he could stand against me. And, therefore, I have no fear from what you've told me."

"All this is nothing," said Agravain, "for it's to happen this way. Now may you give up this battle."

"I won't," said Gawain, "for it won't come true."

"That would please me greatly," said Agravain.

Thus they rode all that day without finding Eric or meeting anyone who could give them news of him, and they were very sorry about it, for they would gladly have found him. Now the story stops speaking of the two of them and returns to Eric, in order to tell by what adventure Gawain killed him.

119. ERIC IS PARALYZED BY THE SPRING OF THE VIRGIN.*

The story tells that after Eric left Gawain, whom he had knocked down in front of many good men,† as the story has already told, he rode all that day, and the next [47] day also, without finding an adventure worth the telling, until he entered the forest. That night he slept at the house of a knight who lived in the forest, who did him great honor, seeing that he was a knight errant. In the morning he left, and he rode all that day until the hour of midday, and then it happened that he found beside the road a beautiful spring, so surrounded by trees on all sides that no one who entered would fear the heat, even though it was August. When Eric, who was in considerable discomfort from the heat, saw the spring so beautiful and the place so well suited to resting, he dismounted to protect himself from the hottest time of the day and to rest a little. He took the bridle off his horse and let it graze. After that he removed his helmet and visor and sat down beside the spring, looking at the water, which was beautiful and clear, and he thought he would rest there until midday had passed.

Then he threw himself down on the grass and began to think very hard, and as he was thinking he turned over on his face. After a little while he found himself so badly affected that he could not move foot or hand or any limb, and he had lost the power of speech. He wondered what it could be, for he saw no man or woman near who could have enchanted him. As he was lying in this distress, he saw coming toward him to the spring three maidens and an old lady on good palfreys. All three of the maidens were dressed as if they were coming from‡ the hunt, for one carried a beautiful, rich horn, the second a bow with a quiver of arrows, and the third a deer trussed up. The lady carried nothing, for she was their mistress. As soon as they reached the spring, they dismounted, and each one tied her palfrey to the trees; then they laid aside what they were carrying in order to rest. They thought Eric was asleep, but the lady, who knew more than they, did not think that; she knew well

*   Corresponds to Magne II:45-59; Bogdanow 1991 427-440; Piel 222-229.
†   "many good men" as in Bogdanow 1991 (427). Magne has "a good man."
‡   "coming from" as in Bogdanow 1991 (428). Magne has "going to."

that he was not asleep. And if anyone wants to ask how it happened that Eric was so badly affected, I will tell him the truth, just as I found it in the true history.

The true history tells us that the spring where this happened to Eric was called the Spring of the Virgin, and this was because of a beautiful adventure that happened to a virgin in the time of Uther Pendragon. [49] There was a king in that land whose name was Nascor. That king in that village was a very good man, and he loved and feared God. He had a beautiful, good lady as his wife, and he had one son and one daughter. The son was the most beautiful young man anyone might see in all the land, and he was sixteen years old. The daughter was the most beautiful creature in all Great Britain, and so great was the fame of her beauty that they came from near and far to see her. Because of her great beauty, they all called her angelic. If she seemed to the people as beautiful as I have told you, she was much more beautiful to Our Lord, for she did secretly all the good works she could do. No one could take such great pleasure in the riches of the world as she took in Our Lord. The truth was that she was marvelously well versed in divine matters, more by grace and Our Lord's concession than by instruction from her teachers. And I tell you that her teachers were from Rome, where at that time lived the priests who had come a long time before from the city of Athens. God had so put His spirit into the maiden that the teachers who taught her were taken aback at the knowledge they found in her. And know that she was familiar with the legend that they call that of the Holy Fathers, which describes a large part of the life of the Holy Fathers and the Trinity.

What shall I tell you? That maiden was a second Catelina in wisdom and goodness, and her* life should be told, for it will be an example and a lesson to all good people who hear of her. When the maiden, whose name was Aglinda, reached the age of fourteen, she was an amazingly beautiful creature and as good as the story has told you. Her brother, who was not yet a knight but was soon to become one, was riding one day through a forest where he had gone hunting and lost all his dogs and men, so that he did not know where they were. He was completely lost in the forest, for the trees were so thick and the paths so bad that he did not [50] know which to take. The young man began to go here and there seeking a path that would take him to the road, but he could find none. All that day he wandered from one place to another, and that night and the next day, and he neither ate nor drank. The forest was a four-day journey long and equally wide, and when he had been wandering three days in distress, the devil appeared to him, as I will tell you.

On the third day it happened that that youth, whose name was Nabor, arrived at that spring, hungry, thirsty, and more miserable than he had ever been before. He was so tired that he almost lost heart, and, furthermore, he was deeply grieved for his men, whom he thought he would never find. He dismounted from his horse, who was already unable to go further, and, seating himself beside the spring, began to think very hard. As he was sitting and thinking, suddenly a devil appeared to him in the semblance of a wise man who was brooding and grieved and sad, and he gave no indication that he knew Nabor but seemed a stranger. He went to the spring and seemed to drink, but he did not drink, for Scripture tells that the devil

---

* "and her" as in Bogdanow 1991 (429). Magne has "she whose."

never eats or drinks; however, Nabor, who was looking at him and still thinking, thought truly that he had drunk.

When the demon, who was thus brooding, had looked a long time at the youth, who was also brooding beside the spring, he did not speak to him but began to lament, and after a while he said, "Wretch! All my efforts are for nothing!"

The youth left his thoughts when he heard this and began to look at him; he saw him attractive in appearance and said to him, "Friend, who are you who say that all your efforts are for nothing?"

The demon, who never tells the truth, replied, "I'm a man from a foreign land, sad in spirit and in deed,* and if in this land I could find [51] counsel in which I could trust, I'd consider myself rich and happy, for I would then have everything my heart desires and be free of all torment and sadness."

When the youth heard this, he desired to know about that man who seemed to him so good, and he said to him, "If you'll tell me about yourself, I'll help you the best I can."

The demon said to him, "I don't want to tell you, for it's an important matter, and perhaps you might reveal it."

"But I won't do so," said the youth.

"And why should I believe that?" asked the demon.

"I'll swear it to you," said the youth, and he swore at once on all Christianity. "But it's necessary," said the youth, "that you tell me all about yourself and who you are and on what you need counsel, for, indeed, I'll help you with all my power."

"I'll do so," said the demon. "Now listen, and I'll tell you all about it The fact is that not long ago I loved a rich and powerful lady of this land, and she loved me as much or more. It happened that that lady had a daughter by me at the same time that the queen of this land also had her daughter. The queen had her daughter killed as soon as she was born, because of a dream she dreamed, that that daughter was to kill her. After she had killed her, she didn't know what to do, for fear the king would kill her, so she took my daughter and had her brought up in the king's presence, making him believe that she was his own. However, before we gave the girl to her, she promised that she would give her back to us whenever we asked for her.

"Thus she took our baby in place of her own, always promising us that she'd give her to us when we wished. Now it happens that I've asked for her, and the queen won't give her to me and denies the whole matter, and moreover she bears me a grudge, and the maiden, who knows truly that I'm her father, won't even recognize me but tells me never to speak to her of it or she'll have me killed. And this is my great sorrow, that [53] my daughter, who's the most beautiful creature in the world and the wisest, nevertheless is so arrogant that she won't recognize me as her father. Now I beg your advice as to what I should do, and you must help me just as you promised."

When the youth heard this, he began to think. He was deeply sorry about his mother, who had raised them, that she had committed the treachery the demon

---

* Literally, "in mind and in life."

said, and, on the other hand, he was deeply grieved because of the maiden he had thought his sister but now thought no kin to him.

The demon said to him again, "What do you say to me about this?"

"Indeed," said the youth, "I don't know how to advise you, for the queen is so powerful that you won't be able to prove what you accuse her of."

The demon said, "You can help me in this, if you wish."

"How?" asked the youth. "Show me, and if I can do it without doing wrong, I will."

"I'll tell you about it," said the demon. "Tomorrow morning I'll take you to the house of your father, who is far from here and deeply troubled about you, for he really thinks he has lost you. When you're there, tell the maiden to come walk with you through the meadow to a good place, and she'll do it willingly, for she loves you so dearly that there's nothing you could tell her that she wouldn't do for love of you. If you bring her here, I'll give you anything you ask for."

Then the youth replied, "I wouldn't do that for anything, for it would be betrayal."

The demon said, "You don't want to do what I'm asking of you?* Now know truly that you've never committed such great folly, and I'll tell you what will happen to you because of it, for you're in this forest in a place so lost and far from all people that you'll never find the road, but you'll remain here, a wretched unfortunate, and die of hunger, and the animals and birds will eat you. Indeed, if you grant me willingly what I ask of you, I will bring you to safety today." [55]

Then the demon left him, in order to increase his distress, and went off by another way. The youth remained at the spring, in greater torment than before from hunger and exhaustion, for it was already three days since he had eaten, but hunger tormented him less than the thought that he would never find human habitation and that the animals, as soon as they found him, would eat him there. Then he began to weep and make such a great lamentation that anyone who heard him would have had to pity him.

Then the demon returned to him in the same semblance as before and said to him, "Unfortunate one, now I see what I wanted to see in you. Now your slight wisdom appears, for you're letting yourself be killed here by hunger and sorrow for a maiden who is no kin."

The youth was greatly tormented and said, "Take me to safety now, and I promise you that four days from now I'll bring her to you wherever you wish."

"Then you'll do it?" asked the demon.

He promised faithfully, and the demon at once guided him to his father's house. The youth found many who received him well in his father's house and who were happy to see him, for they had felt great sorrow because of him.

On the third day it happened that King Nascor went to hunt in that same forest, taking with him the queen and many maidens to enjoy themselves and be entertained with him. The youth did not forget what he had promised the demon, but he thought about how he could accomplish it. He went with the king and queen as far as the forest.

---

*   Literally, "You don't want to do it for anything, and I am asking it of you?"

Then he returned to his sister and said, "Sister, mount, and take one of your teachers with you, for the queen commands you to follow her to see the pleasure of the hunt."

Not daring to say anything against her mother's command, she mounted, although she was not used to it. After they had started on their way, the youth went off in another direction, not the way the hunters had gone, and he went directly to the spring to fulfill his promise. He rode along the way, looking at his sister, and he felt such great delight in her, and she seemed to him so beautiful that there grew in him the unreasonable wish to possess her. Then he began to think that it would be bad and senseless if he did not fulfill his wish with such a beautiful maiden to whom he was in no way kin, and moreover that he was going to put her into the hands of one who would take her where he would perhaps never see her again, and he knew he would never find another so beautiful.

Thus the youth rode, thinking the whole way, and as soon as they arrived at the spring he said to his sister, "Let's dismount here and await the others, for they'll soon be here."

When they had dismounted, the youth took the sword he bore and killed the teacher.

The maiden, seeing this, was badly frightened and said, "Oh, brother! Why did you do this? By God, you've done wrong."

"I'm not your brother," he said, "and don't call me brother, for I have no other tie to you than custom. I'm as much kin to you as to the most alien woman in the world. Therefore, I've brought you here so far from people because I want to lie with you before someone else has you, and if you won't do it, I'll do to you as I did to your teacher."

When the maiden heard this she was badly frightened, for she saw her brother ranged with the devils, and she said, "Oh, brother! For God's sake, mercy! Remember who you are and who I am!"

"This is a waste of time," said Nabor. "Nothing you say will help you."

And he went to take her by force. When the maiden saw that she was on the verge of losing body and soul, she prayed to Our Lord to deliver her from that misfortune. As soon as she did that, the youth at once fell dead to the [57] ground. When the maiden saw her brother dead by such misfortune, she was very sad.

While she was considering by what adventure this had happened, a voice said to her, "Good and worthy maiden, the demon has done this to you in order to take away from you the crown of virgins, if he could." Then it revealed to her the whole business, as it had happened, just as the story has already told. While the maiden was thinking about what she had heard, suddenly her father arrived there with all his company, after having lost the deer he was following.

When the king saw his daughter, he wondered who had brought her there, and he went running to her and said to her, smiling, "Daughter and friend, who brought you here?"

"My lord," she said, "sins and the devil, who labors always to confound Christians." Then she told him the whole adventure as it had happened and showed him her teacher and her brother dead.

The king said angrily, "Now it seems that my son served a bad lord, who gave him a bad reward. This place is bad, and bad is the spring where the demon lives."

"From now on," said the maiden, "it will be even worse, for never will a knight come here, unless he's a virgin, but he'll lose the power of his body and all his limbs while he is here, nor will he ever move from here except with a woman's help. This will be in remembrance of the sin by which my brother was killed, and this remembrance of me and my brother will last until the Good Knight comes who will bring to an end the adventures of the kingdom of Logres. For my sake* this spring will be called, from now on and while the world lasts, the Spring of the Virgin."

So it happened as the maiden had said, for from that time on it was called the Spring of the Virgin. It has this name yet today, and never a knight came there during that time who did not expect to die, except for Perceval and Galahad, for no knight came there who was not tainted by sensuality in some manner. Because of this adventure was Eric reduced to such a bad state when he came there, because he was not a virgin.

But now the story stops speaking of this adventure, for it has spoken about it enough, and returns to the lady and the maidens who arrived at the spring when Eric lay there in such a bad state as I have told you.

Here the story tells that after the maidens had come to the spring, they began to look at Eric, who lay as if dead.

"Oh, God!" said one of them, the youngest. "Who can this be whom adventure has brought here?"†

"I don't know," said the second.

"Nor I," said the third.

"I'll tell you," said she who was their lady. "This is Eric, who doesn't break a promise and who killed his sister recently in order not to be caught breaking a promise."

"Oh!" they said. "This is misfortune, and may ill luck come to him! Killing his sister—and moreover such a beautiful maiden—is the greatest betrayal a knight ever committed, and may he soon come to where his evil‡ act may be avenged."

"You do great wrong to curse him so," said the lady, "for that vengeance that you so desire will come to him so soon that all who hear of it will wonder, and it will be a great pity that he'll die so soon, for I haven't seen a better knight or a better man than he in a long time. Indeed, if I could prevent his death and extend his life, I'd do it gladly, but I can't do it, for it doesn't please Our Lord." [59]

---

*   All three texts have "by me."

†   "Who ... brought here?" as in Bogdanow 1991 (439). Magne has "what can this be? Who brought this knight here?"

‡   "evil" as in Bogdanow 1991 (439). Magne has "mad."

This the lady said of Eric, and Eric understood it clearly but could not reply. After the maidens had looked at him a long time, they grasped him from all sides, some here and others there, and carried him a good bowshot away from the spring.

After he was that far away, his strength and power returned to him just as before, and he said to the maidens, "Thank you for bringing me here,* for I think I would have died, had I lain any longer beside the spring. But, for God's sake, pardon me, and abate the hatred you feel toward me because of my sister, for, indeed, what I did there I did very unwillingly, but I had to do it."

They made no answer but went for his horse and his arms and gave them to him. He thanked them fervently, and they returned to the spring. He prepared his horse and armed himself, and then he mounted and left there, cursing the spring, for he had never had an adventure in which it seemed to him that he was so badly or shamefully treated.

120. Eric Defeats Sagremor, Kills Yvain of the White Hands, and Is Attacked by Gawain.†

So Eric rode, thinking hard about what had happened to him, just as I have told you, and he slept that night in a valley of the forest, with nothing to eat or drink. He was especially tormented because he had heard his death predicted, and he deeply regretted the loss of Meraugis's company, for, if Meraugis were with him, he would not fear that the knight could kill him in combat. However, he thought about this until it seemed to him that if the knight did not kill him by stealth or treason—if he died in combat—it would be more because of his sin toward his sister than because of any lack of skill at arms, for he knew few knights whom he would fear one on one. This comforted him somewhat,‡ but all the while his heart told him that it would be his misfortune to die and that it would be because of his sister.

That night he slept not at all but kept thinking about this. A little before daybreak,§ his heart began to weep in his chest so hard that the tears were forced to rise to his head and come out of his eyes.¶

When he saw that his heart, which had never been afraid, had begun to know fear and that he wept and did not know why, he said, "My lady, Saint Mary, Mother of pity, succor me and don't let me die yet, if it please You, until I may expiate on earth the sin I've committed against my sister. And You, Father Jesus Christ, wellspring of pity and compassion, Savior of the world, have pity on this wretched son of a king, who has offended You more than any other sinner. Don't regard my sin,

---

* "Thank you for bringing me here" as in Bogdanow 1991 (440). Magne has "Your mercy has brought me here."

† Corresponds to Magne II:56-69; Bogdanow 1991 440-453; Piel 230-235.

‡ "This comforted him somewhat" added by Bogdanow 1991 (441).

§ "daybreak" as in Bogdanow 1991 (441). Magne has "he went to sleep."

¶ "his heart … eyes" as in Bogdanow 1991 (441). Magne has "his heart began to weep until the tears came out of his eyes."

which is so vile that all the angels in heaven are frightened, but be my protector, as You are True Father and True Protector, who rejoice in the sinner when he calls You with a true heart, and, however gravely he has sinned against You, You will have mercy on him. My Lord, as I call You with a good heart and a pure [61] will and recognize truly that my sin has killed and confounded me unless Your mercy helps me, my Lord, have pity on this wretch! Whatever misfortune comes to my body, blessed Father, when my miserable and sorrowing soul, which has had no part in my evil deeds, leaves this wretched, painful vessel,* Lord, receive it and shelter it in Your lodging and in Your holy house, where are all joys and good fortunes."

After Eric had said this prayer, he lay down stretched out in the form of a cross facing east. He said his prayers the best he knew how and lay thus until it was full day. After that he took his helmet, shield, and lance, got on his horse, and went his way through the forest. That day it happened, between prime and tierce, that he met Sagremor, fully armed and wanting to joust, if he had someone to joust with, for it was a long time since he had done any deed of arms. He was greatly pleased when he saw Eric coming toward him, for he did not recognize Eric or Eric him.

He said in a loud voice, "Sir knight, you have to joust; defend yourself against me."

Eric heard that Sagremor was asking for a joust, and he did not dare refuse him, for Sagremor would think it wrong of him. Then they charged at each other and gave each other the greatest blows they could. Sagremor broke his lance, and Eric, who was stronger and might well think[†] himself one of the best knights in the world, struck Sagremor in the chest with such a great blow that he knocked him over the horse's rump to the ground, but he did him no other harm. After that he passed by him and did not look at him again.

When Sagremor found himself on the ground, he was deeply ashamed and stood up quickly.

He got on his horse and rode after Eric, calling out, "Turn, knight, turn, for although you've knocked me down, you haven't beaten me."

When Eric heard this, he did not know what to do, for if he refused the battle he would be shamed; he turned, took his sword, and said, "Sir knight, this is wrong, what you're doing to me, forcing me to fight with you. Indeed, if harm comes to you from it, no one should feel sorry for you or blame me."

Then he charged at him, sword in hand, and gave him such a great blow on the helmet that neither helmet nor iron coif protected him, but Eric made him feel the sword in his head. But Sagremor was lucky in that the wound was not mortal. The sword was good, the blow was great and struck with great force, and Sagremor was so badly hurt by it that he could not hold himself in the saddle but fell to the ground, so stunned that he did not know if it was night or day. When Eric saw him on the ground, he put [63] his sword in its scabbard and went away at once, in a greater hurry than before, for he feared that this knight was of the Round Table.

After Eric had left Sagremor, as I have told you, he had not gone far when he overtook Yvain of the White Hands. The knights' horses were not tired, and as soon

---

*   "Whatever … vessel" from Bogdanow 1991 (442). Magne's reading is confused.
†   "might well think" as in Bogdanow 1991 (443). Magne has "thought."

as they saw each other they whinnied. Then Yvain looked behind him, and as soon as he saw Eric, he recognized him, for the day before Gawain had informed him what arms Eric bore and had complained to him of the dishonor Eric had done him before so many good men, and Yvain had promised to avenge him if he could find Eric. As soon as he saw Eric, he remembered what he had promised Gawain and wondered if he should attack Eric at once or later. What shall I tell you? Finally, he decided to attack him at once, as the demon counseled him to his misfortune, which was fated to happen there.

He turned his horse's head and called out, "Eric! evil, treacherous knight! Defend yourself against me, for I challenge you."

When Eric heard himself called evil and treacherous, he wondered who it could be, and he answered, laughing, "Indeed, sir knight, I'm not such as I should be, but from you, God willing, I'll defend myself against the charge of treachery, for I have none of it."

When this had been said, they charged at each other and struck each other so brutally that neither shields nor hauberks could protect them, but they put the points of their lances into each other's naked flesh and knocked each other to the ground, their horses on top of them, so badly hurt that they had considerable need of a doctor, for both were badly wounded, one mortally—and this was Yvain of the White Hands—the other not so badly—and this was Eric. They got up, angry and sorrowful, for both were of great heart* [497] and wanted to avenge themselves. They let go their lances, since they were so heated that they did not feel their wounds. Then they took their swords and attacked each other like lions, giving each other such great blows that it was a marvel. They fought at a rapid tempo, so that each of them had seven wounds before they separated the first time. However, Eric was not so badly wounded nor so badly hurt as Yvain, since he was a much better knight and Yvain had borne great toil in the Round Table.

The first fight went on so long that they badly needed to rest, and they drew apart a little. As they were standing there looking at each other, Eric, who respected Yvain greatly because he saw him so valiant and skilled, although he did not recognize him, spoke first to Yvain, since he suspected that he might be of the Round Table and, if he knew it, he would not fight with him for anything, unless destiny made him do it.

He said to him, "Sir knight, I've fought with you for a good period of time, enough to see that you're one of the best knights I've seen in a long time here, and, because of the knightly skill I see in you, and not because I fear you any more than you fear me, I ask you for God's sake and by your courtesy to tell me your name, since you could be such that I would yield you this battle and surrender myself conquered, and you could be such that I would do my best to defeat you as you would do to me."

Then Yvain of the White Hands answered and said, "This you may not know at this time from me, since I hate you so mortally that I won't tell you my name, nor can there be any other outcome but that I'll kill you or you me. And know that this

---

* Beginning of lacuna. Magne (11:497-498) supplies the text from the Spanish version.

battle is inevitable and that, in whatever manner, [498] one of us must die, and therefore ask no more of me."

"My lord," said Eric, "I've certainly understood what you say, that no good will come of this battle, and, nevertheless, what I said to you I said out of courtesy and good will, not out of any fear I might have of you, and I'll certainly show you that, God willing, before this battle is over, since you want the matter to proceed to its end."

After this they began to fight again so violently that both of them lost a great deal of blood. Then Yvain began to tire rapidly and lose his breath, so that anyone who saw him would have thought his defeat a certainty. Eric, who was such a good knight that his fame ran far and wide, went to him and would not let him rest but gave him many and frequent blows, and Yvain drew back, for he could not endure. When Eric saw that Yvain was already badly hurt, he raised his sword, but not to kill him, for he would not willingly have killed him or anyone else, except by mistake; however, the blow was so violent and deadly that Yvain fell face to the ground, as if he had suffered and endured unto death.

When Eric saw Yvain so badly hurt that he truly believed he would never again get up from there, he put his sword in the scabbard sadly, because he had killed him, and then he bent down to Yvain and said, "Sir knight, I ask you for God's sake and by your courtesy to tell me who you are, for know that your death will grieve me greatly because of the great skill I've found in you."

Yvain, on the point of death, made an effort and said, "Oh, Eric! Know that I'm Yvain of the White Hands. I'm a companion of the Round Table, and many times you have seen me do deeds at arms."

When Eric heard this, he felt such grief that he did not know what to do, and he said with great anger, "For sure, Sir Yvain, you acted unworthily when you concealed your identity from me this way, and because of this you will die and I am forsworn."

After Eric had said this, he looked at Yvain, who lay stretched out in his death agony. When he saw that Yvain was dead, he mounted, for he did not want anyone to see him there, for if they knew it in King Arthur's house, they would think he had done wrong, and they would not believe how it had been. He went away from there and into the forest with at least ten wounds or more, and they were so large that another knight would think himself dead of the least. What hurt him more was the large amount of blood he was losing, so that any man who came after him would have found him by the trail of blood.* [65]

After Eric left the place where Yvain lay dead, it was not long before chance brought Gawain that way, riding alone, for he had left his brother Agravain that day when their road divided into two.†As soon as he arrived where the battle had been and saw Yvain lying dead and recognized him, he dismounted and ran to him with such sorrow that he truly thought he would go mad.

He said, "Oh, Yvain, good knight! What a pity that such a man is lost! And, indeed, many good men will be deeply grieved by your death, and the Round

---

*   End of lacuna; the text returns to Magne II:65.
†   Presumably after the events narrated in chapter 118.

Table should complain bitterly, for those who belong to it can truly say they are impoverished by the loss of one of the best knights in the world. Indeed, since you are dead, and that so recently, I won't ever be happy until I have avenged you, and I'll certainly be able to do it, I believe, for I don't think the man who inflicted this loss on us can have gone far."

Then he left Yvain and rode as fast as he could. He found the horse's trail and recognized it as the right one because he saw it was full of blood, for the knight who was riding ahead of him was grievously* wounded. Gawain was happy at this fortune, for he was sure it was none other than the man who had killed Yvain. He hurried, and he had not gone far when he overtook Eric, riding at a walk, as he needed to rest more than to ride.

As soon as Gawain saw Eric, he recognized him; however, he knew so well that Eric was a loyal knight and good that he could not for anything believe that he had killed Yvain. Then he began to consider what he would do, whether he would attack him at once or leave him for another time. He decided to leave him at that time, for he did not then find a good excuse to attack him. However, if he could somehow be sure that Eric had killed Yvain, nothing in the world would keep Gawain from avenging him. As soon as he reached Eric, he greeted him well and appropriately, and Eric, who had not yet recognized Gawain, returned his greeting and asked him who he was.

"Don't you recognize me?" asked Gawain.

"No, indeed, my lord," said Eric.

"Then know that I'm Gawain," he said, "King Arthur's nephew."

"So?" said Eric. "In God's name, you are welcome."

"And who has wounded you so badly?" asked Gawain.

"My lord," said Eric, "sin and misfortune, which confound many good men."

"Sin?" said Gawain. "For God's sake, tell me how."

"My lord," said Eric, "I'll tell you, and I won't lie to you about it in any detail, for I love you with such great love that I won't hide from you anything I could reveal to a friend. Know that Yvain of the White Hands did this to me."

Then he told him in what manner.

"And I swear to you truly, my lord, by the faith that I owe to all the knights of the Round Table, that if I had known him as he knew me, I would rather have been struck through the heart with a lance than to have laid a hand on him, and no one should blame me for it, for his arrogance and bad judgment killed him." [67]

"How do you feel?" asked Gawain.

"My lord," he said, "I'm very badly wounded and have lost so much blood that it's nothing short of amazing. Nevertheless, if I were somewhere where I could rest and find a doctor who would see to my wounds, I'm sure I'd recover."

"I don't know how you feel," said Gawain, "but if you were the healthiest and best rested you have ever been, I wouldn't fail to challenge you at such a time, for, indeed, you have wronged me so much that I wouldn't for anything in the world fail to kill you, since you killed Yvain of the White Hands, and men would think

---

*   "grievously" as in Bogdanow 1991 (449). Magne has "mortally."

me a bad knight and a coward if I didn't avenge a kinsman so killed.* Therefore, I challenge you! Defend yourself against me, for be well advised that I'll kill you if I can overcome you."

When Eric heard what Gawain was saying, he was shocked, for he had truly believed that Gawain loved him with all his heart, and what is more, he had thought him so loyal that, if Eric had wronged him even more, he would not have laid a hand on him, if for no other reason, because they were both of the Round Table.

Then he said to him, "Oh, Sir Gawain, what are you saying? Remember the oath and pledge of the Round Table, in which we are brothers and companions, and don't disgrace yourself for such a man as I am. For, indeed, if you kill me you'll be forsworn and disloyal and will never have honor from it, since I am such as I am, but shame and dishonor will come to you from it, for I'm wounded and stricken in so many places that I have as much strength as a dead knight."

"What you say to me is less than nothing," said Gawain. "You must fight and defend yourself, or else I'll kill you."

"What, my lord?" said Eric. "So you want to do it?"

"Yes, indeed," said Gawain. "You may be sure of it."

"Indeed," said Eric, "that grieves me, for if you were to attack me while I was sound, I'd certainly expect to defeat you because of the great skill at arms that God has given me."

Then he took his sword and said again, "Sir Gawain, you have attacked me wrongfully and at a time when I have no strength to defend myself. May God help right, and He will do so, I know, but I realize that I've been condemned to death here in vengeance for what I did to my sister."

Then he commended himself very humbly to Our Lord God. Gawain attacked, giving him a sword blow on the helmet, the hardest he could, so that Eric was stunned and bewildered by the blow. However, he held himself in the saddle, although with great difficulty, for he had lost so much blood that almost all his strength had left him. Nevertheless, he defended himself so well with what strength he had that anyone who had seen him and known in what condition he was would have thought it the greatest marvel in the world. And Gawain, who was rested, kept giving him the hardest blows he could, wherever he could reach him. Eric returned [69] them the best he could, putting forth all the force and skill at arms he could muster, for he realized clearly that death was near. This made him fight beyond his strength, and Gawain found such great resistance in him that he was amazed, for however lively and agile he was and however frequently he struck, Eric struck him as often, although not with such great blows as was his wont, for he was bleeding freely. What shall I tell you? Eric defended himself so marvelously, like one who was still hot with blood and anger and was going, as the proverb says, for "double or nothing," that Gawain was greatly afraid that after all he would not be able to defeat him. And the true story bears witness that Gawain would not have defeated him were it not that he killed Eric's horse and Eric fell to the ground.

---

*   "All three texts have "wounded."

121. ERIC'S DEATH; HECTOR AND MERAUGIS TAKE HIS BODY TO CAMELOT.*

When Eric found himself on the ground, he could not help saying, "Indeed, Sir Gawain, now I see a streak of cowardice and evil in you, since you've killed my horse.[†] Now you can't say, when you see me dead, that you've killed me; rather, the failure of my horse did so. But I don't care what happens to me in this battle, for until now I've had the honor of it and you the shame."

Gawain, who was still afraid,[‡] did not wait when he saw Eric on the ground but went to strike him with his horse's chest and knocked him to the ground.[§] Eric fell on his face and fainted with pain; his sword fell from his hand and his shield on the other side. Gawain dismounted, as soon as he saw him lying so, went to him, raised the bottom of his hauberk, and drove his sword through his body, and Eric stiffened in his death agony.

When Gawain realized that he had killed him, he was very happy, for it seemed to him that he was well avenged. He put his sword in its scabbard, got on his horse, and went away as quickly as he could by another road, because he would not for anything have had people know that he had done this deed, for he knew well that he would be blamed for it by all who heard of it. He left Eric lying there, for he thought certainly he was dead, but he was not dead yet but had all his senses as before. He had no strength but lay as he had fallen, but in this he was fortunate that, although his body was tormented, wounded, and stricken, he all the while kept his heart so fixed on his Savior that he could not forget Him but forgot all other things in order to remember Him.

He begged mercy of Him, weeping, and said the best he could, "Jesus Christ, Father of pity and good will, have mercy on this wretch, [71] who in this torment calls You Father of pity. I thank You for having given me such a death, for, indeed, I truly recognize that I've deserved, for my sin, to die a harsher death than this. My Lord, keep me, by Your pity, in this my last day and hour, when my comfortless soul must leave my wretched body and go, I don't know where. My lord, by Your pity, comfort it, for it will have to go to the unfortunate house, if Your mercy does not call it back."[¶]

After Eric had said his prayer, he began to weep hard, afraid for his soul, for he saw clearly that he was close to death. As he was weeping, suddenly Hector and Meraugis appeared by chance. When they saw Eric lying face down, his shield and sword beside him, they did not recognize him, for he had changed from the arms with which they had seen him.

---

*   Corresponds to Magne II:69-81; Bogdanow 1991 453-465; Piel 235-243.

†   "you've killed my horse" as in Bogdanow 1991 (453). Magne has "you kill me for want of my horse."

‡   "still afraid" as in Bogdanow 1991 (453). Magne has "in a great hurry."

§   In chapter 27, during his first adventure, Gawain swore he would never attack on horseback an opponent on foot.

¶   "call it back" as in Bogdanow 1991 (454). Magne has "turn it away." Magne records a marginal note: "Here it tells the prayer that Eric said when Gawain killed him."

Nevertheless, because they thought he was a knight errant, they stopped and asked, "Who is this knight?"

"By God," said Meraugis, "whoever he is, he was good, for it's apparent from his weapons that he defended himself until his death."

"Never believe me," said Hector, "if this isn't one of the knights of the Round Table, and know that many good men will be grieved by his death. Now let's dismount and see who he is, for my heart tells me that we'll be grieved by it, and that he's one of our friends."

Then they both dismounted and tied their horses to two trees, and Hector went to Eric, fell on his knees beside him, and took off his helmet as gently as he could. Eric moved only a little, for death was very near. Meraugis came as close as he could, sat down, took his head and put it on his knees, and began to wipe his eyes, which were full of blood, and his face, which had already darkened with pain, and he found him so badly wounded that he was very sorry for him.

Hector, who was looking at him all the while, said to Meraugis, "Friend, what do you think of him?"

"He's still alive," said Meraugis,[*] "but I know he won't live until nightfall, for he's very badly wounded, and that seems to me a great pity, for I know truly that he was a good knight by what I see he has suffered."

"Now ask him who he is," said Hector, "and see if you can get anything from him by which we may recognize him."[†]

Meraugis asked him, "Sir knight, who are you? For God's sake, tell us that if you can."

Eric, who understood clearly what Meraugis was asking him, answered the best he could, but that was very weakly, "I'm Eric, son of King Lac, and I was of the Round Table, and Gawain has just now killed me through arrogance and treachery. He attacked me when I had just defeated [73] two knights, knowing truly who I was, and he wasn't as loyal to me as he should have been. May Our Lord forgive him, for I do."

When Meraugis heard this, he let himself fall on him[‡] with such great pain and grief that he wished he were dead at that moment, for he loved Eric deeply.

When Meraugis could speak, he said, "Oh, wretch! What loss and pain are here! Oh, Gawain, may God give you misfortune and death, for you've killed the best friend I ever had and the truest knight I ever saw.[§] May God reward you for it."

When Hector knew it was Eric, his favorite foreign knight, he was as deeply grieved as possible, and he cursed Gawain and prayed for great misfortune to him and all his kin.

After that he said with great sorrow, so that the tears fell down his cheeks, "Sir Eric, do you think you can recover?"

---

[*]   The change in speakers is taken from Bogdanow 1991 (455). Magne gives this whole dialogue to Hector as one speech.

[†]   "and see ... may recognize him" as in Bogdanow 1991 (455). Magne has "if we may know him."

[‡]   "on him" as in Piel (237). Magne has "flat," and Bogdanow 1991 (456) has "backward."

[§]   "the best friend ... saw" as in Bogdanow 1991 (456). Magne has "my friend and the most loyal knight I have ever seen."

Eric spoke as well as he could, being of great heart, and said, "Sir knight, who are you who question me?"

He said, "I'm Hector of the Fens, your companion and friend, who feels such grief at your misfortune that I'd swear never again to bear arms if it could undo what has happened to you. This other who suffers for you is Meraugis of Portlegues, who has been looking for you, as I have."

When Eric heard that they were his friends, he said, "You are welcome, for I'm very happy at your coming, and it pleases me very much that you'll be present at my death, for you are the two men I've trusted most in the world. However, before I die, I ask you as friends and companions to take my body to King Arthur's house and give it as a gift to the Round Table, of which Our Lord made me a companion, as you know. And after you place me in the seat, the king will do as he likes with me, but in any case don't fail to tell in court Gawain's disloyalty to me."

"Don't worry about that," said Hector, "for I promise to avenge you and dishonor him so in King Arthur's court that many good men will speak of it after your death."

After this Eric said, "Jesus Christ, Father of pity, filled with all compassion, have mercy on me and judge me not by my sins but by Your mercy." [75] Then he said further, "You're my companions and my friends; I ask you to remember me in your prayers and charities, for I'm a great sinner, and this misfortune has undoubtedly come to me because of my sin."

As soon as he had said this, his soul left his body.

Meraugis and Hector made a great lamentation, and Meraugis said, "Oh, God! How much better it would have been for Gawain the disloyal to receive death in this battle rather than this man, who was so good and able and worthy and more loyal than all the other knights I've ever seen! Oh, Gawain, disloyal, brutal knight! I ask God to please let you fall into my hands. Indeed, I wouldn't take all the world, if they gave it to me, for your head."

"Oh, Lord God," said Hector, "what kind of heart have You to let such misfortune come to such a good man as this!"

They mourned and wept and lamented for him, for they both loved him dearly. Suddenly as they were making their lamentation, Gawain's brother Gaheriet* arrived. When he saw them, he recognized them, and he stopped, amazed at seeing them making such a lamentation.

Hector, who recognized him, could not help saying to him, "Gaheriet, now you can see the great treachery of your brother, who has just killed one of the best men of the Round Table, Eric, son of King Lac, who lies here." Then he told Gaheriet all about how Gawain had killed Eric.

When Gaheriet, who was a very loyal knight, heard this news, he was deeply grieved by it and said, "Who told you that it was so?"

"Eric told us," said Hector, "whom one should believe sooner than another, for you know well that he has never wittingly lied."

---

*   Only Bogdanow 1991 (458) gives his name at this point. Magne has simply "Gawain's brother."

"By God," said Gaheriet, "I wonder how this happened, for, so help me God, I thought that my brother Gawain was one of the most honorable knights in the world, and I still believe it, except for this news that you've told me."

"So help me God," said Hector, "if you weren't my companion of the Round Table, I'd avenge this deed on you with all my might, since I don't find your brother."

Gaheriet, who was deeply grieved, kept silent.

Meraugis, who wanted to honor Eric, said to Hector, "How can we fulfill Eric's request?"

"The only thing we can do," said Hector, "is to prepare a bier and lay it on our horses. We'll follow him on foot until God gives us some help in the form of beasts of burden."

Hector said that was good, and Gaheriet asked them where they wanted to take him.

"We want to take him to King Arthur's court," said Hector, "and there we'll tell about Gawain's faithlessness and in what manner he killed him, for Eric asked us to do so at his death."

When Gaheriet heard this, he felt sadder than before, for he understood clearly that by this his brother would be shamed and proclaimed faithless by everyone when this deed was known at court. He wept a great deal for him, and, because of the great sorrow he felt, he left Hector and Meraugis without taking leave of them.
[77]

When Meraugis saw that Gaheriet was going away, he took his helmet and laced it on. Hector asked him why he was doing that.

"I want to go after this knight," he said, "and avenge my grief on him, since I can't find his brother."

"You shall not do it," said Hector, "for what guilt does he have in his brother's treachery? I tell you truly that it grieves him as much as it does us, for, so help me God, he's one of the most loyal and courteous knights I know. I ask you to let him go in peace."

Because of what Hector said, Meraugis stayed and did not go after Gaheriet.

After they had arranged how to carry Eric, they disarmed him and laid him on the bier in the best and most appropriate way they could. They went on foot to a nearby castle, where the people gave them horses and everything else they needed. And know that they then arranged the body in such a way that they could carry it as far as they wanted.

In this way they left the castle and traveled until they arrived at Camelot, where King Arthur and his company were very sad. When Hector and Meraugis got there, everyone at Camelot was deeply grieved, so that they were never happy and never thought of anything but weeping and mourning. Whoever was there then and saw the great lamentation the ladies made—those who were awaiting their lovers who had gone on the quest—would have a hard and brutal heart if he were not sorry for them, and the king's grief grew from day to day so great that he would rather have been dead. And if anyone asked me why this was, I would answer as the true history tells.

Unquestionably King Arthur, who loved the knights of the Round Table as much as if they had been his sons, felt very sad because they had left him. Because of this he had such a desire to know how things were going for them that he went each day, before he ate, to see the seats of the Round Table. He looked at them, and when he found a name that should be there, then he knew that the knight who was lord of that seat was alive. When he found no letters there, he knew he was dead. Without fail, the Round Table was so marvelous that wherever, near or far, someone died, at once his letters died, too, and this was demonstrated by the deaths of many good knights.

Just as I tell you, King Arthur knew the truth about the death of each of the knights of the Round Table the very day he died. And so did many good men, who believed in this sign as much as he did, for there was not the least man there who had not some relative in the quest. Therefore, each week they made a great lamentation, for there were few weeks when one or two did not die. The king was sad at the death [79] of Yvain the Bastard and Yvain of Cenel, for the latter's sister had already come to court and told in front of all the barons there how Gawain had let her brother be killed in the castle and how he had killed Patrides, King Bademagu's nephew, knowing when he killed him that Patrides was a companion of the Round Table.

King Arthur, who was as deeply grieved as he could be at this news, said to the maiden, "My lady, if it is as you say, he deserves to be shamed and to lose his seat at the Round Table."

And everyone else there condemned him, too. The king was grieved by the death of these three, but when the death of King Bademagu was known throughout the house, they were all so deeply grieved that for two days something happened that had never happened at court before, for no table was laid before the knights. They all said that this was a great loss and cursed Gawain for having started that quest. The king and all the others were deeply grieved by King Bademagu's death. But when Eric died, then began greater lamentation than before; the king wept for him and so did the barons, the knights and the ladies and the maidens. For him the lamentation in Camelot was so great that thunder would not have been heard; for him the wise and the foolish wept, the old and the young. And know that his death was known in Camelot five days before they brought him there. When he got there, the grief had somewhat subsided.

On a Monday the two knights who brought Eric's body arrived at Camelot, and they rode so sadly and with such grief that anyone who saw them when they rode through the village would have felt great sorrow.

When they arrived at the rich palace where the Round Table was, they lowered the bier, took Eric's body in their arms, weeping hard under their helmets, and said, "Oh, good knight! What sorrow and loss is your death!" They carried him to the seat that God had granted him forever, seated him in it, and then said weeping, "Oh, my lord! What grief that you aren't sitting here as whole as you were on other occasions, for the whole kingdom of Logres would be worth more because of it!"

King Arthur and the barons who were there, when they saw this, went in that direction to see what the two wanted to do. They did not recognize Hector because he had changed his arms. Meraugis they could not recognize because they had never seen him. Eric they did not recognize because his face was colored and darkened by death.

The king asked Hector, "Friend, for God's sake, tell me why you've put this dead knight in this seat?"

"My lord," said Hector, "because at his death he asked us to bring him here, put him in this seat, and complain to you for him—for he can't say it to you—about Gawain your nephew, who falsely and treacherously killed him, and we'll tell you in what way he killed him, for otherwise we wouldn't complete what he asked of us." [81]

Then they began to tell before the king and the whole court, which was already assembled, how Gawain had attacked Eric after he had fought with two knights, and how he had killed him, even though Eric had told him his name and begged mercy of him.

When those who were present to hear this story understood that this was Eric, son of King Lac, and that he had had himself brought from such distant lands, such a great and wild lamentation began as if they had found all their friends dead before them.

Meraugis, who felt the greatest grief possible, said to them, "My lords, he couldn't come here alive to complain to you of Gawain, so he had himself brought here dead. Now do with him what you should do with a king's son who has died by treachery."

The king, as grieved as if it had been his son, replied, "Cursed be the hour in which Gawain became a knight, since he's committing so many treacherous acts. He himself is lost, and all his kindred will be shamed. And if this is so, he should lose his seat at the Round Table."

Great were the sorrow and grief they all felt at Eric's death.

Meraugis said to the king, "My lord, this isn't the first wrong your nephew has done, for on this quest he has killed one* more of our companions for you, for whom one should not mourn less than for this one."

"Which one?" asked the king.

"King Bademagu,"† said Meraugis. "And of this one I know truly that your nephew Gawain killed him. This death I would have avenged, had it not been for Eric, who came on the scene and separated me from him."

"Cursed be the hour Eric arrived there and you didn't kill Gawain," said the king, "for he certainly deserved it, since he had killed such a man as King Bademagu."

The king had Eric taken and such honor paid to him as one owed to a king's son and such a good knight as he had been. He had him put in a rich tomb in the church of St. Stephen, where they were laying the other companions of the Round Table.

---

*   "one" as in Bogdanow 1991 (465). Magne has "two."

†   "King Bademagu" as in Bogdanow 1991 (465). Magne has "Patrides and King Bademagu."

Great was the weeping and mourning of knights, ladies, and maidens. That day you could not have found a man or woman in all the city of Camelot who was not very sad. The king, who was of greater heart than any other man of his house, wept bitterly for Eric, when he saw him put in the tomb.

122. HECTOR AND MERAUGIS AT COURT WITH CLAUDIN AND ARTHUR THE LESS.*

When King Arthur returned to his palace and recognized Hector, he had him disarmed, embraced him, and said to him, "I'd give you a good, joyful reception, but the death of these good men has taken joy and pleasure from me. Nevertheless, tell me some news of your brother and your other kindred, and of Galahad, if you know any."

"Indeed, my lord," said Hector, "I believe that my brother is healthy and happy, as well as all our kin." [83]

"And how have they done in this quest?" asked the king.

"My lord," he said, "they've found many adventures and marvels that they didn't accomplish, for it didn't please Our Lord; however, that isn't because they aren't good knights, as you know."

"Indeed," said the king, "I know well that they are all good knights, and if anyone is to do well in this quest, they'll be among the best, for no other kindred is their equal in chivalry. But what can you tell me about Galahad, who accomplished the Perilous Seat?"

"Indeed, my lord," said Hector, "without doubt he's the best knight in the world. I've seen so much of him that I know truly that he won't through any lack of chivalric ability fail to bring the adventures of Logres to an end."

"May God aid him," said the king. "Indeed, it would make me very happy, if it pleased God, to see him in my house as I saw him once before. And Gaheriet, my nephew—have you seen him in this quest?"

"Yes, my lord," he said, "we saw him when Eric died. Know that he was deeply grieved by Eric's death."

"Indeed," said the king, "I know it well. As God is my help, he's the most valuable and praiseworthy knight of my kindred."

Then he asked who Meraugis was.

Hector said, "A foreign knight whom I met by chance in this quest, and we became companions. He's a good knight, marvelously brave, but he has never been able to find out what lineage he's from or who his father and mother were; they told him he would learn the truth about it in your house, and this is why he came to the kingdom of Logres."

"By God," said the king, "that's amazing, that he's such a good knight and doesn't know any man of his lineage."

---

* Corresponds to Magne II:81-87; Bogdanow 1991 465-471; Piel 243-246.

"It's just as I've told you," said Hector.

"And where did he live," asked the king, "before he came to this land?"

"In Cornwall," said Hector, "with King Mark, who made him a knight not yet two years ago."

"And he would stay with us?" asked the king.

"I think so," said Hector, "at least until he knows the truth about his lineage, for he's to learn that here, as they gave him to understand."

"And will you remain with me?" asked the king. "Since it seems I have lost the rest of your kindred, if you can remain with me without breaking the oath you made when you started on the quest, I'll thank you for it; however, even if you break it a little, you should remain because of my asking."

"My lord," said Hector, "I'd do what you ask in anything else, but I'd rather have my head cut off than stay at this time."

When the king heard this, he didn't ask again, for he realized it would do no good.

Then he turned to Meraugis and asked, "Friend, what is your name?"

Meraugis gave his name.

"And where are you from?" asked the king.

"From Cornwall," he said.

"And have you come to stay with us?" asked the king.

"My lord," he said, "I'll stay with you until God gives me counsel in that for which I've come here."

"You are welcome," said the king. "I'm very happy at your coming, and you'd certainly find men here who would honor you and rejoice over you, but you see that they are all sad and full of grief at the misfortune they've seen happen to the good men of this house." [85]

"My lord," he said, "if you feel grief at it, that isn't surprising, for because of the good men you had, your court was until now feared and respected, and its fame went throughout the world."

That day Hector praised Meraugis a great deal and described his skill at arms and spoke much good of him to all who asked him. That day the king and the queen asked Hector so many times that he agreed to remain with them for two days.

The next day at midday, when the king came from the church and seated himself in his palace, there came into his presence one of the clerks whose duty it was to write down the adventures of the knights errant, and he fell to his knees before the king and said to him gently, "My lord, if you wish, I'll show you something that will please you."

"Then show it to me," said the king.

"Come with me, my lord," he said.

Then he took him to the Round Table, to Eric's seat, and showed him new letters that said, HERE SHOULD SIT MERAUGIS OF PORTLEGUES.

When the king saw the letters, he called Hector and many other good men who were there, showed them the letters, and asked, "What do you think of that?"

Hector, who loved Meraugis and was happy at this adventure, spoke first: "My lord, it seems to me that he has earned the honor of the Round Table, for these letters show you that."

All the others agreed, and the king said, "May Jesus Christ be praised and blessed, who so quickly takes thought for the honor of the Round Table with such a man as this."

Then he was happier and more content than before, and he went to Meraugis, took him by the hand, and said to him, "Friend, you are welcome. If we didn't know you, God knows you, and you may see that by the seat at the Round Table that God has given you; on His behalf we put you in possession of it, and may He in His mercy grant that you be as good as its former occupant."

Meraugis answered, "May God do so."

And all the others said the same. Then the king went to seat Meraugis in the seat that had been Eric's, and then there began throughout the palace great rejoicing and celebration, but not such as it would have been had they not felt the grief they did.

The very day that Meraugis received the seat at the Round Table, it happened at the hour of nones that two armed knights arrived, one with white arms, the other with black. And if anyone asked me who they were, I would tell him that the one with black arms was Claudin, son of King Claudas, and the other, with white arms, was the one Perceval would not knight.[*] They would have arrived at court a long time before Hector, but they had been hindered by many things, which had delayed them more than they had wished. They dismounted [87] and entered the palace, armed just as they were. When they had come into the king's presence, the knights greeted the king and his company and asked if Meraugis was there.

"Yes," said the king, "there he is."

"Now have me disarmed," said Claudin.

And they disarmed him. He took a letter, which he bore in his breast, gave it to Meraugis, and said to him, "A recluse sends you this letter, one whom I met not long ago a great distance from here. That lady is Perceval's aunt,[†] and she commands us to tell you that this letter will enlighten you about the thing you desire most in the world to know, for you'll know the truth about your lineage."

When Meraugis heard this news he was as happy as he could be, and he took the letter and said, "You've done me such a great service[‡] that I could never reward you for it."

Then he put the letter into his breast, for he did not want to read it before so many good men. The king asked Claudin who he was and from which land, and Claudin told him the whole truth of the matter. The king was greatly pleased with him, for he respected him highly for his goodness and chivalry. The king also had the knight with white armor disarmed and paid much honor; then he turned to Claudin again and asked how he had left the kingdom of Gaunes, and he told the whole truth of the matter, just as the story has already told.[§]

---

[*] Chapter 106; the youth whom Perceval would not knight is Arthur the Less.

[†] See chapter 105.

[‡] "done me such a great service" as in Bogdanow 1991 (470). Magne has "shown me such great love."

[§] Chapter 108.

As they were rejoicing and celebrating in honor of the foreign knights, one of the queen's ladies, who was well educated, came to the king at the hour of vespers and said to him, "My lord, on King Bademagu's seat and on that of Yvain of the White Hands there are new letters. I believe that the seats have received lords."

The king was very happy at this news and went there, and he found Claudin's name on King Bademagu's seat, and on the seat of Yvain of the White Hands he found letters that said, THIS IS THE SEAT OF ARTHUR THE LESS. This was the knight with the white armor, and may all who hear this story know that he was King Arthur's son, and I will tell you under what circumstances King Arthur begat him, for you could not know in any other way.

123. ARTHUR THE LESS AND MERAUGIS LEARN WHO THEY ARE AND RETURN TO THE QUEST WITH HECTOR.[*]

It is true, and the true history tells it, that, a little after Queen Guenevere had found Lancelot with King Pelles's daughter,[†] King Arthur had gone to hunt in the forest of Bretheam. That day as he was hunting, it happened that he lost his whole company and all his dogs and the stag he was following, so that he wandered lost through the forest, now here, now there, for he had not often hunted in that forest. He wandered [89] lost, as I have told you, and chance brought him to a spring on the edge of a plain. That spring was very beautiful, and he found a maiden there alone, the most beautiful creature he had ever seen. She was dressed and adorned so richly that it was nothing less than a marvel. When the king saw that the maiden was so beautiful, he believed truly that she was a fay, because she was alone. He dismounted and tied his horse to a tree, ungirding his sword and putting it and his bow and arrows on the grass, for he bore that many weapons and no more. After that, he went toward the maiden and greeted her, and she stood up facing him and greeted him fittingly. The king sat down, and she did likewise, and they began to talk together. The king found her marvelously wise and well-spoken, and he was so pleased with her that he lay with her by force. She was a young girl and still knew nothing of such matters, and she began to cry out while he was lying with her, but it did her no good, for the king did what he wanted anyway, and at that time he made in her a son. After he had had his pleasure and wanted to take her with him, suddenly there appeared a knight of some considerable age, who came out of the forest unarmed just like King Arthur, and know that he was the maiden's father. When he found his daughter in tears, he guessed at once that the knight had lain with her by force.

He dismounted, drew his sword, and said to his daughter, "Either tell me why you're crying or I'll cut off your head."

---

[*]   Corresponds to Magne II:87-99; Bogdanow 1991 472-483; Piel 246-252.
[†]   End of chapter 60.

She was afraid of dying and told him what had happened to her. The knight, deeply grieved by it, looked at the king with great anger, until he began to wonder if he was the king.

He was not sure, but because he feared it, he said, "So help you God, sir knight, tell me who you are."

"So help me God," said the king, "never have I denied my name through fear, and I won't do so now. Know that I'm Arthur."

"So help me God," said the knight, "that grieves me, for if you were someone else, I'd avenge my dishonor, but I'd be a traitor to kill* you, for you are my lord. But I will do this much to you: I'll never love you, for you've done me base dishonor, since you've forced my daughter."

The king, who knew well that he had wronged him, said to him, "Here I am, ready to atone to you for it at your will; I want to marry your daughter to one of the greatest and most consequential knights of my house."

"I don't want that at this time," said the knight, "and I'll tell you why: you've lain with my daughter, and perhaps she is pregnant by you. If someone else married her immediately, although the child was yours, neither you nor anyone else would believe it. Therefore, I want to keep her awhile, and if by chance she's pregnant, I'll let you know, and if not, I'll do with her what I think will be to my profit." [91]

Thus the king left the knight and went to look for his company until he found it. The knight took his daughter and had her well guarded. When he saw that she was pregnant, he was happy about it and went to tell the king in secret.

When he saw that it was time for her to have her child, he went to the king again and said to him, "My lord, what shall my daughter's child be named?"

The king said, "If it's a girl, let her be named Guenevere, and if it's a boy, let him be named Arthur the Less in remembrance of me, who am Arthur of such great power, and it's for this reason that any Arthur who comes after me should, in comparison, be called Arthur the Less."

The knight gave the name Arthur the Less to the boy, just as the king had commanded. The knight had a son, a very good knight whose name was Danor, and the father's name was Tanas. The son had as a wife a beautiful lady, marvelously gifted, and it happened that Tanas loved her more than anything else. Because he saw that he could not have his sinful pleasure with her while his son was alive, he killed him one night as he lay with her. After that he lay with her, and she did not dare do anything else, for fear of death. And know that this was the same day that Arthur the Less was baptized.

When the mother of Arthur the Less knew that her father had killed her brother, she could not keep from saying, "Indeed, you've done wrong in killing my brother. I'll very soon have you shamed and destroyed for it."

He was frightened by this threat, for he knew that King Arthur loved her so much that he would quickly do what she said, all the more because he saw clearly that he deserved death.

He answered her, "Daughter, you won't make me die, for I'll do to you as I did to your brother."

---

*   "to kill" supplied by translator.

Then he drew his sword and cut off her head, there where she was lying with the infant she had had the day before.*

Then he began to look at the boy, who lay wrapped in silk cloth, and he said to him, "You must die, for if I let you live, as soon as you were a knight, you'd certainly learn how I killed your uncle and your mother—for such great treachery as this couldn't go unknown—and you'd kill me, for it couldn't happen otherwise."

Then he seized the boy and took him to an inaccessible mountain where there was a lake, and he left him beside the water for the wild beasts to eat. But Our Lord, who did not forget His creature, sent there that lady of whom I have already told you,† who raised him until Tristan came that way and made him a knight. When Tanas realized that he had committed such a great sin, he doubtless thought that if he lived in the land any longer and King Arthur knew it, the king would condemn him to death.

The king, who later found out, was greatly worried about the boy and had him sought, but he could not learn anything about him except through Morgan the Fay, who sent word to him: [93] "Arthur, know that your son Arthur the Less is alive and well, and he'll come to court the year that the great quest for the Holy Grail begins."

And this comforted King Arthur greatly.

Now I have told you how Arthur the Less was King Arthur's son, just as the true history of the Holy Grail tells it.

When King Arthur saw the letters that said, THIS IS THE SEAT OF ARTHUR THE LESS, he drew aside a little, totally speechless with the great joy he felt, for at once his heart told him that this was his son. However, he did not want anyone else to know it, for he did not think it good for others to know.

After he had thought about this a great while, he asked the others, "What do you think of this?"

"We see clearly," they said, "that Claudin has gained this seat, but we know nothing of Arthur the Less."

The king said, "I really think that he's this other knight."

Then they asked the knight, "Friend, are you Arthur the Less?"

He said to them, "My lords, I'm a knight, and I tell you truly that I don't know who I am or who my parents were or what my name is."

They marveled much at that and said to the king, "My lord, what do you say to that? For it doesn't seem to us that we should grant him the seat until we know more about him."

"I'll tell you what we'll do," said the king. "Let's neither take it from him nor give it to him, but let him stay with us, and I'll send to a place I know, from which they'll send me word if it is he."

They all agreed to that, and Arthur the Less stayed. The king sent a messenger to his sister Morgan, asking that she send definite information about that knight concerning whom the whole court was in doubt.

---

*   "she was lying ... the day before" as in Bogdanow 1991 (475). Magne has "that of his son, whom he had killed the previous day, was lying."

†   Chapter 106.

She said to the messenger, "Without doubt, this is Arthur the Less, and tell my brother that just as the father fails to recognize the son, so the son fails to recognize the father."

Thus the messenger left Morgan, returned to court, and told the king everything Morgan had said to him. Then the king knew for certain that this was his son; he put him into the seat at the Round Table, with everyone's agreement, and he did the same to Claudin.

The next morning Arthur the Less said to the king his father, "My lord, for God's sake, since you have informed me about my name, I ask you to give me counsel about something I'll tell you."

The king asked, "About what?"

"My lord," he said, "that I may know the truth about my lineage, for there's nothing in the world I desire so much to know. And they told me I was to learn about it here."

"You shall certainly learn about it," said the king, "before you leave me." Then he drew him into one of his rooms in private and asked him, "Are you already a knight?"

"Yes, my lord," he said, "thanks be to God."

"Now," said the king, "I want you to swear to me on the Holy Gospels, as [95] a knight, that as long as you live you won't reveal to any man or woman what I'll tell you."

He fell to his knees, held out his hands toward a shrine, and swore just as the king had told him.

Then the king raised him up and said to him, "Now I'll tell you what you've asked me. Know that you're my son and that I fathered you a long time ago on a very beautiful maiden."

Then he told him all about it, just as the history has already told. After he had told him all his own story and how Tanas had acted, he said to him, "Son Arthur, although I don't want people to know you're my son, I don't love you the less for that, for I fail to tell it so that people won't know my offense and sin, for, since God has chosen to put me in such a high place, I should hide my wretchedness with all my might, however much of a sinner I may be."

When Arthur the Less heard this news, he was as happy as he could be and said, "My lord, you know that this won't be revealed during my lifetime, but I tell you this much, that this news puts such great pride and strength into my heart that I'd rather die than fail to surpass all my companions in chivalry, and nothing in the world could bring me such great honor as this news, for the great height from which I come will make me accomplish everything my heart dares undertake, or die."

Then he fell to his knees before his father and said to him, weeping, "My lord, from now on I want to be a knight, since you have received me as your son."

The king lifted him up, kissed him, and said to him, "Son, may God make you the kind of man I'd wish. But for God's sake, to preserve your life and because I ask it, don't ever start a fight with King Ban's kindred, for they are all exceptionally good knights, and if by chance you killed one of them, neither I nor anyone else could keep them from killing you for it, and I love you so much that I'd strive to avenge you, but I couldn't do that without great loss to myself and my people, for they are marvelously many and good."

He promised his father that he would do so, but later he fell short of his promise, for later Blioberis the good knight, Lancelot's cousin, killed him.* Great loss resulted from his death, for Arthur the Less was a good and brave knight. And know that he was not smaller† than his father and was certainly as strong and good a knight as he.

After they had spoken of this, they returned to the palace.

Claudin asked Arthur the Less, "Did you find out what you wanted to know?"

He said, "I learned something just now because of which I'll be worth more all the days of my life." [97]

Meraugis said to him, "Arthur, do you like this court?"

"Indeed," he said, "so much that not for the best city in Logres would I wish that I hadn't come here."

"By God," said Meraugis, "I say the same to you of myself, for I've learned what I desired most in the world to know, my lineage: the letter that Claudin gave me told me about it. Blessed be this house, for no one ever comes here so without counsel that he doesn't depart well counseled."

Without question, in the letter that Claudin gave him was written how he was the son of King Mark and his niece and how the king had killed his mother and‡ hung him from a tree. Everything the tale has already told was in the letter. He was sad when he learned what King Mark had done to his mother and his condition when the mountaineer found him hanging from the tree. That day he had a little case made of silver into which he put that letter in order to carry it always in his breast suspended from his neck, so that each time he saw it he would remember the sin in which he had been born and by what chance he had been rescued and so that he would, therefore, amend himself toward God and the world and be more humble. For this reason Meraugis bore with him the letter in which his birth was written.

Seven days Arthur the Less, Claudin, and Meraugis stayed in King Arthur's house because of the honor of the Round Table, which God had given them. Meraugis had begged Hector to stay for love of him, but first he had to promise him that he would leave on the eighth day, and then Hector stayed there to wait for him.

On the eighth day, the king had men look around the Round Table at the seats, to see how many of its knights had died since the quest had begun, and those who had to look said to him, "My lord, there are twenty-one of them dead."

"Which ones?" asked the king.

---

*   In chapter 157 Arthur the Less attacks Blioberis, who kills him.
†   "smaller" as in Bogdanow 1991 (480). Magne has "less."
‡   "killed his mother and" added by Bogdanow 1991 (481).

They said, "Yvain the Bastard, Yvain of the White Hands, Yvain of Cenel, Calogrenant, Patrides, King Bademagu and Donadix his brother, and Peliaz the Strong. These three Gawain killed, and Mordred his brother and Agravain." After these eight they found that Alma of Camelot was dead, and Luzes of Camelot, and Tanadal of Camelot. These three were brothers; they were very good knights and brave, and they were the sons of a nobleman of Camelot. Then they found that Bridalam was dead, and after that Selitom and Sadalom. These two were first cousins and were the most [99] fashionable of the court. After that they found that Loc the Little was dead, and Carmoisim the Great, and Anselian the Poor, and Caligant the Poor, and Baram.* All these had died in the quest for the Holy Grail, but I will not tell you how, for I did not find it in the French, nor does Boron tell it, who found more of it in the great history in Latin than I am telling you.

When the king heard that so many were dead, he bowed his head with great sorrow and after a while said so that most of those there heard him, "Oh, Gawain! May you be cursed, for I've lost all these good men through your doing. There's no court in the world so rich that it wouldn't be honored by such a company. You've done me great wrong. May you receive the gift on this quest of never returning from it."

This the king said of his nephew, for he was deeply grieved at the death of those good men. That evening Claudin, Arthur the Less, Meraugis, and Hector said to the king that they should go the next morning in order to start on the quest for the Holy Grail, and they took leave of the queen and the ladies. The queen had spoken much with Hector that week about Lancelot, and she gave him a ring to give to Lancelot; she told him that as soon as he saw the ring he should return to court immediately.[†] Hector promised to fulfill her mission as soon as he found Lancelot, and thus he parted from her.

The next day without delay the four companions left King Arthur's house. The king went with them as far as the forest. After that he commended them to God and turned back, and they rode into the forest to seek adventures, just as knights errant ought to do.

But now the story stops speaking of them and returns to speak of Galahad, for it has been a long time since it has spoken of him.

---

*   This list contains nineteen names. Bogdanow 1991 (482) says that twenty-two have died and adds three names to make that total: Sarras, Eric, and Brequean.

†   "return to court" as in Bogdanow 1991 (483). Magne has "do only what came to him." If Hector gives the ring to Lancelot, it is not narrated in the Post-Vulgate, nor is the reason for Lancelot's eventual return to court.

124. GALAHAD AND TRISTAN RIDE TOGETHER.[*]

The story says that after Galahad left the tournament where he wounded Gawain, just as the story has already told,[†] Tristan, who had a great desire to know him, because of the marvelous feats of arms he had seen him do in that gathering, went after him. He rode more than a league and did not dare speak to him, because he saw that Galahad wanted to hide his identity. Galahad, who was riding as rapidly as he could and did not believe anyone was near him, rode until almost night, when he reached a forest called Aacena. When he was about to enter the [101] forest, Tristan, who feared to lose him either in the darkness, which was increasing, or in the forest, which was thick, hurried to catch up, and overtook him at the edge of the forest.

Galahad turned his head when he saw Tristan approaching, and Tristan greeted him at once, saying, "My lord, God guide you."

"My lord," said Galahad, "God give you good fortune."

Galahad said no more to Tristan but fell silent; he was sorry the other man had caught up with him because, having seen him at the tournament, he knew Tristan had been following him.

"Oh, my lord," said Tristan, "who are you?"

"My lord," said Galahad, "I'm a knight."

"My lord," said Tristan, "I know quite well that you're a knight, and you're the best in the world. For the sake of God and courtesy, don't hide your identity from me, but tell me something about yourself, for, so help me God, I never saw a knight whose acquaintance and company I'd rather have."

"And who are you," asked Galahad, "who have such a great desire to know me?"

"My lord," he said, "I'm a knight of Cornwall whom they call Tristan, and I've been in King Arthur's house."

"You are welcome," said Galahad. "I've heard you praised so highly by many good men that I will in no way conceal my identity from you, especially since you've followed me so far in order to meet me. Know that I'm Galahad, son of Sir Lancelot of the Lake, who is such a knight as all the world knows."

When Tristan heard this, he bowed low and said, "Oh, my lord! You are very welcome! God be praised that I've found you in this quest. For the sake of God and courtesy, let me keep you company until chance parts us."

"My lord," said Galahad, "you ask of me a favor that I should ask of you. Indeed, you're such a good knight that I desire your company no less than you desire mine."

And Tristan thanked him warmly for that.

After they had said this, they went on through the forest together, and as they rode they began to speak of many adventures that had happened to them in the quest.

---

[*]   Corresponds to Magne II:99-103; Bogdanow 1991 484-488; Piel 252-254.
[†]   Chapter 110.

"Sir Galahad," said Sir Tristan, "I know well that you've done more in this quest than any other knight and have found more marvels and adventures. For God's sake, tell me if you ever saw the Questing Beast, for Gaheriet told me about it one day when we met him."

"Indeed," said Galahad, "I've seen it."

"And did you see the knight who follows it?" asked Tristan. "I've heard him highly praised for knightly skill."

"Indeed," said Galahad, "he's a very good knight. If he were a Christian, one would have to value his chivalry highly. But I'm very sad about him, and indeed I hate him because he is a Saracen."

Then he told Tristan everything he had heard about him. Tristan crossed himself at the [103] marvelous things he heard of him and said it was a great loss that he was not a Christian, since he was such a good knight.

As they were speaking about these things, night came on them so far advanced that they were unable to see their way. Then they found an old house where a mountaineer had lived a long time ago, and it was somewhat fallen down.

Tristan said, "Let's stay here, for if it rains or the weather is bad, we'll lie better in this house than outside."

Galahad agreed. They dismounted and let their horses graze, for they had no grain to give them. After they had taken off their helmets, they began to speak about what delighted them most, the adventures of the kingdom of Logres. As they were speaking of this, they heard a horse coming at a walk, whinnying.

"Some stranger is coming," said Tristan.

"Perhaps it's some knight errant," said Galahad.

"It may well be," said Tristan.

At that the knight reached the other side of the house, intending to stay there that night. He dismounted and let his horse graze.

Then Tristan said to Galahad, "Let's keep still now and see what this knight will do, for he doesn't know we're here."

125. GALAHAD AND TRISTAN OVERHEAR PALAMEDES'S CONFESSION OF LOVE FOR ISEUT; TRISTAN, FURIOUS, FOLLOWS HIM.*

When the knight† was disarmed, he began to think very hard. After he had brooded a great while, he gave a deep sigh; after that he began to weep with great sobs, so that those who heard him were frightened by it.

Then he began to lament, saying, "Oh, love! You have mortified and mistreated me. I truly believed you'd bring me happiness and joy, but now I see you bring me only pain and harm, sorrow and misfortune."

---

*   Corresponds to Magne II:103-109; Bogdanow 1991 488-495; Piel 254-257.
†   We learn in the next chapter that this is Palamedes.

Then he said further, "Oh, knight, unfortunate, wretched, and poor, why did you set your heart in such a high place, from which you can never obtain anything? Why did I see her, when it brings me only confusion and death? For I'll die for having loved well, and I'll never have any reward from love but death."

Then he said further, "Oh, Queen Iseut, the most beautiful woman a man ever saw, queen of queens, lord of lords, source and mirror of beauty, such a beautiful creature and of such grace, so courteous and so highly prized that the whole world is worth more because of you and is lighted by* your beauty; lord,[†] after whose death all the world will be able to boast that there was none so beautiful before you, nor is there now, nor will there be later! Now may it please the King of Kings that you wish me as well as you [105] do the handsome Tristan. So help me God, I'd think myself more fortunate than if all the world were mine."

After he had said this, he fell silent. After he had brooded for a long while, he again began his lamentation, and after a great while he said, "Oh, Queen Iseut, whose beauty is to kill me, for I can't live long, to you I commend my soul, to you I render up my body, to you I give my spirit; yours be my eyes, yours be my going, yours be my speech, yours be my thoughts, yours be my sleep, yours be my waking, yours be my labor, yours be my rest, yours be my death, yours be my life; and may God not wish it otherwise."

After he had said this, he fell asleep, for he was very tired. For a long time after this neither Galahad nor Tristan slept, for they were waiting for him to say something more.

When they realized that he had fallen asleep, Galahad said to Tristan, "Did you ever see such a mad knight?"

Tristan, who was very angry at what he had heard him say, said, "My lord, I don't believe he yet knows his madness, but I'll make him know it before he leaves us. In an evil hour did he feel love for Iseut, for he'll die for it, unless he's a companion of the Round Table."

Galahad kept still, for he did not dare fault Tristan for this. And Tristan said that, were it not for his love for Galahad, he would go kill the knight at once. Tristan brooded a great deal that night on the matter and desired greatly to know who that knight was who loved Iseut so much. After he had brooded a long time, he fell asleep, but Galahad did not do the same, for as soon as he felt Tristan sleep, he drew away from him a little, fell on his knees on the ground, and began to say his prayers and to ask Our Lord God by His pity to keep and sustain him in such deeds that he would not fall into mortal sin, and to guide him, if it pleased Him, in such a way that he might see something of the secrets of the Holy Vessel, if it was an adventure that a sinful knight might be allowed to accomplish. After he had been a great while making his orisons, somewhat near daylight he commended himself to Our Lord and lay down to sleep on his shield, and he slept until it was full day. [107]

When Galahad awoke from sleep, he found beside him Tristan, sleeping as soundly as if he had not slept in four days, but the other knight was not doing the same, for he was already armed and on his horse. When he saw Galahad and

---

*   "lighted by" as in Bogdanow 1991 (489). Magne has "famous for."

†   As earlier (p. 21), the masculine is used to indicate deference or devotion.

Tristan, he was very sorry, for he well knew that they had heard what he had said. For this reason, he hurried to leave as quickly as he could. Know that he bore a black shield with a white lion, and if anyone asked me who that knight was who loved Iseut so much, I would tell him that it was the good pagan knight, the knight of the Questing Beast. And whoever wants to know how he first fell in love with Iseut and how much he did and suffered for her, the great tale of Tristan will tell him.* But at this time know that he was passing by Joyous Guard and saw Iseut, and because of the great beauty he saw in her, the love he had for her renewed itself in him and began to grow more and more, so that he loved her more than anything else. And nothing else made him despair of having his love but that Tristan was one of the handsomest and best knights in the world. These two good qualities that he knew in Tristan were killing him with grief and envy, for he well knew of himself that he was not handsome, but he considered himself a good knight.

After the knight had mounted his horse, he left at great speed. Then he rode until he met Hebes the Famous, a knight of the Round Table, strong and brave.

When the knight of the black shield saw him, he said to him, "Sir knight, you have to joust."

Hebes, who had already been in many such spots since he had become a knight, charged at him. The good knight struck Hebes so violently that he knocked him to the ground, and he bent down and took Hebes's shield and left him his. He did this because he had said to himself that if anyone were blamed for his words of the night before,† the blame would fall on the one who bore his shield.

Galahad had seen him leave the place where he had lain; when he knew that the other was some distance away, he woke Tristan. And if anyone asks me why he had not wakened him while the knight was there, I will tell him that he did not do it so that Tristan would not kill the knight in his presence for such a poor reason as the love of Queen Iseut. When Tristan woke up, he looked around him, fully expecting to find there the knight who loved Iseut.

When he did not see him, he was very sorry, and he asked Galahad, "My lord, did you see the knight when he went away?"

"I saw him," said Galahad, "and it isn't long since he went."

"Now I ask you," said Tristan, "by the faith you owe to your father Lancelot and to all the knights of the Round Table, to tell me what shield he bears and which way he went." [109]

"You've asked me in such terms," said Galahad, "that I'll tell you, but it grieves me, for I know well that no good will come of it either to you or to him. I tell you that he bears a black shield with a white lion, and he went that way," and he showed him which way.

"I ask no more of you," said Tristan.

Then he armed himself, prepared his horse, and mounted.

Galahad did the same and said to Tristan, "Where do you want to go?"

"I want to go after the knight with the black shield," he said, "and, if it pleased you, I'd like you to go with me."

---

*   The Post-Vulgate does not include this information.
†   "for his words of the night before" supplied by Bogdanow 1991 (493).

"I won't do so at this time," said Galahad, "for I have much to do elsewhere."

Then they parted. Galahad went off across the forest, glad to escape from Tristan's company, and Tristan rode with great sorrow and anger along the main road of the forest. He had not gone far when he met Hebes the Famous.

When Hebes saw Tristan, he recognized him, but Tristan did not recognize Hebes, and he called to him loudly, "Defend yourself against me, knight, for I challenge you to the death."*

126. Tristan Wounds Hebes and Fights Palamedes; Blioberis Makes Peace.†

When Hebes heard this, he was thoroughly alarmed, for he well knew he should not lay a hand on Tristan for any provocation. Tristan, who did not recognize him and hated him mortally because of the shield with the white lion that he saw him carrying, lowered his lance and charged toward him.

Hebes began to cry out, "Stop, Sir Tristan, stop!"

But he did not stop, and he struck Hebes so violently that he broke through his shield and hauberk and drove his lance through his chest, so that the point appeared on the other side, and he knocked Hebes to the ground so badly hurt that he needed no doctor. As soon as he saw Hebes on the ground, Tristan dismounted, for he hated him so much that he would not consider himself satisfied unless he cut off his head, and he took his sword and cut the straps of Hebes's helmet.

Hebes opened his eyes, and when he saw that Tristan wanted to kill him, he said to him, "Oh, Sir Tristan, mercy! I was your companion of the Round Table; why have you killed me? God knows I never deserved it of you."

When Tristan heard this, he drew back much alarmed and asked him, "Who are you?"

"I'm Hebes the Famous," he said. "For God's sake, tell me why you've killed me."

"I've killed you," he said, "because of my lady Iseut, whom you love."

"Oh, my lord, mercy!" said Hebes. "I'm dying. But may God never have mercy on my soul if I ever loved her or even saw her."

"What?" said Tristan. "Aren't you the knight who slept here last night near a ruined house?"

"No, my lord," he said. "Gaheriet and I slept in a castle near here. I think that he'll come along this road, and he'll tell you the truth about it."

"Now I don't know what I can do," said Tristan, "for I was seeking one who bore such a shield as yours, and because of this I thought you were he."

---

*   "I challenge you to the death" as in Bogdanow 1991 (495). Magne has "there is nothing here for you but death."

†   Corresponds to Magne II:109-121; Bogdanow 1991 495-512; Piel 257-263.

"Oh, my lord," said Hebes, "he jousted with me today and knocked me down and took my [111] shield and left me his. In an evil hour did I see that exchange!"

"Is that the truth?" asked Tristan. "I'm very sorry, so help me God. But now tell me what your shield was."

"There's a field of silver and a serpent's head."*

While they were speaking, suddenly Gaheriet arrived. When he saw Tristan, he recognized him easily and greeted him. Tristan greeted him also with great sorrow.

"Oh," said Gaheriet, "who has killed Sir Hebes?"

"I killed him because I failed to recognize him," said Tristan. "May God have mercy on me; it grieves me greatly. For God's sake, take care of him, and if he dies of this wound, let him have an honorable tomb, such as a knight errant should have. I'd stay here with you, but I'm following a knight, a stranger, and I'll never be happy until I find him."

Gaheriet said he would do Hebes all the honor he could, and he stayed with him, full of sorrow at his death. He said that if Tristan were not of the Round Table, he would avenge Hebes the best he could. He stayed there until Hebes died, and he took him up and carried him to an abbey. He had him buried as honorably as possible and had letters written on the tombstone that said, HERE LIES HEBES THE FAMOUS, WHOM TRISTAN KILLED. And Tristan, who had left Gaheriet, rode at a great pace after the knight.

He had not gone far when he met Dondinax, who asked him, "Sir Tristan, where are you going so fast?"

"I'm going after a knight who bears a shield of silver with a serpent's head," he said. "They told me that he was going along this road, by which you have come; did you meet him?"

"Yes, I met him," said Dondinax, "in an evil hour for me, for I jousted with him, and he gave me such a fall that it still hurts me."

"Can he have gone far?" asked Tristan.

"No,† indeed," said Dondinax, "if you hurry a little, you'll catch up with him, for he's riding at a walk along this road."

"Now I commend you to God," said Tristan.

And then they parted.

Tristan went after the knight as fast as his horse could carry him. He had not gone far when he caught up with him in a valley. The knight cast a glance behind him when he heard Tristan coming after him, and he stopped, for he understood clearly that Tristan was coming only to fight.

When Tristan got closer, he said to the other knight, "Defend yourself against me, for I challenge you."

The knight, who saw and understood clearly that he could not leave any other way, lowered his lance, and the two struck each other so violently that they knocked each other to the ground, their horses on top of them, but they did each other no other harm, [113] for both had very good hauberks. Although they were bruised

---

* "serpent's head" as in Bogdanow 1991 (497). There is some confusion in the Portuguese.
† "No" added by Bogdanow 1991 (499).

and badly hurt by the fall, they got up lightly, for each one was deeply ashamed to have been knocked down by a single knight. They took their swords and charged at each other, giving each other the greatest blows they could with all their force, so that they made their helmets and shields and hauberks worse than before. What shall I tell you? The two of them carried on that first encounter—and this was because each one thought himself good and valiant—until Blioberis arrived, who was of the Round Table and first cousin of Lancelot of the Lake, and he was a marvelously good knight at arms.

After Blioberis had looked a little at the knights who were still fighting and had seen them so good and lively, he was amazed that they were such as they were, and he was grieved by the battle because of the skill he saw in them, for he could only believe they were of the Round Table. Therefore, he would willingly have stopped the battle, could he have done so to the honor of both. He waited until they were both tired and drew apart from each other, badly hurt and fatigued, for they had endured much. However, Tristan was not as badly hurt as the other knight, for he was stronger, and because of the great vitality he felt in himself he wondered especially how the other knight could endure so long against him. The other thought the same thing, for he personally had hurt and defeated so many good men that he wondered who his opponent could be, for he saw clearly that this was doubtless the best knight he had ever met. Then he thought in his heart that this was the Very Good Knight who was to bring the adventures to an end or Lancelot or Tristan. If it was Galahad, he considered himself a dead man, for he knew well that Galahad was a better knight than he. If it was Lancelot and Palamedes killed him, he feared he would die for it, for Lancelot had among his kin the best knights in the world, who would avenge him. If it was Tristan, he thought that he had done him a great wrong by laying hand on him, for at least he should have kept him safe for love of Iseut, whom he loved so much.

The pagan knight was thinking this through when he drew aside from the battle.

Blioberis, who would gladly have parted them, approached them and said, "Oh, my lords, for the sake of God and courtesy, tell me who you are."* [115]

"Why?" asked Tristan. "This isn't courteous, to ask their names of strange knights who for a long time have been seeking adventures and don't want anyone to recognize them."

"My lord," said Blioberis, "that's true, but, nevertheless, it's the custom that, if one knight sees two very good knights come together in battle through anger and ill will, if he doesn't recognize them and wants to ask their names, because of the skill he sees in them, and asks them about themselves, they shouldn't consider it discourteous of him. Indeed, I believe that if you now saw the two best knights in the world in battle on a field, you'd never be happy until you knew them."

"That could well be," said Tristan.

"Then," said Blioberis, "don't blame me if I ask you, for know that if I didn't see more skill in you than in seven others, I wouldn't ask you. And, therefore, I ask you to tell me who you are."

---

*   "tell me who you are" as in Bogdanow 1991 (502). Magne's text is confused at this point.

"I'll tell you," said Tristan, "but be assured that I don't consider you courteous to ask this; rather, you are a rude and ignorant knight. However, I'll tell you. I'm Tristan."

"Oh, my lord, mercy," said Blioberis. "Don't be so angry with me, but forgive me this wrong, and if you don't want to do it for my sake, do it for the love of my kin, who love you very much."

"And who are you?" asked Tristan.

"My lord," he said, "I'm Blioberis. You should certainly know me."

"Yes, I do," he said, "and because I know you, I forgive you the ill will I bore you."

Blioberis thanked him warmly for that.

Then he turned to the other knight and said, "My lord, I ask you for courtesy's sake to tell me who you are."

"I'll tell you gladly," he said. "Know that my name is Palamedes the Pagan, the Knight of the Questing Beast. I was good to you, some time ago, when Gawain's brothers wanted to kill you, and if I hadn't been there they would have killed you.* Now be good to me in something I'll ask of you."

"Speak," said Blioberis, "for there's nothing in the world I wouldn't do for you, to which I wouldn't immediately recognize myself obliged, because of what you did for me."

"You see here," said Palamedes, "Sir Tristan, who has attacked me without reason. Unquestionably, he's a very good knight, much better than I, but if he were the worst in the world and I held him near defeat, I'd yield him the battle, since I know him, for I'm one who wouldn't fight with him for anything. God knows my wish in this matter. Now beg him to leave off this battle."

"I'll certainly do this for you," said Blioberis. Then he said to Tristan, "My lord, I ask you, for the sake of God and courtesy, to leave off this battle now for my sake, for you're both such good knights, and it would be a great pity to lose one of you. What's more, the knight asks you to do it, and so you have the honor, since he's asking for peace while you haven't yet wounded him in such a way as to have conquered him, and, moreover, he pardons you the wrong [117] you did him when you attacked him without cause."

"Oh, Blioberis," said Tristan, "for God's sake, don't speak to me of peace. Know that there are in the world but two men who could make peace here. I hate this man so mortally that I'll kill him or he me. Therefore, I ask you not to try to make peace here, for it cannot be, and may God prevent it,† until one of us is dead."

"Oh, my lord," said Blioberis, "God willing, you won't do this, for since the knight wants peace, you can't rightfully refuse him."

Then Palamedes came closer and said, "Sir Tristan, I've fought with you until now, knowing that you're one of the best knights in the world. I've tested this well, and I'm not yet so badly wounded that I'd ask for peace, were there not two things that forbid me to fight: one is your good chivalry, and I wouldn't tell you the other for anything."

---

*   Not narrated in the Post-Vulgate as we have it.

†   "and may God prevent it" as in Bogdanow 1991 (505). Magne has "nor is there any use of saying it."

"This won't help you," said Tristan. "You have to die."

But Blioberis, who had already dismounted and put himself between the two of them, said, "Oh, Sir Tristan, I would never have believed that you'd refuse to do something I asked."

"There's no one," said Tristan, "for whom I'd do anything in this case."

Palamedes fell to his knees in front of Tristan and said to him, "Now you may do as you like with me, for I yield myself defeated in this battle, and you see here my sword, which I give you, for know that I have neither power nor strength to defend myself any longer against you. Now have mercy on me, if you please, or kill me, if you please."

When he heard this, Tristan was so grieved by it that he wished he were dead, because he had never hated a knight so mortally as this one, and he could not avenge himself on him without being forsworn and disloyal to the Round Table, for it was the custom that any knight who was a companion of it should not lay hand on a knight who had given him his sword, however much he had wronged him.

Because of this custom, Tristan had to give up that battle then, and when he saw that the knight was giving him his sword, he said with great anger, because he could not fulfill his will, "I don't want your sword or anything of yours. I'll leave off the battle for you, but I swear this much to you, that I won't ever be happy until I'm avenged on you, for in the first place where I meet you, be assured of battle and death, if I can do more than you."

Palamedes answered, "I'll be sorry when you attack me."

Then Tristan said to Blioberis, "You've taken away from me here my vengeance on the one man in the world to whom I wish most ill, [119] and therefore I tell you that I wouldn't be sorry at any harm that came to you."

Blioberis replied, "I'm sorry about your anger, but know that this knight has done so much for me that if I let him die where I could help him, all the world would think it wrong of me."

Tristan went to his horse and mounted, and then he said to Palamedes, "Here you have nothing to fear, but know for sure that in the first place where I find you, you won't escape without my killing you or you me."

Palamedes said, "I don't know how it will happen, but I'll do as much as I can to prevent a fight between us."

Then Tristan went away, sad and angry that he had not killed Palamedes. Palamedes also mounted as quickly as he could and went away in another direction, but he thanked Blioberis repeatedly for what he had done for him and said he would gladly reward him for it if he had the chance. And Blioberis also started out in another direction.

Tristan rode that day until night came on him at the entrance of a castle—called Sagremor's Castle, because King Arthur had given it to Sagremor—which stood on a little plain.

That night Tristan stayed there, and he was served and honored to his satisfaction, for the castle's inhabitants were accustomed to serving knights errant the best they could, because their lord was a knight errant, but they served this one even better than they served others, knowing that he was Tristan, whose great fame ran through the whole kingdom of Logres. The next day, after he had heard Mass, he mounted and rode until midday. Then he emerged from the forest, and he met a fully armed knight who was of the Round Table, and his name was Lambeguez. As soon as they saw each other, they recognized each other, and they embraced and were very happy.

Tristan said, "Sir Lambeguez, what news?"

"Good news," he said.

"How has it gone with you since you started on this quest?" asked Tristan.

"Very well, my lord," said Lambeguez, "thanks be to God, for I've found many adventures, good and bad, but today something happened to me worse than has happened in a long time."

"How?" asked Tristan.

"By God," said Lambeguez, "I was passing near a castle, which you'll find before you today, if you go by this path. There's a large crowd assembled there in tents and huts—I don't know why—and when I got there, I wanted to pass by the tents. Then a knight came against me [121] fully armed and asked a joust of me. I didn't want to refuse it, because it's the duty of any knight not to refuse a joust with one knight or with two, and I knocked him down. Then another good knight came and knocked me down, and by his courtesy he gave me back my horse. After I had mounted, I demanded battle of him, and he told me he wouldn't do battle with a man who had been knocked down. Then I left him."

"Do you think," asked Tristan, "that if I go this way I'll have to joust?"

"Yes, without doubt," said Lambeguez.

"Then I commend you to God," said Tristan, "for I won't leave my path because of such a threat."

"My lord," said Lambeguez, "have you any news of King Ban's kindred?"

"Yes," said Tristan, "Blioberis left me yesterday and Galahad shortly before. I know nothing of the others."

"Do you know where* I could find Blioberis?" asked Lambeguez.

"I don't know," said Tristan, "so help me God."

Then they commended each other to God and parted.

127. PALAMEDES RESCUES TRISTAN AT THE CASTLE LESPAR; GALAHAD RESCUES THEM BOTH.[†]

Lambeguez went off in one direction after Blioberis, as chance guided him, and Tristan went to the castle Lambeguez had shown him. That castle was beautiful and rich and stood on a large, strong, deep river. That day they were holding a great feast there for the king's son, who was to be crowned the next day. There were in the tents a good twenty armed knights, who waited there for chance to bring to them some of the knights of the Round Table, for they well knew that these knights

---

* "know where" as in Bogdanow 1991 (511). Magne has "think."
† Corresponds to Magne II:121-131; Bogdanow 1991 512-523; Piel 263-268.

were on the quest for the Holy Grail and were seeking adventures near and far throughout the kingdom of Logres. As they were waiting, suddenly Tristan arrived there alone and thinking deeply, unable to forget Palamedes, who had thus begun to love Queen Iseut; nor had any adventure in a long while caused him such sorrow as he felt because he had not killed Palamedes.

As Tristan was riding and thinking, approaching the tents, an armed knight came out to him and said, "My lord, are you of King Arthur's house?"

He raised his head and said, "Yes, I am, certainly."

"Then defend yourself against me," said the knight, "for there's nothing in the world I hate so much as those of that house."

Tristan said, "You've conceived such a foolish hate that no good will ever come to you of it."

Tristan charged at him at once and struck him so that he drove his whole lance into him and laid him on the ground, mortally wounded; he drew out [123] the lance, which was unbroken, for it occurred to him that he would yet need it.

When the men of the tents saw that one lying on the ground, and he showed no sign of getting up, they said, "He's dead! He's dead!"

One of them quickly mounted a strong, agile horse and charged at Tristan, and Tristan, who was already riding away, turned toward him and struck him so that he laid him dead on the ground.

When the king, who was to crown his son the next day and who was in the tents with his company, saw those two blows, he said to those who were armed, "Stay there, and let the knight go in peace, for he has acquitted himself well of his duty. So help me God, he's good!" Then he said to one of his brothers, who was unarmed, "Mount quickly and go after him and tell him that I ask him to tell me his name."

The knight mounted and went to Tristan, saying to him all the king had commanded.

Tristan, who was a little angry, answered, "My lord, I'm a foreign knight; ask me no more, for you may know no more about me."

"Oh, sir knight," he said, "God willing, you won't do this discourtesy, to refuse to tell my lord the king what he's sent me to ask you."

"Not for you or anyone else," said Tristan, "will I tell you more than I've already told you."

"No?" said the knight. "Then you respect me little. So help me God, now we'll see what you'll do." Then he took him by the bridle and said to him, "Sir knight, now you're in my power. Your pride won't keep you from telling me what I came here for. I'll take you captive."

"You've spoken well," said Tristan, "and don't you think I'll be free of this captivity as soon as I wish?"

The knight held him all the while.

Tristan said to him, "You're acting foolishly and, indeed, were you not unarmed, you'd pay for it."

Then the knight led his horse toward the tents.

Tristan grew angry and said, "Either you let me go or I'll kill you. And thus the dishonor will be mine, because you're unarmed, and the loss yours, because you're foolish."

He said, "You're wasting your breath,* for you'll come with me anyway."

"I don't yet see anyone here who will take me by force," said Sir Tristan, "and I tell you that I'll go no farther from here."

Then he pulled on the reins, raised his lance, and said, "So help me God, I'll kill you if you don't let me go."

The knight would not let him go, and Tristan brandished the lance and struck him so that he laid him dead on the ground. Then he said to him, "Now I'll go away against your will, and you'll remain, if others don't pick you up." [125]

When the king saw his brother fall, he thought he was mortally wounded and cried to those with him, "Now go after the knight who has killed my brother, for he has betrayed and slain me by taking from me the best friend I had."

Then you would have seen more than a hundred knights ride out after Tristan. Eighteen of them were fully armed and the others armed only with shields and lances. When Tristan saw that the contest was so unequal, that he had to defend himself against them all, he was not very happy about it; nevertheless, he was of such great heart and strength that he never feared anything he saw. He turned his horse's head toward them fiercely, bravely, and with anger and struck the first one he reached so that he knocked him from his horse to the ground, and then the second, and then the third, and then the fourth. Then his lance broke, and he took his sword, like one who wanted to avenge his own death, and went in among them; he knocked down knights, killed horses, and did so much with his own hand that anyone who saw him would have thought it a marvel. He would have defended himself further, but a knight killed his horse.

When Tristan found himself on foot[†] among his mortal enemies, he did not lose heart, for he had been in greater danger, but he defended himself like a wild boar among dogs. Nevertheless, he was not so whole that he did not already have more than seven wounds, of the least of which another knight would have died, and this was something that made him grow weaker. Thus he defended himself among so many knights, each of whom wanted to cut off his head. All the same, he would certainly have died, for he could not endure against such a large crowd. But at that moment chance brought that way Palamedes, the good pagan knight.

When he saw Tristan, he recognized him, and when he saw him defending himself so marvelously in such an unequal battle, he said, "Indeed, Sir Tristan, now I see that you're the best knight I ever met. Now all the world would think it wrong of me if I didn't do everything in my power to help you, and I'll consider not the great

---

*   Literally, "all that you are saying to me is nothing."

†   "on foot" supplied by Bogdanow 1991 (517).

hatred you bear me but your great goodness, for all the world would be diminished by the death of such a man." [127]

Then, sword in hand, he charged at them all and struck the first man he reached so that he knocked him from his horse to the ground, dead.

He took the horse, led it to Tristan, and said to him, "Mount, my lord, and see to defending yourself, for it seems to me that you have great need."

Tristan mounted while Palamedes defended him, to the annoyance of his enemies, and when Tristan saw Palamedes, whom he had promised to kill and who had now been so good to him, he thought it the greatest marvel in the world and thought that if he got the chance, he would reward him for it.

Palamedes said to him, "Sir Tristan, now do your best!"

He did not answer, for he had no leisure, but he began to strike great blows of the sword. Thus the two knights defended themselves in front of the castle that was named Lespar, but their defense would have been in vain, for they would ultimately have been killed or captured, since they could not long hold out against so many people, were it not for the chance that at that moment brought that way the More Than Good Knight Galahad. When he saw the two knights surrounded by such a large crowd, he waited no longer but let his horse gallop in order to help them. He struck so fiercely that he laid the first man he reached on the ground, and before his lance broke he did more than anyone else could have done. After his lance broke, he took the sword he had taken from the stone* and began to give great blows to all those who stood to meet him, and he was so brave and so agile that all who saw him were afraid of him, for no man he reached with a blow was protected by his armor from being wounded or knocked to the ground.† He did so much in a short time, by the great blows he gave, that the best and bravest were aware of‡ his knightly skill, so that they saw clearly that they could not in any way stand against him, and in their fear they left the field and fled to the tents. When the king saw this, he was amazed and asked his men why they were fleeing.

"Why?" said one. "Because of a knight who came on us, who strikes so immoderately with his sword that no armor can endure against his blows, and if a hundred of the best knights in the world were against him, he would ultimately kill and defeat them all."

When the king heard this, he said, "So help me God, I won't believe this unless I see it." [129]

Then he got on a horse, took a shield and lance, and had his sword girded on. He struck the horse with the spurs, went out from among the tents, and saw Galahad, who was knocking his knights down as easily as if they could not hold themselves

---

*   Chapter 75.

†   "was protected by his armor from being wounded or knocked to the ground" as in Bogdanow 1991 (519). Magne has "could they later heal, but Galahad killed or cut or wounded him or knocked him to the ground." Both Magne and Piel (266) include the word "killed," which is missing from the French. It is notable that Galahad is usually saved from the "misfortune/sin" of killing the knights he fights, especially if they are of the Round Table.

‡   "were aware of" as in Bogdanow 1991 (313). Magne has "felt."

in the saddle.* He was doing such damage to them that anyone who saw him would have been frightened.

After the king had watched him a little, he said, "Oh, we have been deceived in not recognizing this man. By Saint Mary, this is the More Than Good Knight who is to accomplish the adventures of the kingdom of Logres. Now I don't feel myself dishonored because he has defeated my men, for no other ability could endure against his.

Then he said to his men, "Come back and let them go, for to try to keep them would be effort wasted."

They came back as soon as they heard their lord's command.

The three knights went to the river and crossed it, and after they had crossed it, Tristan said to Galahad, "You are welcome. Your coming was fortunate for me."

As soon as they had crossed the river, Palamedes the good knight took leave of the other two and went away in another direction. After he had gone a little distance away from them, Galahad asked Tristan about him, and Tristan told him everything about him, whatever he knew and had seen, and said that that was the good Knight of the Questing Beast.

"Indeed," said Galahad, "he's of good character and did a great courtesy when he came to your aid against so many people, knowing that you hated him so much. Indeed, I'm sorry he isn't a Christian."

"By my faith, so am I," said Tristan.

Speaking of this, they rode all that day until they reached a little castle that stood on a mountain. There they were well served, for a beautiful, noble maiden, sister of Dodinel the Wild, who was lord of the castle, worked hard to do for them whatever would please them, because they were of the Round Table. She asked them a great deal about her brother, and they told her what they knew about him. That night they slept comfortably, and the next day, as soon as it was [131] light, they commended the maiden to God and departed. When they had started on their way as before, they began to seek adventures and to ask wherever they went for news of the others. Three days they rode together without finding an adventure, and know that for those three days Tristan was in considerable pain, for he was wounded so badly that, had he not been of greater strength and heart than another, he would not have been able to endure so much torment.

On the fourth day he stayed very unwillingly in an abbey, and an old knight there, who knew a lot of such doctoring, looked at him and said, "Sir Tristan, know that you're in danger of dying because you didn't have your wounds looked at sooner; nevertheless, I'll do what I can for you, for love of Our Lord and for your sake, for you're a good knight, but I don't promise to heal you, for, so help me God, your wounds are so large and perilous and you've borne them so long† that I'm fearful."

"My lord," said Tristan, "for the sake of God and courtesy, whatever happens to me because of it, care for me, for my heart tells me that I'm not to die of it."

---

* "they could not hold themselves in the saddle" as in Bogdanow 1991 (521). Magne has "he were not in the saddle."

† "borne them so long" as in Bogdanow 1991 (523). Magne has "brought so many of them to be healed."

"May God make it so," said the good man.

128. GALAHAD AT KING PELLES'S CASTLE.[*]

Galahad stayed with Tristan two days, but because he could not stay there until Tristan was healed, he urged the brothers to care for him and to be sure much good would come to them if he got better, for Tristan was one of the best and ablest men in the world.

They promised him that they would. Thus Tristan remained, and Galahad went on. He went seeking the adventures of the kingdom of Logres, now here, now there, as chance directed him. When he arrived at two leagues from Corbenic, there in a field he saw rich, beautiful huts, tents, and pavilions. The people of Corbenic were celebrating the beginning of the good season in the month of April, and everyone in the land was present at that celebration, because on such a day as that King Pelles had been crowned, and each year they held such a celebration on the day on which he had been crowned.

On that day when Galahad passed near the tents, it could have been midday. The king was sitting at the table, his barons with him, and they were eating luxuriously, but not through the grace of the Holy Vessel, for the Holy Vessel never emerged from Corbenic by human agency. However, unquestionably, all those who ate [133] in the Palace of Adventures were given an abundance of everything they needed, provided that they prayed for its coming. King Pelles had with him then a magician, who was performing such marvels that all were amazed. When the knights who were closest to the king saw Galahad coming armed, they recognized clearly that he was one of the adventuring knights from King Arthur's house, and they went toward him on foot and begged him so courteously and humbly to dismount and stay with them that he dismounted, disarmed himself, and went to seat himself at the table with the other knights fairly near King Pelles, who had the magician beside him.

When he saw Galahad, Pelles did not recognize him, because Galahad was dark and stained by his armor, and he said to the magician, "Perform one of your tricks before this foreign knight, who perhaps will speak of it in King Arthur's house when he goes there, for I know well that he's from there."

But the magician, who had lost his knowledge and power at the coming of the Good Knight—a holy creature—replied, "My lord, I can't do anything while he's here."

"What?" asked the king. "Does he take your powers away from you?"

"Yes, my lord," said the magician.

"How?" asked the king. "He isn't a magician."

"No, my lord," he said.

"Then how would he take them away from you?"

---

[*]   Corresponds to Magne II:131-143; Bogdanow 1991 523-539; Piel 268-274.

"My lord," said the magician, "that I can't tell you."

The king told him again to perform some of his enchantments, and he said he could not. The king grew angry and said, "Either tell me why you've lost your power or I'll have you killed right now." He commanded his men to seize him and cut off his head if he did not do what the king ordered, and they seized him at once.[*] When the magician saw that it had come to that, he said that they should let him go, and he would do what the king commanded.

Then he turned to the king and said, "King Pelles, now I'll tell you who I am and why I can't perform my enchantments as I did before this knight came."

"Then tell me," said the king.

The magician began, "King Pelles, I'm a native of Barbary, nobler than you think, but chance cast me into this land poorer than was good for me. I was a pagan, but Nascien the hermit baptized me, and after I received baptism I began to sin against my Creator more than another sinner would dare to do, and I'll tell you how. One day I was riding through a forest, despairing at my great poverty, so that I didn't believe in God or man. Then there appeared to me a demon, whose name is Dagon, and he's one of the favorites of hell. He appeared to me in the guise of a rich and powerful man. He asked me who I was, and I told him about myself. He said to me, [135] 'If you'll become my vassal, there's nothing you can ask of me that I won't give you.' I told him that I'd be his vassal if he showed me how I could become rich, and he said to me, 'I'll teach you so much that you'll consider yourself well satisfied with me.'

"I promised him that I'd be his and at once denied my Creator and my Christianity and became a servant of the devil, and he quickly taught me all the power of enchantments that a mortal man could know. I relied so much on his care that whenever I asked for food or drink or anything else, he would appear before me. Although I have told you some things that were done in secret, I really knew nothing of them except what he told me to tell you. Now it happened, when this knight arrived, that the demon by whom I performed the marvels left me, for he couldn't be in the place where there was a man so holy and so much loved by Our Lord, for he is such a holy creature that whether he sleeps or wakes or moves about, he's always accompanied by angels who guide him. Therefore, I lost all my ability to perform the enchantment."

"By God," said King Pelles, "I do believe that he's a good man, but not such as you tell me."

"No?" he said. "By God, he is. Do you want to prove it? Tell him to go some distance away from here, and then you'll see that I'm telling you the truth."

King Pelles, who desired to know if this was true, said to Galahad, "Sir knight, for the sake of God and courtesy, go a little away from here now, until we find out if what this man says about you is true."

Galahad did as the king told him, so they wouldn't think him proud, and went from that tent to another. At once a marvel occurred that afterward was told throughout all King Arthur's land and many other kingdoms, for the magician began at once

---

[*]   "said ... and they seized him at once" as in Bogdanow 1991 (526). Magne has "commanded that his head be cut off if he would not do it."

to burn, as if he were dry firewood, and he was taken up into the air so high that he seemed to be reaching the clouds.

As the devils were thus taking him, he began to cry out, "Oh, Galahad, holy knight, pray for me, for I would yet find mercy if you'd pray for me."

Thus the devils took the magician in the presence of King Pelles and many other good men. When they could no longer see him, they crossed themselves in their amazement. They got up from the tables, went to Galahad, and paid him as much honor as they could. [137]

The king, who had a great desire to know him because of what he had heard the magician say, fixed his eyes on him and looked at him until it seemed to him that it was Galahad, his grandson.

Then he said, "Sir knight, I ask you by your courtesy to tell me who you are."

"My lord," he said, "I'll never conceal my identity from you. I'm Galahad."

The king, as happy as he could be, said, "By Saint Mary, I thought so. Praised be the Holy Spirit who gave us such a man in our lineage!"

At once he began to embrace him and rejoice over him.

Galahad said to him, "My lord, I ask you not to tell anyone who I am."

"What?" asked the king. "Do you want to hide your identity from my men?"

"Yes, for now," he said. "But when it pleases God that chance brings me to Corbenic with my companions, then I don't care if they all know who I am. Do you know why I ask this of you? If your barons recognized me, they wouldn't let me go from here today, and this I don't want for anything, for I want to go away at once."

"What?" asked the king. "You've just come, and you want to go away at once?"

"Yes," he said, "by all means."

"That grieves me," said the king, "but since it pleases you, I commend you to God."

"I ask you," said Galahad, "by that love you must have for me, not to tell anyone who I am."

He agreed. At once Galahad took his arms and mounted his horse, and so he parted from them.

After Galahad had left King Pelles, the knights who had seen the king rejoicing so over him asked him who he was.

He said, "You may not know at this time, and it grieves me greatly that I can't tell you his name."

Eliezer, King Pelles's son, having seen that his father received that knight so well and was so pleased with him, wondered who he could be, and he went to his father and asked him earnestly to tell him who the knight was.

His father said to him, "Son, I can't tell you, for I promised him I wouldn't reveal his identity to anyone here."

When Eliezer, who was a good knight, brave and highly respected, saw that his father did not want to tell him what he asked, he said, [139] "My lord, since you don't want to tell me, I'll do what I have in mind, for perhaps the knight is so good that I'd be worth more for knowing him."

"I don't know what you'll do," said the king, "but at this time you may not find it out from me."

Then Eliezer left his father and armed himself; he mounted a good horse and took a shield, but not one with his own device, so that his father would not recognize him when he left the tents.

When Eliezer was equipped with all he needed, he left his company, asking them not to tell his father. After that he went after Galahad, and he had not gone far when he caught up with him. They did not recognize each other, although Galahad would easily have recognized Eliezer if he had borne the shield with his own device, for he had seen it many times. As soon as Eliezer caught up with Galahad, he came up beside him and greeted him. Galahad greeted him, too, appropriately.

"My lord," said Eliezer, "I ask you by your courtesy to tell me who you are."

"My lord," he said, "I'm this knight you see; you shall not know more at this time."

"My lord," said Eliezer, "you won't commit the discourtesy of not telling me something about yourself."

"I won't tell you for anything," said Galahad; "be sure of that."

Then Eliezer grew angry and said, "Indeed, this is the greatest arrogance of which I ever heard. So help me God, since you won't tell me willingly, I want to find out in spite of you, for I'd rather fight with you than not know. Therefore, I offer you a choice; either fight with me or tell me who you are."

"My lord," said Galahad, "you're the most foolish knight and the most ignoble I ever saw, wanting to find out about me by force. Now I tell you that you won't find it out; rather I'll defend myself against you if you want to attack me."

"Then defend yourself against me now," said Eliezer, "for you're in a battle; never have I wished a knight such great ill as I wish you."

After this, without further delay, they charged at each other as fast as their horses could carry them. Eliezer struck Galahad first, so hard that he broke his lance, and Galahad, who neither recognized nor feared him, struck him so violently that he broke through his shield and hauberk and put the point of his lance into his right side, but not far. He knocked Eliezer from his horse to the ground, drew the lance out of him unbroken, and, [141] when he saw him on the ground, did not even look at him again but went his way. When Eliezer found himself on the ground at the hand of a knight he did not know, he felt such grief that he wished he were dead, for he thought himself such a good knight that he did not expect to find a knight who could ultimately stand against him. He got on his horse, badly wounded as he was, and thought that he would be disgraced if he did not avenge himself.

As soon as Eliezer was mounted, he went after Galahad, crying out to him, "Turn, sir knight, for, by Saint Mary, you won't go away like this. You must defend yourself with the sword, for I summon you to battle."

When Galahad heard this, he turned and said, "Knight, you're seeking your own hurt when you trouble me with battle. This isn't courteous, for you're comfortable and rested, and you go about annoying foreign knights who ride in toil day and night, seeking the adventures of the kingdom of Logres. I well believe that if you rode in such toil you'd have no desire for battle."

"Oh, sir knight," said Eliezer, "you'll never escape by this bravado."*

"I ask you to leave me in peace," said Galahad, "and you'll do a courtesy, for what you're doing—attacking me gratuitously and without reason—is very ignoble."

Eliezer took his sword and said, "Sir knight, if I believed you, you'd keep me talking all day."

Then he charged at him and gave him the hardest blow he could. When Galahad saw that he had to defend himself, he took his sword and said, "Knight, I won't forbear any longer, for I see clearly that you won't respect my request."

He took his sword and gave Eliezer such a hard blow that neither helmet nor iron cap protected him, but Galahad cut him to the skull; Eliezer was fortunate that the wound was not mortal, for his helmet was so good that it checked the blow a little. The blow was hard and administered with great force, and it stunned him, so that he flew from his horse to the ground and lay as if dead. Galahad, who thought that he was dead, stopped to see if he would get up. After a long time he got up, and when Galahad saw that he was not dead, he put his sword in its scabbard and went his way. When Eliezer got up, he also put his sword in its scabbard and mounted, and because he saw that he could not stand up to the foreign knight, he returned to the tents in the greatest possible sorrow, [143] for it seemed certain to him that he would never have honor, since he was thus abased by the hand of a single man, and until then he had been considered one of the best knights in the world.

As Eliezer was approaching the tents, his father saw him returning, but he did not realize it was he because of the shield he had changed, and he asked who it was; his men denied knowing him, because Eliezer had forbidden it. The king told them to go after him, for he wanted to see him, and he said this because he saw that Eliezer was coming from the direction of the road by which Galahad had gone, and he guessed that Galahad had knocked him down. They went to Eliezer and gave him his father's summons.

Eliezer said with great sorrow, "I'll go there, since it pleases him, but I see clearly that all this is happening to me for my greater dishonor."

Then he went to his father, and when his father saw him so badly wounded, he asked what had happened to him. Eliezer told him everything, just as you have already heard it.

"Son," said the king, "now may you see that you've met a better knight than yourself. From now on, don't be so mad as to go attack strange knights, for there are many better than you think. And if they weren't better than others and more

---

* "bravado" from the 1944 edition of Magne. The 1955 edition is somewhat confused. Bogdanow 1991 (535) has "such words."

experienced in trials and battles, they wouldn't have undertaken to ride through strange lands seeking adventures."

"My lord," said Eliezer, "that's true, and if I've acted discourteously this time, I will from now on be careful never to wrong* a knight errant. I'm very sorry for what I've done, not so much because I'm wounded as for the discourtesy I committed and for the courtesy I found in the knight."

So the king spoke with his son, very happy at the goodness he heard of Galahad. But now the story stops speaking about King Pelles and his son and returns to Galahad.†

129. A MAIDEN TAKES GALAHAD TO CURE A MADWOMAN.‡

The story says that after Galahad left his uncle Eliezer, his mother's brother, he rode all that day without finding an adventure, and the next day, too, and on the third day at evening chance brought him to the house of a hermit, who received him well because he saw that Galahad was a knight errant. He disarmed Galahad so he could rest and gave him bread and water, [145] for he had nothing else, and he questioned Galahad a great deal about himself, asking him for God's sake to tell him in confession all that he had passed through in the quest. And Galahad did so, hiding nothing from the good man, for he loved him dearly.

That evening, after the good man had written down everything Galahad had told him, he said to him, "Son Galahad, beautiful creature, fortunate knight, tonight you'll leave me, and I know that I won't see you for a while. I ask you for God's sake not to forget me, for I'm a great sinner."

"My lord," said Galahad to the hermit, "I'll pray for you, and you pray for me, too, as a father for his son, that Our Lord may let me perform in this quest service that pleases Him and that may profit my soul and the kingdom of Logres."

"Son Galahad," said the good man, "may it happen so for you; I'll pray for you."

When it was time to lie down, Galahad lay down on a bundle of grass and the good man on the ground, and they went to sleep.

While they were sleeping, a maiden came and called at the door, "Galahad! Galahad!"

She called so loudly that the hermit woke up and went to the door, asking who was there who wanted to enter at such an hour.

---

* "wrong" as in Bogdanow 1991 (539). Magne has "fight with."

† This is the end of the first volume of Bogdanow's text. It is a source of deep regret to this translator that more of this edition was not yet available, when this translation was prepared, not only because of the excellence of the editor's work, for which scholars for years to come will be grateful, but because it incorporates so many fragments from the French, which are considerably better than the corresponding Portuguese, often somewhat expanded, and almost always clearer.

‡ Corresponds to Magne II:143-151; Piel 274-277.

"My lord," she said, "I'm a foreign maiden and have come to speak with a knight who is sleeping here. Wake him for me quickly, for I have great need of him."

He went to wake Galahad and said to him, "Galahad, my son, get up, for a maiden stands outside waiting for you, and she says she has great need of you."

Galahad got up at once, went to the door, and asked, "My lady, what do you want with me?"

"I want you to take your arms," she said, "get on your horse, and follow me where I'll take you, and I tell you that I'll soon show you the greatest and most beautiful adventure a knight ever saw in your time, and you'll accomplish it, God willing."

When Galahad heard this, he took his arms at once and got ready as quickly as he could, and the good man, who was helping him, said to him, "Son, this is the parting I was telling you about. I know well that we won't see each other again for a long time. For God's sake, remember me."

"My lord," said Galahad, "know that I can't forget you, for you are one of the men in whom I trust most in the world."* [147]

After Galahad was armed and mounted on his horse, he emerged from that place, and he made before himself the sign of the holy, true cross and commended himself to Our Lord.

Then he said to the maiden, "Now you may go, for I'll follow you wherever you go."

The maiden turned and rode away at once, as fast as the horse could carry her, and he after her. They rode until it began to grow light. When it was full daylight, they entered a large forest, which stretched to the sea, and that forest was called Caloise. They rode along the main road all that day, without eating or drinking. At evening after vespers they arrived at a castle, which stood in a valley, strong on all sides and encircled by a wide river, a tall, strong wall, and deep ditches. The maiden rode ahead all the while.

They entered the castle, and all the people of the castle said to them, "My lady, you are welcome. Is this the knight we have awaited so long?"

She did not answer but went toward the fortress. When those inside the fortress knew she was coming, they came out to meet her and received her well, for she was their lady's† first cousin.

She said to them, "See to this knight, for know that he's the best knight who ever bore arms in Great Britain."

They came to his stirrup, made him dismount, and took him to a room and disarmed him.

He asked the maiden, "My lady, are we to stay here?"

"My lord," she said, "I don't know yet, but according to the adventures that happen to us here, we'll do as we like."

Then she asked another maiden, "Has my cousin recovered?"

"No," she said, "rather, she is worse than usual."

---

*   Although never identified explicitly, this sounds like the hermit who first brought Galahad to Camelot (chapter 75).

†   Magne has *seu senhor* ("their lord"). Piel (276) has *sa senhor* ("their lady"). What follows seems to indicate that she is cousin to the madwoman, the lady of the castle.

"Then take us there," she said.

"Gladly," said the maiden.

Then the first maiden said to Galahad, "My lord, do you know why I've brought you here?"

"Not yet," he said.

"There is a lady here of great consequence," she said, "and because of what misfortune I don't know, two years ago she went mad, so that no one could stay with her until they put her in chains, and many good men have tried to cure her if they could. The other day a lady of a religious order came here and said to us, 'If you can find the knight who [149] is to accomplish the adventures of the kingdom of Logres, he is so good and has such grace from Our Lord that I know this lady will be cured as soon as she sees him.' Therefore, I've brought you here; you must go see the lady, and if she can be cured, I'll be happy about it."

Then he went to the room where the lady was lying, and they found her still lying in her chains.

As soon as she saw Galahad, she began to say, "Oh, Galahad! Holy creature and fortunate person, flesh pure and filled with holy grace, blessed be the hour of your birth, and praised be God who has brought you here, for I have so benefitted from your coming here that I'm free of the evil companion I had, who was with me a long time. This was the devil, who has held me two years and more and has done me much harm. Free me, if you please, from these chains, for, God willing, they'll never again have to put me in them, thanks to God and to you."

Galahad thanked Our Lord fervently for this and said, "Oh, my lady! Thank not me but Jesus Christ, who has done all this for you, for He has pity on sinners when He pleases."

Then they took the lady out of the chains, and when she saw herself free, she cast herself down at his feet and kissed them, although he did not want her to, and she wept from the great joy she felt. After that she went to the church to give thanks to Our Lord for the great mercy He had shown her.

The news ran throughout the castle that its lady was cured, and everyone went there as soon as possible to see if it was true. When they saw that it was so, they praised the King of Kings and the hour in which the knight was born, and amazing numbers of men, great and lowly, went there. Then Galahad was served and honored there, much more than he wanted, and that night they made for him such a good and rich bed as if he had been in King Arthur's house. He lay down in it, but as soon as they all went away, he lay down on the ground, and he did not return to the bed again. For most of the night he was praying and begging Our Lord that God would have him do such works as would please Him. The next morning he went to hear the Mass of St. Mary; after that he asked for his arms, and when the people of the castle saw that he wanted to go, they asked him repeatedly to stay with them. He said he would not stay for anything, for he had more to do elsewhere than there. Then they gave him [151] his arms and his horse, and they were very sad because he was not staying with them.

After he was armed, he mounted and said to the maiden, "Mount."

She mounted, and thus the two of them left the castle. When they arrived at the edge of a little forest, they met Blioberis, Lancelot's first cousin. As soon as he and Galahad saw each other, they recognized each other and greeted each other, and they were very happy together, asking each other about their deeds and what had happened since they had parted.

130. GALAHAD REPELS ATTACKS BY ENVIOUS KNIGHTS AND CURES A WOMAN OF LEPROSY; HIS COMPANION IS IDENTIFIED AS PERCEVAL'S SISTER.*

While they were talking, suddenly five knights of the Round Table, skilled and marvelously brave, approached. They were five first cousins, and because of the knightly ability they knew they had, they mortally hated King Ban's lineage, who were better loved and enjoyed King Arthur's favor more than they. The first was named Taulat the Great of Desert; the second Senela, his brother; the third Baradam; the fourth Damas; and the fifth Damatal. All these five were knights of great deeds, but they were poor, and therefore they envied King Ban's lineage, for the latter were rich and honored, and it seemed to the five that they did not get as much honor or love as they deserved. When they saw Galahad and Blioberis, they knew who they were at once, for they had heard of them many times and of what arms they bore.

When they recognized them, they stopped, and Senela, Taulat's brother, spoke first and said, "See, here come two of King Ban's kin. Let's kill them, for by that kindred are we diminished, and if we kill them their kindred will be diminished and ours exalted."

"Oh, brother," said Taulat, "what are you saying? So help me God, never, by my advice, will you meddle with them, for if there were no one but Galahad alone, who's the best knight in the world, as you know, he alone would defeat us and cast us into misfortune, and all the more as he has with him Blioberis, who's one of the best knights in the world."

"Oh, Sir Taulat," said Damas, "I've never seen you so afraid of nothing. Know that we'll defeat them if we attack them."

The others said the same, but Taulat did not think it good and [153] repeatedly forbade them to do it.

When Senela saw that his brother was against it, he said to the others, "My lords, what do you think of this?"

"Let's go to them," they said, "and you'll see that we won't fail you† this side of death, and that we'll conquer them quickly, for they are only two and we are four.

---

* Corresponds to Magne II:151-165; Piel 277-284.
† "you" added by Piel (278).

If Taulat wants to help us, he'll do well, and if not, let him be still, for, God willing, we'll do our deeds well without him."

When Taulat saw that they were agreed on this and would not give it up for him, he was very sorry, for he knew they could not get out of it without loss.

After this, without waiting any longer, Senela called out, "Galahad, and you Blioberis, defend yourselves against us, for your lineage has never loved ours, nor do we love yours."

Galahad asked Blioberis, "Who are these knights who know us so well and challenge us?"

"My lord," said Blioberis, "they are five cousins of Desert, a city of the kingdom of Logres, of which they are natives, and they're all of the Round Table, but through envy they hate all those of our lineage, because we're better loved and enjoy greater favor than they. And it seems to me that because of that they want to fight with us in order to kill us."

"That grieves me deeply," said Galahad, "for, since they're of the Round Table, we shouldn't lay a hand on them nor they on us. But because it's right that every knight defend his life at need, I'll defend mine as well as I can."

Blioberis said the same. He was glad of the battle, since he actually preferred war with them to peace—for his lineage and theirs had never wished each other well.

After that, without further delay, they charged, one side against the other, but Taulat would have no part of it. Galahad knocked one down so badly hurt that he could not get up, for he was stricken with a great stroke of the lance, but he would still have been healed, could he have escaped from there. This was Senela, the marvelously good knight. Blioberis struck Damas with such a great lance stroke that he laid him dead on the ground. Then Galahad charged at Damatal and struck him so hard that he could not hold himself in the saddle but fell to the ground, badly wounded. Baradam charged at Galahad and gave him such a lance stroke on the shield that he splintered his lance; Galahad knocked him to the ground badly wounded in his left side, and he was so badly hurt, between the blow and the fall, that he could not get up. [155] Blioberis, who hated him bitterly, dismounted, took off Damas's helmet, and gave him such a blow with his sword that he split him to the teeth, and Damas died instantly. After that he went to the others and killed them.

Then he said, "My lord, Sir Galahad, now we can truly say that our enemies are dead. Of these four, there's no one left for King Ban's lineage to fear."

When Taulat saw his cousins dead, he felt such grief that he truly wished to die, and he said to Blioberis, "Defend yourself against me, for I'd rather die than not do my best to avenge us, although I see clearly that I'm wrongfully making war on the Round Table. But I do it in order to hasten my death and because I know that I'll never return to the Round Table."

Then they charged and struck each other in such a way that neither shields nor hauberks kept them from putting their lances through each other. Blioberis was badly wounded, but he was of such great heart that he did not feel it, and Taulat had such a large lance wound that the iron point appeared on the other side of his spine, and he died as soon as he fell.

When Blioberis saw this, he said to Galahad, "My lord, now we can go, for there's no longer any one of these for King Ban's lineage to fear."

"Because they were of the Round Table," said Galahad, "I wish that it had been otherwise."

"So help me God," said Blioberis, "I'm more pleased with them dead than alive, for they have always envied us since we came to King Arthur's house."

"What shall we do?" asked Galahad. 'We should bury them, since they're knights."

"Let's have done with the battle," said Blioberis, "and go our way, for chance will bring some good man here later who will see to them."

Blioberis spoke so persuasively to Galahad that they left there and entered the forest. They rode until near nightfall and arrived at the house of a knight who lived on the mountain. There they took shelter, and they found there three knights of the Round Table. One was named Amatin the Good Jouster, because he was one of the best jousters in the world at that time; the second was named Agamenor, the man with the beautiful lover; the third was Arpian of the Narrow Mountain. When the knights saw one another, they greeted one another well, and know that they were well served with everything the host had, for he had a son who was a knight errant, and because of that he loved all the others. Those three knights of whom I told you were brothers with the same father and mother, and they were good knights, courageous and skillful, except that they were more brutal than other knights when they saw a knight better than they were. That evening they [157] repeatedly asked Blioberis if Galahad was as good a knight as people said, and he confirmed to them that nobody's skill approached Galahad's skill at arms. When they heard this, it grieved them very much, for they did not love King Ban's lineage. This was only from envy.

They began to speak about it among themselves maliciously, until Amatin the Good Jouster said, "Let's get him.* We here are three brothers and such good knights that we're known throughout the whole world for our skill at arms. Galahad will leave Blioberis tomorrow and go away with this maiden. Let's go on ahead and see if he is such a good knight as they say, and if we aren't fainthearted, we'll easily be able to defeat him, for we are three and he one, and if we destroy him, we'll thereby diminish King Ban's kindred forever."

And the other two agreed.

Thus the three brothers spoke about Galahad with envy, from which misfortune came to them later.

Where they were lodging there was a maiden, their host's daughter, who had been very beautiful, but ten years before—I do not know by what misfortune—she had become a leper. The maiden who was traveling with Galahad was Perceval's sister. When she heard that there was such a maiden in the house, she went to see her in a room where she lay secluded and asked her how long she had been ill with that disease. The other said that it had been a full ten years and more.

"And do you think," asked Perceval's sister, "that you can be cured of it?"

---

*   *Façamo-lo bem,* "let's do it to him well."

"Indeed, I don't know," said the other. "It's all up to God. However, not seven years ago a hermit came here, a very good man of holy ways, and he said to me, 'Fear not, for you will be cured when the Good Knight comes here who is to accomplish the adventures of the kingdom of Logres, and I'll tell you how. When he comes here, ask him, in the name of Him whose servant he is, to let you wear the garment he wears next to his skin, and he'll give it to you. And know that you'll be cured as soon as you put it on.' This the hermit told me, but I don't understand how it can be, for I don't know how I can find that knight, and even if I found him, perhaps he wouldn't do what I ask."

When Perceval's sister heard this, she said to the maiden, "Now be joyful! You are fortunate, for the Good Knight about whom the hermit spoke to you is here; now ask him to see to you."

When the sick maiden heard this, she held up her hands toward heaven and said, "Oh, Jesus Christ, King of pity! Have mercy on me, and may it please You that I be cured."

Then she sent for her father and said to him, "Oh, father! The Good Knight by whom I'm to be cured is here. For God's sake, go to him and bring him to me, for I wouldn't dare appear there before these knights."

"Daughter," he asked, "how do you know that the best knight in the world is here?" [159]

"I know it," she said, "because this maiden told me."

"Oh, my lady," said the host, "for God's sake, point him out to me."

"Gladly," she said.

Then she went to point Galahad out to him, and the good man fell to his knees before him and said, "My lord, for God's sake, come inside here with me, for we are in great need of you."

Galahad raised him to his feet and said he would go gladly, and the good man took him to the room where his daughter lay and showed her to Galahad, as sick as she could be. As soon as she saw him, she let herself fall at his feet and asked him, weeping, by that God whose servant he was, to give her a gift. He agreed willingly.

Then she thanked him and said, "You will let me put on the garment you wear next to your skin."

He was deeply embarrassed, for he did not want anyone but his abbot to know that he wore a hair shirt.

However, because he had promised the maiden, he could not get out of it, and he said to her, "You may have it, but I don't want anyone but you to know what it is."*

"Agreed," she said.

He made all the others go out of the chamber; then he undressed, gave her the hair shirt, and asked her by the faith she owed to God not to tell anyone, and she promised. After that she remained alone and put it on next her skin, for Galahad went away to the knights, but he told them nothing of all that, for he did not want

---

*   "what it is" added by Piel (281).

anyone to know. And the maiden who had put on the hair shirt was at once as healthy as if she had never been sick.

When she saw what a miracle God had worked for her, she sent for Galahad.

When he came, she locked the door, threw herself down before him and kissed his feet, and said to him, "Very holy knight, look at the good God has done me by your coming. I'm cured of all the illness I had."

"Give thanks to Him who did it for you," he said, "for I did not do it, since I'm a sinner like any other man. And I ask you, by the faith you owe to Him who has shown you such wonderful mercy, not to reveal it while I'm here, for I don't want these knights here to know about it. But after I go away, then you may tell about the mercy God has shown you."

She said she would do so, and he took the hair shirt and put it on and then returned to the knights, and he did not tell them anything about the beautiful adventure that had happened to the maiden. When it was time to sleep, each one lay down in his bed except Galahad, who did not usually sleep there, for most of the time he slept on the ground. That night he was most of the night in prayer, asking Our Lord by His great pity to grant him to do such service as would be to the profit of his soul and the kingdom of Logres. [161]

The next morning all five knights armed themselves, and Galahad went one way with the maiden and Blioberis another. The three brothers followed Galahad, wanting to harm him if they could.

After they had gone as much as a league, they came into a clearing, and they called out to Galahad, "Galahad, defend yourself against us, for we challenge you."

He turned his head and saw them, and he wondered what could be the matter, for he knew them to be of the Round Table.

He said to them, "Oh, my lords! What is this you want to do? You know well that I'm of the Round Table like you, and never, to my knowledge, have I done anything for which you should hate me. By your courtesy and goodness, let me go my way in peace, for I ask nothing of you, nor do I wish you harm."

When they heard this, they truly thought he said it out of cowardice, and they said, "You have to defend yourself, or we'll kill you."

"I wouldn't for anything let you kill me," he said, "but not for anything would I fight with my brothers of the Round Table. Nevertheless, since I must do it, I'll defend my life."

Then he went to strike Amatin the Good Jouster so violently that he drove the point of the lance through his arm and body and knocked him and his horse to the ground; when he withdrew his lance, Amatin fainted. The other brothers struck Galahad and broke their lances on him, but they could not move him from the saddle, and he drove against them both so hard with shield and body that he gave them each a hard fall to the ground, by which they were so bruised that they could not get up for some time afterwards. When Galahad saw that he was free of them, he looked at them no more but turned to his maiden.

She, very happy at this adventure, said to him, "Sir Galahad, now you may see the envy of the Round Table. They began this out of envy, and it has turned out that they had the shame and harm of it."

"So help me God," said Galahad, "it grieves me that they tried it and that I had to lay a hand on them. But since it's so, let's go, lest they come after us, for they're so aggrieved that they'll want to avenge themselves if they can."

Thus Galahad went off as fast as he could, for he did not want the brothers to catch up with him. They, staying behind, were so sad and angry because they had been defeated by a lone knight, that they truly wished to die. They went to Amatin and asked him if he could be healed, and he said there was nothing wrong with him except anger and grief.

"But let's all mount," he said, "and go after Galahad, for if he escapes us, we'll have lost honor forever."

Then he got up without even looking at his wound, so angry was he and full of [163] malice. And as they were getting on their horses and preparing to ride after Galahad, they saw coming toward them two knights of the Round Table; one was named Acorante the Agile and the other Danubre the Brave. They were brothers, sons of the same father and mother, and of King Ban's lineage. When the three brothers saw those two knights coming, they recognized them at once.

Then they said among themselves, "See here two knights of King Ban's lineage, which we hate so much. Now we can avenge on them what Galahad did to us."

Then they called out to them, "Defend yourselves against us, for we challenge you."

When the two brothers heard this, they were amazed, for they knew well that the others were of the Round Table.

Then Danubre said to them, "My lords, why will you attack us? You'll be forsworn, for we're of the Round Table like you. Therefore, you shouldn't lay a hand on us for anything."

"All this won't help you," they said, "for you have offended us so much that you may not part from us without a fight."

"That grieves me," said Danubre, "but since it's so, we'll defend ourselves the best we can."

Then they charged at each other, and Danubre gave Amatin such a great blow with his lance that he laid him dead on the ground. When Arpian saw his brother dead, he took his sword and charged at Acorante and gave him such a great blow on his helmet that he split him to the teeth.

When Danubre in turn saw his brother dead, he took his sword and struck Arpian so wrathfully that he made his head fly more than a lance length from his body, and he said, "Oh, Arpian, you've killed my brother, but you haven't gained anything by it."

Then he said to Agamenor, "Forsworn and faithless knight, now you may see what comes of your treachery. Your two brothers are dead. But I've gained nothing by it, for I have lost the man I loved most in the world. But I'll avenge myself well for this death."

"Avenge yourself?" said Agamenor. "Your death is as near to you as I am."

Then he gave him such a great blow that he put his sword into his brain, and Danubre fell, mortally wounded. Agamenor stood over him and began to unlace his helmet in order to cut off his head. Danubre, who saw clearly that he would die and wanted to avenge his death, when he saw that Agamenor planned to remove his helmet, raised the bottom of Agamenor's hauberk and drove his sword through him, and Agamenor stretched out in the agony of death and fell dead on the other side.

When Danubre saw Agamenor beside him, he said, "Agamenor, you haven't gained much by what you did, for [165] you are dead and we, too, and King Ban's lineage won't be dishonored here, for we were only two and you three."

After he had said this, he stretched out in his death agony, and his soul left him. And know that these two brothers who died here were the first two knights of King Ban's lineage who died on the quest for the Holy Grail.

But now the story stops speaking of them and returns to Galahad.

131. GALAHAD AND PERCEVAL'S SISTER JOIN PERCEVAL AND BORS ON THE BARK; THE SHIP OF FAITH; SOLOMON'S BED; THE SWORD OF THE STRANGE STRAPS.*

When Galahad left the two brothers he had fought, as the story has already told, he and the maiden rode until they reached the sea, where they found Bors and Perceval in the bark. The voice had assured them that they would not wait there long and that the first knight to reach the bark would be Galahad.

When they saw him, they said to him from as far away as they thought he could hear them, "My lord, you are welcome. We have awaited you until God in His mercy has brought you here. Now come aboard, for there's nothing left but to go to the high adventure God has prepared for us."

When Galahad heard them speak so, he wondered who they were, for it was already so dark that he could not recognize them, and he greeted them and asked the maiden if they should dismount.

"Yes, my lord," she said, "and we'll leave your horse and my palfrey here."

Then they dismounted and went on board the ship, and the others received them the best they could. As soon as they were on board, a wind struck the ship so hard that it quickly took them far from land, and they went like this until day broke.

When Galahad recognized those with whom he was traveling, he said, "Now God has satisfied a great part of my desire."

Then they began to weep with pleasure because God had brought them together. Galahad at once laid aside his helmet and sword but not his hauberk. When he saw the bark, so beautiful within and without, he asked them if they knew where

---

*   Corresponds to Magne II:165-173; Piel 284-290.

such a beautiful bark had come from. Bors said that he knew nothing about it, and Perceval told him what he knew.

"And know," he said, "that they told me I'd soon have you both for company.* But they said nothing to me about this maiden, and, therefore, I wonder that Providence has brought her here."

"Indeed," said Galahad, "to my knowledge I wouldn't have come here if it hadn't been for her. Therefore, I can truly tell you that I've come more because of her than anyone else."

They laughed with him and began to tell their adventures, and Bors said to Galahad, "If your father Sir Lancelot were here now, it would seem to me that we lacked nothing."

Galahad answered, "It can't be so now, since God doesn't wish it."

Then Sir Perceval said, "Oh, Sir Galahad, in my opinion you've seen many good knights on this [167] quest. Who do you think has the greatest knightly ability of all those you've seen?"

"Indeed," said Galahad, "I've seen many good knights. But more than all the others, I've given my respect and acclaim to Sir Tristan, and after him to Palamedes, who rates little less in chivalry than Sir Tristan."

And both the others agreed to that, for they had already experienced it.

They spoke much that day of the adventures of the quest and the good knights who were going on the adventures and of the marvels that were happening there. Speaking of this, they traveled over the sea until the hour of nones. Then it seemed to them that they were far from the kingdom of Logres, for the ship ran always before a strong wind. When it was exactly the hour of nones, they reached harbor between two spits of land in a strange place, marvelously secluded. When they reached harbor there, they saw another ship between other spits of land, where they could not go, although they wanted to, except over all the rocks.

"My lords," said the maiden, "on that ship is the adventure for which God brought you three together. You must leave this one and go to that one."

"Gladly," they said.

Then they went out onto the rocks, helped the maiden out, and tied the bark so it could not drift away.

After they had left the ship in which they had come, they went toward the other and found it richer and more beautiful than the one from which they had come. But they wondered greatly that they saw neither man nor woman on board. They drew closer to see if anyone were inside. When they wanted to go on board, they looked toward the end of the deck and saw an inscription written in Chaldean, which said something terrifying to anyone who wanted to go on board. And know that Galahad did not know how to read the letters, but that Lord who had performed a beautiful miracle for him and given him wonderful powers showed him then such a great sign of love: He instantly made him know Chaldean, and he read the letters, which spoke thus—and know that they spoke as if the ship spoke for itself: OH, YOU MAN WHO WANT TO ENTER INTO ME, TAKE GOOD CARE NOT TO ENTER INTO ME UNLESS YOU ARE FULL OF FAITH, FOR KNOW WELL THAT THERE IS NOTHING IN ME EXCEPT FAITH. AND IF YOU

---

*   Chapter 109.

ENTER HERE AND YOUR FAITH IS WANTING, AS SOON AS YOU ENTER, I WILL FAIL YOU, FOR I WILL NOT ENDURE YOU BUT WILL LET YOU FALL INTO THE SEA.

As soon as Galahad had read the inscription, he drew aside a little, as if frightened, for he was greatly amazed at what the letters said. Then he thought a little and told the others what the letters said, and he said he had never heard of such an entrance to a ship.

They replied, "My lord, this is the noblest adventure and the most beautiful that we've [169] ever found. And since the entrance is so marvelous, the inside must be more so."

"My lords," said the maiden, "know that this is the test of the true knights and loyal servants of Our Lord who go on this quest, for no knight in a state of mortal sin enters here who is not instantly lost."

"That is true," they said.

"Then," she said, "let's see what you'll do about it, for by this test I'll know if you are as good as they say."

They said, "We aren't as good as we should be."

Galahad said, "Now let's see who is good or bad, for if we are bad, we'll be lost here, unless God's mercy helps us. And if we are good, we'll go here safely."

The others said, "My lord, we want to enter. If we are bad and disloyal, we'll be lost here. And if there's no one bad here and we are good, Our Lord will have pity on us and make us go in safety."

"Now," said Galahad, "my advice is that we go inside, and we'll see the adventure for which God has brought us together."

They all agreed to that. Galahad went first, making the sign of the cross and commending himself to Our Lord, and entered. After him Perceval entered, then Bors, and then the maiden. Once they were inside, they saw the ship to be marvelously beautiful and rich and well furnished. What shall I tell you? They found it arranged in all respects just as on that day when Nascien entered it, for this ship was that same one, and they found there the bed about which the story has already spoken to you where it spoke to you about Nascien.* But now I will not speak to you about him, because I have already told you about him. They found the sword that lay across the bed, that sword that was of such great wonder and power as the story has already told you. And they found the crown King Solomon had put there and the letter, so that they could learn the truth about the ship and the sword.

After Galahad had read the letter, so that the others would know how and why everything about the ship had been made and put there, Perceval said, "Father of heaven, may You be praised, who have been pleased to show me such beautiful marvels as these."

The others said the same.

Then the maiden said, "Sir Galahad, do you see that sword?"

"Yes," he said.

---

* See *The History of the Holy Grail* chapters 19-23. That narration is considered part of the Post-Vulgate as well as the Vulgate.

"Because of it I've brought you here," she said. "You must see if you can draw it from its scabbard, and, if you draw it, know that you are the Very Good Knight who is to bring the adventures of the kingdom of Logres to an end."* [171]

"Indeed," he said, "if I could be such as you say, I should give great thanks for it to Our Lord."

"I believe that you are such," she said. "Now try it, for by this sword you'll be able to know. If you can draw it from the scabbard without harm, you may be sure that you are the one of whom I tell you."

"I'll try it," he said, "since it pleases you. But I ask these others to try it first."

"My lord," they said, "why should we try it, since you're with us? It would be wasted effort, for we know truly that you are a better knight than we."

"I don't know that," he said, "and even if I am such as you say, I ask you to try it first."

They consented when they saw that he insisted on it so much.

After that, without waiting any longer, Perceval went to the sword and tried to draw it, but he could not. And know that when he grasped the sword, it seemed to everyone that the ship was about to sink into the sea, so violently did it shake from side to side.

When Perceval saw that he could not draw the sword, he said to Bors, "Now you try it."

Bors tried to draw the sword, but he accomplished as much as Perceval.

After they had seen that they were getting nowhere with it, they said to Galahad, "My lord, now see, if you please, what honor God wants to give you here."

Then Galahad held up his hands toward the sky and said, "My Lord, Father Jesus Christ, if You please, grant me by Your pity to be able to draw it."

Then he crossed himself and drew the sword from the scabbard as easily as he wished. After he had drawn it, he held it up and looked at it. He found it as beautiful and clean as if someone had just cleaned it, and after he had looked at it well, he prized it more than any other sword he had ever seen.

Perceval, who also looked long at it, said to Sir Galahad, "Now you may well say that you have the best sword in the world and the richest that ever was, to my knowledge, in the kingdom of Logres. And it seems to me that it is rightfully yours, for you're the best knight in the world, and it's the best sword in the world. But one thing is missing, which grieves me, and which won't, I think, be so easily achieved."

"What's that?" asked Galahad.

"It's about this belt," he said, "which, as you see, is so poor and feeble that it couldn't last half a day. And this letter tells us that this belt has to be taken from it by a king's daughter and a virgin, and that she'll put there beautiful and suitable straps, as rich as are appropriate to such a rich sword. And she must make them of the thing she loves most about herself. Then it's necessary that that maiden put a

---

*   There is an obvious parallel between this sword test and the sword Galahad drew from the stone when he first came to Camelot (chapters 74-75), as well as with the one Arthur drew from a stone to prove his worthiness to be king (*The Story of Merlin,* chapter 5).

name to this sword.* We are missing all this, for we don't know who the maiden is or what her name is or where we can find her."

"Don't let it worry you," said Galahad, "for God, who has helped us until now, will continue to help us." [173]

After that, without waiting any longer, the maiden said, "My lords, don't worry. Know that I am that maiden who has the adventure of this sword."

"What?" asked Perceval. "Are you a king's daughter and such as is necessary to this sword?"

"That you'll see," she said, "God willing."

Then she drew from her breast a small silver purse, rich and well engraved, and she took from it a belt with as many straps as were necessary, the richest and most beautiful anyone ever saw in the kingdom of Logres, and they were worked with gold and precious stones and silk and the maiden's hair.

"My lords," she said, "you see here the straps of this sword."

They looked at them and said that without question they were the richest and most beautiful they had ever seen.

Then she said to them, "Know that they're made of the thing I loved most in myself, and if I loved it greatly, it isn't surprising, for, since King Arthur began to reign, nobody has seen such beautiful hair as I had. All the knights and ladies who saw it said this. But for this belt and these others that take the place of straps, I had myself shorn, and I found myself none the worse for it, since thereby I have brought such a beautiful adventure as this to a climax."

Then she took from the sword the other belt it had and put this one with it.

After that she said to Galahad, "Ungird your sword, and I will gird this one on you."

He did as she told him; at once she girded the good sword on him and asked him, "Do you know with what sword I have armed you?"

"No," he said, "not unless you tell me."

"Know, now," she said, "that I have armed you, by the strange straps, with the best sword a knight ever bore, the one with the greatest power."

"My lady," he said, "my thanks to you; you've given me a rich gift. But I ask you to tell me who you are, so that I'll be able to give some information to whoever asks me about the one who gave me such a sword."

"I'll tell you," she said. "Know that King Pellinor was my father, and Sir Perceval here is my full brother. Because I didn't want him to recognize me until I had accomplished this adventure, I concealed my identity from him as long as I could."

Then she removed from her face the piece of silk she had worn over it, and Perceval recognized her at once and was as happy as he could be; he went to embrace her, and the others were also wonderfully happy.

---

*   The sword is subsequently called the Sword of the Strange Straps, but there is no indication that Perceval's sister gives it this name or any other.

132. GALAHAD, PERCEVAL, AND BORS ENCOUNTER CAIAPHAS.*

Great was the joy they all felt over Perceval's sister, for it was a long time since they had seen her.† They sat down and began to speak of many things. Galahad, who felt a desire to sleep, went to lie in the bed, which was so beautiful and rich that they had never seen another like it.

When the maiden saw this, she said to the others, [175] "Now it seems to me that the letter is fulfilled, for I see that the Good Knight has laid himself in the bed that Solomon prepared for him a long time ago."

They said, "God has shown us a beautiful marvel here."

"He'll show you yet greater," she said, "if He pleases."

That day and night they stayed on the ship, and they spoke of many things.

When Galahad woke up he said, "Are we still at the bank where we found this ship?"

"No, my lord," they said, "it's a long time since we left it, and, therefore, we think that we're far out at sea."

"May God guide us," he said, "to a place where our souls may be saved, for I'm not worried about our bodies."

They spoke a great deal that night of many things, until day came, at which they were very happy.

When the day began to grow lighter, they found themselves at the edge of the sea beside a narrow spit of land, but it was so high and pointed that it seemed to reach the clouds. There was on that spit a great abundance of trees. When they saw the spit so high and narrow, they said they had never seen anything like it. As they were standing looking at its crest, they lowered their eyes and saw before them, at its foot, so near the sea that it could be reached with two casts of a lance, a man so old that no one would believe there could be anyone older in the world. He had hair as white as snow and locks so long that they reached the ground. And know that he had lived so long on this spit of land that he had nothing with which to cover himself except his hair. When they saw him, they wondered what he was, although they realized he was a man or a woman.

Galahad said to the others, "Let's go see who he is, and if he needs our help, let's help him, because he's God's creature as we are, and in my opinion he needs it greatly. I think that he has lived longer on this rock than he had wanted."

The others agreed to that, for it certainly seemed to them that he spoke the truth. Then all three left the ship, leaving the maiden on board, and they went along the spit to the man who was sitting between two trees. They realized that he was a man, but he was so old that they did not think anyone could live long enough to reach such old age. He wanted to stand up to meet them, but he could not.

Galahad asked him, "Where are you from? I ask you to tell us the truth about yourself and your age, what adventure brought you here, how you live, and if you've been here long."

---

* Corresponds to Magne II:173-179; Piel 290-292.

† We last saw her (chapters 67-69) on an island trying to get someone to kill Gawain in revenge for his killing of her family.

Then he said in the low, feeble voice of great age, [177] "I'm a man who has lived long and has had much labor and suffering and little good. Caiaphas is my name. I was bishop of Jerusalem in the time when Titus was Emperor of Rome. But for something the Jews did to a prophet who was called Jesus, we were all lost and destroyed. On me—who truly had not deserved as much as the others—Vespasian, Titus's son, had greater mercy, for he didn't want to kill me like the others but had me put alone in a small boat, without sail or oars, and had me sent out to sea to receive the kind of death God wanted to give me. Once I was on the sea, I went more than two hundred years without eating or drinking or finding people who would receive me into their company. Rather, they reviled me and cursed me as soon as I told them about myself, and I didn't find a single one who took pity on me or who would kill me, for I'd gladly have had them kill me, since they didn't want me in their company.

"In this way, as I've been telling you, I drifted in torment upon the sea more than two hundred years, for I could neither drown myself in the sea nor die of the great hunger I felt. I drifted that way until Providence brought the boat here to this spit of land where I am now. And when I found myself here, I was very happy, for I truly thought that people lived here who would do me some good. After I had gone around the spit and seen that no one lived here, I returned to my little boat, for I imagined that I'd have help sooner on the sea than on a spit of land. And when I got to where I had left it, it was already so far distant on the sea that I couldn't see it. So I remained here, and it's a very long time that I've neither eaten nor drunk nor seen anyone who would succor me. Although I've lived until now in a state of ravenous hunger night and day, I can't die, but I live in such misery as you can see, for, if I could die like any other sinner, I would prefer death to life, for such a life is worse than death."*

When they heard this, they crossed themselves in amazement, for they did not believe a mortal man could live so long without eating.

Perceval said, "Sir Galahad, what shall we do with this man? Shall we put him in our ship and take him to the kingdom of Logres in order to show off this marvel?"

"That may not be," said Galahad, "for he may not enter in that ship, which signifies Holy Church, for he [179] who is to enter there must be filled with faith and belief. Therefore, I tell you that this man may not enter, for he has neither faith nor belief, nor will he ever have; rather, he has sinned in consenting to the death of the Lord of the world and the King of Kings, and he agreed to the great treachery that was committed then. Therefore, I say in just counsel that we leave him here, for I truly believe that the reason he has suffered this torment until now is because Our Lord wants him to be lost as vengeance for the great wrong he did to the Son of God."

Then the others said that Galahad spoke justly.

"If it pleases Our Lord that he be saved, He will save him, and if it pleases Him that he be lost, we have nothing to say about it, for he isn't of our faith."

---

* For the origin of Caiaphas's punishment, see *The History of the Holy Grail* chapter 3.

Then they let him be thus between the two trees* and returned to their ship. After they were on board, the wind struck them so that it took them over the sea, far away from the spit of land. They commended themselves to God, and each one said such prayers as he knew. After that they recounted to the maiden the adventure they had found on the spit of land, and she crossed herself with amazement and said that she had never heard an adventure of such great wonder.

"And indeed," said Bors, "King Arthur and his court will wonder greatly at it, if by chance God wishes us to go there at some time and to tell it there."

133. GALAHAD, PERCEVAL, AND BORS FREE THE CASTLE OF THE COUNT ARNAULT.†

Speaking of this, they started over the sea as chance took them, the maiden with them, from whom they received great kindness. One day it happened that chance took them close to a castle that stood by the sea.

As soon as they saw it, Perceval said, "If it please God, I would much prefer to land in another place than this one, for my heart tells me that some grief will come to us here."

"We can land only where God wishes," said Galahad, "for He, who has brought us here and wants us to land here, will help us in everything."

As soon as they had said this, they found themselves on the shore. They took their maiden, left the ship, and entered the castle, for they could not go in any other direction. They blessed the Lord God and praised Him because He had brought them safely to port and made them pass through so many adventures in peace. As soon as they had entered the castle, fully armed but for shields and helmets, Galahad looked at the front of an ancient church and saw his shield leaning against the door.

He pointed it out to the others and said, "Praised be God, for He hasn't forgotten my shield but, by His mercy, has given it to me." [181]

They said that it was a beautiful miracle. He went to the shield, took it, and slung it at his neck, and thus they all went on foot through the village.

They had not gone far when they met a large, fierce squire who asked them, "Where are you from, sir knights?"

"We're from King Arthur's house," they said.

"You should be sorry for that," said the squire, "for in this castle they hate no people in the world as much as those of King Arthur's house. Therefore, I assure you that you've come to an evil shelter, which you won't be able to leave without dishonor."

"We don't know about that," they said, "but know that if anyone expects to dishonor us, he'll find himself the worse off for it."

---

*   "trees" as in Piel (292). Magne has "ships."
†   Corresponds to Magne II:179-189; Piel 293-298.

Then they began to ask in the village for lodging, for they wanted to stay there until they had horses.

A man came to them and said, "My lords, you labor in vain, for there's no one in the village so bold that he'd dare shelter you. You must go to the fortress, and there they'll shelter you in some manner."

When they heard this, they went there and found a great court of knights and ladies, maidens and other people. And where they expected to find someone who would receive them well—as it was the custom at that time for knights errant to be received in foreign places—they saw coming toward them three armed knights, large, brutal, and fierce. And know that they were brothers. When they reached them, they did not greet them, but one of them went to the maiden, because she seemed beautiful to him, and seized her.

Perceval, who was very brave, stepped in front of the others and said, "Sir knight, let go of the maiden, since she isn't yours, for we have had her with us for a long time, and you won't carry her off as you think."

"Is that so?" he said; "and do you want to take her from me? In an evil hour have you thought of it."

Then he went to a sword, which was suspended from a pillar, and charged at Perceval to hit him on the head, which was unarmed except for his iron cap. But Bors, who loved Perceval dearly, would not permit it and gave the knight such a great blow on the head that he split him to his belt, and he instantly fell dead in the middle of the palace.

When the other two brothers saw this blow, they did not dare stay there any longer, because they were unarmed, and they turned to the others and cried out, "To arms! To arms!"

Then they and all the others armed themselves, and they had a horn sounded so that everyone from the village would gather at the palace.

When Galahad saw that they were arming themselves, he said to Perceval and Bors, "My lords, I see clearly that we can't leave here without a fight; let each of us take helmet and shield and defend himself bravely to the best of his ability, for it seems to me that we have great need."

They said they would do so. Then they went to a room that contained the [183] arms of the castle's people. After they had taken helmets and shields, the best they could find, they returned to the palace and found that the castle folk had already begun fighting against Galahad, and that there were already more than a hundred armed men there. But he was defending himself so marvelously that he had already killed fifteen* of them, and he was so lively and agile that he was going through them as if there were no one there, nor was there anyone there so strong or so well armed that he could stand against Galahad's stroke, nor would armor serve him, because the good sword that Galahad bore cut everything according to his wish. Therefore, they came to know him so well in such a short time that there was no one there who would dare await his blow. When the other two arrived and saw Galahad doing so well, they took their swords, entered the press, and began to give

---

* This is one of the few occasions on which Galahad kills his opponents, and he is deeply troubled about it later. See also chapter 134.

blows to right and left and to deal out such death in a short time that as quickly as possible more than sixty of the knights were dead and a large part of the other men. What shall I tell you? So many were the dead and wounded there that it was a marvel. The cries were so great that all the people of the village gathered there, and the knights defended themselves so well and bravely and helped each other so well that not one of those who had expected to kill or capture them came among them without finding death or a mortal wound. When the two brothers saw that they could not stand against these foreign knights, who had already killed almost all their men, they wanted to leave the palace in order to flee, but they could not, for the three knights went to them and killed them as well as all who came to their aid.

When they saw that they had cleared the palace of their enemies, the three knights said, "Let's go outside, if we can find more of these people, for they're a bad sort and possessed of the devil."

Then they went seeking here and there, and they reached an isolated chamber near a garden. Then they heard a man making a great lamentation, so that he seemed to be in great torment.

Galahad stopped and said to the others, "Do you hear that lamentation?"

"Yes," they said, "do you know who's making it?"

"Yes," he said.

"Know," said Galahad, "that this is Count Arnault, a very good man who has led a moral life; he greatly loves his Creator and honors Holy Church. But from these bad sons of his, whom we have just killed, he received dishonor and grief. Therefore, God wanted them to have this bad death." [185]

Then they entered the room and found the count lying in chains, mortally injured. And know that Galahad knew about him not from any living person in the world but by the will of Our Lord.

They reached him and said to him, "My lord, how do you feel?"

The count, who was close to death, asked them, "Who are you who question me?"

"We're foreign knights," they said, "whom perhaps you don't know."

"Yes, I do," he said. "I know you much better than you think. Take me to the palace, and in that field outside the castle go find me a hermit with whom I may speak, for I've forgotten to tell him things about which I feel myself guilty toward my Creator."

They did as he told them. After they had taken him to the palace, Bors and Perceval went on foot, still armed, to summon the hermit. And know that the people of the village who saw them going through the streets did not appear in front of them but fled as fast as they could. Then they went to the hermit and told him about the count's summons and all the events in the castle.

"My lords," said the hermit, "blessed be the hour in which you were born, for what you've done greatly pleases Our Lord, and for this He brought you here, to destroy these people, who were the worst, most evil men in all the kingdom of Logres."

Then he came with them to the count.

When Galahad saw him, he fell to his knees before the hermit and said to him, "My lord, mercy! Give us counsel about this deed we've done here today, about these men, all of whom we've killed. We did it defending ourselves, but it can't be that we haven't committed a great sin."

"Oh, my lord!" said the good man, "don't think that, for, so help me God, by killing them you did the best deed that knights errant ever did, and much more by killing the three brothers. That was a beautiful miracle, for they were the most evil, brutal knights in Great Britain, and, because of their treachery, all the other men of this place were of such evil habits that they were worse than heretics, and they never did anything that wasn't against God."

Then he made Galahad get up from before him.

"For God's sake, my lord," said Galahad, "all this grieves me greatly, because to me they seemed Christians."

"Don't let it grieve you," said the good man, "for, so help me God, Our Lord thanks you for everything you've done here. Know that He sent you here for nothing else but to kill them, for [187] they aren't Christians but the worst men in the world, and I'll tell you how I know.

"A year ago now, Count Arnault here was lord of this castle. He had three sons, good knights at arms, and a daughter, one of the most beautiful maidens in the kingdom of Logres. All three brothers loved their sister with carnal love so much that they had to lie with her, and because she told her father, they killed her. When the count, who was a very good man, saw the wrong that his sons had done, he felt such grief that he wanted to drive them from the land, but they wouldn't let him. They went to him by night and wounded him very badly, and they would certainly have killed him were it not for two of his nephews who freed him. When they saw that their father had escaped death that time, they seized him again and threw him in prison, and they've held him there until now. Once they were lords of the castle, they committed all the treacherous acts one can imagine. What shall I tell you? They did so many false deeds that it was a wonder this castle didn't fall into the abyss.

"Yesterday morning it happened that the count here sent word that I should come to him and bring the Body of Christ. I did it gladly, for I loved him. When I got here, they gave me more mockery and grief than pagans or heretics would have done. I endured it gladly for the honor of Him for whose dishonor they did it. After I reached the count and he had confessed and received the Body of Christ, I told him what they had done to me.

"He said to me, 'Endure, for your dishonor and mine will be avenged soon by three servants of Jesus Christ. The High Master sent this word to me.' And by this you may realize and be sure that Our Lord sent you here specifically to kill them.'"[*]

---

[*]   Location of quotation marks as in Piel (297). Magne ends the count's discourse after "Jesus Christ."

Then the hermit approached Count Arnault, and the count said to him, "My lord, you are welcome. I sent for you in order to tell you something I had forgotten."

Then the others drew aside, and the count said to him, "My lord, I feel myself guilty toward King Arthur, whose vassal I am, for I've known and seen his wife's and Lancelot's treason and have never told him. Now I'm telling you, and I ask you to tell King Arthur. If you tell him, I think he'll have his wife guarded in such a way that she won't ever again commit such a sin."

The hermit answered him, "I'll think it over, and if it seems wise to tell the king, I'll tell him." [189]

"I beg you to do so," said the count.

Then he turned to Galahad and said, "Galahad, holy creature, I've long awaited you, and now, thanks to God, you're here. For the sake of God and courtesy, let me lean against you, and my soul will be happier when it leaves my body beside such a man as you are."

Galahad did so with a very good will.

When he had put the count's head on his chest, the count shut his eyes, expecting death, and said as well as he could, "My Lord Father Jesus Christ, into Your hands I commend my soul and my spirit."

Then his head dropped, and he lay a long time, so that the others thought he was dead. But after a while he said, "Galahad, servant of Jesus Christ, the High Master sends you this word through me, that you have avenged Him well today on His enemies, and all the company of angels is joyful about it. Now you must go as quickly as you can to the house of the Fisher King, who has awaited you so long, so that he may be healed. All three of you depart as soon as chance permits."

The count said this much and no more, for at once his soul left his body.

134. THE ADVENTURE OF THE WHITE STAG; THE DEATH OF PERCEVAL'S SISTER; GALAHAD, PERCEVAL, AND BORS PART.*

When those who remained alive in the castle saw that the count was dead, they raised a great lamentation, for they had loved him dearly, but they had not dared show it for fear of the three brothers. They buried him with great honor in a hermitage. The next morning Galahad, Bors, and Perceval took whichever horses they wanted and a good palfrey for the maiden, for they could find many horses and weapons there, and they mounted and set out. They rode until they reached a forest. They had not gone far in the forest when they saw pass before them a white stag, guarded by four lions. It went in front of them, cutting across the forest.

"Now," said Galahad, "I see an adventure that I've seen before,[†] because of which I exerted myself a little. Now may it please God to let us learn something about it before the stag leaves us."

---

*	Corresponds to Magne II:189-207; Piel 298-307.
†	Chapter 84.

"By God," said the others, "we, too, have seen this stag before."

"Now let's go after it," said Galahad, "for my heart tells me that this time we'll learn something about it," and the others agreed.

Then they went after the stag. They entered a valley and saw amid some low hills a little hermitage where there lived a [191] good old man who had been living a holy life, serving Our Lord there for a long time. The stag and the lions went into the hermitage. When the knights saw this, they dismounted in front of the hermitage. They went to the chapel and found the good man, who was already dressed to say the Mass of the Holy Spirit. When they saw him, they laid aside their lances, shields, and helmets and said they had arrived at a good time. When the priest got to the secret of the Mass, they saw something at which they wondered more than at anything else they had ever seen, for they saw—or so it seemed—that the stag turned into a Man and seated Himself on the altar in a rich, beautiful chair. Then they saw another marvel, for they saw that the four lions turned into four different figures, one into the figure of an angel, the second into the form of a lion a thousand times more beautiful than it was before, the third into the figure of an eagle, and the fourth into the figure of an ox. Each of them had four wonderfully large wings, with which, it seemed to the onlookers, they could well fly if they wished. After that these four each took a leg of the chair where the Man sat, and they went out with it through a pane of glass in the apse of the chapel, so that the pane of glass neither broke nor was any worse than it had been before. Then they saw nothing of the Man or the others.

They heard a voice, which said to them, "In such a way did the Son of God enter into the Blessed Virgin, so that neither her virginity nor the Blessed Virgin herself was hurt or spoiled."

When they heard this voice, they fell to the ground stunned, for the voice was so loud that it seemed to them that the whole chapel had fallen and the voice had been heard by the whole world. After they had returned to their senses, they saw that the good man had already said Mass. Then they went to speak with him, and they asked him for God's sake to tell them the meaning of what they had seen.

"What did you see?" he asked.

"My lord," they said, "we saw a stag, which we afterwards saw change its shape. And four lions, which kept the stag company, were also changed," and they told him how.

When the good man heard this, he said, "Oh, my lords, you are welcome! Now I know by what you've told me that you're the good men and knights who will accomplish the quest for the Holy Grail and who will suffer great trials and labors in achieving its adventures. You are those to whom Our Lord will reveal His great secrets and hidden things. He has already shown you a large part of it, for when He changed Himself from Stag to Man, He showed you that, as a Man, He suffered [193] mortal torment when, by dying, He conquered death and gave life to the world. And He should indeed be represented by the stag, for just as the stag, when it is old, becomes young, leaving its earthly flesh, so Jesus Christ came from death to life when He left His earthly flesh, for He left His mortal body, which He had taken within the Blessed Virgin. And because this blessed Lord had never a stain of sin, He appeared in the likeness of a white stag without any spot. By the four in His company you should understand the four evangelists, the four blessed persons who put some of Jesus Christ's works into writing, what He did and what He said while He was among men as an earthly Man. And know that never may another knight know the truth of it as you now know it. Thus the blessed Lord has revealed himself many times in this land to good men and knights in the semblance of a white stag. But know that He won't appear in such a likeness again. He may show himself to His friends in other ways, but not again in this."

When they heard this, they wept in piety and gave thanks to Our Lord for what He had shown them. All that day they stayed with the good man in order to hear the good deeds about which he told them, and they took great pleasure in them. The next day, after they had heard Mass, when they had to move on, Perceval took the sword that his sister bore, which was from Merlin's stone, the one Galahad had given up for the sword of the strange straps.* He said he would bear it from then on for love of Galahad, and he left his in the good man's house. Then they left there and rode until midday. They arrived near a strong, beautiful castle, but they did not enter it, for their road did not lead through it.

After they had drawn away from it a little, they saw a fully armed knight coming after them, who asked them, "My lords, is this young lady who is traveling with you a virgin?"

"Yes," said Bors, "truly."

Then the knight took her by the bridle and said, "So help me God, you shall not go until you satisfy the custom of this castle."

When Perceval saw that the knight was taking his sister away, he said to him, "Sir knight, you're neither wise nor courteous to say this, for a maiden should be able to go anywhere freely,† and all the more such a noblewoman as this one, who is a king's daughter."

As he was saying this, suddenly ten armed knights emerged from the castle, and there came with them a young lady who bore a silver basin.

They said to the three knights as soon as they reached them, "My lords, this maiden must perforce observe the custom." [195]

"And what's the custom of this castle?" asked Galahad.

"My lord," said one of them, "each maiden who passes by here must give this basin full of the blood of her arm, and no one passes by here who doesn't give."

"May harm come to him who established such a custom," said Galahad, "for such a custom is especially dissolute and filthy. However others may have observed the custom for you, she shall not do so: as long as I have a soul in my body, she won't do what you ask, believe me."

"God forbid!" said Perceval. "I'd rather die," and Bors said the same.

"By God," said the others, "it's death for you, for in this castle there are so many good men to see this matter through that if you were the best knights in the world, you couldn't stand against them."

Then they charged at one another, and in the joust it happened that the three knocked down all the others before their lances broke. Then they took their swords

---

* Galahad took the sword from Merlin's stone in chapter 75 and gave it up for the sword of the strange straps in chapter 131.

† literally, "free of everything, wherever she goes."

and went among them, knocking them down and killing them as if they were beasts, and they could have killed them all, had they wished. When the inhabitants of the castle saw this, more than forty armed knights came out to help their comrades.

Before them came an old man, who said to the three, "My lords, for God's sake, have pity on yourselves and don't get yourselves killed like this, for that would be a great loss, because you're good men and good knights. Therefore, I beg you, before anything more happens, let the maiden give what we ask of her."

"Indeed," said Galahad, "your efforts are vain, for, as long as she listens to me, what you want cannot be."

"What?" he asked, "do you want to die, then?"

"Not yet," said Galahad, "but, so help me God, since we're in this difficulty, I'd rather die than permit such great treachery as you seek."

Then the battle began among them, and those from the castle were already at least forty, for they increased constantly. But Galahad, who had the sword of the strange straps, struck to the left and right and killed all those he reached, and he performed so many marvels among them that no one who saw him would have thought him mortal man but some strange marvel, for he performed in such a way that he never gave ground but constantly gained on his enemies, and it was worth much to him that the other two defended him to the right and left, so that no one could reach him except from in front.

Thus the battle lasted until night, for aid to those of the castle [197] increased constantly. But the three knights, who in skill at arms were such that there were none better in the world, defended themselves all the while so well that they never had the worst of it or lost ground. They held on so long that dark night arrived, so that they had perforce to part. And know that of those of the castle a full hundred lay on the field dead or wounded.

Then the old knight went to the three and said, "My lords, we beg you by your honor and courtesy to come lodge with us tonight, and we promise you in good faith that tomorrow we'll return you to this field just as you are now. Know that we'll do you as much honor and service as we can—not less than they would in King Arthur's house, if you were there—for we know you're from there. And do you know why I ask you to be our guests? Because I know well that as soon as you know the truth about this custom, you'll quickly agree to let the maiden give of her blood to us. Come along, since they ask you."

They agreed. Then they called a truce and entered the castle together. You never saw greater joy than the hosts showed at having the three as guests.

After the three knights had supped, they asked the others how this custom had been established and why. One of them said, "This I'll certainly tell you. Know that there is a lady here, our lady and that of all this land. This castle is hers and many others. It happened that she contracted leprosy. We sent near and far for all the doctors we knew, and not one of them knew how to help her. At last an old, wise man said to us that if we could obtain blood from maidens who were virgin in will and deed and who were daughters of kings and queens, and if we anointed our lady with that blood, she'd be cured at once. When we heard this, we immediately established a custom that every maiden who passed by here would give us a basin full of blood from her arm,* and we set guards at the doors to capture all who passed by in order to have blood from them until we find that one by whom our lady is to be cured. Then the custom began. Now you've heard how this was established and what we're asking of you. Now do what you please about it."

Then the maiden said in a whisper to Galahad, Bors, and her brother, [199] "My lords, you've certainly heard how this was established. I tell you that I'll heal this lady, if it pleases you for me to observe the custom of this castle, and I'll do it gladly, if you wish. Now tell me your pleasure."

"Indeed," said Galahad, "if you do it, I tell you that you are dead, for you are very young."

"By God," she said, "if I die in order to cure her, it's to my honor and my family's. If for no other reason, I ought to do it for you and for them, for if you meet in battle tomorrow as you did today, it can only be that greater loss will result than from my death. Therefore, I want to do what they want, so that this battle may be called off. I ask you by God and Saint Mary to let me."

They agreed, sadly and reluctantly.

Then the maiden called the other knights and said, "My lords, be joyful, for the battle you were to have fought tomorrow has been called off, for I promise you that tomorrow morning I will observe the custom the other maidens observed."

When they heard this, they thanked her and were very happy.

That night the three knights and the maiden were well served, and they would have been much better served had they wished to receive all the service the inhabitants of the castle wanted to do them.

In the morning, after they had heard Mass, the maiden went to the palace and said to the people there, "Go for the lady and bring her here, and these knights will see her."

At once they went for her. When the three knights saw her, they wondered greatly, for her face was so disfigured and she was in such pain that the maiden said it was a great wonder how she could live. The lady told the maiden to give her what she had promised, and she said she would do so gladly. Then she had them bring the silver basin. After that they lanced her right arm with a blade such as is suitable to that purpose. Her blood began to flow, and she crossed herself and commended herself to Our Lord.

Then she said to the lady, "I'm dying to cure you. For God's sake, pray for my soul."

When the basin was full of blood, she fainted. The three knights went to her, stanched the bleeding, and closed up the cut.

After she had lain unconscious for a long time, she came to and said, "Brother Perceval, I'm dying in order to save this lady. I ask you not to bury me, but, as soon as I'm dead, take me to the nearest seaport, put me in a little bark, and let me go just as chance [201] takes me. And I tell you truly that you won't come to the city

---

* In chapter 18, we saw Balin's maiden observe this custom and live to go on.

of Sarras, where you are to go with* the Holy Grail, so quickly that you won't find me at the foot of the tower.† Then do this much for me and for your honor: have me buried in the Spiritual Palace. Do you know why I ask this of you? Because Sir Galahad is to lie buried there, and you, too, brother."

When Perceval heard this request, he granted it, weeping, and said he would do it willingly.

She also said to them, "My lords, depart tomorrow at the hour of prime, and let each one take his own way until God brings you together again in the house of the Fisher King. And you, Sir Galahad, who are now the best knight in the world and the one to whom God has given most grace, for God's sake, hurry back to Camelot, for know truly that King Arthur desperately needs you to return to him, and if you don't go, he'll suffer such a great loss that it won't be easily amended."

After she had said that, she kept silent a little to rest, and after a while she said, "Have my Savior come to me."

They sent for a hermit who lived near the castle, and he came quickly, since he saw that they had such great need. After she had confessed, she received her Savior. After that, she arranged her hands in a cross on her breast, and her soul left her. And the three knights felt such grief that they did not expect to be comforted soon.

On that same day, the lady was cured, for as soon as they bathed her in the blood of the holy maiden, she was clean of all her leprosy. At this the three knights were happy, and all the others from the castle. After that, they returned to the palace where the maiden was, to carry out her request. They had a beautiful, strong bark found and covered with rich silken hangings, so the rain could not bother her. Then they took a bed, as rich and beautiful as if it had been for the body of King Arthur, and they put it in the bark and laid the maiden on it. After that they pulled the bark to the sea.

Bors said to Perceval, "It grieves me that we aren't putting beside her a letter by which people will know where she was from and how she died, if by chance she reaches some strange land."

"I'll tell you," said Perceval, "that I laid at her head a letter that sets forth her whole lineage, how she died, and all the adventures she helped to accomplish."

"Indeed," said Galahad, "you've done well, for someone may find her now [203] who will do her greater honor after he knows about her."

As long as the people of the castle could see the bark, they stood on the shore, weeping and saying that the maiden had done a very good deed in order to cure a strange lady. When they could no longer see the bark, they returned to their castle. The three knights said they would not enter the castle again and for the others to have them given their arms and horses, which they did gladly.

After they were armed and ready to ride, they saw the sky grow dark, and it began to produce rain and lightning and thunder. When they saw this, they went into a chapel that stood in the middle of the road, because of the bad weather they saw coming, and they left the horses in a porch. After this the weather grew violent; it began to rain hard, with a great deal of thunder and lightning, and sheet lightning

---

*   Both texts have "after." Galahad, Perceval, and Bors will take the Grail with them on a ship to Sarras in chapter 151.

†   Chapter 151.

began to fall so thickly about the castle that it was amazing. All that day the tempest lasted, so great and wild that it knocked down half the walls of the castle, at which the knights were badly frightened, for they would not have believed those walls could be knocked down in two years by any harm that could come to them.

When it was the hour of vespers and the bad weather had stopped, they saw coming toward them an armed knight, badly wounded in the body and head.

He was saying over and over again, "Oh, God! Help me, for I have great need!"

After him was coming a knight with a black shield and a dwarf, who were calling to him as they rode, "By my faith, you're a dead man, and you won't be safe there."

Again the knight said, "Oh, my Lord, Father Jesus Christ, help me. Don't let me be lost at this time."

When the three knights saw how that knight pleaded with Our Lord, they felt pity for him, and Galahad said he would like to help him.

"My lord," said Bors, "let me do it, not you, for you don't have to go for just one knight."

Galahad agreed, since it pleased Bors. Bors mounted.

Then he said, "My lords, I'm leaving you, and tomorrow you'll ride on and try to go to where we three are to meet: the house of the Fisher King."

"Yes, we'll do so," they said.

Then they parted. Bors went after the knight to deliver him from the man who was following him. But now the story stops speaking of him and turns to Galahad and Perceval, who remained in the chapel. [205]

The story tells that Galahad and Perceval stayed all night in the chapel, and they prayed fervently to Our Lord to guard and guide Bors wherever he went. The next day, when it was fully light, they got on their horses and returned to the castle to see what had happened to the people inside. When they arrived at the gate, they found it burned and the walls knocked down. Then they went forward, and they found no man or woman alive and no house not burned and collapsed. When they reached the palace, they found everything on the ground and all the knights dead, some here, others there, just as Our Lord had killed them because of the evil He had found in them. When they saw this, they said that it had been the Lord God's vengeance.

As they were speaking of this, they heard a voice, which said to them, "This is vengeance for the blood of the good maidens whom they captured in this castle for the earthly health of a false sinner, for Our Lord's vengeance is beautiful and marvelous, and the man is foolish who goes against Him even in a matter of life and death."

When they went through the castle, looking at the damage that had occurred there, they found beside a chapel a beautiful cemetery where there were many trees and good green grass, and there were as many as sixty gravestones. The place was so beautiful that there seemed to have been nothing of the storm there, and unquestionably it was so, for there lay the bodies of the maidens who had died for the evil lady.

When they entered the cemetery on horseback, just as they were, they found on each gravestone letters that told the name of the maiden who lay there. They went around the cemetery until they found that twelve daughters of kings lay there. When they saw this, they said that the people of the castle had upheld an evil custom and that the people of the land had done great evil by enduring it so long, for many good men could have sprung from these maidens. Until the hour of tierce they remained there, looking at those marvels. When they left, they rode to a nearby forest.

When they reached the edge of the forest, they stopped, and Perceval said, "Sir Galahad, now the time has come for us to part and for each to go his own way. I pray to Our Lord to guide us so that we may meet again soon, for, so help me God, I never found company in which I had so much pleasure as in yours. Therefore, this parting is more grievous to me than you know. But it must be, since it pleases Our Lord."

Then they embraced each other and wept hard, as they had to part, for they loved each other from the heart, and this became apparent at their death, for one lived only a little after the other.* Thus they parted at the edge of the forest called Aula. [207]

But now the story stops speaking of Perceval in order to tell what happened to Galahad when he returned to the kingdom of Logres and how he delivered King Arthur and the land of Logres from the Saxons who had come there in league with King Mark of Cornwall. But before it speaks of Galahad, it tells briefly by whose counsel they had come there and in what manner.

135. KING MARK OF CORNWALL INVADES LOGRES, BESIEGES ARTHUR IN CAMELOT.†

At this point the story and true history tell that King Mark of Cornwall had heard that his nephew Tristan had gone to Great Britain, taking Queen Iseut with him and leaving her at Joyous Guard. King Mark loved Iseut so dearly that he could not forget her, but he was as miserable as he could be because of her, and many times he had wanted to send word to King Arthur to return her, but he did not dare, for he knew that Tristan loved her so much that King Arthur would not send her back for anything, and even if he wanted to do so, he would not, for love of King Ban's lineage, all of whom loved Tristan dearly. In this pain and grief King Mark lived two years without Iseut, and because of her he hated King Arthur so much that if he could have annoyed him in any way, he would have done so gladly.

When the quest for the Holy Grail began and the knights of the Round Table took their oath and left King Arthur's house, the news ran far and wide in many lands, and there were many, natives as well as foreigners, who told more lies than truths. Thus it happened that they said in Gaul and Gaunes, in Little Britain and in Cornwall, that all the knights of the Round Table had died in the quest for the Holy Grail. The people of Gaul and Gaunes and Benoic were deeply grieved by that, for

---

*   Chapter 152.
†   Corresponds to Magne II:207-217; Piel 307-312.

they would have died for love of Lancelot and King Ban's lineage. News of their grief reached King Mark.

When he saw that they confirmed the rumor as true, he said, "Now King Arthur may well say that his power has come to naught, since the knights of the Round Table are dead."

Then he took counsel with Aldret about what he could do, for there was no one in the world he hated as mortally as King Arthur, and he would gladly have gone to do him harm at such a time, if he had thought he could accomplish it.

Aldret, who was full of deviltry, said to him, "I'll show you how you can destroy him as he is now. [209] You know that the Saxons are a great people, powerful in lands and friends, and they hate King Arthur so mortally that if they could do him harm and take the kingdom from him it would give them the greatest possible pleasure. Send someone to tell them how King Arthur has lost the company of the Round Table, and make them understand that, if they want to come to the kingdom of Logres under such circumstances, they can easily conquer it. And know that they'll come there gladly as soon as they get your message. Let them know that you'll be there with them, to help them, with all the strength you have; set a day, and know that they'll be there with you on time."

King Mark did just as Aldret had advised him, for he sent them that news the best and fastest way he could, and the Saxons, who hated no one in the world so much as King Arthur, were delighted when they heard the news. They gathered all their strength, got into ships and galleys, and crossed to Great Britain, landing in Osinedot. King Mark, who had plotted all this treason, started on his way with all his people and met them at the very place where they landed, and they were pleased with each other. That day they rested in a forest near the sea, and they stayed there as secretly as they could so they would not be discovered. When night came, they took to the field and began to march toward the city of Camelot, for the moon was bright. There they thought to find King Arthur, because he stayed there more than anywhere else. So the Saxons went, resting by day and marching by night, until they arrived on a Saturday at Joyous Guard.

King Mark, who knew well that Queen Iseut was there, took as many as fifty well-armed men from among his knights and the Saxons and said to them, "Let's go to that castle, but as silently as we can."

They did just as he instructed them. The inhabitants of the castle, who had not feared anything in a long time, were not on guard but kept the gates open night and day. In this way King Mark entered with all his knights. They were all on foot, for if the horses had made a noise and the people inside had sent someone to lock the gates before the invaders got inside, they would not then have feared anything, for the castle was extremely strong. King Mark went directly to where he knew the queen was and took her by force from a room where she was sleeping with a large company of [211] ladies and maidens. Then he had fire set to the village and slaughtered so many of the men there that few of them were left alive. After they had killed the people, burned the village, and taken plunder, they left and went on their way, happy with the great booty they had taken.

And know that King Mark wanted none of that booty, since he had Queen Iseut, but he said to them, "Now plan to ride to where King Arthur is. If we proceed wisely, he with his few men won't be able to stand against us."

And they said that they would do exactly as he wanted.

Thus King Mark expected to take King Arthur by surprise, and it would certainly have been so. But news, which runs quickly, reached Camelot, where King Arthur had been very sad since he learned for a truth that many of the knights of the Round Table were already dead in the quest for the Holy Grail, and he cursed the quest and the man by whom it had been begun.

As he was standing thus sadly, he saw before him a squire from Joyous Guard, who said to him, "King Arthur, I bring you terrible, sad news."

"By God," said King Arthur, "if you brought me good news, it would be a great wonder, for it's a long time since I've heard any but bad. But whatever it is, tell me."

"I tell you," said the squire, "that King Mark of Cornwall, with all his forces and those of the Saxons, has invaded your kingdom, destroyed the land in many places, and killed many of your men. The castle of Joyous Guard, which feared nothing, is destroyed and burned, and know that they'll be here with you within three days."

"Is that true?" asked the king.

"Yes, unquestionably," said the squire. "I saw them at Joyous Guard, from which I escaped by great good fortune."

Then the king began to think, and after he had thought a long while, he said, "Oh, House of Camelot! How you were feared and respected as long as the good knights of the Round Table were here! Those who start this war against me would never try it if they knew that those knights were here."

Then a knight from Ireland stood up, a good knight at arms and very brave; he was the brother of one of the knights of the Round Table, Dinadas of Garlot.

He said to King Arthur, "My lord, until now you have been the most redoubted king in the world and the most famous, and you are still. If the knights of the Round Table have left our house, our house has not thereby become deserted, for there are still [213] some of the best knights in the world here, excepting always those. For, indeed, there are so many good men here that the army will be extremely great, and you won't have to order it to retreat from the field as long as God wishes you no harm. Therefore, I tell you not to be frightened by such news, for you have until now been thought one of the best men in the world. But if you fall short of your reputation, we'll think you one of the worst. Send for your knights and your men, of whom you have many round about Camelot, and move confidently against your enemies. Indeed, if you bear yourself forcefully, fortune—which favors the brave—will help you, and it should comfort you greatly that you are right and they are wrong."

The knight said so much that the king took heart and sent word throughout his whole land, as quickly as he could, to all those who held land of him, to come with great haste to help him. They did so as quickly as they could, for they loved him greatly. There gathered in Camelot more than two thousand mounted and armed men and a very great company of others.

On the fourth day, at the hour of prime, two armed knights came to the king where he was hearing Mass and said to him, "My lord, your enemies are coming. Already more than ten thousand men, mounted and armed, have emerged from the forest."

"Go," said the king, "and organize your men into battalions, and wait outside in the field, for I wouldn't want our enemies to find us shut in. But above everything else, take care not to scatter."

They did just as he commanded, for they made of their people ten battalions in which there were many good men and knights. But they were extremely few compared to the enemy, and because of that they took such losses that day as King Arthur would not have wanted for half his kingdom. What shall I tell you? After the king had heard Mass, he came out of the chapel, had himself armed as well as possible, and got on a horse he trusted. A good two hundred knights rode out with him, of whom the most cowardly was a very good knight at arms. After they had emerged from the village, they found that the others were already fighting. But there were so many against the king that his men could not hold out, and great numbers of them had already been killed, for they would not leave the field for death or [215] life. When the king saw his men in such difficulty, he sighed for the knights of the Round Table, and he struck his horse with his spurs and went to strike the enemy with great anger and desire to avenge his men, whom he saw being killed in front of him. He encountered a kinsman of King Mark and gave him such a blow with his lance that he laid him dead at his feet. The cries were loud, for the Cornish recognized King Arthur, and more than twenty of them charged toward him. He took his sword, which was good and sharp, and he was very bold and brave, defending himself so well that all who saw him said that that was certainly King Arthur; even his enemies praised him and respected him greatly, so well did they see him defend himself. King Arthur did many deeds of arms that day, although it was going ill for him, for his men were so few that they could not be seen among the others. But King Mark, who recognized him and hated him mortally, gave him such a great lance stroke in the left side that neither shield nor hauberk could keep the point from appearing through the shoulder on the other side. King Mark was so strong that he knocked Arthur and his horse to the ground, and in the fall the lance broke off, so that King Arthur lay there with the broken shaft in him.

When King Arthur's vassals saw their lord on the ground, they were so grieved that they put everything at risk. Then you would have seen good knights. Then you would have seen the bold. Then you would have seen the brave. Then you would have seen the faithful. Then you would have seen how they showed him the true love they had for him, for where he lay on the ground so badly wounded that he could not get up, they drove in among their enemies until by force they reached him, put him on his horse, and took him to the city, to the great displeasure of King Mark and his company. But know that they left so many of their friends dead on the field that their loss was very great. There were so many Saxons and Cornishmen dead that one could hardly count them, but the invaders cared nothing for any loss they might incur, for they were sure King Arthur was mortally wounded and could not live three days, and they praised King Mark for the blow he had struck and said that he was certainly worthy [217] of a king's crown who knew so well how to avenge himself on his enemies.

The Saxons also said, "Now the kingdom of Logres can't escape us, but we'll conquer it, for after King Arthur's death we won't find anyone to oppose us."

Then they ordered their tents and huts set up around the city and said they would not remove from there until they had conquered it.

Great was the sorrow and weeping among the people of the city when they saw King Arthur wounded, for they truly thought that he was mortally wounded. And no one saw the equal of the queen's grief. But after they had looked at the wound they were comforted, for the doctor said the wound was not mortal and he would soon have the king healed of it.

But now the story stops speaking of them and returns to Galahad.

136. GALAHAD, ON HIS WAY TO HELP KING ARTHUR, IS FOLLOWED BY PALAMEDES AND ARTHUR THE LESS.*

Here the story says that after Galahad left Perceval, he rode all that day without finding an adventure to tell of. The next day† at midday he happened on two knights who were fighting on foot, their horses tied to two trees, and nearby a knight on horseback was watching the battle. And if anyone asked me who these knights were, I would tell him that one of those fighting was Arthur the Less and the other Palamedes, the good pagan knight, and the third knight was Esclabor the Unknown, Palamedes's father.

At the moment when Galahad reached them, it happened that the two knights had stopped their fight to rest, for they were so weary that they could endure no more.

As soon as Palamedes saw the white shield with the red cross, he knew that the man who bore it was Galahad, the Very Good Knight, and he could not help saying to the man with whom he fought, "Indeed, knight, now I can truly say that if there were as much knightly ability in me as in that knight I see, I'd have defeated you in a short time, even had you had the skill at arms of four knights such as yourself."

Arthur the Less was amazed when he heard that, for he could not believe that there was in the world such a knight as Palamedes said.

Therefore, Arthur said at once, "Which is the one of whom you say that?"

Palamedes pointed him out. [219]

"Misfortune take me," said Arthur the Less, "if he'd conquer three such as I."

"Indeed," said Palamedes, "he'd do so, for he'd defeat five such."

"So help me God," said Arthur, "I wouldn't believe that until I saw it."

"Then I'll tell you what to do. You attacked me in order to see if you were a better knight than I, and it happens that you don't yet have any advantage; indeed,

---

*   Corresponds to Magne II:217-233; Piel 312-320.

†   Text reads, "the next day, on the third day."

perhaps you have here more of loss than gain. Leave this battle, if you please, and go test yourself against him. And if you don't find him such as I told you or better, don't consider me a knight."

"I agree to that," said Arthur, "but I don't want our fight to be abandoned thereby, for if you leave me now, know that wherever I find you, I'll call you back to it."

Thus the fight between Arthur the Less and Palamedes ended. As soon as Galahad saw that the fight was over and they would do no more there, he left that place and began to ride fast, for he was impatient to get to Camelot.

As soon as Arthur the Less was mounted, he began to ride after Galahad, and he said to Palamedes, "We are parting; remember our agreement."

"Don't speak of that," said Palamedes, "for if I ever knew the knight of the white shield and the red cross, he'll avenge me on you and destroy your arrogance easily."

Arthur the Less answered not a word to this but rode as fast as he could after Galahad, who was already some distance off.

Palamedes got on his horse and said to his father, "Let's follow them, and we'll see this knight's pride and foolishness broken."

"What?" asked his father; "do you know so well this knight who's riding away, that he's a better knight than this one who fought with you?"

"My lord," said Palamedes, "I tell you that he's the best knight in the world."

"This I'd gladly see," said his father.

Arthur the Less, riding forward ahead of them, said to Galahad when he reached him, "Sir knight, defend yourself against me. You must joust."

Then Galahad looked behind him, and when he saw Arthur, whom he did not recognize, asking a joust of him, he turned his horse toward him and struck him so hard that he knocked him and his horse to the ground, and Arthur was badly bruised, for the fall was great. Nevertheless, because he was of great heart and strength, he got up faster than another knight would have done and got on his horse with sorrow at what had happened to him. Galahad, who did not look at him again while he was mounting, had ridden a full three bow shots away from him.

Meanwhile, Palamedes had caught up with Arthur the Less and said to him, [221] "Now you know how the knight jousts, and if you don't want to die or be shamed further, stay away from him from now on, for, indeed, there's no way you can stand against him. And if he had wanted, he would already have killed you, but he stopped short more because of his goodness than because of yours."

Arthur the Less, who was sad and angry at what Palamedes had said to him, replied, "If he's a better knight than I, I'll demonstrate it to you clearly by sword play; follow me and you'll see."

"Indeed," said Palamedes, "you aren't as courteous as you should be, and I'll tell you why. You're unquestionably a good knight, and with your knightly ability you should be courteous and of good will, but you're evil and scornful, and because of your envy of good knights you go around attacking them and think that's courtesy. Indeed, if he who is now the best knight in the world had your bad habits, he'd be less worthy because of them."

To this Arthur the Less replied, "You shouldn't blame me if I go around attacking you and the other good knights, for I'm a young man and a new knight who needs to win praise and acclaim, and if I don't win them now, when will I win them? For a young knight shouldn't rest but do, while he is young, that for which he may be praised in his old age."

"You speak the truth," said Palamedes, "but all the same, he shouldn't do ignoble deeds after he has become a knight."

After this, Arthur the Less did not want to delay any longer with Palamedes but went after Galahad, and as soon as he caught up with him, he drew his sword and said, "Defend yourself against me, sir knight, for you may not leave me so."

When Galahad saw that the other knight would force him to fight against his will*, he leaned his lance against a tree and took the sword with the strange straps; when he approached Arthur to strike him, he said, "So help me God, knight, you aren't as courteous as you should be, for you're detaining strange knights, who perhaps are in greater distress than you, if they were to tell about it. If harm comes to you because of it, no one should pity you."

Then he charged at Arthur and gave him one blow on his helmet so great that Arthur could not keep himself in the saddle but fell to the ground so stunned that he did not know if it was night or day. And Galahad put his sword in its scabbard, took his lance, and prepared to leave. [223]

Then Palamedes caught Arthur's horse and brought it to him, saying, "Now you can mount," and he mounted. "Now tell me," said Palamedes, "could you agree to what I said to you, that this is the best knight in the world?"

"Indeed, no," said Arthur. "There are better, nor will he be so bold as to say of himself what you say of him."

"That's true," said Palamedes, "for if he praised himself, people would think it unworthy of him, but just because he doesn't say it, he doesn't cease to be the best knight in the world, and he is that, without doubt."

"May God never help me," said Arthur, "if I let him go until I've seen more of his skill than I have so far."

"I tell you," said Palamedes, "that soon you'll be able to see it, if you want to ride with us."

"Where are you going?" asked Arthur.

"Indeed," said Palamedes, "I've heard that King Mark and the Saxons have besieged King Arthur in the city of Camelot. I love and value the king so highly that I want to go with my father to help him, and I know well that this knight is going there in order to destroy the Saxons and help King Arthur. If you are before the city of Camelot on the day he arrives there, you won't then think me a liar in what I tell you of his skill, for I know well that he alone will want to attack the entire army, and I know that he'll perform there the greatest marvels and most skillful feats of arms that ever any earthly knight did."

"Since you're going to Camelot to help King Arthur," said Arthur, "from now on there may not be a quarrel between you and me, for I couldn't hate anyone who loves King Arthur. Therefore, I want to ride with you, if it pleases you."

And they said that it would please them.

---

*   Literally, "had him in such a predicament that he would force him to fight."

Thus the three knights rode after Galahad, speaking of him all the while. Galahad, who was riding ahead and did not know they were following him, rode until the hour of nones, when he arrived at a bridge over a river. The bridge was high and the water deep, boiling, and wild. It happened that Galahad had slept only a little the night before, and riding onto the bridge he fell asleep. The wooden bridge was wide and strong, and on the other side there waited a well-armed knight on a large horse, holding the bridge so that no one passed without jousting. And know that this knight's name was [225] Guinglain, son of Gawain.

When Guinglain saw Galahad reach the bridge, he said to him, "You may not ride onto the bridge, for I forbid it."

But Galahad, who was sound asleep, did not hear him, and his horse crossed the bridge. Guinglain, who truly thought that Galahad had heard him, charged at him and gave him such a blow with his lance that he knocked him from his horse and from the bridge into the water. And if the water had been deeper where he fell, he would have been lost because of his armor, which made him sink to the bottom.

When Galahad found himself in the water, he got up as quickly as he could. By good luck he had fallen near the bank, and he came out. When he saw that he had been knocked off the bridge and was not hurt, he thanked Our Lord fervently.

Guinglain, who did not know him, said, "Indeed, knight, you have come close to paying dearly for your folly, for I was telling you to turn back, and you wouldn't turn."

"Indeed," said Galahad, "I didn't hear you."

"No?" said the knight. "Then were you asleep?"

"It may be," said Galahad. "But since it has happened, I ask you to give me my horse."

"I'll give it to you," said Guinglain, "on one condition: that you don't pass over this bridge."

"I don't care how I pass," said Galahad, "for I'm in such a great hurry that I can't stay here long."

And Galahad mounted and rode through the water, leaving the bridge to Guinglain.

When Arthur the Less saw this, he said to Palamedes, "Now misfortune take me if I say of this man that he's the best knight in the world, for now I know well that I've found a better knight than he who through cowardice failed to pass over the bridge."

"Indeed," said Palamedes, "I don't know what to say to you about it or why he did it. But I still tell you and will tell you that he's the best knight in the world, and if here and now something happened to him that shouldn't have happened, it isn't surprising, for there's no one in the world so good that misfortune doesn't come to him sometimes."

"That's nonsense," said Arthur. "That misfortune came to him only because of his cowardice. And because he didn't dare go over the bridge, I want to go over."

Then he struck his horse with his spurs and lowered his lance.

Guinglain, who saw him coming, said to him, "Turn back, knight; I forbid you the bridge."

Arthur the Less answered, "I don't yet see why I should leave it."

Then he let his horse charge at Guinglain and gave him such a great lance stroke that he knocked him and his horse into the water, and Guinglain would certainly have died, for the water was deep, but he grabbed a branch and then had help from some people. [227] Arthur the Less, who cared nothing whether Guinglain lived or died, did not look at him again but passed over, and Palamedes and his father did the same.

Arthur the Less said to Palamedes, "Indeed, if he who is going from here were such a good knight as you say, he wouldn't have been knocked down by one worse than I."

"Don't say that," said Palamedes, "for it sometimes happens that a bad knight knocks down a good one."

"That's true," said Arthur, "and, therefore, I'll keep still."

Speaking of such things, the three knights rode as long as the light lasted, and it happened that at night they came to the house of a widow, where Galahad had stopped. When she saw them, she received them well and did them great service.

When Arthur the Less saw Galahad disarmed, he looked at him a long time and then said, "Indeed, it would be very wrong if this knight weren't better than any other, for he's without exception the most beautiful and strongest for his age I've ever seen."

"Don't worry about it now," said Palamedes, "for if God brings you to Camelot, you'll be able to value and praise him more than now."

The next day the knights left there and rode until they came to an abbey where Simeon, the father of Moses, lay in the fire in the cloister of the chapel, where he had lain in that torment from the time of Joseph of Arimathea until then, just as the history has already told.*

When the knights were passing in front of the abbey, a brother came out to them and asked, "My lords, are you knights errant?"

"Yes," they said, "but why do you ask?"

"Because," he said, "there's an adventure at which many good men have tested themselves, but they could never accomplish it. Now we think that it may soon be accomplished, for the Good Knight, best of all those who now bear arms, is to come here to accomplish it. We don't know who he is, and, therefore, we ask all the knights who pass by here to come in (for we would gladly know him), so that in our presence he may accomplish this adventure at which many good men have failed."

"Sir Galahad," said Esclabor, "let's go see this adventure, and I think that God will do you† greater honor there than he has done to the others."

"My lord," he said, "let's go, since it pleases you." [229]

Then they went to the abbey and dismounted. Palamedes stayed in the corral, not daring to enter the church, because he was not a Christian. The other three went

---

*   See *The History of the Holy Grail*, chapter 38.

†   "you" as in Piel (318). Magne has "us."

in and said their prayers, asking Our Lord by His pity to grant that this adventure be accomplished at their coming. After they had made this petition, they left the church and went into the crypt underneath.

As they were entering by the stairs, they saw a great fire, and one of the brothers said to Galahad, "My lord, this fire is to die down at the coming of the Good Knight."

"Where did this fire come from?" asked Galahad.

"I'll tell you what I know of that," said the brother. "Within this fire there's a tombstone, and under that tombstone there's a living man named Simeon. I don't know for what sin he was put there, so that he doesn't die but will live in this torment until the Good Knight comes here."

"You've told me enough," said Galahad. "Now I pray to Our Lord that, if this torment is to come to an end in the time of the King of Adventures, it come to an end this very day, and that this fire die down and I may know for what sin this amazing adventure happened."

Then he crossed himself, entered the crypt, and prayed to Our Lord to show him the truth of the matter.

While he was saying his prayer, the fire died down and a cloud of smoke came from it, so that they saw nothing while it lasted.

Then a voice said to him, "Oh, Galahad, servant of Jesus Christ, true knight and truly good man! Praised be God who has brought you here. Your sanctity and true way of life have freed me of the great torment in which I've lived longer than you could believe, and because of your prayer my body and soul are saved, which were nearly lost because of my sin."

"It pleases me greatly that you're saved," said Galahad, "since it pleases the Savior of the world. But now tell me the truth about yourself and how it happened that you were put in such great torment."

Then the voice began to tell the whole truth about Simeon and Moses, just as the story has already recounted.

"And how could I find Moses, your son?" asked Galahad.

"You'll find him in the Perilous Palace," said Simeon, "in the forest of Arnantes.* There he has lived in the torment of the fire fully as long as I. But by God's mercy I'm free, for after the great torment I've had, I've found rest, and my soul will soon be in the great joy that will never fail, and this will happen because of your prayer, not because of my deserving." [231]

Then the voice was silent, and the cloud of smoke dispersed so that they could see clearly into the crypt.

Galahad called the others and said to them, "Come, let's raise this stone, and we'll see what's under it."

They went down, and he grasped the stone and raised it high, and he saw underneath it a body so burned and tortured by fire that anyone who saw it would have to pity it.

The brother said to Galahad, "Now you may see the body of Simeon, who has suffered such torture for so long."

---

*   Chapter 147.

"Whatever torture he has suffered," said Galahad, "much good has come to him, since he has found pardon for his offense."

Then he returned the stone to its place, and, after he had covered the body, he and the others went out of the crypt.

The news swept through the abbey that the adventure of Simeon was accomplished and the fire was dead, and they all came running to see if it was true. While they were doing this, Galahad mounted and left, for he did not want them to honor him for the good God had done him.

When Palamedes heard that Galahad had accomplished that marvelous adventure, he said to Arthur the Less, "What do you say about this knight? Do you still not want to believe that he's the best knight in the world?"

Arthur replied, "Indeed, I truly believe that he's the best knight in the world. However, I won't say so yet, until I know more of the truth about him."

"Now be still," said Palamedes, "for you'll say so as soon as you reach the army of Camelot with him. But let's mount and go with him, for if we lose his company, we'll be the poorer for it."

Then they mounted and went after him, and they caught up with him. They all rode together until the hour of nones, when they reached a spring that rose at the foot of a tree called a sycamore. When they got there they found a knight, fully armed except for shield and helmet, which he had beside him, and he still held his sword in his hand, but he was mortally wounded in the head, and he lay writhing in his death agony. When the four knights saw this, they dismounted to find out if they knew him, for they feared that he might be of the Round Table.

Galahad approached him and said to him, "Sir knight, who are you?"

He did not answer, for he could not; however, Galahad asked him so insistently that he answered as well as he could: "I'm a sinful knight, ill favored by Providence, and, without doubt, death has come to me because of my sin. My name is Arciel. I'm a companion of the Round [233] Table. By ill luck it happened today that my brother Sanades and I met a maiden. I wanted to have her, and so did he. We fought over her like enemies, and in the end I killed him and cut off his head, and he gave me this mortal wound, although when I left him I didn't know I was mortally wounded. After I had killed him, I brought the maiden here, and later, when I saw that I was mortally wounded and could go no farther, I dismounted at this spring and said to the maiden, 'Since I've killed my brother, and I am dying, I don't want you to live or other knights to kill themselves for you.' Then I took my sword and wanted to cut off her head, but she fled as fast as she could, and I remained, for I couldn't go after her."

After the knight had said this, he stretched out in his death agony and died at once. When Galahad saw him dead, he took him up before him and bore him to the house of a religious order nearby where he had him buried in sacred ground, because he was of the Round Table, and he had it written on the stone how he had killed his brother Sanades and how he, too, had died.

137. DEFEAT OF KING MARK.*

That day the four knights remained there in order to bury Arciel. The next day they started and rode until they were six leagues from Camelot. They were riding along the main road of the forest, talking of many things. Then it happened that they met one of King Mark's knights, who was riding through the forest in the company of four Saxon knights. They were very well armed.

Arthur the Less stopped as soon as he saw them and said to the others, "Here are some of our enemies, who hold King Arthur besieged. Now, at them! They are five and we're four. Each one knock down his own, and I'll knock down two."[†]

They agreed to this. Then they called to them to defend themselves. Arthur the Less spurred his horse ahead of the others and gave the first such a lance stroke that he knocked him down dead. Palamedes killed his knight, and Esclabor his, but Galahad did not kill his knight, who ducked behind his saddle[‡] to protect himself from death. And this was King Mark's knight. After each one had struck his blow, Arthur the Less took his sword in order to keep his promise; he charged at the fifth man, who was seeking to flee, and struck him so hard that he knocked his head more than a lance length away from his body.

When Palamedes saw this blow, he said, "Arthur the Less, you have kept your promise well!" [235]

Arthur replied, "I tell you that it would please me if one of them were alive and we could get news of the besiegers and defenders."

While they were speaking of this, he saw that King Mark's knight, whom Galahad had knocked down, had stood up and wanted to take to his horse in flight.

As soon as Arthur the Less saw him, he ran to him and said, "You can't be safe there!"

The other, in fear of death, drew his sword and gave it to Arthur.

Then Arthur said to him, "Now tell me who you are and how King Arthur is getting along, and what the besiegers have done since they encircled Camelot."

"I'll tell you all this," said the knight, "but on condition that you promise me that I won't die."

"I promise you," said Arthur the Less.

"Now I'll tell you what you ask," said the knight. "Know that I'm King Mark's knight, a member of his household. King Mark has besieged Camelot with a great force of Cornishmen and Saxons, so that he can't fail to take it, unless help comes to King Arthur from somewhere else and unless that help is so great that it can dislodge an army. King Arthur, who is besieged inside, is very badly wounded with a wound King Mark gave him the first time they clashed."

"And what are those on the inside doing?" asked Galahad. "Do they come out at times to fight with their enemies?"

"Yes," he said, "but not often, for they're so few against those on the outside that they can't stand against them, and, therefore, they lose each time they encounter

---

*   Corresponds to Magne II:233-250; Piel 321-330.

†   This remark recalls Kay's at Queen's Ford (chapter 34).

‡   Literally, "held himself so badly in the saddle."

them. Nevertheless, I know for sure that they'll come out tomorrow morning to attack our forces in an all-out battle, whatever happens to them because of it, for today King Caradoc Shortarm came to their aid with a fairly large army. Because of this, they sent word to us that they would join battle with us, and it's set for tomorrow."

"And do you think," asked Galahad, "that the defenders can hold out against the attackers?"

"No," he said, "there's no way this could happen, for the defenders are very few and the attackers are a great army."

Palamedes approached and said, "Do you have any news of my lady, Queen Iseut?"

"Yes, my lord," he said. "She's already in Cornwall, for King Mark sent her with a large escort of knights more than a month ago."

When Palamedes heard this news, he was so sad that he would gladly have died at that moment, for he saw clearly that his love could not be accomplished if he was not where she was. [237]

Palamedes was angry and deeply grieved at the news he had heard of the woman he loved more than himself.

Arthur said further to the knight, "You are among the men to whom I wish most ill in the world, and yet I don't want to kill you, for I promised. But mount and go where you wish."

The knight mounted and went to the army happily, for he had been in great fear of death. He told King Mark how he had escaped and the others had been killed. Know that a great lamentation was made for them there, for they had been rich and of high lineage. That night the four knights took shelter in a hermitage that stood at the edge of the forest on the side toward the city, so near the army that there was not half a league between them. That night they spoke of many things among themselves and took counsel as to what they would do in the morning.

Galahad said, "I think we should wait until those from the city come forth and the battle is begun. Then we'll go and strike the enemy, and if God wishes us to defeat them, that fortune will be beautiful, and we'll have to thank Our Lord fervently and pray to Him for it."

The others agreed to this. That night Galahad beseeched Our Lord to give aid to the distress of the kingdom of Logres, for he knew well that if King Mark could accomplish what he had started, all the good men of the kingdom of Logres would be tortured and destroyed, for he knew well that at that time the Holy Church was neither so highly honored nor so well established in any other land as in Great Britain, nor were there in all the rest of the world such good knights or as many good men as there were there. And because of this, it seemed to him that it would be a great pity if such a prosperous, respected kingdom were delivered by some ill fortune to destruction and confusion.

Galahad thought much about this that night, and the next day, when the sun had risen, he armed himself, and the others, too, and they went to hear Mass. After that, they mounted and went along the main road of the valley until they emerged from the forest. As soon as they reached the plain, they saw Camelot and the tents and huts of the army. Those from inside had already ridden out, their battalions ordered, and joined battle with their enemies, but they were so few that they were in great danger. King Caradoc, who was acting as lord and leader of those from the city, was doing it so well that anyone who saw him [239] would have thought him a good knight at arms. He had good men with him who were helping him greatly, but he had so few men in comparison to his enemies that it was a wonder how he could stand his ground. As soon as the four knights arrived near where the battle was, they met a knight who had left it badly wounded.

Arthur the Less went to him and asked, "Who are you?"

He was frightened and wanted to flee, but Arthur held him by the bridle and said to him, "You're a dead man if you don't tell me who you are."

"I'm from Camelot," he said, "and I've received so many blows and wounds in this battle that I couldn't endure any longer. I'm leaving in order to go die somewhere else, for I know I'm mortally wounded."

"Which side is getting the worse of it?" asked Galahad.

"No one should ask that," said the knight, "for those from inside are so few that they can't hold out long."

"Now you may go," said Galahad, "for you've told us enough."

He rode away. The four knights entered the battle on the city's side, and they got there just when King Arthur's party was close to being defeated.

Galahad said to the others, "My lords, what do you think?"

"Indeed," said Palamedes, "King Arthur's men are badly hurt, and they'll be defeated if they don't get help soon."

"Now may we do our best,"* said Galahad, "and if we're only three, Our Lord, if it pleases Him, will be the fourth of our company, for He'll be worth more to us than a hundred thousand knights."

"What?" asked Palamedes; "aren't we four?"

"No," said Galahad, "for you aren't of our company, since you aren't a Christian."

"No?" he said. "Then seek whoever will aid you, for I will only hinder you from now on, since you've cast me out of your company."

At once he defied his father, Galahad, Arthur the Less, and all those of King Arthur's side, and he said to Galahad, "My lord, you value me little when you don't want to count me as a knight. So help me God, I'd rather die in this battle than fail to show you whether I'm a knight or not."

Then he went to King Mark. Thus Palamedes left his companions when they most needed him.

Galahad said to the others, "My lords, we're few, but don't be distressed by that, for be sure that Our Lord will help us if we put our hope in Him." [241]

Esclabor said to him, "My lord, go strike them, for we won't fail you this side of death."

Then he spurred, charging where he saw the greatest press of King Mark's knights, and he struck the first so hard that he knocked him and his horse to the ground. After that he spurred to the others and, before his lance broke, he had knocked down a full seven of them. Arthur the Less also did so well that none of them could

---

*   Literally, "may we do that well."

stop him. Esclabor the Unknown did the same, and all three accomplished so much on their first foray that they frightened more than two thousand of the enemy.

King Mark said to those near him, "Now you may see three good men. These are among the knights of the quest for the Holy Grail, brought here by chance. If they live long, they'll do us great harm. Now at them without further delay."

When Esclabor, who was nearest to King Mark, heard what he was saying, he charged at him, striking him so hard that he broke through shield and hauberk and drove his lance through Mark's left side. The wound was deep but not fatal. The king, who was very strong, gave Esclabor a great fall to the ground.

But when Palamedes saw his father on the ground, he said, "King Mark, I would have served you, but you've given me a poor reward for it, and I'll give you another such."

Then he turned toward King Mark among his men and struck him so hard that he knocked him off his horse to the ground, but he did him no other harm because of Mark's armor, which was very good, except that the king was stunned by the fall. When King Mark's knights saw their lord on the ground, they were all frightened. Then more than ten of them spurred toward Palamedes; they killed his horse and wounded him with many wounds, and they would have killed him then, for he could not defend himself on foot, but Galahad, who valued him highly for his chivalry, took the sword with the strange straps and began to give out such great blows that he knocked men down wherever he went. He did such great damage that everyone, however brave, was frightened at the prodigies they saw him perform, for he reached no knight, no matter how well armed, whom he did not lay on the ground dead or mortally wounded or crippled. They all drew back from before him as soon as they had a little experience of him, for there was clearly no knight on the field who had not in a short time seen that he performed the greatest prodigies with weapons that were ever performed in the kingdom of Logres. And there was something else [243] about Galahad, which caused greater fear to his enemies, that he never stayed in one place, but you would have seen him now here, now there, now far, now near, now on your right, now on your left, so that he was encircling all the battalions so marvelously that hardly a man could escape him. When King Mark's knights saw this marvel—that he crippled every man he reached and that no weapon could stand against his sword—they drew back with all the dignity they could muster, and they thought only to save their lives, for everyone, no matter how brave, feared death or dishonor before he got through that day.

When Arthur the Less saw the great prodigies Galahad was performing, he said, "Oh, God! What can I say of this man? By my faith, no mortal man could do what he's doing. Truly, all the other knights in the world are nothing compared to him, for if everyone else in the world were a knight and he faced them all in one place, I think he would defeat them all, for it doesn't seem to me, from what I've seen, that he could grow weary from striking during the lifetime of one man. Now may I have ill fortune if I don't from now on call him the best knight in the world and the best of all those who now bear arms, for I see well that he deserves it."

Thus spoke Arthur the Less, so astonished at the marvels he had seen that he could not believe that ten of the best knights in the world could do what Galahad was doing. And Galahad, who neither stopped nor grew tired, harried the Saxons and Cornishmen so badly with his trenchant sword that they saw clearly they could find no safety from him there. Therefore, they took to their tents as secretly as they could, but their circumspection did them no good, for when King Arthur's men saw that they were going that way, they charged at them, and neither tents nor huts nor anything else could protect them. Then began a great slaughter; more than ten thousand were killed there, not counting the wounded and crippled, who could not be counted, for the army that surrounded the city was very large. In this way the barons and knights—the army of Saxony and Cornwall—were defeated and killed.

King Caradoc said to his men, "See that none of them escapes you, not for booty or for anything else, but kill them all."

They obeyed his command, for as each one reached the man he had marked, [245] he cut off his head, and he would not have stopped for the man's weight in gold. Doubtless they would have killed them all had it not been for the forest, which was close, into which they who escaped the killing fled.

What shall I tell you? The defeat and slaughter were the greatest there had ever been in the kingdom of Logres, for more than thirty thousand died there that day. King Mark fled and Aldret with him; they were terrified of dying and fled into the forest where they saw it thickest, and thus they escaped.

When Galahad saw that the Cornishmen and Saxons were dead and defeated and that the city had nothing to fear, he went away as fast as he could ride, not toward the city but toward another part of the forest, not where the pursuit was. When King Caradoc, who had clearly seen the prodigies Galahad had performed that day and knew well that his enemies had been defeated by him, saw Galahad riding off, he went after him to bring him back to the king, if he could, or at least to learn his name, in order to tell it to the nobles of Logres.

As soon as he caught up with Galahad at the edge of the forest, he greeted him and said, "Oh, sir knight! For God's sake, don't let what I say grieve you."

"My lord," said Galahad, "it won't grieve me. Say what you like." He knew well that this was King Caradoc.

"My lord," said King Caradoc, "you're doing a great wrong and a great sin in leaving us without speaking with my lord King Arthur. For God's sake, when he knows what you've done for him and that you've left and didn't want to see him, he'll be so deeply grieved by it that I don't know who may comfort him. Therefore, I ask you, by God and by the courtesy that must be in you, to return with us to Camelot to see King Arthur, who's the best man in the world—you know that well. Indeed, if you don't do that you'll be very discourteous."

"Oh, my lord, mercy!" said Galahad. "Know that I wouldn't return for anything, and I ask you not to let that grieve you, for I have so much to do elsewhere, where I'm in a great hurry to go, that I wouldn't delay here for anything."

"Indeed," said King Caradoc, "your going grieves me, and it will grieve King Arthur when he knows. However, since you won't stay at my asking, I beg you to tell me your name."

"My lord," he said, "I'll tell you. Know that my name is Galahad."

"What?" said King Caradoc. "You're the man who accomplished the adventure of the Perilous Seat?"

"Yes, my lord," he said.

"By my faith," said the king, "your knightly career began more beautifully than that of any other knight ever did, and you [247] are continuing well in what you have begun. It seems to me that King Ban's lineage, where there are the best knights in the world, won't be degraded by you. Go, now, since you want to go, and may Our Lord guide you and give you the power to accomplish the adventures of Logres, as we believe that you are to do."

Galahad replied, "May God do His pleasure in that."

After that they parted. Galahad rode into the forest where he saw it thickest, for he did not want anyone to follow him to keep him company, for from that time on he wanted to do his knightly deeds so covertly that the fewest possible would know anything about them. King Caradoc returned to his company, who had taken so much booty from King Mark and the Saxons that they were rich all their lives, and the city was the richer for it for a long time. The news reached King Arthur where he lay wounded that the outsiders had been defeated so that few of them were left alive.

King Arthur, very happy at this news, asked, "Oh, God! How could this be, since our men were so few compared to theirs?"

"By God," said those who were telling him the news, "one single knight defeated them all. And know truly that never in the kingdom of Logres has there been such a good knight, for by his hand alone there are more than seven hundred either dead or wounded."

The king crossed himself in wonder at what he heard, and he said, "Praised be God who has shown us such mercy. Truly this kingdom is rightfully called the Kingdom of Adventures, for such great good fortune and such marvels don't happen anywhere else as they do here, and for this adventure, by which God helped us, saving us from shame and peril of death, we should thank Him fervently all the days of our lives."

Then he asked who the knight had been who had done such wonders, and they said, "We left him in the field, and we think King Caradoc is bringing him to you."

"Oh!" said the king; "wasn't he coming here?"

As they were speaking of this, King Caradoc came in, happy at his good fortune. As soon as the king saw him, he asked, "Where's the Good Knight?"

"My lord," said Caradoc, "so help me God, he wouldn't stay for any petition I could make but left us as soon as the battle was over. I went after him to bring him back, but I couldn't, for he said he was in a great hurry to go elsewhere."

"Now tell me," said the king, "do you know his name?"

"Yes, my lord," said Caradoc. "He is Galahad, the Good Knight who accomplished the adventure of the Perilous Seat." [249]

"By God," said King Arthur, "now I well believe it, for that's the knight who is to be the best of the best, but it grieves me very much that I didn't see him in order to ask him about Lancelot and the other knights of King Ban's lineage. But now tell me, is King Mark dead or taken?"

"No, my lord," said Caradoc, "for he fled from the battle."

"That grieves me," said the king. "I'd rather have had him than all the others, for I would have executed him as a traitor should be executed."

King Arthur was sad that King Mark had escaped. On the other hand, he was happy at the great good that God had done him. Then there began throughout Camelot such great feasting and rejoicing as if Jesus Christ had descended among them.

The king asked, "Did Galahad come alone or with another?"

"My lord," they said, "three knights, who were marvelously good, came with him."

"Where have they gone?" asked the king.

"My lord," said Caradoc, "I'll bring them to you soon, for I brought them here almost by force and had them taken to my lodging to be disarmed, and they'll be here any minute."

"That pleases me greatly," said the king, "for now we'll have news of the knights of the quest."

At that the three knights entered, richly dressed.

When the king saw his son, he recognized him and said, "Arthur, you are welcome."

Arthur fell to his knees before the king and kissed his foot, and the king received the others very well. After that they seated themselves near him. The king, who knew Esclabor the Unknown well, welcomed him with great pleasure, telling him he was sorry about the loss of his sons.

"My lord," said Esclabor, "thus it pleased Our Lord, but all the same, by His mercy, with all that great loss that I suffered, one son remains to me in whom I hold myself well satisfied and who comforts me greatly, for because of his reputation at arms and his chivalry he is praised and respected throughout many lands—may God be thanked for it."

The king asked where he was.

"My lord," said Esclabor, "here he is."

The king looked at Palamedes and saw him so well made and handsome that he seemed a marvelously good man. He asked him his name, and Palamedes told him.

"Oh, Palamedes!" said the king. "I have often heard you praised as a very good knight, and I value you for your chivalry over all others [250] who don't believe in God. I've never seen in you anything in which anyone could fault you, except that you aren't a Christian. For God and your salvation, and for love of me, receive baptism."

Palamedes replied, "My lord, I didn't come here for that, nor, by my will at present, would I do it for anything, but know well that if I were to do it for any man's asking, I'd do it for you, for you're the man for whom one should do most in the world."

The king said further, "Do what I ask you and I'll give you this city of Camelot, which is the city I love most in the world."

"Oh, my lord," said Palamedes, "for God's sake, don't ask me, for there's nothing for which I'd do it now, for my heart doesn't consent."

The king spoke no more to him of it, seeing that it did not please him. After that, he began to ask them for news of the Round Table, and they told him what they knew. The king asked King Caradoc and the others who had been in the battle how Arthur the Less had done there, and they said they had never seen a man do so well after being a knight such a short time.

The king was happy at this news and said, "Arthur, work at being good, for you won't lack the crown of a rich kingdom, if I see that it will be well employed by you."[*]

Arthur thanked him warmly for that.

That day they feasted and rejoiced in Camelot, and the king moved throughout the palace to honor the good men who had been in the battle. The king and queen asked much about Lancelot that day, but nobody could tell them anything about him. For seven days the three knights were at Camelot, and then they departed, for Palamedes was frequently asked to become a Christian, but he did not want to, so he went his way, saying that from now on he would renew the search for the Questing Beast and that he would never leave it, except for death or for company in which he was satisfied, until he brought it to an end. Then he parted from his father and Arthur the Less in order to go on his quest alone, as was his wont.

But now the story stops speaking of them and returns to Galahad.

138. KING MARK TRIES TO KILL GALAHAD.[†]

Now the story says that after Galahad parted from King Caradoc, he rode all that day. At evening he arrived at the house of an order of white brethren, which stood in a valley. When he got there, the brothers received him well and welcomed him as a knight errant; then they asked him where he was coming from. He said he was coming from Camelot.

"By God," they said, "can King Arthur hold out against his enemies?"

"I'll tell you as much as I know of this," said Galahad. "Know that King Mark and all his company have been defeated, and the siege is lifted. I don't think anyone ever saw such a great slaughter of knights in one day in the kingdom of Logres as there was today in Camelot. Soon you'll be able to learn the truth about it from others and news of the great good fortune God gave to this land today."

When they heard this news, they held up their hands toward heaven, praising God for showing such great mercy to the kingdom of Logres, and they asked why he thought they were defeated.

"My lord, where are you from? If you are of King Mark's party, leave here."

---

[*] This promise is not kept in the Post-Vulgate as we have it.
[†] Corresponds to Magne II:251-261; Piel 330-335.

"Indeed," he said, "I am not of King Mark's company; rather I've given him more hindrance than aid, and I tell you that I'm a knight errant and of the Round Table."

"Then you may command here as in King Arthur's house," they said, "for know truly that we'll do you all the service we can and all you can ask."

Galahad thanked them warmly for that. So Galahad stayed with those brothers, and after a little while there came to the abbey a knight of the Round Table whose name was Faram the Black; he was of King Lac's lineage, a very good knight and a good man, and he was going to Camelot to help King Arthur.

When the brothers learned that he was a knight errant and of the Round Table, they told him the news that Galahad had told them.

He was very happy and asked them, "Who told you such good news?"

"It's true," they said, "and the knight is still here; he was in the battle in which King Mark was defeated with all his company."

"Oh," he said, "for God's sake, point him out to me, for, if he's of King Arthur's house, I'll certainly know him."

Then they took him to a room where Galahad lay, tired from his great labor [253] that day. When they went inside, Galahad got up to meet them, for he recognized that this was a knight, and he seated Faram beside him.

"My lord, in God's name," said Faram, "tell me if you were at the defeat of King Mark."

"Yes," he said, "today I saw Mark and all his company defeated, and know that King Arthur's men gained great wealth there."

"And King Mark?" asked Faram. "Was he killed?"

"Indeed, I don't know," said Galahad, "for I didn't want to stay there once I saw that they were all defeated, and I didn't ask, either."

"And who are you?" asked Faram.

"I'm a knight errant of King Arthur's house," he said, "but you may not know my name at this time."

Faram left it at that, but all the while it was in his mind that he had seen him before, but he could not remember when or where, nor did Galahad ask him anything about himself, so he could not ask Galahad about himself.

As they were speaking of this and of many other things, King Mark arrived there, and he brought with him ten of the knights of Cornwall, who had escaped, wounded and badly hurt, from the rout and had caught up with him in the forest; they were accompanying him to guard him the best they could, in case by chance anyone wanted to attack him.

When King Mark dismounted there, the brothers began to ask those who were traveling with him, "My lords, where are you from?"

Afraid to be recognized, they said, "We're of the kingdom of Logres, and we come from Camelot."

"And what news do you bring us?" they asked. "Is it true that King Mark is defeated?"

"Yes," they said, "you may be certain."

"You are welcome," said the brothers. "Blessed be this news!"

The brothers made them dismount and took them to a room in order to disarm them, and they saw to their wounds. After that, they took them to another room, not the one where the other two were. For as soon as they heard that there were knights of King Arthur's house there, the Cornish knights were afraid of being recognized; therefore, they kept apart from the others as much as they could. When it began to grow dark, King Mark happened to pass by the room where Galahad [255] lay; he cast an eye inside and saw Galahad's shield hanging from a pillar. As soon as he saw it, he knew that that was the shield that had been greatly feared that day.

He pointed it out to his knights and asked them, "Do you recognize that shield?"

"Yes," they said, "as soon as we saw it; truly, we know it well. Cursed be the knight who bears it, for he alone defeated and destroyed us today."

"Now tell me," said the king, "what we can do about it, for there's nothing in the world I'd do with a better mind than kill him, for the whole rest of the world hasn't done me as much harm as he alone, and I know well that he's one of those two, but I don't know which."

"My lord," they said, "you'll never be able to avenge yourself on him as well as now, for if we take our arms and go to them while they're unarmed, we'll kill them."

"Not that way," said the king. "I'll avenge myself in another manner as soon as we know which he is. Now one of you go ask which it is who bears the white shield with the red cross."

Immediately one went into the room and asked them, and Galahad replied, "Sir knight, I've borne it until now, but why do you ask?"

"My lord," he said, "in order to make your acquaintance. So help me God, I rejoice to know a man such as you, and whoever knows you will always be worth more as a result, for, unquestionably, you are the best knight in the world."

Galahad was greatly embarrassed by the other's excessive praise, and he fell silent and said nothing to him. The knight returned to his lord and told him what he had learned.

"Now keep still," said King Mark. "I'll avenge myself, for I'll make him die a hard death, but the vengeance won't be as great as he's deserved, for he has destroyed me and so many good men that if a hundred knights like him were killed for it, we wouldn't be avenged."

So spoke King Mark, and so he hoped to do; the story tells in what manner he expected to accomplish his vengeance, and I will tell you how.

Galahad was wounded with many wounds, large and small, but none was mortal, and Faram, too, was wounded [256] from a battle in which he had been.

Therefore, King Mark came to them and said to Galahad, "My lord, are you badly wounded?"

"I am not," he said, "thanks to God, for I have no hurt because of which I'd have to interrupt my journey."

"I say it for your good," said King Mark, "and so that my coming may benefit you, for I have a remedy such that there's no man in the world so badly wounded— as long as he isn't dead yet—who, if he drinks it, won't be whole in two days. I'll give you some of it before I leave you, and to your companion, too, for love of you, for I have heard you praised so highly for knightly skill that I'd be the falsest man in the world if I didn't wish for your health."

Galahad, believing that he said it for his good, thanked him warmly.

King Mark made Galahad believe this, but he had something else in mind, for the potion he wanted to give Galahad was a poison so strong that anyone, having drunk it, would die instantly. Know that he had brought it to the kingdom of Logres in order to kill his nephew Tristan with it, for he could see no other way to kill him, because Tristan was an exceptionally good knight, feared by all. There was no one in the world whose death King Mark desired as much as Tristan's. He had already had him sought by his men throughout the whole kingdom of Logres in order to give him that potion to drink, but he had not been able to find him, because Tristan still lay badly hurt with the wounds he had received the day Palamedes and Galahad had rescued him.* What shall I tell you? When they lay down, King Mark took the poison he was carrying for his nephew Tristan and gave it to Galahad and Faram the Black to drink. Once he had done this, he returned to his men with great pleasure, for he truly thought himself avenged. But things did not come to pass as he had thought, for it did not please Our Lord, but a beautiful miracle came of it, as I will tell you and as the true history tells.

A little after Galahad had said his prayers and lain down, he fell asleep, and as he lay sleeping there came to him a marvelously large, beautiful man, who said to him, "Galahad, son of Holy Church, true knight of Jesus Christ, because you serve so loyally Him who [257] made you a better knight and more gifted than any other known, great good luck has come to you, for where any other man would have died, you have escaped."

Galahad asked him, "My lord, how can this be?"

"I'll tell you," he said. "Know that tonight King Mark has given you a deadly poison, and its result will appear in your companion, but not in you, for you'll find him dead, because he was in a state of mortal sin, and you will escape, because the Great Master has found you living a virtuous life."

This the good man said to Galahad where he lay sleeping, but he did not wake up because of it but slept until dawn. Then he woke up and commended himself to Jesus Christ; he crossed himself and got up and said his prayers and orisons. After that he went to Faram to see if what he had heard in his dream was true. He tried to waken Faram but could not, for Faram had been dead for a long time.

Galahad said with great sorrow, "Oh, God! What treachery this was! Oh, King Mark, how many evil deeds have you done!"

Then he went to his armor and armed himself alone the best he could. After that, he opened the doors and saw that it was already full daylight. He turned to Faram and found him yellow and black, so swollen it was a marvel.

Galahad said, "Oh, God! What a great wrong the man has done who made you die such a death!"

Then he went to King Mark's room and found that he and his knights had already risen and that he was preparing to arm himself. Galahad, who did not recognize

---

*   Chapter 127.

King Mark, said to them, "Which of you is King Mark? Tell me quickly, or you're all dead."

They knew very well that he was the Good Knight, and they feared death, for they knew they could not defend themselves against him.

Because they did not wish their lord to die, they said, "Oh, my lord, mercy! We know nothing of King Mark. Know that he isn't among us."

"You're wasting time," said Galahad. "You must tell or you're dead men."

Then he struck one of them such a blow with the flat of the sword that he knocked him to the ground so stunned that the victim truly thought he was dead.

Galahad said to them again, "Tell me quickly which of you is King Mark, or you're all dead men." [259]

One of them, who did not love King Mark, feared for his life when he saw this blow, and he answered, "My lord, will you protect me if I tell you which he is?"

"Indeed, yes," said Galahad.

The other pointed him out at once.

Galahad went directly to him, naked sword in hand, and said, "King Mark, false, treacherous knight, what did that knight do to you for which you killed him? And you also hoped to kill me with the poison you gave us last night. You're a dead man, for no one but God can save you, if you don't admit before these your knights and before these monks the treachery you've committed."

Then he raised his sword and made as if he wanted to cut off Mark's head.

King Mark, who truly expected to die, fell to his knees before Galahad, raised his clasped hands, and said, "Oh, good knight, mercy! Don't kill me! I promise you that there's nothing you can tell me that I won't do to have your favor and to make up to you for the offense I've committed against you."

"You're wasting time," said Galahad. "Like it or not, you must admit the treacherous act you've committed, and then, if I find it in my heart to spare you, I'll spare you, or, if not, I'll make you die a hard and shameful death and reward you for your great treachery."

When King Mark saw that he had to say it, he said, "Oh, good knight, mercy! I put myself in your power. Now do with me what you will, for I'll do whatever you command."

Then Galahad sent for the monks, and when they were all assembled, he said to them, "My lords, you see here King Mark, whom you sheltered here and didn't know it. Know that this night he has committed great treachery against a knight of the Round Table, whom he killed, and he wanted to kill me. I want him to tell you how, and then, if I find it in my heart to kill him, I'll kill him, and if not, I'll let him go."

When the monks heard this, they marveled, for they did not believe that such a man as King Mark had killed any man by treachery. [261]

Then Galahad said, "Now, King Mark, tell it all as it was, and don't lie about anything, for know truly that if you lie I'll kill you at once."

In fear for his life, King Mark began to tell it all as it had happened.

"And," he said, "I have never seen anything at which I marveled so as at the fact that you didn't die as your companion did—for I didn't think anyone in the world could escape."

After he had told it all, just as the story has already related it, Galahad answered, "I've never killed a man willingly. However, I've never seen—or thought a man could see—another who deserved death so much. I won't kill you, and I will let you go, not for any pity or love I have for you, but for love of Him who, by His mercy, in this peril and in many others, protected me. But just because I let you go, Our Lord won't forget this matter but will reward you for it in such a way that He'll confound you along with those who meddle in treachery. Now you may go when you like, you and your men, for I'll consider not your treachery but the fact that I shouldn't lay a hand on a king except to defend my life or for my earthly lord, for, although you are treacherous, you are not less a king because of that, and this is a source of great shame to all the kings of the world."

139. GALAHAD CONFOUNDS ENVIOUS KNIGHTS.*

When the king heard this, he was wonderfully happy. He took his arms and armed himself, and all the others did the same, and after they had mounted, they departed, happy that they had escaped so well. After they had left, they entered the forest where they saw it thickest, for they greatly feared to meet someone who might harm them.

Galahad, who stayed with the good men, angry and sad over Faram's death, cursing King Mark and his whole company, said that God should soon reward the king for his treachery. He had Faram buried there with as much honor as possible and had letters made on the stone that told how King Mark had killed him. And know that the monks thought this such a great miracle that the abbey, which had previously been called "The Uther Pendragon Abbey" because Uther Pendragon had built it, had its name changed at that time, for from then on [262] it was called "Galahad's Miracle," and it is still so called and will be as long as God is worshiped there. Galahad was there all that day, and the next day he left by the main road through the forest, in order to hear some news of Camelot from those who might come that way. That day he rode without finding any adventure to tell about. At the hour of midday, when it was already very hot, it happened that a squire caught up with him and greeted him, and Galahad greeted him in return.

"My lord," said the squire, "it's very hot and you're laden with weapons. I ask you to accept my service, to give me your shield, lance, and helmet. I'll carry them for you, and thus you may ride better."

Galahad agreed, because the heat was tormenting him.

He gave the squire his helmet, shield, and lance, and they rode on speaking of many things. Galahad asked him where he was from.

---

*   Corresponds to Magne II:261-277; Piel 336-345.

"My lord," he said, "I'm from Gauna, son of Frollo, a prince of Lamanha who held Gaul from the Romans, and King Arthur killed him before the city of Paris when he besieged it.* I was born then, and I've been in that land until now. This past Easter† I conceived a desire to come here, because this land is renowned for chivalry above any other, and I thought that here I'd serve some good man who would make me a knight. However, I wouldn't want to receive such a high order as knighthood except from the hand of a good man."

Then Galahad fell silent. That day the two of them rode until the hour of vespers. Then they arrived at a castle that stood in a beautiful, rich field. Galahad had already laced his helmet back on, because the heat had somewhat abated. Having arrived there, they saw coming from the other direction three knights who wanted to take shelter there that night, and know that they were Gawain's three brothers, Guerrehet, Agravain, and Mordred.

As soon as he saw them, the squire said to Galahad, "My lord, three good knights are coming this way."

"What do you know about them?" asked Galahad.

"My lord," he said, "I know them well, for they are Gawain's brothers," and he named them.

"I truly believe that they are good knights," said Galahad.

As they were speaking of this, Agravain, who was proud and scornful, called to him, "Be on guard against me, sir knight; you must joust."

"My lord," said the squire to Galahad, "be on guard against this knight; take your shield and lance and defend yourself." [263]

Galahad answered, "It doesn't please God for me to take arms against him."

"What?" asked the squire. "Won't you have the courage to defend yourself?"

"Not against him," said Galahad.

"Now ill fortune take me," said the squire, "if I ever heard of such a cowardly man; poorly would you defend me, if I needed it, when you don't want to defend yourself, and because of the great fault I see in you, I don't want to serve you any longer. For what I've done so far I find myself worse off, but a squire isn't dishonored by serving a knight until he sees his fault."

Then he threw the shield and lance he carried to the ground and said in great anger, "Now, sir knight, serve yourself as you can, for, so help me God, I won't ever serve such a bad knight."

Then he spurred and rode away from Galahad, calling to Agravain, "Sir knight, turn back, and don't bother to attack this bad knight, for he has admitted that he wouldn't dare face you in a joust."

Agravain stopped and said, "Since he refuses to joust out of cowardice, I won't attack him."

Then he turned back and told his brothers what had happened; they laughed together and said, "Let's await him and learn who he is."

They stopped and waited until Galahad reached them. He greeted them and they him, and they asked him where he wanted to take shelter.

---

* Chapter 60.
† "This past Easter" as in Piel (336). Magne has, "The other day, in sorrow."

"In this castle," he said, "is someone who will shelter me, and in the morning I'll be on my way again."

The squire said to him, "Indeed, sir knight, you're traveling poorly, since you have to carry your own shield and lance. Those who are good knights don't do so."

Galahad replied, "He is not a knight errant who does not gladly travel without company."

Guerrehet, who was very courteous, said to his brothers, "Let's ride together, and let's not laugh at this knight, for he is perhaps a better man than we suspect."

They arrived at the entrance to the castle, and when they wanted to enter, they saw emerge from inside four armed knights, who said to them, "Knights, you must joust if you wish to take shelter here."

When Guerrehet heard this, he went to strike one of them; he knocked him to the ground, and Agravain one, and Mordred the third, and all were so badly wounded that they could not get up. When Galahad saw this, he thought they were dead, and he was sad about it and feared that if he struck the fourth he would kill him.

Therefore, he said to him, "Sir knight, you see how it goes with your companions, and if you're wise, you'll give up the joust."

The other, who was a very good knight, [265] replied, "I want to joust, but, although I have the desire, I'll give up the joust, if you wish."

"I do wish," said Galahad, "for I believe that no good can come to me or you from this joust."

The knight put down his lance and began to smile, for he truly believed that Galahad had refused the joust out of cowardice. Then the three brothers began to mock him and laugh at him, saying that he was without exception the worst and most cowardly knight they ever hoped to see.

Then they went into the castle. At the entrance they were asked for their names, and they had to name themselves.

When Mordred heard that the man who was traveling with them was named Galahad, he crossed himself in amazement and said to his brothers, "What shall we do? The Very Good Knight who is supposed to bring the adventures of the kingdom of Logres to an end is named Galahad and bears a shield like this one. Maybe this is he."

"No," said Agravain, "be sure that it isn't he, for many knights are called Galahad, and many bear arms with the same device."

The other two agreed with him. Thus speaking, they rode through the castle until they arrived at the chief fortress. They dismounted there, and the three brothers were well received when people knew of what lineage they came, but Galahad was little honored and poorly served, and there was no one there who did not despise him, believing that he had given up the joust out of cowardice. Nevertheless, as soon as they saw him disarmed and saw how he was built and how handsome he was, they said that God had committed a great wrong when He had put cowardice in such a beautiful body, that he should have been called Handsome rather than Galahad, the gallant one.*

---

* Translation of this phrase was suggested by Samuel N. Rosenberg.

Agravain said, "If his name is Galahad, don't be surprised, for where there are many similar things, it can only be that some of them are bad. There are many knights throughout the world who are called Galahad, and there are good and bad among them, and just as the very good Galahad, who is to put an end to the adventures of the kingdom of Logres, is the best knight of all those who are named Galahad, so this Galahad is the worst and most cowardly." [267]

At this they all laughed (except Galahad, who thought them bad and envious), and they said that Agravain had spoken well.

That evening, after they had sat down to eat, a maiden came to Galahad and began to look at him, and after she had studied him a long time, she said to him, "Oh, knight! How much it should grieve you that you're so handsome and so bad. Cursed be the beauty that was given to such a bad person as you."

Somewhat angry, he began to smile and said, "My lady, it doesn't seem to me that you have a good reason to say that, for you never yet saw anything in me because of which you should insult me so."

"Indeed," she said, "that's true, but all who are here say so much ill of you that I can't help saying it to you."

"My lady," he said, "so help you God, tell me now, if I were as good a knight as I am handsome, what would you say to that?"

"So help me God," she said, "I would say that you'd be the best knight in the world, for you're unquestionably the handsomest, and because despite this, you're more than bad, you cause yourself to be scorned and insulted."

Galahad fell silent, deeply embarrassed at what the maiden had said to him.

One after another, they spoke much about Galahad, but not to his honor. He bore it all well, being more patient and moderate than any other knight known to man and moreover not wanting to start a fight with them, because they were of the Round Table, for, if he did so knowingly, he would be forsworn. That night he put up with it well, making no reply to anything they said to him. After they had made his bed for him—not such as they made for the others—he put out the candles, for it was his custom not to lie down until he had said his prayers; most of the night he remained in prayers and petitions to Our Lord to let him do such deeds in this quest as would be profitable to his soul. The next day, as soon as it was light, he got up and went to a chapel there and heard the Mass of St. Mary. He returned to the palace, took his arms, and found that [268] the others were already arming themselves to leave. When they were all armed, they took leave of the people of the castle and departed through the gate by which they had entered.

Galahad asked them, "Which way do you want to go?"

"We want to go to Camelot," they said, "to help King Arthur, for they tell us that King Mark has him besieged."

"Don't go there for that reason," said Galahad. "King Mark and all his company are defeated, and he's fleeing back to his land as fast as he can. I was present at his defeat."

When they heard this news, they were so happy that they could not believe it, and they asked him when that defeat had taken place. He told them the day on which it had occurred.

"Oh, for God's sake," said Agravain, "if it isn't true, don't make us think it is, for in that way you'll destroy us."

"I tell you," he said, "and I swear on my faith that I saw King Mark defeated before the city of Camelot and so many of his people killed that few were left alive."

When they heard this, they praised God and said, "We won't go to Camelot, since King Arthur is freed of the siege, for they would think us bad knights, especially since we haven't yet accomplished anything."

"Indeed," said Mordred, "that's true, and, therefore, I recommend that we return to our quest," and the others agreed.

Then they asked Galahad, "Sir knight, which way do you want to go?"

"I don't know," said Galahad, "except that I'd like to go to the kingdom of the Strange Land."

"We, too," they said, "for we know well that the Maimed King is in this land. Now let's go together," they said, "until chance parts us."

"Let's go," said Galahad.

Then all four set out along the great road, and they rode until they reached a small forest. They had not gone far through it when the road on which they were riding divided into four ways.

Galahad stopped at once and said to the three brothers, "Now we must part, for these four ways tell us so."

They valued his company little, and they said to him, "Go where you wish, for we don't wish to part."

Galahad went along the path he saw to be narrowest and they by the widest, speaking of him and saying that they had never met such a bad and cowardly knight. [269]

"Oh, God!" said Agravain; "what a difference there is between this Galahad and ours!"

"Indeed," said Mordred, "we were wrong not to take from him the shield he bore, for we shouldn't have let such a bad knight bear a shield like that of the best knight in the world, for this man is the shame of all good knights and the dishonor and scorn of all knighthood."

The others agreed and said it would have been well if they had taken it from him so that he could never again bear such a shield.

Speaking of this, the three brothers rode until the hour of tierce, and then it happened that they met Gawain, Kay the Seneschal, and Brandeliz. These three knights were riding toward Camelot as fast as they could, for they had heard that King Arthur was besieged, and therefore they were riding far each day in order to come quickly to his aid. As soon as they recognized one another they were very happy, for they had not seen one another in a long time.

Guerrehet asked them, "Where are you going in such a hurry?"

"To Camelot," they said, "for people told us that King Arthur was besieged."

"You can turn back," said Guerrehet, "for King Mark has been defeated, and the siege is already lifted. We learned this from a knight who was there."

When they heard this, they raised their hands toward heaven and said, "Praised be God, who has shown such great mercy to the kingdom of Logres."

Gawain said to Brandeliz, "Shall we go to Camelot or turn back?"

"What will we go and do at Camelot," asked Brandeliz, "since King Arthur is delivered?"

"I fear that it may be a lie," said Gawain.

"It isn't," said Brandeliz. "Rather, it's the truth, for yesterday a knight who was coming from there told me, but because I didn't believe him, I didn't dare tell you."

"Then let's turn back to our quest," said Gawain, "for we haven't yet done anything in it to increase our worth."

Then all six* companions turned back.

Guerrehet asked Gawain, "My lord, do you have any news of Gaheriet?"

"No," he said, "it's a good half year since I've seen him, but I've often heard news of him."

Then Kay said, "Not two months ago I saw him whole and happy before the Tower of Maidens. He asked me for news of Galahad, and I couldn't say anything about him, for I've seen him seldom in this quest."

When Mordred heard them speaking of Galahad, he said to Brandeliz and Gawain, "Don't you know? Last night the best adventure in the world happened to us." Then he began to recount to them [271] everything they had seen of Galahad the Bad, and he swore that never had such a bad knight borne arms. When Gawain heard this tale, he believed it and felt great chagrin because such a bad knight bore the arms of such a good man as Galahad.

He could not keep from saying, "Indeed, when you saw him lacking, you were wrong and at fault not to take the shield from him. I don't know who this knight is, but if chance brings me to him, he won't bear the shield away, and what's more, if he doesn't promise me as a knight that he won't ever bear it again, I'll mutilate him."

And Kay and Brandeliz said the same.

That day they all six rode until the hour of nones, and it happened then that they saw Galahad riding ahead of them.

When the first three saw him, they said to the other three, "Now you may see the knight about whom we have been speaking all day today."

Kay charged toward him at once, saying, "Sir knight, give up the shield you bear, or beware of me!"

Galahad, not recognizing him, said, "I won't give up the shield as long as I can defend it."

He turned his horse's head toward Kay and rode to strike him so that he knocked him to the ground considerably wounded; after that he drew his lance out of him.

When Gawain saw that blow, he said to his brothers, "By Saint Mary, he isn't such a bad knight as you say."

---

*   "six" as in Piel (341). Magne has "four."

Brandeliz, who was deeply grieved by what had happened, for he knew that Kay had been knocked down because of his love for King Ban's lineage, charged at Galahad, and Galahad, not recognizing him, struck him, too, so hard that he knocked him and his horse to the ground, and Brandeliz was so stunned by the fall that he did not know if it was night or day.

Gawain, who was afraid of being mortally wounded, said to his brothers, "You've misled us by what you made us believe; this knight is much better than you said, for were he not of exceptionally great ability he wouldn't have knocked Brandeliz down."

"My lord," they said, "don't worry about that, for we'll avenge that blow."

Then Mordred charged at Galahad, and Galahad knocked him over his horse's rump to the ground. Then he knocked Guerrehet down and after that Agravain.

When Gawain saw this, he was so frightened that he did not know what to do except to say, "Saint Mary! What's this I see? But I'd rather be knocked down or killed than not do my best to avenge my companions." [273]

Galahad was already riding away, for he had no desire to joust, and Gawain called to him, "Turn back, knight, for you must joust."

When Galahad heard that he had to joust, willing or not, he turned and said, "Saint Mary! What do these knights hope to accomplish, not letting me go my way in peace? I never offended them, and they attack me gratuitously."

Then he turned to Gawain and did to him as he had done to the others and worse still, for he gave him a great wound in the left thigh and knocked him down so violently that Gawain thought he would be permanently crippled by it. When Galahad saw that he had nothing more to fear from them, he started on his way and began to ride as fast as he could, not out of fear but to free himself of the quarrel, and also because he thought they were of King Arthur's house.

As soon as Brandeliz found himself and the others on the ground, he stood up and said to them, "We've been misled and deceived. Know that this is Galahad, the More Than Good Knight, Lancelot's son. Let's mount and ride after him and beg his pardon for having attacked him without reason."

"Let's go," said the others.

Gawain, who was hurt worse than the others, got up the best he could and said, "We've erred badly in attacking him because of our pride. Now he may well laugh at our mistake, he and all those who hear of it."

Then all six mounted as well as they could and rode at a gallop after Galahad, so that they caught up with him. They begged his pardon for having attacked him without reason, but know that the three brothers thought themselves demeaned by everything they said. After Galahad had pardoned them, and they wanted to leave him, suddenly Hector of the Fens and Meraugis of Portlegues rode up. When Hector saw Galahad, he recognized him, and Galahad Hector, and they were so happy that they slung their shields at their sides and went to embrace each other, and they greeted each other well, saying that they had greatly desired to see each other, for they had not seen each other in a long time. Great was the joy and pleasure one friend had with the other. Galahad asked Hector who Meraugis was. Hector told him what he knew, and Galahad received Meraugis well, for [274] he had already heard of his ability and chivalry in many places. Meraugis bowed deeply to Galahad when he found out who he was, for he knew well that this was the best knight in the world. Great was the joy of the three knights together.

Meraugis, who was more talkative than Hector, asked Galahad, "My lord, who are these knights?"

"They are all our brothers of the Round Table," said Galahad, and he immediately told him each one's name.

"Oh, God," said Meraugis, "may You be praised, since it has pleased You to let me find Gawain the Treacherous. Indeed, if Eric isn't avenged now, I never want to bear arms again," and Hector said the same.

Hector went to Gawain at once and said to him, "Beware of me, for I defy you. Falsely and treacherously did you kill Eric, King Lac's son, the truest knight in the world and one of the men I loved most in the world. By your evil you killed him, for you killed him by treachery, and I'll kill you by right."

When Gawain heard this, he did not know what to reply. He knew well that Hector was telling the truth, and he was badly frightened, for he saw that Hector was a good knight, and he saw Galahad and Meraugis, who were on Hector's side, and he knew himself badly wounded and Hector whole. All these things made him afraid, and that was not surprising.

Then Meraugis said to him, "What, Sir Gawain, won't you defend yourself against Sir Hector's accusation of treachery?"

"Meraugis," said Gawain, "there's no knight in the world so good that he could accuse me and I wouldn't defend myself, but I know that there can be no battle between Sir Hector and me because of the companionship of the Round Table that is between us, and, moreover, he knows it as well as I. I marvel at what he would do, for he couldn't lay a hand on me without being strangely forsworn. On the other hand, if I now wanted this battle, he shouldn't want it, for he'd have no honor from it, for he's whole and I'm wounded. But I'll tell him what he'll be able to do about it to his greater honor. He's of King Arthur's house, and I am, too. Leave this battle now and confront me in King Arthur's house, where there are [275] many good men. I'll defend myself there. If I can't defend myself successfully against him, let me die like a traitor, and if I conquer him, let him know that I'll deal with him as with a false accuser."

"Oh, false knight," said Hector, "you're wasting time. You must defend yourself here among your brothers; either I'll kill you or I'll make you admit the treachery you committed in killing Eric."

Gawain answered, "This may not be. You can't force this battle on me here, for, since you're whole and I'm wounded, you can't hasten this trial but must let me have a delay of forty days, and then, without fail, once the day of battle is set, if I'm not there, you may attack me, armed or unarmed, well or ill, in the first place in which you find me, and nobody will hinder you in anything you do to me. Such is the custom of the knights of the kingdom of Logres, and you want to lay hands on me in defiance of this. For that I accuse you of treachery and oathbreaking, and forty days from today I'll answer in my uncle's house and prove that you should lose your place in the Round Table. And I tell you that here in front of Galahad."

When Hector heard this, he did not know what to say, but he answered, "Gawain, Gawain, much do you know of evil. Great is your treachery, secret and hidden!

I see clearly that this battle can't take place now, for it would offend against the sacrament of the Round Table. But if God brings me to the king's house and I find you there, I'll make you see that you never killed a man whose death will be so well avenged as Eric's will be."

Then he turned to Galahad and said, "My lord, leave the company of this false knight, for no man can be with him without being the worse for it."

"Sir Hector," said Galahad, "don't say that. If Sir Gawain has offended any of his companions through ill will or mistaken identity, he'll avoid it better another time. Indeed, I never before heard so much ill said of him as you're saying, and, therefore, I don't know that I can believe it."

Then Meraugis said, "Gawain, Gawain, neither did a place at the Round Table avail Eric, nor that he was so badly wounded, nor that you recognized him, nor that you greeted him. You killed his horse,* and then you killed him, too. And now you're so innocent of it that you won't answer the accusation. Know that if Sir Galahad weren't here, I'd hope to prove easily the treachery of which Sir Hector accuses you, for I know well that you acted faithlessly in this matter, and I'll never meet you in any other place without proving it [277] on you."

Then Galahad, Hector, and Meraugis left there, and the others went off, too, in the other direction.

"Sir Hector," said Galahad, "where do you want to go?"

"My lord," he said, "let's go to Camelot, for people have told us that King Arthur is besieged there."

"Turn back," said Galahad, "for I'll tell you good news about that."

Then he told them everything he had seen. When they heard that King Mark and the Saxons were defeated, they held up their hands toward heaven and thanked Our Lord fervently.

Then they asked Galahad, "My lord, where do you want to go?"

"I'd like to go to the kingdom of the Strange Land," he said, "for I've heard it said that the greatest adventures of the kingdom of Logres are happening there."

"That's true," said Hector. "I've heard of it from many good men, and I know that road well."

"Now may Our Lord bring us there," said Galahad, "to the salvation of our souls."

140. GALAHAD, HECTOR, AND MERAUGIS IN THE CASTLE OF TREACHERY.†

Then they went along the main road, and they rode four days without meeting any adventures. Know that in those four days they drew far away from Camelot, for they slept little, riding for long periods and changing animals frequently. On the

---

* "greeted him. You killed his horse," as in Piel (345). Magne has "spared him and killed his horse."

† Corresponds to Magne II:277-287; Piel 346-353.

fifth day it happened that they approached a castle that was called the Castle of Treachery. That castle was master of the surrounding land for a long day's journey in all directions.

As they were riding, they met a beautiful, well-dressed maiden. She had a sparrow-hawk on her hand, and a young man was with her. The young lady was on foot, strolling along the bank of a river.

When the knights came up to her, she said to them, "Sir knights, turn back, for you're following a foolish course. If you go forward, you won't be able to leave without loss of life, for this is the Castle of Treachery, from which no knight or maiden who enters comes out again, but all remain captive."

"Why?" asked Galahad.

"Because of evil customs that prevail there," she said, "and cursed be all those who established them and uphold them, for many good men and maidens have fallen into misfortune there."

"My lady," said Galahad, "we won't turn back for anything until we learn what it is, for we came from our own lands for no other reason than to see the [279] marvels of the kingdom of Logres."

Then they left her and went to the gate.

Know that the castle stood on a high mountain and was so strong that it feared nothing. This castle had been built by Galamanasar, a relative of Priam, king of Troy. This Galamanasar was a good knight at arms and had sons who were good knights, who held the land after him in such peace that no neighbor dared make war on them. Rule of that land passed from father to son until the Christians came, and neither King Mordrain nor Nascien, when they came to Great Britain, could bother them, nor could Joseph of Arimathea or his son Josephus convert them to Christianity, nor could St. Augustine, who was in England at that time. Rather they mocked him, so that it came to pass, because St. Augustine found there the most treacherous men he had ever met, that he named the castle "Castle of Treachery," so that it never afterwards lost this name.

Thus pagans lived in this Castle of Treachery when all the rest of the kingdom of Logres had converted to faith in Christ. Customarily all the lords of that castle, as son succeeded father, were good knights at arms, as if they inherited the ability. When King Uther Pendragon reigned, he beseiged that castle for a long time, but he could not take it. So pagans had lived in that castle from the destruction of Troy until the time of King Arthur, and they certainly never met anyone who could cause them much trouble. The men of the castle were not famous before King Arthur's time, for they stayed in their own land, but when they learned the truth about the Round Table—with how much pride it had been made and the names of its knights who had to go throughout the world seeking marvels and adventures—and saw that King Arthur was more powerful than any other Christian king, the man who was lord of the Castle of Treachery wondered how he could destroy King Arthur. Then in the field at the foot of this castle, on a richly worked block of marble, he had letters cut that said, You, KNIGHT ERRANT WHO RIDE IN SEARCH OF ADVENTURES, IF YOU DARE GO UP ABOVE AND PUT AN END TO THE ADVENTURE OF THE CASTLE, YOU WILL GET EVERYTHING YOU ASK FOR, and there were other letters that said, You, MAIDEN IN DISTRESS, WHO RIDE IN SEARCH OF THE HELP OF AN ADVENTUROUS KNIGHT OR SOMEONE

ELSE, IF YOU DARE GO TO THAT CASTLE, YOU WILL NOT LEAVE WITHOUT BEING HELPED AS YOU WISH. [280]

This said the letters on that stone, which were made so in order to trap the knights and maidens who passed by there, and they were indeed trapped, for as soon as the knights climbed up there, they were put in prison and remained there until they died. But the castle's rulers did not do so to the maidens, for they kept them as concubines, and after they tired of them they made them learn to embroider on silk and kept them as servants forever. In such a manner as I have told you did the lord of the castle have the stone made, so that many good men died there and more than five hundred women were captives there. The great evil that came from that castle was not known in the kingdom of Logres, for the men of the castle would not tell, lest they lose it, and the knights who entered there all died, and the women were so closely guarded that they could not get out.

In this way Arpian, who was lord of the Castle of Treachery, thought he could take from King Arthur all his good knights, but he could not, for Our Lord did not want that treachery to endure forever. Therefore, He wanted the Very Good Knight to come there and bring to an end the great wrong. When the three knights—who had not seen the stone, for they had not come by the road where it stood—climbed the mountain and arrived at the gate, they found no one to forbid them entrance, but, as soon as they had entered, a hanging gate of iron fell shut and gave off such a great sound as if the whole castle had fallen.

Then they looked behind them and said, "Evil men live in this castle. They already think they've captured us."

"Don't be afraid," said Galahad, "for Our Lord will bring us out of this with honor."

Then they went along the main street of the castle, directly toward the fortress, and as they passed from street to street they heard everyone speaking the pagan language.

"By God," said Galahad, "these aren't our people. Now let each of us hope to do well, for I know that we can't leave here without a fight."

"We aren't afraid as long as we're with you," said the others.

Saying this, they reached the fortress, which stood in a little field and was beautiful and well placed. When they reached the door, they found it open. They entered the corral, and the people of the castle received them well, [281] held their stirrups, helped them dismount, and showed them great friendship, but in their hearts they felt something else.

When they had taken the knights to the palace, they showed them such an infinity of love and rejoicing that the knights thought it a good hour in which they had come there. The hosts had the knights disarm at once and asked them where they were from, and the knights said they were from King Arthur's house.

"You are welcome," they said. "We love you much more because of that."

After they had been disarmed, an old knight came to them and said, "Will you come with me, and I'll show you a knight of the Round Table who lies here sick?"

"Let's go," they said, "for we'll gladly see him."

He went ahead and led them to the tower. There was a small iron gate there, and he opened it and said to them, "Go in and wait for me inside there, and then I'll show you what I promised."

The knights, expecting no treachery, entered, and the man pulled the gate to and locked it.

Then he said to them, "Now make the best of it, for you'll never get out of here except in death, and this is your last adventure."

When they saw that they were thus locked in, they said to each other, "Oh, God, what great treachery we have here! We won't ever get out of here unless the one who put us here lets us out."

"Don't be afraid," said Galahad. "Know that if, in this quest, we've served to His liking Him for love of whom we started on it, He won't forget us but will get us out of here despite everyone in the castle, for He's the true Shepherd who will deliver His sheep from all peril."

Meraugis said, "May He deliver us as He can, for great is our need."

"Oh, God," said Hector, "My Lord, don't forget us."

Thus they spoke together of their adventure, and they said that that castle should certainly be called the Castle of Treachery, for truly there were here the most treacherous people they might ever expect to meet.

Speaking about this, Hector and Meraugis fell asleep, for they were very tired. But Galahad did not sleep, for he was thinking of something else much more than they were; he fell to his knees* and remained most of the night in prayer, begging Our Lord with many tears to help him, by His pity, and to bring him out of that prison, for otherwise he had no way to [283] get out.

After he had said his prayers to Our Lord, he slept, and there came to him a beautiful man, in appearance the same as the one who had appeared to him on another occasion, and he said, "Galahad, don't fear but be confident, for tomorrow you'll be delivered, for the High Master has received your prayer. But when you're freed, destroy this castle and all who are in it, except the women who lie in prison here; free them, for God doesn't want them to suffer that misfortune any longer."

This was said to Galahad in a dream, which he remembered clearly after he woke up.

The next day, when the sun had already risen, he woke up and said, "Oh, Lord and Father Jesus Christ, don't forget us but come to our aid, if You please."

Meraugis said the same, and Galahad comforted them and said to them, "Have no fear, for Our Lord will come to our aid very soon."

"Oh, God!" they said. "And how can that be? For we're locked in among our mortal enemies and in such a castle that all the world couldn't get us out by force."

As they were complaining, they saw that the weather was changing. It was growing dark, as if night were approaching, and there began to be a windstorm and thunder, and sheets of lightning fell throughout the castle on all sides so thickly that anyone who saw them would have to have been badly frightened.

---

*   literally, "to knees and elbows," prostrate.

"Oh, God, Father Jesus Christ," said Hector, "have mercy on us and don't make us pay for the treachery of the false people of this castle."

Meraugis said the same, for he was in terror of imminent death. Galahad kept comforting them, but they were so terrified that it did them little good.

After that tempest had lasted from prime until tierce, such a great marvel happened that it should well be put into the story, for, without question, it was one of the most beautiful miracles that ever happened in the kingdom of Logres in the time of the adventures, for the tower, which was marvelously strong—that tower where the three knights were—split from its top to its foundation, so that one part of it fell to the right and the other to the left, killing many of those evil folk. When the three knights who were in prison saw the tower fall, they were so badly frightened that they fell [285] to the ground unconscious. Know that the tower fell in such a way that it did no harm to any of them. After they had come to and seen that they were not hurt and that they could walk out of there, they fell to their knees on the ground, holding up their hands toward heaven, and thanked Our Lord fervently from their hearts.

After they had been a long while in prayer, Galahad said to them, "Up, now, and let each of us take his arms, and let's kill all we find in this castle, except the maidens who are prisoners, for so Our Lord wishes."

They did just as Galahad had said, for they emerged from there whole and bold and went toward where they had left their arms. When they reached the palace, they found all the knights and men lying unconscious because of the great fright they had had.

"Oh, God," said Galahad, "what shall I do without my sword? Lord Jesus Christ, may it please You to let me have it."

As he was saying this, a beautiful maiden came to him and said, "Sir Galahad, my lord, you are welcome. Praised be God, who has brought you here, for by you will the captive maidens be freed." Then she gave him his sword and said to him, "Here's your sword. Keep it well from now on."

He took his sword and thanked her warmly for it; then he asked her, "Do you know where our arms* are?"

She took them to a room where they were. After they were armed, they turned to the people of the palace, who were already getting up, and began to knock them down and wound them and make an amazing slaughter. After they had killed them all, they went to the village and set fire to it on all sides, so that in a short time it was completely burned, and they killed all who escaped from the fire, so that by the hour of vespers not one man was left alive.

In the middle of the castle there was a large tower, which contained a large open space. In that tower were the captive maidens. That tower remained whole and all the maidens who were there, for it did not please Our Lord to let them die yet.

When Galahad saw that every part of the castle was destroyed except the tower, he said to the others, "Let's go see what's in that tower."

---

* Both editions have, "where your sisters are," but what follows suggests that "arms" is the correct reading.

They went there and found in a palace a good three hundred maidens unconscious from fear of the violent storm. They brought them all back to consciousness and told them not to be afraid, for the [286] bad weather had passed and they were free. After that, they told the maidens who they were and why they had come there. Then they went to another palace and found there a good two hundred maidens, some alive, some unconscious, some dead. They brought some of them to consciousness and comforted them as they had the others.

The maidens had never felt so pleased as when they heard this news, and they asked, "Is Sir Galahad here? For we know we're to be freed by no other."

Meraugis pointed him out to them, and they fell to their knees before him and said, "My lord, you are welcome. Praised be God, who has brought you here, for now we know truly that we'll be delivered from the torment and misery in which we've lived."

He raised them and said, "Give thanks to Our Lord for it and to no one else." After that he said further to them, "Look and see how many maidens are dead."

They counted them and found that they were fifty. Then they returned to the palace where they had gone before and found the other maidens rejoicing so much that it was a marvel, for they already knew that Galahad was there and that they were free, and, therefore, they were so happy that each one thought she was a queen.

Great were their festivity and rejoicing over Galahad.

He asked them, "How did you know that I was to come here and you were to be freed by me?"

"My lord," they said, "from a maiden, daughter of the king of Lomblanda, who within this past year was here with us in prison. She fell sick and died, and when she was about to die, she said to us, 'Maidens who are here in prison, don't lose heart but be glad, for I bring you good news: Sir Galahad, the Very Good Knight, he who is to put an end to the adventures of the Grail, is coming here, and as soon as he comes you'll be freed from this prison, and this castle will be destroyed and emptied forever.' This the maiden said to us of you, and thus has it come to pass, may God be thanked!"

All that day the maidens were full of joy, and at night Galahad said to them, "What can we do with you, for we can't remain here long?"

"We'll stay," they said, "until we've taken up our companions who are [287] dead, to bury them in a consecrated place, near or far. After we've done that, we'll go to King Arthur's house in order to tell him the marvels Our Lord has done here for you." For they already knew how the tower had fallen and how God had protected them at its falling.

"If you go to King Arthur's house," said Galahad, "greet him well for me and all those of his house, and say that, if it please God for me to return to the Round Table, I'll be very glad, for I've never been in a company that so satisfied me."

They said they would do it if God brought them there.

That night Galahad and the others were well served by those maidens, and in the morning the three departed. They rode many days without finding an adventure worth the telling, and they made it known throughout the land that the unbelievers of the Castle of Treachery were all dead and the castle destroyed. This news was soon known throughout the whole land, and everyone came there to see if it was true. When they saw the marvel that had happened with the castle and the tower, those who had not believed before believed at once and had themselves baptized, saying that God had truly had His vengeance there. The maidens who remained there, after they had had their companions buried, all went to Camelot on foot, and know that there were four hundred fifty. After they had told the king, who was healed of his wound, everything that had happened at the Castle of Treachery and the marvel of the tower, he held up his hands toward heaven and thanked God fervently for it, saying that this was one of the most beautiful miracles he had ever seen.

Then the king sent the maidens each to her own land, as well adorned as she could wish. The others, who wanted to stay with the queen, were without exception well served and honored for love of Galahad and married when it pleased them. The king left Camelot then with a great army and went to the Castle of Treachery.*
[498]

He went up into it, seeing how it had been destroyed and how the tower had been split down the middle, and he said, "This was Our Lord's vengeance and a prodigious miracle."

He sent throughout the whole land for all the master builders who knew how to build towers and castles, saying that since the original inhabitants had [499] left he would have the castle populated with good, believing folk, if God pleased. For this reason, he ordered so many people to go settle there that it became a great issue, but it did not please God to have the tower inhabited: one morning they found a good two thousand five hundred men suddenly dead, and those who remained alive fled when they saw this.

It seemed to the king, when he saw that the men he had ordered to inhabit the castle were dead, that it did not please Our Lord to have it inhabited, and he left it deserted. He said that he wanted to rebuild the tower, but God performed a great miracle, for whatever the king built in fifteen days all fell down in one night.

The king was sad and said in anger, "This is no use!"

He ordered it begun again. When he had finished a great part of it, it all fell to the ground.

When the king saw this he said, "I see clearly that Our Lord doesn't want this tower to be raised by me. Nevertheless, I'll try again," and he ordered it begun again.

One night as King Arthur was in his bed, thinking about the tower that had fallen so many times for him, a voice said to him, "Arthur, stop trying to raise the tower, for it doesn't please God for it to be built by a man as sinful as you are, nor will it ever be done by you or anyone else until there comes a king of Gaul who will bear the name Charles. He will turn to the faith of Jesus Christ a greater people than you have done, and he won't be so greatly honored or so powerful, nor will he have such a good body of knights as you, but he'll be a better Christian and more faithful to Holy Church, and he'll bring under his rule the whole kingdom of Logres† and

---

* The text from here to the end of the chapter is taken from the Spanish version (Magne II:498-500).

† Spanish text has "kingdom of London."

many other kingdoms, and that king will come from the lineage of King Ban, a lineage of knights."*

All this that I tell you, the voice said to King Arthur while he was thinking about the tower that had fallen, and in the morning, before he got up, messengers arrived who said to him, "My lord, the tower has fallen again. Don't try any longer to build it, for you can't succeed."

"You're right," answered the king, "since I've had true tidings about this, that never in our time will it be built up. Therefore, I want to leave it."

Thus the king left the Castle of Treachery. When he arrived at Camelot, he ordered put in writing the name of King Charles and everything the voice had said to him, and he ordered the written record kept in a chest at the Cathedral of Camelot. It was kept until the coming of Charlemagne, who conquered England and many other kingdoms, just as the true history tells. Exactly as the king ordered it written down, it later came to pass, since it happened, when Charlemagne conquered England, that he heard of that tower of the Castle of Treachery, which Our Lord had split down the middle in order to free Galahad and his companions. He went there and said that he wanted to raise that tower for love of the Good Knight, if it pleased God. Then he built it up, and it is not found that he made another tower in all of England. After raising the tower, he had a knight made of gold, worked and engraved as well as possible, and he had a shield and armor made like Galahad's. He had a seat of gold made, so beautiful and rich that it was a marvel. After all this was done, he had the seat put on top of the tower and had seated in it the knight that was made in honor of Galahad, and he ordered a stone canopy built over it, so that the rain could not strike it from any direction. That image was in that seat in such a way that it could not fall unless people knocked it down by force, and it held in its right hand a gold sword pommel to signify that Galahad had been the best knight in the world. There were yet other riches in that [500] image: it had in the middle of its chest a stone so brilliant that, however dark the weather, one could see by its light more than half a league in the direction from which one had come, so brightly did the stone shine. Thus Charlemagne made the image of Galahad, and that image was there more than two hundred years, and afterward it was taken away because of the evil men of England who fell into poverty of spirit through failure of chivalry.†

---

*   This tower that will not stand echoes a similar tower being built by Vortigern in Merlin's youth (*The Story of Merlin*, chapter 2).

†   End of the excerpt from the Spanish.

141. LANCELOT, ON THE BARK WITH PERCEVAL'S SISTER'S BODY, MEETS HIS GRANDFATHER GALEGANTIN, THEN IS JOINED BY GALAHAD.*

After Lancelot had boarded the bark,[†] where he found Perceval's sister dead and the letter giving news of Bors and Galahad, he was happy that Bors and Galahad were together.[‡] Then he put the letter where he had found it, went to the edge of the bark, fell to his knees, and prayed to Our Lord to show him his son Galahad before the quest was over, so that [289] he might know him and speak with him and enjoy his company. As he was making this petition, he looked and saw that the ship was beaching beside a cliff, and at the foot of the cliff there was a little chapel. At the entrance to the chapel an old man was sitting, white of hair and trembling with age. When Lancelot reached him, he greeted him, and the old man returned the greeting more strongly than Lancelot would have thought possible; he stood up from where he was sitting, approached the bark, and asked Lancelot what adventure had brought him there. At once Lancelot told him all about himself and how the bark had brought him where he did not think he had ever been before.

"What's your name?" asked the good man.

Lancelot gave his name, and when the other man heard that he was Lancelot of the Lake, he raised his hands toward heaven and said, "Father of heaven, may You be praised, since it has pleased You to let me see before my death the knight I desired to see most in the world. Oh, son Lancelot, much have I desired to see you. Do you know who I am?"

"No, my lord," he said, "not unless you tell me."

"Know, then," he said, "that I am King Galegantin.[§] Your mother, Queen Elaine, and another woman, her sister,[¶] were my daughters. When they were very young, I gave one to King Ban and the other to King Bors in marriage. After I had married them off, I set sail on the sea and came here to be a hermit because of a sin in which I felt myself guilty toward my Creator. A long time have I lived here in this misery to expiate that sin. But even here, so far from men, I've heard news of you from many good men who have told me that you were the best knight in the world and the most famous, and, therefore, have desired to see you, so that the first prayer I uttered each day to Our Lord was not to let me die until I had seen you. Since I now see you—may God be thanked for it!—I'm happy and ask nothing more but the death of this world and the life of the other. Nevertheless, however much the life may please me that I've led here hoping for Our Lord's mercy, I weep and grieve for the sin [291] you've committed with Queen Guenevere since you became a knight, for by it you're a traitor to your Lord in heaven and your earthly lord. Be sure that that betrayal has made you so unworthy of all good adventures and has

---

* Corresponds to Magne II:287-298; Piel 353-359.

† At the end of chapter 104, we left him on a river bank with no mention of the bark or Perceval's sister (last seen chapter 134).

‡ This first sentence from Piel (353); not in Magne.

§ In the Vulgate Galegantin is not Lancelot's grandfather but just a knight (see *Lancelot,* chapter 162).

¶ Evaine, mother of Bors and Lionel (see *Lancelot,* chapter 4).

so excluded you from them that you aren't to achieve the adventure of the sword with the strange straps,* not because you aren't a good knight but because of your sin and your great betrayal of your lord. Unquestionably, this sin has taken from you the chance to accomplish this and many other things, and I'm deeply grieved about that. Nevertheless, however much you've sinned until now, if you'd correct yourself and keep yourself from mortal sin, you'd still find forgiveness and mercy in Him in whom is all pity. But now tell me how you came onto this bark."

Then Lancelot told him all the adventures through which he had passed since he had confessed his sin with Queen Guenevere.

"Son Lancelot," he said, "know truly now that Our Lord showed you a great deal of good will when He put you in the company of such a holy maiden. Now take thought how you may be chaste, in thought as in deed, so that your chastity may match the maiden's, for thus your companionship with her may continue."

Lancelot promised him this with a good heart and promised that with every thought he would keep from doing anything in which he might sin against his Creator.

"Go, then," said the good man; "you are not to delay, for soon you'll be in that house where you desire to go, the house of the Fisher King."

"And you," asked Lancelot, "what will you do? Will you stay?"

"Yes," said the good man, "never, God willing, will I leave here until I receive the great reward that they should receive who put themselves totally at their Creator's service. Son, look to yourself, for I want to look to myself, knowing well that I'm not to be here long. When I leave here, may Our Lord receive me into His holy glory, if it please Him."

As they were speaking of this, the wind struck the bark and made it leave the bank. When they saw that they were drawing apart, they commended each other to God and wept, for they knew well that they were never to see each other again.

Galegantin said to Lancelot, "Oh, Lancelot, servant of Jesus Christ, remember me, and ask Galahad, the Good Knight, with whom you'll soon be, to pray to Our Lord for me."

When Lancelot heard that he would soon be [292] with his son Galahad, he was overjoyed. He fell to his knees[†] in the bark and began to pray that God would take him where he could do Him service.

Thus Lancelot sailed in the bark a long time and never left it. And if anyone asked me what he lived on, I would tell him that that Lord who gave manna to the people of Israel in the desert and made water come out of a stone for them to drink—that Lord gave to this knight what he needed.

Every morning, when Lancelot got up and said his prayers, he said at the end, "Oh, my lord Jesus Christ, do not forget me, and give me today my daily bread, just as a father should do to his son."

Each time he uttered this prayer he found himself so filled with the grace of God that it seemed to him that he had eaten of all the foods in the world.

---

*   Achieved by Galahad in chapter 131.
†   Literally, "his hands and knees."

After he had sailed on the sea for a long time as chance took him, it happened one night that the bark landed at the edge of a forest. But now the story stops talking about him and returns to Galahad, Hector, and Meraugis.

When Galahad left the Castle of Treachery with his company,* he rode for many days without finding an adventure worth the telling, until chance took him to where Tristan lay wounded with the wounds he had received when Galahad and Palamedes had rescued him, just as the story has already told.† When they met Tristan, they were very happy and rejoiced over him, and Tristan over them, and he asked them for news. Galahad told him how King Mark with his full strength and that of the Saxons had besieged King Arthur in Camelot because he had heard that all the knights of the Round Table had died in the quest for the Holy Grail.

"But it wasn't as he thought," said Galahad, "for he was so badly defeated that he'll never recover from the loss he suffered there, for few escaped being killed or captured. At the end, he was lucky to escape from the battle with a few of his companions."

"What?" asked Tristan. "Is it true that this happened to my uncle, King Mark?"

"Yes," said Galahad, "I saw it, for I was in the battle."

"And do you have any news of Queen Iseut?" asked Tristan. [293]

"Not really," said Galahad, "except that I know that King Mark went to Joyous Guard, went inside by night, and inflicted a great loss of men when he found her. He took her with him for a while and then sent her to Cornwall before he went to besiege Camelot. That much I know for truth and no more, except that I imagine that Iseut is in Cornwall."

When Tristan heard this news, let no one ask if he was grieved by it, and in his grief he stiffened and all his wounds broke open—he had already been partially healed—and he fainted and lay a long time unconscious as if he were dead. The others went to him and found the place all covered with blood.

"Oh, Sir Galahad," they said, "you've done wrong. Your news has killed Sir Tristan."

"So help me God," said Galahad, "I'm sorry I told him. But he won't die of it, be sure of that."

Then they lifted Tristan and took him to a bed. They undressed him and found all his wounds reopened. This grieved them very much, and they stanched the blood as quickly as they could.

For a long time Tristan lay unconscious, and when he came to and could speak, he said, "Oh, wretch! I'm finished! I've lost everything, since I've lost my lady!‡ Oh, fortune, cursed, treacherous thing, how you have come upon me this time! You've confounded and killed me."

From this news such a great illness took Tristan that he lay sick with it half a year and more, so that he could not ride or go out of that place. The other three stayed there with him four days and then departed. They rode together many days without finding an adventure worth the telling. And since they saw that together they were finding nothing, they separated, and each went his own way. Then Galahad rode for

---

*   Chapter 140.

†   Chapter 127.

‡   The quotation up to this point from Piel (356), not in Magne.

many days and found nothing. One evening chance brought him to an old, ruined chapel, which was on the verge of falling down. He dismounted in order to rest there that night, and after saying his prayers, he fell asleep.

As he lay sleeping, he heard a voice, which said to him, "Galahad, get up quickly, take your arms, mount, and ride to the sea, and you'll find an adventure with which you'll be well pleased."

When he heard this, he got up, crossed himself and commended himself to God, and did what the voice had commanded. He went through the forest as chance took him, for he certainly did not know where he was to go. After he had ridden thus all day and most of the night, he came to the sea and found a bark on the shore. Know that that bark was the one in which were Perceval's sister and Lancelot. [295] As soon as Galahad saw the bark, he dismounted in order to go see who was inside.

When Lancelot, who was at the side of the bark, saw him he said, "Sir knight, you are welcome!"

Galahad said, "And may you have good fortune, my lord!"

Lancelot asked him, "Who are you, sir knight? Tell me, so help you God."

"My lord," he said, "I'm a foreign knight, and perhaps even though I tell you my name you won't know me. Nevertheless, I'll tell it to you. My name is Galahad."

"Galahad?" said Lancelot. "My name is Lancelot. May God be praised who has united us, for I've never desired anything in the world so much as to have your company."

Then they held out their arms and embraced each other and felt the greatest joy possible. Galahad laid aside his helmet and shield in the bark, and he was as happy as could be that God had brought them together. They both wept with joy, and it was already so near dawn that the father recognized the son and the son the father. Each asked about the other, and each told what had happened to him since they had left court.

When the daylight became full and they could recognize each other better, they began to rejoice again, and when Galahad saw the maiden, he recognized her at once and asked Lancelot if he knew who she was.

"Yes," he said, "very well, because of the letter I found by her head. But for God's sake, is it true that you achieved the adventure of the sword with the strange straps?"

"Yes," said Galahad, "and if you've never seen it, see it now."

As soon as Lancelot saw the sword, he recognized it, and he took it and kissed it repeatedly. He asked Galahad to tell him how he had found it, and Galahad told him the whole truth about the ship, how Solomon's wife had made it and all the things there were on it, just as the story has already told.* After he had told Lancelot the truth about the ship and the letter he found there, Lancelot said that such a beautiful adventure had never before happened to a knight.

Lancelot and Galahad were together a long time on the bark, each serving Our Lord from his heart. Often they landed on strange islands, where there was nothing but deer and where they found many adventures, which they accomplished, either by their knightly skill or by the grace of the Holy Spirit, who helped them

---

* Chapter 31. See also *The History of the Holy Grail*, chapters 20-22.

everywhere. And of those adventures the history of the Holy Grail tells nothing, for it would delay the story to tell everything that happened to them during this time. [297]

In the season when the birds begin to sing and the trees and meadows to grow green and put out flowers—at this season, when all creatures are happiest, it happened one day at midday that they landed at the edge of a forest, before a cross, and they saw emerge from the forest a knight with white armor, mounted on a very good horse and leading a white horse on his right. When he saw the bark, he went to it and greeted the knights on behalf of the Great Master, and they greeted him in return.

"Galahad," said the knight, "come off this bark and get on this horse, which is good and beautiful, and take your arms and go where chance leads you, seeking the adventures of the kingdom of Logres."

"My lord," said Galahad, "who are you, who order me to do this?"

"I am a man," he said, "and you may not know more now. But do what I tell you."

When Galahad heard this, he went running to his father and kissed him and said, "My father and lord, I don't know if you will ever see me again. But I commend you to the true Person of Jesus Christ; may He keep you in His service."

Then they both began to weep from the very heart.

After Galahad had left the bark, taken his arms, and mounted, a voice said, "Now let each of you try to do well, for you will never see each other again until the terrible day when Our Lord will give to each one what he has deserved."

When Lancelot heard this, he said, weeping, "Son Galahad, since I'm parting from you forever, pray to Jesus Christ for me, that He not let me depart from His service but keep me in such a way that I may be His earthly and spiritual servant."

Galahad answered, "My lord, no other prayer can avail you as much as your own, and, therefore, remember yourself."

Immediately, they parted, and Galahad went into the forest seeking the white knight, who had already left him. And the wind again struck the bark, where Lancelot was, so hard that in a short while it had taken it so far from the bank that he could not see land in any direction.

But now the story stops speaking of him and turns to Galahad in order to relate something of his adventures, for unquestionably the greater part of the quest was his.

After Galahad had left his [298] father and gone into the forest, fully expecting to find the knight with the white armor, he rode until the hour of vespers, and he happened on the house of a hermit with whom he stayed that night and with whom he spoke at length about confession and the good of his soul. In the morning, after he had heard Mass, he departed, and he rode all that day without finding an adventure worth the telling. That night...*

---

* Lacuna in the Portuguese. Magne summarizes from the Spanish: Galahad reached an abbey where Mordrain lay, "blind and crippled in all his limbs, eagerly awaiting the coming of the good knight. On hearing the long-desired news, Mordrain asked Galahad, pure and virgin above all knights, as is the lily, symbol of virginity, to hold him in his arms and, having uttered an ardent prayer to Our Lord Jesus Christ, commended his soul to God, whom he had served for so long." There follow the adventures of

142. GALAHAD, BORS, AND PERCEVAL DEFEAT COUNT BEDOIN.*

When Bors and Perceval saw Galahad's shield hanging in front of the hut,[†] they stopped, and Bors said to Perceval, "Isn't that Galahad's shield?"

Perceval said, "It certainly is."

Then they went toward the shield, and they found Galahad trying to get on his horse in order to attack them, since he thought that surely they were men of the castle, not recognizing them by their arms, which they had changed. As soon as they reached him, they greeted him. He asked them who they were, and they gave their names and dismounted quickly. Galahad took off his helmet and they theirs, and they welcomed one another with the greatest good will in the world.

"My lord," they asked, "what are you doing here?"

He told them everything, as the story has already told.

"And I'm waiting here in case someone from the castle comes out, for never will a knight or anyone else come out of there but I'll kill him, until the count makes peace with his sister to my liking."

"In God's name," they said, "since it's so, we'll remain with you, and if we don't avenge as best we can the Round Table that he hates, may we never have its company."

Thus the three knights besieged the Castle of the March, where there were more than three hundred armed men who thought very little of this, for they could not believe that three knights would dare undertake such a great enterprise. When the three knights had made another hut, at which they gathered, suddenly there appeared a squire, who came riding on a great nag.

As soon as he saw Galahad, he recognized him, and he fell on his knees before him and kissed his feet, saying, "Oh, Good Knight, for the sake of God and pity, grant me a favor."

Galahad looked at him and recognized that he was Frollo's son, who the other day had thrown his shield and lance to the ground in scorn,[‡] and he replied, "I grant you what you ask of me, if it's something I can or should give, but I shouldn't, because the other day you behaved very discourteously toward me."

"Oh, my lord," he said, "mercy! I didn't recognize you. For God's sake, forgive me!" [299]

"I forgive you," said Galahad. Then he made him get up and said to him, "Now tell me what you want."

"My lord," he said, "I ask you to make me a knight."

"I agree to that," said Galahad, "but wait until we can get horse and armor for you."

---

the Perilous Wood, the burning spring, Simeon, and others that the Portuguese omits or relates in other places. Piel's summary (359), for which he gives no source, fits better with what follows: Galahad finds shelter with a widow, disinherited by her brother, Count Bedoin. Galahad promises to help her, goes to the count's castle, and threatens him.

*   Corresponds to Magne II:298-307; Piel 359-365.

†   How they got here is not told; perhaps it is in the lacuna at the end of the last chapter. We last saw Bors and Perceval in chapter 134 after the death of Perceval's sister.

‡   Chapter 139.

Thus Samaliel, King Frollo's son, was hopeful that Galahad would make him a knight.

A short while before, it had happened that three fully armed knights came out of the castle and were going to entertain themselves in the forest. They were armed, not because they feared anyone but because at that time it was considered ignoble of a knight to ride without arms.

When Bors saw them emerge from the castle, he said to Galahad and Perceval, "Here come three of their knights. For the love of God, grant me this joust, and let me attack them alone, for I tell you that they won't stand against me."

They agreed, with the proviso that they would help him if they saw reason.

Then Bors charged toward the three knights, saying, "Defend yourselves against me, for I defy you."

When they saw that he was alone and heard him defy them, they thought it amazing, and because they would have thought it cowardice if all three had attacked him, one came forward. Bors gave him such a great lance stroke that he knocked him to the ground, but he did him no other harm because of his hauberk, which was good. After that, Bors charged at the second, who was already coming toward him, and struck him so hard that he knocked him to the ground, with his horse on top of him, and the knight was knocked unconscious by that fall. When the third saw this, he fled, for he feared to lose his life if he awaited a blow from this knight, and therefore he fled back to the castle as fast as his horse could take him. Bors did not want to follow him, and he turned back to the others, who were lying on the ground.

Samaliel came running to him and said, "Sir Bors, let me take the arms of one of these knights."

Bors agreed, and Samaliel went to one, unlaced his helmet, and unbuckled his sword. The knight, who was afraid of dying, begged mercy.

"If you don't want to die," said Bors, "you must let this squire take your arms and horse." [301]

He agreed gladly when he saw that he would be spared for so little. The squire disarmed him, took his horse and all his armor and weapons to Galahad, and asked him to make him a knight.

"I'll do it gladly," said Galahad, "but not today, for it's late, but tomorrow morning, whenever you like."

He thanked him fervently, and Bors, when he wanted to leave the knights, said to them, "I won't harm you this time, but go and say to your lord the count that it was an evil hour when he disinherited his sister, for he'll be disinherited for it and reduced to poverty and misery, and he'll never emerge from the castle without receiving mortal dishonor."

Then he left the knights and returned to his companions.

They came forward to receive him and said, "By Saint Mary, you've done well! You've begun this enterprise well; God grant that the end be good."

They made him disarm at once, and the two knights who had been knocked down both got on one horse. They went to their castle and told their lord what Bors had done and said to them. When he heard about Bors, he was not as confident as he had been before, for he had heard many knights say that Bors of Gaunes was one of the best knights in the world. He did not know what to do, for if Bors were to die there, King Arthur would come to avenge his death, and all the men of King Ban's lineage would soon reduce him to destruction and misfortune.

He asked them, "Where did Bors of Gaunes come from when he came to you?"

"My lord," they said, "from a hut at the edge of that forest. Two knights were with him, fully armed, but I don't know if there were more."

"Leave it now," said the count, "for we'll soon avenge ourselves very well."

Thus the count spoke, but he thought otherwise, for he feared King Arthur might have sent Bors and the other two knights to begin a war.

Then in secret he called a good, agile young man who was his [303] relative and said to him, "Go to those knights errant, see how many they are, and learn if they have more of a company than what they show us. If they ask you whom you serve, don't tell them, for I fear they may hurt you."

The young man left him by night on foot and went to the huts. He found the knights sitting in front of them in the moonlight, which was very bright. They were talking about their adventures to comfort themselves, because they had nothing to eat, nor had any of them eaten or drunk that day.

And know that they had a great many such days. When the young man reached them, he greeted them as fittingly as he could. They asked him where he was from, and he said he was from the kingdom of Logres, from King Arthur's house.

"You are welcome," they said. "What are you seeking?"

"I won't tell you that," he said, "unless first I know your names, for you may be such that I'll tell you all about myself, or such that I won't."

The knights, who had a great desire to hear news of King Arthur's house, gave their names.

He asked them, just as if he knew nothing about it, "And what are you waiting for here?"

They told him, just as the story has already told.

"And are you no more than three?" he asked.

"No, truly," they said.

He crossed himself in wonder at that and said, "By my faith, I never saw such ignorant or insane knights, for you are only three and have besieged a castle such as this is. Here there are more than three hundred armed men, who will kill you as soon as they wish."

"Don't worry about that," they said. "But now tell us what we ask you: where did you leave King Arthur, and what are you seeking?"

"It's not more than a month," he said, "since I left King Arthur at Camelot with a great company of rich men and knights, and I left at his command to go look for Sagremor wherever I might find him, for the king summons him to court immediately. For God's sake, if you know anything about him, tell me, for I can't return to court until I find him."

They said that they knew nothing about Sagremor and that it was a long time since they had seen him.

"I'm very sorry," said the young man, and then he took leave of them.

"Where will you go to take shelter," they asked, "since it's so late?"

"I don't care where I go," he said, "as long as I hear news of the man I seek."

Then he left them and returned to the castle, and the knights, who did not suspect a thing, remained. [304]

When the young man reached his lord, he told him everything he had found out, and when the count heard him speak of Galahad, who he knew truly was such a good knight that hardly anyone could defeat him, he was so disconsolate that he did not know what to do, except that he said to the squire, "Keep quiet, for I don't want anyone to hear this news."

Then he went to lie down in a chamber alone, for he did not want anyone to keep him company. He began to think very hard, not knowing what to do in such a predicament, for he had heard such great wonders of Galahad that he knew truly there was no army in the world by which he could be defeated, both because of his skill as a knight and because of the two knights who were with him. After he had thought about this for a great while, he got up from his bed, called his chamberlain, dressed himself, and asked for his arms. He did not want anyone to know what he was planning except for two knights who were his first cousins. He had them take their arms and told them to come with him to a place where he had to go, and they did so gladly, for they loved him dearly. After they had mounted, they rode out through a little gate in the fortress, and the count forbade the chamberlain to say anything to anyone.

As soon as they had emerged from the castle, the count said to the knights, "You're my friends and my cousins, and, therefore, I won't conceal from you anything I want to do. The situation is that out here before us there are three knights errant from King Arthur's house who have done us dishonor and will do more if we let them. But we wouldn't have to let them do this if we destroyed them, and so that King Arthur won't bear me a grudge because of their death or disinherit me for it, I want to kill them so secretly that no one knows it except the three of us."

"My lord," they said, "we'll do whatever you say."

"Then let's go to the huts where they are," he said, "for there we'll find them disarmed, and we'll kill them and hide them in this forest."

They agreed to that.

Thus the count rode toward the huts, and this was at the hour of midnight. Bors and Perceval were sleeping, but Galahad was not sleeping, for he was longer at his prayers and thought more about Our Lord than the others. When he saw the three knights coming, he realized immediately why they were coming. He took his helmet and laced it on as [305] quickly as he could. He was fully armed except for his shield and lance, and he got on his horse and tried not to wake the others.

When the count saw that Galahad was on horseback, he drew aside a little and said to the others, "What shall we do? They're awake, and they're very good knights. I fear that if we engage them we'll get the worse of it."

The other two, who were very good knights, said, "My lord, don't worry, for they're no more than we are. Attack them confidently, for we'll defeat them."

Reassured, the count charged at Galahad and struck him so hard that he broke his lance on Galahad's chest, but he did him no other harm, and Galahad, who was used to giving great blows and who had by now taken his shield and lance, struck the count so violently that he put the point of his lance through his sides and knocked him from his horse to the ground. When he drew out the lance, the count fainted, and Galahad did not look at him again but charged at the other two and with one blow knocked them both to the ground, one badly wounded in the chest and the other so stunned that he did not know if it was night or day.

After he had dealt this blow, Galahad returned to the huts, dismounted from his horse, and fastened it so that it would not wander. He left his lance there and, in order to find out who they were, returned to where he had left the knights. When he reached the count, he took off his helmet and began to give him great blows on the head with the pommel of his sword.

When the count felt this, he was afraid of dying, and he begged for mercy and said, "Oh, sir knight, don't kill me, for you'll gain nothing by my death, but let me live, and I tell you that profit and honor will come to you."

When Galahad heard this promise, he understood that the other man was of noble birth, and in order to learn more of the truth about him he said, "Tell me your name, or you are a dead man."

"Oh, my lord," said the count, "I'll tell you on condition that you don't take it amiss."

"You have to tell," said Galahad, "willing or not."

"Oh, my lord, mercy," he said. "I am Count Bedoin."

When Galahad heard that he was the count, he was wonderfully happy, for he saw at once that the lady's war was won.

He pretended to be very angry and said, "Not for anything in the world will I let you live; count yourself a dead man."

The count raised his clasped hands toward Galahad and said, "Oh, good knight, mercy! Don't kill me, for I'll do anything you command me."

"Then swear it to me," said Galahad, "and then, if my companions agree, I'll let you live, and if not, you're a dead man."

Bedoin swore in great fear.

"Now," said Galahad, "come with me." [307]

Bedoin did so with great difficulty. His two knights, when they saw him being taken away, did not dare help him, for they knew they would be no use to him, nor did they dare return to the castle, for they knew that the people in the castle would kill them when they saw them return without their lord. Therefore, they went off into the forest however they could.

When Galahad reached the huts, he woke up the others and said to them, "Get up and see what a beautiful adventure God has sent us."

They got up and asked him, "My lord, what is it?"

"See here Count Bedoin, whom I bring you," he said. "By God's mercy we've now ended our war. Let's mount and take him to his sister and put him into her hands, and she'll do as she likes with him."

"Oh, my lord, mercy," said the count. "I'd rather have you kill me here than take me there, for she hates me so mortally that I know well she'll make me die a more painful death than I have deserved."

"Indeed," said Galahad, "you have to go, whether you wish or not, to endure what she wishes to do to you."

When Bedoin saw that he had no choice, he mounted one of the horses of the knights who had gone away; the others also mounted, and they left there, the squire with them.

When they had ridden until it was day, Galahad said to his companions, "Take this count to his sister," and he told them where she was. "And I ask you," said Galahad, "to stay with her until she is possessed of all her lands and he has amended to her satisfaction all the offense he has done her, according to what he can do and what you see to be good. I'll go to some place near here where I can make this squire a knight, just as I promised him."

143. ADVENTURES OF SAMALIEL.*

Thus Bors and Perceval left, taking the count. And Galahad went to a hermitage he knew near there and asked the hermit to sing Mass for him, and he did so. After he had heard Mass, Galahad made Samaliel a knight, and know that Samaliel was the largest knight in all King Arthur's house, and God had endowed him correspondingly, for he was a very brave, skillful knight, so that many said that he was one of the best knights in the world.

When Galahad made him a knight, just as the custom was at that time, he said to him, "Act so that you become such a good knight that your noble kindred won't be dishonored by your deeds as a knight."

"My lord Sir Galahad," he said, "I should be very joyful because I've received the order of chivalry from such a good man as you are. I know well that you are the best knight in the world, and since God wanted me to be honored by being made a knight by such [309] a man as you, I promise God that I'll never rest until I know if I'll be able to resemble my father in chivalry. If within this year I'm not such that men in this kingdom and in many others consider me a skilled knight, may God never help me if, after that, I bear shield or lance, whatever difficulty I may have."

Galahad said, "You've made a noble pledge.† May God make you such as I would wish."

Such a promise did Samaliel, son of King Frollo, make on the day he became a knight, and after he had made it, he said to Galahad, "My lord, I want to go away. I commend you to God."

"May God guide you," said Galahad.

Then they parted, each armed to his satisfaction. Galahad went off seeking the adventures of the kingdom of Logres, for he had plenty to do. On the third day he

---

*   Corresponds to Magne II:307-319; Piel 365-372.

†   Literally, "You've said a great deal."

happened to find Samaliel in a valley, badly wounded with many wounds, his horse so tired that it was almost falling.*

As soon as they saw each other, they recognized each other and said, "My lord, you are welcome."

"Who has wounded you like this?" asked Galahad.

"My lord," said Samaliel, "a knight of the Round Table whom they call Yvain, son of King Urien. He attacked me just now up there on that knoll, and I don't know why, so help me God, but he gained nothing by it, for I left him lying on the ground, and I don't know if he was mortally wounded or if he could be healed."

"And where are you going in such a great hurry?" asked Galahad.

He said, "I'm following a maiden who carried off a sword of mine, which belonged to my father, who gave it to me last night.† I had hung it from a tree when Yvain attacked me, and she took it while we were fighting. I wouldn't lose it for anything, and, therefore, I must leave you. I commend you to God."

"Be commended to God," said Galahad, "but take care not to ride far, for it will be dangerous for you."

"I will," he said.

Then they parted from each other.

Galahad went toward where he thought he would find Yvain, and when he got to where Yvain lay, he found him so badly hurt that he had no strength to get up. Galahad dismounted in order to see how he was and removed his helmet so he could rest better.

Yvain, who was in great distress and [310] had many perilous wounds, opened his eyes and asked, "Knight, who are you?"

"I'm Galahad," he said, "a knight who is grieved by your misfortune. For God's sake, tell me if you think you can escape death."

"Yes, my lord," he said, "certainly, for I have no mortal wound. Oh, Sir Galahad, long have I desired to see you, for I've heard much about you, and you are welcome. I can tell about myself more confidently to you than to anyone else. I have so many wounds large and small that I barely‡ expect to escape from them. I ask you for God's sake to help me get on my horse, and I'll go to an abbey near here, whether I die or live."

Galahad went to look for the horse and brought him to Yvain. He helped him mount and went with him to the abbey. There he had him dismount and had his wounds cared for by an old knight who was a brother there and who assured him that Yvain would not die of those wounds but would soon be healed of them, with God's aid. Thus Yvain found help for the wounds Samaliel had given him. Galahad stayed there four days for love of Yvain, and on the fourth day he asked him why that battle had taken place between him and Samaliel.

"Indeed," said Yvain, "it was because of Lucan the Wine Steward, whom he knocked down and to whom he gave a great wound. I followed to avenge Lucan,

---

*   Compare this incident with Galahad's meeting with the badly wounded Meleagant, whom he had recently knighted (chapter 82).

†   "last night" is probably a corruption, since King Arthur killed Samaliel's father some time previously (see chapter 39 and below in this chapter).

‡   Text has "don't," which contradicts his earlier statement.

and you see what happened to me, but I tell you this much good about the knight, that to my knowledge he's one of the best knights in the world, and he strikes well with the sword."

In the morning Galahad left him and again set out to seek the adventures of the kingdom of Logres as he was wont to do. But now the story stops speaking of him and returns to Samaliel.

After Samaliel parted from Sir Galahad, he rode, wounded as he was, until he caught up with the maiden. He took the sword from her and hung it from the cantle of his saddle.

She said to him, "Sir knight, you've taken the sword from me by force; know that if I find you where I have the upper hand, I'll make you pay dearly for it."

He made no reply to anything she said. At evening he came to a house where Kay the Seneschal was lodging. When Kay saw him with two swords, he wondered, for it was not then the custom for any knight in the kingdom of Logres to bear two swords unless he had made a promise or taken an oath.* And if anyone [311] were so bold as to bear two swords habitually, he could not refuse if two knights called him to battle. Therefore, Kay marveled at Samaliel, that he bore two swords, but he kept still, waiting for an opportunity to ask him about them. That evening, as they were sitting at the table, Kay looked a great deal at Samaliel, for he seemed to him a good knight.

When Kay saw a chance to ask Samaliel, he said to him, "Sir knight, I'd like to ask you, by your courtesy, to tell me who you are."

Samaliel answered, "My lord, I'm a foreign knight who has lived so briefly in the kingdom of Logres that I haven't yet any reputation, nor should anyone blame me for it, for it's only a little while since I became a knight."

"Then how are you so bold as to bear two swords?" asked Kay. "Don't you know the custom of wearing two swords?"

"No," said Samaliel, "but tell me about it, so help you God."

Then Kay told him about it, just as the story has already told.

"Indeed," said Samaliel, "I've never heard that, but I was bearing one for love of my father, to whom it belonged, and the other for love of the man who made me a knight, who girded it on me, and I love them both so much that I can't give up either, since it happens that I'm bearing them and I didn't know I was doing wrong. I promise God that I'll always bear them as long as I live by the laws of chivalry."

"Indeed," said Kay, "you've said too much. It's such a difficult thing that you've begun that I think harm will yet come to you."

"I don't know now what will happen to me because of it," said Samaliel, "but since it's so, may God let good come to me from it."

Then he asked Kay, "So help you God, tell me who you are."

"Indeed," he said, "I'm Kay, King Arthur's seneschal, and I'm of the Round Table."

When Samaliel heard him speak of King Arthur, he bowed his head and began to brood, so that Kay saw clearly from that brooding that the news had grieved him.

---

*   See Balin's two swords, chapter 8.

After a while Samaliel said, "You serve the man to whom I bear the greatest ill will, for he killed my father and that day inflicted such a great loss on me that where I had had a large portion of worldly good fortune, he reduced me to poverty and misery, from which I still suffer and will suffer as long as I live." [313]

"Who was your father?" asked Kay.

"My father was Frollo," he said, "the prince of Germany who was king of France, whom King Arthur killed on an island in Paris,* and because of this I could never love him but will hate him as long as I live."

When Kay heard this, he could not help saying, "Sir knight, I'm King Arthur's man, and I'm so much his that I would be disloyal if I didn't avenge him on all his enemies with all my strength. For love of him I say to you that you have no greater enemy in the world than I. I'll demonstrate that to you as soon as you leave here, but here you should fear nothing, since we're eating together."

Samaliel replied, "When you attack me, I'll defend myself if I can."

They said that much that night and spoke no more about it. And know that after he became a knight, Samaliel seldom ate anything but bread and water, except to keep someone company, nor did he ever want to kill anyone except in self-defense.†
The next day, when he had taken his arms, he set out to seek adventures as the other knights did. He had not gone far when he met Kay, who was a little way off the path waiting for him.

When Kay saw him approaching, he called, "Sir knight, defend yourself against me, for I don't want to attack you without defying you," and he lowered his lance to strike Samaliel.

Samaliel, who was agile and very brave, gave him a lance stroke that knocked Kay and his horse to the ground but did him no other harm, for his hauberk was good; however, he was badly bruised in the fall by his horse, who fell on top of him. The man who had knocked him down did not look back but passed by him and rode away, and know that he was riding with great difficulty because of his wounds, of which he had yet taken only little care. This was something that bothered him so much that, had he not been of great heart, he could not in any manner have endured it.

Samaliel rode all that day with great difficulty. At evening he reached the edge of a forest and took shelter there in a mountaineer's house, and he stayed there one month. After he was healed of his [315] wounds enough so that he could ride, he left and set out to seek adventures as before. One day, riding thus, he happened to meet Gaheriet and Girflet.

They stopped as soon as they saw him wearing two swords, and Gaheriet said to Girflet, "Now I see something I haven't seen in a long time."

"What is it, my lord?" asked Girflet.

"This knight who wears two swords, and he isn't one of the most cowardly in the world. I believe that if he were not better than anyone else, he wouldn't begin such a noble undertaking. Let's attack him, for we are two, just as the custom dictates."

---

*   In the Vulgate *Lancelot* (chapter 176) but missing from the Post-Vulgate as we have it; mentioned in chapter 60.

†   This is a notable characteristic of Galahad, as well.

Gaheriet said, "Please God, I won't attack him with another's aid, since he's alone. If he has begun his career so nobly, I shouldn't fault him for it, for I know well that his great heart led him to do it. But if you have a mind to joust, attack him by yourself, and if he knocks you down, I'll do my best to avenge you."

Then Girflet called to Samaliel, "Sir knight, you have to joust. Defend yourself!"

When Samaliel saw that he could not get away by any other means, he charged as fast as the horse could carry him and struck Girflet so hard that neither shield nor hauberk kept him from giving Girflet a great but not mortal wound. He knocked Girflet to the ground, and when he drew out the lance, Girflet gave a cry of agony, for he felt himself badly hurt.

When Gaheriet saw this, he said with sorrow, "Girflet, you have started a foolish enterprise. I don't think we'll come out of it with honor, but whatever happens to me as a result, I'll see if I can avenge you."

Then he charged at Samaliel, saying, "Defend yourself, knight!"

Samaliel, seeing that he must, turned toward him. Gaheriet struck him so that he gave him a great wound in his chest, but he did not move him from the saddle, and his lance splintered. Samaliel, who was stronger, did better,[*] for he struck Gaheriet so violently that he knocked him and his horse to the ground, but he did not wound him, for his hauberk was good. After that, he passed by. [316] When he realized he was wounded, he wanted to return to Gaheriet and kill him, but then he reflected that it would be the greatest villainy in the world if he laid a hand on a knight after he had knocked him down, unless the knight called him to battle, and therefore he went away.

When Girflet saw him go, he got up and went to Gaheriet, who had also stood up, and said to him, "Sir Gaheriet, let's go after him, for we'll be at fault if he escapes us thus."

"Sir Girflet," said Gaheriet, "you may do as you like, but I won't go after him at this time, for he has so well acquitted himself of his obligation to us that it would be a great villainy to ask more of him. I don't say that if I meet him another time I won't do my best with a sword, but at this time I'll do no more."

Thus spoke the two knights, and Samaliel went off riding one way and another, seeking adventures, and he did so much in a short time that his reputation became great, as well in King Arthur's house as in many other lands, and all those who saw him said that Frollo's son, if he lived, would be one of the best knights in the world.

King Arthur, hearing this, said, "If he has become a good knight, it's no wonder, for his father was a very good knight."

One day it happened that Samaliel was riding through the forest of Camelot alone. This was at the beginning of winter. King Arthur had gone to the forest that day to hunt, and all his men had become separated from him except one squire. The king was weary from his hunt, and he dismounted beside a spring and lay down to sleep, and the squire took care of his horse, leading it back and forth so it would not founder. As the king was lying asleep, Samaliel happened to arrive there armed.

---

[*]   Literally, "reached him better."

As the king was lying down, and because he did not recognize him, he asked the squire, "Who's that knight sleeping there?"

The squire, suspecting nothing of the true situation, replied, "This is King Arthur."

"So?" said Samaliel. "This is blessed news! Now may ill fortune take me if I don't avenge my father, whom he killed."

When the squire heard this, he was badly frightened for his lord because of the knight, who was armed, and he called to the king, [317] "Oh my lord get up, get up, for this knight wants to kill you!"

The king was sleeping so hard that he did not awaken. When Samaliel heard the squire crying out, he took his sword and pretended he wanted to cut off his head.

The boy, who feared to die, clasped his hands toward the sword and said, "Oh, my lord, mercy! I'll be still, and so will the whole world after you have killed such a man as this, for after his death they'll have nothing to talk about."

When Samaliel heard this, he was frightened and changed his mind, for he considered King Arthur one of the best men in the world, and he thought how he welcomed all the good men who came to him. Nevertheless, he dismounted, tied his horse to a tree, and held in his hand his naked sword, the one that had belonged to his father.

He went thus to King Arthur and stood looking at him, and when he saw him to be so large and well built, he said, "Indeed, if he weren't good, it would be a great wrong, for of all the kings I have seen, he seems most endowed with good qualities."

Then he began to consider whether he would kill him or spare him, and he said in his heart, "He killed my father, and if I don't avenge his death, after I've prepared for it, everyone will blame me. On the other hand, if I kill King Arthur, who's the best king in the world and always supports chivalry better and more honorably than any other king, this will be the greatest misfortune and sin that ever happened on earth."

Thus Samaliel thought about these things, as he held his sword in his hand. He wanted to avenge his father's death, but he could not, for the knowledge deterred him that such great loss could not come to the world from the death of any other single man.

Then he called the squire and asked him, "Do you know who I am?"

"No, my lord," he said.

"Know, then," he said, "that I'm Samaliel, son of Frollo King of Gauna, whom King Arthur killed near Paris. I wanted to avenge my father's death and had a great desire to do so when I came here. But the great good that men tell of King Arthur has taken away my will to do it, and, therefore, I'll rather let him live. But so he may know the good deed I have done here, I'll take his sword and leave him my father's, so it may remind him of my courtesy and moderation when he finds it."

Then he took the sword the king bore and left his, and after that, he got on his horse and went his way. [319]

Now the story stops talking about Samaliel and turns to King Arthur.

After King Arthur had slept a long time, he awoke and asked the squire for his horse, which the boy brought, and the king mounted.

When he got ready to belt on his sword and saw that it was not his, he asked the squire, "Who has changed my sword on me?"

The squire answered, "Oh, my lord, you don't know what happened to you just now while you slept. Never, to my knowledge, has such a marvelous adventure happened to anyone, for you were in danger of death."

Then he told him everything he had seen and what he had heard from Samaliel.

"Indeed," said the king, "if he had killed me, it would be no great wonder, for I certainly killed his father. But for such great courtesy and kindness as he has done me, I would gladly reward him, if the chance arose. And in remembrance of his moderation, I'll bear this sword always, unless I'm forced to change it for another, better one."*

The king was happy at this adventure that had happened to him, and he wondered about Samaliel, how, being so young, he had known how to show such great courtesy. King Arthur thought much about this that day. When he arrived at Camelot, he told everyone at court, and everyone who heard it said Samaliel would never fail to be a good man. The king had this put in writing in the great book of the adventures.

But now the story stops talking about King Arthur and Samaliel and returns to Lancelot.

144. LANCELOT, HECTOR, GAHERIET, AND GAWAIN AT CORBENIC.†

After Galahad had parted from his father, just as the story has already told,‡ Lancelot remained on the bark and sailed many days across the sea as chance took him. One night the bark happened to land at Corbenic near the gate. After Lancelot had looked closely at the castle, he recognized that it was Corbenic, and he thanked Our Lord fervently for this adventure, for it seemed certain to him that his quest would be finished, either to his honor or to his shame. When he had taken his arms, he commended himself to Our Lord, left the bark, and went to the gate. As soon as he left it, he saw the bark sail away as fast as if all the winds of the world were taking it. After he had stood until he could no longer see it, he went over the bridge on foot and armed, entered the castle by a little gate, and went to the great palace. He found no one to challenge him, for it was already past midnight and everyone was asleep. [321] When he reached the palace, the one they called the Palace of Adventures, he found the gate open. He crossed himself, commended himself to God, and went inside, thanking Our Lord for having brought him there.

And if anyone asks me why the knights errant could not go to Corbenic, since they knew that the Holy Grail was there, I will tell him just what the true history tells. The castle of Corbenic never moved, but Tanabos the Enchanter, who lived before King Uther Pendragon and who was the wisest necromancer there ever was

---

*   Excalibur does not seem to be an issue in this incident.
†   Corresponds to Magne II:319-333; Piel 372-380.
‡   Chapter 141.

in the kingdom of Logres, except Merlin, established that castle in such a way that no outside knight who sought it could find it, unless chance took him there, and if he had been there a hundred times, he would not know how to go there more quickly. And if anyone who knew the way wanted to take a stranger there, he would not know how to do it. All this Tanabos had done because of his wife, who was very beautiful and whom a knight loved, from which it happened that, after Tanabos had made the enchantment, the knight could not go to the lady or the lady to him. Therefore, they both died when they saw that they could not see each other. That spell lasted from before Uther Pendragon's reign until the coming of Charlemagne, who had the castle pulled down and destroyed, and never after was it rebuilt. Now that you know this, I will return you to my subject.

When Lancelot entered the Palace of Adventures, he walked through it until he reached a room where he saw a great light. He went in to see what was there, and he found nothing but two thick candles burning. He went on from room to room until he reached the chamber where the Holy Grail was, and he saw such a great light as if it were midday. He looked at the room and saw it to be so beautiful and rich that he had never seen anything else that seemed so good to him. In the middle of the room was a table of silver in place of an altar, with the Holy Vessel on it, covered as richly as it had been on the day when Joseph was the first bishop and sang Mass.* When Lancelot saw the place where the Holy Vessel stood covered, at once he knew that that was the Holy Grail.

He said, "Oh, God! How fortunate the man would be [322] who could now see that vessel that stands there covered, because of which so many great marvels have come to pass in the kingdom of Logres!"

Then he looked all around to see if he could see anyone who would keep him from entering, for he wanted to go to the holy table and unveil the Holy Vessel, to see what was there.

Then he heard a voice that said to him, "Lancelot, do not enter, for it is not granted to you."

But he was so eager to see that for which so many good men were striving that he threw himself into the room as far as he could. He did not go far, for he felt many hands, which seized him by the body and arms and hair and pulled him out, and they gave him such a great fall to the ground that he thought he was dying, and he lay unconscious until it was full daylight.

In the morning, when the knights came in and found the armed knight lying in front of the door to the room of the Holy Grail, they all crossed themselves and looked to see if they could recognize him, and they found him so badly hurt that he could not move foot or hand. They disarmed him completely and took him to the king's palace, but no one there could recognize him, not even King Pelles, although he had seen him many times. But the king did recognize that the man was not dead, but he fully expected that he would soon die, because he did not move any of his limbs. Therefore, he had him watched all that day. Toward evening it happened that King Pelles's beautiful daughter came to see Lancelot; after she had looked at

---

*   *The History of the Holy Grail,* chapter 7.

him a long time, she recognized that he was Lancelot, the man she loved most in the world.*

When she saw him like that, she felt great grief, and she said, "Indeed, my lord, if you die it will be a great pity and loss to the world."

After she had said this, she went away, and those who remained understood that she had recognized him. After she had reached her room she began to make the greatest lamentation in the world. The news reached the king that his daughter had recognized the knight, and the king sent for her and told her to tell him who the knight was, and she told him. [323]

"Oh!" he said, "I'm very sorry about his affliction."

Then he had Lancelot taken to a room and undressed, and know that when they found him wearing a hair shirt, they marveled greatly at it, because they knew about Lancelot's luxurious lifestyle, and they could not believe he would wear such a harsh garment. After they had undressed him, they laid him in a room far from people; the king had him watched closely, and the king himself stayed there, because he imagined that Lancelot would soon die.

What shall I tell you? In this way Lancelot lay there twenty-four days without eating or drinking, and no one saw him make any sign that he would not soon die. On the twenty-fifth day there came there a hermit of very holy life, to whom Our Lord had revealed many of His secrets.

When the king saw him enter, he went to do him honor, and after they had talked a long while the king said, "Let's go see a marvel that I want to show you."

The hermit said to him, "Is it Lancelot that you want to show me?"

He answered, "My lord, you speak the truth. And, for God's sake, if you know why he endures so long in such great distress, tell me."

"My lord," said the hermit, "he has well deserved what he's suffering. It's twenty-five days today that he has been suffering this distress, and he'll soon be free of it. These twenty-five days stand for the twenty-five years that he has been a knight of Holy Church, and were it not for one sin, in which he has so long persisted, he wouldn't fail to have honor and praise in this quest."

This the good man said of Lancelot, and he was telling the truth.

The next day at the hour of prime Lancelot spoke and asked where he was, for he did not remember that he was in the house of the Fisher King.

The king, who was standing nearby, said, "You're at Corbenic."

Then Lancelot remembered the room where he had seen the Holy Grail, and what the voice had said to him.

The king asked him, "How do you feel?"

"I'd feel better and be better if I could stay forever in the pleasure I've seen. But it grieves me that they've taken me from it."

"And do you think you'll recover?" asked the king.

"I am recovered," he said, "for I feel nothing wrong." [325]

Then he had himself dressed, but he was much grieved that they had taken the hair shirt from him, and in his embarrassment he did not dare ask for it. The news

---

*   This episode echoes Elaine's recognition of Lancelot in his madness and his cure in the Grail castle (chapter 65).

swept through the castle that the knight who had lain unconscious so long was well again, and all came to see the marvel. Nobody knew who he was except the king and his daughter, but before the day was far advanced, most of them knew, and they honored him more than before.

On the third day it happened that King Pelles was sitting at his dinner in the Palace of Adventures, and they had all been served already by the grace of the Holy Vessel. As they were sitting, all the windows and doors of the palace began to shake and to close, with no one touching them, and they shook as if there were a storm.

Lancelot, who was sitting near the king, asked him, "My lord, what's happening here, just as if there were a storm?"

"I'll tell you," said the king. "This is a sign that Our Lord shows frequently to the knights of the Round Table who start on the quest for the Holy Grail without being confessed, and they have themselves called servants of Holy Church, but they aren't. Our Lord demonstrates this fact here to them in this way, that when they come here and want to enter this palace, which is named the Palace of Adventures, all the windows and doors shake, and they close against them. And by this sign I know truly that some adventurous knight is at the door and wants to enter but can't."

As the king was speaking of this, they heard a knight at the door calling out, "Open! Open!"

The king said to Lancelot, "Now you may hear what I was telling you. That is one of the knights of the Round Table."

"Oh, my lord," said Lancelot, "have him come in!"

"I couldn't do that even if I wanted," said the king. Then he called one of his knights and said to him, [327] "Go tell that knight who's outside to go his way, for he can't enter here."

The knight went to the window and opened it, and he saw waiting in the courtyard Hector of the Fens on a marvelously large horse.

He said to him, "Sir knight, go your way. You won't enter here, for you have aspired too high."

He said this to the knight to mock him. As soon as Hector heard it, he instantly remembered the dream he had dreamt and how the good man had interpreted it for him,* and then he was so sad that he wished he were dead, for he saw clearly that not for anything he had done in the quest for the Holy Grail would he have reward or praise when he returned to court, but shame and dishonor. The knight asked him what his name was.

"My name is Hector of the Fens," he said, "and it was an evil hour for me when I first picked up a shield, for I'm so shamed this time that I won't ever receive honor."

Then, weeping hard, he turned away and went off through the streets of the castle with such great grief that he wished he were dead. The knight turned back to King Pelles and told him that the knight was going away, and then he told them that it was Hector of the Fens.

---

*   Chapters 91-92.

When the king heard that it had been Hector, Lancelot's brother, he said to his knights, "Go after him, for, just because he may not enter this palace, I won't fail to show him honor and love."

Then most of them mounted. They caught up with Hector outside the castle and told him what the king had sent them to say, and he said he would not return for anything.

"My lord," they said, "you'll at least do so for love of your brother Lancelot, who is there and who sent you word by us."

"What?" he asked. "Is my lord and brother there?"

"Yes, certainly," they said.

Hector was so deeply grieved by this news that he said, "Now I never want to bear arms again, nor may it please God that I be able to, for I'll never receive honor for anything I can do when my brother knows the dishonor that has come to me here."

Then he left them and went off as fast as the horse could carry him, cursing the hour of his birth and that in which he had become a knight and taken arms, for his [328] lineage, in which were the best knights in the world, would never receive honor because of him but dishonor and degradation.*

Thus Hector went away lamenting. He had not gone far when he met Gawain and Gaheriet, and they greeted him, for they had recognized him from far off. He stopped and greeted them sadly, a man full of grief. When Gawain saw that he was greeting them so sadly, he thought it was because of Eric's death, at which he became very angry and passed him by. Gaheriet, who loved Hector well, stopped and asked him, by his faith and the friendship there was between them, to tell him the truth about what he had found.

"For I know well," he said, "that where you are coming from you've found something at which you are grieved."

Hector told him everything that had happened to him at Corbenic.

"And I wouldn't have cared at all," he said, "had it not been for my brother, who was there and saw my misfortune."

Gaheriet, who loved him well, comforted him as much as he could, saying, "Oh, Sir Hector, don't grieve so. Know that many adventures worse than this have happened on this quest to many good men of the Round Table. And since you have so many companions in loss and misfortune, you should take comfort."

Hector said he would do so, but he was very sad about it.

"Now I ask you," said Gaheriet, "to go relax at a castle near here, which belongs to a relative of mine, and wait for me there until I return from Corbenic, and know that I'll return to you and tell you what happens to me and my brother."

Hector said that he would not await him more than two days.

Then they parted. Hector went where Gaheriet had told him, and Gaheriet went after his brother. After he had caught up with him, they set out toward Corbenic.

---

* "for his [328] lineage, in which were the best knights in the world, would never receive honor because of him" as in Piel (377). Magne has "as well as his lineage, in which were the best knights in the world, for they would never receive honor...."

They had not gone far when they saw the castle, and Gawain said, "Oh, God! Lord, if it pleases You, let me enter this castle and come out of it with greater honor than last time."*

"What?" asked Gaheriet. "Were you dishonored here?"

"Yes," said Gawain, "and I've never been worse in any place where I've been."

"Now don't worry about it," said Gaheriet, "for if you didn't have good fortune then, you will now." [329]

Then they entered the castle and went to the fortress. When they reached the Palace of Adventures, they could not enter, for they found all the doors and windows locked. When Gaheriet saw this, he knew at once from what Hector had told him that he could not enter, and he was so deeply grieved that he wished he were dead.

Gawain began to call out, "Open! open!"

After a little, a maiden came and said to him, "Who are you, knight, who want to enter?"

He gave his name, and she said, "Sir Gawain, you may go away, for neither you nor your companion can enter here. But if you please to take shelter in this castle, you'll find many there who will show you honor and love."

"What?" asked Gaheriet. "Can't we enter here?"†

"No," she said, "for it doesn't please Our Lord, and by this you may see that you haven't served Our Lord in this quest as you should have."‡

Gaheriet answered sorrowfully, "My lady, that grieves me."

Then Gawain said to Gaheriet, "Brother, let's turn back, for I wouldn't stay here any longer, since I can't go inside."

Gaheriet said the same. Then they turned away, and the maiden asked Gaheriet what his name was.

He said, "I know that you ask me that in order to mock me. Nevertheless, I'll tell you. My name is Gaheriet."

Then he went off after his brother. As they went along the street, they met many men and women who laughed and mocked them because they were returning so quickly from the Palace of Adventures. After Gawain got out of the castle, he began to curse it and all who lived in it and wished that a bolt of lightning would strike it and knock it to the depths of the abyss.

"Oh, my lord," said Gaheriet, "you speak wrongly. You know well that the Holy Vessel is there, because of which God has performed such a beautiful miracle for the world."

He answered, "For the Vessel I pray only for honor and good, but I'd wish that the castle were knocked down by lightning, for I've never come here without leaving in shame and sorrow."

"Oh, my lord," said Gaheriet, "for that we must blame not the castle but ourselves, for we've done bad deeds, because of which we can't have honor there."

---

*   Not in the Post-Vulgate as we have it.

†   "enter here" as in Piel (378). Magne has "stay here."

‡   In the Vulgate *Lancelot* (chapter 137), Gawain saw the Grail at Corbenic but failed to recognize it. Moreover, he was not fed from it because, as he later learned, he lacked humility.

"Now tell me," said Gawain, "what shall we do? For it seems to me that [331] from the beginning we've followed the quest for the Holy Grail in vain, for I see that we are at the peak of all the honor we'll have from it. And, therefore, I'd think it good for us to return to Camelot."

"My lord," said Gaheriet, "that would be to our shame, for I see that none of the questors of this quest is there yet, and if we're the first to return, we'll always be condemned for it."

"Then what shall we do?" he asked.

"My lord," said Gaheriet, "let's go to seek adventures, as we were doing before, and let's ride for a year or two. When we learn that some of our companions are at court, then we can go without blame."

As they were standing talking about this and taking counsel, suddenly a maiden approached, saying as she reached them, "Gawain! Gawain! Now your evil deeds become apparent. Much wrong have you done in this quest, and many good knights have you killed treacherously and treasonably. Indeed, if the men of the castle knew the brutalities you've committed since you left court, they wouldn't let you go but would make you die a hard death. Be informed that Perceval, the true knight, whose father you killed, will enter the Palace of Adventures with greater honor than you, and, therefore, his goodness will be more to him than your evil to you, for you conceal your evil as much as you can, but his goodness and his good life can't be concealed, but Our Lord will make them known."

And know that the maiden who said that was Yvain's sister.*

Gawain made no reply, feeling himself guilty of everything she said, and he said to Gaheriet, "Brother, let's go."

Gaheriet agreed, and he could not for anything believe that Gawain had done so much wrong in that quest as he had. The maiden returned to the castle, and the brothers rode all day and reached the place where Hector was awaiting Gaheriet.

"My lord," said Gaheriet to Gawain, "we must see Hector, who is waiting for us here."

"I won't see him," said Gawain, "for he hates me because of Eric's death, in which, [333] so help me God, I'm not so guilty as he says. But you go, if you wish."

Then Gawain went his way, and Gaheriet entered the castle and went to where Hector awaited him. When Hector saw him, he received him well and asked him how it had been for him at Corbenic.

Gaheriet told him everything, and Hector took some comfort and said, "Now I can't be alone, since I have you as a companion in this misfortune."

As they were speaking thus, suddenly Lancelot came in. It was already completely dark, and the people of the castle, who were accustomed to honoring and serving knights errant, took him to a room and disarmed him. After that, they took him to where Gaheriet and Hector were sitting, and when they saw him they were happy and asked him how it was with him.

Gaheriet said, "Oh, Sir Lancelot, I've never seen a man so tormented by grief as your brother has been today because of the adventure of the palace where he

---

* Chapters 88, 89.

couldn't enter, while you were inside. But he shouldn't grieve much over it, because the same thing happened to me and to Sir Gawain."

Lancelot said, "I left Corbenic only to catch up with him and comfort him, for I knew well what would happen to him there, and I want him to take comfort and not care a straw about it, for many men have failed to enter there since this quest began, men I consider as good knights as he is."

Hector replied, "My lord, know that I felt such grief not because I had failed to enter but because I was shamed before you, for I thought you'd think ill of me because of it."

Lancelot said, "I don't blame you for it, for of the questors there will be few who can enter there."

Then Hector was much consoled, since his brother comforted him so well.

145. GALAHAD DEFEATS PALAMEDES, WHO IS THEN BAPTIZED AND SEATED AT THE ROUND TABLE.[*]

Early the next morning they departed. Gaheriet had wanted to speak of peace between Hector and Gawain, but he dared not at that time. That day at midday they chanced upon a forest, and they saw the Questing Beast come out of a valley. They saw a good sixty dogs after it, some beagles, some bulldogs, some very good greyhounds, and they were barking so hard after it that the whole valley echoed. [334]

"Now after it," said Lancelot. "Evil to him who lets it go if he can help it."

Then they struck the horses with their spurs, and they had not gone far when they heard Palamedes coming after them, calling out, "Turn back, my lords, turn back! Don't take my quest from me, for no good can come to you of it."

Gaheriet looked behind him; he pointed out Palamedes to Lancelot and Hector and said, "Oh, God! What a good knight is coming!"

"Who is he?" asked Lancelot.

"He's Palamedes the pagan," said Gaheriet, "one of the best knights in the world, who has already carried on the hunt for this beast a good fourteen years and more."

Hector called to him, "Sir knight, will you joust?"

"Yes," he said, "since you wish it."

They charged at each other as fast as their horses could carry them, and they struck each other so violently that both of them were badly wounded, but from that blow Hector fell, his horse on top of him. Gaheriet charged at Palamedes, who did the same to him as to Hector, or even worse.

When Lancelot saw these two blows, he said in his heart, "Gaheriet spoke the truth. If this isn't one of the best knights in the world, I'll never believe what I see. I don't know what will come of it, but I'll joust with him, although I do a great

---

* Corresponds to Magne II:333-357; Piel 380-393.

discourtesy, for after two such blows he should be free of any other claim. But in any case I'll do all I can to avenge my brother and my companion, for if I didn't avenge them, people would think it wrong of me."

Then he called to the knight, "Defend yourself against me, for you must joust."

Palamedes replied, "I have no need to joust now, for I've done enough this time, and if you wish to force me beyond that, people won't think it courteous of you."

"You're wasting time," said Lancelot. "Whatever discourtesy I may do you, you must joust, like it or not."

"That grieves me," he said, "but if I must, I will."

Then they charged at each other and struck each other so violently that neither shield nor hauberk kept them from feeling the lance points in their bodies, and, if the lances had not broken, they could both have died. Each knocked the other down, his horse on top of him, but both were of great [335] skill and courage, and they got up quickly.

Palamedes went to his horse, mounted, and said to Lancelot, "My lord, I've acquitted myself well toward you. Now I ask you, by your courtesy, to let me go."

"And how do you feel?" asked Lancelot.

"You and that other, your companion," he said, "have wounded me badly."

"Then you may go now," said Lancelot, "since you're wounded. If I called you to a sword fight to your sorrow, I'd commit a great discourtesy."

Palamedes went away at once, and Hector and the other two mounted.

Gaheriet said to Hector, "My lord, how does that knight seem to you?"

"He can only seem good to me," said Hector, "for without doubt, this is the best knight I've ever met, except for Galahad and Tristan."

"Indeed," said Lancelot, "were he not wounded as badly as he is, and would he not think it a discourtesy in me, I wouldn't for anything let him go without calling him to battle, but because of that, and because he did very well among us, I don't want to. Now may he go to good fortune, for I'll always speak well of him."

Thus spoke Lancelot about Palamedes, and Palamedes left the road and went where he thought he would soonest find his beast, and he had not gone far when he met Gawain, who was following the beast at great speed.

As soon as Palamedes overtook Gawain, he said, "Sir knight, what necessity makes you ride so fast?"

"My lord," said Gawain, "I'm following a beast that I saw pass by me just now. It's so strange and bizarre that the desire took me never to leave it until I've caught it."

"Now I'm hearing marvels," said Palamedes. "I've never before heard of a house where there were so many mad knights or so many wise ones as in King Arthur's house, and the wise ones surpass in skill and fame all the other wise knights in the world, and the mad ones surpass in madness all the other mad knights in the world."

"Why do you say that?" asked Gawain.

"For God's sake," said Palamedes, "I say it because of you and the other madmen who have begun the quest for the Holy Grail—none of you may come to the end of it, nor [337] have you yet received anything from it except shame, but along with that quest, in which you've done nothing from which honor might come to you,

you've begun another quest. Isn't this extremely great madness, that you leave what you've begun and start on quests that foreign knights have been following for a long time? Wouldn't it be better first to bring to an end the quest you've begun than to meddle in another? You're one of those people who meddle in everything and leave each thing with shame."

When Gawain heard this, he said, "Are you the foreign knight who has conducted the hunt for this beast so long?"

"Yes," he said, "I am."

"You speak not to your honor," said Gawain, "but to your shame, when you say that you've been following this beast so long, for, indeed, if you were a good knight, you'd have brought it to an end long ago."

Palamedes answered, "One can't find a good knight as quickly as you think."

"Indeed," said Gawain, "there's no knight in King Arthur's house so bad that, had he ridden as long as you have in this quest, he wouldn't have completed it."

"Yes, there are some," said Palamedes, "and if you yourself had followed this beast as long as I, you wouldn't yet have caught it, for in my opinion I'm as good a knight as you, and I've been laboring a long time and haven't yet accomplished anything."

"What?" asked Gawain. "Do you think you're as good a knight as I?"

"Yes," he said.

"In God's name," said Gawain, "then defend yourself against me, for I want to see this at once, and if you're a better knight than I, I'll leave you your quest."

"Indeed," said Palamedes, "I wouldn't now refuse to joust, were it not that I'm badly wounded. Therefore, I ask you to let me go, for if you have the better in the joust, there will be no honor for you, since I'm wounded and you're whole."

"This may not be," said Gawain, "since you've challenged me in chivalry. Either joust with me or I'll kill you."

"Indeed," said Palamedes, "I have no need to joust at this time, but I'll do it, since I have no choice." [339]

Then they charged at each other and struck each other with all their strength. Gawain, who did not have Palamedes's skill, fell to the ground, badly wounded. Palamedes passed by him without looking at him again and, although he was wounded, rode off after his beast just as if he had been whole.

Gawain, who remained on the ground, was so deeply grieved that he could find no consolation, and he called himself star-crossed, wretched, and unfortunate. As he was standing and lamenting under an oak tree, suddenly along came Galahad, whom chance brought there at that time. When Galahad saw him, he recognized Gawain by his arms, for he had had them newly painted with his insignia. Galahad was amazed to see Gawain making such a lamentation, for he knew that it was not without a good reason. When Gawain saw Galahad, he knew him by his shield, for no other knight bore such a shield, and he was much pleased, for he imagined that he would be avenged on the knight who had put such grief in his heart.

Galahad said to Gawain as soon as he reached him, "Sir Gawain, God be with you. How are you?"

"Ill, my lord," he said, "for a brutal, arrogant knight, who is riding away from here, has shamed and wounded me. And I'm grieved not so much for myself as for a knight of the Round Table whom he killed just now, one of the best friends we had."

"What was his name?" asked Galahad.

"Lionel," said Gawain, "Sir Bors's brother."

Gawain made this accusation in order to create mortal hatred between Galahad and the Knight of the Questing Beast.

Galahad really believed that Gawain was telling the truth, and he was deeply grieved by this news and asked, "Who's the knight who did this?"

And Gawain told him enough about the knight that Galahad realized it was Palamedes.

Then Galahad asked which way the knight had been going, and Gawain showed him which way he had gone.

Galahad said, [340] "He has made me lose a knight I much loved, and I think he'll find himself the worse for it."

Then he rode off as fast as he could. He found Palamedes beside a spring where he had dismounted to bind up his wounds. When he saw Galahad coming so fast, he realized at once that he was not coming for his welfare, and his heart failed him,* for he well knew that he could not stand against Galahad, whom he considered to be the best knight in the world.

Galahad called to him, "Palamedes, defend yourself against me, for I challenge you, because you've killed one of the knights I loved most in the world, and be sure that I'll do the same to you, unless you can defend yourself against me. Mount quickly, or I'll strike you as you are."

When Palamedes heard this, he did not know what to say, for he knew well that if they came to battle, the result was a foregone conclusion.

Therefore, he replied the best he could, "Oh, Sir Galahad, my lord, mercy! Know that I have never knowingly killed a man of your lineage and that even if I had killed him and you, therefore, wished to fight with me, you should look for a day and time that would be to your honor, so that, after you had conquered me, you wouldn't be shamed or blamed for it. But, indeed, if you make me fight with you now, you'll have no honor thereby, for you are completely whole, and I'm very badly wounded—amazingly so—and have lost so much blood that all strength has failed me, so that it would happen that any good man who heard it would consider you wrong and at fault, and thus you could lose your honor for nothing."

"This is a waste of time," said Galahad; "you have to fight."

"That I cannot do," said Palamedes, "and even if I wanted to, I couldn't, and therefore [341] I tell you that at this time you may well kill me, for I won't lift a hand against you."

"Then what will you do?" asked Galahad. "Will you yield yourself vanquished without a blow, being such a good knight as you are?"

"I won't yield myself as vanquished," said Palamedes, "as long as I have my soul in my body. But since you have such a wish to fight with me, give me respite until I'm healed, and let us set a day and place to meet, and if you defeat me there, you'll earn honor and praise."

---

* Literally, "his mind and his heart changed."

"Indeed," said Galahad, "since you are as badly wounded as you say, I'd give you a brief truce, if I thought you'd come at the end of it."

"I promise you as a knight," said Palamedes.

"Now I tell you," said Galahad, "twenty days from today be beside this spring at the hour of prime, and if I don't arrive at that hour, await me all that day, and come prepared to defend yourself against me."

Palamedes promised Galahad he would do it. After they had exchanged oaths, Galahad went away to seek adventures, and Palamedes mounted, rode to his father's house, dismounted, and had himself disarmed.

When his father saw him so badly wounded, he felt such grief that he began to weep and said, "Son, your knightly skill has been your undoing, for you'll die for it before your time."

Palamedes made no reply to anything his father said to him, and he went to lie down in a room. His father, who knew a great deal about it, had his wounds attended.

After he had seen to them, he said to Palamedes, "Son, don't be afraid of these wounds, for you'll certainly recover from them."

Palamedes made no reply, for he was thinking hard about his battle and about Galahad, for he knew well that it could only end in his death, and he was in the greatest distress over it that he had ever known. Two days he lay without eating or drinking; they could not get a word out of him, and he was always brooding.

His father, who recognized [343] quickly that his brooding was not the result of pain or fear of death from his wounds, said to him, "Son, what are you thinking? Whenever I've seen you, I've seen you happier than other knights, and now I see you so sad and pensive that I'm amazed, and I ask you to tell me the source of this brooding."

Palamedes loved his father very much; when he saw him so distressed by his brooding and by the desire to know its source, he said, "My lord, if I'm pensive it isn't surprising, for since I became a knight I've never begun anything I didn't finish with honor, except the quest for the Questing Beast, to which I couldn't put an end, and I see clearly that such a noble adventure isn't to be accomplished by me. But now there has come to me a frightening adventure, in which I'll meet my death, unless I'm saved by great good luck."

"What is it?" asked his father.

"I have to fight with Sir Galahad," he said, "the best knight in the world."

When his father heard this, he fell unconscious to the ground, such grief did he feel.

After he had come to and could speak, he said, "Oh, son! Bad luck has come to you!"

"I know," said Palamedes, "that no good can come to me from this fight. However, I can't get out of it, for I've promised."

"Son," said his father, "you know how Jesus Christ, the kind and merciful Father, has until now been Father and Friend to you, and you've always been an enemy to Him. Of His wonderful grace He has given you knightly skill* and better fortune,

---

*   Literally, "He gave you such wonderful grace of knightly skill."

judged according to your sinful state, than to any other knight I know. What shall I tell you? He has shown you wonderful love and greater kindness than to any other sinful knight, for He has always delivered you from all perils with honor. He has done so much for you, and you nothing for Him, and He wants to show you this now, for when you have greatest need of His mercy, He'll fail you, so that you'll die in this battle unpleasantly and shamefully, and whatever skill at arms you have always had will be dead and turned to nothing."

When Palamedes heard this he said, "My lord, you speak the truth, but give me your advice about [345] this, for the battle can't be called off unless I die before the end of the period of truce."

His father said to him, "Son, if you'll receive baptism and turn to the law of the Christians, I know well that Our Lord Jesus Christ will give some great help to your situation, so that you'll get out of this battle with your honor and Galahad's friendship. And know that if you don't do it, you'll die with dishonor, and I, who am your father and love you more than myself, will die of grief, for after you have left me, I'll know no happiness."

"What?" asked Palamedes. "Are you telling me as my father that if I receive baptism, I'll get out of this battle with honor?"

"Yes, son," said his father, "I tell you that as your father and your friend."

"And I," said Palamedes, "now promise to Our Lord Jesus Christ that, if He gets me get out of this battle in one piece, I'll receive baptism at once and, from that time on, I'll be a loyal knight of Holy Church."

"Son," said his father, "it's so with mortal things, that if you're alive today, you don't know if you will be tomorrow. Therefore, I advise you, for the profit of your soul and the honor of your person, to have yourself baptized as soon as you can, for mortal flesh, as you know well, has no truce beyond its appointed lifespan."

Palamedes answered, "As I have promised God, so shall I do without fail."

The father, who loved his son with paternal love, dared say no more to him against his will but comforted him as much as he could and said to him, "Son, have no fear, for the promise you've made Our Lord will get you out of this battle happy and with honor."

"May God do it," he said, "if it pleases Him."

Thus Palamedes remained with his father during that truce, brooding all the while and more and more sorrowful. He was fortunate that before the twenty days were up he was fully recovered and able to bear arms. During this respite he had all his arms made fresh, the best the people of that land knew how, and their covers were all black. The day before the battle was [346] to be, he had himself armed in the presence of his father, who might see if he was lacking anything, and be sure that his armor was the best one could find.

When his father and the people of the house saw that he lacked nothing, the former said, "Wear it confidently, for you'll lose nothing because of your armor."

Palamedes replied sadly, "May He help me to whom I've promised to hold to His true belief; may He help me at this time, for I truly believe that He'll be worth more to me in this great need than all the armor I bear."

This Palamedes said, having already turned his belief to the true faith of Jesus Christ.

That night Esclabor was very sad and worried about his son, for he knew well that Palamedes was not such a knight as Galahad. The next morning Palamedes got up and had himself armed. After he was armed and had mounted the best horse he could find, he parted from his father.

At their parting, Palamedes saw him weeping, and he said, "My lord, why are you weeping? Now it seems to me that you don't have enough faith in Jesus Christ, for if you truly believed, you wouldn't fear for me, since I've made Him such a promise."

"Son," said his father, "You're right. Go, now, and may He who can deliver you from all peril come to your aid."

After that, he made the sign of the cross over him and commended him to God, and he said further, "Son, I command you, as a father should command his son, to come see me, if you can, today by nightfall at the latest, for I'll never be happy or well until I see you."

And Palamedes promised him that he would do so.

After this, the son left the father and went toward where the battle was to be. He had not gone far when he met Gawain. When Gawain saw Palamedes, he did not recognize him, because Palamedes wore different armor, but Palamedes recognized him.

Gawain said to him, "I ask you to joust."

Palamedes did not reply. Gawain thought him disdainful and said to him, "What's this, knight? Don't you hear what I'm saying to you?"

Palamedes heard him well, but he did not [347] answer him but went his way. Then Gawain became angry, for it seemed to him that Palamedes was doing it for some evil reason. He got in front of Palamedes, took him by the bridle, and said to him, "I'm taking you captive, knight; either joust with me, or yield yourself defeated in the joust."

Palamedes replied, "Let me go, sir knight, and don't force me to it, since it doesn't please me. Know that I won't joust with you today."

"Why not?" asked Gawain.

"Because it doesn't please me," he said. 'You won't make me joust by force."

"That's true," he said, "but since you're a knight errant like me, and you fail me in the joust, I consider that you do it from cowardice and lack of skill."

"You don't speak truly," said Palamedes, "and it isn't courteous to say grievous things to a strange knight whom you don't know. However unskilled and cowardly I may be, if you had as much to do today as I do and knew your peril to be as great as I know mine, indeed, you aren't so brave that you would dare go there, for you have neither courage nor strength nor skill by which you could escape without loss of your life. And I tell you this because of the discourtesy I find in you."

Gawain, who was very angry, replied, "Knight, you despise me greatly, and that grieves me, for I'm sure that you've never seen me joust. Nevertheless, however unskilled I may be, I ask you by the faith that you owe to all knighthood to joust one time with me, and, by my faith, I'll ask no more of you."

"So pressingly have you invited me," said Palamedes, "that I'll do it, even though it isn't in my best interest, for I have much to do elsewhere."

By then they were both angry, and, much aggrieved, they charged at each other. Palamedes struck Gawain in such a way that he knocked him and his horse to the ground. He went to him and took Gawain's lance in place of his own, which had broken in Gawain, for without a lance he did not want to go where he was going. After that, he rode away, and he did not look back. Gawain got up, got on his horse, and went after him, saying that he would rather die than not do him some dishonor.

When he caught up with Palamedes, Gawain said, [349] "Turn, knight; you may not go off this way, for it takes no great skill at arms for one knight to knock another down, but good knights are recognized by their swordplay."

Palamedes replied in anger, "Sir Gawain, why are you so rude and envious? You have no reputation, and you're one of the most discourteous knights in the world. So help me God, I'm much amazed, for you know the terms that you just now established with me, and yet you call me to battle. Let me go now in peace, and you'll be doing a courtesy, and later, in the first place where you find me, call me to battle, if you see any advantage to yourself in it, and I promise you that I won't deprive you of it."

"If I thought," said Gawain, "that you wouldn't fail me the first time I called you to battle, I'd let you go."

"I promise you," said Palamedes.

"Then tell me your name now," said Gawain.

And Palamedes gave his name.

"By Saint Mary," said Gawain, "you're one of the men I hate most in the world, for you have so much offended me and my relatives and friends that you may be sure I'll take vengeance for it as soon as I get the chance."

Palamedes made no reply to anything Gawain said to him. Then they parted. Gawain had not gone far when he met Gaheriet, his brother, and their joy at meeting was great. Gawain related to Gaheriet everything that had happened to him with Palamedes.

"Oh, my lord," said Gaheriet, "what are you doing? Take care, as you love your life, not to meddle with Palamedes, for know that he's a better knight than you."

"I don't care about that," said Gawain, "for he has offended me so much that I wouldn't for the kingdom of Logres fail to make him die a hard death."

"May God keep you from killing such a good knight," said Gaheriet, "for that would be an extremely great loss, and, so help me God, no knight in the world, however ignoble— unless he were falser than any other knight—knowing Palamedes's skill and prowess as I do, would want to kill him."

"He has so shamed me,"* said Gawain, "that I would reward him for it." [351]

So the two brothers spoke.

After Palamedes had parted from Gawain, he rode until, just before tierce, he reached the spring where the battle had been set, but he found no one there. He dismounted and laid aside his shield, lance, and helmet in order to refresh himself in the breeze. After he had rested awhile and laced his helmet on again, he looked toward the main road and saw Galahad coming. When Palamedes saw him, he was

---

*   "so shamed me" as in Piel (389). Magne has "so honored me," possibly sarcastic.

not confident, for he knew that Galahad was the best knight in the world. Then he got on his horse and waited until Galahad arrived.

Galahad said to him, "Palamedes, they give me to understand that you've killed one of my kin, whom I loved dearly. I didn't take vengeance for it when I told you, but you left me under such an undertaking as you know, and now I call you to battle for it, and we'll see how you do."

Palamedes replied that he was prepared for the battle, since he could not get out of it. Then one charged at the other, they struck each other with all their force, and Palamedes crashed to the ground, badly wounded. As soon as Galahad saw him on the ground, he dismounted, tied his horse to a tree, took his sword, and went quickly toward Palamedes, who had already stood up and drawn his sword.

When Palamedes saw Galahad coming toward him, his sword raised in his hand, he said in great fear, "Oh, My Lord Jesus Christ, don't let me die here, but save me from this with honor."

Galahad gave him such a great blow on his helmet that he could not keep his feet and had to fall to both knees on the ground, and had his helmet not been especially strong, he would have split him to the shoulders. Palamedes got up quickly and lightly, put his shield over his head, and defended himself as long as he could, but this could not be for long, for nobody's skill approached Galahad's, and although Palamedes endured as much as he could, he had already lost so much blood and had so many wounds, large and small, that it was a wonder how he could lift his shield.* The field around him was all stained with blood, so that he awaited only death, and nevertheless, all the while he suffered and endured, for he was great of heart. [352]

When Galahad saw that Palamedes could no longer defend himself, he took pity on him because of the knightly virtues he knew in him and because of his great skill at arms. Then he thought that, if he could make him a Christian, he would have great joy and good fortune. He went to Palamedes, seized him by the helmet, and pulled on it so hard that he lifted it off his head and gave Palamedes such a fall that he was completely stunned.

Galahad placed himself above Palamedes and said, "You're a dead man unless you yield yourself defeated."

Palamedes had never offended in chivalry or done anything that could be counted ignoble and was of great heart because of the good fortune he had always had until then; he replied, "Sir Galahad, your threat has no force.† Certainly, the fear of death won't make me say anything by which anyone might think me a coward, but I can't deny that you're a better knight than I and than all those who ever bore arms in the kingdom of Logres. Therefore, it doesn't much bother me to die at your hands, for thus they can never say that a worse knight than I am killed me."

"That's not it," said Galahad. "You must admit yourself defeated."

"But it's foolish of you," said Palamedes, "to think that I'll do anything that could redound to my shame out of fear of death, which will pass in a short while. You have a good sword; kill me if you wish."

---

* Literally, "how his shield could still endure."
† Literally, "what you ask of me is nothing."

When Galahad heard this, he did not know what to do, for he hated him mortally and, on the other hand, respected him and his chivalry so much that he saw clearly that if he killed him it would be a great loss.

Then Galahad said, "Palamedes, you see that you're dead, if I wish."

Palamedes replied, "That's no great shame to me, for all those who know you know truly that you're the best knight in the world."

"If I'm a good knight," said Galahad, "your situation is that much worse, for I'll kill you if I wish. But now do one thing that I want to ask of you for your benefit and honor, so that I may be your companion and friend while you live."

"Indeed," said Palamedes, "as to what you say, as long as it redounds to my honor, there's nothing in the world I won't do, primarily in order to save [353] my life, and then for you, and I'd think myself fortunate in anything I did for you. Tell me what it is."

"I tell you," said Galahad, "that if you'll leave your faith and receive baptism, I'll forgive you whatever quarrel I have with you, and I'll freely become your vassal, so that from now on, in whatever place you find me, you'll be able to put me into any danger to defend your person."

When Palamedes heard this he said, "Then let me up, and I'll do what you ask of me on the terms you've given me, and know that I never had a greater desire to do anything in the world than now to receive baptism and believe in the holy law of Jesus Christ, first because I promised it to Him, and second because of your request."

Thus ended the enmity between these two, and both agreed to keep their promises. Then Galahad stood up and asked Palamedes if he could ride.

"Yes, my lord," he said, "for I feel considerably better."

Galahad went for Palamedes's horse and brought it to him.

Palamedes mounted and asked Galahad, "My lord, what do you wish us to do?"

"I'd like us to go to some place where you may be baptized," said Galahad.

"Then, my lord, let's go to my father's house," he said.

Galahad mounted, and they rode until they came to the house of Esclabor the Unknown.

Then they dismounted, and the father, seeing his son so badly wounded, began to weep and asked, "Son, how do you feel? Do you think you'll recover?"

Palamedes said not to fear, for he did not feel badly hurt.

Then Esclabor asked Galahad, "On what terms was your fight ended?"

Galahad told him, just as the story has already related, and the father held up his hands toward heaven and wept with pleasure, saying that now all his desires were fulfilled, since his son had agreed to receive the Christian faith.

By such an adventure as I have told you did Palamedes become a Christian, and he was called in baptism by the same name he had had before. When he stood in the holy water, a marvel occurred, which men thought a great miracle, and even today they speak of it in the land. The marvel was that Palamedes was healed of all his wounds as soon as he entered the holy water of baptism, so that Sir Galahad, a bishop, and many other people, who saw him go in wounded and emerge whole, gave thanks to Our Lord. This miracle [355] was proclaimed throughout the whole kingdom of Logres, and as soon as King Arthur knew about it, he had it written in the book of adventures. Palamedes stayed three days in his father's house after he became a Christian, happy and whole and with great pleasure, for all the people of the land came there to honor and celebrate him, in pleasure that he was a Christian.

On the third day Sir Galahad said to him, "Sir Palamedes, I've stayed here longer than I should have, for I have much to do elsewhere, but I delayed for love for you and because of the honor God has done you. Now I would go."

"My lord," said Palamedes, "let's go when you wish."

"What?" asked Galahad. "Do you want to go with me?"

"Oh, my lord," said Palamedes, "why not? Didn't you promise me your company?"

"Yes," said Galahad, "for, so help me God, I love and value your company very much, for I well know your knightly qualities and your skill, so prepare yourself and let's go in the morning."

Palamedes said that he was ready.

That evening Palamedes took leave of his father and the others of his house and said that he wanted to go in the morning in Galahad's company, and his father said that he was glad of that company. The next morning Palamedes had himself armed with good, rich arms, and Galahad also.

After that, they started out, and Palamedes said to Galahad, "My lord, for a new man, new deeds. I'm a new servant of Jesus Christ, and I want to place myself in His service, for I want to start on the quest for the Holy Grail, if you recommend it."

Galahad answered him, "You can't become a true companion in the quest for the Holy Grail unless you are first a companion of the Round Table. Therefore, I'd advise you to go to Camelot, and you'd see that in this quest they keep account of those knights of the Round Table whose seats are empty. I truly believe that if you went there Our Lord would honor you with one of the seats; then you could start confidently on the quest."

"Then you advise me to do so?" asked Palamedes.

"Yes," said Galahad.

"I want to do it," said Palamedes.

Then they embraced each other and parted. Palamedes went off to Camelot, with wonderful joy and pleasure that he was a Christian, and he met no hermit to whom he did not make confession nor a man of a religious order from whom he did not ask [357] counsel about his way of life, and he met many who told him not to bear arms any more, for because of them he could frequently fall into mortal sin.

"I can't give up bearing arms," he said, "not for anything, for I could better give up everything else."

What shall I say? Palamedes reached Camelot, where they already knew that he was a Christian and the marvel that had happened to him. As soon as he got there, he found many who honored and loved him, for all men and women greatly esteemed his chivalry and courtesy.

Then another marvel happened to him, for, where he was sitting at the table among the knights who were not of the Round Table, a knight came to the king and said, "My lord, let's be glad. The Round Table has one more knight, at which everyone should be glad."

"May God be praised," said the king. "Which is he?"

"My lord," he said, "Sir Palamedes. I just now found his name written on one of the seats of the Round Table."

The king was glad at this news and commanded Palamedes to get up from where he was sitting and go to the seat at the Round Table. Palamedes did so and was glad of the honor God had so quickly done him, and he thanked Him for it.

146. GALAHAD AND PALAMEDES AT THE SPRING OF HEALING, WHERE THEY FREE GAWAIN, GAHERIET, BLIOBERIS, AND SAGREMOR FROM THE GIANT'S TOWER.*

In such a way as I have told you did Sir Palamedes get a Round Table seat. While he stayed there five days, the king had great pleasure in asking for news of Galahad and the other good knights of the quest. Palamedes began the quest after the others, and he rode for a full year without meeting Galahad, until one day at the beginning of May he met Galahad, who had dismounted to rest by a spring near a tower.† When Palamedes saw him, he dismounted from his horse, put his shield and lance on the ground, and went running to embrace him, and Galahad did the same to him.

Palamedes said, "My lord, Sir Galahad, how have you been since we parted?"

"Very well," said Galahad, "thanks to God. I've met many adventures since then and many marvels, which God by His grace had me accomplish, but I'm amazed and glad about you, and I'm happy that you're of the Round Table, as I've since heard."

After the two companions [358] had talked a long time, Galahad asked Palamedes, "Have you heard news of my lord, Sir Lancelot?"

"Yes, my lord, certainly, many times," said Palamedes. "Know that he was in the house of the Fisher King, but he accomplished nothing there."

"So it is with adventures," said Galahad. "He didn't fail because of any deficiency in his deeds or because he isn't a good knight, but Our Lord wishes it so."

After they had talked much together, they mounted and rode until they reached the Forest of Serpents. They stayed that night in the house of a religious order, which King Ban of Benoic had built in a valley there when he was a youth. That evening Galahad asked for the road to the Giant's Tower, where he wanted to fight with the Knight of the Spring.

---

* Corresponds to Magne II:357-365; Piel 394-399.

† Three sentences combined for smoother construction.

The brothers showed him the road but said, "If you want to fight with the Knight of the Spring, it will be great madness, for no man has ever fought with him who hasn't left with dishonor and shame."

"That may well be," said Galahad, "but however it may be, we want to go see him."

After this, both knights went to lie down, but Palamedes did not forget about the skill of the Knight of the Spring, and he thought that, if God led him to the knight, he would ask Galahad to grant him this battle. The next day they went to hear Mass. After that, they armed themselves, mounted, and went off, and they rode along the road the people had shown them until they reached the tower that men called the Giant's Tower. Galahad recognized the tower as soon as he saw it.

"Sir Palamedes," said Galahad, "you see here the tower I was seeking. Now you may be sure that you'll see the greatest marvel you ever saw from one knight."

"What marvel is that?" asked Palamedes.

"I'll tell you," said Galahad. "If you fight with him, I know you're such a knight that you'll defeat him, and if he leaves you, so badly wounded that you can't believe he'll be able to bear arms for a long while, then you'll see him return to you, more whole and rested than you found him at the beginning. He'll recover his strength many times in this way, so that finally he'll defeat you."

"By God," said Palamedes, "this is the greatest marvel I ever heard of. And since we're so near him, I ask you to grant me this battle."

When they reached the tower, Galahad said, "I don't know where we can find the knight of this place, since he isn't here."

"Let's not be impatient," said Palamedes, "for if he's here, he'll come out."*
[359]

As he was saying this, they saw a squire emerge who came to them and said, "My lords, are you knights errant?"

"Yes," they said, "but why do you ask?"

"Because if you wish to joust, you'll find here someone with whom to do so," said the squire.

"Who?" asked Palamedes.

"The lord of this tower," said the squire, "who's the best knight in the world."

"I want to," said Palamedes.

At once the squire sounded a horn, and after a little they saw an armed knight come out of the tower, fastening on a green shield with two red bands on it.

Palamedes said to Galahad, "This is the knight who defeated Sir Gaheriet,[†] one of the best knights of the Round Table. Indeed, I'll avenge him if I can."

Then he turned his horse's head toward the knight.

When the knight saw this, he said, "Stop, knight, for we won't joust here, but let's go to a place nearby that's better prepared for knights' jousting than this."

Then they went to a small meadow near a thick forest. Through the middle a channel ran from a nearby spring, but it arose among some trees so thick that it could not be seen from the meadow. Know that that spring was of great power, for

---

*   "if he's here, he'll come out" as in Piel (395). Magne has "he's here and will come out."

†   As told by a maiden in chapter 91.

any man, however badly wounded, if he drank of that water, would be healed at once. But strangers who passed by there did not know this, so that when the Knight of the Tower was wounded and about to be defeated, he would ask for a stay to rest and get his breath; he would go to the spring, and as soon as he drank of the water, he would regain his strength and be as whole as before. This he would do as often as he wanted, and because of this he defeated all those with whom he fought. The story tells this where it speaks of three marvels—the Questing Beast, the old lady of the chapel (she whom Helain the White saw living on the bread of the angels*), and the spring that was called the Spring of Healing. The Maimed King told the truth about these three things to Galahad, when he was at Corbenic with Bors and [361] Perceval,[†] who saw the Holy Grail, which mortal man could not see.[‡] There it tells how these three marvels came to be and in what manner. But now I return you to the battle of the knights.

When both knights were in the field near the spring, they charged at each other and struck each other so hard that both lances splintered. The Knight of the Tower, who was not as good as Palamedes, crashed from his horse to the ground, but he got up quickly, being very brave. He was angry about that fall, and he took his sword and charged at Palamedes, who was on horseback.

Palamedes drew aside and said to him, "Go your way, knight, for I can't lay a hand on you, I being on horseback and you on foot."

Then he dismounted and tied his horse to a tree. He took his sword and went to give the knight the greatest blow he could on top of his helmet, and after that another. The knight was strong and defended himself marvelously well, but before the first stage of the battle was over, he was so badly hurt, both with wounds and loss of blood, that he could hardly stand. Unquestionably, Palamedes was of great heart, skilled at arms, and much stronger than he. When the Knight of the Spring saw that he could do no more, he drew aside a little and asked a respite to rest, and Palamedes gave it to him. At once he went to the spring and drank, and he felt himself as whole and well as before. He returned to Palamedes, called him to battle, and began to give him heavier blows than before.

When Palamedes saw this, he was amazed and said in his heart, "What can this be? Earlier this knight was as much as defeated, and now he's stronger than I've seen him yet today. This is the greatest marvel in the world. Now I see what Galahad told me."

The knight began to torment him and give him heavy, frequent blows on his helmet. But Palamedes was very [363] able and could not be defeated so easily; he defended himself well, but with great effort. Five times he saw the knight come back to the battle whole and agile. By the fifth time, Palamedes was exhausted. Galahad said in his heart that he could not believe Palamedes was such a knight that he could endure as much as he had from the Knight of the Tower, who had already been defeated five times. When Galahad saw him return to the fray as whole and

---

*   Chapter 91.
†   Chapter 150. Actually the conversation takes place after Pellehan, having been healed, has left Corbenic to live out his life at a hermitage nearby.
‡   "see" as in Piel (396). Magne has "believe."

rested as at the beginning, Palamedes was already so tired and badly hurt and had lost so much blood that it was a wonder he had not died some time ago.

When he saw the knight coming toward him and summoning him to battle, he said to him, "Sir knight, you've tricked me five times. By Saint Mary, you won't trick me again; you won't leave me until you defeat me or I you. For your going has been causing me great annoyance."

The knight made no reply but began to give him the greatest blows he could. Palamedes defended himself as one who was of great heart and strength, and he did so much, in spite of his exhaustion, that he brought the other knight close to defeat. The knight wanted to go to the spring when he felt himself so badly hurt, but Palamedes seized him by the helmet, pulled the knight to him, and put him on the ground.

He stood over him and said, "By Saint Mary, you won't escape without owning yourself defeated and telling me whence this wonder comes to you."

Then he removed the helmet from his opponent's head, threw it far away, and pretended to be ready to cut off his head. The knight, from fear of death, begged him for mercy, to spare his life, for he would own himself defeated.

"I won't do it," said Palamedes, "until you tell me what I ask you."

"I'll tell you," he said, "since I see that I can't do otherwise. Now let me go."

Palamedes let him go. The knight asked Palamedes his name, and Palamedes told him.

"Oh, Palamedes," said the knight, "much have I heard of you, and great is your fame throughout all this land. And since I'm defeated, it pleases me greatly that I'm defeated by [364] such a knight as you. Now I'll tell you what you ask. My name is Atamas, the Knight of the Spring, because I guard a spring that has been here a long time, which has the virtue that any man who drinks of it, however tired or badly wounded he is, will at once be recovered and whole, just as before."

"So?" said Palamedes. "Show me this spring."

Then Atamas got up and took Palamedes by the hand. He led him to the spring, which rose at the foot of a tree called a sycamore, and the knight drank of that water and Palamedes, too, and they were both as whole and rested as before. Then Palamedes saw that Atamas was telling him the truth.

"Oh, Sir Galahad," said Palamedes, "now we may see that for the sake of which we have traveled so long through the kingdom of Logres without finding it—the Spring of Healing.* Here it is!"

Galahad replied, "Many times have I heard men speak of it. Praised be God who has shown it to me."

Then he asked Atamas, "Tell me how this power came to the spring."

"So help me God, I don't know," said Atamas. "I haven't been able to find anyone to tell me that, but I'll tell you as much as a woman, who brought me to this spring, explained to me, that no one could know the truth about this except from the Maimed King. He'll describe this adventure, how it happened, to the Good Knight who is to put an end to the adventures of the kingdom of Logres."

---

* Palamedes actually calls it the Spring of Adventures, but that name was given to the spring where Gawain, Yvain, and Morholt met their damsel guides, chapter 53.

Palamedes said to Galahad, "My lord, you've heard enough about it. Now let's go when it pleases you, for we're to know the truth about this adventure only through you."

Galahad was silent, for he did not want Atamas to know who he was.

Then Palamedes said to Atamas, "We want to go. And you, what will you do? Will you stay?"

He said, "I'll stay here and guard this spring as long as I can wield a sword."

Galahad said to Palamedes, "Let's not go away without first going to see the tower, if there is some knight of the Round Table imprisoned there, for many good men have told me that this knight, after he defeated them, put them in prison." [365]

"That's a good idea," said Palamedes.

Atamas replied, "My lord, if I hold prisoners in my house, it's none of your concern. I ask you not to force me."

"By God," said Palamedes, "you must release them, either through force or for love."

Atamas replied, "You've done to me what no other man could do, and, therefore, I'll do for you what I wouldn't do for anyone else."

Then they went to the tower, and they found enough people to show them honor and love, for Atamas had so commanded them.

"Now," they said, "if there are any prisoners here, have them come."

"There are four here from the Round Table," he said, "whom I had wanted to kill in prison. And because of a wrong they did me, I've made their captivity so disagreeable that I hardly believe they'll ever be able to recover their strength."

"So be it," said Palamedes. "Have them come, and we'll take counsel about them."

Then Atamas sent for them, and they were brought in, in such bad condition that they were hardly recognizable. And know that they were famous: one was Gawain, the second was Gaheriet, the third was Blioberis, and the fourth was Sagremor. All four had been defeated by Atamas, but that is not surprising, for he could recover his strength and be healed of his wounds, just as I have already told you. When Galahad and Palamedes received the four knights, they wept hard, for they felt great pity for them.

When Gawain saw Galahad he said, "Oh, Sir Galahad, welcome! I said all along that we'd never be freed from prison if not by you. Praised be God who has brought you here."

Galahad said, "Thank not me but Sir Palamedes here, who defeated the Knight of the Spring, by whom you are freed. How do you feel?" he asked them. "Will you be able to recover?"

"Yes," they said, "for the pleasure we feel at being freed has healed us."

Galahad and Palamedes stayed in the tower until the four knights recovered, and then all six departed from the tower well equipped, as Atamas gave them everything they needed. They rode together for two days and then separated, and each one went his own way.

But now the story stops talking about them and returns to Galahad.

147. GALAHAD ACCOMPLISHES THE ADVENTURES OF THE BURNING TOMB AND THE HOT SPRING; PALAMEDES KILLS THE QUESTING BEAST.*

After Galahad had left the others, he rode alone seeking the adventures of the kingdom of Logres everywhere he heard of them, so that chance brought him to the forest of Arnantes, where the Perilous Palace was. [367]

There he found the tomb of Moses, Simeon's son, which burned constantly, as the story has already told,† and just as Simeon was delivered from the fire by Galahad's coming,‡ so was Moses freed in the same way. This miracle was put in writing at the big church of Camelot. After he had accomplished this adventure, he rode day after day until chance brought him to the Perilous Forest. There he found the spring that boiled, where Lancelot had killed the two lions that were guarding the tomb of King Lancelot, King Ban's father, just as the great history of Lancelot tells.§ He brought to an end the adventure of that spring that had already boiled so long, and I will tell you how.

One day it happened that Galahad was riding through the Perilous Forest, and he overtook a knight, with whom were riding a squire and a maiden. He greeted them, and they stopped and greeted him, asking him where he was from, and he said that he was from King Arthur's house.

The heat was great, and the knight said to him, "My lord, it would be good for us to rest during this heat."

Galahad said that this would please him. Then both knights dismounted in order to rest, and they laid aside some of their armor.

Then the maiden said to the squire, "I have a great desire to drink; see if you can find water here."

The squire went looking in all directions, and he found a beautiful spring. He did not look to see if it was hot or boiling, but returned to the maiden and told her that he had found the most beautiful spring in the world. She, being very thirsty, went to the spring, bent down to drink, and fell in. The water, which was so hot it was boiling, killed the maiden instantly, but as she was about to die, she gave a cry that the knights heard. They came running and found the squire, who dared not put a hand in the water, which was already scalding him.

The knights asked the squire where the lady was.

"She's in this spring," he said. "The water is so hot that I can't get her out."

The knight, in sorrow for his maiden, put in his hands to draw her out, but he could not, for he burned himself and said, "Oh, God! How I'm hurt!"

"What's wrong?" asked Galahad.

"What's wrong, my lord?" said the knight. "I've found the greatest marvel that ever [369] a man saw: this spring, which is as hot as if all the fire in the world were heating it."

---

*   Corresponds to Magne II:365-371; Piel 399-403.
†   *The History of the Holy Grail,* chapter 35.
‡   Chapter 136.
§   Not in the Post-Vulgate as we have it.

"So?" said Galahad. "This is the spring that boils? I've heard many good men speak of it."

Then he crossed himself, commended himself to Our Lord, and said, "My Lord, Father Jesus Christ, if you please, let the heat of this spring have an end in my time; let it grow cold."

Because of this petition Galahad made, the spring at once became as cold as any other spring. The knight, seeing this marvel, was frightened and did not realize it had happened because of Galahad's goodness. Galahad gave thanks to Our Lord, took his leave, and went away.* The knight, after he had pulled the maiden out and had her buried, went to King Arthur's court and related this adventure there, how it had been accomplished by a knight with a white shield with a red cross on it. Immediately everyone realized that it had been Galahad, and they said it had happened not because of his knightly skill but through the great love God had for him, and they had that adventure written down with the others. Those of Galahad's adventures that are missing here are in the *Tale of the Cry.*†

After Galahad had left the knight, he rode for many days through many places that I won't tell you, for I would have too much to do if I were to tell you all of Galahad's marvels, and moreover, the last part of my book would be longer than the first two. But what I leave out of this last part is in the *Tale of the Cry.*

After Galahad had gone about the kingdom of Logres so much that he had accomplished more adventures and caused himself to be widely talked about throughout the land, one day it happened, where he was going through the Deserted Forest, that he met the Questing Beast, and fully twenty pairs of dogs were chasing it. The beast was moving fast, but it seemed tired.

When Galahad saw it before him, he said in his heart, "Now it will be wrong of me if I fail at least to accomplish this adventure, since so many good men have labored at it and not been able to do anything."

Then he went after the beast, but he had not gone far when he saw two other knights chasing it; one was Palamedes and the [370] other Perceval. When they saw Galahad, they knew him by his shield, but he did not recognize them, for it was a long time since he had seen them, and they had changed their arms. As soon as they reached him, they made themselves known to him. He was very glad and embraced them, and they him.

"Sir Galahad," they said, "how have you been since you left us?"

"Very well," he said, "thanks to God. I've found many marvels in the kingdom of Logres, and, thanks to Our Lord, I haven't yet found an adventure so difficult that I couldn't accomplish it except this one of the Questing Beast. I met this beast long ago and have never been able to do anything about it. Therefore, I'm following it, for it seems tired to me."

"By God, my lord," they said, "we've been chasing it for more than a month. Nevertheless, since you've taken on the quest for it, we'll leave it to you, if you like."

"Don't do that," he said. "I'd rather you bear me company and I you."

---

*   "took his leave, and went away" as in Piel (401). Magne has "and went away amazed."
†   See chapter 37.

Then they promised one another that they would never leave that quest as long as they could keep to it.

That day the three knights started hunting the Questing Beast, and they followed it wherever they thought it was going, but they could not find it that day or see it, so far distant from them had it gone. They slept that night in the forest in a hut they found there; they neither ate nor drank, but they saw to their horses as well as they could.

The next day they started out again, and Galahad said to the others, "I think we're nearing the end of our quest."

"How do you know, my lord?" they asked.

"I believe it to be so," he said.

"May God make it so," they said.

They rode thus until midday, and they found a good twenty dogs dead.

"The beast is going this way," they said, "and it killed these dogs here."

As they were speaking of this, they met a squire on foot, and they asked him if he had seen the beast.

"Yes," he said, "in an evil hour for me, for it killed my horse, and I have to walk."

"Which way is it going?" asked Galahad.

And he showed him the path it was following.

After they had left the squire, they went in the direction he had shown them. They had not gone far when they entered a deep valley, and in the middle of that valley there was a small, deep lake. In that lake [371] was the beast, who had just arrived, weary and breathless, and had entered the water to drink, for it was very thirsty. On the bank were the greyhounds; they encircled the lake on all sides, and they were barking in such a way that the knights who were following the beast heard the barking.

Galahad said to Perceval, "Do you hear the cries of those dogs?"

"Yes," he said, "it's the beast. Let's go there." Then they rode as fast as they could. When they reached the lake, they saw the beast in it, but it was not so far from the bank that they could not hit it if they wished by throwing a lance. As soon as they saw it there, they went toward it as quickly as they could. Palamedes was very brave; he had a mind to kill it and had already taken great pains to that end. He went into the lake just as he was, on his horse, and struck the beast in such a way that the lance passed through both its sides, and the point, with a great deal of the shaft, appeared on its other side. The beast gave a cry so loud and frightful that it frightened Palamedes's horse and those of the others so that they could hardly hold them. But when the beast felt itself wounded, it went under the water and began to make such a great tumult all through the lake that it seemed that all the devils of hell were there in the lake, and it began to throw and shoot forth such flames on all sides that anyone who saw it would have thought it one of the greatest marvels in the world. That fire did not last long, but a marvel resulted from it that still endures there now: that lake began to grow hot and to boil in such a way that it never stopped boiling, but it boils still and will boil as long as the world lasts, or so men believe. That lake, which got its heat from such a marvel as I have told you, is still called the Lake of the Beast.

148. GALAHAD AT CORBENIC; THE QUEST IS ACCOMPLISHED.*

After the knights had stood a long time by the lake watching those marvels and the beast had not reappeared, they said, "This is the greatest marvel in the world." [373]

Galahad said, "This lake is much changed, for before it was cold, and now it's hot. This marvel won't fail in our time. Now we can go, for this adventure is unquestionably finished. Now what I told you this morning has come to pass. Never will anyone see more of this beast than he has already seen, and Palamedes should have the honor and praise for it. We'll bear witness to it, for we saw him. And now let's praise Our Lord, who has shown us such a marvel."

They did so, and they left the lake. They went to a hermitage, where they disarmed themselves and stayed to rest that night. Afterwards, all three rode together, and they found many adventures that the history does not relate here, but you will find them in the *Tale of the Cry*. They rode in this manner from land to land until they arrived at Corbenic.

When Galahad saw the castle, he recognized it and said, "Oh, Corbenic, how long have I been seeking you, and how much have I labored to find you, and how many days and nights have I ridden in order to see the marvels there are in you! Praised be God, who is pleased to let us see you, because of the great marvels and adventures from which, by His mercy, He has delivered me whole and happy and to the honor of chivalry."

When the others understood that this was Corbenic, where they knew truly that the Holy Grail was, for which they had taken all that trouble, they raised their hands toward Our Lord and praised Him,† for it seemed to them that they had accomplished the quest.

Galahad said to them, "Do you want to go in at once or shall we wait and enter by night?"

"My lord," said Perceval, "by my counsel, we won't wait, but since God has brought us so near, let's go there and see what God wishes to do with us, for we're still lively. And if it pleased Our Lord to let us receive the holy food we received at Camelot, I wouldn't wish to live any longer."

Galahad replied then, [375] "May Our Lord regard not our sins but our desires."

Then they rode until they entered the castle.

As they were going through the streets, the villagers said, "See here the knights who have labored so long in the quest for the Holy Grail," and they held up their hands toward Our Lord because He had brought the knights there.

After that, the knights went to the fortress, then to the Palace of Adventures, which was rich and beautiful.

"My lords," said Galahad, "now you may see the proofs of our deeds. No knight may enter this palace unless he conducts himself toward Our Lord as a knight of Holy Church. If we are knights of the Holy Grail, the doors will open to us, and if we aren't, we won't enter there."

---

* Corresponds to Magne II:371-382; Piel 403-410.

† "praised Him" as in Piel (404). Magne has "blessed themselves."

"Oh, God," said Palamedes, "be our help in this situation, for without Your mercy, all chivalry is nothing."

When they had dismounted, they went to the door of the palace, and the door opened to them, not by the hand of any man but by the pleasure of Our Lord, who knew each one's deeds and thoughts. As soon as they were inside, the doors shut after them.

Galahad said, "Let's disarm ourselves, for here we'll do nothing by arms but by the mercy of Our Lord, who will be able to help us here more than all the arms in the world."

They did just as he told them, and after they had been disarmed in one of the rooms there, they saw nine knights of the Round Table whom chance had brought there that same day. One was Bors of Gaunes; the second was Meliagante of Dinanarca, whom Galahad had made a knight at the beginning of his career.* And if I have not spoken to you of Meliagante in this history, do not blame me, for I left him out, not because he did not do many good knightly deeds in this quest, but so that my book would not be too long, but whoever wants to know about his accomplishments will find them in the *Tale of the Cry.* The third was named Helain the White, the fourth Arthur the Less, the fifth Meraugis of Portlegues, the sixth Claudin, son of King Claudas, a good knight who led a good life, the seventh Lambeguez (that knight was old but his life was very holy); the eighth was Pinabel of the Island, and the ninth Persidos of Calaz. [376]

These were the nine knights whom chance had brought there because the adventure of the Holy Grail was to be accomplished. When they saw one another they were very glad.

Galahad said, "God, blessed be Your name, for it pleases You to let me see Your nine knights. Now I see clearly that in this coming will be accomplished the task of which people speak so much throughout the kingdom of Logres."

Then they began to ask one another for news of the quest. They told one another what they knew about it, and whoever had been there then would certainly have been able to hear much news and many beautiful marvels and fine adventures related.

As the knights were talking of this, an old man came to them, who said, "Which one is Galahad?"

They pointed Galahad out to him.

"Sir Galahad," said the good man, "we've awaited you for a very long time. Much have we desired your coming, and thanks be to God that we have you. Come with me, and we'll see if you're such as the good men say you are."

Galahad went with him, and they went from room to room until they arrived where the Maimed King lay. This was the very room where the Holy Grail was.

The good man said, "Sir Galahad, I can't keep you company any farther, for I'm not such as should go inside, but you enter in order to heal the Maimed King, for it's a long time ago that he was maimed, not because he deserved it but because of another's sin."†

---

*   Chapter 82.
†   By Balin in chapter 20.

Galahad made the sign of the cross before himself, commended himself many times to Our Lord, and went in. He saw in the middle of the room, which was large and rich, a table of silver where the Holy Vessel stood in such honor as our history has already described. He did not dare approach it, for it seemed to him that he was not worthy to approach it, but when he saw it he fell to his knees and prayed to it, weeping from his heart. He saw on the table the lance with which Jesus Christ's holy flesh was wounded, and the lance stood upright, point down and shaft up. And know that from the point it shed drops of blood, which fell down thickly into a silver basin, but as soon as they fell into it no one knew what it did with them. [377]

When Galahad saw this marvel, he thought that this was the lance with which Jesus Christ was wounded. He prayed for a long time and was so glad that God had showed it to him that he wept with great joy and thanked Our Lord fervently.

As he was thus on his knees, he heard a voice, which said to him, "Galahad, get up. Take that basin from under the lance. Go to King Pellehan* and spread it on his wounds, for thus is he to be healed by your coming."

But when Galahad took the basin, he saw that the lance went away toward heaven, and it mounted up so that neither he nor anyone else ever saw it again in Britain. When he took the basin, he saw nothing inside it; nevertheless, he was sure that there was a great deal of blood in it, as he had seen the drops falling thickly.

He said then, "Oh, my Lord God, how marvelous are Your powers!"

The room was wonderfully large, made in the form of a square, and so beautiful that one could hardly find its equal. King Pellehan, for whom God had performed many miracles, had not emerged from that room for a good four years and had never had anything else to eat but was sustained by the grace of the Holy Vessel; he was so badly hurt that he had no strength to rise but remained always lying down.

When he saw Galahad, who was bringing the basin from the lance, he cried out to him, "Son Galahad, come here and see to healing me, since God wills me to be healed at your coming."

When Galahad heard what the king was saying, he knew at once that this was King Pellehan, for whose injury everyone mourned. Then he went directly to him, the basin in his hands.

The king held up his clasped hands toward the basin, uncovered his thighs, and said, "You see here the Dolorous Blow that the Knight with the Two Swords struck. Much harm came from this blow, and I'm grieved by it."

And know that the wounds were as fresh as on the day he was stricken. Galahad tipped the basin, in which he thought there was nothing, over Pellehan's thighs, and when he tipped it he saw three drops of blood fall onto the thighs, and just as quickly the basin went out from between his hands, so that he had no power to hold it, and went off toward heaven. It happened just as I have told you with the Lance of Vengeance and the basin that stood under it, for they departed from the kingdom of Logres, with Galahad watching, and went off to heaven, just as the true history testifies. We do not know for sure if that holy lance and basin went to heaven, but it

---

* "Pellehan" as in Piel (406). Magne has "Pelles" throughout this section, but the manuscript has *peleã*, whereas it uses *pelles* for Pelles. Apparently Magne has misread.

was God's will that nobody in England after that time could say he had seen them.
[379]

King Pellehan was immediately healed of the wounds he had had for so long, and
he went to Galahad, embraced him, and said, "Son, holy knight, holy creature, filled
with great righteousness, truly you seem to me true rose and lily, because you are
clean of all sensuality. A rose you truly seem to me because you're more beautiful
than any other knight, better and of better grace, filled with all good powers and all
the good habits in the world. You are Jesus Christ's new tree, which He has filled
with all the good fruits man may have."

After Pellehan was healed, he prayed for a long time. Then he and Galahad left
the room, and Pellehan said, "Son Galahad, since God has shown me such great
mercy, I'll never leave His service. I'll leave here without speaking to anyone, go
to a nearby hermitage, and be a hermit for the rest of my life."

Then he went to the knights inside the palace, gave them the kiss of peace, and
told them about the great mercy Our Lord had shown him at Galahad's coming,
and they gave thanks to Our Lord for it. The king went away at once, without
anyone knowing,* and he went to the hermitage and stayed there more than half a
year in the service of Our Lord, so that Our Lord worked many beautiful miracles
for him.

The twelve knights whom he left in the Palace of Adventures stayed there until
vespers. Galahad told them what he had seen of the Lance of Vengeance and the
basin into which the blood fell.

After that, they heard a voice, which said to them, "Knights filled with faith
and belief, chosen over all other sinful knights, enter the chamber of the Holy
Vessel, and you'll receive an abundance of the food that you've sought and so
much desired."

When they heard this voice, they fell to their knees and wept with joy, giving
thanks to Our Lord.

Then they said to Galahad, "My lord, go ahead and guide us."

He did so, since he saw that they wished it, and Perceval followed him and then
Bors, and then all the others. After they had entered the chamber and seen the most
Holy Vessel standing on the rich table† of silver, everyone recognized it as the Holy
Grail, and at once they fell to their knees on the floor, so full of joy at what they saw
that it seemed to them that they would never die. [381]

As they were thus at their prayers, they saw above the silver table a man dressed
in white robes, but none of them could see his face, for it was of such brightness
that mortal eyes could not look at it but fell humbly, so that no one's eyesight could
look at this celestial marvel.

The man, who was above the table, as I have told you, said, "Come forward,
knights filled with faith and belief, and you shall have the food you desire so much.
And you, son Galahad, whom I have found truer and better than any other knight,
come forward."

---

*   "without anyone knowing" as in Piel (407). Magne has "so that no one in the castle who knew
him saw him."
†   "table" as in Piel (408). Magne has "crown."

He stood up and approached the table, but the brightness was so strong that he could hardly see where he was going.

The man said to him, "Open your mouth."

He opened it, and the man gave him the Host, and he did the same to each one. But know that each one of them thought he was putting a living man in his mouth, and each one thought he was not on earth but in heaven. Thus they felt such joy as mortal heart could not imagine. After they had been filled with the holy food and the glorious grace of the Holy Grail, as I have told you, they again fell to their knees before the table and began to ask one another how they felt.

Claudin answered, "I feel so filled with good nourishment—which belongs not to sinners but to the just, is not terrestrial but celestial—that I say that never, to my knowledge, have sinful knights received during their lifetime such a great reward as we have in His service, if it pleases Him, for this food is joy and pleasure and spiritual grace."

And each of the others said the same. Then they knelt again before the table, remaining in prayer and orison until midnight, so joyful that no mortal man could tell you of their joy.

At midnight, after the knights had asked Our Lord to guide them to the salvation of their souls, a voice said to them, "My sons (for you are not my stepsons), my friends (for you are not my enemies), go out from here—go where chance wishes you to do most good. Do not draw back, for at the end you will be well rewarded."

When they heard this, they replied with one voice, "Father of heaven, may You be praised who take us as Your sons. Now we know that our efforts are not wasted."

Then they left the chamber and went to the Palace of Adventures, and they embraced one another and took leave of one another, weeping, because they did not know when they would see one another again.

They said to Galahad, "Know that never have we had such pleasure as since we've been in your [382] company for this great feast and glorious food. This is the last feast of the kingdom of Logres. Against our great joy, we feel at the same time great sorrow, because we're parting. But thus it pleases Our Lord."

"My lords," said Galahad, "if you like my company, I like yours as much. But since I see that we have to part, I commend you to Our Lord and ask you, if you come to King Arthur's court, to greet him and my father Lancelot and all the knights of the Round Table for me."

They said they would do so. Then they armed themselves, and it happened that each one found his horse in the fenced enclosure. After Galahad had mounted and was holding his lance and shield, Palamedes, who was very sad at this parting, went to him, embraced his armored leg, and began to kiss his foot, weeping hard.

He said, "Oh, Sir Galahad, holy knight, holy person, holy flesh! This leave I'm taking from you is killing me, for I fear God won't let me see you again, and if that's so, I ask you to remember me. You've brought me from suffering to great good fortune, and, therefore, I ask you to pray to Our Lord not to forget me and to keep me so that He may have my soul after my death."

Galahad replied, "I won't forget you. Don't you forget me."

Then they all parted and rode out of Corbenic, and they met no one to challenge them. Galahad went off by one road, Bors by another, and Palamedes and Perceval by another, and they had not gone far when chance brought them* together again. When they saw this, they were glad and praised God.

I will tell you about these three whom Our Lord reunited, what happened to them and how Galahad and Perceval died and Bors returned to the city of Camelot. Of the others in this adventure, I will tell you nothing more. Certainly I will tell you about Palamedes, what happened to him and how Gawain killed him and by what treachery. Whoever wants to hear what happened to the other eight may go to the *Tale of the Cry.* But now the tale stops speaking of all of them and turns to Palamedes.

149. THE DEATH OF PALAMEDES.†

When he left Corbenic, Palamedes rode a long time without finding an adventure to tell about. [383] One day he happened to dismount beside a spring in order to drink, and after he had drunk, he sat down to rest. As he was sitting there, Lancelot and Hector came along.

Lancelot, recognizing Palamedes's shield, said to Hector, "Brother, do you see that knight?"

"Yes," said Hector.

Lancelot said, "Know that you are seeing one of the best knights in the world. It isn't long since I tested him with a lance, and I had no advantage over him. Therefore, I want to test him with a sword, to see if he's as good at that as he is with a lance, but not if he doesn't want to." He added, "Now go to him and tell him that I call him to a sword fight, but tell him in such a way that he'll find nothing to complain of."

"What's his name?" asked Hector.

"I'll tell you another time," said Lancelot.

Then Hector went to Palamedes and said to him, "Sir knight, you see here an unknown knight who asks you for a sword fight. Believe me, and defend yourself against him."

"Who is he?" asked Palamedes.

"This you may not know at this time," said Hector.

"Why does he summon me to a fight?" asked Palamedes. "Have I offended him?"

"It seems so," said Hector.

Then Palamedes got on his horse and took his weapons, and as soon as Lancelot saw Palamedes on horseback, he took his sword and went toward him, and

---

*   We learn at the beginning of the next chapter that Galahad, Bors, and Perceval are reunited, while Palamedes continues on his own.

†   Corresponds to Magne II:382-394; Piel 410-416.

Palamedes did the same. Then there began between them a battle so ferocious that it seemed to Hector that one could find no two better knights in the whole world. Their swords were so good that their armor could not prevent them from inflicting on each other many wounds, large and small. The fight between those two lasted until they were forced to rest, for the more whole and bold had lost much of his force. Lancelot had a slight advantage in the fight, but not much. After they had fought until they had to rest, they drew apart from each other. Palamedes began to look at Lancelot, and when he saw him so large [385] and found in him such skill at arms, it suddenly struck him that this was one of the knights of the Round Table, and if he fought with him he would be forsworn and false.

He said, "Sir knight, I've fought with you until I can fight no more, and I've found such skill in you that I strongly desire to know you. Therefore, I ask you to tell me your name, before we do any more, and if by chance I've offended you in anything, I'll make it up to you to your satisfaction."

"Indeed," said Lancelot, "you've never offended me, Sir Palamedes, nor do I hate you, nor did I begin this battle because of any hatred I had for you. I began it in order to learn if you are as good a knight with a sword as you are with a lance, and I've seen so much in you at this time that I know that you're one of the best knights in the world. Because I summoned you to battle, I know I've wronged you, and I want to make it up to you to your satisfaction. If it pleases you that the battle stop at this point, it pleases me. I know your skill better than before and you mine."

"What?" asked Palamedes. "For this you began the fight and for no other reason?"

"Indeed, no," he said.

"By God!" said Palamedes; "this is a great matter. But now tell me what your name is."

He told his name. When Palamedes saw that it was Lancelot, the most famous man in the world and the one with greatest exploits, except for Galahad, he threw his shield and sword to the ground and said, "Oh, my lord! I yield myself defeated to you. For God's sake, if I've wronged you in anything, forgive me."

Lancelot said that Palamedes had never wronged him. "But because I fought with you, knowing who you were, forgive me, for I've certainly wronged you greatly."

Palamedes forgave him. Then they both dismounted and Hector, too, who was pleased that the battle was over.

After they had sat down to talk of their adventures, Lancelot asked Palamedes, "How do you feel from the battle?"

"From this battle, very bad," he said, "but I'll recover. Nevertheless, I tell you truly [387] that you've wronged me badly, for I'm your brother of the Round Table, so that you shouldn't lay a hand on me for anything."

Then he told Lancelot how he had received a seat at the Round Table.

"I certainly see that I've wronged you," said Lancelot, "but I ask you to forgive me."

And Palamedes forgave him gladly.

"Now tell me," said Lancelot, "do you have any news of Galahad?"

Then Palamedes began to tell how the twelve companions went to the house of the Fisher King, the beautiful adventure that happened to them there, and how they subsequently parted, and know that all the while the account lasted, Lancelot and Hector wept with joy at the news of Galahad and Bors, of whom they had not expected to hear. After Palamedes had told them his news, they disarmed themselves. Palamedes had his wounds tied up the best he could, and Lancelot, who was badly wounded, did the same. After that they mounted and rode together, but they had not gone far when they separated where the road divided into three ways.

Palamedes went off to the left through a forest at the foot of a mountain; he was badly wounded and had lost so much blood that it was a wonder how he could stay on his horse. As he was riding thus, fortune and ill luck, which were at work there, brought it about that he met Gawain and Agravain, who hated him. They were whole and rested, for it was a long time since they had fought or found an adventure that amounted to anything. As soon as Gawain saw Palamedes, he recognized him, and when he saw him riding feebly, it seemed to him that Palamedes was not very well.

He pointed him out to Agravain and said, "There you see the knight to whom I wish most ill in the world, who has wronged me the most."

"I say the same," said Agravain, "but I don't know what we can do about it, for I know well that he's one of the best knights in the world and that if we attack him he'll fight and defend himself better. Now be careful what you try to do to him, for it's no small matter to attack a man who is an especially good knight."

Gawain said, "We [388] can attack him safely, for I see clearly that he's badly wounded."

"I don't know what will happen," said Agravain, "but since you want to attack him, so do I." Then he called to Palamedes, "Defend yourself against me, for I challenge you."

Gawain said the same. When Palamedes saw the two brothers coming, he recognized them, and he did not know what to do, for he knew they were of the Round Table, and if he laid a hand on them he would be forsworn and disloyal.

He said to Agravain, "Wait while I tell you something."

Agravain waited.

"Tell me," said Palamedes, "aren't you of the Round Table?"

"Yes," said Agravain.

"And companions of the Round Table may never come together in battle through ill will without being forsworn?"

"No," said Agravain.

"Then," said Palamedes, "this matter is ended, for I'm of the Round Table like you," and he told them how and where he had become so.

Gawain came forward past Agravain and said, "Palamedes, this is a waste of time. Indeed, you're a dead man, for no one but God will give you life."

"Oh, Sir Gawain!" said Palamedes; "you won't commit such a base wrong. I haven't deserved death from you, and I'm your brother of the Round Table."

Gawain replied, "Defend yourself against me if you wish, and if you don't dare defend yourself, let yourself be killed, for without question, to this have you come."

Palamedes said, "This very day there was a time when, had you attacked me, I'd have thought nothing of it, for I'd have expected to defend myself against you both, but Sir Lancelot, from whom I've just now parted, has wounded me so badly that it will be no wonder if you kill me now, for you'll find slight defense in me. Nevertheless, I'll defend myself as long as I can. But if I die, I die wrongly, and whatever happens to my body, may God have His part in my soul, if it pleases Him." Then he took his sword and said, "Now whichever of you wants to be forsworn first, come ahead."

Gawain said, "You're wasting time." [389]

He went to give Palamedes the hardest blow on the helmet he could, and Agravain did the same. They began to harass him with their swords in every way they could. He defended himself amazingly well with what strength he had, and he exerted himself so much in his own defense that all his wounds broke open, so that in a short while the field was red all around with his blood. Because of this, he soon lost all his strength, for his heart and all his limbs failed him; his sword fell from his hand, and he fell to the earth as if dead. As soon as Gawain saw this, he dismounted and took off Palamedes's helmet in order to cut off his head.

"Oh, brother," said Agravain, "do him no more harm, for he's certainly a dead man. You don't want to cut off the head of such a good knight. Let's go, for we've done enough to him."

Gawain replied, "If you don't wish, I won't cut off his head, but he won't get off like this."

Then he raised the edge of Palamedes's hauberk and drove his sword through him.

Palamedes, feeling the wound, gave an agonized cry and said, "Oh, my Lord, Father Jesus Christ, have mercy on my soul!"

Then he stiffened with the agony of death, which he felt within him.

When Gawain saw this, he got on his horse and said to Agravain, "Now let's go, for we're sure about this one, that he won't dishonor us."

"Let's go," said Agravain, "but, so help me God, it grieves me greatly, because he was such a good knight, and such a loss will be hard to conceal."

Then they rode off and left Palamedes, as I have told you. Gawain was happy about it, but Agravain was grieved, because he thought Palamedes a good knight. They had not gone far from him when Lancelot and Hector arrived and found Palamedes lying face down on his shield. As soon as they saw the shield, they recognized it, and they removed it and his helmet and mail cap. When they saw that it was Palamedes, they fell on him and began to make a lamentation as great and sorrowful as if they had all their kindred dead before them.

They said, "Oh, God! What a great and sad loss there is here! How the man has diminished the Round Table and the good body of knights of the Kingdom of Logres who killed such a knight as this!" [391]

As they were saying this and weeping copiously, they saw that Palamedes was still alive. After he had listened to them a great while and heard how they wept, he suddenly realized that they were not Gawain and his brother, and he made a great effort and opened his eyes so that he could see them. When he saw them, he recognized them, and tears came to his eyes, for it was hard for him to leave such companions.

After a while he said, "Oh, my lord, Sir Lancelot, I'm dying! For God's sake, remember me, for you're the man I love most in the world, except for Sir Galahad, and may you not be forgotten by him after my death. And you, Sir Hector, if you ever wished me well in my lifetime, remember me after my death."

"Oh, Sir Palamedes," said Sir Lancelot, "for God's sake, tell me who did this to you!"

"Gawain," he said, "who killed me without reason. May God forgive him as I do. Agravain helped him, but he was more grieved than pleased."

"Do you think you can recover?" asked Lancelot.

"No," he said, "I'm certainly dying. When you go to King Arthur's court, greet him well for me and all my companions and brothers of the Round Table."

Then he struck his chest with his fist, proclaiming his guilt, and began to weep hard for his sins.

After a while he said, "Oh, Jesus Christ, Fountain of pity and compassion, have mercy on my soul and, as I've been serving You loyally and with good will since I received baptism, have mercy on my soul at this time when I need nothing but Your mercy." He was silent a long time, and then he said, "Oh, death, if you had waited a little, I could have been a good man in the sight of God and the world."

Then he raised his clasped hands toward heaven and said, "Oh, Jesus Christ, Father and Lord of pity, into Your hands I commend my soul and my spirit."

Then he arranged his arms in the form of a cross on his breast, and immediately he died. Lancelot and Hector made a great lamentation all that day and night, so that they neither ate nor drank nor did anything but lament.

"Oh, God!" said Lancelot. "What great sorrow and loss this is! Who could ever conceal such destruction and loss?"

"Indeed, no one," said Hector, "for there wasn't a better knight in the world, save Galahad."

What shall I tell you? The two brothers made a great [393] lamentation all that day and night, for they loved and valued Palamedes marvelously well.

The next day, when the sun was up, Esclabor, Palamedes's father, arrived and asked the knights whom they were mourning so, and they told him. When he heard that it was his son, the creature he loved most in the world, his heart constricted so that he could not speak, and he fell to the ground from his full height. They, not recognizing him, went to him, removed his helmet, and found him unconscious.

When he came to, he cried as loudly as he could, "Oh, my son and friend! What bad news this is!"

Then he threw himself down on top of his son and began to kiss his mouth, which was full of blood and dust. When the brothers saw this, they realized that it was Esclabor, and they began to lament with him as before.

They mourned all that day until the hour of nones, when Esclabor said, "Oh, my lords! I'm a dead man. Never will I know joy or wellbeing, now that I see my son, the creature I loved most and the best knight in the world, dead before me. I've lived too long. However, before I let myself die, I want to ask you to take my son's body to an abbey near here, for I'm so old and feeble and sorrowful that I couldn't carry him there, and I want him to lie in the abbey because I built it."

They said they would do it gladly, and they did. They got on their horses, and Lancelot put Palamedes in front of him and carried him to the abbey, but no one ever saw such grief as the father's.

When Palamedes had been buried, the two knights told Esclabor who had killed him; after that they left him. The father had the tombstone covered with silver and carved with beautiful work, so rich that one could find no better in the kingdom of Logres. And each day he went to lament over it so bitterly that the most hardhearted man in the world would have been saddened by it. The monks, who knew well that Palamedes had been one of the best knights in the world and who had heard how he had died, said that they would make letters on the tombstone that would describe his virtues and his death.

"Of what?" asked the father.

"Of gold," they said, "for that [394] is appropriate to his virtues."

"Oh, my lords," he said, "since you wish this, I ask you to grant me a favor."

And they agreed.

"Now know," he said, "that you have agreed to make these letters tomorrow of what I send you."

Then he left the abbey and took with him a squire. He took shelter that day among some cliffs in a mountain a league away.

The next day, when the sun had risen, Esclabor sighed, took his sword and helmet, and said to the squire, "You'll take this helmet full of my blood, carry it to the abbey, and tell the brothers from me to make the letters on my son's tombstone with it, so that by those letters they can see the memorial of the son's death and the father's, for after the death of such a good son, I don't want to live on, old and feeble and in such bad condition as I am. I ask you to have my body laid near my son, not, however, with him, for I'm not worthy to lie with such a good knight as he was."

After he had said this, he took his sword and drove it through himself; he filled the helmet with his blood, gave it to the squire, and said, "Do what I've asked of you."

The squire was frightened when he saw this and said sorrowfully that he would do this errand. Then he took the blood, went to the abbey, and did everything just as Esclabor had told him. Thus were the letters made on Palamedes's tombstone, telling how he had died and by what treachery, and how his father had killed himself in his grief at Palamedes's death, because he valued him greatly for his chivalry. When King Arthur learned of it, he was deeply grieved and said that such a great loss from the death of one man would not come to the kingdom of Logres for a long time. He asked God never again to bring Gawain to his house, for he had hurt the court beyond belief by the many good men he had killed.

What shall I tell you? Great were the lamentation and sorrow at Palamedes's death. But now the tale stops speaking of him and returns to Galahad and Perceval.

150. PELLEHAN EXPLAINS THE QUESTING BEAST, THE SPRING OF HEALING, AND THE LADY OF THE CHAPEL.*

Now the tale tells that after Galahad, Perceval, and Bors were reunited, as the story has already told,† [395] they rode for many days, now one way, now another, as chance led them. Riding along, as I have told you, thinking they were going toward the sea, they found themselves near Corbenic at that hermitage King Pellehan had entered as a hermit. When he saw Galahad, King Pellehan was glad and received him and the others well. Because it was late, they stayed with him, and they dined on such food as the good man had.

Then Galahad said to him, "My lord, for God's sake, tell me one thing that I long to know, and I'm quite sure that I can learn about it only from you."

"Gladly," said King Pellehan, "if I know it."

"My lord," said Galahad, "in this forest I've seen three marvels; one was the Questing Beast, the second the Spring of Healing, and the third the lady of the chapel," and he described how he had seen them.

King Pellehan said, "Without doubt, these are some of the adventures of the kingdom of Logres, and it's a long time since these marvels came about. I'll tell you the truth,‡ as I know it, and I'll speak to you first of the Questing Beast, because you called it first to mind.

"There was a time when there was in this land a king whose name was Hipomenes. That king had a daughter, the most beautiful in all the kingdom of Logres. The maiden had a brother whose conduct was good and glorious in Our Lord's sight, and with all this he was so handsome and wise and of such good grace that everyone who knew him marveled at his conduct and his deeds. He was well educated, but the maiden was more so, for she had surrounded herself with the best masters in the world, who taught her as much of the seven arts as they could. When she reached the age of twenty, she was so wise and intelligent that everyone marveled at her knowledge, and they could ask her nothing about church matters to which she could not reply comprehensively, but she studied no other discipline so gladly as necromancy. The maiden was elegant and merry; she had a greater taste for the world than she should, and when she learned to [397] love, she loved her brother because of his beauty and goodness. What shall I tell you? She loved him so much that she couldn't bear not to tell him.

"He was a virgin and wanted to remain so all his life, devoting himself to serving Our Lord with all his strength; he was very sad and said to his sister to frighten her, 'Go, unfortunate creature, never say that to me again, or I'll have you burned.'

"She was frightened and shamed by his threat and fell silent as if paralyzed and distraught, but although her brother threatened her, she loved him no less than before but more. What shall I tell you? She tried all the marvels she could, ecclesiastical as well as other kinds, to see if she could have him, but she couldn't.

* Corresponds to Magne II:394-406; Piel 416-423.
† End of chapter 148.
‡ As promised in chapter 146.

"Then she said, 'Better to kill myself than live in this torment.'

"Then she took a knife that she kept in her coffer. She left her ladies and maidens, went to a garden of her father's, to a spring, and there wanted to kill herself in order to escape from the torment. And the devil appeared to her in the semblance of a marvelously handsome man.

"When he saw that she wanted to kill herself he said, 'Oh, my lady, don't kill yourself. Wait while I talk with you.'

"She was frightened, but not much. She checked her blow and asked him, 'Who are you?'

"'I'm a man who loves you greatly,' he said, 'and who values you above all the maidens I know. It grieves me a great deal that you can't have what you want.'

"She was thoroughly frightened when she heard this and said, 'And you, who are you, who know what I want and can't have?'

"'I know it well,' he said, 'and I'd tell you if I knew it wouldn't grieve you.'

"'Tell me,' she said. 'I ask you to.'

"'Gladly,' he said, 'since it pleases you. You love your brother so much that you're close to being lost for him. Therefore, I've come here to you. If you'll do what I ask of you, I'll help you to have him at your will, and that soon.'

"When the maiden heard this she said, 'I know that you're wiser than anyone could believe, for you know what no man or woman but my brother and I could know. Therefore, I agree to do whatever you want and tell me,' and she promised.

"Then he said to her, 'Now I beg you to give me your [399] love as the price of having what you so desire.'

"'Oh,' said the maiden, 'how could I do that? You already know that I love my brother so much that I'm dying for him.'

"'It can't be otherwise,' said the devil. 'Either do what I tell you or you'll never have him.'

"She was full of sin and misfortune, and she agreed, although very unwillingly. It helped that the devil appeared handsome to her.

"So she granted her love to the devil, and he lay with her, just as Merlin's father lay with his mother.* And when he lay with her, she experienced such pleasure that she forgot her love for her brother as completely as possible. One day she was standing by a spring with her lover the demon, and she began to think very hard.

"He asked her, 'What are you thinking? Are you thinking how you could kill your brother?'

"'By God, yes,' she said. 'And now I see clearly that you are the wisest man in the world. I ask you by the love you have for me to show me how I may kill him, for there's nothing in the world that would please me so much.'

"'I'll show you,' he said. 'Send for your brother to come speak with you in a room, and once you are there, lock the door and then ask what you wish of him. He won't want to do it. Grasp him and lean hard against him, and he'll quickly grow angry so that he'll hurt you, but not much. Cry out, and all the other knights will come. Then you can say that he raped you. The king will have him taken and executed, and so will you be avenged.'

---

*   *The Story of Merlin,* chapter 1.

"She did just as the devil had said. She sent for her brother, and when she tried to speak of that matter to him, he gave her such a slap that her whole face and chest were covered with blood.

"Then she began to cry out, 'Help me! Help me!'

"All the palace folk came running, and King Hipomenes, too, and broke down the door of the room. When the king saw his daughter like that, he was deeply grieved and asked her who had done it to her.

"'My lord,' she said, 'my brother, who has shamed me.'

"'How?' he asked. 'Did he lie with you?'

"'Yes,' she said, 'against my will.'

"At once the king had his son seized and put in a tower.

"Then he asked his daughter, 'Did he lie with you today?' [400]

"'No,' she said, 'some time ago, but I dared not tell you for fear you'd kill me.'

"She said that to him because she thought she was pregnant, so that everyone would blame her brother.*

"Thus King Hipomenes put his son in prison because of his daughter's treachery. The boy defended himself the best he could, but it did him no good, for his father and all the others believed it had happened just as she said.

"King Hipomenes was so deeply aggrieved by this event that he called his barons and made them swear that they would judge his son according to the law, and they decided that according to the law he must die. The king asked his daughter by which death she wished him to die.

"'I wish them to throw him to the dogs,' she said, 'when the dogs have fasted for seven days.'

"Just as she had commanded, the king had it done, and the young man, who was so handsome and good, was brought to the dogs, who were dying of hunger.

"But when he saw that they were decreeing death for him and he couldn't escape, he said to his sister before his father and all the barons who were there, 'Sister, you know that you're making me die wrongfully and that I haven't deserved this death you're making me die. It grieves me not so much because of the pain as because of the shame.† You're shaming me undeservedly, but He who takes vengeance on the great shames and treacheries of the world will avenge me. At the birth of what you're carrying, it will become apparent that it wasn't mine, for never of man or woman was born such a strange thing as will be born of you, for the devil made him. You carry a devil, and a devil will come forth in the semblance of the most grotesque beast anyone ever saw. Because you're having me given to the dogs, that beast will have inside it dogs who will bark constantly in remembrance of and reference to the dogs to which you're having me given. That beast will cause much loss among good men. It will never stop doing evil until the Good Knight, who like me will be named Galahad, [401] joins the hunt. By his hand and at his coming, the dolorous fruit that will come forth from you will die.'

"This the young man said to his sister, and after that they threw him to the dogs, who ate him at once.

---

*   Literally, "so that whoever wished could understand it."
†   Literally, "because of the shameful death you are making me die."

"The king had his daughter cared for until it was time for her to bear the child. The ladies who were with her at the birth found, where they thought to find a child, the most grotesque and ill-favored beast, as you have already heard, and they experienced such great fear that they all died except her and one other lady. The beast ran away, so that there was no one in the palace or the castle who could bring it back, and it ran uttering the greatest barking in the world. When the king learned of this, he realized at once that what his son had said at his death had been true, and he tortured his daughter so that she had to tell him the whole truth, how she had had her brother killed wrongfully, and how the demon lay with her without her knowing he was a demon, although later she knew.* Then the king had her seized and made her die a worse death than her brother.

"In such a manner, Sir Galahad," said King Pellehan, "as I have told you, the Questing Beast was made, and because it's a child of the devil, so many misfortunes have come about because of it in this land and so many good men and knights have died, as you've already heard. Now I'll tell you about the Spring of Healing, how it happened to have such marvelous power.

"It's true—and good men still testify to it—that in the time of Joseph of Arimathea there came to this land King Mordrain and his brother-in-law Nascien.† Nascien feared and loved his Lord Jesus Christ above everything else in the world. When he reached Camelot, King Camalis came out against them in battle and defeated the Christians in the field, and the pursuit lasted more than a day, until he caught up with King Mordrain and Nascien before the Tower of the Giant and locked them inside it so that they couldn't go anywhere. King Camalis was a marvelously good knight at arms and knew well that Nascien was the most famous knight in the world. He sent word to Nascien by one of his men that he would fight with him, one on one, on the understanding that if he defeated Nascien, Nascien and his whole company would become his vassals, and if Nascien defeated Camalis, Camalis would do the same. Camalis asked for this [403] battle because it seemed to him better for one of them to die than for so many people to be lost. At the time when the battle was requested, Nascien was so badly wounded that he could hardly ride, and because of this he didn't know what to do, from fear not for himself but for his people, for he knew well that Camalis was a marvelously good knight.

"His companions asked him, 'Nascien, what will you do in this situation?'

"'Indeed,' he said, 'I wouldn't agree to undertake a battle, but since he asks it of me, I'll put myself in the power and at the mercy of Jesus Christ in order to save this people.'

"Then he said to the man, 'Now you may tell your lord that tomorrow at the hour of prime he'll find me in front of this tower, prepared for battle, on such an understanding as you have said to me.'

"Then the man returned to his lord.

"So the battle was arranged between Camalis and Nascien before the Giant's tower. That night Nascien thought much about how he was badly wounded and had to fight with such a good knight, and he thought that, if he were defeated, Jesus

---

* "and how the demon lay with her ... later she knew" as in Piel (420), not in Magne; "he was a demon" added by translator.

† *The History of the Holy Grail* chapters 28-31.

Christ's people would be wholly lost and reduced to slavery. That thought threw him into the greatest fright that ever was.

"As he lay thinking of this, a voice said to him, 'Do not fear, Nascien, for Our Lord will help you, and I'll show you how you'll be healed of your wounds. In the morning, plant your lance in the ground where you want the battle to take place, and when you draw the lance out, a spring will arise, and that spring will be of such great power that any man who is wounded and drinks of it will at once be whole, and for that power it will be named the Spring of Healing.'

"When he heard this, Nascien was glad and gave thanks to Our Lord. He did just as he had been told, and he was healed of his wounds and defeated the king who didn't believe and made him and his whole company believe. Just as I've told you was the Spring of Healing created, and it still exists, as you know, but it won't exist after this, for Our Lord doesn't wish it. Now I'll tell you about the lady of the chapel.

"That lady was called Queen Guenevere. She was queen of a large and good land and lived such a good and glorious life that, living among her people, she loved Our Lord deeply and showed it to Him in many ways. And know that she was an ancestor of Sir Perceval here. The lady had four sons and a beautiful daughter. The maiden loved one of her father's knights more than herself or [405] anything else. She loved him so much that she couldn't hide it, and she told her father and asked him to give her the knight as a husband. Her father didn't want to grant her this, for the young man wasn't as highborn as he should be to marry a king's daughter.

"The king said to her, 'You're mad! Don't even think of it or I'll make you die a hard death, for I don't want to debase my lineage for you.'

"Fearing her father, she kept still, but she loved the knight no less because of it but much more.

"One day the knight and the maiden were alone, and the knight said to her, 'My lady, what shall we do?'

"'Indeed,' she said, 'I don't know, for you can hope for no better while my father lives, but if he were dead, I know it would please my mother and my brothers.'

"'What?' he asked, 'can't I have you except after the death of your father?'

"'No, indeed,' she said.

"'Then I'll try to work out how he may die,' he said.

"A little while after this, when the king lay sleeping with his wife in his room, the knight went in to him as if he were his most intimate friend; he went to him and put his knife through his heart, so that the king died at once, without speaking or moving, and the queen didn't wake up. He was so frightened at what he had done that the knife fell from his hand on top of the queen, and he went out of the room, so that no one heard him except the maiden. She realized at once that her father was dead, and she gave such a great wail that everyone lying round about heard her. The king's sons, who slept in the palace, got there first and found their mother sleeping beside the king, the knife on top of her. When they saw this, there wasn't one of them who didn't believe truly that she had killed the king, and, therefore, they took her and entombed her alive, putting over her a stone such as the story has already told.*

"Thus the sons thought to kill their mother. But Our Lord, whom she had served with all her heart, didn't forget her where she lay imprisoned but began to work for her such beautiful miracles and exercise such powers that people came there from all parts of the kingdom of Logres. And no one came there so feeble or infirm, or however badly hurt, that he wasn't [406] healed. Along with all this, Our Lord sustained her, where she lay, on heavenly bread until you arrived at Corbenic. But I don't know if she is now dead or alive."

"Why not?" they asked.

"That I'll certainly tell you," he said. "While I was in the chamber of the Holy Grail, I knew the greatest marvels of the kingdom of Logres, for the holy voice revealed them to me, but since I left there I know only as much as other men. Now I've told you the truth about the three things you asked me."

"Indeed, my lord," they said, "very well and much to our pleasure."

151. GALAHAD, PERCEVAL, AND BORS TAKE THE HOLY GRAIL TO SARRAS ON SOLOMON'S SHIP; BURIAL OF PERCEVAL'S SISTER.†

In the morning, they left, and they never again saw King Pellehan, nor did King Pellehan see them. They rode for many days until they reached the edge of the sea, and they found there on the beach the beautiful ship that Solomon and his wife had built.‡ They went on board and found on the bed in the middle of the ship the Holy Grail, covered over with a silk cloth so beautiful and rich that it was a great marvel.

They pointed it out to one another and said, "What good fortune has come to us, since we have what we desired in our company. Let's go with it wherever it may please Our Lord to have us stay."

After they had gone on board the ship, the wind struck it so hard that it drove it away from the beach and onto the high sea. Thus they went for a long time, not · knowing where God wanted to take them. Each time Galahad lay down or got up, he prayed to Our Lord that whenever he might ask for his death, He would give it to him.

He said this prayer until the holy voice said to him, "Galahad, Our Lord will do as you wish in this, for at whatever hour you ask to die, you shall, and you shall find the life of the soul and eternal joy."

Perceval heard this prayer that Galahad made many times, and he asked Galahad to tell him why he asked for such a thing.

---

* Chapter 91.
† Corresponds to Magne II:406-411; Piel 423-426.
‡ *The History of the Holy Grail*, chapters 22-23.

"This I'll certainly tell you," said Galahad. "At the time when we saw a part of the marvels of the Holy Grail, which God of His mercy showed us, I saw some marvelous hidden things that aren't shown to all men. I saw such things as tongue cannot tell nor [407] heart imagine, and my heart knew such joy and delight that, if I had died then, no man would ever have died in such delight as I. For I saw such a great company of angels and so many things of the spirit that, had I died at that moment, I would have gone at once to the eternal life of the glorious martyrs and true friends of Our Lord. Therefore, I was making the request you heard, and I'll go there at a time when I can go with the marvels of the Holy Grail before my eyes."*

Thus Galahad described his death to Perceval, as it was to be, just as the holy voice had told him.

That night it happened that Galahad lay sleeping, and a beautiful man, dressed in white clothes, came and said to him, "Galahad, I know what you were thinking when you fell asleep."

"How do you know that?" asked Galahad.

"I know it well," he said.

"Then tell me," said Galahad.

The other replied, "You are wondering if you or the Holy Grail will ever return to the kingdom of Logres. I tell you that you and Perceval will never return to the kingdom of Logres, but Bors will. Nor will the Holy Vessel, which has done so much good in the kingdom of Logres, ever return there, for they haven't worshipped or served it there as they should, nor, in spite of all the good they had many times from it, have they stopped sinning. Therefore, they'll be deprived of it and never have it again."

Thus Galahad learned that the Holy Vessel would not return to Great Britain.

In this way, as I have told you, did the people of England lose the Holy Grail— they who had often received great benefit from it and who had many times been filled by it, so that never, while it was in the kingdom of Logres, was there famine in the land. But as soon as it left them, a famine began that lasted three years, and it was so widespread that many people died of it and so severe that people nearly ate one another. Then they agreed about the Holy Grail and said that they had suffered a great loss and that it had happened because of their sin and misfortune.

When King Arthur saw this famine [409] in the land, he said, "Indeed, we deserve this famine and suffering for our sins, and it has certainly come about because of the Holy Grail. Just as Our Lord gave it to Joseph and the other good men who were to come of his lineage, because of their goodness and prowess, so He has taken it from us because of our evil and our bad conduct, and by this may one see that the bad heirs have lost by their evil what the good acquired† by their goodness."

But now the story stops speaking of King Arthur and his company and turns to the three knights.

For a long time the three knights traveled on the sea. One day Galahad happened to go to the side of the ship to see if he could see land. He looked and saw the city

---

* "I will go there at a time when I can go" from Piel (424). Magne's reading is confused, and the manuscript is nearly illegible.

† Literally, "kept, maintained."

of Sarras. He pointed it out to the others, and they were greatly pleased, for it had been a long time since they had seen land in any direction.

Then they heard a voice, which said to them, "Go forth from this ship, knights of Jesus Christ, and take this silver table, just as it is, and carry it to the city, but under no circumstances set it on the ground until you reach the Spiritual Palace where our Lord made Josephus the first bishop."

They wanted to take the table at once, and they looked across the water and saw a bark coming, the one in which they had placed Perceval's sister.

When they saw this, they said, "Faithfully has this maiden kept her promise* to us!"

When they reached the shore, they took the table and removed it from the ship. Bors and Perceval held it from in front and Galahad from the other side, and thus they went toward the city. When they reached the gate, Galahad was a little tired. In front of the gate lay a crippled man, asking alms of passers-by, and when he had to walk, he made use of two sticks.

Galahad said to him, "Man, come here and help me carry this table, and let's put it in that palace."

"Oh, my lord," he said, "I can't do that, for it has been a good ten years since I could move a single step without someone's help."

"I care nothing for that," said Galahad. "Get up and have no fear, for you are whole." [411]

As Galahad was saying this, the man tried to see if he could get up, and he found himself whole as if he had never had any infirmity. Then he ran to the table and grasped it on the side where Galahad held it, and when he entered the city, he told everyone he met the beautiful miracle that Our Lord had worked for him. When they entered the palace, they placed the table in front of the rich chair that Our Lord had made for Josephus, and at once all the people of the city came running to see the man who had been crippled and was now sound.

After the three knights had done what had been commanded of them, they returned to the sea, took the maiden from the bark, carried her to the palace, and buried her there as richly as a king's daughter should be buried. When Escorante, who was king of the city of Sarras, saw the three knights, he asked them where they were from and what they bore on the silver table. They told him the truth about everything he asked them, including the power and virtues God had placed in it. That king was more brutal and treacherous than any other man in the world, being of the cursed lineage of the pagans. He refused to believe any of what they told him and said that they were liars and troublemakers; he waited until he saw them disarmed and then ordered them taken and thrown in prison, and he kept them there a year. But Our Lord did not forget them, for at once He put the Grail in with them, by which they were given in abundance everything they needed while they were in prison.

---

*   Chapter 134.

152. Death of Galahad and Perceval; Bors Returns to the Kingdom of Logres.*

At the end of a year, Galahad made this petition to Our Lord: "My Lord, it seems to me that I've lived long enough in this world. If You please, take me soon."

The very day that he made this petition, King Escorante lay on his deathbed. He had Galahad come before him and begged his forgiveness for what he had done to him, for having wronged him so badly without cause. Galahad and the others forgave him gladly. When Escorante was dead and buried, the people of the city were in great distress because they did not know whom they would make king, since he had no son.

They spoke about this [412] for a long while, and as they were sitting in council, a voice said to them, "Take the greatest of the three foreign knights, who will guard and support you well as long as he is with you."

They obeyed the voice's command and chose Galahad, making him king and putting the crown on his head, whether he would or not. It grieved him greatly, but because he saw that they would kill him if he did not do it, he agreed, and once he was king, he had a curved vault made over the table where the Holy Grail stood, of gold and precious stones richer than anyone had ever seen before. Galahad and the others, each time they got up, went to the Holy Vessel, fell to their knees before it, and said their prayers and orisons.

When, at the end of a year, the anniversary came around of the day on which he had taken the crown, Galahad got up in the morning, and the others, too. When they entered the Spiritual Palace, they looked and saw in front of the Holy Vessel a man dressed as a priest of the Mass on his knees before the table. He was striking his chest with his hand, proclaiming his guilt, and around him was a large company of angels. After he had been on his knees for a long time, he stood up and began his Mass of the Glorious Lady.

When the good man came to the part after the consecration, when he took the paten from on top of the Holy Vessel, he called Galahad and said to him, "Come forward, servant of Jesus Christ, and you shall see what you have always so much desired to see."

Galahad approached at once and looked at the Holy Vessel, and after he had looked a little, he began to tremble hard, as his mortal eyes[†] began to see spiritual things, and he held up his hands toward the sky and said, "Lord, to You I give thanks and to You I pray and to You I give praise, because You have shown me such great mercy that I see openly what mortal tongue could not tell nor heart imagine. Here I see the beginning of the great fervors. Here I see the cause of the great marvels. And since it is so, Lord, that You have satisfied my wish and let me see what I have always so much desired, now I beg You that in this hour and in this great joy it please You to let me pass from this terrestrial life and go to the celestial."

---

*   Corresponds to Magne II:411-417; Piel 426-430.
†   Literally, "flesh."

As soon as Galahad had petitioned Our Lord, the good man who was singing the Mass took the Corpus Domini and gave it to him. [413]

Galahad received it with great humility, and the good man asked, "Do you know who I am?"

"No," said Galahad, "not unless you tell me."

"Know, then," he said, "that I am Josephus, the son of Joseph of Arimathea, whom Our Lord has sent to you to keep you company. And do you know why He sent me rather than another? Because you are like me in two respects: because you've seen the marvels of the Holy Grail, just as I did, and because it's right that a virgin bear company to another virgin."

After Josephus had said this, Galahad turned to Perceval and kissed him, and then he said to Bors, "Greet Sir Lancelot, my father and my lord, well for me as soon as you see him."

Then he turned back to face the table and fell to his knees. He had only been there a short while when he fell to the ground; his soul went out of his body, and the angels carried it away, rejoicing loudly and praising Our Lord.

As soon as Galahad was dead, a great marvel occurred, for Bors and Perceval saw a hand come from the sky—but they did not see the body to which the hand belonged—and take the Holy Vessel and bear it off toward the sky with such a great singing and rejoicing that never did a man hear anything more delightful, and never afterwards could anyone on earth say in truth that he had seen it there. When Perceval and Bors saw that Galahad was dead, they were as sad as they could be about it, and if they had not been such good men and led such good lives, they would have fallen into despair, so great was their sorrow. The people of the land were also very sad, because Galahad had led such a good life and been a very good king to them and upheld their honor and the honor of the land.

After Galahad had been buried in the Spiritual Palace as honorably as the people of the City of Sarras could manage, Perceval installed himself as a hermit in a hermitage outside the city, and this greatly grieved the people of the city, who had already proposed among themselves to make him king, but he did not want this, saying God should never make him king so far from his friends and the kingdom of Logres. Bors went with Perceval, but he did not change his secular dress, for he had it in mind to return yet to King Arthur's house. One year and two months Perceval lived in the hermitage. Then he passed from this world, and Bors had him buried in the Spiritual Palace with his sister and beside Galahad. When Bors saw that he had lost Galahad and Perceval and that he was in a land as distant and alien as the land of Babylon, he was so deeply grieved that he could not [415] console himself. He left Sarras so secretly that no one knew it, for if they had known they would not have let him go, because of the knightly virtues they knew he had. When Bors left Sarras, he went armed to the sea, boarded a ship, and had such a good wind that in a little while he was in the kingdom of Logres. Then he walked until he found someone who would give him a horse, and he mounted and rode by the most direct route he knew toward Camelot. When he was four days' journey away, he sheltered in the house of a mountain man, where he met a knight who had arrived there a little before he had.

After they had eaten, Bors asked the strange knight where he came from.

"My lord," he said, "I come from Camelot, and it's not seven days since I left there."

"Was King Arthur there?" asked Bors.

"Yes," he said. "I left him at court with a good twelve knights of that lineage, but they were sad and grieved over Bors of Gaunes, for they said he had died in the quest for the Holy Grail, and over Galahad the Good Knight and Perceval. King Arthur was deeply grieved by the loss of these three knights."

"How are things going at court for King Ban's kindred?" asked Bors.

"Very well," said the other, "except for two things: one, that King Arthur has a complaint about Hector of the Fens, who, after he returned from the quest for the Holy Grail, accused Gawain of Eric's death and also of Palamedes's, and he wants to prove that Gawain shouldn't be a knight or a companion of the Round Table. There was to have been a battle, and it wouldn't have failed because of Hector, but the queen and Sir Lancelot made peace between them, but they'll never love each other. The other matter, by which King Arthur's lineage is dishonored—and they say it in secret, but I don't know if they tell the truth—is that Sir Lancelot lies with the queen, and they want to tell the king in order to cause mortal hatred between him and King Ban's kindred."

"What do you think about it?" asked Bors. "So help you God, do you think it's true?"

"I think so," he said. "I've heard it said by so many men who are to be believed."

That night Bors asked eagerly for news of his kindred. The next day he took leave of his host and the knight and rode far each day until he reached Camelot. Never was such great rejoicing seen anywhere for a man, for he was greatly loved by all the men and women in the kingdom of Logres. But the pleasure King Ban's kin felt had [417] no equal, for they considered that they had in their ranks one of the best knights in the world. And however great was their pleasure, equally great was Gawain's grief, for King Ban's kindred was growing stronger.

King Arthur, when he saw that Bors was rested from the great labors he had endured, summoned him one day and said, "I charge you, by the oath you took when you left here, to tell us all the adventures* you encountered in this quest where you remained so long."

Bors, who was a good man and led a good life and who would not for anything be forsworn, told all the adventures he had encountered as he remembered them, and how Galahad and Perceval had died. And know that if you had been there to hear it all, you would have seen many good men and knights weep when they heard how Galahad and Perceval passed away. King Arthur had all the adventures Bors told him written down. And know that these three knights were the most widely praised of the quest: Galahad, Bors, and Perceval. Bors tried to make peace between Hector and Gawain, but it could not be, for Hector was of great heart and could not acquiesce in anything that would be to Gawain's profit, for he thought him disloyal. He had loved Eric so greatly that he could not forget his death and said that it would yet be

---

* "to tell us all the adventures" supplied from Piel (430) and Magne 1944:11:315; omitted from Magne 1955, in which the following line has been doubled.

avenged. What shall I tell you? Bors remained at court until he realized that Lancelot loved the queen, and this grieved him greatly.

But know that the knight of his kindred most grieved by this fact was Lionel, for he was wiser than many, and when he drew apart with his kin where no other was present, he would say, "Grief and loss will come to us from this love, and in an evil hour was it begun. Lancelot has already stuck to this love to the point that there's no knight in King Arthur's house who doesn't know something about it, and they conceal it from the king only because of their fear of King Ban's kindred, for they know that whoever tells him will die. And the men of King Arthur's house who know it best are Gawain and his brothers, but they don't want to tell him because they know that much evil will be born of it."

But now the story stops speaking of the news Bors found at court—of Galahad, Perceval, the Holy Grail, and the wrong-doing of the queen and Lancelot—and turns to Agravain in order to tell how he exposed Lancelot and the queen to the king.

The Post-Vulgate, part III
The Death of Arthur

TRANSLATED BY MARTHA ASHER

The Death of Arthur

153. Lancelot's Disloyalty Revealed to King Arthur.*

One day, says the story, the brothers had drawn apart into a room and were speaking ill of the queen and [418] Lancelot. Gawain, who was wiser than the others, said, "Keep quiet. There's no point in that, for if we tell the king, such war may be born of it that more than sixty thousand men may die, and for all that our dishonor couldn't be avenged, for the power of King Ban's house is very great, and God has placed them in a position of such honor and power that I don't think they can be brought down by anyone. Therefore, let's leave it, for bad luck could come of it. And I say this not because I don't wish more evil to King Ban's line than you can imagine. If I saw my chance, you'd see what I'd do."

After Gawain had said this, Gaheriet replied, "Whatever you say among us, I don't agree that we should harm them, for they are all very good men and great of soul, and our lord the king has given them such great honor and power that they can't be brought down by anyone. Therefore, I tell you to beware of declaring war against them, for they are such good knights and have so many friends that great harm and dishonor could quickly come to us from it, and perhaps the kingdom of Logres would be destroyed."

On this Gawain and Gaheriet agreed, but not the other three; rather, they said that they would let the king know and that they would rather die than endure any longer such great abuse of their lord and his lady.

"Don't do it," said Gaheriet, "for if you do, you'll bring about your death and ours. Now look: you can't find in all of King Ban's line one knight who isn't worth two of the other kind, and they are so much loved that, if they wanted to leave here today, you'd see that more than half the knights of the Round Table would go with them. The grace God has given them is no trifle but a great wonder, as they are bringing everyone under their influence, and they'll certainly do it if they live long. Therefore, I counsel you, for the sake of God and your honor, to beware and keep this a secret, as you value your lives."

But they would not agree to anything the other two said to them.

* Corresponds to Magne II:417-430; Piel 430-438.

As they were talking about this, the king entered and heard Gawain saying to Agravain, "Be still; no more of that."

"My lord and brother, Sir Gawain, so help me God, I won't keep still, but I'll tell the king. God help me all the same."

Hearing this, the king approached and asked, "Agravain, what is it that you'll tell me?"

"My lord," said Gawain, "it's nothing but good. Leave us; in this lies nothing but good for you."

"All the same," said the king, "I want to know." [419]

"My lord," said Sir Gaheriet, "don't worry about it. Never by my advice will you learn any more, for no good can come from everyone knowing about it. And know that Agravain is only telling the greatest jest and lie in the world."

"By Saint Mary," said the king, "I want to know. I charge you by your homage and the oath you have sworn to me to tell me."

"My lord," said Gawain, "why do you always burn so to hear new tidings? Know that you won't hear it from me or from Gaheriet. And if someone else tells you, harm will come to him and worse to you."

"So?" said the king. "Now, on my soul, I want to know, no matter what."

"Good luck," said Gawain, "for, God willing, you won't hear it from me, for neither profit nor honor will come of it to me or anyone else, and, without question, I'd ultimately have your hatred because of it, so that you'd wish me worse than to anyone else, for it happens thus in such a matter."

Then he and Gaheriet left the room, both deeply grieved, and they said that it was an evil hour in which this matter was raised, for, if the king found out and quarreled with Lancelot, the kingdom of Logres would be destroyed by it, for it could not be otherwise.

The king remained with his other three nephews, locked the door, turned to them, and said, "Tell me what you were talking about just now."

"So help me God," said Agravain, "I'll tell you nothing more about it."

"By Saint Mary, you will!" said the king.

He ran to a sword, drew it from its sheath, and said to him, "Tell me or you are a dead man."

He raised the sword to strike him, and Agravain said in fear, "My lord, stop! I'll tell you."

Then he told him what they had been talking about and that it was the truth.

The king had several times already heard people say that Lancelot loved the queen, but he had not been able to believe it, so much did he love him, so that each time he had replied to those who told him, "Indeed, if Lancelot loves Guenevere, I know well that it isn't by his will. The power of love—which alone makes the wisest man in the world foolish and the most faithful knight faithless—makes him do it, and, therefore, I don't know what to say to you, for I wouldn't for anything believe that such a good knight as he is would be able to commit treason."

This the king had said of Lancelot, for he could not believe that it was true. But when his nephews bore witness to it, he knew grief greater than all other griefs, for he loved the queen without measure, so that he could not love more.

Then he began to think, and he stood a great while and said nothing.

Mordred said to him, "My lord, we concealed it from you as long as we could, and we tell it to you now against [421] our will. Now do what seems best about it, and may no harm come to our land or our friends."

"Whatever happens to me as a result," said the king, "I'll be avenged in such a way that people will always talk of it, and, if you wish me well, I ask you to catch him at it."

They promised they would do so, and the king promised them that he would exact such justice that he and his kin would always be honored. Then they left the chamber and went to the palace, but it was quite apparent that the king was angry.

All that day the king was very sad. At the hour of nones it happened that Gawain and Gaheriet came into the palace. When they saw the king so sad, they realized at once that he already knew about Lancelot and the queen, and, therefore, they went not where the king was but elsewhere.

Gaheriet said to Gawain, "An evil day has come to Camelot today. If I've ever known the pride of King Ban's line, the kingdom of Logres will pay dearly for what has been told to the king."

All the courtiers except those five brothers kept still and dared not speak, because they saw the king so sorrowful.

Then a knight entered and said to the king, "My lord, I bring you news of the tournament of Carael, where the men of the kingdom of Sorelois and the Land Laid Waste were defeated."

"Now tell me," said the king, "among those knights was there anyone from here?"

"Yes," he said, "Lancelot was there. He defeated them all and bore away the prize for it and the praise from all sides."

When the king heard this, he bowed his head and began to brood; after a long time he got up, as sad and tormented as he could be, and said so loudly that they could all hear him clearly, "Oh, God! What torment and loss that treason is lodged in such a man."

He went to his room and threw himself on his bed, so sad and tormented that he did not know what to do, for he knew well that, if Lancelot were taken or killed in this affair, never would such great harm have resulted from the death of one knight; however, he would rather have died there than not have his dishonor avenged.

Finally he sent for his nephews and said to them, "I want you to bring this matter to a head and prove it."

They said, "My lord, it's up to you, and we'll tell you how it may be done. Tonight, tell your knights that tomorrow you want to go hunting, but don't let Lancelot go with you, for we're sure that if he stays here he'll go to the queen, and we'll watch him closely."

The king agreed to this plan.

Gawain and Gaheriet arrived, and when they saw that the others were speaking about this, Gawain said [423] to the king, "My lord, may God make this plan turn out well for you and for others, for, indeed, I fear much harm may come of it. Agravain, my brother, I ask you not to begin something you can't finish or to say anything about Lancelot that you don't know for a fact, for, indeed, he's a much better knight than you."

"Gawain, Gawain," said the king, "go away from here, for I'll never trust you. You've done me much harm in this matter by knowing of my shame and not telling me. Indeed, anyone who looked to justice should treat you as a disloyal knight and a traitor."

"My lord," said Gawain, "you'll say what you please to us, but you've never seen treason in me, and if I've committed treason, I never committed it against you or to your harm."

Then he left the king's presence, saying, "Agravain, I'd care nothing about this, but I know for a truth that great harm is yet to come of it and that many good men, who never deserved harm, will die for it."

"Now," said Gaheriet, "whatever good may come to the king and to you, my brother, I'll never meddle in this matter, for I know for a truth that never, if a man quarrels with King Ban's kindred, can he bring it to a good end."

"By God!" said Gawain; "there are no men in the world whom I hate so much. But they are so many and so strong that my hatred bothers them very little, and, therefore, I'll leave them alone until I see my chance."

Then they went out of the room and went to Gaheriet's lodging. As they were going through the village, they met Lancelot, Bors, Lionel, Hector, and Blioberis with a large company of knights.

They greeted one another well and with great joy, and Gaheriet then said to Lancelot, "I ask you to sleep tonight in my lodging, and be sure that I say it for your benefit."

Lancelot agreed. He turned back with Gaheriet, and they went to Gaheriet's apartments and disarmed themselves. In the evening, they went to the king, and, as they were sitting at the tables, the king told all the knights that he wanted to go hunting in the morning.

Lancelot said, "My lord, I'll keep you company, if you please."

"No," said the king, "for you need to rest more than to hunt, for today you arrived exhausted from the tournament; therefore, I want you to stay behind."

Lancelot dared not disobey the king's command and said he would stay, but he [424] realized clearly that the king was showing him no sign of love or favor* as was his wont, and he wondered why, for he did not suspect that he had been betrayed.

That night, when they returned to Gaheriet's apartments, he said to Bors, "Did you see the countenance the king showed me today? I'll never believe but that he's angry about something."

"Be sure," said Bors, "that he has heard about you and the queen. Now think what we'll do, for we're beginning a quarrel that won't die down for a long time. May God grant that we do well in it, for greatly is King Arthur to be feared."

"Oh, God!" said Lancelot; "who was brave enough to tell that news to the king?"

"If it was a knight," said Bors, "it was Agravain, and if it was a woman, it was Morgan, who hates you mortally, as you know. None but these two would dare tell him."

---

*   Literally, "of good chivalry."

The next day Gawain said to Lancelot, "Gaheriet and I want to go to the hunt with these other knights; do you want to go?"

"No," said Lancelot; "I have no desire to go this time."

Then they followed the king, and he stayed behind.

As soon as King Arthur had left for the hunt, the queen sent word to Lancelot to come to her without fail. He was glad and said he would go as secretly as possible, and he asked Bors how he could do it.

"Oh, my lord," said Bors, "for God's sake, don't go, for if you go, you'll regret it, for my heart—which never yet feared for you—tells me so."

Lancelot said he would not for anything fail to go.

"My lord," said Bors, "since you won't stay, I'll show you how you may go there secretly. You see here a garden, through which you may go, so that no one will see you. But in any case, take your sword, for one never knows what may happen."

Lancelot did so, and he went to the queen's room. But be assured that Mordred and his brothers with many other knights followed him. As soon as he entered the room, he lay down with the queen, but he had not lain there long when those who were spying on him came to the door.

They found it locked and said, "Agravain, what shall we do? Shall we break down the door?"

"Yes," he said.

When they struck the door, the queen heard them, and she sprang up half paralyzed and said to Lancelot, "Oh, friend! We are dead!"

"Why?" he asked. "What's this?"

He listened and heard at the door a great uproar and loud cries of men trying to break down the door.

"Oh, friend," she said, "now the king will know [425] my deeds and yours. Agravain has arranged all this for us."

"So help me God," he said, "I'll arrange his death." Then he got up. "My lady," he asked, "is there some hauberk here?"

"No, indeed," she said, "for God wishes us both to die. However, if it pleased God to let you escape from here in one piece, there is no one who would dare kill me, knowing that you were alive, but I think our sin will be our ruin."

Then Lancelot went to the door and called to those outside, "Evil, cowardly knights, wait a little, for soon you'll have the door open, and I'll see who will be the brave one who will enter first." Then he opened the door and said, "Now enter."

A knight who was named Einaguis entered first, for he hated Lancelot. Lancelot, who held his sword raised and ready, struck him with all his strength, so that the armor Einaguis wore did not keep him from being split to his shoulders and laid dead on the ground. When the others saw this blow, there was no one brave enough to enter, but they drew back so that the entrance was cleared.

When Lancelot saw this, he said to the queen, "My lady, this battle is already over. When you please, I'll go."

She said, "If you're safe, I'll have no fear for myself."

Then Lancelot drew the knight he had killed toward him and locked the door so the others would not enter.

He disarmed the knight, armed himself in that armor the best he could, and said to the queen, "My lady, now I can go in safety, God willing, for I think I'll deliver myself well from all those who lie in wait for me here."

"Then go," she said, "and think of me, for I know well that I'll soon have need of your aid."

"Well, then, I'll certainly go," he said, "but if you like I'll take you with me, for there's no man here because of whom I would leave you."

"I don't want that," she said, "for thus would our deed at once become more widely known. God will arrange it better."

Then Lancelot opened the doors and said he would stay in captivity no longer. He struck the first man with such a great blow that he fell stunned to the ground, and the others, seeing this, drew back, and there was no one who would not leave him a path. Lancelot went to the garden and from the garden to his apartments, and in a room he found Bors, who had feared that Lancelot might not be able to return at will, for his heart had told him that King Arthur's kin would take him with the queen if they could. [427]

When Bors saw his lord armed, who had been unarmed, he knew at once that there had been some encounter, and he asked him about it. Lancelot told him everything, how Agravain and Mordred and Guerrehet, with a large company of knights, had wanted to take him with the queen, and how he had defended himself so that they could not take him.

"Oh, my lord," said Bors, "now it's going badly; now the affair is revealed; now a war will begin that will never end, and as much as the king has loved you until now—from his heart, more than any other man who was not of his kin—so much will he hate you from now on, once he knows truly the wrong you've done him with his wife. Now see what we may do about it, for I know well that from now on the king will be our mortal enemy. But for the queen, who will be condemned to death because of you,* I'm sorry, and I'd gladly have us take counsel how she may escape."

Hector happened upon this discussion, and he was very sad when he knew how the quarrel stood. He said, "My lord, since it's so, let's go to that forest and hide there, and when the queen is condemned to death, they'll bring her outside the village to burn her. Then we'll come forth and rescue her, and we'll take her to Benoic or Gaunes, and we won't fear the king after that."

Lancelot and Bors agreed to this plan, and they mounted immediately with twenty-seven good knights who were present. Then they left their lodgings, went to the forest, and established themselves in its outskirts where they saw the trees to be thickest, and they stayed there until night. Then Lancelot chose one of his young men and sent him to Camelot to learn news of the queen. The youth left them, mounted his horse, and went to the palace.

Now the story stops speaking of him and returns to the three brothers from whom Lancelot had parted.

The story tells that when Lancelot escaped from those who wanted to take him with the queen, they entered the room and took the queen. They dishonored and

---

*   "you" as in Piel (436); Magne has "us."

grieved her greatly, and they told her that now her treachery had been proved and she would die. She wept so hard that those who were leading her away should certainly have felt sorry for her.

At the hour of nones the king returned from the hunt. As soon as he had dismounted, they told him the news of the queen, whom they had found with Lancelot and who had been taken. Let no one ask if he was deeply grieved when he heard this. He asked if Lancelot had been taken.

"No, my lord," they said, "for he defended himself more determinedly than any other man has ever done." [429]

"Then," said the king, "he isn't here; you'll find him in his apartments. Have knights armed and go take him and bring him to me. I'll execute him and the queen together."

Then a good thirty knights went to arm themselves, not willingly but because the king commanded. They went to Lancelot's apartments, but they did not find him, and everyone there was glad at that, for they knew well that they would find in him a fight to the death. Then they returned to the king and told him, and the king said he was sorry, but since he could not avenge himself on Lancelot, he would avenge himself on the queen.

King Iom asked him, "My lord, what do you want to do?"

"For this disloyalty," he said, "I want to inflict on her such a sentence that all other women will be punished by it. I command you, King Iom, first, because you're a king, and all the barons here, too, by the faith you owe me to see by what death she should die, for she shouldn't escape death, even though you might think so."

"My lord," said King Iom, "it isn't the law or custom of this land to dispense justice after nones, especially the death of a man or woman and especially of such a noble lady as the queen. But tomorrow morning, if you so command, we'll do it."

Then they stopped talking about it, and the king was so deeply grieved that all that day he neither ate nor drank, nor did he want the queen to come before him.

In the morning at prime, as soon as the barons were gathered, the king ordered Mordred and Agravain and all the barons to say what they were to do with the queen in true justice.

They went out to confer, and Agravain and Mordred said, "This is true justice—there is no other choice: since she has put another knight in the place of such a noble man as King Arthur, she should be burned."

They all agreed to this, gladly or under constraint.

When Gawain saw that they were giving such a verdict, he said, "God willing, I'll never be a part of such a verdict, in which I'd see the death of the one lady in the world who has always honored me most."

Then he went to the king and said to him, "My lord, I give back to you all that I hold of you, and never as long as I live will I serve you again."

The king was not swayed by anything he said, for he had his heart firmly set on something else. Gawain left him then and went to his apartments, lamenting bitterly. The king ordered a great fire made in the field outside the village. Throughout the village there was as much grief as if the queen had been everyone's mother. The king [430] sent for the queen to come into his presence, and she came weeping, dressed in a garment of red silk. She was such a beautiful lady and so appealing that one would not have found another such of her age anywhere in the world. When the king saw her, he felt such grief for her that he could not take his eyes off her, and he ordered them to take her from him and go do to her what they had decided.

As soon as the queen left the palace and they took her through the streets of the village, you would have seen young and old, men and women, rich and poor, running out from all directions, crying out and wailing, making the greatest lamentation in the world.

They all said with one voice, "Oh, good lady, endowed with all good qualities, more courteous and better instructed than any other lady, where from now on will the poorest find help and pity? Oh, King Arthur, you're having her killed treacherously and brutally; may you be sorry for it, and may you be deprived of your kingdom for it, and may the traitors who are making you do it die a hard death!"

Thus spoke all the people of the village, as she passed among them, and after that they all followed her, crying out as if they were out of their minds.

154. Lancelot Rescues the Queen, Takes Her to Joyous Guard; Death of Agravain, Guerrehet, and Gaheriet; King Arthur's Grief.*

The king ordered Agravain and his brothers to take eighty knights to guard the field where the fire was, so that if Lancelot came, he could not rescue her.

"My lord," said Agravain, "if you want me to go, order my brother Gaheriet to go with us."

The king ordered Gaheriet to go, and Gaheriet said he would not; however, the king threatened him so much that he said he would go. Then he armed himself, as did all the others Agravain chose, and Agravain armed himself, too.

After they were armed and had come out of the village, Gaheriet said to Agravain, "Do you think I'm coming here in order to fight with Lancelot if he comes to the queen's aid? Know that I'll have no part of it, for, so help me God, I'd rather have him take her alive than find her dead here."

Speaking thus, they reached the fire.

As soon as Lancelot, who was hidden in the forest, saw his squire returning, he asked him, "What news of the queen?"

"Bad news, my lord," he said, "for they're bringing her to be burned."

"So?" he said. "Now let's mount, for he who thinks to kill her will die for it. And may it please God, if He ever heard a sinner's prayer, that I meet Agravain there, who brought this about." [431]

Then they mounted. They counted and found themselves to be thirty-three. They rode, as well armed as possible, toward where they saw the fire.

---

* Corresponds to Magne II:430-443; Piel 438-447.

When the people in the field saw them coming, they called out to those who were guarding the queen, "Flee! Flee! See, here is Lancelot coming to rescue the queen."

Lancelot, who was riding ahead of the others, charged at Agravain, for he knew him well by his armor, and struck him so hard that neither shield nor hauberk prevented his putting the lance through him so that the point appeared on the other side; he knocked Agravain to the ground, and in the fall his lance broke. Bors charged at Guerrehet and struck him such a blow with his lance that he knocked him to the ground, beyond the need of a doctor. The rest of Lancelot's men went to strike the others and knocked down a great many of them; then they took their swords and began a hard, brutal fight. When Gaheriet saw that his brothers were on the ground, he was angry, for he was sure they were dead. Then he charged at Meliaduc the Black, who was trying hard to help Lancelot to avenge the queen's honor, and he gave him such a blow with his lance that he knocked him and his horse into the fire. Then he took his sword and struck another man such a blow that he laid him dead at Sir Lancelot's feet. When Hector,[*] who cared a great deal for Gaheriet, saw that he was doing them such harm, he said in his heart that if this lasted much longer, he would do great damage to them, and, therefore, it would be better if they killed him if they could, although he was the knight at court best loved by King Ban's line. Then he went to give him such a great sword stroke that he knocked the helmet from his head to the ground. When Gaheriet felt his head uncovered, he was completely taken aback. And Lancelot, who was going from group to group and running to the battalions first on one side, then on the other, and who did not recognize him, struck him so hard on his head that he split it to the teeth and knocked him dead to the ground. This was a great loss, for Gaheriet was one of the best knights of the court, and he had always loved Lancelot more than any other knight of the court that he had ever seen. By this blow was the king's party [433] scattered and defeated, so that of the eighty there had been, there escaped only three, who fled to the city. One was Mordred, and the other two were of the Round Table.

When Lancelot saw this, he went to the queen and said, "My lady, what do you want us to do with you?"

She replied happily, "I'd have you take me to some place where the king could do me no harm."

"My lady," he said, "mount, and let's go to that forest, and there we'll decide what will be best."

She agreed. They put her on a horse, of which there were many without masters; then they went to the forest, to where they saw it thickest. They counted their company and found four missing, and they asked one another what had become of them.

Hector said, "I saw Gaheriet kill three of them."

"What?" asked Lancelot, "was Gaheriet there in that battle?"

"What are you asking me?" asked Hector; "you killed him."

---

[*]   Both editions have *este* ("he"), which seems to mean Lancelot, but that makes no sense in view of what follows. In the Vulgate *Death of Arthur* (chapter 12) it is Hector.

"Now," said Lancelot, "we may well say that we'll never have peace with the king or with Gawain because of Gaheriet's death, at which I'm deeply grieved, so help me God. And now a war will begin that will not end during our lifetime."

Lancelot was deeply grieved by Gaheriet's death, for he was among the knights Lancelot had always loved most.

Bors said to Lancelot, "My lord, the queen will need to be in safety in a place where she'll have no fear of the king."

Lancelot said, "If we could get her to a castle that I have conquered, she'd be safe there, for the castle is wonderfully strong and so situated that it can't be besieged, and once we're there and have provisioned it, we can send for help to many knights whom I have helped or conquered, and we're so many that, if I have their help and we're in that castle, we can easily carry on a war with a man of great power."

"Where is this castle?" asked Bors.

"It's near the city of Longueson, and its name is the castle of Joyous Guard, but when I conquered it a long time ago, when I was newly a knight,* its name was Dolorous Guard."

"Oh," said the queen, "I've seen that castle, and truly it's so strong that it need fear nothing but treason."

They agreed to this, and they rode [435] until they reached a castle that stood in the forest and was named Caleque. Its lord was a count, a good knight and powerful, who loved Lancelot greatly. When he knew that Lancelot was coming, he was glad of it, and he received him well, doing him all the honor and service he could, and promised that he would help him against King Arthur.

He said to Lancelot, "My lord, my lord, I give you this castle, you and the queen, and you should accept it because it's so strong that here you'll have no fear of King Arthur."

Lancelot thanked him warmly but said that they wanted to go elsewhere.

The next day he parted from Count Dangis, who gave him forty knights and exchanged oaths of mutual aid with him. Then they left him and rode until they reached the castle of Joyous Guard. When the inhabitants of the castle knew that Lancelot was coming, they came out to receive him, rejoicing and celebrating as if he were God. When they learned that he was going to stay with them and why, they swore to help him against the whole world, and he was much strengthened by this. He sent at once for all the people of the land, and they came there, and they were many. Then he had his castle well provisioned.

But now the story stops speaking of him and turns back to King Arthur.

The story says that when King Arthur saw his nephew Mordred returning with few companions, he was amazed and asked how it had come about.

A young man who had been present where the battle took place said to him, "My lord, I'll tell you bad news, by which you and everyone here will be grieved. Know that of all the knights who took the queen to the fire, only three escaped, and of those three who escaped, one is Mordred. I don't know who the other two are."

"Oh!" said the King. "Then Lancelot was there?"

---

* Not in the Post-Vulgate. See the Vulgate *Lancelot,* chapter 24.

"By God, yes, my lord," he said, "and he did more yet, for he took the queen with him into the forest."

Having heard this news, the king was so sad that he did not know what to do.

At this point Mordred arrived and said to the king, "My lord, things are going badly! Lancelot has defeated us all and taken the queen away with him."

"Now after him," said the king, "for he won't get away if I can help it."

Then he had knights, men at arms, [436] and everyone with him armed, and they mounted as quickly as they could, went to the forest, and looked everywhere, but they did not find Lancelot. Then the king ordered them to go off in many directions, to see if they could find the fugitives.

King Caradoc said, "My lord, I don't think this is good, for if they split up and Lancelot finds them together, he'll kill them all, for he leads a large company of good knights."

"Then what shall we do?" asked King Arthur.

"My lord," he said, "I'll tell you. Send your men to everyone in this land with your orders that no one be so bold as to let Lancelot or any of his company pass. Thus he'll have to stay in the land, and when he has settled down and we know where he is, we'll move against him. You'll be able to take him easily, and you'll be avenged on him."

The king wrote his orders to this effect and sent them to all the ports of Logres, that no one be so bold as to let Lancelot or any of his company pass. After he had sent the messengers, he turned to where the defeat had taken place and saw his nephew Agravain, whom Lancelot had killed. He had a piece of the lance through his chest, so that the point showed on the other side. The king was so deeply grieved that he could not hold himself in his saddle. He fell unconscious on top of his nephew and lay there a long while.

When he came to and could speak, he said, "Oh, good nephew! He who gave you this blow hated you mortally, and he who took away such a knight from among my kin put great torment in my heart."

After he had said this, he removed the helmet from Agravain's head and kissed his eyes and his mouth. Then he had him carried to the city. He went to see all the others, and he found Guerrehet, whom Bors had killed, with a lance wound in his chest. There you would have seen the king lament and beat his hands and say that he had lived too long when he witnessed the death of the men he loved most in the world, the source of such grief. Then he had Guerrehet lifted up on his shield. He went about looking at the others, and he looked to the left and saw Gaheriet, whom Lancelot had killed, and this was the nephew he loved most, except for Gawain. When he saw the one he loved so much, his grief for the others was nothing to his grief for this one. He went to Gaheriet, embraced him, and fell unconscious on top of him, so that those who were present thought he was dead.

After he had lain [437] thus for the time it would have taken to go half a league, he came to and said, "Oh, death! How impatient I am for you, for it seems to me I've already lived too long. Oh, Gaheriet, my nephew, if I am to die of grief, I'll die of grief for you, for I've never seen another death that grieved me so much. Good nephew and friend, in an evil hour was that sword made that thus wounded you, and cursed be the arm that gave you such a blow, for it has confounded me and all my kindred."

Kissing Gaheriet's eyes and mouth and face, bloody as they were, he made a great lamentation, for they had all loved and valued Gaheriet, such a good knight and courtier was he.

Great were the lamentations and cries that most of them made, either for relatives or for friends, and they took Gaheriet up on his shield and bore him to the village. When the villagers knew that this death had taken place, you would have seen savage lamentation, and they took up their friends* and bore them to the palace. At these cries Gawain came out of his apartments, for he really thought the queen was already dead and that this great lamentation was for her.

As he was standing in the street inquiring, they said to him, "Oh, Sir Gawain, if you wish to know your great grief and the destruction of your kindred, go to the palace, and there you'll see the greatest grief you ever saw."

He was deeply grieved by this news and did not reply to anything they said to him. He bowed his head sadly and began to go toward the palace, but he still thought the lamentation was only for the queen. He look to the right and the left and saw all the people weeping and wailing.

Each one said to him, "Go, Sir Gawain, go, and you'll see the cause of your great grief and mourning."

When he heard what they were all saying to him, his sorrow grew much greater, but he dared not show it, and he went along sad and pensive. Entering the palace, he found them all making such a lamentation as if they saw all their kin in the world dead before them.

When the king saw Gawain, he said to him in a loud voice, "Gawain, Gawain, see here your great sorrow and mine; see here lying dead your brother Gaheriet, the most highly esteemed knight of our line."

He showed Gaheriet to Gawain, all bloody, just as he held him against his chest. Seeing this, Gawain had no strength to speak or stand, for his heart and body failed him, and he fell as if dead in the middle of the palace and lay unconscious a long time. When the barons, who were so deeply [439] grieved that they thought they would never be happy again, saw that it was Gawain, they went to take him up.

They held him in their arms weeping from the heart and saying, "Oh, God! What a great loss there is here on all sides!"

After Gawain had lain thus a long time and come to, he got up and turned to Gaheriet, who lay dead. He took him from the king, embraced him, and began to kiss him. Such deep grief seized his heart that he could not stand, and he fell with Gaheriet to the ground and lay longer than before.

When Gawain came to, he sat up and began to look at Gaheriet, and, seeing such a great wound in him, he said, "Oh, good brother! Cursed be the arm that gave you such a blow, for its owner has wrongfully killed me and all my kin, and he isn't worth more thereby, for, after what I see here, I don't want to live, good brother, except long enough to avenge you on the traitor who did this to you and has inflicted such torment on my heart."

---

*   Literally, "each one took up his friend."

Thus Gawain lamented, and he would have lamented more if he could have, but his heart was constricted with grief, so that he could do it only later. After he had sat thus a long time, he looked to his right and saw Guerrehet and Agravain before the king, where they lay on their shields on which men had brought them in.

Recognizing them, he said in a loud voice, "Oh wretch! In an evil hour have I lived to see my brothers thus dead of a terrible death!"

Then he went to them and let himself fall on them, embraced and kissed them, bloody as they were, and fainted several times over them, so that the noblemen who were present thought he would die among his brothers.

The king, who was so tormented that he did not know what to do or say, asked the barons, "What shall we do? For if we leave Gawain here much longer, I think he'll die of grief."

"My lord," they said, "we think it would be good to take him away from here and keep him in a room until these men are buried, for unquestionably, if he's here much longer, he'll die."

The king agreed to this plan, and the barons carried him, unconscious as he was, to a room. All that day and night he lay without speaking. During that whole time there was great mourning in the palace and throughout the village. The dead knights were disarmed and buried, each according to his rank. For Guerrehet and Agravain they made such beautiful, rich tombs as [441] there should be for a king's sons, and they put the two of them side by side and laid them inside the monastery of St. Stephen of Camelot, which at that time was the principal church. Thus they buried those two, and at their heads they put another tomb, better and richer than either, and they had Gaheriet put there, but as he was being buried you could have seen great lamentation and wailing, for all the bishops and archbishops of the land had come there, and all the good noblemen who could do so had arrived at the tomb and paid as much honor as they could to the dead, but most of all to Gaheriet. Because he had been such a good man, they had his monument raised more than all the others and had letters written on it, which said, HERE LIES GAHERIET, NEPHEW OF KING ARTHUR, WHOM LANCELOT OF THE LAKE KILLED. Similarly they had written on the others' stones the names of the men they believed had killed them.

After the archbishops and bishops and priests had done all they should, the king returned to his palace and seated himself among his barons; his sorrow would not have been greater had he lost half his kingdom, and all the others were equally sad, so that they did not know what to do or say. All the barons were seated in the palace, and many other knights and people with them, but they were so quiet that it seemed there was no one there.

The king was sitting sadly at the head of the palace, and after he had sat for a long time, he said so loudly that everyone heard him, "Oh God, how long have You upheld me in honor and exaltation, and now in a short time I am brought low by bad fortune. Never has a man lost as much as I have lost, for this is a loss greater than all other losses, for if a man loses land, he can sometimes recover it, but if a man loses friend or kinsman, there's no way he can get him back. My lords, I've suffered this loss, as you see, not through the will of Our Lord but through the arrogance of Lancelot of the Lake. If this loss had come to me through God's vengeance, I'd bear it more to our honor, but it has come to us through one whom we had put in the place of highest honor we found, and whom we received in our land with as much honor as if he were my son. He has caused us this loss and dishonor. You all hold land of me and are my vassals, and you have sworn to me the pledge and oath of vassals, and, therefore, I ask you, by the right that you ought to do, to aid and counsel me as good men should counsel their [442] lord, in such a way that my dishonor may be avenged and you may have honor in breaking and destroying those who caused me this dishonor."

Having said this, the king fell silent and waited for his barons to reply. They began to eye one another and tell one another to speak.

After they had sat silent a great while, King Iom stood up and said to the king, "My lord, I'm your vassal, and I should gladly advise you what may be to your honor and benefit and that of the kingdom. Our honor, unquestionably, lies in avenging this as well as we can, but he who would look to the profit of the kingdom would not, I believe, start a war with the kindred of King Ban of Benoic, for we see that Our Lord has so exalted them over all other known kindreds in the strength of their people, their knightly skill, and their good lineage that there isn't now, in my opinion, any man in the world so high born that he could bother them much, were they in their own country, except only you. Therefore, my lord, I ask you, for God's sake, not to start a war against them unless you see that you can finish it well, for indeed, in my opinion, they will be hard to defeat."

Here the uproar in the palace was tremendous. They said that what King Iom had said was wrong and that he was saying it out of cowardice.

"Indeed," he said, "I don't say it from fear greater than any of yours, but I know truly that, once a war has started, if they take to their land, they'll fear us much less than you think."

"Indeed, Sir Iom," said Mordred, "never did such bad counsel come from such a good man. But if the king listens to me, he will in no way fail to go there and to take you with him, although it may grieve you."

"Mordred, Mordred," said King Iom, "indeed, I'll go there more willingly than you. Let the king go when he likes, for I'll gladly go with him."

"What are you fighting about?" asked Mador of the Gate. "If you want a fight, you'll find it nearby, for Lancelot is in a castle he conquered when he first became a knight and went on adventures for the kingdom of Logres. That castle is named Joyous Guard. I know it well and where it is, and so I should, for I had been a prisoner there a long time and was afraid of dying when Lancelot freed me—me and other knights from here who were prisoners there!"*

"By God!" said the king, "I know that castle well, but do you think he's there, and the queen with him?"

"My lord, I tell you truly that the queen is there, and Lancelot with all his kindred, just as he was here. I don't advise you to go there now to harm them, for the castle is so strong that no one has ever besieged it, and they're such good knights that they won't fear to make war on you and dishonor you." [443]

When the king heard this, he answered, "By my faith, Mador, you're telling the truth about the castle, that it's strong, and about their arrogance. But you and

---

*   See the Vulgate *Lancelot,* chapters 27, 30.

everyone here know well that since I became king I've begun no war that I didn't bring to a close to my honor and that of my kingdom. Therefore, I tell you that I won't for anything fail to start a war against those who have committed treason and caused me such great loss, and I ask you first, all you who are here, to help me, according to my trust in you. I'll also send word to those who are farther away, who hold land of me, and once all our forces are assembled—that can be fifteen days from now—then we'll move. And because I don't want you to hold back, I want you all to swear to me as my vassals and promise me that you'll help me carry on this war with all your strength until our dishonor is avenged."

At once he had the Holy Gospels brought and promptly received their solemn oath and promise. After that he sent word throughout his whole land, near and far, to those who held land of him, to come to him, and he set a day on which they were to be with him at Joyous Guard with all their troops. All agreed to this and prepared to go, and there they expected to accomplish easily what they had said.

When Lancelot heard this news, he sent word to the kingdoms of Benoic and Gaunes and to the barons who held land from him to furnish the castles well, so that if, by chance, they had to leave Great Britain and go to Gaul, they might have their castles well furnished against King Arthur. Then he sent the queen to the kingdom of Sorelois, and he sent to the Strange Land and to all the knights he had helped and who had often professed their love for him, to come help him against King Arthur. Because he was the knight who was most loved in the world and who had most honored and loved the other knights, and because of that request he made of them, so many knights came to his aid that, if Lancelot had been a crowned king, he would have been hard put to gather such a force of knights as he assembled at Joyous Guard.

But now the story stops speaking of them and returns to King Arthur and his company.

155. War Between King Arthur and Lancelot in Britain and Gaul; Gawain Receives His Death Wound; Arthur Defeats the Romans.[*]

The story tells that on the day when the king had ordered his barons to assemble at Camelot, they went there, and such a large body of knights had not assembled in a long time. Meanwhile, Gawain, who had been very ill with grief over the death [445] of his brothers, had recovered.

On the day they assembled, they said to the king, "My lord, before you leave here, we'd think it good if from among these nobles here you chose replacements for those who were killed for the queen and gave them seats at the Round Table, so that the number of one hundred fifty may be complete. We tell you truly that if you do this, our company will be more feared."

[*]   Corresponds to Magne II:443-453; Piel 447-452.

The king agreed to this and said it was good. He called his barons and commanded them, on the oath and promise they had made to him, to choose the best knights they could find as to skill and good habits, not passing over anyone because of poverty or low birth, and to seat them at the Round Table. They drew apart and asked how many were lacking. They found by tally that seventy-two were missing, and they chose that many who were deserving. But without doubt, there was no one so bold that he dared sit in the greatest seat of the Round Table, which they were used to call the Perilous Seat. A knight named Elians sat in Lancelot's seat,* and he was the best and most famous knight in all Ireland, son of the king. In Bors's seat sat another knight whose name was Balinor, son of the king of the Strange Isles. He was unquestionably a good knight, and at his friends' request he won Bors's seat. Hector's seat went to a man from Scotland, a good knight, strong in weapons and friends, large of body and marvelously bold, and his name was Vadaans the Black; he was a man of great consequence but more brutal and envious than any other knight they knew. Gaheriet's place was taken by a young and good knight named Gaheris of North Wales. After that they put the best knights they found among the remainder into the other seats.

When they had done this and the tables had been laid, they sat down to eat, and seven kings, his vassals, served at King Arthur's table. That day they set their affairs in order, as they would move out the next morning. The next day they heard Mass and then rode out, and during this day they reached a castle named Lambor. The following day they went on, and they rode far each day [447] until they arrived at half a league from Joyous Guard. Because they saw the castle so strong that it feared no strength of men and could only be besieged from a distance, they camped there on the bank of the Humber, and while they were readying themselves, they placed armed knights before their position so that, if the men from the castle came, they would be received as enemies should be. In this manner the men of the army prepared to receive their enemies. But those of the castle, who were experienced, sent a large part of their knights to hide themselves in a forest nearby, in order to prepare an ambush for the army, when they saw that it was ready, so that the army would be attacked by men from the forest and from the castle, who cared nothing for the siege but let the army camp in complete peace, planning to attack the next day.

The knights of the forest were two hundred by count, good knights and brave, and Bors and Hector were their captains. Those of the castle had arranged with them this signal: in the morning, as soon as they saw a red banner in the tallest tower, they would ride out at once and fall on the army, for those of the castle would also ride out immediately, so that the army would be attacked from both sides. They did as they had said. When the army saw that Lancelot's forces were letting them camp in peace, they were more confident, and many of them said that, if Lancelot had had a large company, he would not for anything have failed to attack the army, for he was not a knight to endure any harm his enemy might do him.

---

*   The author does not tell us if the magical name-writing on the seats confirmed this redistribution of seats belonging to living knights who had fallen from royal favor.

When Lancelot saw that King Arthur—the man he had loved most in the world and who had honored him most—had him besieged, he was so grief-stricken that he did not know what to do, not from fear but because the king had loved him more than any other man who was not his kin.

Therefore, he took a maiden aside into a room and said to her, "My lady, you'll go to King Arthur and say to him on my behalf that I wonder greatly why he has begun this war against me, for I truly don't think I have ever offended him so that he should do it. If he says to you that he has done it because of the queen, and that I have wronged her, as some say, tell him that I'll defend myself against the two best knights of his court who may accuse me falsely of this sin, and for his honor and love, which I lost by false slander, tell him that I'll place myself under the judgment of his court, if it [448] pleases him. And if he says that he started this war because of the death of his nephews, tell him that I'm not to blame for that death and that he should not hate me so mortally, for they themselves were to blame for their deaths. My lady, say to my lord the king for me that I don't feel myself so guilty toward him that I wouldn't place myself under the judgment of his court for it. And if he won't agree to any of these things that I send you to say to him, I'll withstand his strength with greater sorrow than he or anyone else would believe, and let him know that, once this war is started, I'll do all the harm I can to his followers. Truly, because I hold him my lord and my friend—although he sees me not as friend but as mortal enemy—I assure him that *he* need not beware of me; rather, I'll always protect him from all those who want to harm him. My lady, say this to him."

She said she would deliver this message so well that they would be able to find no fault with her. The maiden left him and went out of the castle without anyone knowing. This was at the hour of vespers. The king was sitting at dinner, and because they realized that she was a messenger, as soon as she arrived they took her to the king. She approached the king and told him everything Lancelot had said to her.

Gawain, who was near the king, heard everything the maiden said to him and spoke before the others could speak, saying so that all the barons heard him, "My lord, my lord, you are on the point of avenging your shame and the great loss of your nephews, which you incurred because of Lancelot, and you have the ability and strength to do what you planned at Camelot, to destroy and reduce to nothing the kindred of King Ban, who by their pride and excess have inflicted upon you such great wrong and loss that it can never be avenged except by God. I tell you this because if you make peace now, when you and your kin are on the point of getting revenge, both your own men and strangers will think it wrong of you."

"Gawain," said the king, "the matter is already such that never, as long as I live, will Lancelot have peace with me by anything he may do or say, even though he's the man in the world to whom I have most obligation to forgive a great offense, for, unquestionably, he has done more for me than any other knight. But finally he has done me such a great wrong that I promise you as king that he'll never have peace with me." [449]

Then he turned to the maiden and said, "My lady, tell your lord that I'll do nothing of what he sent you to tell me, nor will he ever, while I live, have peace with me."

"Indeed, my lord," said the maiden, "this is a great loss, more for you than for anyone else, for you, who are now the most powerful and renowned man in the world, will thereby be destroyed and killed, and the wise men who have spoken much about your end weren't wrong, for this is certain, that those wise prophets who have lived in our time, who know a great deal about events that are to come, have said that at the end King Ban's lineage will endure wrong and conquer and overcome all their enemies. And you, Sir Gawain, who ought to be wise, are more ignorant than I thought, for you are seeking your death even though you are able to see it."

Then the maiden left the king, went to her lord, and told him everything the king had said to her, and he was deeply grieved.

The next day at dawn Lancelot had the red banner raised over the tower. The men in the forest saw it at once and rode out, and at the same time Lancelot rode out of the castle, and they attacked* the army violently from both directions. King Arthur lost much in that battle, much more than the other side, for the men of King Ban's lineage were so skilled at arms that neither the king nor his men could stand against them without losing heavily each time they met, and this was frequently. In the end the king would have lost everything were it not for the archbishop of Canterbury, who was related to the queen; he excommunicated the entire kingdom of Logres because the king would not take back his wife. When the king saw that Holy Church was pressuring him, he took her back, and he was much happier than he showed, for he loved the queen more than anything else in the world.† And know for a truth that Lancelot would not have given her up were it not that men would have thought that what was being said was true. And he excused himself for this many times with many good men.

After Lancelot gave back the queen, he left the kingdom of Logres entirely with all his kindred. He crossed the sea to Gaunes and had his cousins crowned kings: to one he gave the kingdom of Gaunes and to the other that of Benoic and all Gaul, just as King Arthur had given it to him. And at that time the people of the kingdom might well say that they were rich, [451] for they had a good lord, who held the land and the kingdom in peace, and a good body of knights. But that peace did not last long, for King Arthur came there subsequently, with his whole army, to avenge the death of his nephews, and this was on Gawain's advice. He besieged the city of Gaunes, where Lancelot was with all his kin. After he had besieged it, he lost more than he gained, for those inside were unusually strong. And if Lancelot had wanted, he could have defeated and captured him many times over, but he did not want to, for he loved King Arthur with all his heart.

When the king saw that in this siege he could accomplish nothing to his honor, he said to Gawain one day, "You've killed me by making me come here, for those inside the city care nothing for us."

---

*   Both editions have *começarom* ("began"), but the manuscript seems to have *cometarom* ("attacked"), which makes more sense.

†   Compare to King Mark, who loves Iseut and wants her back, although she has betrayed him (chapter 135).

When Gawain heard this he was deeply grieved, and so great was his sorrow that he sent word to Lancelot: "Lancelot, if you maintain that you didn't kill my brothers by treachery, I'll prove it against you."

When Lancelot heard this, he was very sad and said that he would defend himself. The battle was before the city of Gaunes, and when they were put onto the field, Gawain made his uncle promise that, if Lancelot defeated him, he would lift the siege of Gaunes and declare Lancelot free of all complaints that he had against him. Similarly, Lancelot made his kindred promise that, if Gawain defeated him, they would all freely become vassals of King Arthur, except King Bors and King Lionel; those two were free of this covenant because they were kings.

Then the two knights attacked each other, and the battle lasted a long time. But at the end Gawain was so badly wounded that he could do no more, and Lancelot would have killed him then were it not for his love of the king and all the barons of the kingdom of Logres. And know that in that battle Gawain received a wound of which he could never be healed, but which eventually brought him to his death.

When the battle was over, King Arthur declared Lancelot and all his kin free of any complaint he had against them.

But now the story stops talking of them and turns back to King Arthur, in order to tell how he fought with the emperor of Rome.*

In this part, the story says that as soon as the settlement between King Arthur and Lancelot was established, news reached him from which he derived much grief and anger, for they told him that the emperor of Rome was in Brittany with a great army, and he wanted to take Gaul and then cross to the kingdom of Logres and conquer it. Many of the king's knights were wounded, and he stayed there until they were whole. When he saw that Gawain and the other knights were healed, he rode forth with his whole army against the emperor of Rome, [453] and he fought and defeated and killed him and captured many of the best Romans, making them swear on the Holy Gospels that they would take the emperor to Rome.

At their departure he said to them, "You'll take the emperor to the Romans from me and tell them that this is the tribute I owe them."

156. MORDRED'S RISING; DEATH OF THE KNIGHTS OF LOGRES; KING ARTHUR IN THE ANCIENT CHAPEL.†

The day the Romans were defeated, very bad news came to King Arthur, for a squire said to him, "My lord, you've lost the kingdom of Logres. Mordred, your nephew, with all the good men of the land, has turned against you and has been crowned

---

* The beginning of this encounter is narrated in chapter 4.
† Corresponds to Magne II:453-461; Piel 452-457.

king of all your land. He has besieged Queen Guenevere in the Fortress of London[*] and threatened to kill her because she wouldn't take him for her husband."

I want to tell you how this happened. I tell you that when King Arthur left the kingdom of Logres in pursuit of Lancelot, he entrusted his land and his wife and his people who remained, without exception, to his nephew Mordred and made them swear on the Holy Gospels that they would do as much for Mordred as for himself. When Mordred saw that the land was in his power, he quickly decided to ensure that his uncle would have no way to return to it. He loved the queen as much as Lancelot had ever loved her. He had false letters written and brought as if from Arthur[†] where he was sitting among the good men of Logres, telling them to make Mordred king and give him the queen as his wife. The people of Logres, who truly believed that things were as the letters said, made Mordred king, but when they wanted to give him the queen as his wife, she refused, for she hated him greatly, and she shut herself into the fortress of London[‡] with people of her kindred. Mordred had the tower attacked but could not take it, for those inside were skillful and defended it well.

This was the treason Mordred committed against his uncle. The king was very sad when he heard of it, and he said, "Now let's ride, for, God willing, I won't rest until I'm in Logres."

Kay the Seneschal had done well in the battle, but he had emerged mortally wounded, as had Gawain and many other good knights. Kay, who saw clearly that he could not go with the army, had himself taken to Normandy to the house of a maiden who had been his fiancée. There Kay died, and for love of him the men of the king's lineage made a village named Caiam. [454]

The king reached the sea and crossed over with all the men he had. Gawain died as soon as he reached land, and they took him to the castle of Cros.

There was much good in Mordred, and as soon as he was elevated to the throne, he made himself well loved by all.

Therefore, they said to him, when they knew King Arthur was coming, "My lord, have no fear, but ride and defend what we've given you, for we're ready to die to defend your honor."

Then Mordred had all his people armed and left London,[§] where he had been besieging the queen. As soon as he left, the queen entered a convent, thinking that if Mordred won he would not be so evil as to take her from there, and if Mordred were defeated, she would go to her lord.

Mordred rode with his whole company until he met King Arthur with many men. When the two armies met, much was said on both sides in an effort to make peace, but this could not be, for the king would not agree. All these things, which it is not fitting that I describe fully to you here, you will find in the *Tale of the Cry,* for I have

---

   *   "London" as in Piel (452); Magne has "Logres." In the Vulgate *Death of Arthur* (chapter 17), the tower is in London.

   †   Both editions have *de carreira* ("from the road"), but the manuscript is hard to make out here. The rendering "Arthur" is logical, even if *de carreira* is in fact correct, the implication being that the letters appear to have been brought from Arthur on his travels.

   ‡   Both Magne and Piel (452) have "Logres."

   §   Both Magne and Piel (453) have "Logres."

not tried to describe the great battles that took place between King Ban's lineage and King Arthur, and the emperor of Rome and King Arthur, because they would be longer than the three parts of the book permit.

When the armies were gathered on the plain at Salisbury, one could see good knights on both sides. Therefore, it happened that, as soon as they struck each other with their lances, you would have seen great numbers of dead and wounded lying on the ground. In that battle were killed* seven kings on King Arthur's side, and the *Tale of the Cry* tells which they were. There Yvain died, son of King Urien. There Kay of Estral died, and Dodinel the Wild, and Brandeliz, and a good twenty from the Round Table, of whom the one who was worth least was considered a good knight and a good man.

In that battle Mordred fought and defended himself so well that everyone who saw him thought him a surprisingly good knight. And know that the story says that in his whole life he did not do as much in arms as on that one day, for with his own hands he killed six companions of the Round Table, whose names and deeds the *Tale of the Cry* relates.

King Arthur also did so well that [455] day that all his men took example from him, and he never tired of wielding his sword.

Therefore, Lucan, who was near him and saw the marvels he was achieving, said to Girflet, "Sir Girflet, let's be confident that we'll win this battle: see King Arthur here, who sets us a good example. He has learned well to destroy and kill his enemies. He should certainly be called king who knows so well how to help his people."

Thus spoke Lucan of King Arthur, when he saw that he was doing so well. King Arthur rode about the battlefield until he met Mordred, and he gave him such a great blow on the helmet that he laid him unconscious on the ground.

He thought Mordred was dead and said to him, "Mordred, much wrong have you done me, but it has brought you no profit."

King Arthur knocked Mordred down, just as I have told you, but Mordred did not stay on the ground for long, for his vassals picked him up. When he was back on his horse, he felt deeply ashamed that he had fallen with his men watching. He charged at Sagremor and gave him such a blow that he knocked Sagremor's head far away, and his body fell to the ground.

When the king saw this blow, he said, "Oh, God, what bad luck! That traitor is killing good and faithful knights!"

The king had already recovered his good, strong lance. He charged at Mordred, who was so courageous that he did not flinch, and struck him so hard that he put the lance right through his chest, and the wood appeared on the other side. And the story says that after he had pulled the lance back out, a ray of sunshine passed through the wound, so bright that Girflet saw it clearly, so that the people of the land, when they heard of it, said that it was a miracle from Our Lord and a sign of grief.

Mordred knew that he was mortally wounded. He struck the king his uncle so hard that neither helmet nor iron coif kept the sword from penetrating to the bone

---

*   "killed" as in Piel (454); not in Magne.

and cutting off a large piece of his skull. With that blow the king fell to the ground, and Mordred, too.

In this way, as I have told you, King Arthur killed Mordred, and Mordred wounded him mortally. And this was a great wrong and a great loss, for there was not, after King Arthur, a Christian king so well favored or who [457] did such deeds or loved and honored chivalry so much.

When Blioberis, who was near him, saw this blow, he said with great sorrow, "Oh, God! Now I see fulfilled the prophecy that the wise men of this land have often uttered, that King Arthur would die by the hand of his son. Oh, God! What pity and loss!"

Then he dismounted, went to the king, and put him on his horse.

The king was still so dazed by the blow that he could hardly hold himself upright, and yet, as soon as he was conscious and saw Mordred lying on the ground, he said, "Mordred, in an evil hour did I beget you.* You have ruined me and the kingdom of Logres, and you have died for it. Cursed be the hour in which you were born!"

At the time when the king said this, the battle was already over, for of sixty thousand who had come together there that day, there remained only sixty alive. After Blioberis, who had done better at arms than anyone else, had put the king on his horse, he dismounted beside Mordred in the sight of everyone there, tied him to the tail of his horse, and began to drag him across the battlefield. He pulled him until Mordred was torn in pieces.

Of Mordred's army, not a man remained alive, and of King Arthur's army only four remained on horseback—the archbishop of Canterbury, Blioberis, Girflet, and Lucan. King Arthur was on horseback, but he knew well that he was mortally wounded.

When they saw that there remained no one with whom they could fight and saw Salisbury Plain covered with dead knights in all directions, they said to one another, weeping, "Oh, God! What a great pity and loss! Oh, God! What greater harm could you have done us, for we see everyone lying dead in torment and sorrow!"

After they had made their lamentation, they left the dolorous plain. The king made such a great lamentation that he could have died of it.

The archbishop comforted him as much as he could and said, "My lord, if you have lost your friends, you have, on the other hand, thanks to God, had good fortune, and you have escaped alive and won this battle and killed your enemies."

"Oh!" said the king, "if I've escaped alive, what good does it do me? My life is worth nothing, for I see clearly that I'm mortally wounded. Oh, God! What suffering and misfortune† have come upon a great land through the treason of one evil man!" [459]

Thus King Arthur left Salisbury Plain. Blioberis was still pulling Mordred's head behind him, for his body had been torn completely to pieces.

The king asked Blioberis, "Do you still have that much of the traitor who has so ruined us?"

---

* Literally, "make you." Magne supplies "a knight," but it is not in the manuscript and is not needed for the meaning.

† Both editions are confused here, and the manuscript is nearly illegible, but this seems to be the gist.

"Yes, my lord," said Blioberis, "this is Mordred's head."

"I'm pleased," said the king. "We'll go put it in a place where whoever wants can see it. You and the Archbishop stay on this plain and make a large tower in which will lie the heads of those who have died here. Hang Mordred's head from the top by a great chain, and have an inscription written there telling how great sorrow came about on this plain because of him, so that when those who come after us learn from the inscription the evil that came about because of him, they'll all curse his soul."

The archbishop and Blioberis did just as the king had commanded, for they made a great tower on the plain and named it the Tower of the Dead. They put Mordred's head there, and it remained hanging there until Charlemagne crossed over to England and came to see the tower. And when Ganelon the traitor, who later did so much harm, as the story tells, knew why Mordred's head was hung there, it seemed to him that it was put there as an affront and warning to all the traitors in the world, and he was deeply grieved by it, for he held himself to be one. He went there by night, cut it down, and put it in a place where no one knew from then on where it was. The tower remained; some of its walls are still there.

But now the story stops speaking of the tower and returns to King Arthur.

Now the story tells that when King Arthur left the field where the battle had taken place, so deadly and so lamentable, and Lucan and Girflet went with him, he rode until he reached a chapel. That chapel was called The Ancient Chapel, but the *Tale of the Cry* tells where it got this name, for it belongs more to that story than to this one.* When they reached the chapel, the king, who felt himself weakening, dismounted. The others entered the chapel with him, and the king fell to his knees in front of the altar. Lucan, who [460] was at his side, also on his knees, had not been there long when he saw the aisle behind the king full of blood. Then he first understood that the king was mortally wounded and that he could not be saved from death.

Lucan could not help saying, weeping, "Oh, King Arthur, what a great loss your death is! Never again shall such a man die!"

The king was frightened by this speech, as a man is when he hears someone speak of his death.

He replied, "The loss won't be mine alone, but many good men will lose thereby."

Then he fell flat. He was large and heavy, and he was armed, and it happened that when he fell he pinned Lucan, who was already disarmed, between himself and the ground. And he fell onto him so violently and pressed him so hard beneath him—not because he was angry with him but because of the agony he felt—that he crushed Lucan, who died at once.

After the king had lain thus a long time, he got up, but he did not realize that he had killed Lucan. Girflet saw that Lucan was dead and told the king.

The king was deeply grieved and said in great anguish, "Girflet, I'm not the King Arthur whom they are wont to call the King of Adventures because of the good

---

* There is an Ancient Chapel in chapter 91, but there is no indication that it is the same one, and the source of its name is not given. In the Vulgate *Death of Arthur* (chapter 24), the dying king goes to the Black Chapel.

fortune he had. But whoever would now call me by my true name would call me ill-fortuned and wretched. Chance, who has become my stepmother and my enemy, has done this to me. Our Lord shows me clearly that it pleases Him to make me live this little time I have left in grief and sadness, for just as He wished—and was able—to raise me up through many beautiful adventures and without my deserving it, so is he now able to bring me down through cruel and evil adventures because of my deserving and my sin."

Thus spoke King Arthur when he saw that he had killed Lucan. He lay there that night in great sorrow and such pain that he knew he would last only a little longer.

When day came, he said to Girflet, "Let's mount and go straight to the sea, for so much misfortune has recently come to me in Logres that I wouldn't die here. Just as my life has always been passed in adventure, so will it be with my death. For my death will be so much in doubt among all men that no one will be able to boast that he knows for certain the truth about my end."

Then they mounted, left the chapel, and went directly to the sea. [461] But now the story stops speaking of King Arthur and Girflet and returns to Blioberis and the archbishop.

157. BLIOBERIS GOES TO LOOK FOR LANCELOT; DEATH OF ARTHUR THE LESS.*

The story tells that after Blioberis and the Archbishop had built the tower just as King Arthur had told them, they left it.

Blioberis said to the archbishop, "My lord, what will you do?"

"Indeed," said the archbishop, "since we began this tower that we're now completing, I have often heard it said by many who were to be believed that King Arthur is dead under such circumstances that they don't know where. And since I know for certain that I'll never again have the company of such a good man, I don't want to live any longer in the world. From now on, the world will be worth but little, since such a man as he was is lost, for he was the pillar of the earth and the honor of the world. Since he's gone, I'll become a hermit in a hermitage, and I'll pray to Our Lord for King Arthur, to have mercy on his soul, and for the other good knights who have died in the dolorous battle of Salisbury."

"I'm not advised to become a hermit," said Blioberis, "for I've heard that my lord Sir Lancelot is soon to cross over here with a large army in order to take this land, which Mordred's sons are already enjoying."

"Then I commend you to God," said the archbishop, "for I'll go to that hermitage," and he told him where the hermitage was.

"I know that hermitage well," said Blioberis, "for I've been there. Know that if chance brought me that way, I'd try to see you."

---

*   Corresponds to Magne II:461-465; Piel 458-461.

In this way the two parted. The archbishop went to the hermitage, and Blioberis went off alone, guided by chance, through the kingdom of Logres, fully armed as a knight errant. One day he happened to meet Arthur the Less, also fully armed. When they saw each other, they did not recognize each other, for they had changed their arms some time back. Nevertheless, each suspected that the other was a knight errant, and as soon as they met, they stopped. Each one was so grief-laden that for a while they did not speak, remembering the agony and torment in which the knights errant and good men of the kingdom of Loges had died and to what the kingdom of Logres was reduced.

Then Blioberis said, "For God's sake, tell me who you are, for much would I like to know, as I think you were one of King Arthur's knights."

Arthur replied with difficulty, for he was deeply grieved when he heard his father's name, and he said weeping, "My name is Arthur the Less. I was a long time at King Arthur's court. I was there so long that it pleased God to make me a companion of the Round Table. Now [463] tell me who you are."

"I'm Blioberis," he said, "whom you should certainly recognize, for like you I'm of the Round Table."

When Arthur the Less heard him, he said, "You're among King Arthur's enemies, for you're of King Ban's kindred. Because of that line, all the men of the kingdom of Logres are dead and destroyed, for they began the war, and for this reason I'm your mortal enemy. I tell you to be on guard against me, for there's nothing but death in this."

When Blioberis heard this he replied, "Oh, Sir Arthur! You won't do this, God willing, for you know that you'd be forsworn and disloyal."

"That doesn't matter," said Arthur. "Defend yourself, if you wish; if not, harm will come to you as a result."

When Blioberis saw that he could not do otherwise, he charged at Arthur. Each struck the other so hard that they knocked each other to the ground, their horses on top of them. They were both badly wounded, but both were of such great heart and strength that they got up as quickly as they could. They took their swords and charged at each other, and they gave each other so many blows that they made each other's shields and hauberks* worth a small part of what they had been before, for anyone who was there would have realized that both knew sword play well.

What shall I tell you? Before they tired of that round, the blows had been such that another knight would have thought himself badly hurt by them. But they had such great hearts and their anger was so immoderate that they did not feel them. When they were tired, they rested in order to recover their strength.

When they were somewhat rested, Blioberis said, "Sir Arthur, you've attacked me gratuitously, and you've fought with me a great while and gained nothing. I ask you, for the sake of God and courtesy, to give up this battle, and I'll absolve you of whatever fault you have in it."

Arthur said he would not do so until one of them was dead.

---

*   "and hauberks" as in Piel (459); Magne has "and lances."

"And if you kill me," said Blioberis, "what good will it do you? For whoever learns of it will consider you forsworn and disloyal, and, what's more, you know well that I've never deserved death from you."

"Yes, you've deserved it," said Arthur, "and I'll tell you how. You know well that it's the custom among knights errant that if some knight is a traitor to his native lord and any man helps that knight against him, he, too, is a traitor. Now tell me," said Arthur, "you know well that you helped Lancelot of the Lake, who was a traitor to his lord, for he was found with Queen Guenevere. You helped him all through that war that began because of him. Aren't you then a traitor for helping the traitor against your lord? Because of this I [465] attacked you just now, and because, before Joyous Guard, you killed the knight I loved most in the world.* And now I find you here and want to reward you for it."

"Indeed, Sir Arthur," said Blioberis, "you're holding to evil counsel. Since I see that I can't make peace with you, I'll tell you something (not to praise myself): I don't fear just you alone, for I know truly that I'm as good a knight as you or better, and I'll certainly show you that that is true, for I'll kill or defeat you before I leave you, and, so help me God, it grieves me greatly, but since I can't do otherwise, I'll do it. I prefer you to die at my hands than I at yours."

After this, without further delay, they charged at each other and with their swords gave each other the greatest blows they could. That battle continued in that manner until both of them were afraid of dying, for both felt themselves wounded, but Arthur the Less was a great deal worse wounded than Blioberis, so that he already saw that he could not escape death, for he had a good twelve wounds, of which the least perilous was mortal.

When he saw that he could no longer endure the battle, he drew aside a little and said, "Blioberis, how do you feel?"

"Well enough, considering the situation," he said, "thanks to God, for I'm badly wounded but not mortally."

"No?" said Arthur. "By God, I can't say the same of myself, for I feel that I'm mortally wounded because of my folly, and I'm less grieved by my death than by the fact that I won't avenge myself."

After he had said this he fell flat on the ground. Blioberis, who was deeply grieved, put his sword in its scabbard, for he did not want to do him any more harm. He went to Arthur and removed his helmet and coif in order to give him some air so he could breathe better.

When Arthur felt this he thought Blioberis was doing it in order to cut off his head, and he said to him, "Oh, Blioberis! Do me no more harm, for you've killed me for my arrogance. If I have wronged you, you've avenged yourself well. Restrain yourself, if you please, and let me be buried whole."

"So help me God," said Blioberis, "I have no wish to do you any more harm; rather, I'm grieved by what I've already done."

"For God's sake," said Arthur, "you shouldn't be blamed for it, for it was all because of my arrogance. But I want to tell you something I've never told anyone else, because I see that I'm dying and I want the world to know it. Know that King

---

*   Not narrated in the Post-Vulgate.

Arthur was my father, and, therefore, I'm called Arthur the Less. Have this written, if you please, on my tombstone."

As soon as he had said this, he died. Blioberis put him in front of himself on his horse, took him to an abbey, and had him buried with great honor. He had what Arthur had asked written on the tombstone and left.

Now the story stops talking about him and returns to King Arthur.

158. The Death of King Arthur.[*]

When King Arthur left the Ancient Chapel, just as I have already told you, he went [466] with Girflet toward the sea, full of grief over the adventures he had seen and the misfortunes that had recently come to him, one after another.

When he reached the sea—this was at midday—he dismounted and seated himself at the edge of the sea. He unbelted his sword, drew it from its scabbard, and saw the blade[†] red with the blood of those he had killed.

After he had looked at it a long time, he said, sighing, "Oh, Excalibur, good and honored sword, the best that ever entered the kingdom of Logres except for the one with the strange straps,[‡] now you'll lose your lord, but where will you ever find a man by whom you'll be as well employed as you have been by me, unless you come into Lancelot's hands? Oh, Lancelot, the best man and the best knight I ever saw, except for Galahad, who was the best of the best! Now would that it pleased Our Lord for you to have this sword and for me to know it! Indeed, my soul would be more joyful forever."

Then he called Girflet and said to him, "Take this sword, and go up there to that knoll, and there you'll find a lake; throw it in, for I don't want the evil men who'll live after us to have such a sword."

"My lord," he said, "I'll obey your command, but I'd rather, if it pleased you, that you gave it to me."

"I won't," he said, "for by you it wouldn't be used as I wish, for you haven't long to live."

Then Girflet took the sword, went to the knoll, and found the lake. He drew the sword from the scabbard and looked at it, and he saw it so good and rich that it seemed to him a terrible waste to throw it in the lake and better to throw in his own, take this one for himself, and tell the king he had thrown it in the lake. Then he took his own sword and threw it in the lake; he concealed the king's sword among the weeds, returned to the king, and told him that he had thrown it in the lake.

"What did you see then?" asked the king.

"My lord, I saw nothing."

---

[*]   Corresponds to Magne II:465-472; Piel 461-465.
[†]   Both Magne and Piel (461) have "belt."
[‡]   See chapter 131.

"Oh," said the king, "you're tormenting me. Go back there and throw it in, for you haven't yet thrown it in."

Girflet went back and took the sword; he looked at it, mourning, and said it would be a great pity if it were thus lost. He thought he would throw the scabbard in and keep the sword, for it could yet be useful to him or to someone else. He took the scabbard and threw it into the lake, and he returned to the king and said he had thrown the sword in. The king asked him again what he had seen.

"My lord," he said, "I saw nothing. What was I to see?"

"What were you to see?" said the king. "You haven't yet thrown it in. Why do you wrong me so? Go and throw it in. Then you'll see what happens to it, for it can't be lost without a great marvel." [467]

When Girflet saw that he had to do it, he returned to the lake and took the sword, saying, "Oh, good and rich sword, what a great pity it is that no good man holds you in his hand!"

Then he threw it as hard as he could, and when it got near the water, he saw a hand come out of the lake, appearing as far as the elbow, but of the body he saw nothing. The hand received the sword by the pommel and brandished it three or four times. After it had brandished the sword, it withdrew with it into the water. Girflet waited a long time to see if it would appear again.

After that, he left the lake and returned to the king. He told him how he had thrown the sword in and what had happened.

"By God," said the king, "I knew all this would happen. Now I know well that my death is fast approaching."

Then tears came to his eyes; he thought a long while and said, "Oh, Girflet, long have you served me and kept me company. But now the time has arrived when you must leave me. You may well boast that you are the companion of the Round Table who bore me company the longest. But now I tell you to go; I don't want you to stay with me after this, for my end is approaching, and it isn't fitting that anyone know the truth of my end, for just as I became king here by adventure, so shall I pass from this kingdom by adventure, and after this, no one will be able to boast that he knows for certain what has become of me. For this reason I want you to go, and after you've left me, if they ask you for news of me, answer them that King Arthur came through God's adventure, and by God's adventure he departed, and he alone was the King of Adventures."

"Oh, my lord, mercy!" said Girflet. "For God's sake, let me keep you company until you reach your end."

"I'll never love you," said the king, "if you don't go, and be assured that harm will come to you if you don't."

"Oh, my lord," said Girflet, "I'll do it, since you wish it, but know that I never did anything that grieved me as much as parting from you, for I've always loved you above everything. But for God's sake and by your goodness, tell me this much, if you please: do you think that I may see you again after parting from you now?"

"Indeed, no," said the king, "you'll never see me again."

Girflet replied, "My lord, so much greater is my grief."

Then he went to his horse, mounted, and [469] said weeping violently, like one whose heart was about to break, "My lord, I commend you to God."

"God be with you," said the king.

And Girflet left him. Then it began to rain hard and to storm. Girflet went toward a hillock as fast as he could, for he thought that from the hillock he might see which way King Arthur went.

When Girflet reached the hillock, he stood under a tree while the rain grew heavier, and he began to weep and to look toward where he had left the king. He had not stood there long when he saw coming across the sea a little bark in which were many ladies. The bark landed near King Arthur, and the ladies emerged and went to the king. Among them was Morgan the Enchantress, King Arthur's sister, who went to the king with all the ladies she led and entreated him to come on board the bark. After he was on board, she had his horse and all his armor put aboard; then the bark began to go across the sea with him and with the ladies, so that no knight or anyone else in the kingdom of Logres might say with certainty that he had seen King Arthur afterward.

When Girflet, who was standing on the hillock, saw that the king had gone on board the bark with the ladies, he came down from there and rode in that direction as fast as his horse could carry him, for he thought that if he got there in time, he would go on board the bark with his lord and that he would not part from him for anything that might happen except death.

When he reached the sea, the bark had already pulled away from the shore. He saw the king among the ladies and recognized Morgan the Fay, for he had seen her many times. The bark was a bowshot away from the shore, and when Girflet saw that he had thus lost the king, he began to make the greatest lamentation in the world. He stayed there all that day and night without eating or drinking, nor had he eaten the day before.

The next day, when the sun had risen, Girflet mounted, tormented and grieved, and left there, and he rode until he reached a small wood. A hermit lived there who was his close acquaintance, and he stayed with him two days because he felt unwell.[*] He told him what he had seen of King Arthur when he had seen him go out to sea with the ladies.

On the third day, he left and went to the Ancient Chapel in order to find out if Lucan was already [471] buried. He reached there at midday, dismounted, tied his horse to a tree, went inside, and found two rich, beautiful tombstones before the altar, but one was richer than the other. On the one that was less rich there were letters that said, HERE LIES LUCAN THE WINE STEWARD, WHOM KING ARTHUR KILLED BENEATH HIM. On the other, marvelously rich one, there were letters that said, HERE LIES KING ARTHUR, WHO BY HIS PROWESS AND ABILITY CONQUERED TWELVE KINGDOMS.

When he had read the letters, he fainted on the tombstone, and when he came to, he kissed it, weeping from the heart. He stood there until evening, when a man who served the chapel altar arrived.

As soon as Girflet saw him, he asked, "My lord, for God's sake, is it true that King Arthur lies here?"

"Indeed," said the good man, "I think it is, for not long ago some ladies brought here on a litter the body of a knight, and they were making a marvelously great

---

[*] "he stayed with him two days because he felt unwell" as in Piel (463); not in Magne.

lamentation. When I asked them who it was for whom they made such a lamentation, they told me that it was King Arthur, and then they put him in this tomb. After that they went away toward the sea, and they didn't return."

Girflet thought that those were the ladies whom he had seen put King Arthur in the bark; nevertheless, he said in his heart that all the same he would like to know for certain if it was King Arthur who lay in the tomb.

Then Girflet went to the tomb, with the good man standing nearby. He raised the stone, and when he looked inside he saw nothing except King Arthur's helmet, the very one he had worn in the dolorous battle.

When he saw that the king's body was not there, he showed the empty tomb to the good man and said to him, "My lord isn't here; I want you to be my witness."

He replaced the stone over the tomb as it had been before and asked again, "Did you see clearly my lord's body put here?"

"By God," said the good man, "we put a body here, and the ladies gave me to understand that it was King Arthur. I can't with certainty tell you anything more about it."

"So?" said Girflet, "in vain will I labor to find out how King Arthur died. Truly he's the mysterious king, whose death no man shall know, and he certainly told the truth that just as [472] he came to the kingdom of Logres in mystery, so has he gone away from it in mystery. But since I see that there's no point in my seeking him, as he can't be found, I'll never live in the world again, but I want to stay here in this hermitage as long as I live."

Then he asked the good man to receive him into his company. Just as I have told you, Girflet stayed with that good man and served God in the Ancient Chapel, leading a good and holy life there, but not for long, for he lived no more than three months after parting from King Arthur.[*]

But now the story stops talking about King Arthur and about Girflet's death in order to tell about Lancelot and Mordred's sons.

159. GUENEVERE'S DEATH; LANCELOT'S LAST DEEDS AND DEATH.[†]

The story tells that, while Girflet was at the hermitage, both of Mordred's sons went to Winchester to fortify the town. When they learned about the deaths of their father and King Arthur and other good men who had died in the dolorous battle, they were greatly comforted. They were both good knights and knew much of evil like their father, and they gave and promised so much to the people of Winchester that the people received them as their lords, just as they had done with their father. They quickly gathered together as many people as they could get and went about

---

[*] "but not for long, for he lived no more than three months after parting from King Arthur" as in Piel (464); not in Magne.

[†] Corresponds to Magne II:472-489; Piel 465-475.

through the land making themselves lords of it. This they could easily do, for all the good knights had died in the battle.

When the queen learned the truth about the battle that had taken place on Salisbury plain, and they told her that the king and all the good knights of Logres were dead, she felt such great sorrow that she wished she were dead. When they told her that Mordred's sons were going about making themselves lords of the land and that they had such a large following that they would soon have the whole kingdom, she was as grieved as she could be, for she feared that they would kill her. Therefore, she took the habit of the religious order and became a nun.

While this was happening, the news reached Lancelot, who was in Gaunes with a large company of good men of his kingdom. Then they also told him how Mordred's sons, who had not been in the battle, were going about making themselves lords of the land. Lancelot was deeply grieved at this news and mourned for King Arthur, for there was no man in the world whom he loved more. [473]

He asked for news of the queen, but the man who had brought him the news knew nothing about her, for there were few in the land who knew what had become of her, since she had tried to hide as well as she could, in fear for her life. Lancelot was deeply grieved at this news, and with King Bors and King Lionel he considered what they could do, for he hated nothing in the world as much as Mordred and his sons.

King Bors replied, "My lord, I'd think it good for us to gather and cross to Great Britain and, if they await us, to kill them in some unpleasant way, for I don't see how we can avenge ourselves on them in any other way."

Lancelot agreed to this plan. Then they sent word to the kingdoms of Benoic, Gaunes, and Gaul and gathered in the city of Gaunes more than twenty thousand men, some on horseback, some on foot. After they were gathered, Lancelot, King Bors, King Lionel, and Hector, with their entire company, left Gaunes and rode long each day until they reached the sea. They found their ships ready and went on board, and they had such a good wind that they landed in Great Britain on the very same day. They disembarked and rested on the shore of the sea.

The next day, the news reached Mordred's sons that Lancelot was in the land with a great army. When they heard this they were badly frightened, and they received advice to assemble and fight with him. To this they agreed, because they had more people than Lancelot. They did just as they had said, for they assembled at Winchester, and they did so much in a short time by their grandeur and prowess that all the men of the kingdom of Logres swore fealty to them, and they had the help of many foreign knights.

When they were assembled, they marched out of Winchester, and the next morning, as they were riding, a messenger reached them who said, "You are defeated and dead men, for Lancelot is coming here with a large company of men, and he isn't more than six leagues from here. I assure you that he'll be with you very soon."

When they heard this, they said that they would await him there and there they would fight with him, and they dismounted in order to rest themselves and their horses. Thus the men of Logres remained before Winchester. Lancelot rode with his entire company, although with great [475] sorrow, for on that day the news had reached him that the queen had died a good three days earlier.

But because our story does not tell how she died, we will tell it here in another manner.

At this point the story tells that, before Queen Guenevere entered the religious order for fear of Mordred's sons, she had always lived in luxury with all the pleasures of the world. Thus it happened that when she had to suffer the deprivations of the religious life, to which she was not accustomed, she fell at once into poor health and weakness, so that all who saw her wondered whether she would live or die. She had with her a maiden of high station who had taken the habit for love of her. This maiden had been engaged to Girflet, son of Doon.* And because the queen had heard that Girflet had kept King Arthur company longer than any other knight, she loved this maiden's company with all the love of which she was capable. They comforted each other and wept together frequently when they remembered the pleasures and the high rank and the great power they had enjoyed, and now they were in a convent in fear of death.

The queen, even though she was in a convent, never stopped mourning for Lancelot and saying from time to time, "Oh, my lord Lancelot, Sir Lancelot! How have you forgotten me, when I believed you'd never leave me. If you believed in your own goodness, your pleasure, and the great power that God gave you, you'd remember me sometimes, and you'd avenge King Arthur's death and conquer the kingdom of Logres, relieving me of this torment in which I live and this alien power in which I've placed myself in fear of death."

This the queen said of Lancelot as she lay sick, and the maiden comforted her as much as she could. She told the queen not to fear, for she knew truly that Lancelot would not long delay in coming, as she had already had news of him.

The queen replied, "How the time drags! I know I'll die of this delay."

In that abbey there was a nun who had entered the convent because she had desired Lancelot, and he would not have her, and she hated the queen with all her heart because Lancelot had renounced her out of love for the queen. She thought that since she could not vent her anger on Lancelot, she would vent it on the queen.

One day it happened that this nun said to [477] Girflet's friend who took care of the queen—and she pretended she did not want the queen to hear her—"Oh, my lady, I bring you bad news. Sir Lancelot, who was coming with a large force to conquer the kingdom of Logres, has been lost at sea with all his men."

"By God," said Girflet's friend, "that's a great loss. But how do you know it's true?"

"I learned about it from one who saw it," she said.

When the queen, who was sick, heard this news, she was so grief-stricken that she almost went out of her mind; nevertheless, she concealed her feelings carefully, out of fear of the woman who had brought the news.

After that woman had left, the queen said in grief, "Oh, cursed sea, full of bitterness and sorrow, evil, unknowing, and unknown, cruelly have you afflicted me who have taken from me the most loyal lover in the world and his love."

---

*   Both Magne and Piel (467) have "Dodinel." Girflet was identified as the son of Doon in chapter 4.

After she had said this, she fell silent in such deep grief that she could no longer eat or drink, and she lay like that three days. On the fourth day, the news arrived that Lancelot had definitely landed in Great Britain with such a large body of good knights that no one dared await him in the field.

The maiden who was caring for the queen was happy when she heard this news; she went running to the queen and said to her, "My lady, I bring you very good news. Be sure that Sir Lancelot is in Great Britain with so many men that in a short time he'll overrun it all."

When she heard these words, the queen, who was near death, replied with great effort, "My lady, you tell me this too late; his coming is of no use to me now, for I'm near death. However, because Sir Lancelot is the man I love most in the world, I beg you, for love of me and of him, to do what I want to ask of you."

The maiden promised faithfully that she would do the best she could.

"Then I'll tell you," said the queen. "I see clearly that I'm dying and that I won't see tomorrow morning, and I tell you truly that I was never so happy at any news as at this. On the other hand, it grieves me exceedingly that I can't see him before I die, for it seems to me that my soul would be happier if I saw him. Because I want him to see and know that I was happy at his coming, and that I died in sorrow, and that I would gladly have seen him if I could, I ask you to take out my heart as soon as I am dead and take it to him in this helmet, which [478] was his, and tell him that, in memory of our love, I send him my heart, which never forgot him."

That same day Queen Guenevere passed away, and the maiden obeyed her command, except that she did not find Lancelot and, therefore, did not accomplish all that the queen had commanded her.

But now the story stops talking about her and turns to Lancelot and Mordred's sons.

Here the story tells that when Lancelot heard that the queen was dead, he was so grief-stricken that it was a marvel; nevertheless, he departed and rode with his company that day until they reached Winchester. The others, who were waiting for them, mounted when they saw them and met them in battle. In that encounter many were killed and wounded, and great was the hatred between them. After they had broken their lances, they took their swords and began to strike as hard as they could, so that you would have seen many dead and wounded on both sides. The battle lasted until the hour of nones. It happened that Mordred's son Melian had a short, thick lance with a very sharp point. He was a skilled knight, and he charged at Lionel and struck him so that neither shield nor hauberk kept the lance from going right through his chest; he knocked Lionel from his horse to the ground, and in the fall the lance broke so that the point and part of the shaft remained in him. King Bors saw this blow and realized clearly that his brother was mortally wounded, and he thought he would die of grief.

Then King Bors charged at Melian and gave him a great sword stroke; he cut through his helmet and coif and split him to the shoulders. He drew his sword back, and Melian fell dead to the ground.

When he saw him dead on the ground, Bors said, "Traitor! How inadequately do I repay the harm you've done me today! Indeed, you've put such sorrow into my heart that it will never come out."

Then he charged at the others, where he saw the thickest press, to knock down and kill [479] as many as he could, so that everyone was amazed at the marvels the knights of Gaunes performed. When they saw King Lionel fall, they dismounted, drew him out of the press, and laid him under a tree. And although they saw him so badly wounded, they dared not lament, lest their enemies take pleasure in it.

Thus was there begun before Winchester an evil and dolorous battle, which lasted until the hour of nones so unremittingly that one could hardly tell who was getting the better of it. After the hour of nones, it happened that Lancelot met Mordred's older son, and he was unquestionably a good knight. Lancelot recognized him because he bore the insignia his father used to bear, and he charged at him, sword in hand. The other did not refuse him but raised his shield against the blow when he saw the sword coming. Lancelot, who hated him mortally, struck him so hard that he split his shield to the boss and cut off the fist with which he was holding it. When he felt that he had lost a hand, he wanted to flee toward a forest nearby, for he knew that he could not endure against Lancelot. But Lancelot kept him so closely engaged that he could not escape and gave him such a great blow that he made his head with his helmet fly from his body to the ground more than a lance length away.

When the others saw that he was dead, they did not know where to turn for help and advice, and they began to flee, with Lancelot's men following them, knocking them down and killing them in the roads. Lancelot, who rode ahead of his whole company, was overtaking them, knocking them down, and wounding and killing them so violently that one could clearly see behind him the trail of those he had knocked down, dead and wounded. He went on like this until he overtook a Duke of Gorre, whom he knew to be a traitor and who had often grieved King Ban's lineage.

When Lancelot overtook him and recognized him, he said, "Oh, faithless traitor! You're surely a dead man, for nothing in the world can save you but God."

The other looked behind him, and when he realized that it was Lancelot who was threatening him, he was greatly afraid, for he knew [481] that Lancelot was the best knight in the world, and he knew that he was a dead man if the other caught up with him. He began to ride toward a mountain as fast as his horse could carry him. He was riding a good horse, and so was Lancelot, so that they galloped a full two leagues. Then the duke's horse grew tired, so that he fell dead beneath him from exhaustion. When Lancelot, who was riding close behind him, saw the duke on the ground, he went to him just as he was on the horse and gave him such a sword stroke on the helmet that he split him to the teeth. He did not look at him again but began to ride as fast as he could, but the more he tried to return to his company, the farther from it he went.

So Lancelot wandered, lost, until he reached a deep valley. There he met a squire coming from the direction of Winchester, and he asked him where he was coming from. The squire said that he was coming from the field where there had been a dolorous battle.

"And in my opinion," said the squire, "no one but you escaped from it alive."

He said this because he thought that Lancelot was of the kingdom of Logres.

"However, I tell you this much, that the men of the other side are deeply grieved for King Lionel, whom they lost in the battle."

"What?" asked Lancelot. "Is it true that King Lionel is dead?"

"It's true," said the squire. "I saw him dead, and you never saw such a great lamentation as his people were making for him."

"Indeed," said Lancelot, "here's a great loss, for he was a good knight. May Our Lord have mercy on his soul." Then he began to weep violently.

The squire said to him, "My lord, where do you expect to lodge tonight, for it's late?"

"I don't know," he said. "I care nothing about shelter, so great is my grief."

The squire asked him his name.

"My name is Lancelot," he said.

The squire fled as soon as he heard him say that he was Lancelot, for he was much afraid Lancelot might kill him. Lancelot began to ride, sad and tormented. He rode that night and all the next day, and neither he nor his horse ate. In the morning, chance brought him to a hermitage, where he found the archbishop of Canterbury and Blioberis, who had placed themselves there to serve Our Lord. When he met them, he was very happy, and they were, too, when they saw him. [483] They received him well and disarmed him. As soon as he was disarmed, he went to an altar of Saint Mary there, fell to his knees in front of it, and swore that, so help him God and Holy Mary and the saints, he would never leave Our Lord's service but would remain in that hermitage as long as he lived. And as he promised, so he did, for he died there in the service of Our Lord.

But now the story stops speaking of him and turns back to Bors and his company.

After the men of Gaunes had accomplished their battle and destroyed the men of Winchester, they saw King Lionel dead. They were deeply grieved and took counsel among themselves what to do.

"Indeed," said King Bors, "I've lost so much in the kingdom of Logres, since I've lost my brother, that I have no desire to stay longer; rather, I want to go from here."

But he did not yet know that Lancelot had left them. He ordered his brother put in a litter and left the field where the battle had taken place.

He rode until he reached the sea, and he wanted to cross it, but the men of his company said to him, "My lord, we've done wrong, for we've been traveling for two days and we've had no word from Lancelot."

Then he ordered half his people to proceed with King Lionel's body, and the other half remained.

"For I never loved this land as much as I now hate it," said King Bors, "because of the death of my brother, whom I've lost here."

They did just as King Bors had commanded them, for half of them stayed with Hector, and the other half went off with King Bors. Those who remained stayed four days in a castle called Ambenic, and they waited there to see if they could get news of Lancelot. Hector stayed with them, in great sorrow over his brother, about whom he could get no tidings.

As they were waiting, suddenly a hermit arrived and said to Hector, "You're waiting here in vain for your brother, for he has no desire to come here. He has entered a hermitage, which he'll never leave, for he has promised Our Lord, and with him are the archbishop of Canterbury and Blioberis. Those two are also hermits."

"Where are they?" asked Hector. "Could I find them?"

"That I won't tell you," said the hermit.

"If you won't tell me," said Hector, "I'll nonetheless go seek him until I find him."

Then he had his whole company come before him and made them swear that they would obey [484] all his commands, and after they had sworn, he said to them, "Now I command you to leave the kingdom of Logres and go to your own lands."

"And you, my lord," they asked, "what will you do?"

"I'll remain," he said, "and if later I wish, I'll follow you."

They did so, for they embarked on the sea and went away to their own lands, and Hector remained behind. Then he begged the hermit for God's sake to take him where his brother was, for he wanted to serve God there with him. Then they left, and the hermit took him to the hermitage where his brother and the others were, as I have told you. As soon as the brothers saw each other, they wept for joy, for they loved each other dearly.

Hector said to Lancelot, "My lord, since I find you in the service of Jesus Christ, and it pleases you to remain, I want to stay with you, in order never to part from you."

When the others heard this, they were happy that such a good knight was entering God's service, and they received him well into their midst, giving thanks to Our Lord. Thus both brothers remained in the hermitage, and from that day they labored to serve Our Lord. Four years and more Lancelot lived in the hermitage, so that no one could endure more effort or labor, for he endured fasting and vigils, prayers and orisons and mortification of the flesh in every way he could.

In the fourth year Hector passed away, and they buried him in the hermitage.

In the fifth year, fifteen days before May Day, Lancelot fell ill. He saw clearly that he could not escape death, and he asked the archbishop and Blioberis to take him, as soon as he was dead, to Joyous Guard and put him in the tomb where Galehaut, the lord of the Distant Isles,* lay. They promised him that they would do so. Lancelot lived four days after this request, and on the fifth day he expired. But at the moment of his death neither the archbishop nor Blioberis was with him. They were sleeping outside under an elm. Blioberis happened to wake up first, and he saw the archbishop lying beside him sleeping, and in his sleep he was laughing and showing the greatest signs of joy you ever saw.

He said in his dream, "Oh, God, may You be praised, for now I see what I've so much desired to see and know!"

---

* Galehaut does not appear in the Post-Vulgate. For an account of his friendship with Lancelot, see the Vulgate *Lancelot,* chapters 72-76, 106.

When Blioberis saw that he was sleeping and heard what he said, he was amazed. [485] He feared it was a demon that had entered into the archbishop, and he awakened him.

"Oh, my lord," said the archbishop, "why have you taken me away from the great joy I was experiencing?"

"What joy were you experiencing?" asked Blioberis.

He said, "I was part of great rejoicing and in such a large company of angels that I have never seen such a crowd of people gathered. And with such great joy and festivity as I've told you, they were taking away Sir Lancelot's soul. Now let's go see if he's dead."

"Let's go," said Blioberis.

They went at once to where they had left Lancelot, and they found that his soul had left him.

"Oh, God," said the archbishop, "may You be praised! Now I know truly that that great rejoicing the angels were making was for his soul. Now I can surely say that penance is better than all other worldly things. From now on, as long as I live, I won't stop doing penance."

"Now it's fitting that we take him to Joyous Guard," said Blioberis, "for we promised him."

"That's true," said the archbishop.

Then they prepared a litter and laid Lancelot's body on it. One took it from one side and the other from the other, and they left the hermitage and went to Joyous Guard. But know that this was with great effort and labor.

When the people of the castle knew that it was Lancelot's body, they came out to meet him with great singing, weeping, and lamenting as if they all saw their kindred dead before them. They bore him to the chief church of the castle and paid him as much honor as they could—as much as they should pay to such a man. The very same day that this happened, King Bors arrived there, in great poverty, accompanied by a single knight and a single squire. When he learned that Lancelot's body was in the church, he went there and had it uncovered, and he looked at it and studied it until he realized clearly that it was his lord. As soon as he recognized him, he fell unconscious on top of him, and when he came to, he began to make his lamentation, the greatest in the world.

All that day and night, the mourning in the castle was great, and they had Galehaut's tomb opened, which was as rich as it could be. In the morning they put Lancelot in it. Then they had letters carved on the stone that said, HERE LIES GALEHAUT, THE LORD OF THE DISTANT ISLES, AND WITH HIM LANCELOT, THE BEST KNIGHT WHO EVER BORE ARMS IN BRITAIN, EXCEPT ONLY GALAHAD HIS SON. [487] After they had put him in the sepulchre, you would have seen more than a thousand mourning round about.

The archbishop asked King Bors how he had happened to arrive at the very moment of Lancelot's burial.

"Indeed, my lord," said King Bors, "a hermit of holy life who lives in the kingdom of Gaunes told me, not a month ago, that, if on this day I could arrive at this castle, I'd find my lord here, dead or alive. And it came about just as he told me. But for

God's sake, if you know where he lived until now, tell me, for I greatly desire to know."

The archbishop related to him the story of Lancelot's life—what he did after he left the battle at Winchester, the beautiful end he made, and everything he had seen of it.

When Bors, who listened gladly to what the archbishop was saying, had heard the whole story of Lancelot's life, he replied, "My lord, since he lived with you until his death, I'll keep you company in his place as long as I live, for I won't ever stop doing penance, but I want to go with you. And I'll live in your company all the days of my life."

The archbishop and Blioberis thanked him warmly. The next day, they left the castle of Joyous Guard, and King Bors sent his knight and his squire to tell the people of Gaul and Gaunes to make whom they would king, for he would never come back there. He went with the archbishop and Blioberis on foot and in poverty, so that whoever considered his high rank and how he was of great consequence and king of such a rich kingdom would well understand that he had a strong wish to serve God.

One day, as they were going to their hermitage, they happened to meet Meraugis of Portlegues, fully armed. When he saw the three good men, although he did not recognize them, he had pity on them, because he saw them walking barefoot, and it seemed clear to him that they were good and well honored, men of good lives.

Still seated on his horse, he asked them, "What men are you?"

The archbishop replied, "We're sinful men who are doing penance for our sins. We'll be fortunate if, by means of such slight suffering, we're able to save our souls."

Meraugis looked closely at him, and he thought he had seen him before on some other occasion, but he could not recognize him.

Therefore, he said, "I ask you, by the faith you owe to Him whom you serve, to tell me who you are."

The archbishop said, "I'm a hermit, but I was once archbishop of Canterbury, and I was still such on the day when the dolorous battle of Salisbury took place, in which the kingdom of Logres was destroyed. Because of that evil day, which I saw, I entered a hermitage, [489] and I've stayed there up to now, and I'll stay there as long as I live."

"And who are these other two," asked Meraugis, "who are veiled?"

He named them. When Meraugis heard this, he was filled with wonder, for he would never have believed that knights so much honored and of such high station would enter so soon into God's service.

He quickly dismounted from his horse and said, "My lords, since I see that you've given up knighthood to serve Our Lord, I'll give it up, for like you I have great need to save my soul, and I won't ever take arms again unless great need makes me do it."

Then he disarmed himself, left all his armor and weapons in the middle of the road, and went with them. When the other three saw this, they were greatly pleased, and they thanked Our Lord. Then they went together to the hermitage. Meraugis asked them if they knew any tidings of Lancelot, and they told him all they knew and how he had been a hermit with them.

But now the story stops speaking of them and turns to King Mark, how he learned something about the deaths of the knights of the kingdom of Logres and that they were all of the Round Table.

160. THE FINAL DESTRUCTION OF LOGRES.*

When the news of Lancelot's death became known throughout Great Britain, Gaul, and Gaunes and in Benoic and Brittany, Scotland, Ireland, and Cornwall, King Mark was still alive. By that time, he was older than any other king in the world. He still rode robustly, and he held his land strongly, so that he feared no neighbor. His line had been diminished by the death of Tristan his nephew, but he was not very sorry about that. About the death of Queen Iseut he was very sad, so excessively had he loved her, but about the death of his nephew he was not sad but happy.

When he heard men speak of Lancelot's death, he was happy and said, "Now I see no one who could keep me from taking the kingdom of Logres, since King Ban's kindred are dead. Even if they were still alive, the death of this one alone would give it to me. But while he was alive, there was no one in the world who could take it."[†]

Then he assembled as many men as he could get, crossed the sea, and went to Great Britain. [490]

When they had disembarked from the ships and unloaded what they had to unload, King Mark said, "Now I'm in the land where I received more dishonor and harm than in any other place I've ever been. Now I wish that they never think me a king if I don't avenge myself."

Then he commanded his men to make a crusade such as no other Christian king ever made, to kill every man or woman they met.

"I don't wish anything to remain of all King Arthur has done," he said, "but let everything be destroyed, including all the churches and monasteries he built, for however many you destroy, I'll build richer and better. I order this destruction because I don't wish anything made by King Arthur to remain in this kingdom after my death."

King Mark ordered this done, from which it came about that the kingdom of Logres was lost and destroyed.

According to his orders,[‡] they began to go through the land destroying everything wherever they went, and they went until at midnight one night they reached Joyous Guard; they went inside and ruined it so completely that it was never afterwards

---

*   Corresponds to Magne II:489-493; Piel 475-478.
†   Literally, "accomplish it," that is, the taking of Logres.
‡   Literally, "after this had been commanded."

worth anything. When King Mark learned that Lancelot's body lay there, he went to see the tomb where he lay.

When he saw it so beautiful and rich, he said, "Oh, Lancelot, how much wrong you did me while you were alive! I could never avenge myself. But now I'll avenge myself as much as I can."

Then he had the monument, which was so rich and beautiful that all the wealth of Cornwall would not equal its value, broken open and cast out of the castle into a lake, from which no one could remove it. He had a great fire made, and he took Lancelot's body, which was still uncorrupted, and commanded that it be thrown into the fire, along with Galehaut's bones, and he let them burn there until they were turned to ashes. And I tell you truly that there were many good men there who were deeply grieved by this.

After King Mark had done this, he went to Camelot, whose people were few in comparison to his own, but they were of great heart and reputation, and they said they would not let themselves be besieged. They all rode forth from the city and fought with the enemy, but they were so few that they were all soon killed, so that none escaped, and certainly their courage brought about their death, because they would not run away. King Mark entered the city and destroyed most of it.

When he came to the Round Table and saw Galahad's place, he said, [491] "This was his place who in a single day destroyed me and the Saxons.* For hatred of him I'll destroy the Round Table, his place first and after that all the others."

He did just as he had said, for he had it completely destroyed, so that nothing was left.

Just when King Mark was doing this, there came to him a knight from Cornwall who had always hated King Arthur and King Ban's kindred, and he said to the king, "My lord, you've done nothing if you don't kill King Bors and Blioberis and the archbishop of Canterbury and Meraugis. They were of the Round Table, and they're living in this land. If they escape you, they'll seek men with whom they'll do much harm to you and all those on your side."

The king asked where they were, and the knight told the king all about those four knights.

"This won't do," said King Mark. "I must avenge my anger on them. Arrange to go seek them; whoever takes me to them, I'll give him such riches that he'll think himself well paid."

Because of that promise, many knights went from hermitage to hermitage seeking them.

There were four knights of King Mark's lineage on that quest. One day it happened that they arrived near the hermitage where the four knights were living. Near a spring they found Meraugis lying asleep, poorly dressed, thin, pale, and much changed from what he used to be, for he had suffered great hardship. They woke him in order to ask him about what they were seeking.

He told them, "You'll find them in this hermitage. I'm Meraugis, one of the four knights you seek."

Then they said, "Take us there."

* Chapter 137.

He did so. When they saw the two companions who had been such good knights at arms and so powerful in every way and who had thus placed themselves in Our Lord's service, they had great pity on them.

They came out of the hermitage and said among themselves, "Shall we kill them or not?"

Finally it turned out that they agreed not to kill them but to tell [493] the king about them. Then they returned to the king and told him what they had found.

"So?" said the king. "This is good news. They've wronged me often; I'll avenge myself."

Then he chose one of the four knights and said to him, "Take me there."

He said he would do so. Then the king, fully armed, left his company. He did not want anyone to know it except the man who was guiding him. He hated those four so much that he wanted to kill them with his own hands. When they reached the hermitage, inside they found a knight of King Ban's line named Paulas, who had just arrived, and he was still armed. When the king saw that he was not one of those he sought, he went out of the hermitage and walked around, looking at the four hermits where they stood rejoicing over the guest who had just arrived. When King Mark had gone on foot to where they were, he asked which of them was King Bors.

King Bors said, "My lord, what's your pleasure?"

"My pleasure is something that will turn to your harm," he said. "Do you know who I am? I'm King Mark of Cornwall, who have come here to avenge myself on you."

Then he drew his sword, and when the archbishop saw that King Mark wanted to kill them, he put himself in the path of the stroke, and the king gave him such a great blow on the head that he killed him.

When Paulas saw this, he stood up in great sorrow and said, "Oh, King Mark, brutal and false! You've committed the falsest act a king ever committed. But you'll lose by it, if I can manage."

Then Paulas took his sword, charged at King Mark, and struck him violently, being very strong, so that neither helmet nor coif kept him from splitting the king right to the teeth, and his body fell to the ground. When the knight who had come with the king saw this blow, he begged Paulas for mercy, not to kill him.

Then promise me," said Paulas, "that you won't tell about this death anywhere."

He promised and left, and the hermits took the body of King Mark and buried it near the hermitage, outside the sacred ground, for they thought him one of the falsest men in the world.

Thus, as I have told you, King Mark of Cornwall died, and the hermits remained in the hermitage in the service of God. And thus we have finished. Amen.